Read SAP PRESS online also

With booksonline we offer you online access to leading SAP experts' knowledge. Whether you use it as a beneficial supplement or as an alternative to the printed book – with booksonline you can:

- Access any book at any time
- Quickly look up and find what you need
- Compile your own SAP library

Your advantage as the reader of this book

Register your book on our website and obtain an exclusive and free test access to its online version. You're convinced you like the online book? Then you can purchase it at a preferential price!

And here's how to make use of your advantage

1. Visit www.sap-press.com
2. Click on the link for SAP PRESS booksonline
3. Enter your free trial license key
4. Test-drive your online book with full access for a limited time!

Your personal **license key** for your test access including the preferential offer

cr6m-fjzx-y53g-bquk

A Practical Guide to SAP® NetWeaver Business Warehouse (BW) 7.0

SAP PRESS is a joint initiative of SAP and Galileo Press. The know-how offered by SAP specialists combined with the expertise of the Galileo Press publishing house offers the reader expert books in the field. SAP PRESS features first-hand information and expert advice, and provides useful skills for professional decision-making.

SAP PRESS offers a variety of books on technical and business related topics for the SAP user. For further information, please visit our website: *www.sap-press.com*.

Ingo Hilgefort
Integrating SAP BusinessObjects XI 3.1 Tools with SAP NetWeaver
2009, 260 pp.
978-1-59229-274-5

Larry Sackett
MDX Reporting and Analytics with SAP NetWeaver BW
2009, 380 pp.
978-1-59229-249-3

Muke Abdelnaby, Subhendu Roy, Hisham Ismail, Vu Pham, and Joseph Chica
Mastering Information Broadcasting with SAP NetWeaver BW 7.0
2009, 220 pp.
978-1-59229-276-9

Daniel Knapp
SAP NetWeaver BI 7.0 Migration Guide
2008, 180 pp.
978-1-59229-228-8

Bharat Patel, Amol Palekar, Shreekant Shiralkar

A Practical Guide to SAP® NetWeaver Business Warehouse (BW) 7.0

Bonn • Boston

Galileo Press is named after the Italian physicist, mathematician and philosopher Galileo Galilei (1564–1642). He is known as one of the founders of modern science and an advocate of our contemporary, heliocentric worldview. His words *Eppur se muove* (And yet it moves) have become legendary. The Galileo Press logo depicts Jupiter orbited by the four Galilean moons, which were discovered by Galileo in 1610.

Editor Erik Herman
Developmental Editor Kelly Grace Harris
Copyeditor Julie McNamee
Cover Design Jill Winitzer
Photo Credit Image Copyright Dole. Used under license from Shutterstock.com.
Layout Design Vera Brauner
Production Editor Kelly O'Callaghan
Assistant Production Editor Graham Geary
Typesetting Publishers' Design and Production Services, Inc.
Printed and bound in Canada

ISBN 978-1-59229-323-0

1st Edition 2010

Library of Congress Cataloging-in-Publication Data
Patel, Bharat, 1967-
A practical guide to SAP NetWeaver BW / Bharat Patel, Amol Palekar, Shreekant Shiralkar. — 1st ed.
p. cm.
Includes bibliographical references and index.
ISBN-13: 978-1-59229-323-0 (alk. paper)
ISBN-10: 1-59229-323-9 (alk. paper)
1. SAP NetWeaver BW. 2. Data warehousing. 3. Business intelligence—Data processing. I. Palekar, Amol, 1979- II. Shiralkar, Shreekant. III. Title.
QA76.9.D37P38 2010
005.74'5—dc22 2009045237

Contents at a Glance

Contents

Preface

Information technology has transformed the way business is conducted today. One of the most dramatic impacts of this transformation is the pace of change. Although not all aspects of change can be captured in the form of trends or projections, it's possible to analyze and manage some aspects using the science of statistics, supported by *business intelligence* (BI) solutions. BI solutions make it possible to analyze consumer spending behavior, key economic indicators, and much more. Companies that possess a deep understanding of their business and the forces impacting it can better navigate the waters of change with ease and predictability. Analysts say that BI solutions are the most promising tool for managing business today.

SAP is the most significant and largest solution in enterprise resource planning (ERP), and its BI solution is *SAP NetWeaver BW*. Recently, SAP also acquired BusinessObjects, a leading BI solution known for its presentation and data extraction components. The integration of the BusinessObjects presentation components into the existing SAP BI solutions has established SAP as a leader in the BI space.

Amol Palekar, Bharat Patel, and I (Shreekant Shiralkar) have been practitioners, trainers, and authors using SAP's BI solutions for many years. Our experience has helped us to develop a deep understanding of the solution, its components, and the aspects of its implementation. Our goal in writing this book is to help you make great leaps in your understanding of SAP NetWeaver BW by offering a unique mode of teaching; a mode that focuses on experiential learning. This book explains the essentials of SAP NetWeaver BW and its applications by the development of a basic sales analytic scenario. We highly recommend that you create the sales analytic scenario that we've provided in your own system and then use it to enhance your learning.

Acknowledgments

We take this opportunity to acknowledge those who significantly influenced us, contents and the book and ensured our interest in bringing this book to you.

Contents of the book were reviewed by our fellow practitioners: Atul Thatte from SAP India, Rakesh Rai from SAP Labs, Sohil Shah from Cognizant, and Upendra

Pateriya from Accenture. We acknowledge their contributions in validating the technical accuracy of the content and their valuable suggestions about topic coverage. Atul has more than 16 years of experience working with end-to-end implementations of SAP NetWeaver BW for large global companies across many industries. Rakesh has been engaged in the development and maintenance of SAP NetWeaver BW as a product from SAP Labs at Bangalore, India for many years. Sohail, currently a consultant with Cognizant Technology Solutions, has over 5 years of experience in Imaging Media & Entertainment and Retail industries. Upendra has more than 14 years of experience, most of it in managing and developing SAP BW solutions for leading Fortune 500 companies all over the world.

We were privileged to be supported by the team at Galileo Press, especially Erik Herman as the Editor for the book, who at times patiently and forcefully at appropriate times ensured a timely navigation of the journey of developing the contents of the book. We are grateful to Kelly Grace Harris (Developmental Editor) who played a crucial role in developing and structuring the contents of the book, and Kelly O'Callaghan (Production Editor) with her timely inputs helped us meet the publication schedule without a glitch.

Bharat Patel would like to thank his wife, Swati, and his son, Akshay, for doing without him almost without complaint for so many weekends/holidays and, nevertheless, actively supporting him in this book project. He also sincerely thanks his colleagues and senior management particularly Mr. K B Narayanan, Mr. J R Akut, Mr.Ratnakar Behera of Bharat Petroleum Corporation Ltd. for motivating and supporting him in this project.

Amol Palekar would like to thank his wife and family who helped him keep his spirits high throughout this endeavor. He is also thankful to fellow practitioner Mangesh Gokhale for his inputs on one of the chapters in the book.

Shreekant Shiralkar would like to express his gratitude to his children Shashank and Rohan who are the reason for everything he does, for their unending support and doing without him on many occasions.

To conclude, we sincerely hope that you enjoy reading this book as much as we've enjoyed writing it and that you find it to be the most simple and effective way of learning SAP NetWeaver BW.

Bharat Patel
Amol Palekar
Shreekant Shiralkar

Book Content Overview

The purpose of this book is to explain SAP NetWeaver BW in a way that allows you to easily understand and use the system. Our explanations focus on simplicity to avoid overly technical explanations but still allow you to take full advantage of SAP NetWeaver BW as an effective BI solution.

Each chapter begins with a chapter introduction that establishes an overall context for the core content and outlines the scope of the subject covered in the chapter. We've structured the topics within chapters in a sequence that makes it easy for you to understand, moving from broad introductions to specific information. Each of the individual topics within a section is explained using illustrations, screen captures, examples, and code.

Chapter 1 outlines the book's case study, based on a typical company (ABCD Corp.), which is used throughout the text as a way to explain the technical aspects of SAP NetWeaver BW as they relate to business requirements and sales analysis. We describe ABCD Corp.'s entities and business processes (specifically the sales and billing process), as well as what ABCD Corp. requires from a BI solution.

Chapter 2 provides an overview of SAP NetWeaver BW as a BI solution and includes a discussion of its benefits, technical architecture, and implementation options. The chapter introduces the system by exploring actual navigation through screens.

Chapter 3 engages you in step-by-step activities that will help you understand the business requirements mentioned in the first chapter. We explain the concept of the InfoObject, the basic building blocks of SAP NetWeaver BW, and how knowledge of InfoObjects is essential to building a strong and reliable solution that will be scalable and relevant for a long time.

Chapters 4, 5, and 6 cover the major building blocks of SAP NetWeaver BW as a data warehousing solution, discussing DataStore Objects (DSOs), InfoCubes, and MultiProviders. We also introduce the most important aspects of InfoSet objects, with a brief mention of VirtualProviders.

Chapters 7 and 8 cover extraction, transformation, and loading (ETL) concepts and their design in SAP NetWeaver BW. Chapter 7 explains the entire ETL process, beginning with data acquisition from source systems to its transformation to the desired format, and concluding with the process of loading to data targets. Chapter 8 explains the detailed process of data extraction from SAP source systems, the activation of SAP Business Content, and the extraction of data from an SAP system using a generic extractor.

Chapter 9 explains the creation of queries using the Business Explorer Query Designer tool, and introduces the various features and functionalities offered by SAP NetWeaver BW to build queries and present data for analysis.

Chapter 10 explains how reporting and analysis in SAP NetWeaver BW. Can be done in two ways; via and Excel Interface (using BEX Analysis) or a web interface (using BEX Web Analyzer).

Chapter 11 covers the BEx Web Application Designer, which is used to build custom web applications in SAP NetWeaver BW. We describe a wide spectrum of ways to perform reporting and analysis in Excel, as well as in a web/portal environment.

Chapter 12 introduces the Integrated Planning functionality offered in SAP NetWeaver BW. We discuss this topic in the context of the planning requirements for ABCD Corp.

Chapter 13 explains how reporting can be done using SAP BusinessObjects and SAP NetWeaver BW.

Chapter 14 explains the administration and maintenance aspects of SAP NetWeaver BW. In this chapter, we move from step-by-step explanations to a do-it-yourself approach, assisted by additional reading and references.

Chapter 15 introduces you to the advanced features of SAP NetWeaver BW. The features we explain in this chapter are meant to get you started in gaining advanced technical understanding of SAP NetWeaver BW as a data warehousing, reporting, and analysis tool.

In addition to what we've presented in this text, please visit the SAP PRESS website (*www.sap-press.com*) for ancillary material related to the book.

References and Recommended Reading

Because this book is designed for beginners, we recommend the following additional reading as you increase your understanding of SAP NetWeaver BW:

- Basic reference: SAP Online Help
http://help.sap.com/saphelp_nw70ehp1/helpdata/en/b2/e50138fed-e083de10000009b38f8cf/frameset.htm
- Reference for specific topics: How-To Guides at SDN
www.sdn.sap.com/irj/sdn/nw-bi?rid=/webcontent/uuid/e02b28a7-0d01-0010-1b87-86c0a91f8359#section2
- Reference for advanced topics: Performance Tuning
www.amazon.com/Performance-Tuning-Shreekant-Shiralkar-Bharat/dp/0977725146

This chapter will establish the context for SAP BW as a BI solution and provide an overview of how information technology is the lifeline of any business.

An Introduction to Business Intelligence

This chapter begins by building a context to help you understand how information technology (IT) has become more than an enabler of efficiency for businesses and their constituents in various forms. We briefly touch on various forms of software applications and then discuss business intelligence (BI) solutions and how SAP NetWeaver BW is positioned within the BI solution space.

Information Technology and Business Intelligence

In the early days of computerization, most companies implemented an *electronic data processing (EDP)* function to leverage computational capabilities. The next phase saw a transformation of this EDP function into computer applications for many of the intense functions a company requires, such as *materials requirement planning (MRP)*. Soon after, this morphed into what is known today as *enterprise resource planning (ERP)*. Information technology has now become an integral component of every company because it enables basic functions such as sales, finance, HR, and so on, and is growing to touch almost all aspects of business: materials management, human capital management, production planning, and so on. Figure 1 illustrates various functions within an enterprise.

The advent of technology proliferates into an array of forms of IT — from basic desktop software application to an enterprise application such as SAP, from a desktop PC to a superdome computer, from a simple LAN to an intranet, from a point of sale application to an RFID-enabled global positioning system, from information security solutions to digitized process controls — any business process can be digitized.

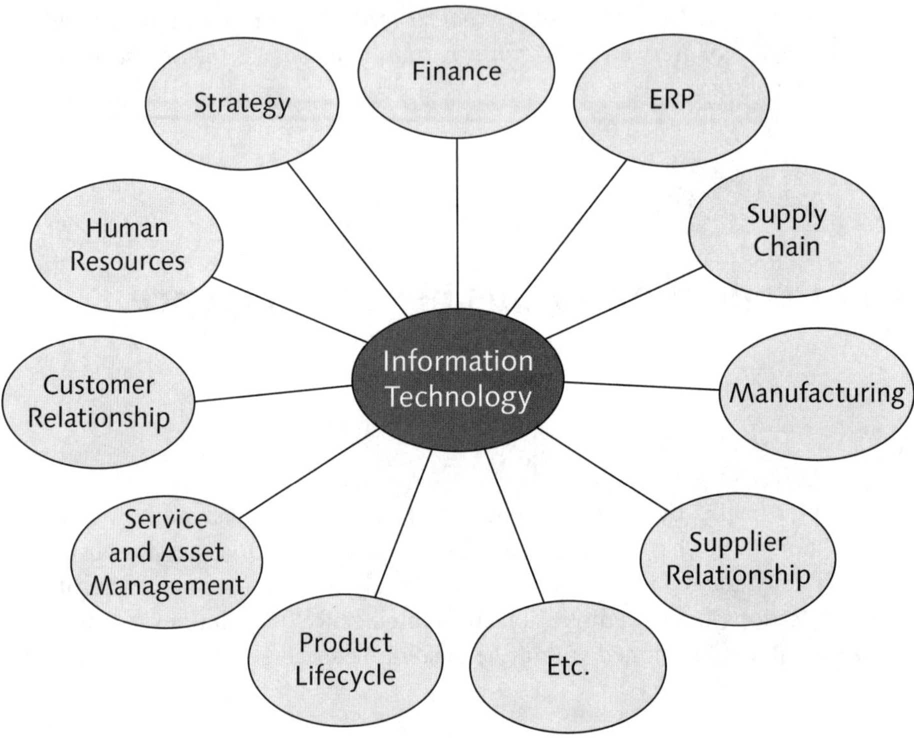

Figure 1 Information Technology in Today's Business

Software applications digitize the business process to make it more efficient and accurate. These applications cover a variety of business tasks and functions, as shown in Figure 2.

Among software applications, *business intelligence* (BI) solutions play a significant role because they enable the decision-making process to be accurate and informed; these solutions are almost like the brain of the company. BI applications cover all aspects of decision making, from basic monitoring of the status, to data mining, to helping unravel hidden trends from static reports, to alerts from the solutions based on occurrence of events related to a specific business process (see Figure 3).

BI solutions exist for supporting the decision-making process within companies, especially in reporting and analysis. As Figure 3 shows, data in a report can transform information into knowledge and intelligence when viewed from different perspectives.

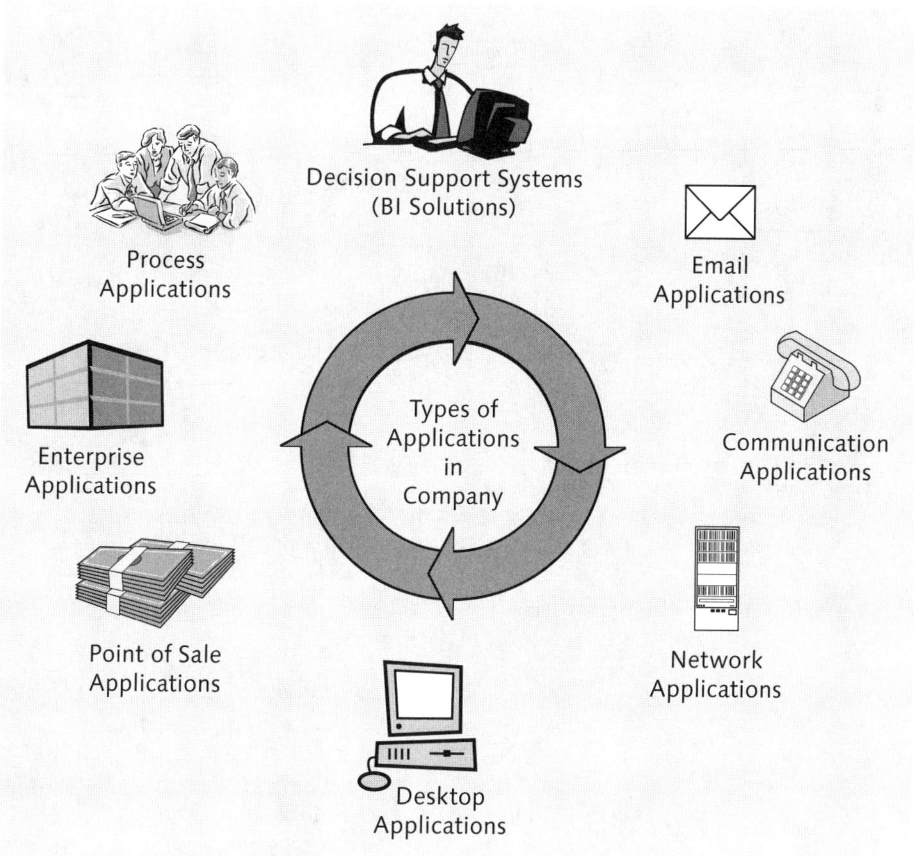

Figure 2 A Multitude of Software Applications

As a rule of thumb, a majority of users require static reports for reporting and analysis. Approximately 20% of users use applications for analysis from different perspectives, which is called *slice-n-dice* reporting. The most demanding users of the solutions are those in the analyst community who dive deeper into data and mine it for otherwise hidden facts. Figure 4 illustrates a generic segmentation of users of BI solutions.

Information needs vary from operational layers to strategic layers of a company. A sales manager might need the status of sales by a store on a daily basis, the head of sales for a company might analyze sales trends over the period of a month, and the vice president of sales might require a projection of sales for a geographic region based on a period of time that could be well over one year.

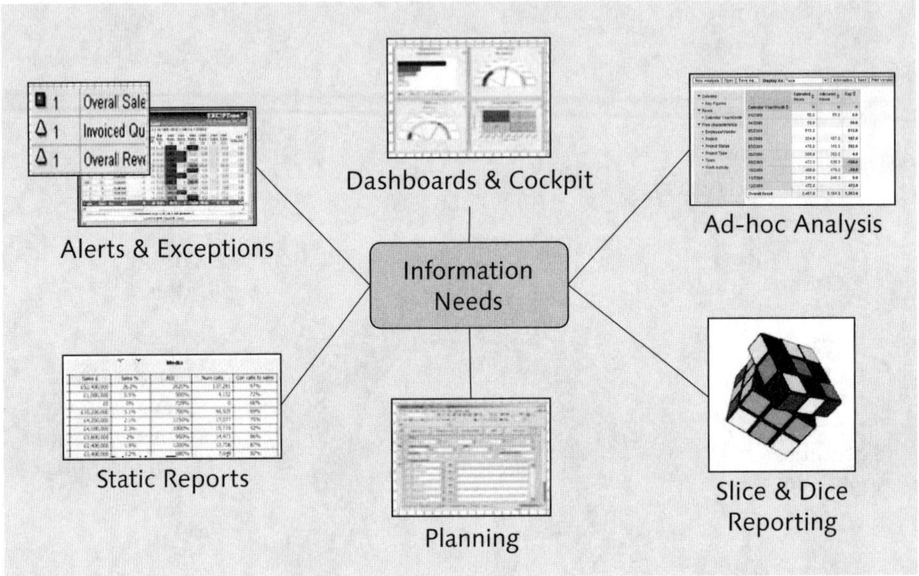

Figure 3 BI Solutions for Decision Making

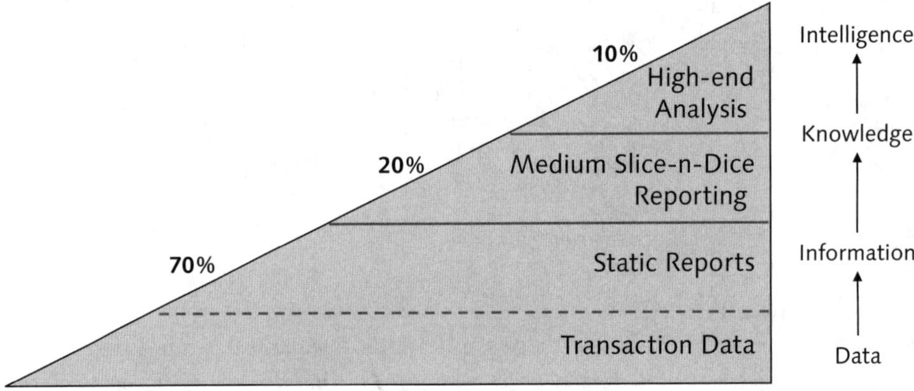

Figure 4 Typical Mix of BI Users

SAP NetWeaver BW Within BI Solutions

SAP NetWeaver BW version 7.0 was released in July 2005 as part of SAP NetWeaver 7.0 (also known as 2004s). SAP then acquired BusinessObjects and has since ensured a tighter integration between SAP NetWeaver BW and BusinessObjects. We estimate that more than 12,000 SAP NetWeaver BW installations exist worldwide.

A multitude of BI solutions in the marketplace compete to provide comprehensive solutions for a company's business intelligence needs; SAP NetWeaver BW has been classified as a leader in this field by Gartner, a group that analyzes available BI solutions. Gartner publishes its report and findings in a quadrant known as Gartner's magic quadrant (Figure 5). As you can see, SAP NetWeaver BW is a best of breed BI solution and is identified as a leader based on SAP's execution and the completeness of their vision.

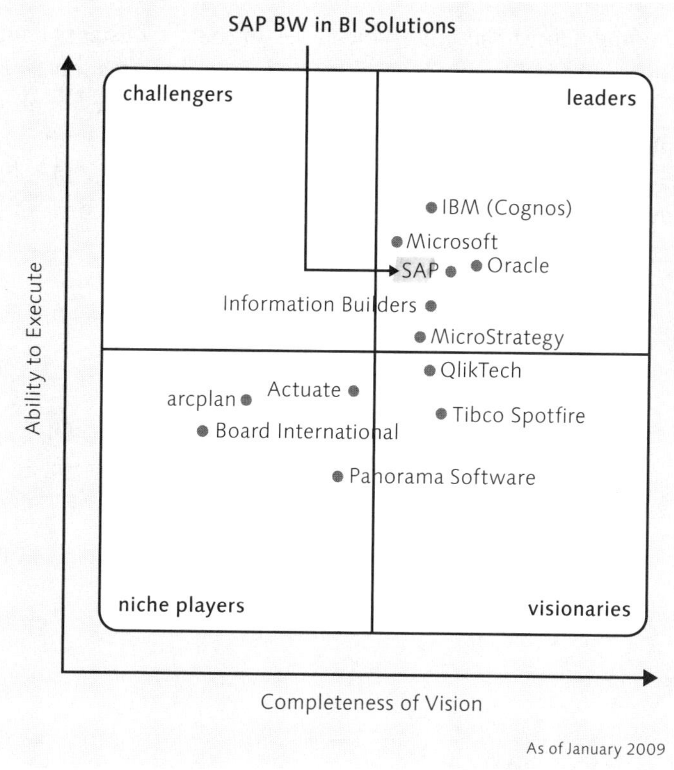

Figure 5 Leading Position of SAP NetWeaver BW in BI Solutions (Source: Gartner)

One of the factors that enables SAP NetWeaver BW's leading position is its rich add-on called *Business Content*, which offers predefined extensible SAP NetWeaver BW data models based on industry best practices. This leads to a faster implementation and facilitates data warehouse design. From an architectural point of view, this is the true value of SAP Business Content, and one of the reasons behind the success of SAP NetWeaver BW.

SAP NetWeaver BW has morphed from a one-off solution to incorporate an architecturally based approach. In this way, SAP NetWeaver BW has set new standards of quality in terms of its positioning within an enterprise. These fundamental advantages of SAP NetWeaver BW have led more and more companies to design their corporate data warehousing strategy around SAP NetWeaver BW.

Summary

In this introduction, we highlighted the importance of IT in today's business environment and the position of BI solutions within the paradigm of information technology. We briefly covered the importance of BI solutions for businesses, typical user groups, and the process of the conversion of data to business intelligence. We concluded by explaining the leading position of SAP NetWeaver BW in the BI solutions area. We also provided an overview of the content found within the forthcoming chapters.

A clear and comprehensive business requirement leads to a better design of a business intelligence solution. In this chapter, we present a basic sales process scenario for a company, which will be used as a reference in subsequent chapters.

1 The Business Scenario: ABCD Corp.

Business managers always prefer making informed decisions, a process enabled by *business intelligence (BI)* solutions. A good BI solution improves the efficiency and transparency of operations, offers better control over the outcomes of decisions, and allows you to fully explore all of the options at your disposal. It can also assist in the automation of managerial processes.

The process of making decisions for sales growth based on quantitative information is *sales analytics*, which forms one of the most common requirements for BI solutions across different companies around the world. For this reason, we've chosen to build a simple sales analytics example for a typical company, called *ABCD Corp.* In the process of building sales analytics for ABCD Corp., we explain all aspects of designing a data warehouse solution based on SAP NetWeaver Business Warehouse (SAP NetWeaver BW) version 7.0.

This chapter describes ABCD Corp. and then describes the entities involved in the typical selling processes. Each entity and the process will be referred to throughout the book as we build different components of an analytics solution using SAP NetWeaver BW (version 7.0).

1.1 ABCD Corp.: Company Overview

ABCD Corp. is a company located in North America with headquarters in New York City. It sells different electronics and white goods (i.e., appliances) to its customers, who are spread all over the world (Figure 1.1).

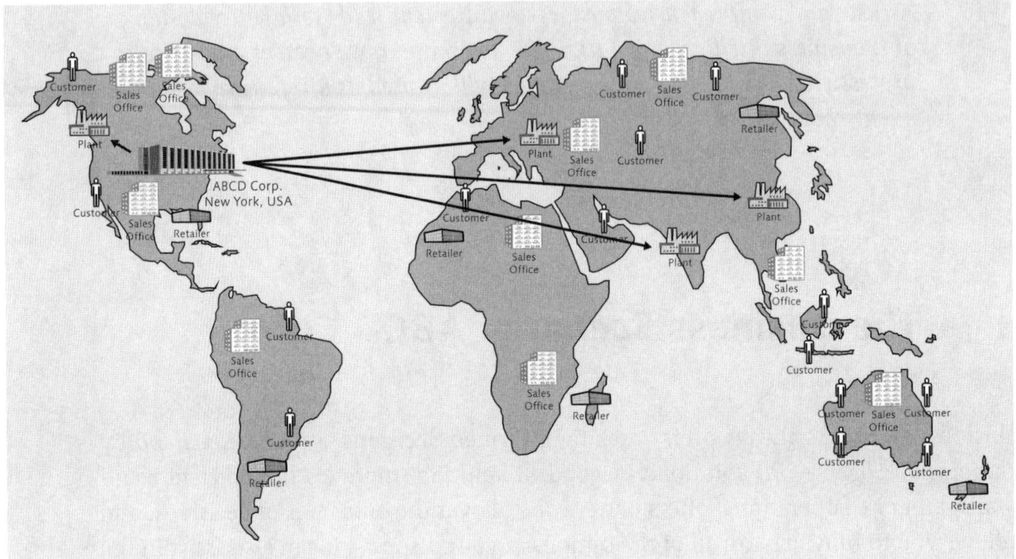

Figure 1.1 Overview of ABCD Corp.

1.2 Marketing Network

ABCD Corp. has more than 90 worldwide customers, which are either retail chains or independent stores (see Table A.3 in Appendix A, Case Study: ABCD Corp.). The company has three main markets — North America, Europe, and Asia-Pacific — and each market has one or more regional marketing offices. Within the US, the customers are grouped by states; outside the US, they are grouped under their respective country or city (e.g., London). ABCD Corp. has sales offices in most cities where customers are located, and the sales offices report to their corresponding regional marketing office. Figure 1.2 shows a hierarchy of the marketing network.

Each sales office has one or more salesperson, and each customer is serviced by a specific salesperson who maintains regular contact with his customers, mainly for the purpose of taking *sales orders* from them. Whenever an order is placed, a *sales transaction* is created in the SAP system located at the sales office. The salesperson then contacts his sales office with the details of the order. If the regular sales office is closed, the salesman contacts a sales office in a nearby country to ensure on-time delivery to the customer. Salespeople are rotated from customer to customer after a certain period of time or after the achievement of set target sales.

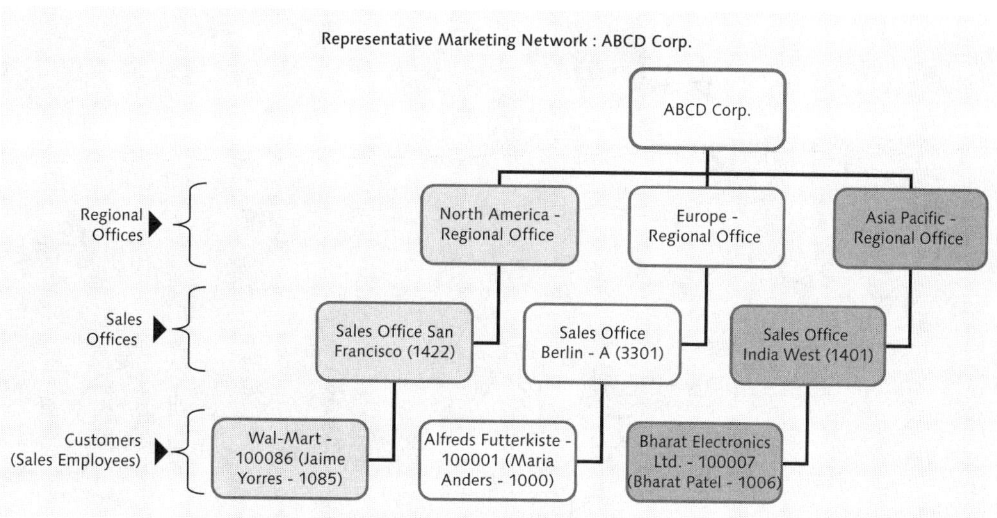

Figure 1.2 Overview of ABCD Corp. Marketing Network

ABCD Corp. has more than 30 products, which are logically grouped into 3 portfolios: Consumer Electronics, Domestic Appliances, and Consumer Lifestyle (see Table A.7 in Appendix A). The company has four manufacturing plants to supply these products (see Table A.2 in Appendix A).

1.3 The Sales and Billing Process

ABCD Corp. sells it products through two different *selling channels*: either *directly* or through the *Internet*. Product sales happen via a *billing document*; a typical flow of information generated by the creation of a billing document is illustrated in Figure 1.3.

Each billing document is represented by a unique number. Within the billing document, one or more products is listed, each of which is identified with an *item number*. In addition to the item numbers, the billing document also lists the quantity sold and a selling price for each product. In most cases, ABCD Corp. receives payment for products sold when they are delivered to the customer; in some cases, larger customers are permitted to make delayed payments.

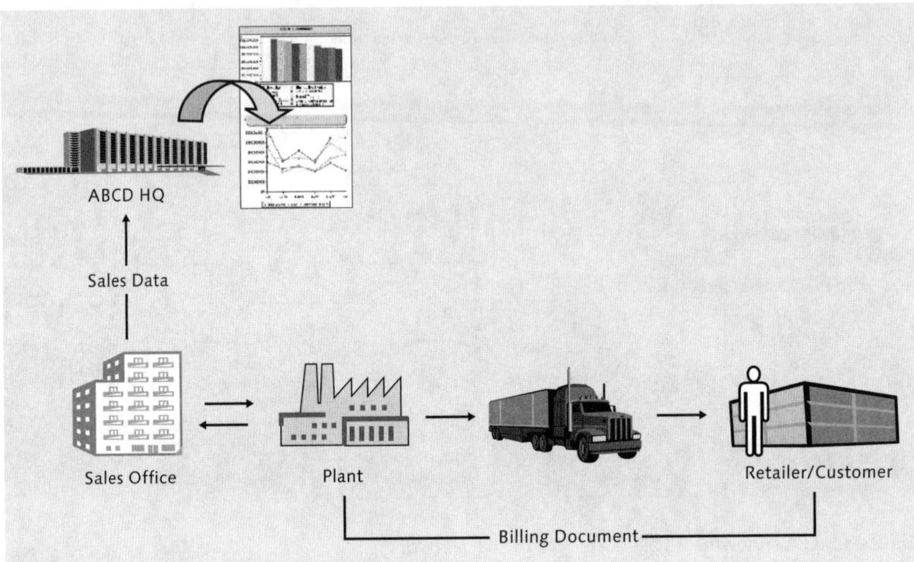

Figure 1.3 Overview of ABCD Corp. Selling Process

The *terms of payment* and *type of billing document* for transactions differ based on the method by which the transaction has taken place. For example, a specific type of billing document is generated if the customer makes the payment using a credit card or any other mode of delayed payment, and a different type of billing document is generated for immediate payments (see Table A.9 in Appendix A).

If the product is sold to a customer outside the US, the corresponding billing document is identified as an export; within the US, it is treated as a domestic sale (see Table A.10 in Appendix A).

Whenever the value of a record in the billing document is more than $10,000 USD, the transaction is identified as a *high-value transaction,* and the billing document is marked with an indicator to differentiate it from those with lower transaction values.

Similarly, if the cost of any item in the bill is listed without a value (i.e., is a free item), the system is designed to identify such a record separately (see Table A.11 in Appendix A). Normally, most items require payment; however, for special occasions (the holiday season, clearing sales, etc.), some low-value products (e.g., cords or batteries) are provided free with a bigger purchase. Such items are listed with an item category of DC, whereas normal items are identified with an item category of NOR. The cost of items under item category DC is recorded on the billing document, but taxes or other costs are not recorded.

Figure 1.4 shows a sample billing document for ABCD Corp.

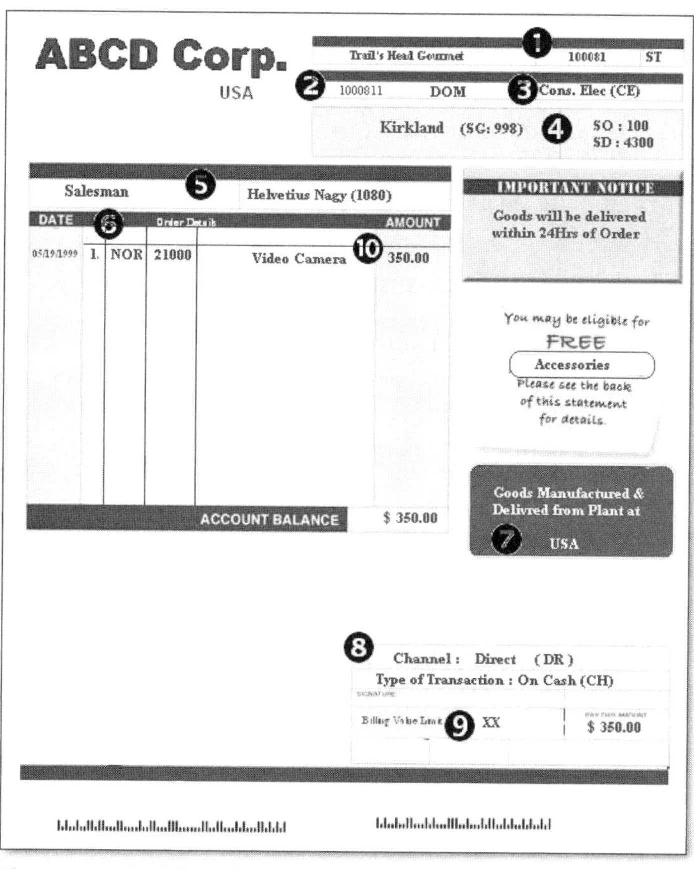

Figure 1.4 ABCD Corp. Sample Billing Document

The sample billing document shows how the business entities and processes are presented. Information such as customer name, customer code, and customer group are captured in ❶ of Figure 1.4; the billing document number and type of billing transaction are captured in ❷; and the product group is captured in ❸.

The billing document also provides information about the sales office, sales district, and sales group that services the customer. The name and code of the salesperson responsible for a specific sale is captured in ❺.

The product, product code, type of item, and product description is captured in ❻ of the figure. Information on the plant that manufactured and dispatched the product is captured in ❼. The type of transaction and selling channel are reflected on the lower section of the billing document (❽), as are the type of billing value and gross billing amount (❾). Finally, each item in the billing document has information such as quantity, cost, and net value in USD.

Returns

For product returns, a credit is issued to the customer. Each item in the return billing document has detailed information about the transaction, such as the quantity, cost, net value, and so on.

1.4 Business Intelligence Requirements

ABCD Corp. wants to have a global BI solution for sales analysis that accesses business transaction data from SAP (as the main data source) and Excel sheets, or *flat files* (as the secondary data source). The goal is to build a robust and scalable BI solution based on SAP NetWeaver BW that has reporting capabilities with the following guiding principles:

- Ease the management of the company at the corporate and local level through improved control and visibility.
- Move to a more digitalized company to support growth and enable quicker integration of new acquisitions.
- Increase return on investments by optimizing the cost and time spent on the design, deployment, and maintenance of the BI solution. Use SAP NetWeaver BW Business Content, which addresses a significant number of sales analysis requirements.

ABCD Corp. wants to analyze its sales process and find answers to the following types of questions:

- What products are selling in different sales organizations?
- Which product lines or specific products are selling highest or lowest?
- How do ABCD Corp.'s current year compare to the previous year?
- What are the top 10 best-selling products?

The *analysts* of ABCD Corp. require the solution to allow them to easily create their own reports when existing reports do not meet their reporting needs. The *auditors* of ABCD Corp. require the solution to provide traceability to specific billing documents for a customer when the need arises to analyze instances of variances; additionally, this sales document level investigation must be addressed in SAP NetWeaver BW, instead of in the transactional system. The *IT team* at ABCD Corp. requires the solution to be automated for most processes, including email alerts of successes or failures of systemic processes; they also require that the existing SAP R/3 system work at optimal efficiency by removing old data related to business-critical transactions from the OLTP (online transaction processing) system. The *head of planning* at ABCD Corp. requires the BI solution to compare actual and planned sales to ascertain and address the causes of variances or to correct plan figures.

In this book, the concept, design, and development of different SAP NetWeaver BW components are explained by using each of these requirements as examples.

1.5 The Business Planning Scenario

Within ABCD Corp., *sales planning* is an annual cycle for all three sales organizations: 1000 (APAC), 2000 (Europe), and 3000 (North America). Each sales organization projects sales figures according to three different divisions or product ranges: Consumer Electronics (CE), Daily Appliances (DA), and Consumer Lifestyle Appliances (CL). This is a high-level plan for the organization, and high-level values for each of the product ranges are transferred to different products belonging to these product ranges.

Each sales organization has a product range manager who is responsible for planning the sales of each product under his assigned product range. The plan for a year (January to December) is divided into quarters; thus, there are four planning periods: Quarter 1 (Q1), Quarter 2 (Q2), Quarter 3 (Q3), and Quarter 4 (Q4). Figure 1.5 is a graphical representation of this scenario.

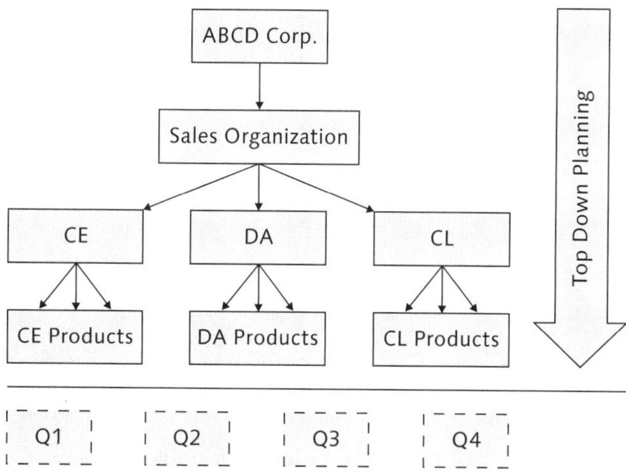

Figure 1.5 Overview of ABCD Corp. Sales Planning Process

This business scenario description should provide you with an understanding of ABCD Corp. and its sales process. In Appendix A, Case Study: ABCD Corp., we provide additional information in the form of tables, which have more details about the business scenario. These tables also include the specific SAP codes used to identify each element.

1.6 Summary

In this chapter, we explained a very basic business scenario for a typical company. We also explained the BI needs for this company, specifically those related to analyzing its sales process. While creating the scenario, we've addressed some aspects with more detail than others; those explained in detail relate to the realization of the technical requirements we discussed in Section 1.4, Business Intelligence Requirements, and are dealt with in subsequent chapters of this book. In the next chapter, we provide a brief overview of SAP NetWeaver BW.

This chapter describes the fundamental benefits of SAP NetWeaver BW as a business intelligence solution, unique aspects of its technical architecture, and different implementation options.

2 SAP NetWeaver Business Warehouse – Overview

Companies employ BI solutions to have visibility and control across their entities, functions, and business processes. This chapter discusses the evolution of SAP NetWeaver BW and its architectural layer, and then describes the basics of navigation within screens. More specifically, we cover the Data Warehousing Workbench (DWW) functions, the activation of SAP Business Content, and the implementation and architecture options of SAP NetWeaver BW. In its concluding section, the chapter lists additional channels of learning for SAP NetWeaver BW.

2.1 Evolution of SAP NetWeaver BW

Up to 1997, SAP had been maintaining and developing its reporting and analysis offerings within the core ERP solution, which included components such as Logistics Information System (LIS), Executive Information System (EIS), and Report Painter. In 1998, SAP launched the first version of product focused specifically on data warehousing and reporting, *Business Warehouse Information System*. Although it experienced several name changes along the way, it has now been integrated with SAP BusinessObjects and is called *SAP NetWeaver BW (SAP NetWeaver Business Warehouse)*. Figure 2.1 shows the evolution of SAP NetWeaver BW.

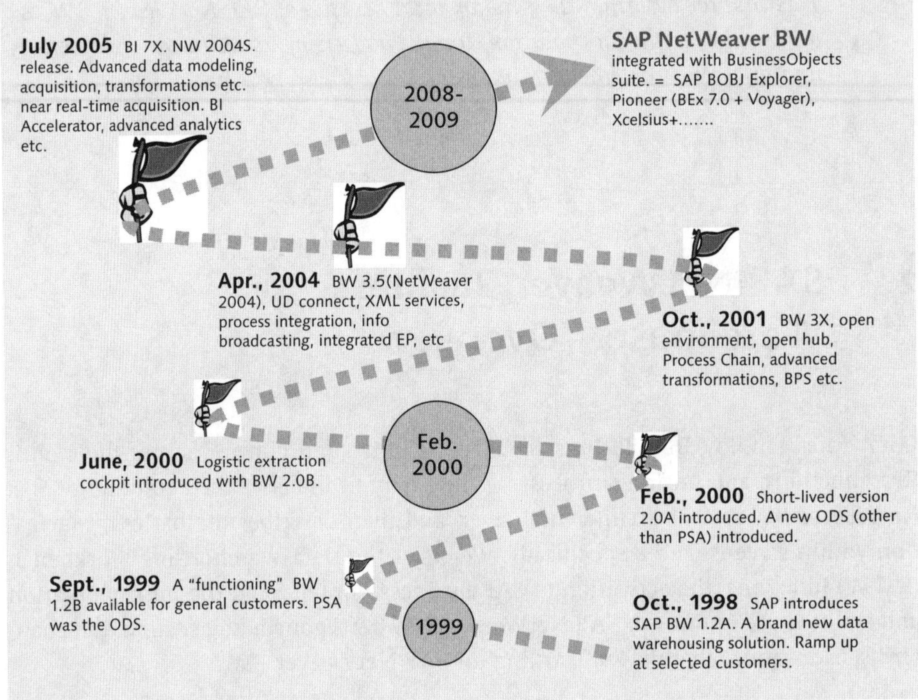

Figure 2.1 Evolution of SAP NetWeaver BW

As a portfolio of products, this state-of-the-art solution is meant to provide a closed loop and tighter integration among strategy, execution, and the ability to respond to results in real time; it's a leading BI solution that provides data warehousing capabilities on a comprehensive platform. Combining a scalable and layered architecture with a rich set of predefined business content, SAP NetWeaver BW is one of the best-of-breed BI solutions and provides the following:

- Tightly integrated and reliable data acquisition from all applications and business processes in the SAP Business Suite, including the ability to acquire data from heterogeneous sources (❶ of Figure 2.2).
- A strong online analytical processing (OLAP) capability, essential for a robust foundation for computing business data across dimensions and hierarchies. This also provides a strong framework for designing planning applications that are tightly integrated with the data warehouse.

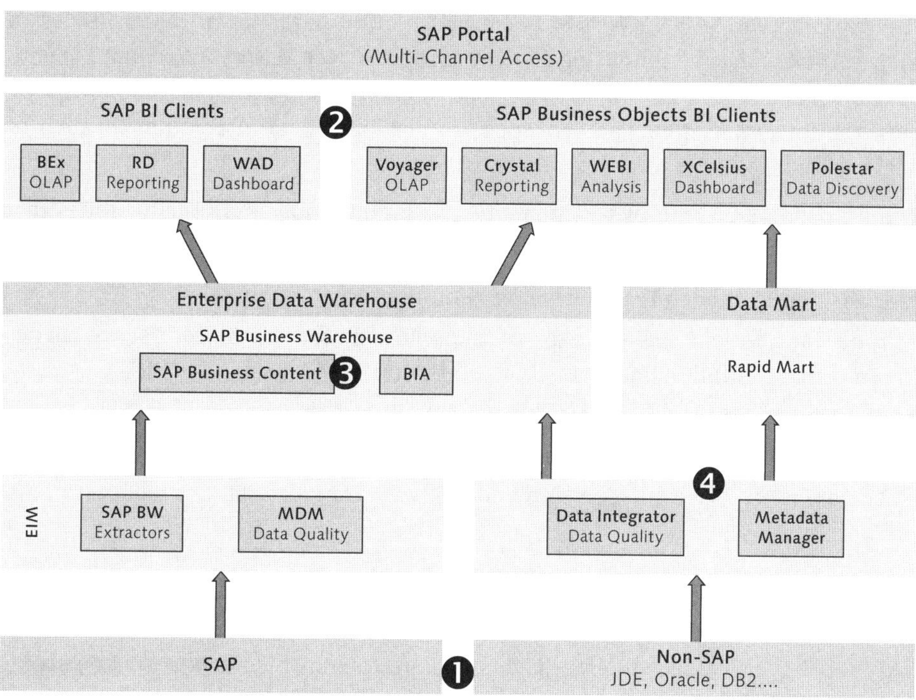

Figure 2.2 SAP NetWeaver BW Architecture and Positioning

- Business-driven models that help in rapid implementation through best practices and rich predefined business content across most industry and business processes (❸ of Figure 2.2).
- State-of-the-art lifecycle management functionality at three levels (❹ of Figure 2.2):
  - System lifecycle management
  - Metadata lifecycle management
  - Information lifecycle management
- Advanced tools and functionalities for optimized operations of administration and maintenance tasks; active push of critical events and actionable recommendations for recovery.

SAP Business Content

With a view to accelerate solution deployment and to offer best practices on industry-specific analytic scenarios, SAP delivers preconfigured end-to-end analytic solutions. All of the underlying components and objects necessary for preconfigured scenarios are also delivered as a collection. This collection of all of the preconfigured scenarios based on best practices and their components is provided as part of the *SAP Business Content solution*.

The advantages of SAP NetWeaver BW have led more and more customers to design their corporate data warehousing strategy using SAP NetWeaver BW, citing the end-to-end conception of SAP NetWeaver BW. In comparison to fragmented technologies, the integrated metadata concept spanning from data integration through to analysis leads to lower total costs for most projects.

The following are some of the high-end and unique tools and functionalities that SAP NetWeaver BW offers:

- User-friendly modeling and development interfaces
- Tools for efficient maintenance of the solution; for example, process chains, remodeling, Administration Cockpit, and so on
- Powerful ad-hoc analysis tools; for example, BEx web analyzer
- Integrated Planning, which assists with a closed-loop planning process
- The ability to perform reporting and analysis from a portal as well as from an Excel interface

2.2 Layers of SAP NetWeaver BW

SAP NetWeaver BW has different layers that are responsible for reliable data acquisition and information processing, along with robust analytical capabilities (Figure 2.3).

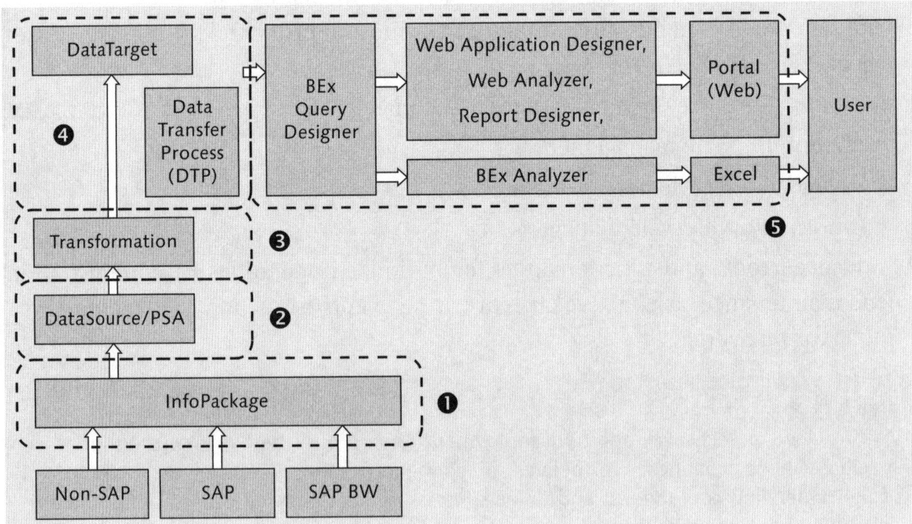

Figure 2.3 Layers Within SAP NetWeaver BW

Based on the functions and applications in the solution, the different layers in SAP NetWeaver BW are listed here:

- Extraction layer
- Staging layer
- Transformation layer
- Loading layer
- Reporting and analysis layer
- Planning and advanced analytics layer

Each of these layers and its function are explained next.

2.2.1 Extraction Layer

The extraction layer (❶ of Figure 2.3) is related to the *extraction process*, which is the collection of data from source systems. It aims to guarantee the integrity of data while eliminating reporting burdens on the source systems. As previously mentioned, SAP NetWeaver BW is capable of acquiring data from a wide spectrum of sources, such as the following:

- **Extraction from SAP systems**
  SAP NetWeaver BW offers predefined, customizable extractors for application data from the entire SAP Business Suite; you can also design extractors for customized SAP applications. Most extractors for SAP application transaction data are delta-enabled, which means that transactions can be written to a delta queue at the time of posting. They are then extracted from this delta queue into SAP NetWeaver BW.
- **Direct extraction from databases**
  These databases are based on table or view definitions using DB Connect and UD Connect extraction interfaces.
  - **DB Connect (Database Connect):** DB Connect permits the extraction from and direct access to data lying in tables or views of database management systems. This feature is available only for some specific databases.
  - **UD Connect (Universal Data Connect):** UD Connect permits the extraction from and direct access to both relational and multidimensional data.
- **Web services**
  These services allow you to push data to the SAP NetWeaver BW system with external control.
- **Flat file interface**
  This interface enables extraction from flat files in ASCII and CSV format.

- **Staging BAPIs (Staging Business Application Programming Interfaces)**
  Staging BAPIs are open interfaces from which third-party tools can extract data from older systems. The data transfer can be triggered by a request from the SAP NetWeaver BW system or by a third-party tool.

Data Extraction Modes

When the data is being extracted into the data warehouse by action triggered on the data warehouse, it's called pull mode; when the data is being exported by the source system based on a trigger outside of the data warehouse, it's called push mode.

Data is acquired from SAP NetWeaver BW using a pull mode, through objects called *InfoPackages*. Parameters for the data acquisition can be set in the InfoPackage. The extraction process is discussed in more detail in Chapters 7, Extraction, Transformation, and Loading, and 8, Extraction from an SAP Source System.

2.2.2 Staging Layer

Extracted data is received and temporarily stored in the *staging layer* of SAP NetWeaver BW (❷ of Figure 2.3). The data staging layer primarily serves the following purposes:

- Stores source data from different operational sources. All needed transformations can then occur without interfering with the operations in the source systems.
- Preprocesses data for cleansing before calculation and/or aggregation based on business requirements.

This layer is mostly represented by the *persistent staging area (PSA)*, where data is stored in SAP NetWeaver BW after it's extracted. The technical structure of a PSA depends on the structure of the DataSource. More details about PSA and staging are discussed in Chapter 7.

2.2.3 Transformation Layer

The transformation layer of SAP NetWeaver BW (❸ of Figure 2.3) facilitates the consolidation, cleaning, and integration of data to synchronize it technically and semantically. It converts data from the source data format into the desired destination data format. Data transformation can involve data mapping, the application of a custom transformation program, and formulas. We cover transformation in detail in Chapter 7.

2.2.4 Loading Layer

The process of adding transformed data to data targets is called the *loading process* (❹ of Figure 2.3). A data transform process (DTP) transforms the data based on the parameters defined between the DataSource and the data target. For more details on DTPs and loading, see Chapter 7.

2.2.5 Reporting and Analysis Layer

The *reporting and analysis layer* (❺ of Figure 2.3) is where data is presented in different forms, such as reports and dashboards (Figure 2.4). This layer allows you to perform analysis on the data stored in SAP NetWeaver BW. Various components that represent the reporting and analysis layer in SAP NetWeaver BW are grouped together as SAP Business Explorer (BEx) components. The reporting and analysis layer is discussed in more detail in Chapters 9, BEx Query Designer, and 10, Reporting and Analysis.

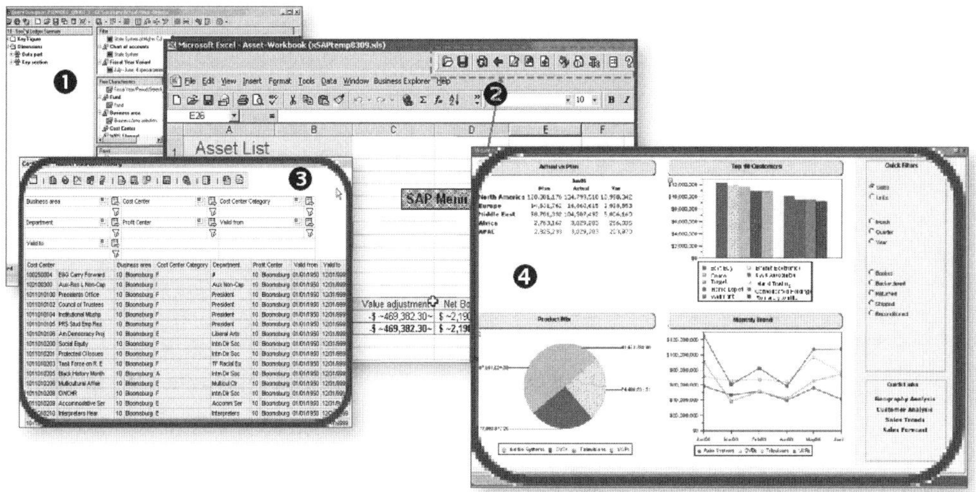

Figure 2.4 Reporting and Analysis in SAP NetWeaver BW

2.2.6 Planning and Advanced Analytics Layer

This layer consists of two different solutions that are integrated in SAP NetWeaver BW to perform planning activities and advanced analysis:

- **Integrated Planning**
  This component allows you to create planning applications (❶ of Figure 2.5) that

are integrated with reporting and analysis functions. The detail modeling and planning methods are designed to be multidimensional, so they are also very flexible.

- **Analysis Process Designer (APD)**
  This component allows you to perform advanced analysis (❷ of Figure 2.5), such as data mining.

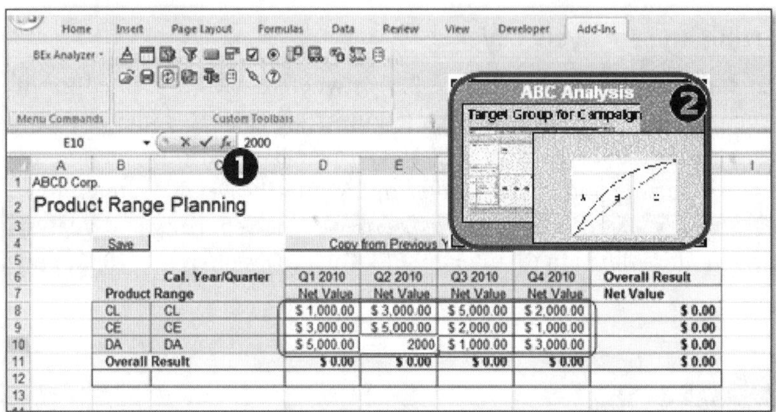

Figure 2.5 Planning and Advanced Analytics in SAP NetWeaver BW

> **Data Mining**
>
> *Data mining* is the process of automatically determining significant patterns and hidden associations in large amounts of data.

APD offers the following data mining capabilities:

- **Decision trees**
  Decision trees display data using (noncontinuous) category quantities. The display rules are determined in training using those sections of historic data where the assignment to categories is already known.
- **Clustering**
  Clustering is used to split data into homogeneous groups. The model looks for a global structure for the data, with the aim of partitioning the data into clusters.
- **Association analysis**
  Association analysis is the search for associations among objects with comparable information content. Statements are formulated about partial structures in the data, and take the form of rules. In contrast to decision tree classification, clustering and association analysis determine the models using data itself. One of the uses of association analysis is to identify cross-selling opportunities.

- **Scoring and weighted score tables**
  In *scoring*, data is displayed using continuous quantities, which allow you to split the data into classes (if needed). The scoring function can either be specified using weighted score tables or determined by using historic data.
- **ABC classification**
  ABC classification displays data grouped into classes (A, B, C, etc.) using thresholds and classification rules. The classified results are displayed in the form of an ABC chart or list.

2.3 Basic Navigation in SAP NetWeaver BW

In this section, we explain how to navigate within SAP NetWeaver BW, including logging on to the system, screen elements, and basic navigation functions in the Data Warehousing Workbench (DWW). We also introduce some specific *terms* used in subsequent chapters of the book.

2.3.1 Logging On to SAP NetWeaver BW

To log on to an SAP NetWeaver BW system, you must have a valid user ID and password, along with the appropriate SAP GUI (graphical user interface) version loaded on your PC. The illustrations used in this book are based on SAP GUI for Windows. Follow these steps to log on to SAP NetWeaver BW.

1. From the Windows START menu, follow the path PROGRAMS • SAP FRONT END • SAP LOGON. You see the SAP logon pad, as shown in Figure 2.6.

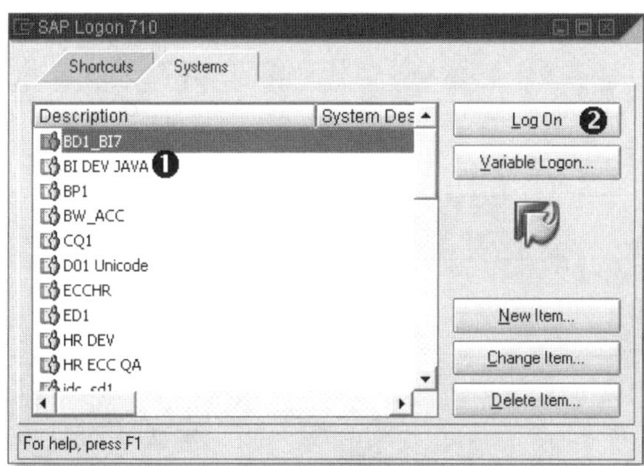

Figure 2.6 SAP Logon Pad

2. The SAP logon pad displays the SAP systems configured for access on your Windows system; select the SAP NetWeaver BW system you want to access (❶ of Figure 2.6).
3. Click on the Log On button (❷ of Figure 2.6), and you'll get the SAP Logon screen, as shown in Figure 2.7.

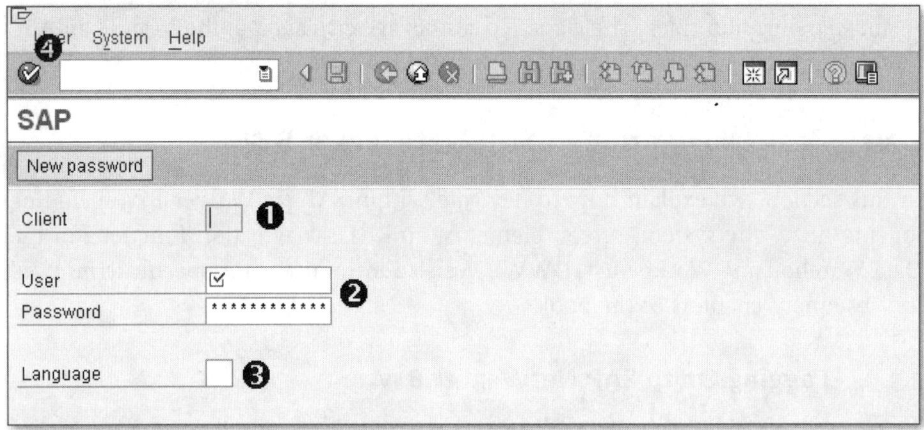

Figure 2.7 SAP Logon Screen

4. Enter the values for the Client field (❶ of Figure 2.7), your user ID and password (❷), and language (❸). All of these values are required and should be available from the administrator of your SAP NetWeaver BW system. Press ENTER, or click on the Continue icon (❹) to log on. A successful logon brings you to Figure 2.8.

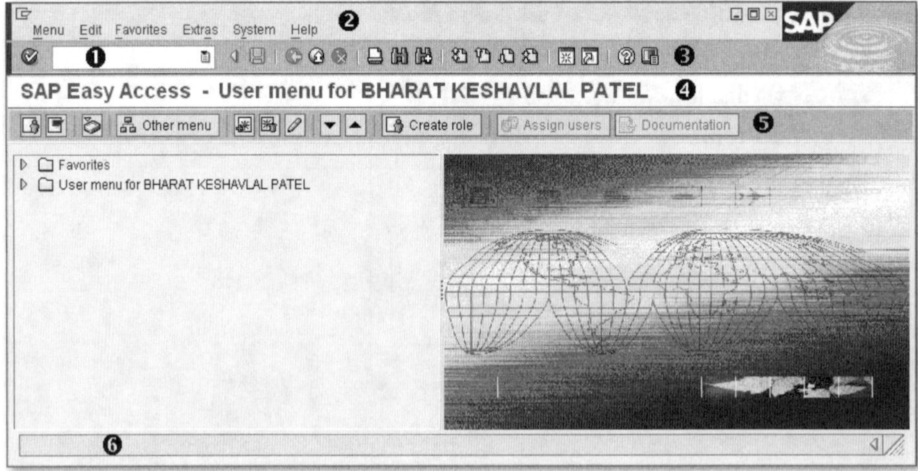

Figure 2.8 SAP Easy Access Screen

Always log off when you've completed your work. To log off, follow the menu path SYSTEM • LOG OFF. You can also use Transaction /NEX.

2.3.2 Screen Elements

The initial screen displayed after logon is known as the SAP Easy Access screen (though this default screen can be changed and customized). The SAP Easy Access screen can contain the following simple screen elements:

- **Command field**
  You can start applications directly by entering the specific transaction code in the command field (❶ of Figure 2.8). Type the code, and press ENTER.

Transaction Code

A *transaction code* gives you a shortcut for accessing an application and is used as an alternative to a menu path. For example, you can call DWW in SAP NetWeaver BW using SAP MENU • INFORMATION SYSTEMS • BUSINESS INFORMATION WAREHOUSE • MODELING • DATA WAREHOUSING WORKBENCH : MODELING — or you can simply call Transaction RSA1 in the command field.

- **Menu bar**
  Different menu functions are available in the menu bar of the SAP screen (❷ of Figure 2.8). The menus shown can change depending on the application you're using. These menus may also contain cascading menus.
- **Standard toolbar**
  The standard toolbar buttons are shown on every SAP screen. Not all of the buttons shown on a standard toolbar are available at all times; depending on the context, the button may be deactivated (❸).
- **Title bar (dynamic menu bar)**
  The title bar displays the function you're currently using (❹).
- **Application toolbar**
  The application toolbar shows the function buttons available in the current application (❺).
- **Status bar**
  The status bar provides general information on the SAP system and transaction or task you're working on. The left side of the bar contains warnings and errors (❻); the right side contains status information. The status information on the status bar can be hidden or displayed using the COLLAPSE/EXPAND icon.

2.3.3 Basic Navigation Functions

The Data Warehousing Workbench (DWW) is the central tool for developer and administrators (Figure 2.9). You can create, maintain, monitor, and administer SAP NetWeaver BW objects using DWW.

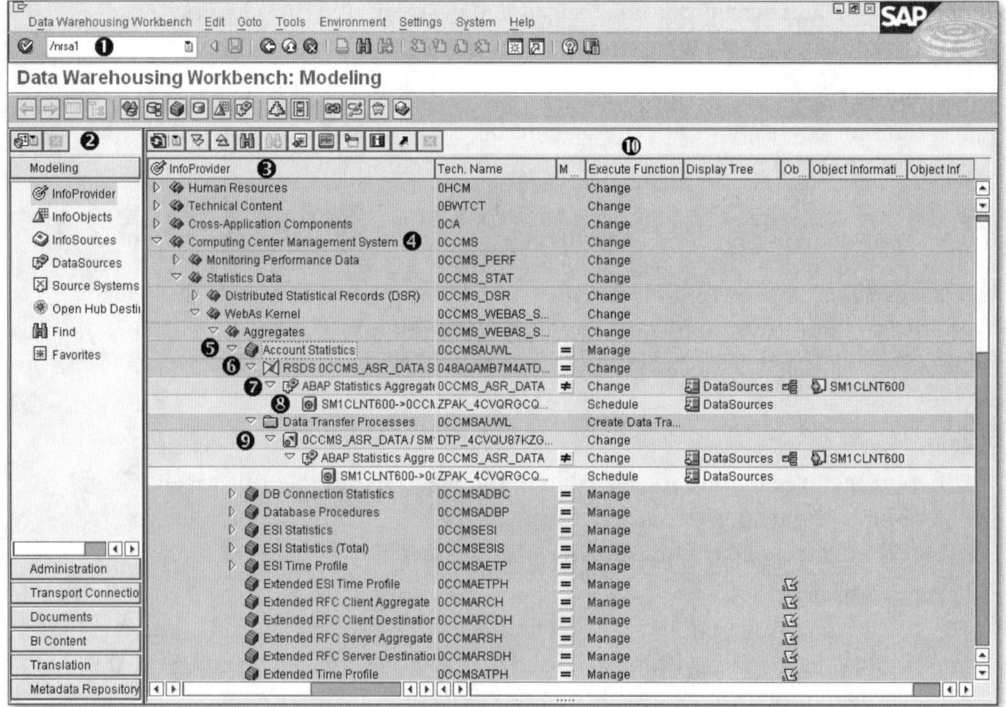

Figure 2.9 The Data Warehousing Workbench

To start the Data Warehousing Workbench, enter Transaction RSA1 in the command field (❶ of Figure 2.9).

/N and /O in Transaction Codes

When you want to call a transaction while you're already working in a transaction, preface the transaction code by either "/N" or "/O." Using the former opens the new transaction in the same session (i.e., the same window); the latter opens the new transaction in a new session (i.e., a new window).

Executing Transaction RSA1 calls DWW (Figure 2.9). The screen is divided into two panels; the left panel (❷) is known as the *navigator section*, and the right panel is known as the *tree* section (❸).

Following are the different options available under the navigator:

- Modeling
- Administration
- Transport Connection
- Documents
- BI Content
- Translation
- Metadata Repository

The tree on the right side of the screen is refreshed based on the option selected in the navigator.

By default, DWW opens with the Modeling option. Different suboptions are available under Modeling, which are different types of objects that can be modeled in DWW. If you select the InfoProvider option, the right side displays the InfoProvider tree (❸ of Figure 2.9), which consists of different objects associated with InfoProviders. Each object has a description and a unique technical name. In SAP NetWeaver BW, different icons are used to represent different objects. Some of these icons are shown in Figure 2.10.

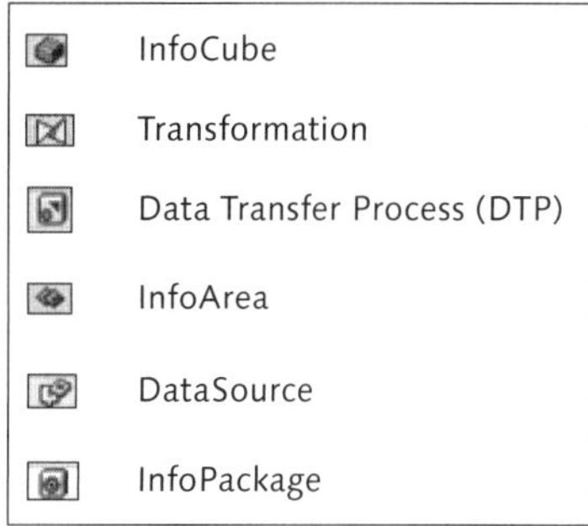

Figure 2.10 Icons for Various Objects in DWW

The InfoProvider tree displayed in Figure 2.9 illustrates the InfoProvider hierarchy. For example, the InfoArea with the *description* "Computer Center Management System" has the *technical name* "0CCMS" (❹ of Figure 2.9). All of the objects related to this InfoArea are displayed under it in a hierarchical fashion, which is an arrangement known as *nesting InfoAreas*. InfoAreas can be nested at multiple levels; under the Aggregates InfoArea, for example, the Account Statistics *InfoCube* (technical name: 0CCMSAUWL) is created as shown in ❺ of Figure 2.9. In other words, we can say that InfoCube 0CCMSAUWL is attached to the Aggregates InfoArea. This InfoCube is a part of the data flow in SAP NetWeaver BW, and all objects related to the InfoCube are displayed under it. The objects marked with ❻, ❼, ❽, and ❾ of Figure 2.9 show the visual data flow from a DataSource to an InfoCube.

Each object supports various functions that you can maintain and configure. To call the list of various functions available for an object, select the object, and call the context menu. The most common function for each object type is available under the Execute Function column in the tree section (❿ of Figure 2.9). You can see that Manage is the most common function available for InfoCubes, whereas Change is the most common function for InfoAreas. By double-clicking an object, you can start the default function available for that object.

When you double-click on InfoCube 0CCMSAUWL, a third panel opens up to the right of the tree section, as shown in Figure 2.11. This third panel shows you the object-specific settings and definitions.

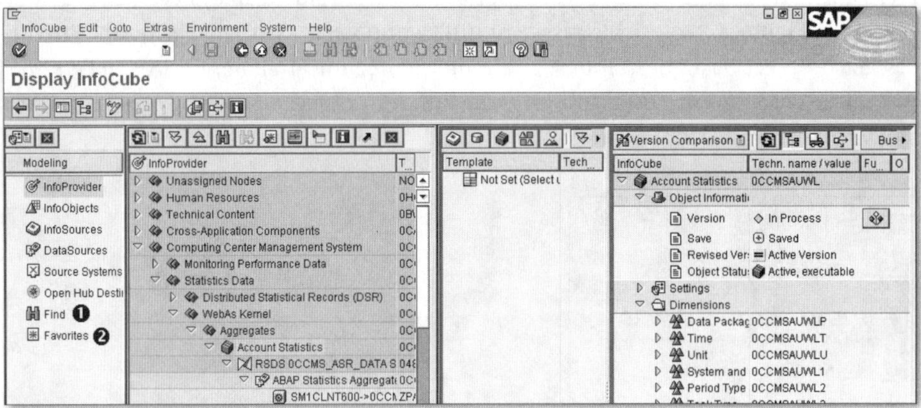

Figure 2.11 Navigation in DWW

Now that you have a basic understanding of how DWW works, let's examine three specific functions it offers: hide/unhide, find/search, and favorites.

2.3.4 Hide/Unhide

You have the option of hiding or unhiding the navigator or tree. These settings are visible after clicking the Setting List icon (icon) (Figure 2.12). Hiding the navigator or tree after navigation is useful if you want to free up some of the display space on the screen (Figure 2.13).

The other option is to hide the tree after navigation. When you double-click on an InfoCube, the tree panel is hidden, as shown in Figure 2.14.

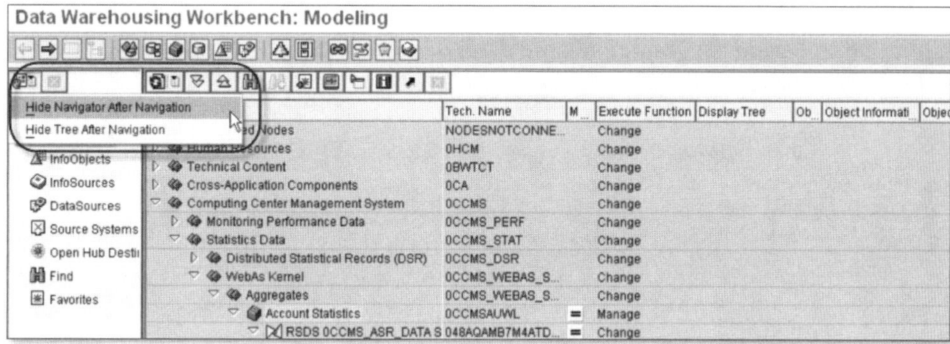

Figure 2.12 Hide/Unhide Navigator

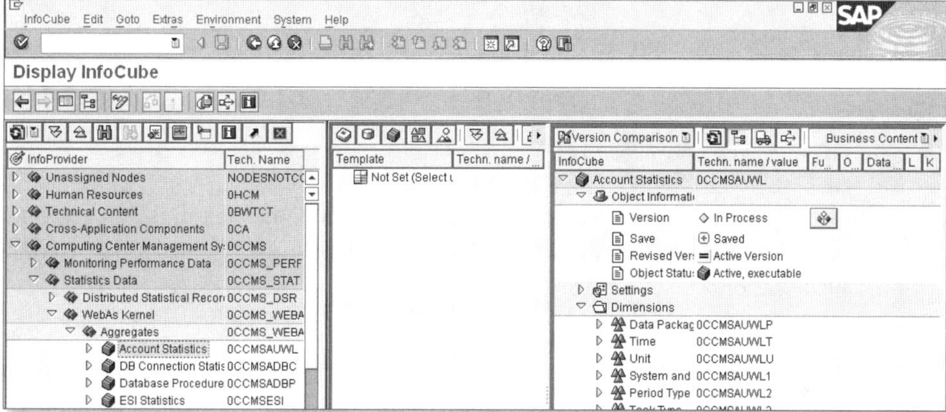

Figure 2.13 Hidden Navigator

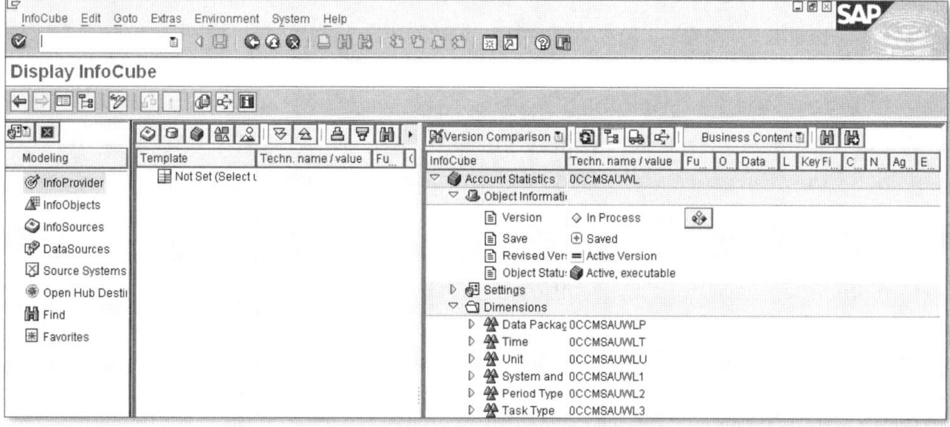

Figure 2.14 Hidden Tree

When you double-click on an InfoCube with both options selected, both the navigator and tree panel are hidden (Figure 2.15).

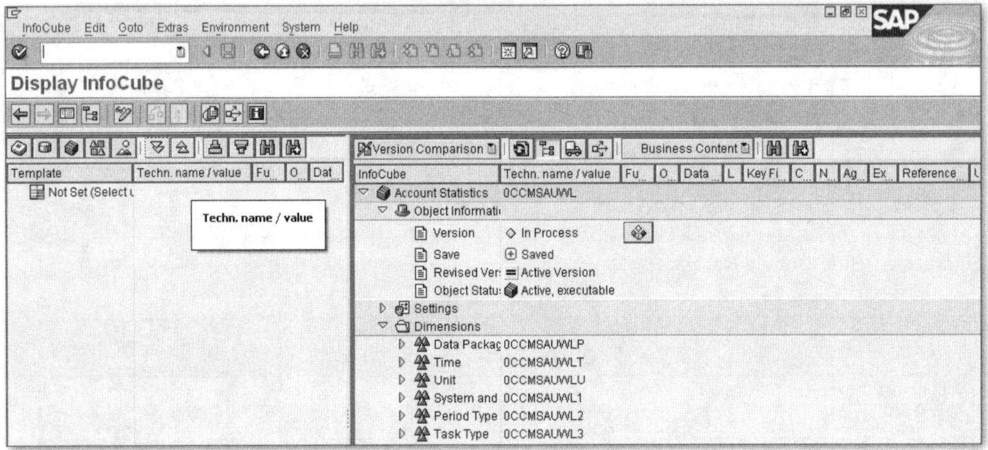

Figure 2.15 Hidden Navigator and Tree

The hide option selected is saved for you in the system. Other features that are very useful while navigating in DWW are Find/Search and Favorites, which are discussed in the next section.

Find/Search

You can find or search objects in DWW by using their technical names or descriptions. Two different options are available for this purpose; the first (the search method) allows you to search for a selected object type from the navigator.

1. Click on the type of object you want to search, as shown in ❶ of Figure 2.16. In the example here, we are searching for InfoCube 0CRM_SALO, so we've selected InfoProvider under Modeling.
2. Click on the Search icon, as shown in ❷ of Figure 2.16. SAP NetWeaver BW displays the Object Search in Tree box, as shown in Figure 2.16.
3. Type the technical name or description of the object you want to search for in the Find box (❸), and indicate which object you're searching for (❹). If you want, restrict your search to an InfoProvider or InfoArea (❺).
4. Click on Search (❻).

If an object is found, it's displayed in DWW; otherwise, an appropriate message is displayed in the status bar.

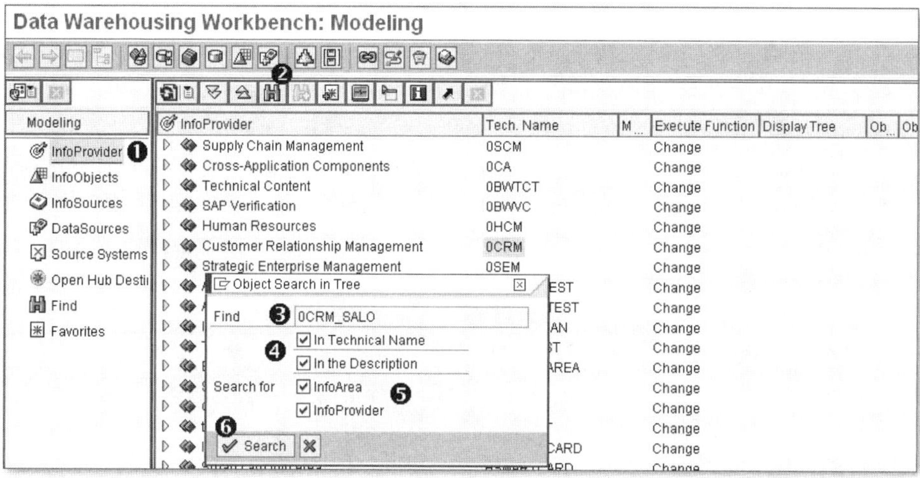

Figure 2.16 Searching Objects in DWW

The second option (the find method) uses the Find option under the Modeling section of the navigator. It allows you to search across all object types at once.

1. Click on Find under the Modeling section of the navigator (Figure 2.16). SAP NetWeaver BW displays a General Search in the Data Warehousing Workbench pop-up box, as shown in Figure 2.17.

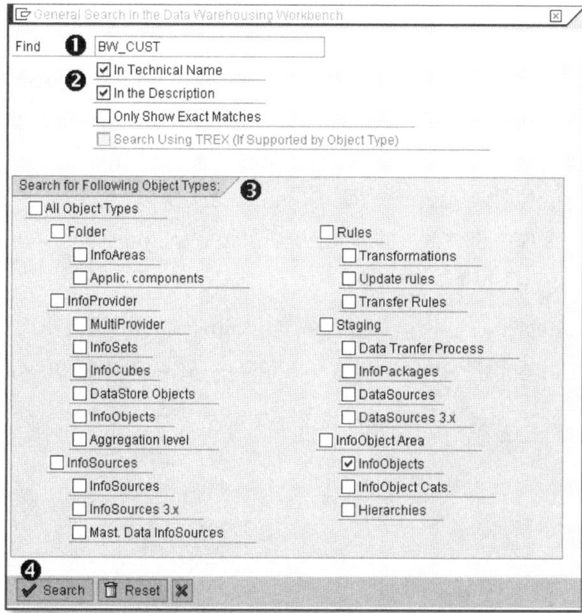

Figure 2.17 General Search in Data Warehousing Workbench

2. Type the technical name or description of the object you're trying to search, as shown in ❶ of Figure 2.17.
3. Select the checkbox indicating whether you want to restrict your search to the technical name or description (❷).
4. If you don't know what kind of object you're searching for, select All Object Types. If you do know the object type, tick the appropriate checkbox (❸).
5. Click on the Search icon (❹). SAP NetWeaver BW shows the result of this search, as shown in Figure 2.18.

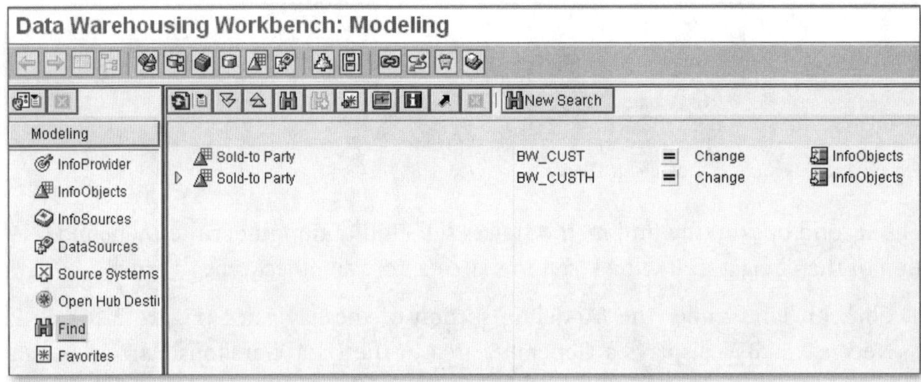

Figure 2.18 Search Results

Favorites

Many objects are available in the SAP NetWeaver BW system, and you'll probably only work with a few at a time. The favorites functionality helps you keep your most commonly used objects in one area. To use this functionality, follow these steps:

1. Select the object you want to mark as a favorite (❶ of Figure 2.19).
2. Click on Add Object to Favorites (❷). SAP NetWeaver BW displays a message stating that the object has been added to the Favorites list.

To view the objects in this list, click on Favorites under Modeling (Figure 2.20). If required, you can also remove the objects by opening the context menu and selecting Delete Object from Favorites.

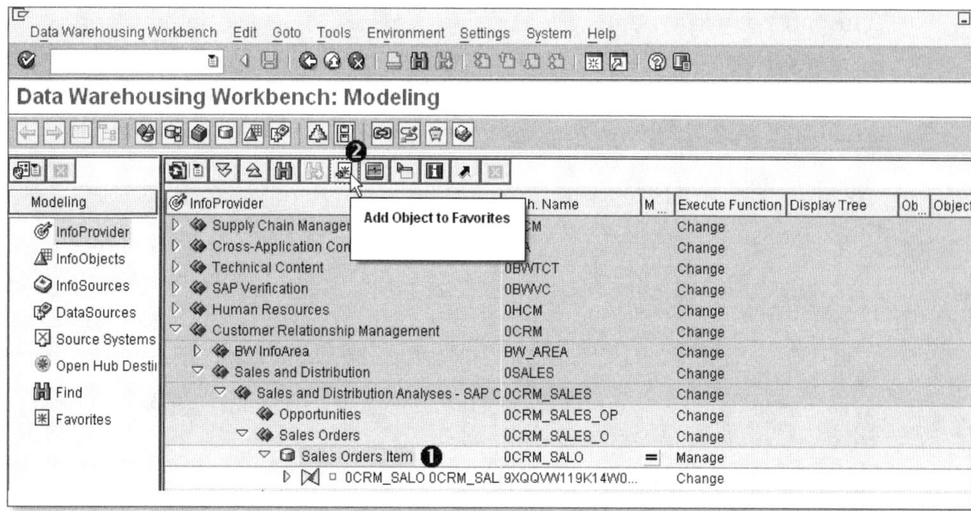

Figure 2.19 Adding an Object to Favorites

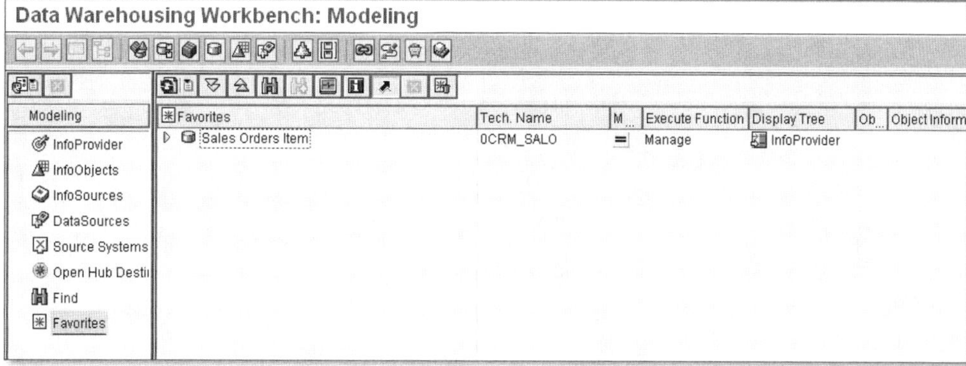

Figure 2.20 Objects Available Under Favorites

2.4 Data Warehousing Workbench Functions

As stated earlier, the Data Warehousing Workbench (DWW) is the central tool for designers and administrators of SAP NetWeaver BW. In this section, we explain the various functionalities available in DWW.

The initial screen of DWW is shown in Figure 2.21 (Transaction RSA1). The sections available in DWW are listed here:

- Modeling (❶)
- Administration (❷)

- Transport Connection (❸)
- Documents (❹)
- BI Content (❺)
- Translation (❻)
- Metadata Repository (❼)

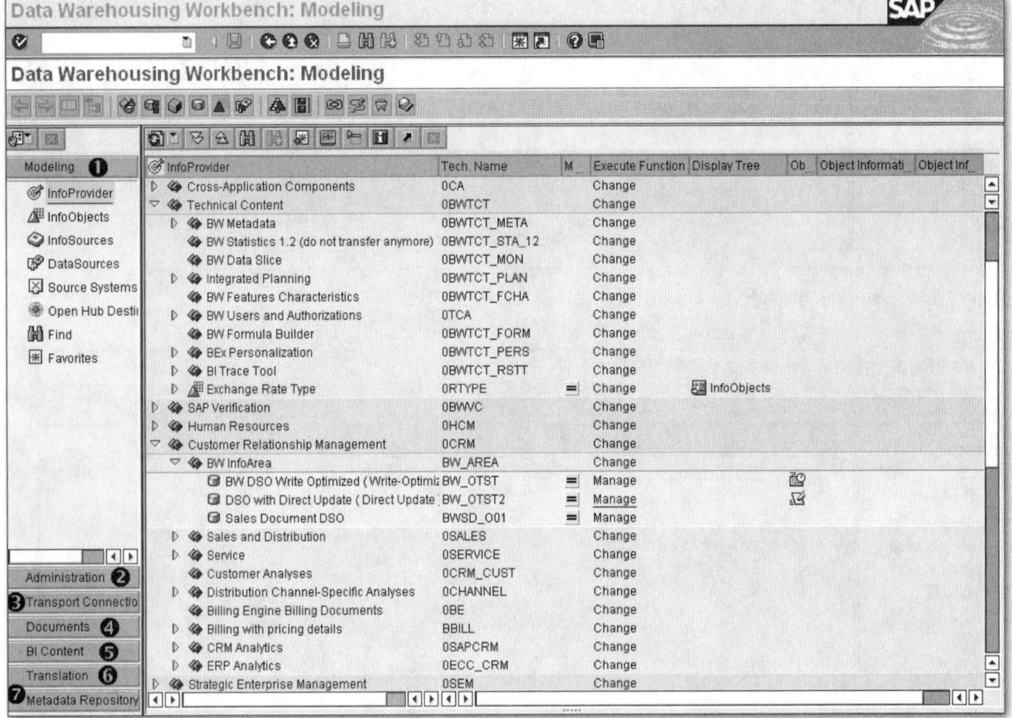

Figure 2.21 Various Functionalities in DWW

The following list explains these functionalities in more detail:

- **Modeling**
  Modeling is a very important section of DWW because it's used for the creation and modification of almost all SAP NetWeaver BW objects, including *InfoObjects, InfoObject catalogs, InfoAreas, InfoCubes, DataStore objects, MultiProviders, InfoSets, InfoSources, DataSources, transfer rules, update rules, transformations, data transfer processes, source systems, open hub objects,* and so on.
- **Administration**
  All of the administrative activities related to SAP NetWeaver BW are combined under this section, including the ability to monitor the data loading process.

Other functions, such as remodeling, repartitioning, and analyzing, are also available here. For complex loading and monitoring of data from multiple sources, SAP NetWeaver BW delivers a tool called *process chain*. Creation and monitoring the process chain is done using the Process Chain option under the Administration section.

- **Transport Connection**
  The design and creation of SAP NetWeaver BW objects is done in the SAP NetWeaver BW development system. After initial testing is complete, the objects are moved to the quality assurance (QA) system for integration testing. This process of moving objects from one system to another is known as *transport*. After integration testing is completed in the QA system, the objects are transported to the production system, which is accessed by end users. The transport connection functionality helps to collect required objects in a transport request, which is then transported to the target system using the Change and Transport Organizer (CTO) tool.
- **Documents**
  You may be required to attach comments to your query output (i.e., your report) that can be viewed by you and other users. This is accomplished by using the Documents functionality (which also allows you to create different versions of the same document). The search functionality is available for retrieving attached documents.
- **BI Content**
  Preconfigured information models based on metadata are available under the BI Content section (note: SAP sometimes refers to Business Content as BI Content), which helps shorten SAP NetWeaver BW project timelines by eliminating the need to create everything from scratch. These objects are marked with a D (for "delivered"); before using them, you must activate them using the activation process (see Section 2.5). Activated objects are available for use, as well as for building your own information models. Activated SAP Business Content can be used in the following ways in SAP NetWeaver BW.
- **Translation**
  Each object in SAP NetWeaver BW contains a technical name and description (short and long text), and the translation functionality helps to translate this text into multiple languages.
- **Metadata Repository**
  All SAP NetWeaver BW objects (those delivered by SAP Business Content as well as those already active in the system), their related objects, and links among these objects, are stored in the Metadata Repository. This is a good place to study SAP Business Content (in delivered status) before activating them. The Metadata

Repository also offers search functionality that allows you to search for a particular object. Finally, you can exchange metadata between different systems and list metadata in HTML pages.

Metadata

Metadata is information about data. For example, the technical name and description of a table that contains data is known as the metadata for that table. Similarly, for a specific field in the table, information such as name, size, data type, and so on represent the metadata for that field.

2.5 Activation of SAP Business Content

SAP Business Content plays a crucial role in any SAP NetWeaver BW project. In this section, we explain the process of activating SAP Business Content. Start DWW using Transaction RSA1, and click on BI Content, as shown in ❶ of Figure 2.22.

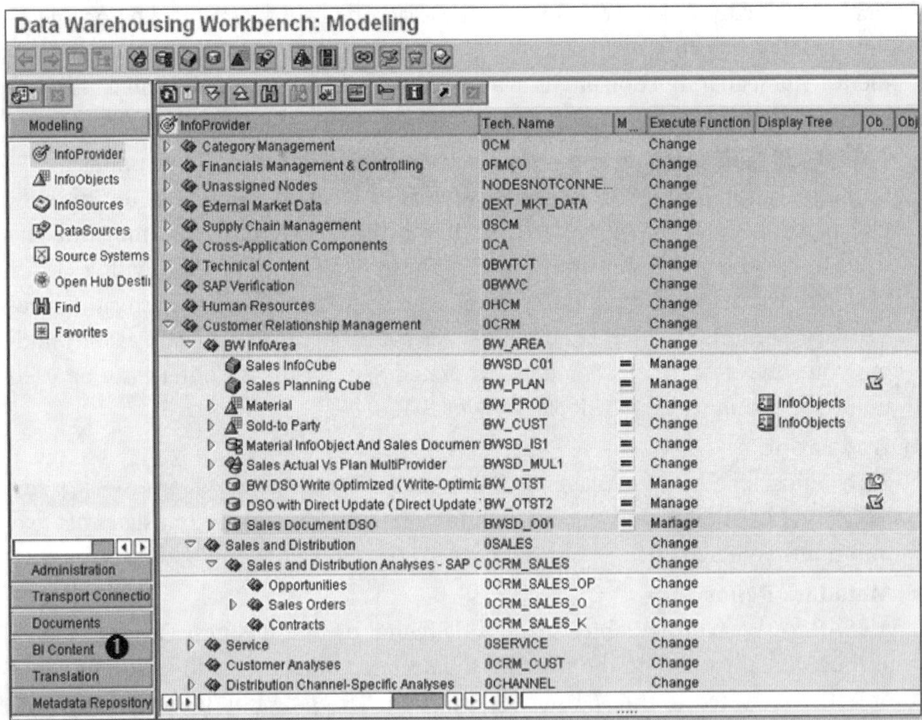

Figure 2.22 Starting Business Content

As shown in ❶ of Figure 2.23, various options are listed under BI Content. The various options allow you to select objects in an effective manner. The right panel shows the screen for collected objects (❷).

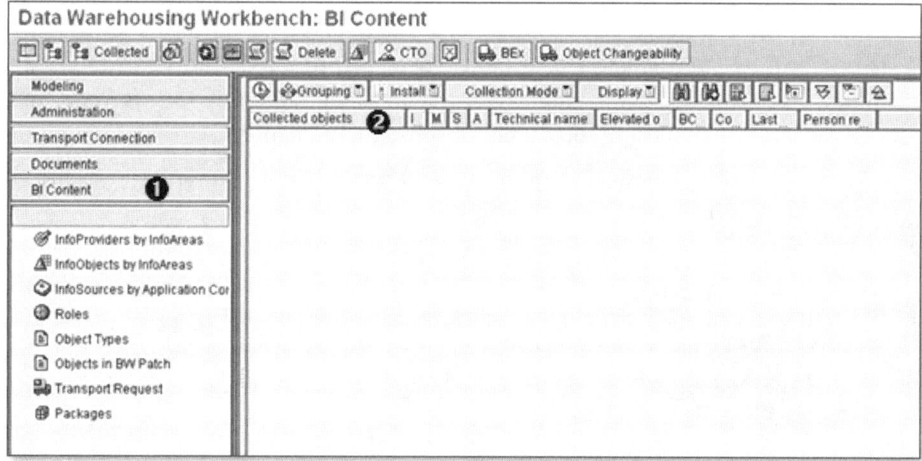

Figure 2.23 BI Content Initial Screen

When you click on InfoProviders by InfoArea, the screen shown in Figure 2.24 appears.

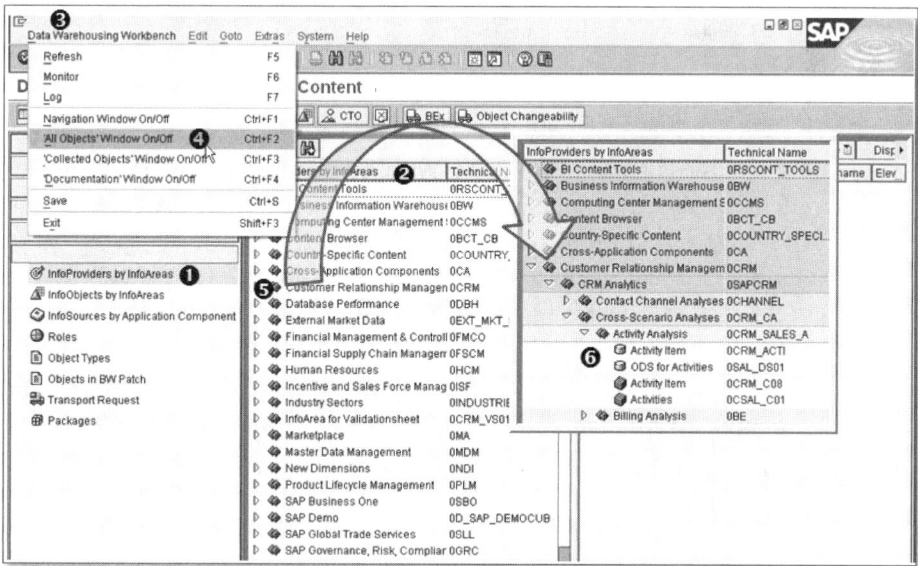

Figure 2.24 Selecting InfoProviders by InfoArea

As shown in ❶ of Figure 2.24, the selected option is now highlighted. On the right side, one more panel — InfoProvider by InfoAreas — opens up (❷). If you're unable to view this panel, click the Data WAREHOUSING WORKBENCH MENU, and select ALL OBJECTS WINDOW ON/OFF, as shown in ❸ and ❹.

All of the InfoAreas offered by SAP Business Content are listed in this panel. Expand *Customer Relationship Management (0CRM)* (❺ of Figure 2.24), and you can see an expanded tree structure displaying InfoAreas and data targets (❻). (InfoAreas and data targets are explained in more detail in subsequent chapters.)

Now click on Roles, as shown in ❶ of Figure 2.25. The right panel shows a list of roles offered by SAP Business Content (❷).

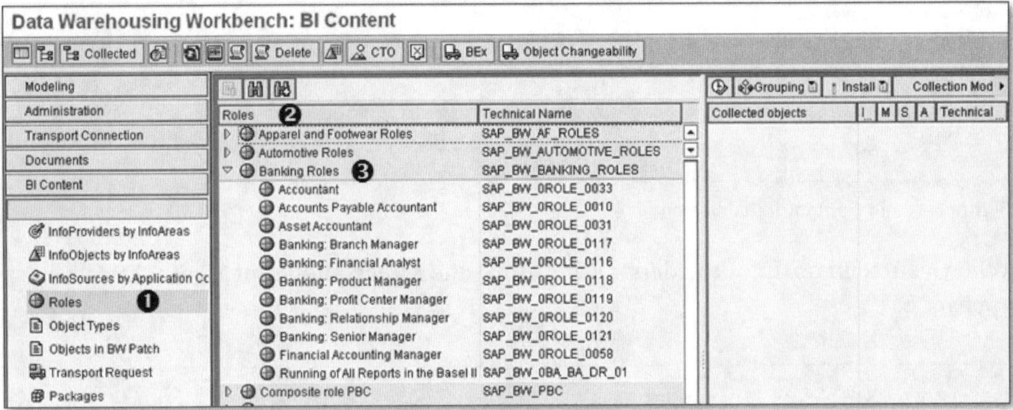

Figure 2.25 Business Content: Roles

SAP NetWeaver BW offers roles for different industries, for example, Apparel and Footwear, Automotive, Banking, and so on. Within industries, various roles are classified for different jobs; for example, some banking industry roles (❸) are accountant, branch manager, and profit center manager. When you activate a role, all of the relevant objects (DataSources, data targets, queries to web templates, etc.) are activated in the system. These activated objects can be used immediately in a productive system.

For demonstration purposes, we've activated a single InfoObject from SAP Business Content, 0AD_AUTHID (Author ID). Click on Object Type under BI Content, as shown in (❶) of Figure 2.26. The panel on the right side now shows different available object types (❷).

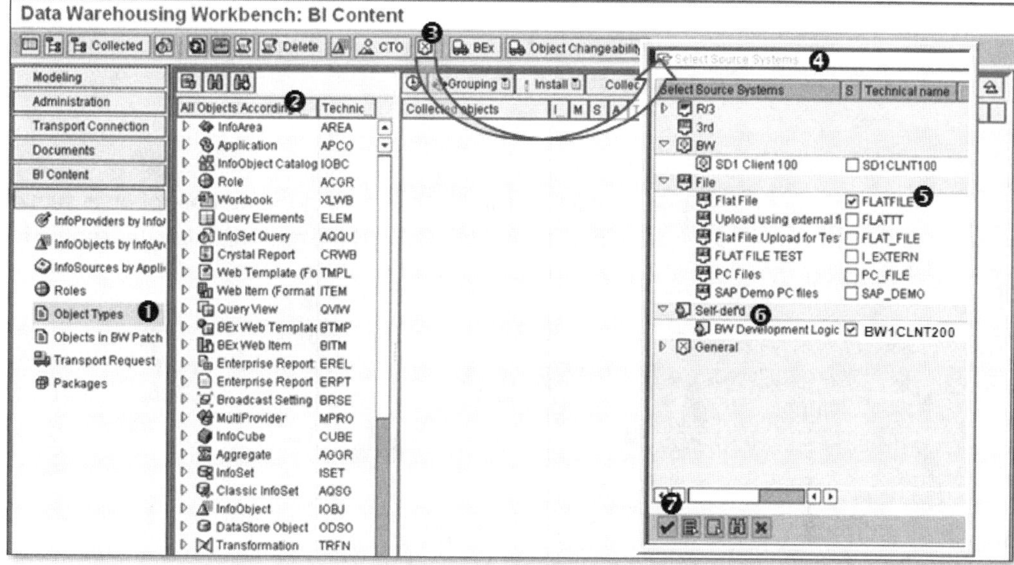

Figure 2.26 Selecting Object Type and Source System in BI Content

SAP NetWeaver BW can extract data from a number of systems, referred to as *source systems*. There may be many source systems connected to SAP NetWeaver BW, and a number of objects may be connected to particular source systems. When activating SAP Business Content, you must inform the SAP NetWeaver BW system about the source system connection because the activation process activates objects related to that source system.

To do this, click the Source System icon (), as shown in ❸ of Figure 2.26. This action results in a pop-up window where you can select from the source systems (❹), which are classified into different categories (R3, SAP NetWeaver BW, File, 3rd party, etc.). There are also different types of file source systems connected as shown in ❺; we explain the process of creating file source systems in Chapter 7.

As shown in ❻, there is a source system called "Self-defd," which stands for *self-defined*. This system is also known as a *myself connection* and is used when loading data from one data target to another data target in the same SAP NetWeaver BW system. For our demonstration, we need only the myself connection, which is set. (The FLATFILE source system isn't required for our demonstration purposes; it's configured just to show that multiple source system connections can be configured). Click on the Continue icon (), as shown in ❼.

Before selecting the object and starting the activation process, you must configure a few more options as discussed in the following sections. After explaining the options, we explain the activation itself.

2.5.1 Grouping

The most important option, which can significantly affect the number of objects that can be activated by the system, is Grouping. Open the Grouping menu, as shown in ❶ of Figure 2.27, to see the four options available (❷):

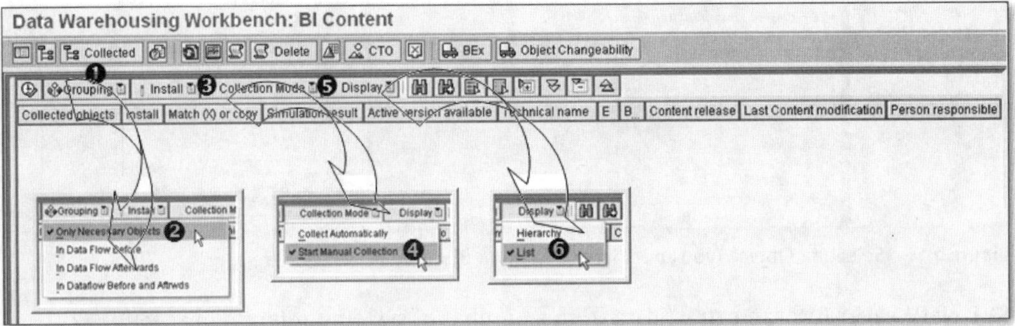

Figure 2.27 Configuring Various Options Before Activating Business Content

- **Only Necessary Objects**
  This option activates the minimum number of objects required to activate the selected object. Thus, if you've selected one InfoObject A, and InfoObjects B and C are attributes of InfoObject A, the system activates all three objects. For this example, we've selected this option as shown in ❷ of Figure 2.27.
- **In Data Flow Before**
  This option activates all objects that are required to supply the data to the selected object. So, when you select InfoCube A for activation, and there are two different DataSources that gives data to InfoCube A, the system activates all of the InfoObjects required to activate InfoCube A *and* the two DataSources.
- **In Data Flow Afterwards**
  This option activates all of the objects that get data from the selected objects. So, if you've selected InfoCube A for activation, and there are two queries that are based on this InfoCube, the system activates all of the InfoObjects required to activate InfoCube A, the two queries, and all of the related objects required to activate these two queries. If these queries are associated with web templates, the system also activates the web templates.

- **In Dataflow Before and Aftrwds**
  This option is a combination of the In Data Flow Before option and the In Data Flow Afterwards options.

2.5.2 Collection Mode

To activate any object, you must first select it from the list and drag and drop it over the Collected Objects area. There are two collection modes, as shown in ❹ of Figure 2.27:

- **Collect Automatically**
  This option starts the collection of other objects as soon as you drop the object in this area.
- **Start Manual Collection**
  This option can be used to select multiple objects (one by one). Drag and drop required objects into the Collected Objects area, and click on the Execute icon ( ) to start the collection. Because we're selecting single objects in our example, either option will work. We've selected Start Manual Collection, as shown in ❹ of Figure 2.27.

2.5.3 Display

The Display option (❺ of Figure 2.27) shows the collected objects in two different ways: Hierarchy, in which collected objects are shown in a hierarchical fashion; and List, in which collected objects are shown in list fashion. We've selected List, as show in ❻ of Figure 2.27.

2.5.4 Activating the InfoObject

Now that the options are set, we can select InfoObject 0AD_AUTHID. Expand the InfoObject tree, and double-click on Select Objects, as shown in ❹ of Figure 2.28. This results in a pop-up box, Input Help for Metadata, as shown in ❺. This pop-up box lists all of the InfoObjects available in the system, both active and inactive. Find the InfoObject 0AD_AUTHID by using the scroll bar or Find icon.

InfoObject 0AD_AUTHID is now available under Collected Objects, as shown in ❶ of Figure 2.29. The Install column shows a tick for this InfoObject (❷). This tick isn't available for editing (in gray) and indicates that the InfoObject isn't active. Click on the Execute icon ( ), as shown in ❸. The system now collects all of the necessary objects that are required to activate InfoObject 0AD_AUTHID and lists them (❹).

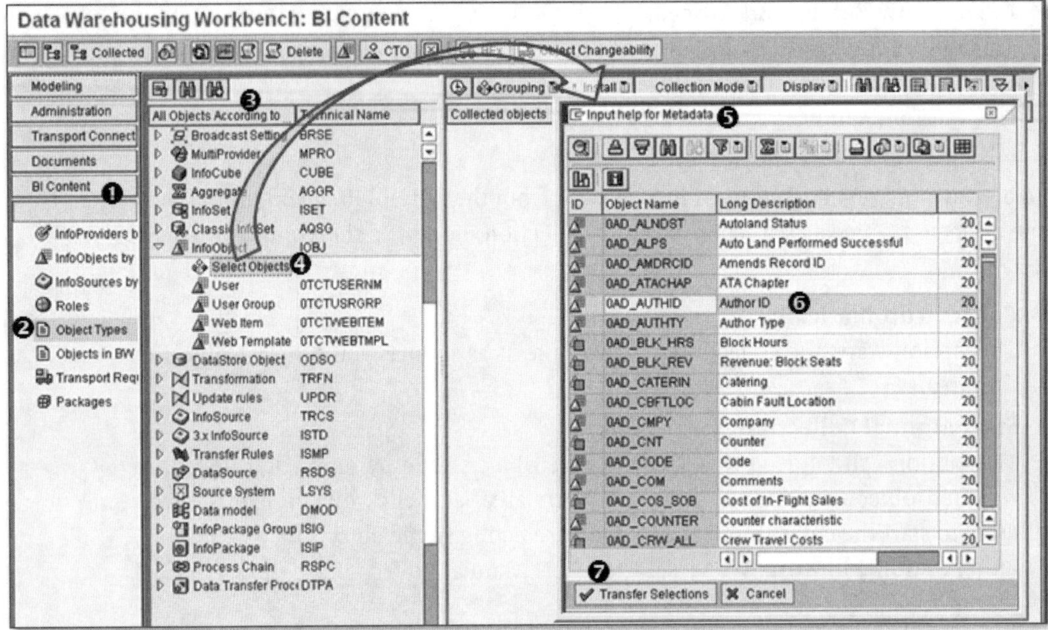

Figure 2.28 Selecting InfoObject for Activation

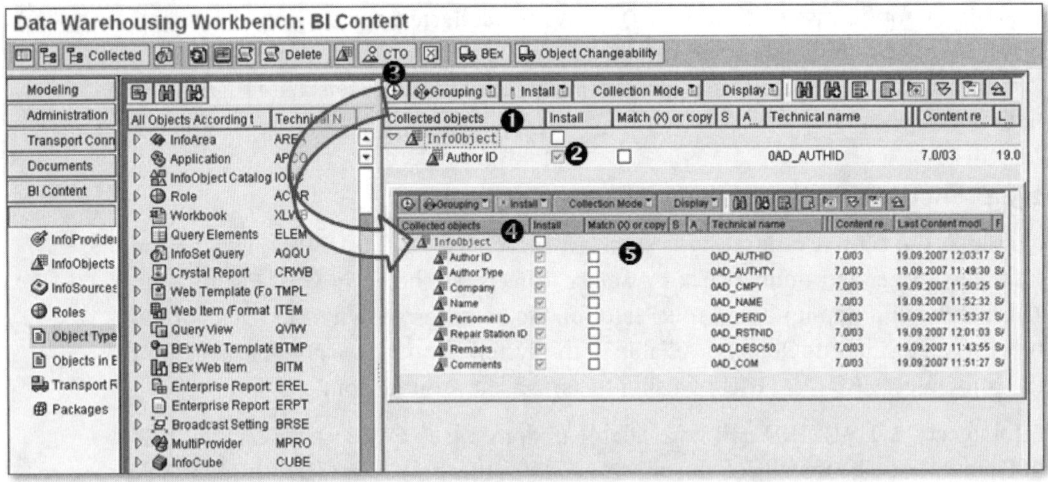

Figure 2.29 InfoObject Selected and Objects Collected

If the list shows an object that is already active, you can re-activate it from BI Content. You can configure this by checking the Match or Copy column, as shown in ❺ of Figure 2.29. There are multiple scenarios when you may need to execute re-activation; for example, you may have modified a BI Content object and then want to revert to the original.

Now select the Install dropdown menu, as shown in ❶ of Figure 2.30. Click on Simulate Installation (❷). Selecting this option simulates the installation of the selected objects and shows the simulation result (❸). The OK icon (✔) shows that the simulation result is positive and that there won't be any errors when actually activating the selected objects in the system.

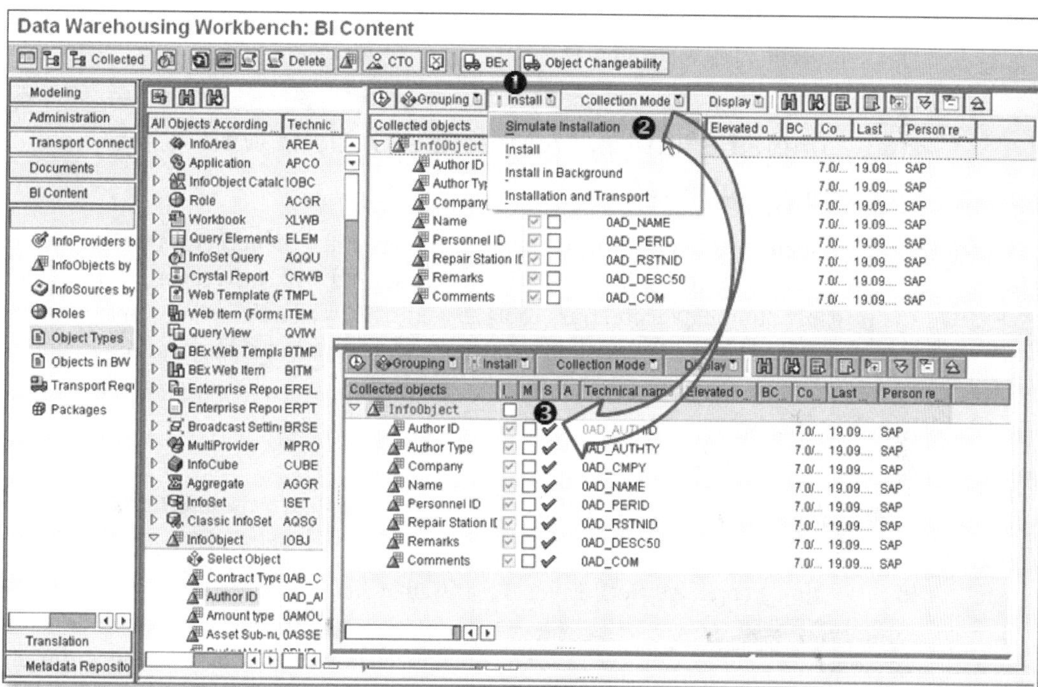

Figure 2.30 Simulating Activation

When the simulation result is positive, you can install the selected objects in the system. Select Install from the Install dropdown menu (❶ and ❷ of Figure 2.31).

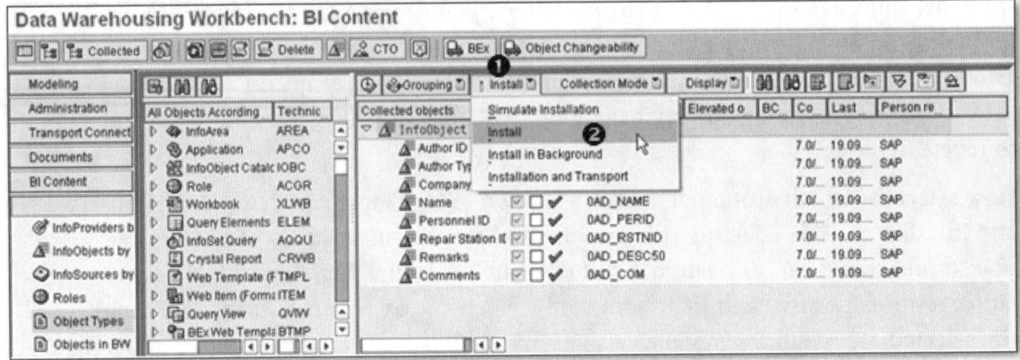

Figure 2.31 Installing Selected Objects

This action activates all of the selected objects in the system.

2.6 Implementation/Architecture Options with SAP NetWeaver BW

Large companies with many business entities or establishments across various countries operating in different time zones may have several SAP NetWeaver BW instances and possibly other data warehouse tools as well. The two landscape options for organizing SAP NetWeaver BW solutions for consistency and company-specific requirements are discussed next.

2.6.1 Core Landscape

A *core landscape* uses SAP NetWeaver BW as the core information hub across the company (Figure 2.32).

In this setup, a core SAP NetWeaver BW instance is implemented. It contains a data warehouse layer as well as data mart layer services and includes operative-level reporting. The core SAP NetWeaver BW instance aims to source all information-relevant and relays-relevant data to local SAP NetWeaver BW instances. The local analytical and reporting needs are serviced by the local SAP NetWeaver BW instances, whereas the enterprise-level analytical needs are met via the core instance, and it's possible to separate reporting and analysis services as load increases. Implementing a core SAP NetWeaver BW instance is always the best option within a single division company with a strong headquarters.

That being said, certain conditions (e.g., a regional enterprise structure without process integration between the regions), coupled with technical and political factors, can cause an enterprise to use the alternative setup, a peripheral landscape.

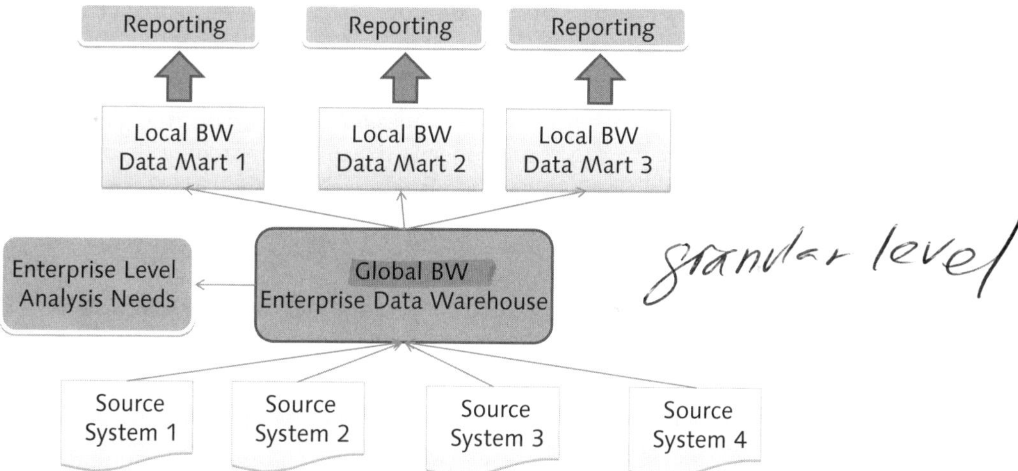

Figure 2.32 Landscape with Core SAP NetWeaver BW Instance

2.6.2 Peripheral Landscape

A *peripheral landscape* is based on local instances of SAP NetWeaver BW within various units of a company, all of which provide and receive data to and from a higher-level global instance of SAP NetWeaver BW, possibly at the company's headquarters (Figure 2.33).

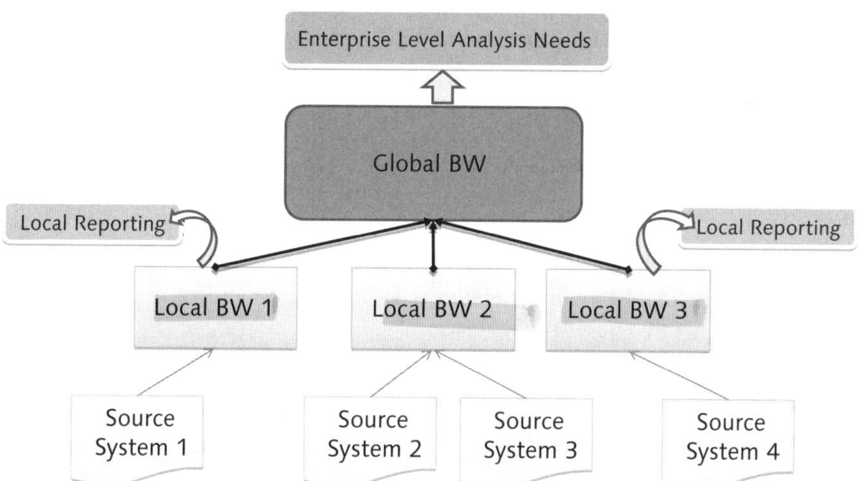

Figure 2.33 Landscape with Peripheral SAP NetWeaver BW Instance(s)

Each peripheral SAP NetWeaver BW instance operates like an enterprise data warehouse for its own area as it sources information from local source systems and meets all of the operative unit-level reporting locally. In this way, the sum of the local enterprise data warehouses forms a quasi-virtual enterprise data warehouse. Having a peripheral landscape architecture means that for over-arching reporting and analysis, at least one additional integration layer is required to consolidate the data from the local SAP NetWeaver BW instances; this is referred to as the *global* SAP NetWeaver BW.

The core enterprise data warehouse requires all corporate data to be integrated at a granular data level; although always preferable, this isn't necessary with peripheral SAP NetWeaver BW instances because each peripheral enterprise data warehouse necessarily ensures a peripheral granular data integration.

A hybrid of both options is also possible and is sometimes used as a result of company mergers and acquisitions.

2.7 Avenues of SAP NetWeaver BW Learning

Many training guides, enhanced documentations, ASAP Accelerators, and how-to guides are available that offer support to SAP NetWeaver BW users. These documents all focus on offering support with concrete challenges that arise during a project (Figure 2.34) and are detailed next.

- **Partner Academy**
  SAP and some of its partners offer educational courses on SAP as part of Partner Academy. These are classroom trainings where the trainer uses a structured courseware and SAP solution to train participants.
- **SAP Help Portal**
  SAP has a dedicated portal for details on its solutions and functionalities.
- **SAP Developers Network**
  A large number of technocrats practicing SAP and implementing SAP solutions collaborate on the SAP Developers Network (SDN) to exchange and grow knowledge. SAP runs and manages this portal.
- **Books and professional journals**
  The growth of SAP has seen an explosion in books and periodicals on SAP and its solutions.

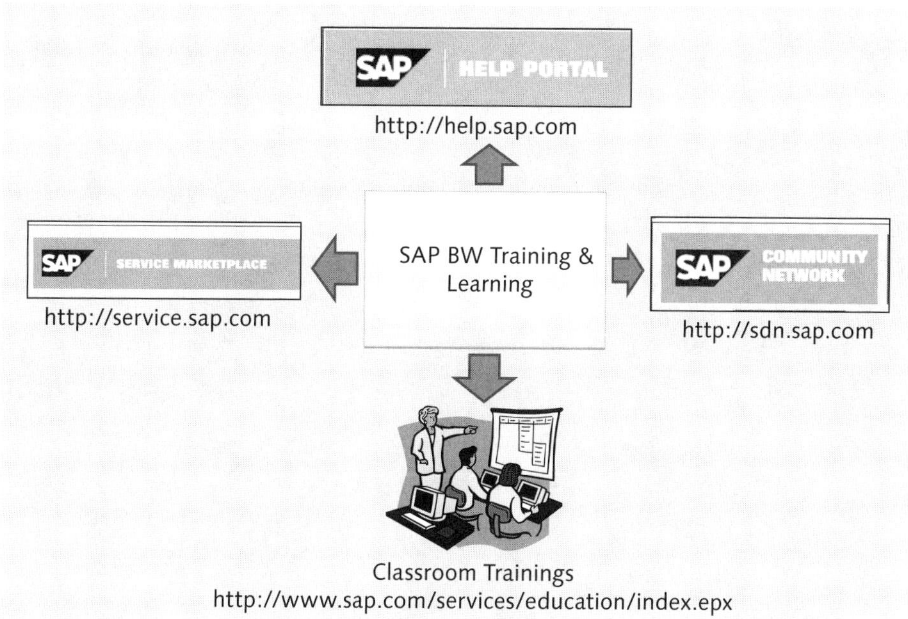

Figure 2.34 Avenues of SAP NetWeaver BW Learning

2.8 Summary

In this chapter, we explained the aspects and components of SAP NetWeaver BW that make it a leading BI solution. We covered its components, its unique architecture, various screen elements, terminology, and relevant navigation modes. We also explained how to activate SAP Business Content, the most distinguishing feature of SAP NetWeaver BW, and the landscape architecture options for a company using SAP NetWeaver BW. Finally, we concluded with a brief list of the different channels of learning available for SAP users.

In this chapter, we explain the concept of the InfoObject, which is the basic building block of SAP NetWeaver BW. Understanding this building block and its configuration will help you create a robust data warehousing solution that is scalable and relevant for a long time.

3 InfoObjects and Master Data

A typical business intelligence solution is comprised of many objects, each serving a specific purpose. For example, there are objects that source and store data (*data targets*), objects that make the data available for analytical purposes (*InfoProviders*), and objects that present data in the form of a report (*queries*). Together, these objects make up the infrastructure of a data warehouse that serves the following purposes:

- Receives and obtains information from its source.
- Modifies and arranges information in the required form.
- Presents and reports information in the desired form.

The basic and smallest building block used in building other objects is called the *InfoObject*.

The Smallest Building Block

In SAP NetWeaver BW, an InfoObject is the smallest building block. You must use InfoObjects to design or configure other SAP NetWeaver BW objects such as InfoCubes, DSOs (DataStore objects), MultiProviders, Queries, InfoSets, and so on.

Figure 3.1 represents how an InfoObject is used in creating all other objects.

We explain InfoCubes and DSOs in subsequent chapters of this book. In this chapter, we focus on the creation and configuring custom InfoObjects. We discuss types of InfoObjects, different organizational entities, and how to create and configure different types of InfoObjects (characteristic, key figure, and unit).

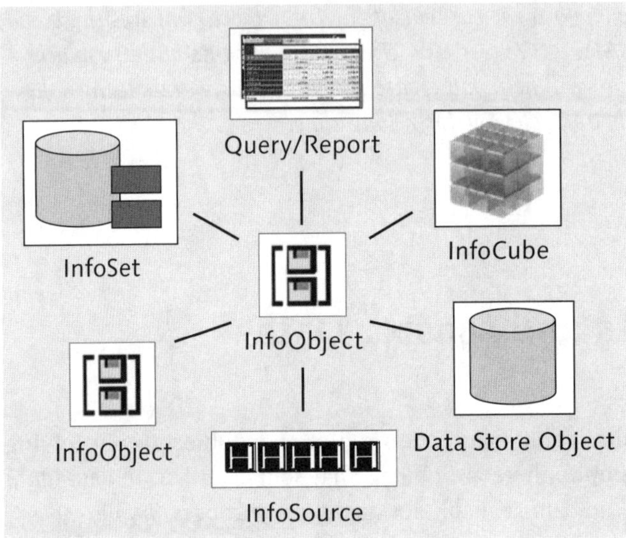

Figure 3.1 InfoObject: The Basic Building Block

3.1 Types of InfoObjects

There are five types of InfoObjects, each of which represents a type of business entity or establishes a relationship between entities. Figure 3.2 shows each type of InfoObject with examples of their relevant business entities or numeric measures.

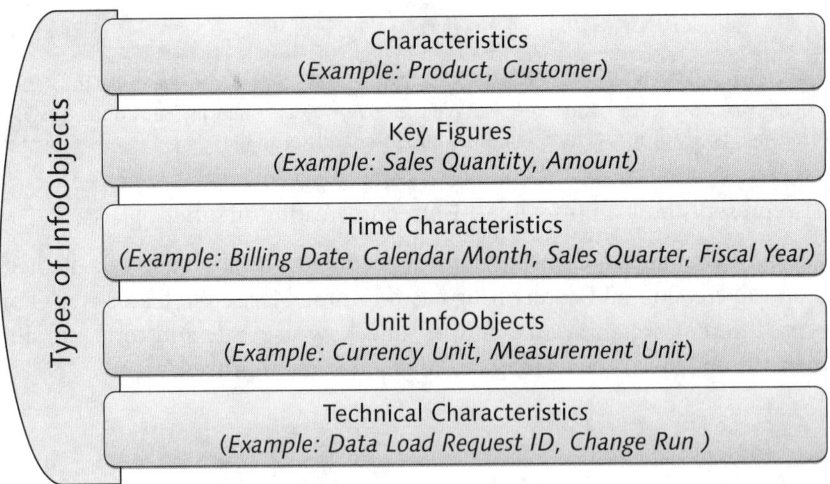

Figure 3.2 Type of InfoObjects

- Characteristics: This type of InfoObject represents business entities that are the subjects of analysis, for example, product, customer, and marketing regions.
- Key figures: This type of InfoObject represents numeric measures of business entities, for example, weight, number, quantity, and amount.
- Time characteristics: This type of InfoObject represents the period of the transaction between entities, for example, date of billing, month of sale, and fiscal year. Time characteristics are delivered by SAP and aren't customizable.
- Unit: This type of InfoObject represents the unit of measure for the numeric measures of business entities, for example, the currency, unit of weight, unit of volume, and so on.
- Technical characteristics: This type of InfoObject represents entities that are internal to SAP NetWeaver BW and are technical in type, for example, a data load request ID. (The data load request ID helps in the maintenance and administration of the SAP NetWeaver BW system.) Technical characteristics are delivered by SAP and aren't customizable.

All types of InfoObjects are delivered by SAP as part of SAP Business Content. If you can't find an appropriate InfoObject in the ones provided by SAP, you can create a custom one (except for time characteristic and technical characteristic InfoObjects). We explain the procedure for creating custom characteristic, key figure, and unit InfoObjects later in this chapter.

SAP Business Content Naming Space

Every component and object delivered by SAP as a part of SAP Business Content has a technical name that starts with a zero. To maintain this technical naming convention and its integrity, SAP doesn't allow you to create an InfoObject or any other SAP NetWeaver BW component with a technical name that has a zero as the first character.

3.2 Creating an InfoArea

A typical data warehouse has large number of objects. To facilitate the task of managing these objects, they are all organized in groups. *InfoAreas* represent the highest level of grouping; for example, all objects related to sales processes are grouped under one InfoArea, whereas all objects related to finance are grouped under another InfoArea.

This logical grouping in the form of InfoAreas is also used for managing the authorization of data warehouse functions. For example, a developer working with sales analytics can't access or change any objects relevant for finance; similarly, another developer designing finance analytics can't access or change any objects relevant for sales. We explain more about authorization in Chapter 14, Administration and Monitoring.

You can also create an InfoArea within an InfoArea, as shown in Figure 3.3. Figure 3.3 represents a structure of InfoAreas: 0CRM_SALES_OP and 0CRM_SALES_O are subsets of InfoArea 0CRM_SALES; and InfoArea 0CRM_SALES is a subset of 0SALES, which is a subset of InfoArea 0CRM. In this mode, you can logically organize and group InfoObjects or other objects.

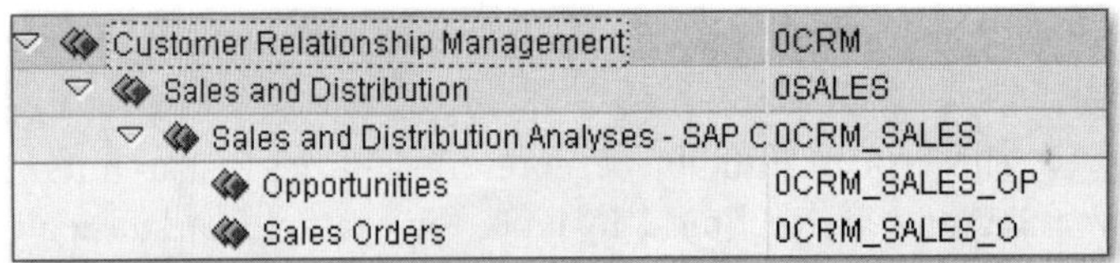

Figure 3.3 InfoArea Tree Structure

Let's now explore the process of creating a custom InfoArea. In our example, we'll use the technical name "BW_AREA."

1. Start the Data Warehousing Workbench (DWW) using Transaction RSA1.
2. Click on Modeling to start the Modeling tasks of the DWW (❶ of Figure 3.4).
3. Within the Modeling tasks, click on InfoObjects (❷). On the right panel of the screen, a tree structure displays existing InfoAreas arranged in a hierarchy (Figure 3.4).

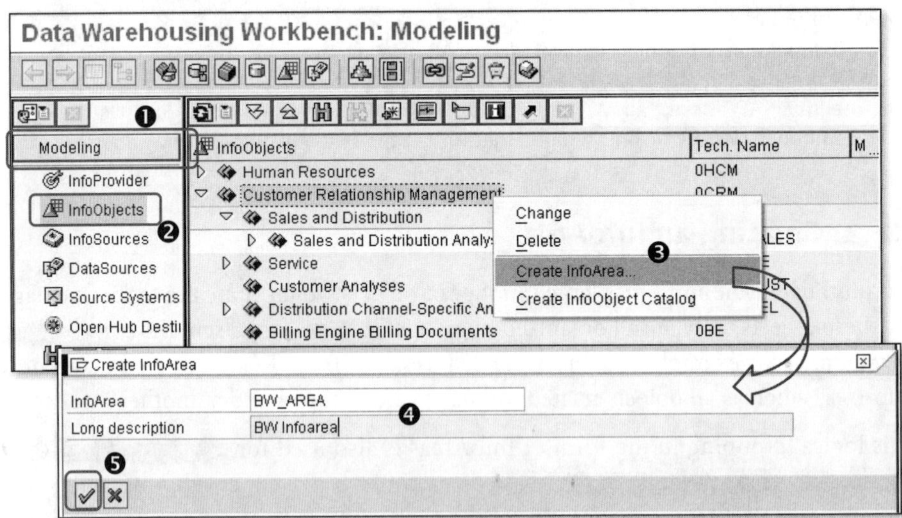

Figure 3.4 Selecting an InfoArea to Create InfoArea

4. Select the InfoArea under which you want to create your custom InfoArea (❸), and select Create InfoArea from the context menu.
5. In the Create InfoArea box, enter the technical name and description of the InfoArea (❹), and then click on the Continue button (✔) or press Enter (❺).

As you can see in Figure 3.5, the structure of InfoArea 0CRM is updated, and an InfoArea titled "BW InfoArea" is visible as a subset.

▷ Human Resources	0HCM
▽ Customer Relationship Management	0CRM
BW InfoArea	BW_AREA
▷ Sales and Distribution	0SALES
▷ Service	0SERVICE
Customer Analyses	0CRM_CUST

Figure 3.5 Newly Created InfoArea BW_AREA Under InfoArea 0CRM

3.3 Creating an InfoObject Catalog

To arrange a vast number of InfoObjects within an InfoArea in a logical group, InfoObjects are grouped in an *InfoObject catalog*. To make a simple comparison, an InfoObject is like a file, and an InfoObject catalog is like a file folder. InfoObject catalogs are created under an InfoArea.

The InfoObject catalogs are shown in Figure 3.6. There are two types of InfoObject catalogs; one groups the characteristic InfoObjects ( ), and the other groups key figure InfoObjects ( ).

▽ Customer Relationship Management	0CRM		Change	InfoProvider
▽ Sales and Distribution	0SALES		Change	InfoProvider
▽ Sales and Distribution Analyses - SAP C	0CRM_SALES		Change	InfoProvider
Opportunities	0CRM_SALES_OP		Change	InfoProvider
Sales Orders	0CRM_SALES_O		Change	InfoProvider
Contracts	0CRM_SALES_K		Change	InfoProvider
▷ CRM Sales: Characteristics	0SALES_CHA01	=	Change	
▷ CRM Sales: Key Figures	0SALES_KYF01	=	Change	

Figure 3.6 InfoObject Catalogs

We recommend that you maintain a naming convention that easily identifies the type of InfoObject Catalog. In our example, the name for the characteristics catalog is "0SALES_CHA01" (CRM Sales: Characteristics), and the name for the key figures catalog is "0SALES_KYF01" (Sales: Key Figures).

Note

It isn't mandatory to create an InfoObject catalog before creating an InfoObject. InfoObjects created without assignment to InfoObject catalogs are grouped under a predelivered InfoObject catalog called "CHANOTASSIGNED."

The following steps explain how to create an InfoObject catalog.

1. Start DWW using Transaction RSA1.
2. Click on Modeling to start the modeling tasks of DWW.
3. Within the Modeling tasks, click on InfoObjects. A tree structure appears on the right side of the screen (Figure 3.7). Click on any row, and the branch opens into the folders or the branches below it.

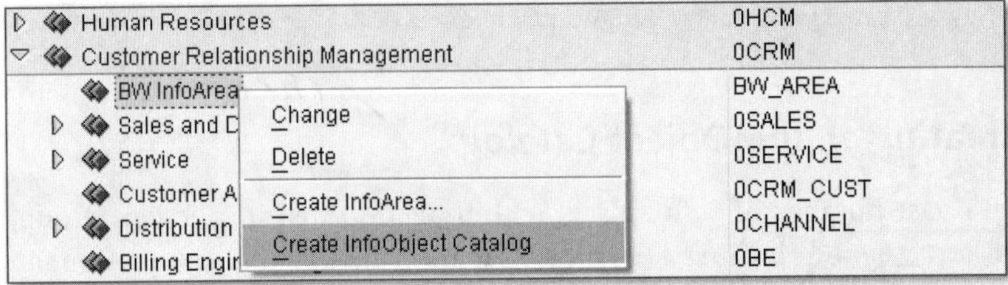

Figure 3.7 Create InfoObject Catalog

4. To create an InfoObject catalog, select the InfoArea where you want the catalog to be created. We chose InfoArea BW_AREA. Use the context menu to select Create InfoObject Catalog (Figure 3.7). The screen shown in Figure 3.8 appears.
5. Enter the technical name of the InfoObject catalog and its text description (❶ of Figure 3.8).
6. Because you're creating a characteristic InfoObject catalog, select the Char. radio button (❷).

Note

You can also create a new InfoObject catalog by copying an existing InfoObject catalog and then modifying it.

7. Having defined the name for the InfoObject catalog, click the Create icon (❸), or press F5 on the keyboard. The system creates the new InfoObject catalog, which is still inactive (Figure 3.9).

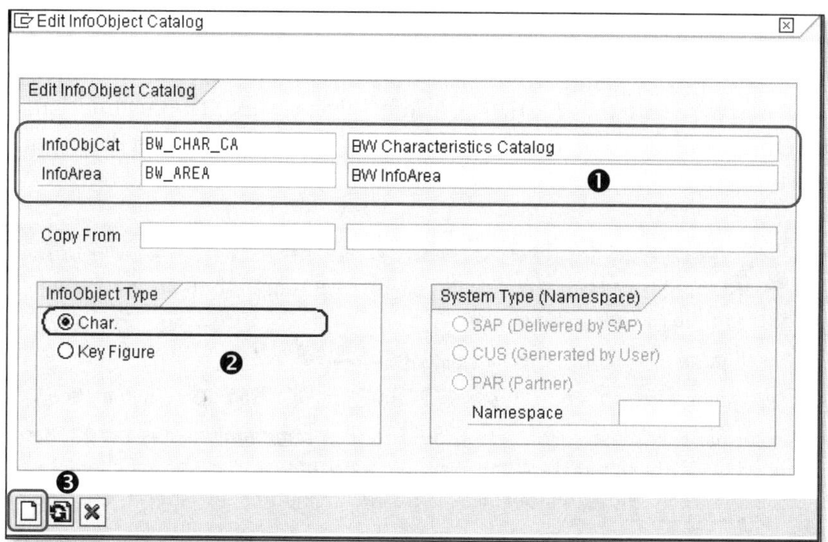

Figure 3.8 Edit InfoObject Catalog

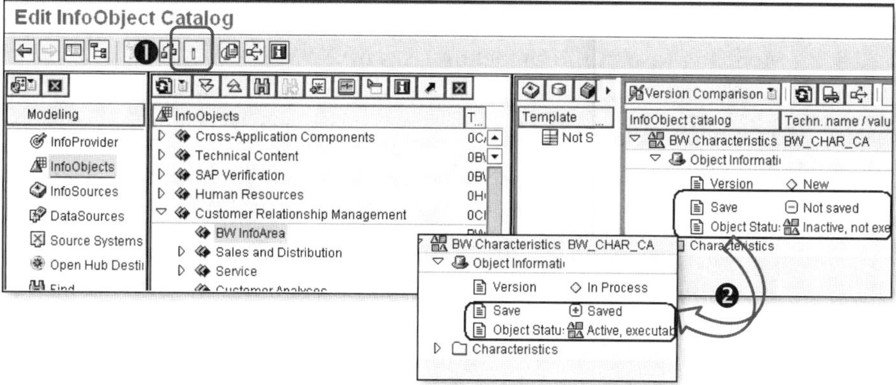

Figure 3.9 Activate InfoObject Catalog

8. Activate the InfoObject catalog using the Activate icon (❶ of Figure 3.9).

After you activate the InfoObject catalog, you'll see a message confirming activation at the bottom of the screen. You can also view your newly created InfoObject catalog BW_CHAR_CA under InfoArea BW_AREA. As you can see in ❷ of Figure 3.9, the InfoObject catalog is listed as Active.

3.4 Creating a Characteristic InfoObject

In this section, we explain the procedure for creating a custom characteristics InfoObject within the newly created BW_CHAR_CA InfoObject catalog. The custom characteristic InfoObject will have the technical name "BW_CUST" and the text description "Sold-to party."

Naming Convention Conditions

To distinguish custom objects from those delivered in SAP Business Content, the following conditions apply to their naming convention:

- The technical name of custom objects can't begin with a zero.
- The technical name of custom objects can't have any special characters (such as * or $).
- The technical name of custom objects should have a minimum of three characters and a maximum of nine characters, for example, alphabets a to z, special characters, and numbers 0 to 9. You can't begin a name with a number or special character, however..

To create a characteristic InfoObject, follow these steps:

1. Start DWW using Transaction RSA1.
2. Click on Modeling to start the Modeling tasks of DWW.
3. Within the Modeling tasks, click on InfoObjects. A tree structure appears on the right of the screen. Click InfoObject Catalog BW_CHAR_CA, and select Create InfoObject from the context menu (Figure 3.10). A screen appears prompting you to enter the name of the characteristic InfoObject you want to create (❶ of Figure 3.11).

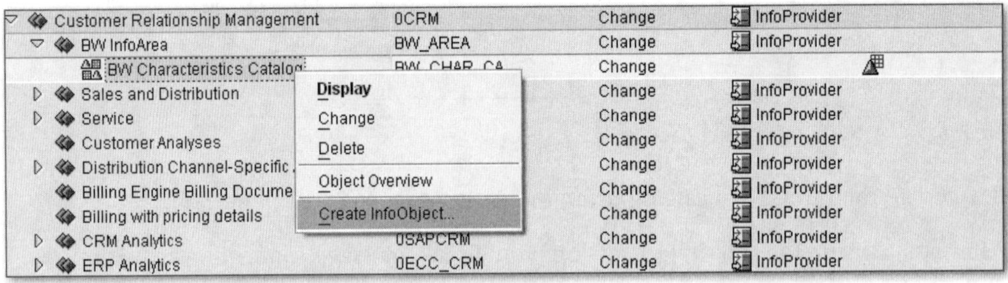

Figure 3.10 Create InfoObject: Context Menu

4. Enter the name of the InfoObject ("BW_CUST") and description ("Sold-to Party"). From ❷ and ❸ of Figure 3.11, you can see that there are two additional fields: Reference Characteristic and Template. We discuss these later in this section.

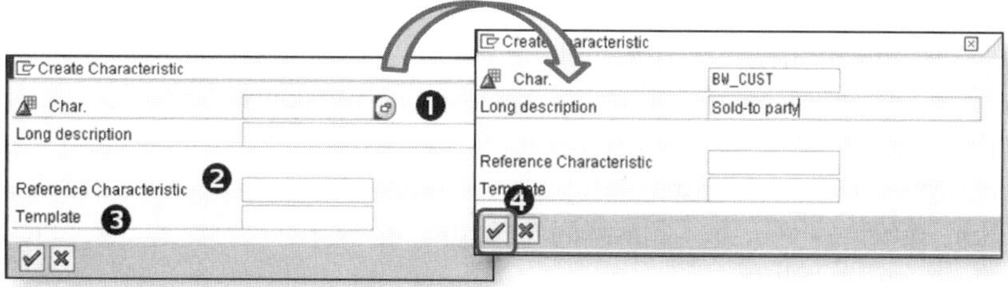

Figure 3.11 Creating Characteristics InfoObject

5. Click the Continue icon.

Next we explain the implications of the Reference Characteristic field and the Template field.

3.4.1 Reference Characteristic Field

To understand how this field is used, assume you have an existing InfoObject (BW_CUST, Sold-to Party) with master data. Whenever this InfoObject is used, its description is listed as "sold-to-party." As the smallest building block, the InfoObject is likely to be used in many InfoCubes (or InfoProviders); because of this, its "sold-to party" description may not always be accurate. For example, a report for the department that collects payments would use customer data contained in the BW_CUST InfoObject, but they would not want customers to be referred to as "sold-to-party"; rather, they would want them to be referred to as "payers." To solve this problem, you can create an identical InfoObject — comprised of the same definitions and master data — with its only difference being the description ("payer" instead of "sold-to-party"). To do this, enter the existing InfoObject into the Reference Characteristic field (❷ of Figure 3.11).

> **Note**
>
> You can't change the technical settings of an InfoObject created by reference to another InfoObject.

3.4.2 Template Field

To understand how this field is used, assume that you want to create a new InfoObject that is similar to an existing InfoObject. Enter the name of the new InfoObject in the Char. field, and enter the name of the already-available InfoObject in the Template field (❸ of Figure 3.11). Click the Continue icon (❹).

The system copies all of the definitions of the existing InfoObject (its data type, length, etc.), saving you the work of defining them individually; if necessary, you can change the copied definitions based on your requirements. Upon activation of the new InfoObject, the system automatically identifies it as separate from the one that was chosen for its template. The master data for this new InfoObject must be loaded separately (the process of loading master data is discussed in Chapter 7, Extraction, Transformation, and Loading).

In our example, we don't use the Template or Reference Characteristic field; so, simply click the Continue icon.

3.5 Configuring a Characteristic InfoObject

Creating a custom InfoObject (without using a template or reference to another InfoObject) involves configuring various settings based on specific requirements. When you click on the Continue icon, the screen shown in Figure 3.12 appears.

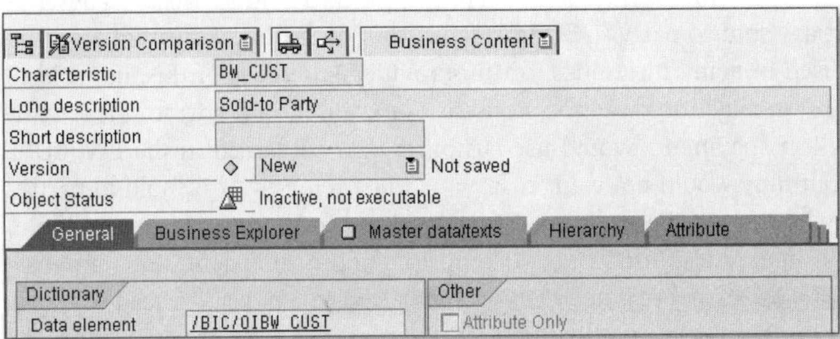

Figure 3.12 Characteristic InfoObjects: Tabs

Six different tabs are available when configuring characteristic InfoObject: General, Business Explorer, Master Data/Texts, Hierarchy, Attribute, and Compounding (not visible in figure). We explain each of these tabs next.

3.5.1 General Tab

Two of the three basic settings you must configure when creating a custom characteristic InfoObject are the *type* and *size* of the data it stores. Table 3.1 lists the four types of data.

Data Type	Explanation
CHAR	Used to store character strings of both numbers and letters, for example, customer numbers, material numbers, vendor numbers, *and so on*.
NUMC	Used to store character strings of only number, for example, item numbers for billing documents.
DATS	Used to store dates; for example, a field of eight characters in length would use the YYYYMMDD format.
TIMS	Used to store times; for example, a field of six characters would use the HHMMSS format.

Table 3.1 Data Types for Characteristic InfoObjects

In our example, the InfoObject stores characteristic customer IDs that are 10 characters in length. Using this information, configure the Data Type and Length shown in ❶ of Figure 3.13.

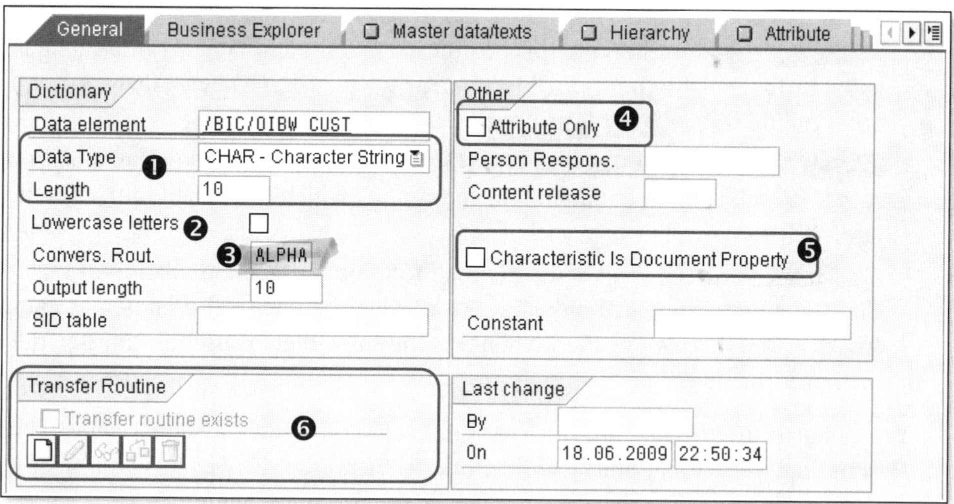

Figure 3.13 General Tab

By default, the conversion routine (Convers. Rout) is supplied as ALPHA for the CHAR data type (❸). The conversion routine determines the following:

- The way data is stored in an internal format, as well as the way the data appears on screen
- That data is stored in an acceptable format in the database

For example, if the length of BW_CUST is 10, and you have an ALPHA conversion routine, a BW_CUST value of 1 is stored as 0000000001; so is a BW_CUST value of 0001, 001, and so on. Without the conversion routine, the system would treat BW_CUST value = 1 and BW_CUST value = 0001 as two different customers.

Let's briefly discuss the rest of the settings in the General tab as shown in Figure 3.13:

- Lowercase Letters **(❷):** This setting determines whether the system converts the text value into uppercase letters. If you check this box, the system uses the value exactly as it's entered; otherwise, the value entered is converted to uppercase letters in the screen template as, for example, a variable (see Chapter 9, BEx Query Designer).
- Attribute Only **(❹):** Checking this box means that the InfoObject can be assigned as an attribute of another InfoObject but can't be used as a navigational attribute. So, it can be a display attribute only.
- Characteristic Is Document Property **(❺):** Checking this box allows an analyst to record and document comments in the report, which is available for reference later.
- Transfer Routine **(❻):** This setting is used to indicate the manipulation of incoming data by custom ABAP code. The ABAP code used here, also known as global transfer *routine*, gets executed whenever the InfoObject is used in transfer rules or transformation.

You can activate the custom InfoObject after filling the three essential fields (Long Description, Data Type, and Length) in the General tab. However, you'll need to evaluate settings in the other tabs to meet business requirements.

3.5.2 Business Explorer Tab

The Business Explorer tab's (Figure 3.14) settings are divided into two main areas: General Settings and BEx Map. Next we briefly explain those that are most useful and relevant.

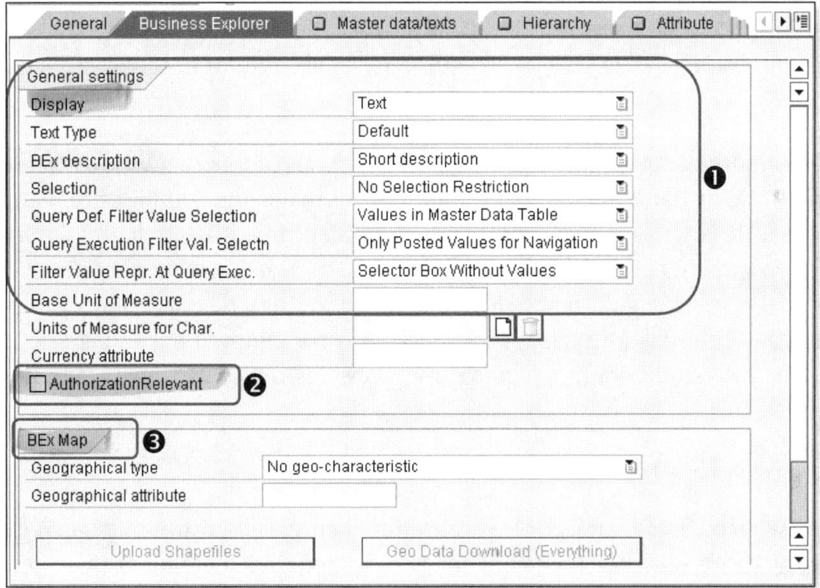

Figure 3.14 Business Explorer Tab

General Settings Area

The configuration settings in this area influence the presentation in a report that uses this InfoObject. By default, the Display field is filled with "Key." This means that, when you execute a report that uses InfoObject BW_CUST, the report displays the customer key. On the other hand, if the field is filled with "Text," the report displays customer text.

We explain this briefly using the sample data from BW_CUST data in Table 3.2. A report with the setting Display = Key would only show 100066, 100006, and 100017; it would not show the text values (Romero y tomillo, Best Buy, and Consumer Electronic Store).

BW_CUST_KEY	BW_CUST_TEXT
100066	Romero y tomillo
100006	Best Buy
100017	Consumer Electronic Store

Table 3.2 Sample Data for Customer Texts

Note

In subsequent chapters dealing with report design, we'll explain how you can change these default values.

One of the important settings in the General Settings section is the Authorization-Relevant flag. As the name suggests, this option is for managing administration and access control. If you're interested in showing limited or no data relating to this InfoObject, you would check this box (❷ of Figure 3.14). Note, however, higher level organizational objects (e.g., a marketing region, marketing office, or plant) generally control the authorizations; also, additional steps are required beyond checking this box. Our case study doesn't require any access restrictions; so, we leave this unchecked.

BEx Map Area

The BEx MAP area (❸ of Figure 3.14) is relevant when you want to use geographical areas as part of your sales analysis. Such analysis requires that you provide geographic information about the objects of analysis; for customers, for example, you might be required to upload the longitude, latitude, and height above sea level for their physical addresses. Our case study doesn't require any edits to this area.

3.5.3 Master Data/Texts Tab

Master data for a business entity such as a customer or material is stored in characteristic InfoObjects. Only in exceptional cases is it stored in a DSO (and our case study is no such exception).

The other purpose of this tab is to configure the way text is stored in the system. Understandably, it's difficult for an analyst to memorize the codes of all products and customers. So, it's important to have text descriptions for the codes of the business entities included in a report. A report can provide text descriptions only if such information is stored in the SAP NetWeaver BW system, and the details of this storage are included in this tab.

Master Data

Master data is defined as a type of data that stores information about a business entity (such as a customer or a product), doesn't change over a long period of time, and is nontransactional. For example, a customer's city is part of the master data for a customer because it provides information about the location of the customer, doesn't change over a long period of time, and isn't about a sales invoice or payment.

Next we discuss the two main areas of this tab, which are configured by selecting the With Master Data flag and the With Texts flag.

With Texts Settings

BW_CUST is configured to store the names of customers, which is indicated in this tab by selecting the With Text checkbox (❷ of Figure 3.15). There are additional steps related to the process of providing text information about business entities in a report, but we'll cover these steps in more detail in Chapter 9, BEx Query Designer.

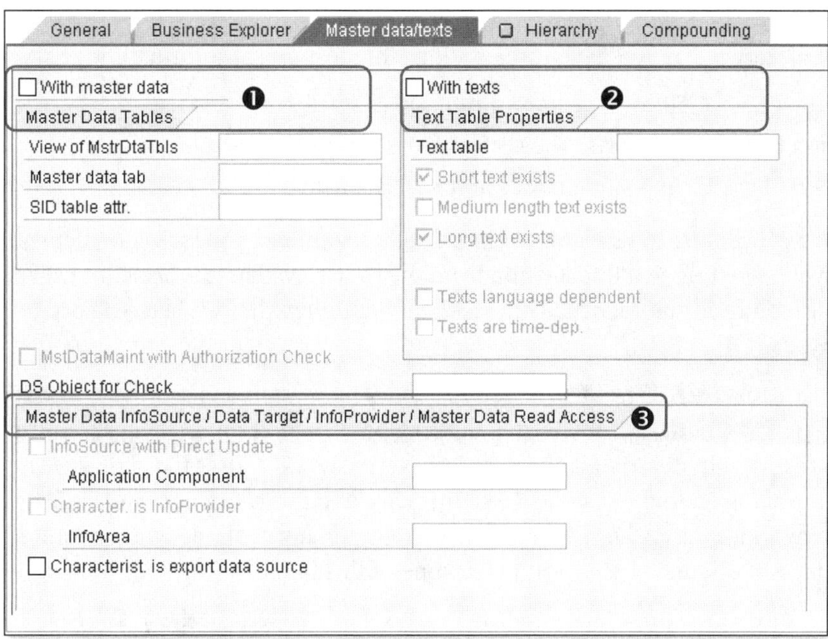

Figure 3.15 Master Data/Texts Tab

Let's explore some of the more important fields of the Text Table Properties area (Figure 3.16), which become editable when you check the With Texts box.

By default, the SAP NetWeaver BW system chooses the Short Text Exists flag (❶ of Figure 3.16) and the Texts Language Dependent flag (❷). This indicates, respectively, that the system receives and stores only short text for the InfoObject; and that the text can be in different languages.

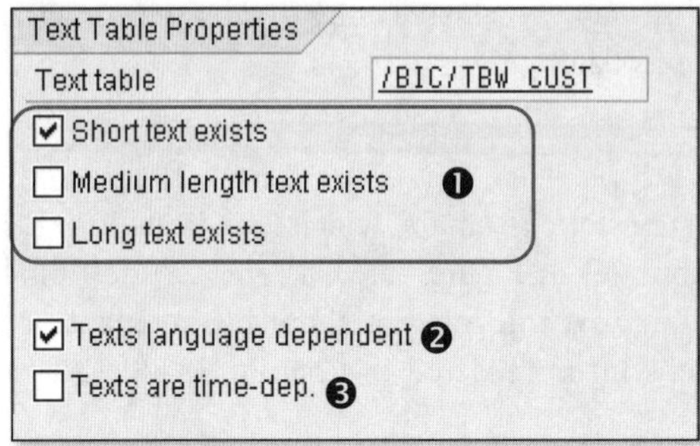

Figure 3.16 Configuring Texts for InfoObject

Figure 3.16 shows that you have three options for storing text information:

- Short Text Exists: The system stores up to 20 characters.
- Medium Length Text Exists: The system stores up to 40 characters.
- Long Text Exists: The system stores up to 60 characters.

You have the flexibility to select one or more of these options; your selection depends on how you're getting text information from the source system (the DataSource) and what you require in the reports. Our case study requires that we select Short Text Exists and Long Text Exists.

If you check the Texts Language Dependent box, the system creates the necessary infrastructure that allows you to load and store text data in different languages. After you load text data in different languages, SAP NetWeaver BW uses the language chosen when you log on to the system. (Note that checking this check box isn't sufficient to enable working in multiple languages; there are many more activities required, but this type of discussion is beyond the scope of this book.)

Another important setting in this tab is the Texts are Time-Dep. box (❸ of Figure 3.16). Imagine a scenario where a customer has changed his name, and the new name of the customer is valid from a particular date. Assume that you've already loaded master data for this customer (along with textual information). If this box isn't checked, and you load the same customer master data with the new name, the old name is overwritten by the new name. Our case study requires you to analyze sales data for both the new name and the former name based on the period of analysis (i.e., before the change and after the change). This requirement is met by selecting this checkbox.

To summarize, for the Master Data/Texts tab, we chose the checkboxes shown in Figure 3.17.

☑ With texts
Text Table Properties
Text table /BIC/TBW_CUST
☑ Short text exists
☐ Medium length text exists
☑ Long text exists
☐ Texts language dependent
☑ Texts are time-dep.

Figure 3.17 With Texts Settings

With Master Data Setting

Before we get into the details of this checkbox, we must explain some basic information regarding master data.

When business analysts analyze customer sales data, they are often interested in relating this sales information to other data, such as the customer's marketing office or city. In SAP NetWeaver BW terminology, this type of information is known as an *attribute*. In other words, attributes provide additional information about characteristics (in this case, an InfoObject).

In the example given in Figure 3.18, the marketing office and city are attributes of the characteristic InfoObject BW_CUST. Attributes themselves are also created (or delivered) as InfoObjects in system.

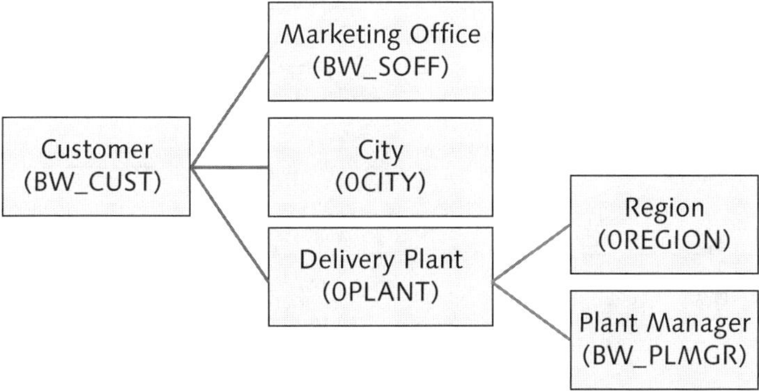

Figure 3.18 Attributes of InfoObjects

Figure 3.18 shows that the marketing office, city, and delivery plan provide information about the customer that is technically replicated in the system by assigning the following three attributes to InfoObject BW_CUST:

- BW_SOFF (Marketing office)
- 0CITY (City of customer)
- 0PLANT (Plant from which products are delivered to customer)

As mentioned earlier, these attributes are also InfoObjects. You can create custom InfoObjects and assign them as attributes (BW_SOFF is an attribute of BW_CUST), and also use SAP-delivered InfoObjects as attributes (0CITY and 0PLANT are SAP-delivered InfoObjects and assigned as attributes to your custom InfoObject).

It's important, as well as interesting, to note that attributes of InfoObjects (which are themselves InfoObjects) can have their own attributes, as shown in Figure 3.18. 0PLANT is an attribute of BW_CUST, while 0PLANT has its own attributes (i.e., 0REGION, which refers to the region in which the plant is located; and BW_PLMGR, the plant manager). In this example, we've attached our own InfoObject (BW_PLMGR) to a SAP-delivered InfoObject (0PLANT).

To create InfoObject BW_CUST with the preceding definition, we need to create two of our own InfoObjects (BW_SOFF and BW_PLMGR) and also activate three predelivered InfoObjects (0CITY, 0REGION, 0PLANT) from SAP Business Content. This brings us back to the subject at hand, which is the With Master Data checkbox: To assign attributes to characteristic InfoObjects, you must check this box (Figure 3.19).

After you check this box, the Attribute tab appears. This tab is explained in Section 3.5.5, Attributes Tab.

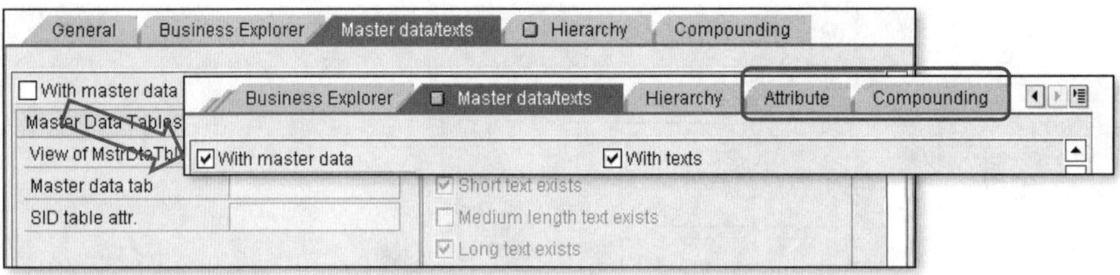

Figure 3.19 With Master Data Checkbox

3.5.4 Hierarchy Tab

Hierarchies are used to display data in tree structures and can have multiple levels with nodes and leaves arranged in parent-child relationships. The data based on a hierarchy is grouped according to the relationship defined in that hierarchy. On the Hierarchy tab, you can define if a characteristic can have hierarchies built on it, and you can also define the type and properties of hierarchies. You can create multiple hierarchies on the same characteristic InfoObject.

Consider an example of customer data where each customer (sold-to-party) is assigned to a specific region. A hierarchy representing this relationship between customer and region can be built on the customer characteristic (Figure 3.20).

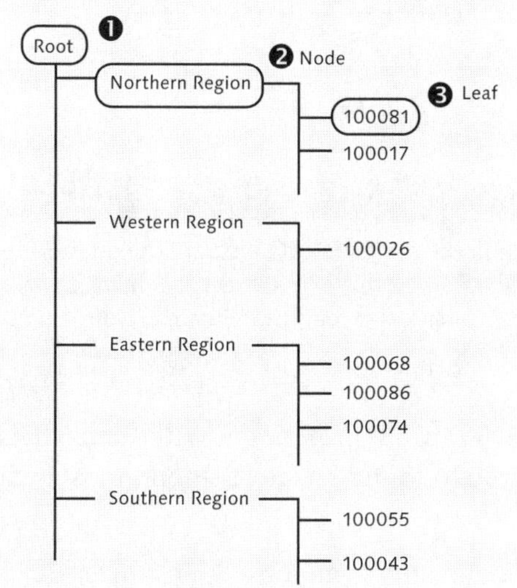

Figure 3.20 Customer: Regional Hierarchy

Check the With Hierarchies box (❶ of Figure 3.21) to enable hierarchies for a characteristic InfoObject.

You can either manually create a hierarchy or load it from the source system. Two types of parent nodes are available in a hierarchy: the text node and the characteristic node. Each hierarchy has a root node. You can add a text node (such as, from our example, Northern region, Western region, Eastern region, or Southern region) and then add a leaf (which is a characteristic value, in this case, because the hierarchy is based on customers) below the text node, as shown earlier in Figure 3.20.

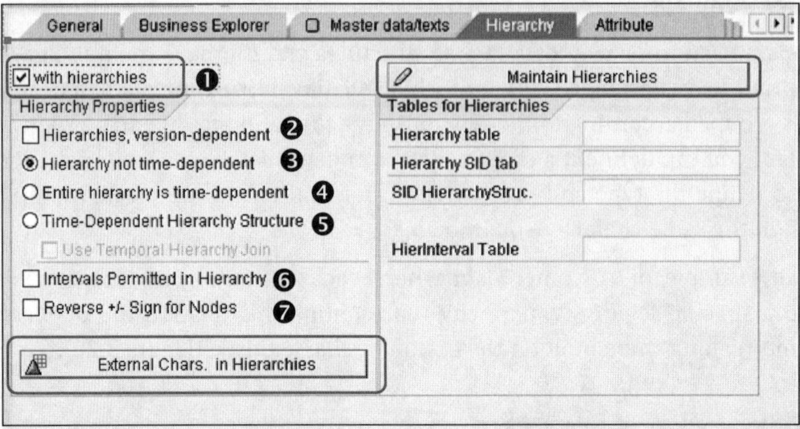

Figure 3.21 Hierarchies Tab

A hierarchy can have multiple levels, at a maximum of 98.

Other Ways to Maintain Hierarchies

The hierarchy for master data objects is available in the SAP ECC system. The SAP ECC configuration menu offers a way to create a DataSource that will extract this hierarchical structure for loading into SAP NetWeaver BW. You can also load the hierarchy from a flat file.

To configure a hierarchy for this InfoObject (BW_CUST), check the With Hierarchies checkbox. SAP NetWeaver BW then allows you to configure the other options shown in Figure 3.21.

Next we divide our discussion into four main topics: multiple hierarchies, time-dependence, intervals, and reversing signs for nodes.

Multiple Hierarchies

To provide analysts the flexibility to analyze data in different ways, it's possible to create multiple hierarchies for a characteristic, as well as multiple versions of the same hierarchy. For example, consider a situation where, due to re-organization, customer 100074 moves from the Eastern region to the Northern region. If your business analyst doesn't want to lose data from the former relationship (i.e., customer 100074 as a part of the Eastern region), you can create a new version of the hierarchy by defining the hierarchy as version-dependent. To do this, flag the Hierarchies, Version Dependent checkbox (❷ of Figure 3.21). You can now add a new version of the existing hierarchy where customer 100074 is assigned to the Northern region (Figure 3.22).

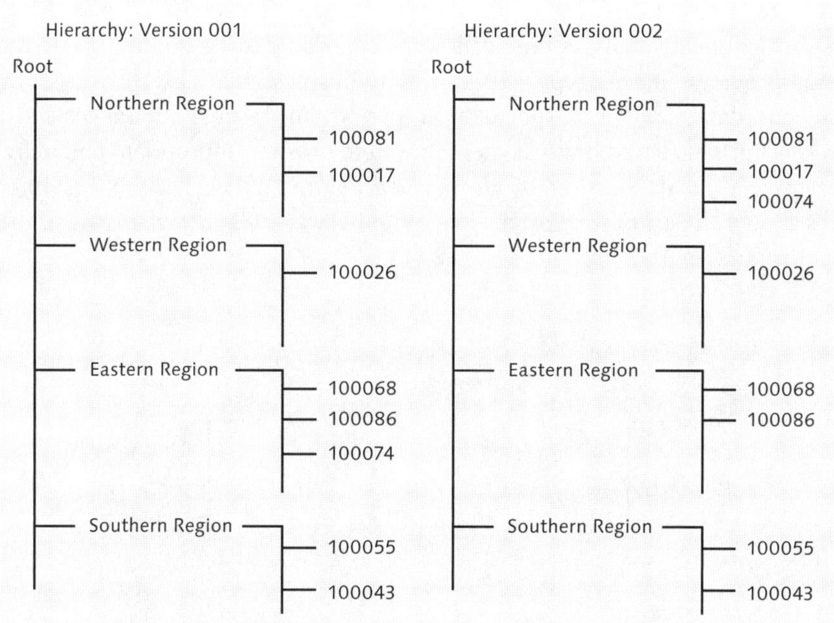

Figure 3.22 Sold-to Party: Regional Hierarchy

When the analyst chooses hierarchy version 001, the sales for customer 100074 are aggregated under the Eastern Region node. When the analyst chooses version 002, the sales for customer 100074 are aggregated under the Northern Region node (Figure 3.22).

Time-Dependency

The Hierarchy tab has settings related to time-dependency. By default, the hierarchy isn't time dependent (refer to ❸ of Figure 3.21), which means that it's valid for all time periods. The other two time-dependent settings are Entire Hierarchy Is Time-Dependent, and Time-Dependent Hierarchy Structure. The key difference between these two options is that, with the former, you create a new hierarchy structure with a new validity period. With the latter, you have a single hierarchy with different nodes/leafs that have different validity periods.

To explain the implication of the time-dependency options, let's once again refer to the example in Figure 3.22, where customer 100074 changes from the Eastern region to the Northern region. Let's also assume that this change of region is applicable from a specific date: April 1, 2009. For this situation, you must enter the validity period, not the version, when creating a hierarchy with a new relationship. This can be done by choosing the Entire Hierarchy Is Time-Dependent radio button (refer to ❹ of Figure 3.21), which means that the time validity is applicable for the entire hierarchy. This option provides another type of flexibility to business analysts: They can now analyze region data based on a specific time period. To do this, the analyst must choose a specific date; based on this date, the system uses the appropriate hierarchy. In our example, if the date chosen by an analyst is before March 31, 2009, customer 100074 is shown as part of the Eastern Region; otherwise, it's shown as part of the Northern Region (Figure 3.23).

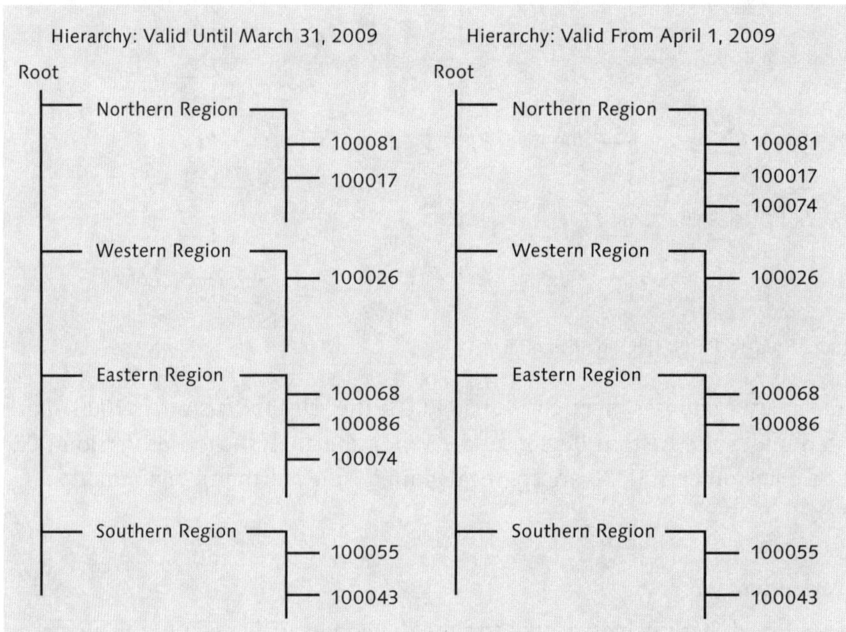

Figure 3.23 Entire Hierarchy Is Time-Dependent

For simplicity's sake, we've shown only two validity periods for the hierarchy. Customer 100074 is now part of the Northern Region (instead of the Eastern Region), which is valid from April 1, 2009. With this setting option, we create a new hierarchy valid from April 1, 2009, onward. We now have three hierarchies, each valid for different periods of time. The appropriate hierarchy to be used in a report depends on the selected date of the query at runtime.

The Time-Dependent Hierarchy Structure option (refer to ❺ of Figure 3.21) is used when you want to use a single hierarchy, but when you also have leaf values (refer to ❸ of Figure 3.20) that change nodes (refer to ❷ of Figure 3.20) based on the time period. For example, assume customer 100074 was attached to the Eastern Region from April 1, 2000 to March 31, 2009, and, from April 1, 2009 onward, is changed to the Northern Region. In this case, the system automatically maintains the end validity date as March 31, 2009. At runtime, SAP NetWeaver BW uses the date chosen in the query to construct the structure of the hierarchy. In Figure 3.24, you can see that customer 100074 is part of two nodes (Eastern Region as well as Northern Region) but with different validity periods.

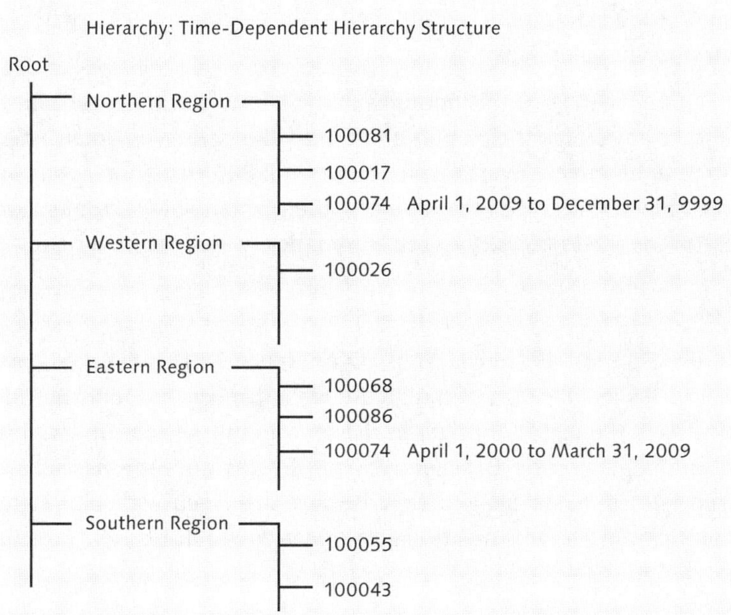

Figure 3.24 Time-Dependent Hierarchy Structure

Note

The Hierarchies, Version-Dependent option is offered as a checkbox, meaning that you can check this checkbox *and* one of the radio buttons, allowing you to configure both versions of hierarchies and time-dependent hierarchies.

Intervals

In some cases, there are such a large number of customers that assigning each one to a node in a hierarchy and then maintaining this data when changes occur is too tedious. SAP NetWeaver BW solves this problem by using the Intervals Permitted in Hierarchy option (❻ of Figure 3.21). By checking this flag for a hierarchy on customers grouped under regions, you can assign customers to specific regions based on their customer key values. For example, assume you've created a hierarchy where customers 000 to 105,000 belong in the Northern Region, and customers 105,001 to 110,000 belong to the Southern Region. All of the customers falling within the range are automatically assigned to their respective nodes; additionally, when you gain a new customer, the customer is automatically assigned to the correct node. For example, customer 102000 is automatically assigned to the Northern Region without specific maintenance for the hierarchy.

In summary, the major advantage of this option is that it allows you to create a hierarchy quickly. Another advantage is that you don't need the entire customer list at the time of creating the hierarchy. Even if you only have 2,000 customers, you can configure nodes for ranges that exceed that number; then, when new customers are added within these predefined ranges, they are automatically assigned to a node.

Reversing Signs for Nodes

When the Reverse +/- Sign for Nodes checkbox (❼ of Figure 3.21) is checked, you can decide whether to reverse the sign of transaction data displayed in reports. This functionality only affects the display of data in the report, and not the underlying actual data. For example, if you have a hierarchy on income and expense where income is displayed with minus signs and expenses are displayed with plus signs (according to accounting norms), this functionality allows you to display the income node with a negative sign.

3.5.5 Attributes Tab

> **Note**
>
> To see this tab, you must check the With Master Data checkbox in the Master Data/Texts tab.

As stated earlier, attributes give additional information about characteristic InfoObjects. Assume that in our case study, we want to analyze sales data for a customer with additional information about that customer, for example, the marketing office of the customer, the group to which this customer belongs, and so on. To meet this requirement, you must add the appropriate InfoObjects (Sales Office, Customer Group, etc.) as attributes of BW_CUST. You can assign multiple attributes to BW_CUST (Figure 3.25).

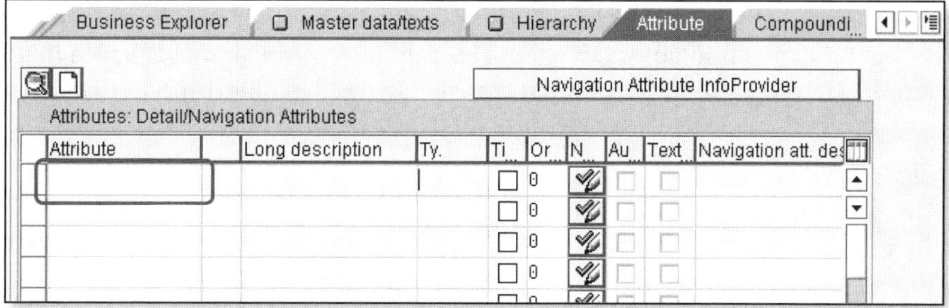

Figure 3.25 Attribute Tab

For our example, assign the following InfoObjects as attributes of BW_CUST:

- 0CUST_GROUP (Customer GRP2)
- 0CUST_GRP1 (Customer GRP)
- 0SALES_OFF (Sales Office)
- 0SALES_GRP (Sales Group)
- 0SALESEMPLY (Sales Employee)
- 0SALES_DIST (Sales District)

Assign each of these InfoObjects under the Attribute column. As shown in Figure 3.26, enter "0CUST_GROUP" and press Enter. SAP NetWeaver BW displays the rest of the column information automatically, that is, Long Description and Ty. (type of attribute).

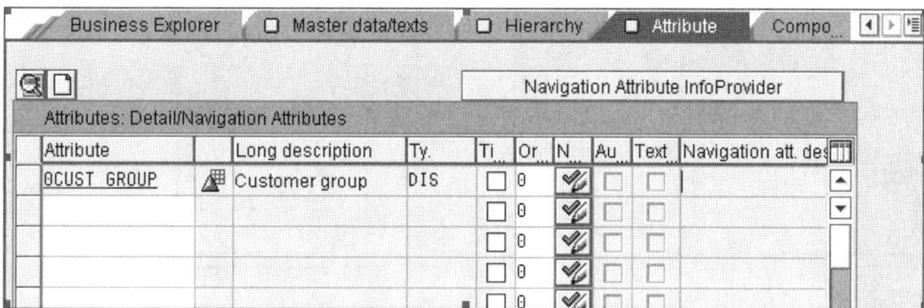

Figure 3.26 Entering Attributes

SAP NetWeaver BW offers two different types of attributes (which are displayed in the Ty. column):

- **Display Attribute (DIS)**
  By default, SAP NetWeaver BW marks attributes as display attributes so that when you analyze a report that contains the InfoObject in question (in this example, the Customer Group InfoObject), you can get additional information displayed in the report. For example, if 0SALES_DIST (Sales District) is the display attribute of BW_CUST, you can display the values of sales district for the respective customer in your report.
- **Navigational Attribute (NAV)**
  Defining an attribute as a navigational attribute enables additional navigational capabilities (such as sorting and drilldown) when the report is executed. SAP NetWeaver BW queries don't differentiate between characteristics (which are part of InfoCubes) and navigational attributes (which aren't part of InfoCubes).

Note

The choice to define an InfoObject as a characteristic or a navigational attribute depends on your reporting requirements, business processes, and SAP NetWeaver BW modeling techniques, as well as SAP Best Practices.

When you enter your attributes, they are automatically defined as display attributes. To change this, click the Navigational Attribute On/Off icon (❶ of Figure 3.27) for the appropriate attribute.

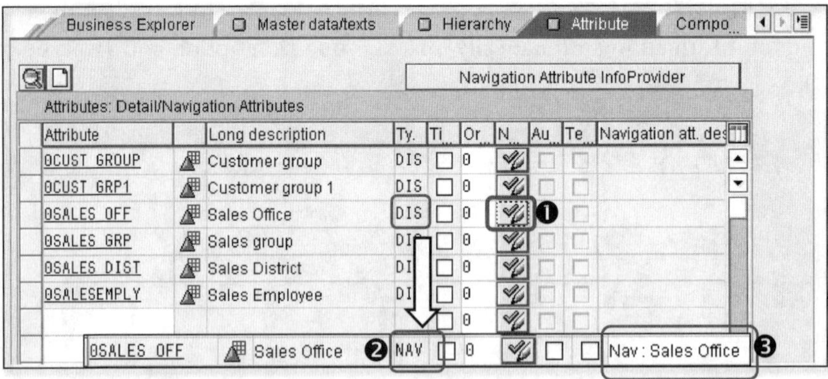

Figure 3.27 Defining Attributes

For our case study, we define 0SALES_OFF as a navigational attribute. When you assign this definition, SAP NetWeaver BW offers you a field for a description of the navigational attribute (❸ of Figure 3.27); you should always fill this out because it helps query designers distinguish whether the InfoObject is being used as a navigational attribute or a characteristic.

For each attribute, you can decide whether to make it time-dependent. You should use this if you want to keep track of specific data changes, for example, when the sales employees attached to certain customers change. If you don't want to keep track of this, leave this checkbox deselected. In this case, the information you load when you first load master data is what is used in reports; if the data is changed after master data is loaded, the old data is overwritten.

If you're interested in keeping track of these changes, you must define Sales Employee as a time-dependent attribute of BW_CUST (Figure 3.28). When any attribute is declared as time-dependent, the system internally uses two InfoObjects, 0DATEFROM (Valid From) and 0DATETO (Valid To), to store the values of dates when changes in the attributes are made. So, when you attach a customer to a sales employee, you must specify the dates for which that attachment is valid.

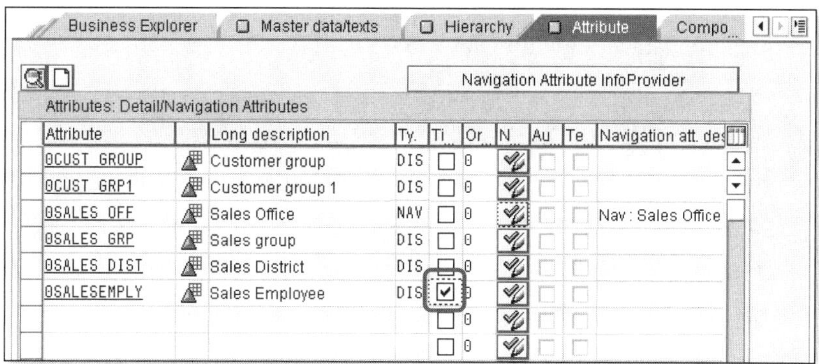

Figure 3.28 Switching Time Dependency

Let's consider a situation where the master data for a customer has the values listed in Table 3.3. (Note: The data here is in a simplified form for the purpose of explaining InfoObjects.)

BW_CUST	0SALESEMPLY	0DATEFROM
100086	12349999	01.01.2008

Table 3.3 Sample Data to Illustrate Time Dependency (A)

When loaded, it's stored as shown in Table 3.4.

Record Number	BW_CUST	0SALESEMPLY	0DATEFROM	0DATETO
1	100086		01.01.1000	12.31.2007
2	100086	12349999	01.01.2008	12.31.9999

Table 3.4 Sample Data to Illustrate Time Dependency (B)

As you can see from Table 3.4, one record becomes two records; due to the attribute's time-dependency, an additional record is created for the time period starting from January 1, 1000 (i.e., the past) up to one day before the Valid From date. This is done to show that the customer was *not* attached to an employee before the Valid From date.

Now, assume that on March 15, 2009, the customer is assigned to a new sales employee. As a result, you would load the new master data shown in Table 3.5.

BW_CUST	0SALESEMPLY	0DATEFROM
100086	67679999	03.15.2009

Table 3.5 Sample Data to Illustrate Time Dependency (C)

The system stores the data as shown in Table 3.6.

Record Number	BW_CUST	0SALESEMPLY	0DATEFROM	0DATETO
1	100086		01.01.1000	12.31.2007
2	100086	12349999	01.01.2008	03.14.2009
3	100086	67679999	03.15.2009	12.31.9999

Table 3.6 Sample Data to Illustrate Time Dependency (D)

As you can see from Table 3.6:

- Record 1 isn't changed.
- For record 2, the value of 0DATETO is changed from 12.31.9999 to 03.14.2009.
- For record 3, the newly added 0SALESEMPLY is valid from 03.15.2009 to 12.31.9999 (i.e., the future).

3.5.6 Compounding Tab

In some situations, BW_CUST doesn't have a unique value of its own but always depends on some other InfoObject for uniqueness. This is true, for example, when you have multiple sales organizations (0SALESORG), and the BW_CUST value is repeated throughout them. Without the value of the sales organization in the report, there's no unique value for BW_CUST. As shown in Table 3.7, BW_CUST = 100086 in 0SALESORG 1000 and 2000; so without including 0SALESORG in the query, the data in the report would be incorrectly accumulated under 100086.

0SALESORG	BW_CUST	BW_CUST (Text)
1000	100086	Wal-Mart
2000	100086	Electronic Shop

Table 3.7 Sample Data for Compounding

It's this type of situation where you need to use and configure the Compounding function. To begin, enter "0SALESORG" in the Superior InfoObject column (Figure 3.29). You do this because, in our example, BW_CUST must be compounded by 0SALESORG. After this relationship is defined at the InfoObject definition level, SAP NetWeaver BW includes 0SALESORG whenever you use the BW_CUST InfoObject (for designing InfoCubes, queries, etc.).

Multiple Superior InfoObjects

You can include multiple superior InfoObjects, if required.

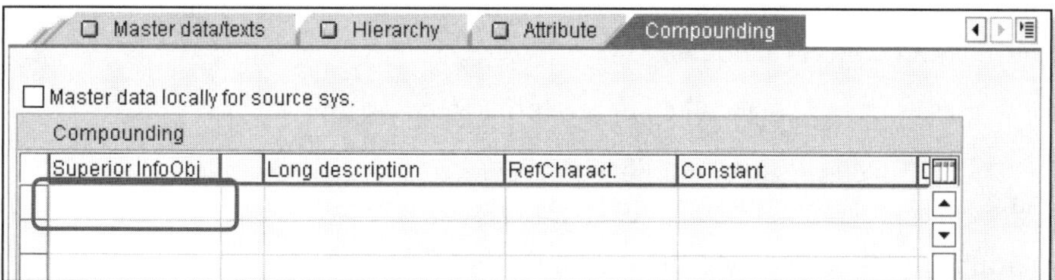

Figure 3.29 Compounding Tab

Note

In a business scenario that requires compounding, we recommend configuring the settings in the Compounding tab first and then configuring the settings in the Attribute tab.

Activate the InfoObject by using the Activate icon. An activated InfoObject can be used for creating other objects, such as InfoCubes, DSOs, and so on.

You've now completed all of the activities required to create and configure a characteristic InfoObject.

3.6 Creating a Key Figure InfoObject

In earlier sections, we explained the creation and configuration of characteristic InfoObjects that relate to business entities such as customers and products. In this section, we explain *key figure InfoObjects,* which relate to numeric measures of business entities in the form of quantities, values, *and so on.*

Key figure InfoObjects are created and stored in a separate InfoObject catalog. Before we explain key figure InfoObjects in more detail, let's first create an InfoObject catalog for key figures; the procedure for creating an InfoObject catalog is explained in Section 3.3, Creating an InfoObject Catalog, of this chapter. Create an InfoObject catalog under InfoArea BW_AREA with the following information:

- InfoObject Name: BW_KF_CA
- Description: BW Key Figures Catalog
- InfoObject Type: Key Figure

Activate the InfoObject catalog. Now you can create custom key figure InfoObjects under this InfoObject catalog.

Follow these steps to create a key figure InfoObject:

1. Start DWW using Transaction RSA1.
2. Click on Modeling to start the Modeling tasks of DWW.
3. Within the Modeling tasks, click on InfoObjects. A tree structure appears.
4. Select InfoObject catalog BW_KF_CA, open the context menu, and click Create InfoObject (❶ Figure 3.30).

In the resulting screen, you're prompted for the technical name and long description of the InfoObject. Additionally, there are two input fields: Reference Key Figure (❷), and Template (❸). We briefly discuss these fields next.

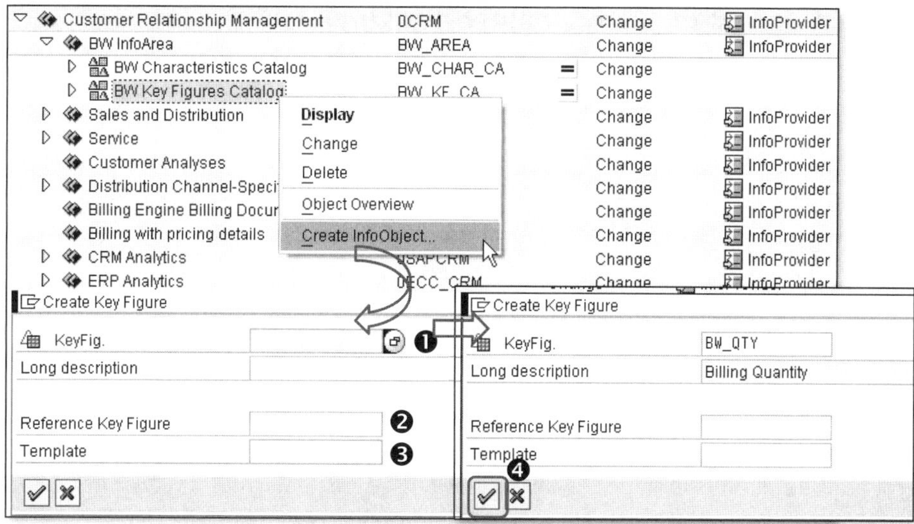

Figure 3.30 Create Key Figure InfoObject

3.6.1 Template Field

If you want to copy an existing key figure as a template for the new InfoObject, enter the name of the original key figure in the Template field. This creates a new key figure, copying all of the settings and properties from the template (which you can then edit, if needed). The new key figure doesn't have any reference to the template key figure.

3.6.2 Reference Key Figure Field

You may want to create a key figure with a reference to eliminate internal business volume; for example, the value of service revenue from internal work must be eliminated when accounting for the service revenue at the company level. When creating a key figure with reference, you see an additional tab page, Elimination. Enter one or more characteristic pairs in this tab regarding the key figure to be eliminated. In doing so, always choose a *sending characteristic* and a *receiving characteristic*. A typical example for such a pair of characteristics is Sending Cost Center and Receiving Cost Center. The characteristics of such a pair must have the same reference characteristic.

Enter the technical name and the long description for the key figure, and create the InfoObject with the following specifications:

- KeyFig.: BW_QTY
- Long Description: Billing Quantity

Click the Continue icon (❹ of Figure 3.30).

3.7 Configuring a Key Figure InfoObject

Creating a custom key figure InfoObject also involves configuring various settings based on specific requirements. The configuration settings are segregated in the tabs:

- Type/Unit
- Aggregation
- Additional Properties

Next we discuss each of these tabs in detail.

3.7.1 Type/Unit Tab

In this tab (Figure 3.31), you choose the Type and Data Type of the key figure InfoObject you're creating. Six types of key figures can be created: Amount, Quantity, Number, Integer, Date, and Time. Next we explain each of these in more detail.

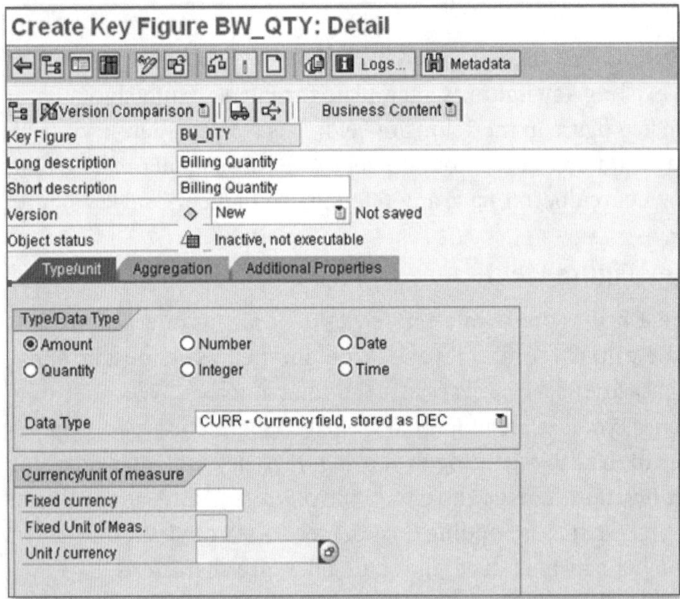

Figure 3.31 Type/Unit Tab

Amount Key Figure

Business measures associated with currency are created using amount key figure InfoObjects, for example, billing amounts, discounts, costs, and so on. Without a currency associated with this type of information, these numbers don't carry any significance.

The data type for a key figure is set by selecting from the dropdown menu shown in Figure 3.32.

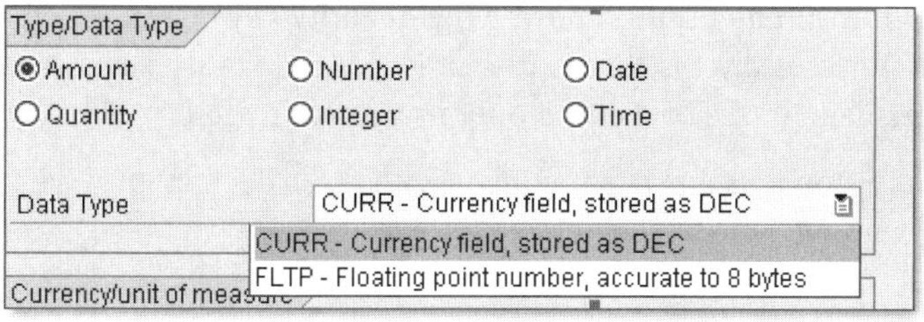

Figure 3.32 Create Key Figure: Data Type for Amount

Two different data types are associated with an amount key figure InfoObject: *CURR* and *FLTP*:

- CURR: The value is internally stored as a packed number with two decimal places and +/- sign.
- FLTP: The value is internally stored as a floating point number having no fixed number of digits, before and after the decimal point.

The definition of an amount key figure InfoObject isn't complete until the currency information is maintained for the InfoObject. You have the flexibility to associate a key figure InfoObject with either a fixed currency (❶ of Figure 3.33) or a variable currency (❷).

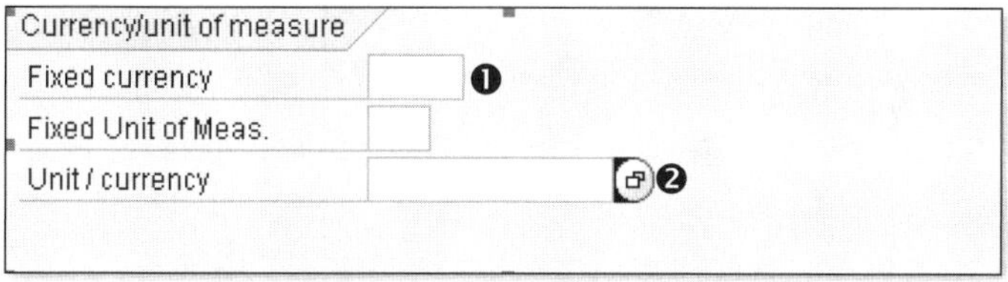

Figure 3.33 Fixed/Variable Currency

Your choice between a fixed and variable currency depends entirely on your business requirements. If all your business transactions are carried out in a single currency, a fixed currency is appropriate. On the other hand, if your business transactions occur in different currencies, you should fill the Unit/Currency field (❷). A unit InfoObject (e.g., 0CURRENCY) should be maintained in this field. This unit InfoObject will store the currency information when the data is loaded for the key figure. (Unit InfoObjects are discussed in more detail in Section 3.8, Creating a Unit InfoObject.)

Quantity Key Figure

Business measures such as billing quantity, net weight, and sales volume are always associated with a unit of measurement. By choosing the quantity key figure InfoObject, the key figure InfoObject is always linked to a unit. For a quantity key figure InfoObject, you can store data in one of the two options shown in Figure 3.34:

- QUAN: Value internally stored as a packed number with three decimal places.
- FLTP: Value internally stored as a floating point number.

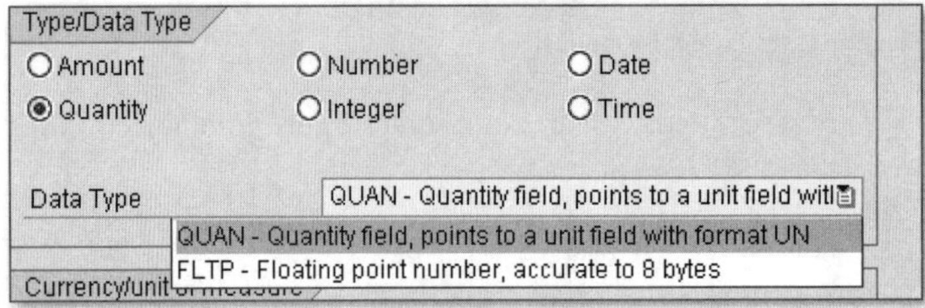

Figure 3.34 Data Type for Unit of Measurement

A quantity without a unit of measure has no meaning. In a scenario where all business transactions use only one unit of measure (meter, kilogram, etc.), you can enter a Fixed Unit of Meas. (❶ of Figure 3.35). Otherwise, you use a unit InfoObject (❷), which can store varying units of measure for business transactions.

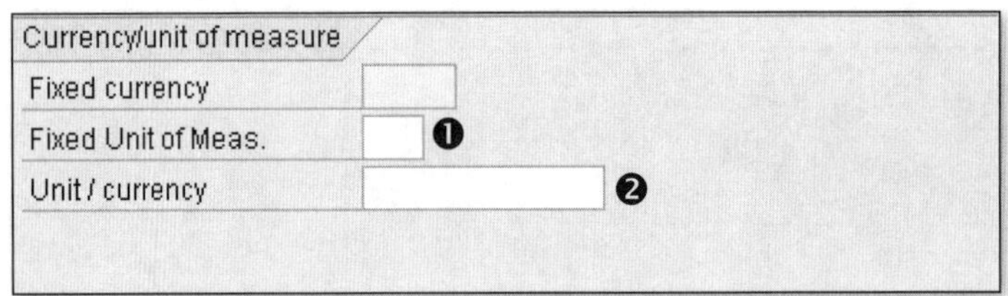

Figure 3.35 Fixed/Variable Unit of Measurement

Number Key Figure

Business scenarios always have some measures that don't have a unit or currency, and, further, may not be a whole number (e.g., exchange rates and interest rates). In this situation, you use a number key figure InfoObject (Figure 3.36). When you select the Number radio button, the Currency/Unit of Measure area is grayed out and becomes noneditable.

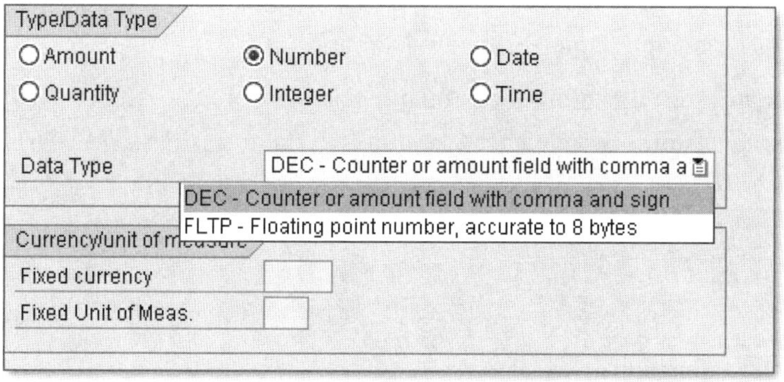

Figure 3.36 Number Key Figure

Your two options of data type are DEC and FLTP:

- DEC: Value internally stored as a packed number with three decimal places.
- FLTP: Value internally stored as a floating point number.

Integer Key Figure

When a business scenario has a measure that is always a whole number (e.g., item positions), you can use the integer key figure InfoObject (Figure 3.37). Again, in this case, the key figure doesn't require reference to any currency or unit of measurement.

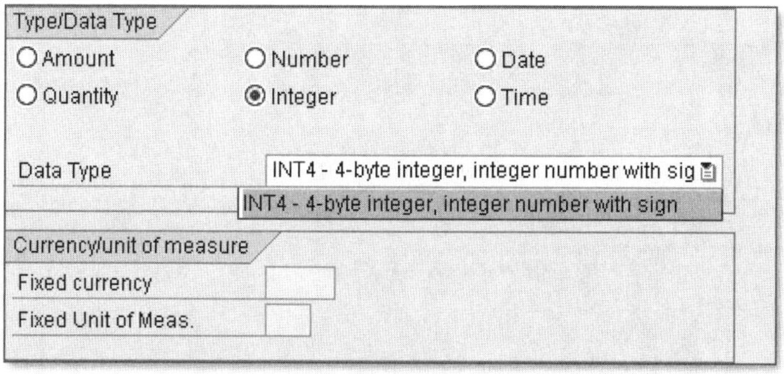

Figure 3.37 Integer Key Figure

Internally, the system stores information in only one format, INT4: 4-byte integers without decimal places.

Date Key Figure

When the business scenario has a measure that is always a date, use the date key figure InfoObject (shipment date, billing date, etc.).

Your two options for Data Type (Figure 3.38) are DEC and DATS:

- DEC: Value internally stored as a number of days, starting from 01.01.0001.
- DATS: Value internally stored as characters, length 8, in the format YYYYMMDD.

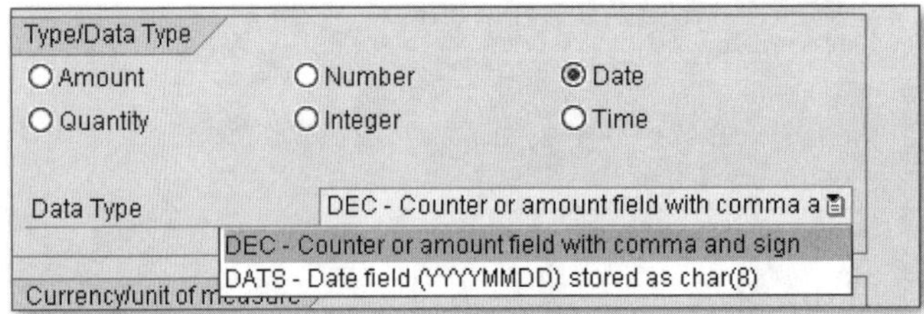

Figure 3.38 Date Key Figure

Time Key Figure

When the business scenario has a measure that is in time, you use the time key figure InfoObject. This is used to keep track of things such as the time a vehicle entered a plant, the time an employee entered the office, *and so on.*

Your two options for Data Type (Figure 3.39) are DEC and DATS:

- DEC: Value internally stored as number of seconds starting from zero o'clock. You can use this for calculation.
- TIMS: Value internally stored as characters, length 6, in the format HHMMSS.

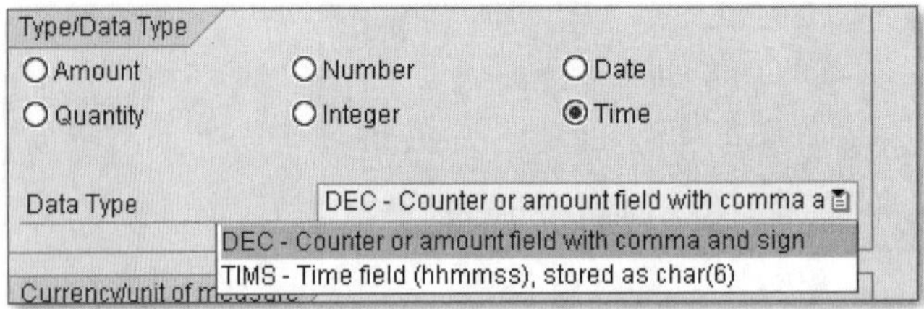

Figure 3.39 Time Key Figure

Our case study requires the key figure BW_QTY to be defined as a quantity key figure InfoObject (❶ of Figure 3.40) because the key figure corresponds to billing quantity (❷).

Because this key figure could have many different units of measure, you should define 0UNIT as the unit of measure (❸).

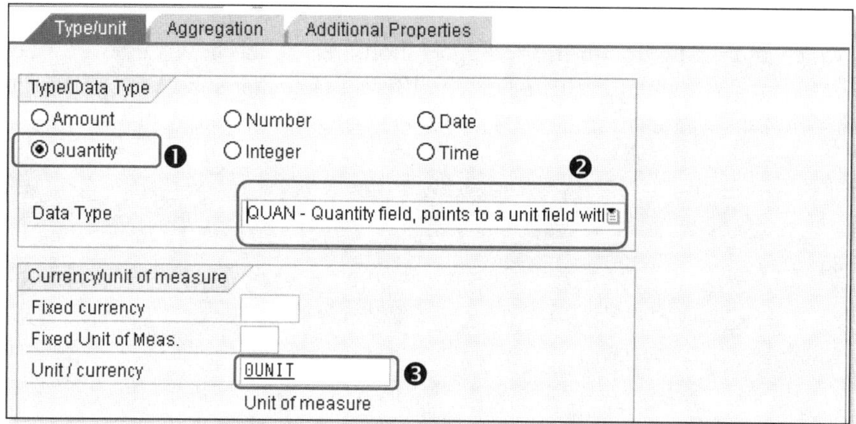

Figure 3.40 Create Key Figure BW_QTY

3.7.2 Aggregation Tab

There are two areas in the Aggregation tab (Figure 3.41):

- Aggregation
- Cumulative/Non-Cumulative Values

Type/unit | Aggregation | Additional Properties

Aggregation
Aggregation: SUM
Exception Aggregat.: Summation
Agg.referen.char.:

Cumulative/ Non-Cumulative Values
Cumulative val
NCum. value with NCum. value change
Non-cum.value change
Ncum. value with in- and out- flow
Inflow
Outflow

Figure 3.41 Create Key Figure: Aggregation

We discuss these areas next.

Aggregation Area

The settings and configuration in the Aggregation area define how values of a key figure are aggregated when evaluated using different characteristics. We explain the implication of the Aggregation field (Figure 3.41) using the sample data in Table 3.8.

BW_CUST	Material	Month	Billing Quantity (in SKU)
100086	38300	01.2009	100
100086	38300	02.2009	120
100086	38300	03.2009	110
100086	42000	01.2009	55
100086	42000	02.2009	58
100086	42000	03.2009	62

Table 3.8 Sample Data for Aggregation Behavior of Key Figure (Main)

In a report based on the data shown in Table 3.8, you decide to remove the month characteristic, so you can focus just on billing quantity and material. Because the aggregation and exception aggregation settings for BW_QTY are defined as SUM (which is the default setting) in the Aggregation field of Figure 3.41, the system adds up the billing quantity for each material (Table 3.9) sold to a customer.

BW_CUST	Material	Billing Quantity (in SKU)
100086	38300	330
100086	42000	175

Table 3.9 Aggregation Behavior of Key Figure (A)

Now, assume that you remove characteristics material from the report to view the data only at the customer level. As a result, SAP NetWeaver BW adds the billing quantity for all of the materials sold to a customer (Table 3.10).

BW_CUST	Billing Quantity (in SKU)
100086	505

Table 3.10 Aggregation Behavior of Key Figure (A)

The aggregation settings for a key figure allow you to define aggregation options such as minimum and maximum value from the range of stored values (Figure 3.42), depending on the scenario in consideration.

Figure 3.42 Create Key Figure: Aggregation

To explain the Exception Aggregation field, we use the sample data presented in Table 3.11.

Country	City	CalYear	Population (in Millions)
USA	New York	2007	10.5
USA	New York	2008	10.9
USA	New York	2009	11.0
USA	Detroit	2007	2.5
USA	Detroit	2008	2.6
USA	Detroit	2009	2.7

Table 3.11 Sample Data for Exception Aggregation of Key Figure (Main)

In this example, assume you decide to remove the CalYear column from the report. If SAP NetWeaver BW followed the same technique of summation as we discussed in the previous example, the resulting data would look like Table 3.12.

Country	City	Population (in Millions)
USA	New York	32.4
USA	Detroit	7.8

Table 3.12 Sample Data for Exception Aggregation of Key Figure (A)

Clearly, this is logically incorrect. This happened because the definition of the population key figure has SUM in both its Aggregation *and* Exception Aggregation fields. When you can't accumulate the value of key figures for different characteristics, you need to use the Exception Aggregation. Instead of SUM, Last Value (i.e., the most recent value) is a more appropriate selection (Figure 3.43).

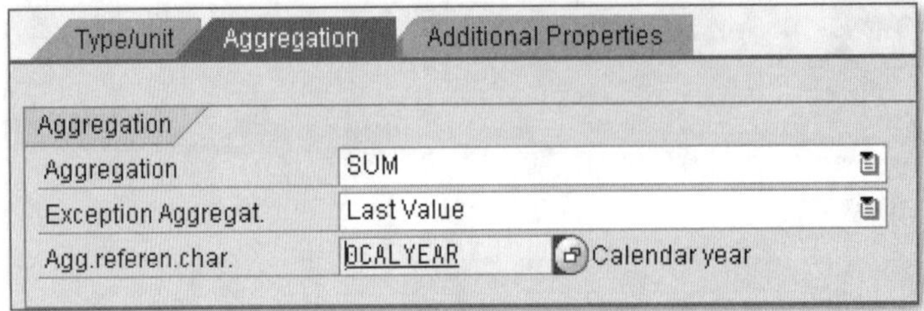

Figure 3.43 Create Key Figure: Exception Aggregation

Using the definition shown in Figure 3.43, SAP NetWeaver BW is instructed to perform the Last Value operation on the population key figure, using the reference characteristics (Agg.Referen.Char.) for exception aggregation. In this example, the reference characteristic is 0CALYEAR. (In most cases, the aggregation reference characteristic is a time characteristic, but not always.)

Now when CalYear is removed from the report, it results in the data shown in Table 3.13.

Country	City	Population (in Millions)
USA	New York	11.0
USA	Detroit	2.7

Table 3.13 Sample Data for Exception Aggregation of Key Figure (B)

SAP NetWeaver BW offers a variety of functions for the Exception Aggregation field, some of which are shown in Figure 3.44.

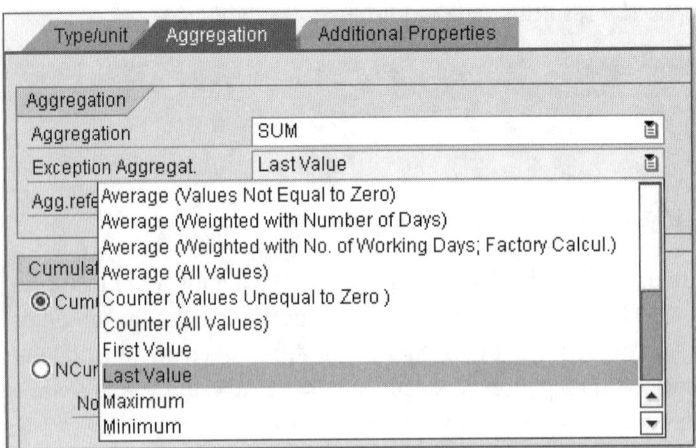

Figure 3.44 Functions Available for Exception Aggregation

Cumulative/Non-Cumulative Values Area

Cumulative key figures are those that can be meaningfully accumulated over a period of time. For example, the billing quantity for a customer over several months can be accumulated to get a total billing quantity for a customer for the quarter. *Non-cumulative key figures* are those that can't be accumulated meaningfully over a period of time; for example, the inventory of a certain material over three months of a quarter can't be added to get the total inventory at the end of the quarter. Such key figures must be defined as cumulative or non-cumulative.

Cumulative Key Figures Versus Exception Aggregation

The concept of cumulative versus non-cumulative key figures differs from the concept of exception aggregation because the latter only works at the report level (e.g., with BEx Analyzer output), while the former relates to data storage.

When you define a key figure as non-cumulative and use it in the definition of an InfoCube, it's known as a *non-cumulative InfoCube*. For non-cumulative InfoCubes, SAP NetWeaver BW maintains a specific feature called a *marker*, which is normally a time pointer. For this marker, the system calculates the value of a non-cumulative key figure; for the rest of the time periods, values are calculated at runtime based on the value at the marker and the non-cumulative value changes. For example, assume the value of a non-cumulative key figure on its marker (January 1, 2009) is 1000. The value of this key figure on December 31, 2009, is calculated by taking 1000 as the baseline and then, at runtime, adding/subtracting the subsequent value changes that have occurred between its marker (January 1, 2009) and December 31, 2009.

Value changes are stored in two ways, depending on how your DataSource supplies the value. The first way uses non-cumulative values to calculate value changes. For example, for inventory balance (which is, as we discussed, a non-cumulative value), the source system sends only the value change of inventory, whether a reduction or an increase, from the base value. If your change value is supplied using only one key figure from your DataSource, define your non-cumulative key figure as shown in ❷ of Figure 3.45. It's essential that the key figure used for the value change is cumulative.

The second way to define a non-cumulative key figure (❸ of Figure 3.45) is to have two cumulative key figures, one that will indicate the addition of value (inflow) and another that will indicate the reduction of value (OUTFLOW). If your DataSource supplies value changes using two different cumulative key figures, you can define your non-cumulative key figure using these settings.

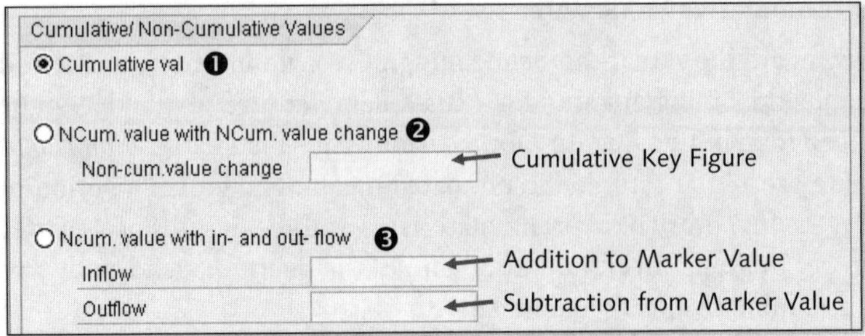

Figure 3.45 Non-Cumulative Key Figure

Non-cumulative key figures add additional processing burden to the system because the values are calculated at runtime and therefore take a longer time to report. We strongly recommend that you don't define a non-cumulative key figure unless your business scenario demands it.

For our example scenario, we retain the Aggregation tab settings for BW_QTY shown earlier in Figure 3.41.

3.7.3 Additional Properties Tab

The Additional Properties tab allows you to set the properties shown in Figure 3.46.

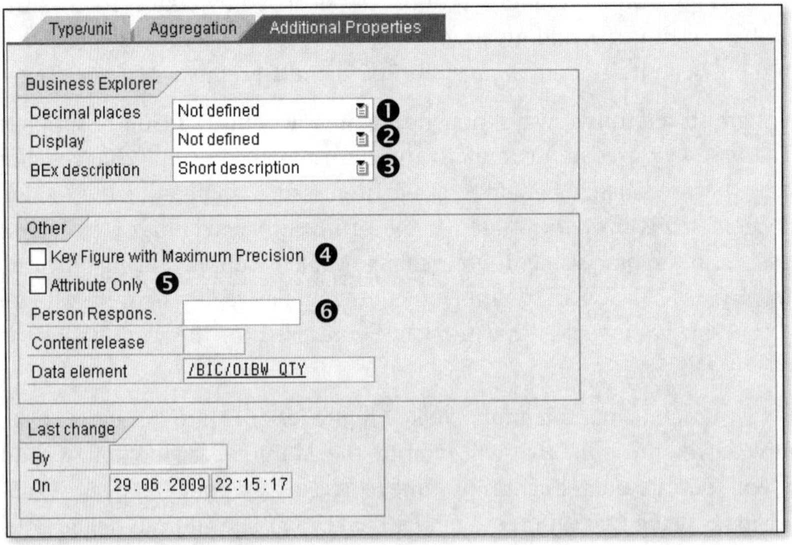

Figure 3.46 Additional Properties for Key Figure

The Additional Properties tab is divided into two main areas, which we discuss next. The last section (Last Change) is self-explanatory, so we won't discuss it here.

Business Explorer Area

The settings configured here are applied in the report only.

- **Decimal Places (❶)**
  You can define how many decimal places key figures can have when displayed in query output. The user of the query can override this setting.
- **Display (❷)**
  When the value of the key figure is large, it's difficult to read. You can solve this by configuring the Display field, which allows you to specify how to display numbers. For example, if you select Thousand, a key figure of 563412 is displayed as 563.412.
- **BEx Description (❸)**
  This indicates whether the short or long description is displayed in query output.

Other Area

The settings in the Other area are described here:

- **Key Figure with Maximum Precision (❹)**
  When you configure this setting for a key figure, SAP NetWeaver BW reduces the rounding issues for floating point numbers.
- **Attribute Only (❺)**
  When you set this for a key figure, you can't use the key figure as a navigational attribute when configuring other characteristic InfoObjects. You only attach this key figure as a display attribute.
- **Person Respons.**
  This field is used to indicate the person responsible for maintaining this key figure. This is used only for documentation purposes (❻).

We don't need to change any settings for our example, so we keep those shown in Figure 3.46.

Use the Activate icon to activate the key figure InfoObject. Figure 3.47 shows the active version of key figure InfoObject BW_QTY.

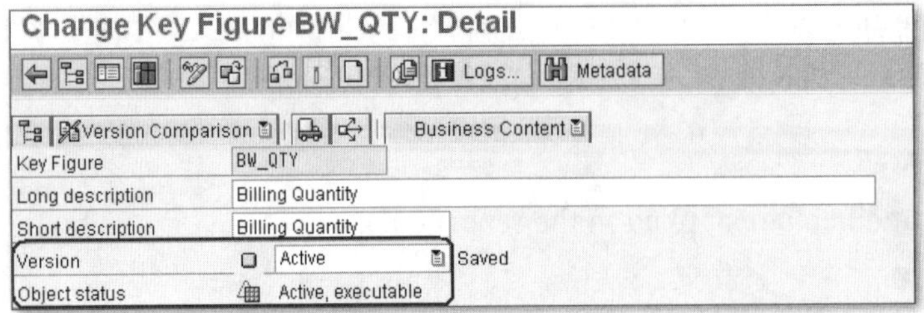

Figure 3.47 Key Figure: Active Status

Using the Back icon to return to the main DWW screen, you can see that your newly created key figure InfoObject is now available under InfoObject catalog BW_KF_CA (Figure 3.48).

Customer Relationship Management	0CRM	Change	InfoProvider
BW InfoArea	BW_AREA	Change	InfoProvider
BW Characteristics Catalog	BW_CHAR_CA	Change	
BW Key Figures Catalog	BW_KF_CA	Change	
Billing Quantity	BW_QTY	Change	InfoObjects
Sales and Distribution	0SALES	Change	InfoProvider

Figure 3.48 BW_QTY under InfoObject Catalog BW_KF_CA

We've now completed the process of creating a key figure InfoObject in SAP NetWeaver BW. In subsequent chapters of this book, we'll use the characteristic InfoObject BW_CUST and the key figure InfoObject BW_QTY to build our example scenario for ABCD Corp.

3.8 Creating a Unit InfoObject

We've now shown you the step-by-step process for creating characteristic and key figure InfoObjects; however, as we've already mentioned, you can't create time and technical InfoObjects. In this section, we conclude our explanation of creating InfoObjects by briefly explaining how to create a unit InfoObject. (Note, however, that we don't require a specific unit InfoObjects to be created or configured for our case study.)

To create a unit InfoObject, follow these steps:

1. Use Transaction RSD1 to open the Edit InfoObjects: Start screen (Figure 3.49).
2. Select Unit from the Type area (❶ of Figure 3.49).
3. Enter the technical name for the unit (❷).
4. Click on the Create icon (❸).
5. In the Create Unit box, enter the long description (❹).

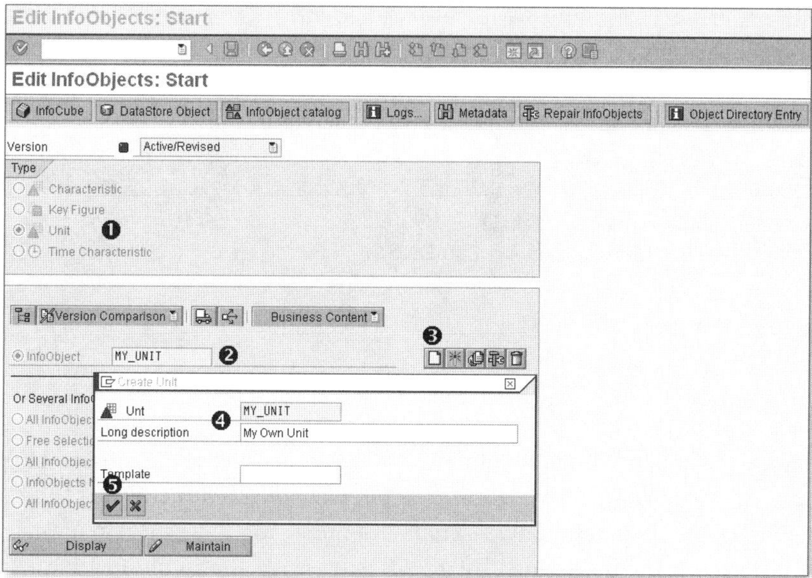

Figure 3.49 Creating a Custom Unit InfoObject

6. Click on the Continue button (❺). The next screen displays the InfoObject definition and the General tab (as shown in ❶ of Figure 3.50).

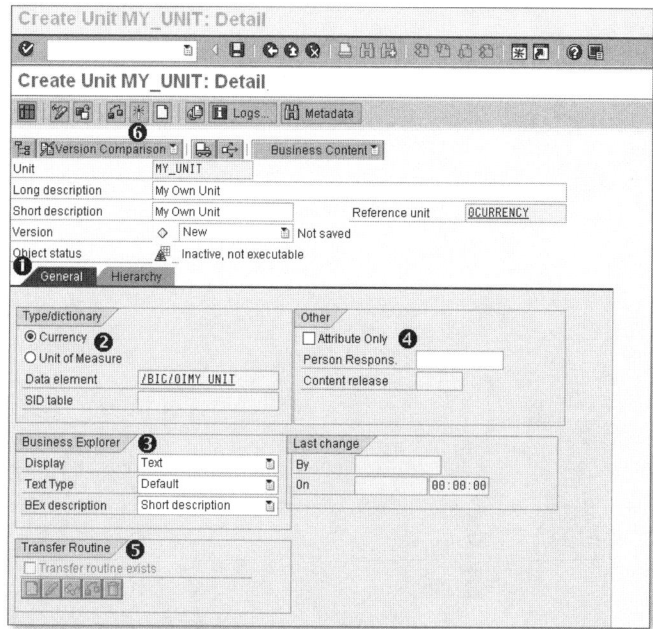

Figure 3.50 Creating a Unit Custom InfoObject

7. Select either Currency or Unit of Measure, as shown in ❷ of Figure 3.50. *Unit* InfoObjects are always created with reference to the SAP-delivered definition of unit/currency. So, if the data type is selected as CURRENCY, the reference unit is always 0CURRENCY. If Unit is selected, the reference unit is always 0UNIT.

Note

Other settings are shown in ❸, ❹, and ❺ of Figure 3.50. These settings have the same meaning as those explained in Section 3.5.1 and 3.5.2.

8. Activate your unit InfoObject (❻).

3.9 Summary

Because they are the smallest building block, InfoObjects are one of the most important objects in SAP NetWeaver BW. In this chapter, we explained the types of InfoObjects, how to create them, and how to configure them. You'll learn the relevance and use of different InfoObjects in subsequent chapters of the book. In the next chapter, we explain the DataStore object (DSO), its architecture, and the different types and application scenarios.

In this chapter, we explain the details of the DataStore object (DSO). DSOs play very crucial roles in the overall design of data warehousing, so understanding how DSOs work will help you design SAP NetWeaver BW solutions more effectively.

4 DataStore Objects

Storing operational data at the most detailed level is an integral function of a typical data warehouse. To this end, SAP NetWeaver BW's technical architecture includes the *DataStore object* (DSO), which stores data at a detailed level, tracks changes to data, and stores master data.

Note

DataStore objects were previously referred to as *operational DataStore objects* (ODS), but the title was changed to eliminate some common misinterpretations and assumptions related to the function and purpose of these objects.

In this chapter, we explain the DSO's architecture, configuration setting options, types, and application scenarios.

4.1 Introduction to DataStore Objects

In this section, we offer a brief introduction to the definition and purpose of DSOs, and then introduce the three types of DSOs offered by SAP NetWeaver BW.

4.1.1 Definition and Purpose

A *DSO* is an object that stores data at the most granular level, for example, storing records by business transactions such as billing documents (Figure 4.1).

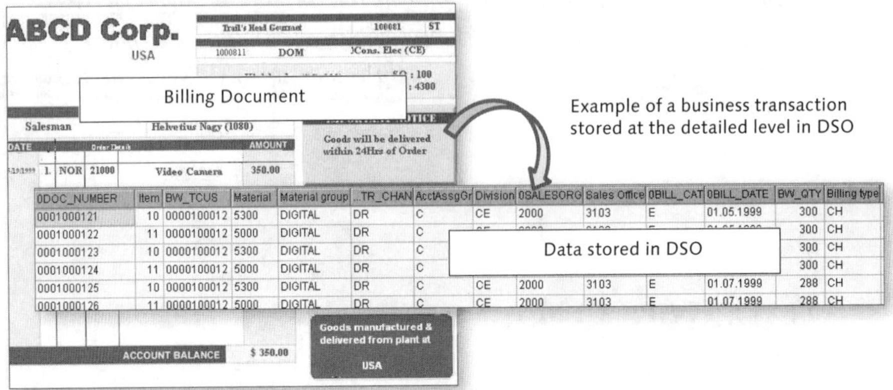

Figure 4.1 Detailed Storage of Business Transaction Data in DSO

In SAP NetWeaver BW, data targets are objects that physically store data. InfoProviders, on the other hand, are objects you can use to create queries for reporting. Queries can also be created on most data targets, so a data target can be an InfoProvider, but not all InfoProviders are data targets. DSOs are data targets but not necessarily InfoProviders. The central data target in SAP NetWeaver BW is an *InfoCube*, which normally stores data at the aggregated level and is used for creating queries (see Chapter 5, InfoCubes, for more details on InfoCubes). In any SAP NetWeaver BW design, it's a good practice to have DSOs as the staging layer, to store the transaction level and/or data from multiple sources, before relaying it onto InfoCubes or other data targets.

One of the major benefits of DSOs is the overwrite capability. Unlike InfoCubes, DSOs are transparent tables and can overwrite stored data for a defined key. In database parlance, a table's *key* uniquely identifies each record in the table. The key for a DSO is a unique combination of key field values. In addition to overwriting, DSOs can be configured to cumulate data for a defined key, just as with InfoCubes.

A DSO serves the following functions of data warehousing:

- Replication of business-critical data from the transactional source system into the data warehouse, which provides flexibility for archiving the data from the source system.
- Flexibility within data warehousing solutions to redesign other data targets, such as InfoCubes, that receive data from DSOs.
- A mechanism to identify changes in the original records for data sources that send entire data sets every time a change is made. This feature helps in transmitting

only relevant records or changes in the record to data targets that are above the DSO in the data flow of the data warehouse.

- A data staging layer within the data warehouse where data validation, cleansing, and synchronization can be managed.

DSOs have two types of fields: key fields and data fields. While the *key fields* uniquely identify a record in a DSO, all other fields are the *data fields*, which can contain both characteristic and key figure InfoObjects. When a DSO is created for a billing document with multiple items, the key fields of the DSO are generally the billing document number and item number. However, if you reset billing document numbers every year (making it possible to have duplicate billing document numbers across different years), the DSO must be identified by the billing document number, item number, and the year.

Data can be loaded into DSOs from any source system, as shown in ❶ and ❺ of Figure 4.2. The data stored in a DSO is normally very detailed and is further extracted to InfoCubes where it's summarized, as shown in ❷ of Figure 4.2. A DSO that is supplying data to an InfoCube can also be an InfoProvider; that is, queries can be created on this DSO (❸). That being said, it isn't *mandatory* to extract data from DSOs to InfoCubes; if you don't, the DSO is the end of the data flow, and queries can be created based on the DSO directly (❻). And you also create queries based on an InfoCube that stores data at a summarized level (❹). Finally, SAP NetWeaver BW offers a function called *report-to-report interface* (RRI), which you can use to jump from an InfoCube query to a DSO query (❼) to view detailed level data.

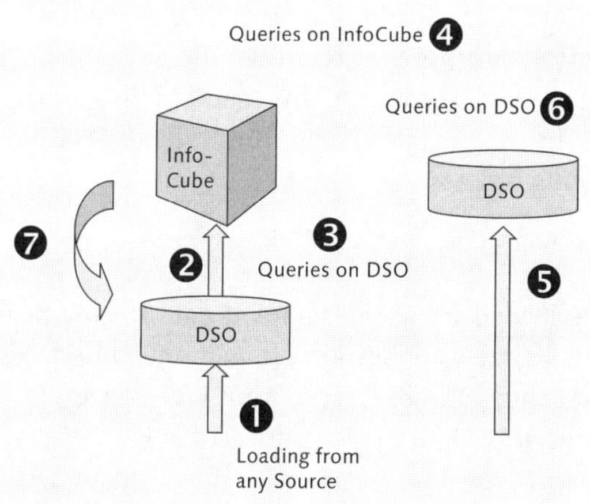

Figure 4.2 Position of DSO in SAP NetWeaver BW

Report-to-Report Interface (RRI)

RRI is a function that allows a BEx query (defined as the sender) to interact with another query, a BEx web application, a transaction code, or an ABAP report. These are known as the jump targets (defined as the receiver) and can be either inside or outside of the SAP NetWeaver BW system. This feature is available in the query navigation context menu, under the Goto function.

4.1.2 Types of DSOs

There are three types of DSOs in SAP NetWeaver BW, as described next.

Standard DSOs

This type of DSO is used most often in the data-staging layer and allows the overwriting of data fields as well as the adding of key figure values. Data in this type of DSO can be loaded using the standard data staging processes (i.e., data extraction, transformation, and data transfer processes), which are discussed in more detail in Chapter 7, Extraction, Transformation, and Loading. It consists of three tables, which are the Activation Queue table, Active Data table, and Change Log table. The Change Log table keeps track of record changes for a record with the same key field values. (Tables will be discussed in more details in Section 4.2, DSO Architecture.) Data from a standard DSO can be loaded to another DSO or to another InfoCube.

Write-Optimized DSOs

The architecture of this type of DSO is optimized for writing data into it and was introduced with SAP NetWeaver BW 7.0. It can load the data more quickly than a standard DSO because it isn't necessary to process the activation of a newly loaded request (this is explained in more detail in later sections of this chapter). This type of DSO consists of only one table: the Active Data table. Data in this type of DSO can be loaded using the standard data staging process.

Direct Update DSOs

The data in this type of DSO can't be loaded using the standard data staging process; instead, SAP NetWeaver BW supplies a few application programming interfaces (APIs). This type of DSO is used as a data target in the Application Process Designer (APD) process. As with the write-optimized DSO, this type consists of only the Active Data table.

4.2 Architecture of the Standard DSO

In this section, we focus specifically on the architecture of the standard DSO because it's the most widely used and is relevant to our ABCD Corp. case study. More specifically, we discuss the types of tables in a standard DSO and its activation process.

4.2.1 Types of Tables

As we've mentioned, the standard DSO consists of three tables: the Activation Queue, Active Data, and Change Log tables (Figure 4.3). These are discussed in more detail next.

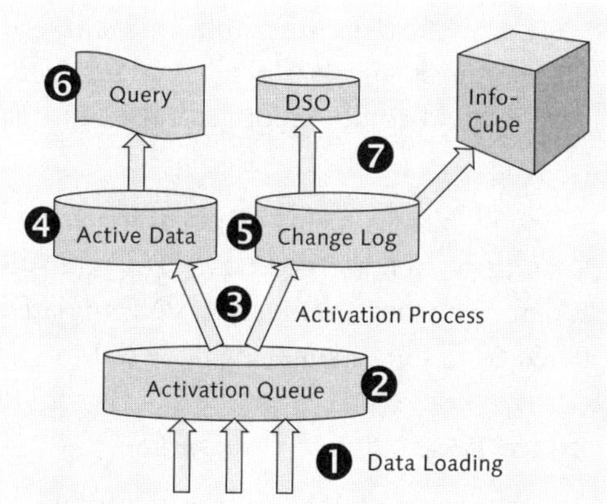

Figure 4.3 Architecture of a Standard DSO

Activation Queue Table

The Activation Queue table is only relevant for standard DSOs. When data is loaded into a standard DSO (❶ in Figure 4.3), it's first stored in this table. The key fields of this table are technical and consist of the request SID (*surrogate ID*), the package ID (data package number), and the record number. The *request SID* is a number given to each new data loading, and each request SID is divided into a number of data sets known as the *package ID*. Individual records in each package ID are assigned a number, starting from 1, and this is the *record number*. The data available in the Activation Queue table is neither available for reporting nor for sending to another data target because data in the Activation Queue table, by definition, hasn't yet been activated. The Activation Queue table is shown as ❷ of Figure 4.3.

Active Data Table

The data from the Active Data table *is* generally used for reporting, as shown in ❻ of Figure 4.3. In some cases, this table also supplies the full data upload to another data target. The key field chosen while designing a DSO is the key of this table. This key is also known as the *semantic key* of the DSO. The activation process (only applicable to standard DSOs) moves the data from the Activation Queue table to the Active Data table and the Change Log table (❸). The Active Data table is shown in ❹. In some cases, an Active Data table also supplies a full upload.

Change Log Table

All of the changes to existing records (i.e., records with the same key field combination) are recorded in the Change Log table. The key fields of this table are technical, so they are comprised of a combination of the request GUID (Globally Unique Identifier), package ID, and record number. This key field combination isn't the same as that for the Activation Queue table.

The Change Log table is related to the other two tables in such a way that the activation process moves data from the Activation Queue table to the Change Log table (❺ of Figure 4.3) and Active Data table (❹). When data from a standard DSO is updated to other data targets, the delta load is supplied from the Change Log table (❼).

4.2.2 Activation Process for a Standard DSO

As we explained earlier, data in standard DSOs are contained within three tables. Data moves among these tables during the activation process (which we explain more thoroughly in Section 4.4, Configuration of the Standard DSO). More specifically, the activation process moves data from the Activation Queue table to the Active Data and Change Log tables, deleting it from the Activation Queue table on successful activation.

Note

Write-optimized and direct update DSOs only have one table: the Active Data table. As such, there is no movement among tables in these two types of DSOs. This discussion of data movement applies only to the standard DSO.

To explain this concept more thoroughly, let's use an example (Figure 4.4). The key field for the DSO in Figure 4.4 is the Document Number field, and its two data fields are customer and amount. The amount field is set to the overwrite mode. The process of configuring the overwrite mode is explained in Chapter 7.

When a request is loaded into a standard DSO, the loaded data gets stored in the Activation Queue table, as shown in Figure 4.4. The key field combination of the Activation Queue table is technical, as stated earlier. At this moment, the Active Data table and Change Log table are both empty.

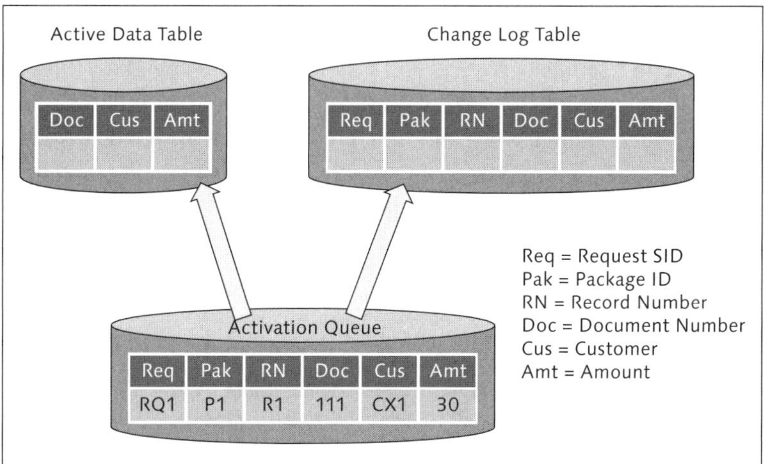

Figure 4.4 Activating a Request in a DSO (Part I)

When a request (let's call it request RQ1) is activated, the data is moved *from* the Activation Queue table *to* the Active Data and Change Log tables (Figure 4.5).

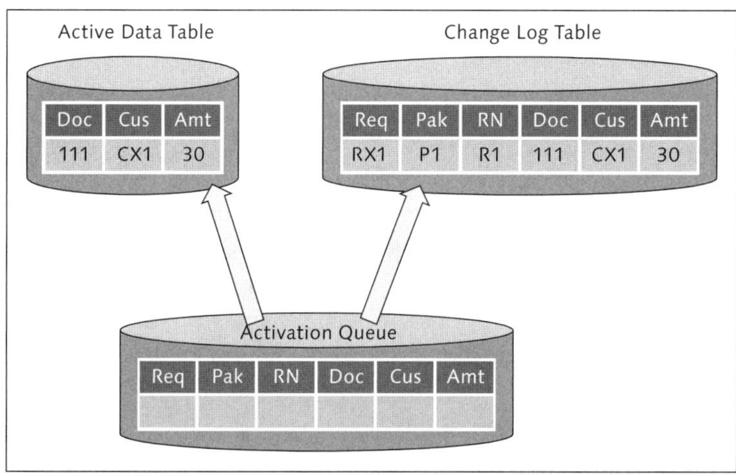

Figure 4.5 Activating a Request in a DSO (Part II)

Because the Active Data and Change Log tables were empty, the records in request RQ1 are inserted into them. The key field combination of the Active Data table is semantic (developer configured), and the key field combination of the Change Log table is technical. The request ID in the Activation Queue table and that of the activated request in the Change Log table are different; in this case, we identify the request in the Change Log table as RX1.

Now assume that a second request, request RQ2, is loaded into the DSO (Figure 4.6). As you can see from the figure, RQ2 shows that document number 111 in the source system has been changed; the amount was 30 and is now 40. Because this request is still not activated, the data in the Active Data and Change Log tables remains unaffected.

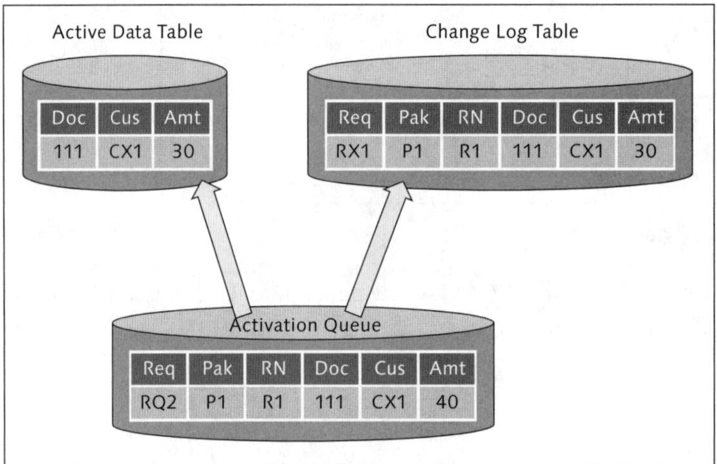

Figure 4.6 Activating a Request in a DSO (Part III)

During the activation process for RQ2, SAP NetWeaver BW checks the existence of the records in the Active Data table. If a record with the same semantic key is found, the values of the data fields are overwritten. To keep track of this change, SAP NetWeaver BW creates two records in the Change Log table. One record is known as the *before image*, which is a copy of the existing record with the key figures negated. The second record is known as the *after image*, which is the latest value in the record.

As shown in Figure 4.7, the Active Data table still shows only one record because the former record was overwritten by the latest value of the amount key figure. The

Change Log table, on the other hand, has three records after activation. The first record is from the previous activation, and the next two records are from the current activation process.

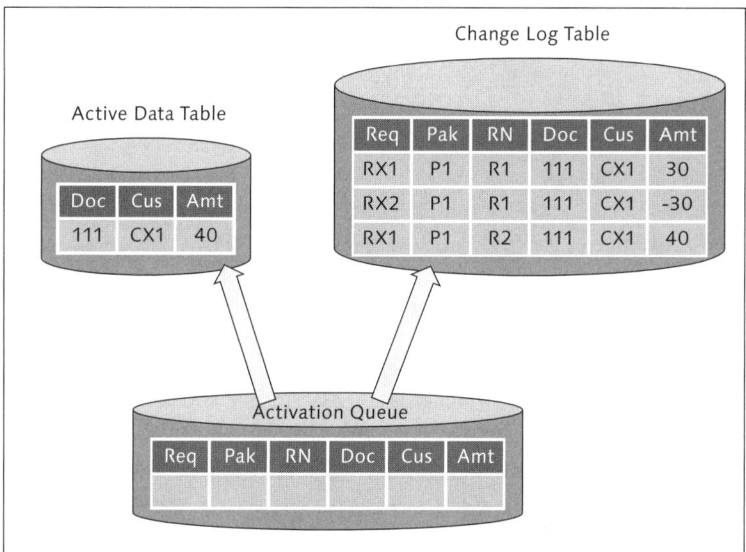

Figure 4.7 Activating a Request in a DSO (Part IV)

In short, whenever any change happens to the existing record of a standard DSO, two records are inserted in the Change Log table, as shown in Table 4.1. The total change in value of the Amount field is 10 (-30 + 40).

	Req	Pak	RN	Doc	Cus	Amt
Before Image	RX2	P1	R1	111	CX1	-30
After Image	RX2	P1	R2	111	CX1	40

Table 4.1 Before and After Image Generated in the Change Log Table

Field changes don't only happen to fields with numeric values (as was the case in this example) but can also happen to non-numeric fields, such as Delivery Date, Status of Record, and so on.

Table 4.2 provides a brief comparison of these three types of DSOs. This table should help you understand the architecture and usage of each type.

Type of DSO	Activation Required?	Active Data Table	Activation Queue Table	Change Log Table	Reporting Possible?	SID Generation
Standard	YES	YES	YES	YES	YES	YES
Write-Optimized	NO	YES	NO	NO	YES	NO
Direct Update	NO	YES	NO	NO	YES	NO

Table 4.2 Comparison of Different Features of DSOs

We now explain the influence of values of InfoObject 0RECORDMODE on the activation process.

4.2.3 0RECORDMODE

When a standard DSO is activated, SAP NetWeaver BW adds the 0RECORDMODE InfoObject to the definition of the standard DSO (in addition to the key fields and data fields) and to all three tables of the standard DSO. This InfoObject is used internally by SAP NetWeaver BW. You can overwrite the existing record for the same semantic key field combination, in addition to adding key figure values for the record with the same semantic key field combination.

SAP Business Content offers DataSources for a number of standard business processes. The DataSource field ROCANCEL, for example, is mapped to the 0RECORDMODE InfoObject in SAP NetWeaver BW. The combination of the update mode (overwrite or add) set in the transformation, along with the value of the 0RECORDMODE InfoObject, helps SAP NetWeaver BW properly treat the incoming record in the Active Data and Change Log tables. For example, consider a situation where you've created and loaded a SAP source system document in the DSO, and now you're forced to cancel this document in the SAP source system. The DataSource sends the reverse image of the document to SAP NetWeaver BW, which is communicated using ROCANCEL and 0RECORDMODE mapping. The treatment given to this record in the Active Data and Change Log tables depends on this value. Alternatively, another DataSource in this situation might send a delete signal using the ROCANCEL and 0RECORDMODE mapping. In this case, the treatment given to the record in the DSO is different. The following are the values for the field ROCANCEL and the meaning that they communicate about the record:

BLANK	The record provides an after image.
X	The record provides a before image.
A	The record provides an additive image.
D	The record must be deleted.
R	The record provides a reverse image.
N	The record provides a new image.

Note on Multiple Requests

When using standard DSOs, multiple requests can be loaded and activated in parallel. While doing so, SAP NetWeaver BW internally sorts the data, first using the technical key and then using the semantic key. This ensures that the records in the Active Data table are updated in the correct sequence. Sequence plays a very important role when multiple changes are made to the same document.

4.3 Designing a DSO

Recall the case study we've been using throughout this book (ABCD Corp.). For the purposes of this discussion, let's assume that the auditors of ABCD Corp. require traceability to a specific billing document. This might be needed to analyze instances of variances, or when aggregated results require billing document level investigation, and the information is contained in the data warehouse solution (as opposed to transactional systems, where records are archived over periods of time). This means that you must have a DSO that stores billing documents at the most detailed level.

With this scenario in mind, this section explains the process of creating a standard DSO and adding InfoObjects to the DSO. Although there are three types of DSOs, the processes of creating all three are similar. The content discussed in this section applies to all three types of DSOs.

To begin, start the Data Warehousing Workbench (DWW) using Transaction RSA1. Under Modeling in the Navigation section, select InfoProvider, as shown in ❶ of Figure 4.8. DSOs are created under InfoArea. From the tree section of the screen, select the InfoArea to which you want to attach your DSO (❷). In this example, InfoArea BW_AREA is selected.

Using the context menu of InfoArea BW_AREA, select the Create DataStore Object option (❸). A pop-up box titled Edit DataStore Object appears (Figure 4.9).

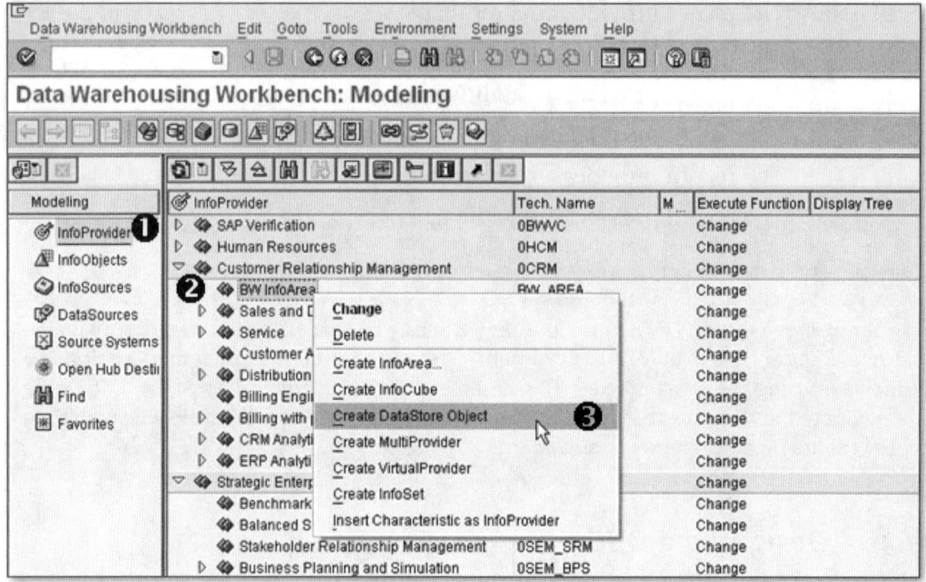

Figure 4.8 Creating a DSO

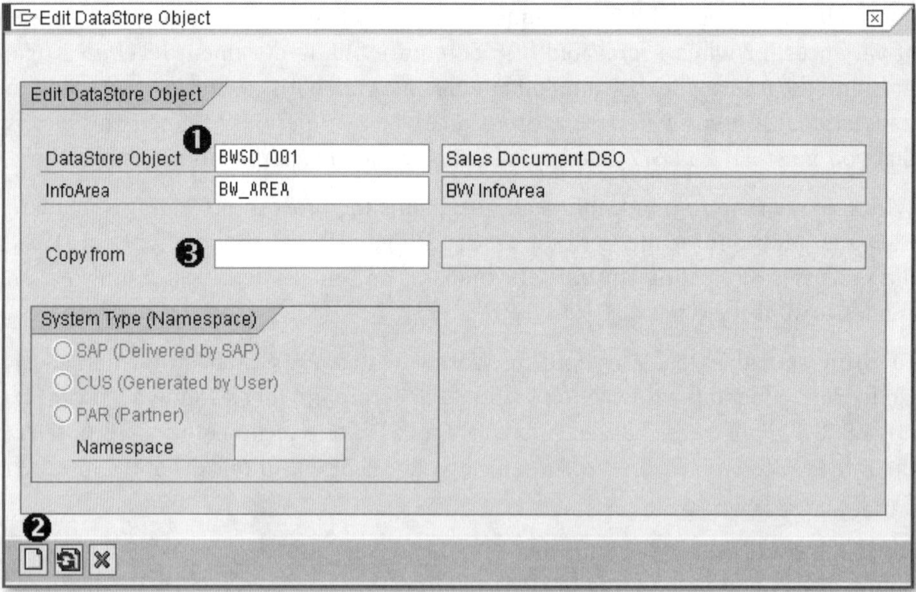

Figure 4.9 Edit DataStore Object: Entering Name and Description

DSOs require a unique technical name and description. In this example, we use the technical name "BWSD_O01" and the description "Sales Document DSO," as shown in ❶ of Figure 4.9. If you're creating a DSO that is similar to another DSO in the SAP NetWeaver BW system, you can copy the structure of that DSO by entering its name in the Copy From field (❸).

Click on the Create icon (❷). The resulting screen is shown in Figure 4.10.

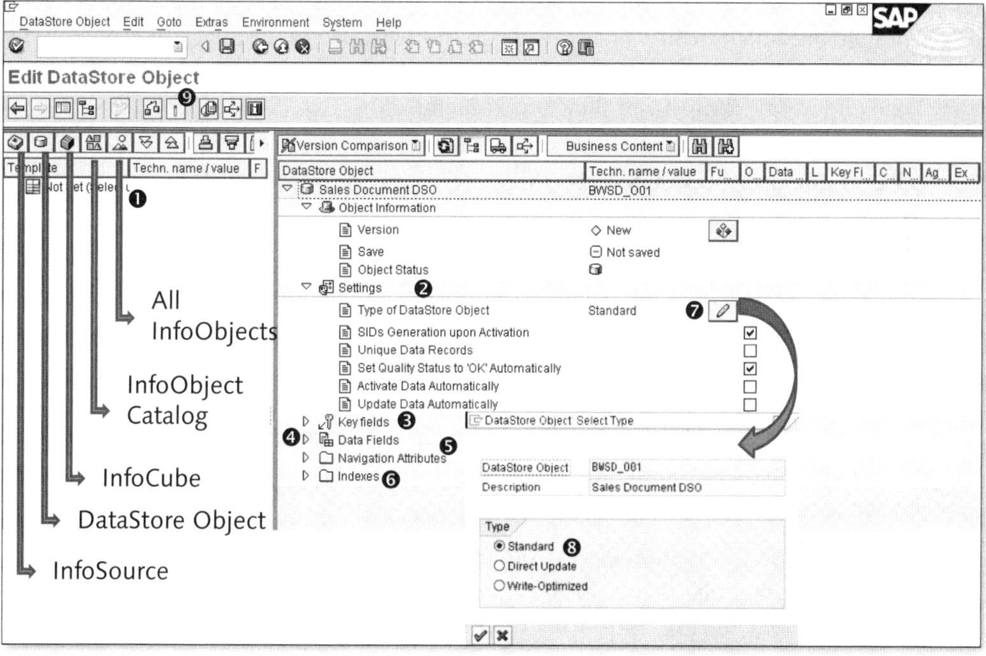

Figure 4.10 Key Settings in a DSO

The settings available when creating the DSO are shown in ❷ of Figure 4.10 and are explained in detail in Section 4.4.1, Key Settings in a Standard DSO. Different sections of a DSO definition are visible as key fields, data fields, navigation attributes, and the index, which are shown in ❸, ❹, ❺, and ❻ of Figure 4.10.

By default, the DSO type is created as the standard type (❼). This can be changed by clicking on the Change icon. The resulting pop-up box (❽) allows you to change the type of the DSO by selecting the appropriate radio button.

4.4 Configuration of the Standard DSO

Although the process of designing a DSO (discussed in Section 4.3, Designing a DSO) is the same for all three types, some of the configuration settings for each one differ. In this section, we explain the configuration settings for a standard DSO.

4.4.1 Key Settings in a Standard DSO

There are a few key settings for a DSO that play a very important role in its overall design and functionality. Figure 4.10 shows the screen with the settings we discuss in this section (❷). You can access this screen by selecting the DSO from the DWW and choosing Change from the context menu.

SIDs Generation Upon Activation

When checked (which occurs by default), the SIDs Generation Upon Activation box causes the system to generate an integer number known as the *surrogate ID* (SID) for each master data value. These SIDs are stored in separate tables called *SID tables*. For each characteristic InfoObject, SAP NetWeaver BW generates a separate SID table. When loading and activating data into a DSO, SAP NetWeaver BW checks the existence of an SID value for each value of the InfoObject (if the InfoObject contains master data) in the SID table. The system then generates a new value of SID if an existing value isn't found. The SID value is used internally by SAP NetWeaver BW when a query is based on a DSO.

There may be a situation where you create and use a standard DSO for intermediate data staging; that is, you create a standard DSO that only keeps data that is sent to another DSO or InfoCube. This DSO may not be used for reporting purposes. In this situation, you don't want the system to look for the existence of an SID value because it's a time-consuming process, so you should uncheck the SIDs Generation Upon Activation box.

Because our case study requires that this DSO be used for reporting purposes, we didn't change this default setting.

Unique Data Records

This setting is used when there's no chance that the data being loaded into a standard DSO will create a duplicate record, and it improves performance by eliminating some internal processes (such as sorting or creating a before image). If this box is checked, and it turns out that there *are* duplicate records, you'll receive an error message. Because of this, you should only select this box when you're sure that you won't have duplicate data For example, when your source system doesn't have the ability to edit, change, or delete created documents, you can safely use this setting.

Set Quality Status to 'OK' Automatically

The Set Quality Status to 'OK' Automatically flag results in the quality status of the data being set to "OK" after being loaded without any technical errors; the status must be set to this to activate newly loaded data in a standard DSO. Only activated data can be passed to further data targets.

This flag is checked by default, and we don't recommend changing this.

Activate Data Automatically

Data loaded in standard DSOs first get stored in the Activation Queue table, which is activated using the activation process. (Only activated data is available for reporting and passing to another data target.) To make this process automatic, you should check this flag. It's unchecked in this example because we're going to explain the manual process of activation in subsequent chapters (Chapter 14, Administration and Monitoring). The process of automatically activating data can also be configured using the Process Chain tool, which is covered in Chapter 14.

Update Data Automatically

Activated data available in a standard DSO can be passed to other data targets, such as another DSO or an InfoCube. This process can be automated by setting this flag. You can also automate this process using the Process Chain tool, which is covered in Chapter 14.

After all of the key settings are configured, you must include InfoObjects in the DSO

4.4.2 Including InfoObjects in the DSO

At this point, you must decide which InfoObjects you want to include in the DSO. The most important decision is to finalize its key fields because combinations of these uniquely identify each record in the DSO. Using the case study scenario we described at the beginning of this section, you design the DSO for storing billing records at the detail level. Billing records contain details such as the sold-to party, material, billing date, billed quantity, billed amount, and so on, and all of these details can be uniquely identified by the combination of a billing document number and its billing item number. In this case, the billing document number and billing item number can be designed as key fields of the DSO, and all other objects can be included as data fields.

The InfoObjects to be included in a DSO can be selected using two different methods — templates and direct input — which we discuss in more detail next.

Using Templates

The left pane of Figure 4.11, allows you to select InfoObjects using the template function (refer ❶ of Figure 4.10). Several types of templates are available for selecting InfoObjects: InfoSource, DataStore Object, InfoCube, InfoObject Catalog, and All InfoObjects.

In this example, we'll use the template called InfoObject Catalog. To do this, select the InfoObject Catalog icon, as shown in ❶ of Figure 4.11. SAP NetWeaver BW displays a pop-up screen titled Select InfoObject Catalog. Select InfoArea (❷). The InfoObject Catalog attached to the selected InfoArea is listed (❸). Double-click on InfoObject Catalog BW_CHAR_CA. The Template area on the screen now shows all of the InfoObjects available under the selected InfoObject Catalog (❹). You can select one or multiple InfoObjects by dragging and dropping over either key fields or data fields (❺).

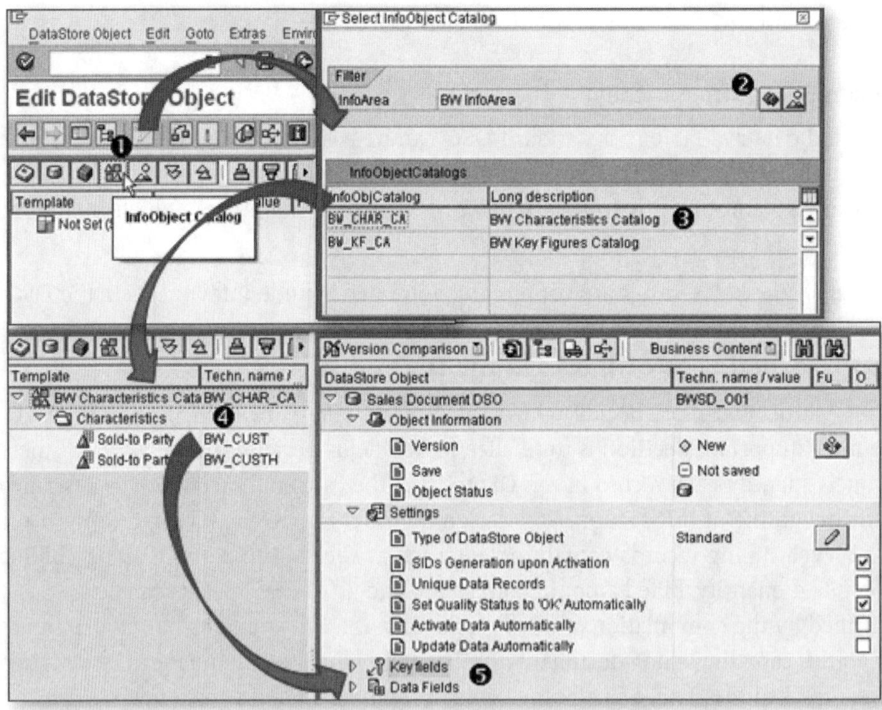

Figure 4.11 Edit Data Store: Using Templates to Include InfoObjects in a DSO

Direct Input

If you already know the technical names of the InfoObjects you want to include in the design of your DSO, you can use this method. Referring back to our case study scenario, the key fields of DSO BWSD_O01 are Sales Document Number (InfoObject 0DOC_NUMBER) and Sales Document Item (InfoObject 0S_ORD_ITEM). Because the names of these InfoObjects are already known, we can use the direct input method. Select the key fields as shown on ❶ of Figure 4.12. Using the context menu, select the INFOOBJECT DIRECT INPUT option (❷).

Type the technical name of the InfoObjects you want to include as key fields of the DSO. Enter "0DOC_NUMBER" and "0S_ORD_ITEM," as shown in ❸ of Figure 4.12, and press Enter. (SAP NetWeaver BW automatically checks the entered InfoObject names and shows the long description if they are validated correctly.) Now click on the Continue icon (❹).

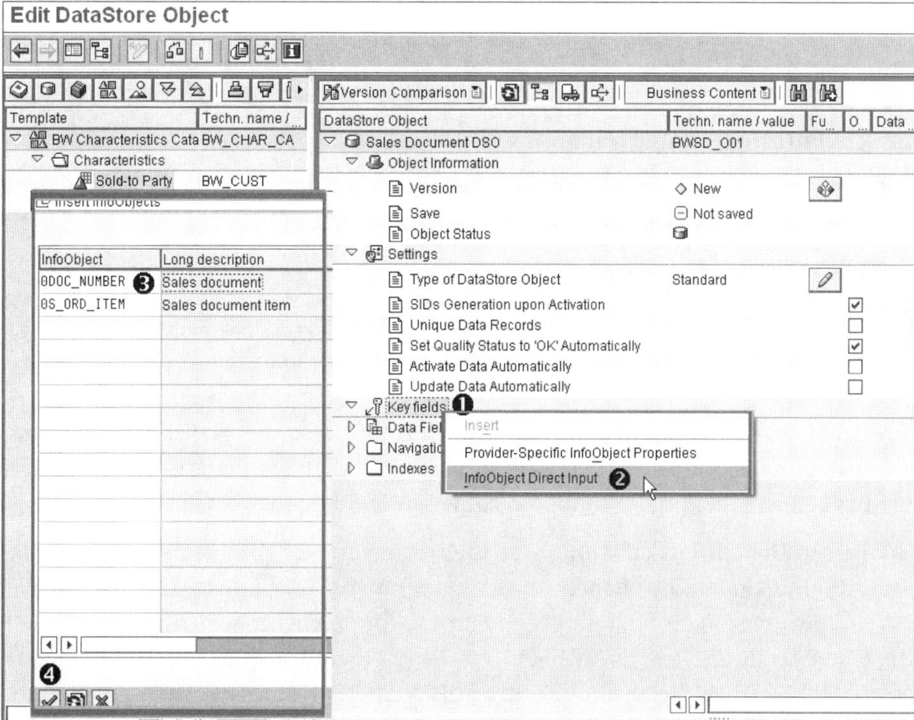

Figure 4.12 Edit DataStore: Direct Input

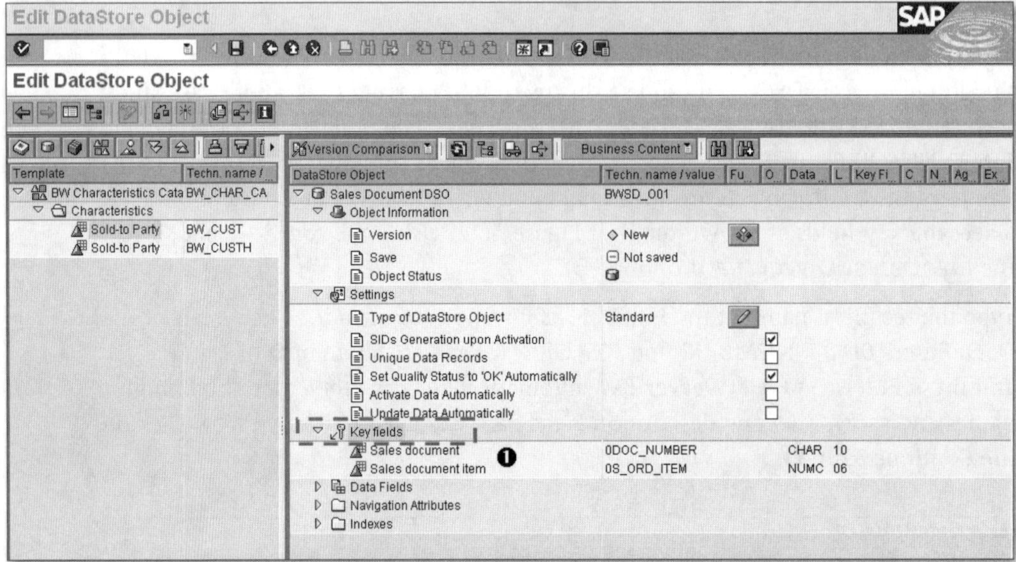

Figure 4.13 Edit DataStore: Key Fields

4.4.3 Entering Data Fields

The next step in configuring a standard DSO is to enter the data fields. The data fields can have both characteristic and key figure InfoObjects.

> **Note**
>
> Including InfoObjects in data fields is accomplished by the exact same process as including InfoObjects in key fields (either by the template or direct input method).

Navigation attributes defined in the included InfoObjects are available for viewing under the Navigation Attrib column. They are included automatically, but you still need to confirm them by selection, as shown in ❶ of Figure 4.14.

The box in the On/Off column (refer to ❷ of Figure 4.14) indicates whether the navigation attribute is switched on (included) or off (excluded). SAP NetWeaver BW follows a standard naming convention for navigation attributes: NAME_OF_CHARACTERISTICS__NAME_OF_ATTRIBUTE. So, for example, the name 0MATERIAL__0DIVISION indicates that 0DIVISION is the navigation attribute of the 0MATERIAL InfoObject (❸).

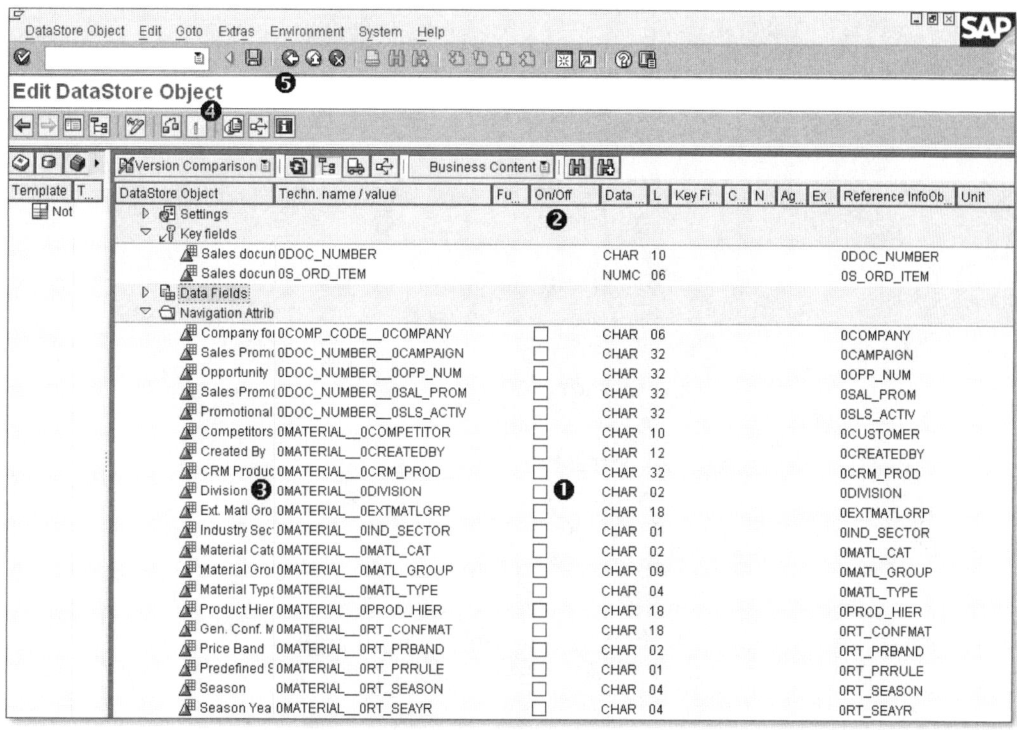

Figure 4.14 Edit DataStore: Navigation Attributes

> **Note**
>
> Reporting performance on DSO is improved by use of secondary indexes. You can create secondary indexes in all types of DSO.

This completes the steps required to configure a standard DSO; the final design of DSO BWSD_O01 is shown in Table 4.3.

Type	InfoObject Name
Key Fields	0DOC_NUMBER 0S_ORD_ITEM
Data Fields	0BILL_TYPE 0ITEM_CATEG 0BILL_CAT 0BILL_DATE

Table 4.3 Design of DSO BWSD_O01

Type	InfoObject Name
Data Fields	BW_CUST 0VTYPE 0CUST_GRP1 0CUST_GROUP 0MATERIAL 0DIVISION 0MATL_GROUP 0PLANT 0COMP_CODE 0SALESORG 0REGION 0DISTR_CHAN 0COUNTRY 0SALES_OFF 0SALES_GRP 0SALES_DIST BW_QTY 0NET_WGT_DL 0GRS_WGT_DL 0UNIT_OF_WT 0UNIT 0DOC_CATEG 0COST 0LOC_CURRCY 0DOC_CURRCY 0ACCNT_ASGN 0CO_AREA 0NET_VALUE 0SUBTOTAL_1 0SUBTOTAL_2 0VALUE_LC

Table 4.3 Design of DSO BWSD_O01 (Cont.)

You can now activate the DSO using the Activate icon, as shown in ❹ of Figure 4.14. Activating the DSO creates the three tables we mentioned earlier: the Activation Queue, Active Data, and Change Log tables.

Return to the initial DWW screen by using the Back icon (❺ of Figure 4.14). As you can see in ❶ of Figure 4.15, the newly created DSO BWSD_O01 is available under InfoArea BW_AREA.

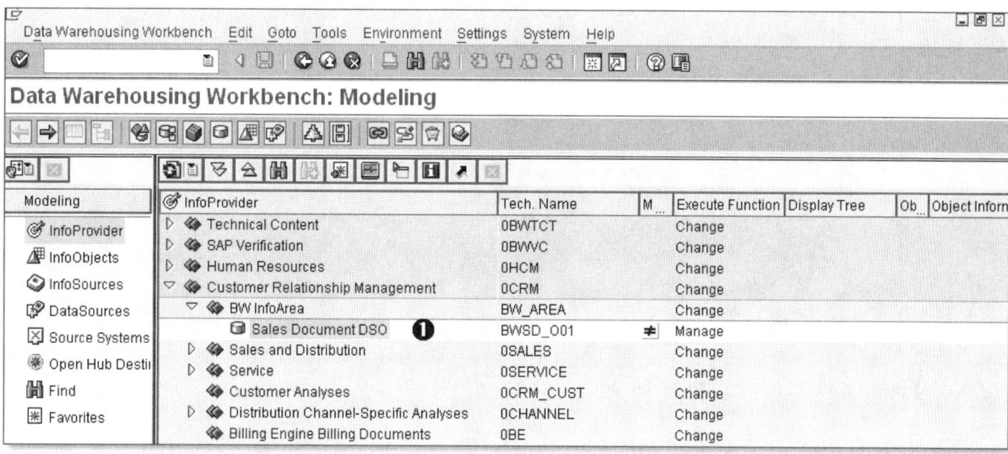

Figure 4.15 DSO BWSD_O01 Under InfoArea BW_AREA

4.5 Configuration of Write-Optimized DSOs

In this section, we explain the configuration details of the second type of DSO, the write-optimized DSO. Write-optimized DSOs consist of only one table, the Active Data table. Because there is no Activation Queue table or Change Log table, there is no activation process; data is loaded directly into the Active Data table. This type of DSO is useful when you have a large amount of data and complex transformations are involved. After data is loaded into this DSO, the transformed data can be loaded into other smaller InfoProviders using different filters. You can also use this type of DSO as your source system copy data; source system data is stored in this DSO without any transformation. This DSO can then be used as a source of data for other InfoProviders.

Compared to standard DSOs, the settings required while creating a write-optimized DSO are much less stringent (Figure 4.16). To access this screen, select DSO from DWW. From the context menu, select change.

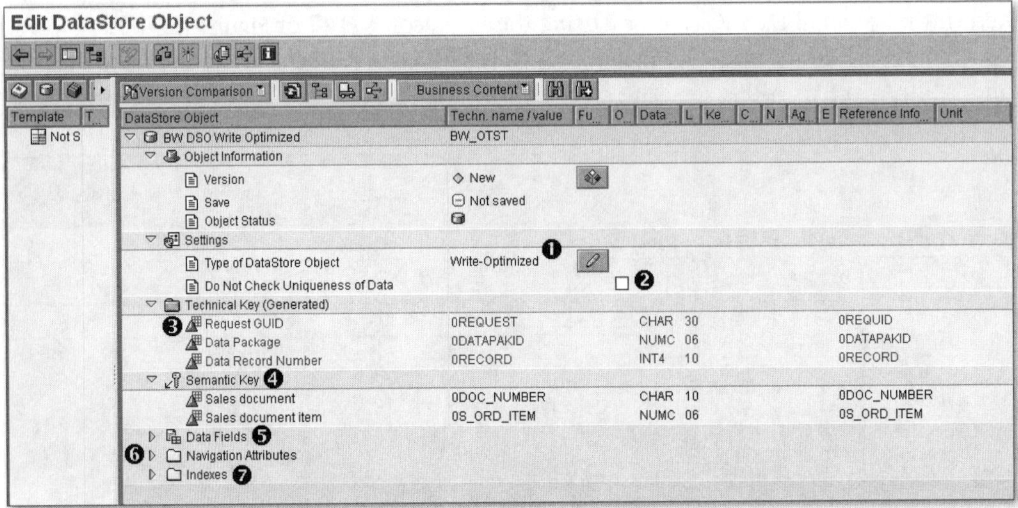

Figure 4.16 Creating Write-Optimized DSOs

The first thing to do when creating a write-optimized DSO is to change the Type of DataStore Object to Write-Optimized, as shown in ❶ of Figure 4.16. The technical key is then generated by the system, which consists of the following fields: Request GUID, Data Package, and Data Record Number (❸).

By default, the Do Not Check Uniqueness of Data setting (❷) isn't checked. In this case, a unique index called Key is created with the fields included in the Semantic Key section (❹). While loading data, Do Not Check Uniqueness of Data is checked with respect to fields in the semantic key. If this indicator is checked, the Key index isn't generated, and the DSO can have several records with the same semantic key value. This significantly improves the loading performance.

As shown in Figure 4.16, you need to maintain the semantic key (❹), data fields (❺), navigation attributes (❻), and index (❼). The semantic key is the same as the key fields of the standard DSO, as are the rest of the settings.

Data can be loaded into a write-optimized DSO using standard data staging, that is, using transformation and DTP (processes that are discussed in Chapter 7). Data from this DSO can be sent to other data targets using the details of the request.

Upon activation (which is accomplished by clicking the Activate icon), a write-optimized DSO is available in the DWW under InfoProvider, as shown in ❶ of Figure 4.17. As you can see, it's indicated with a special icon (icon) that appears to the right of its technical name.

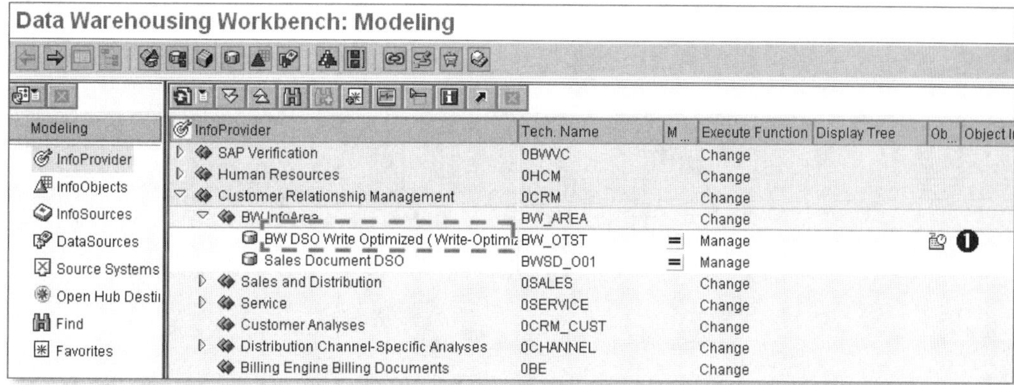

Figure 4.17 Write-Optimized DSO in DWW

4.6 Configuration of Direct Update DSOs

In earlier versions of SAP NetWeaver BW releases, the direct update DSO was called the *transactional DSO*. Like the write-optimized DSO, it consists of only one table: the Active Data table. Data can't be loaded into this type of DSO using data staging, but there are special APIs available in SAP NetWeaver BW that can write into it (even from an external system). Additionally, multiple users can simultaneously write into this DSO, and the newly written data is immediately available for further usage. This DSO is mainly used as a data target in the APD (Analysis Process Designer) process. (APD is the tool that supports complex analysis tasks; as a part of this process, you can merge, manipulate, and transform data from different sources.)

When creating a direct update DSO, first change Type of DataStore Object to Direct Update, as shown in ❶ of Figure 4.18. This type of DSO contains a semantic key, which is defined while creating the DSO (❷). No other settings are available while creating a direct update DSO. You must also select the data fields (❸), navigation attributes (❹), and indexes (❺).

Once activated, the direct update DSO is available in DWW under InfoProvider, as shown in ❶ of Figure 4.19. As you can see, it's indicated with an icon [icon] that appears to the right of its technical name.

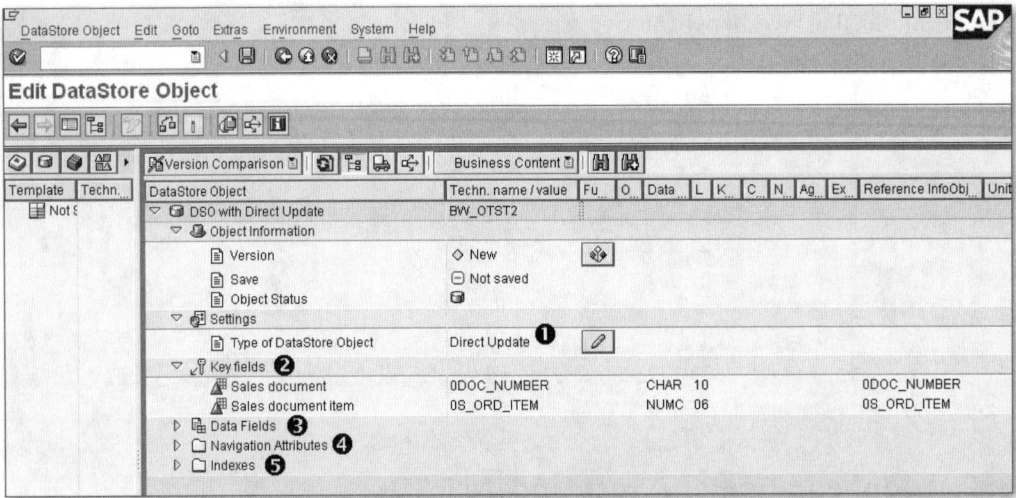

Figure 4.18 Creating a Direct Update DSO

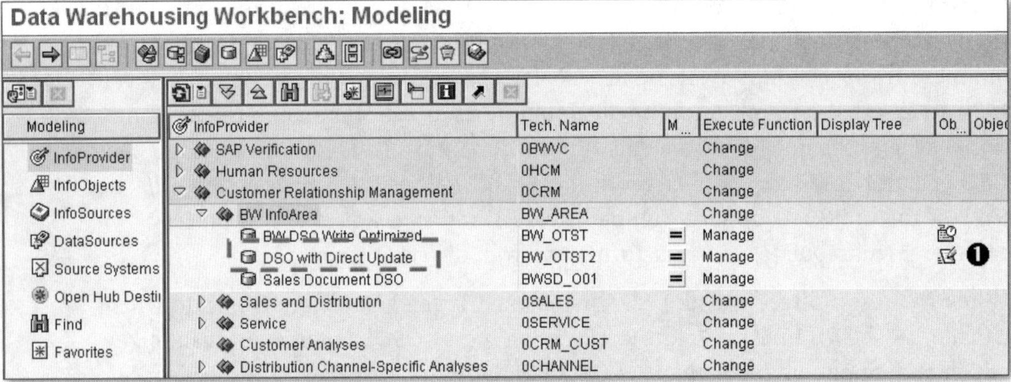

Figure 4.19 Direct Update DSO in DWW

Now that we've explained different types of DSOs, we'll now briefly introduce the application scenarios that require specific types of DSO.

4.7 Usage Scenarios for DSOs

The technical architecture of a DSO enables it to fulfill the requirements of data warehousing. In this section, we briefly explain some of the application scenarios for DSOs.

4.7.1 Data Staging

Some typical business processes require a DSO for storing data before transmitting it to an InfoCube and serving as the data staging layer. There are scenarios where data from multiple source systems is extracted and stored in DSO, and a harmonized and synchronized set of data is transmitted to InfoCube or other data targets as a delta load. For example, this is true of SAP Business Content DataSources for Accounts Payable, Accounts Receivable, and SAP General Ledger in Financial Accounting, all of which need a DSO as a staging layer before data flows as a delta load to their respective InfoCubes.

4.7.2 Temporary Storage Area

Other business scenarios require dealing with extremely large sets of data. When executing complex transformations in such a scenario, use a write-optimized DSO because the system doesn't generate SIDs, and the request to the DSO doesn't need to be activated, which means you can save and further process data quickly.

4.7.3 Analysis Process Designer

There are certain requirements where you might want to perform calculations or analysis on the SAP NetWeaver BW query output (or on other sources of data in SAP NetWeaver BW). SAP NetWeaver BW provides the Analysis Process Designer (APD) for just this purpose. In this case, a direct update DSO should be used to store data.

To give you a more practical example, let's say our example company ABCD Corp. uses queries based on data from different systems to calculate organizational-level performance metrics. Because these metrics change every day, senior management wants to track how they change over a period of time. You need to persistently save the data from these queries together for future analysis. To do this, you can build an analysis process where you merge the results from all needed queries and then store the data in a direct update DSO. The details about APD are explained in Chapter 15, Advanced Features.

4.7.4 Pseudo-Delta

We explained the data activation process earlier in this chapter. The typical architecture of the standard DSO enables it to identify changes in original records for the data sources that send entire data sets every time a change is made. This feature helps in the transmission of only relevant records to the data targets above the DSO in the data flow of the data warehouse. To explain this further, let's take a very simple scenario in which SAP NetWeaver BW receives billing document 123456 with a quantity of 10, and then the quantity is changed to 12. The DSO transmits only delta for the changes in the data field value, which is +2 in this case (Table 4.4).

Sequence from Source	Data from Source		Net Result in DSO Tables		Net Transmission to InfoCube
	Key Field of DSO Billing Document No.)	Data Field of DSO (Quantity)	Active Table in DSO	Change Log in DSO	
First Time Receipt	123456	10	10	10	10
Second Time Receipt	123456	12	12	+2	+2

Table 4.4 Illustration of Delta Functionality by Use of a DSO

These four application scenarios explain how the unique technical architecture of a DSO provides a variety of application options, besides its predominant use as a data-staging component.

4.8 Summary

In this chapter, we introduced you to the basic concepts involved in DSOs. We began our discussion with some information about DSOs in general and then moved on to an explanation of their respective architectures. After that, we explained the process of setting up a DSO (which is common to all three types of DSOs) and then went into the individual configuration details for each type. In the next chapter, we explain the InfoCube, the central object in SAP NetWeaver BW.

Understanding the InfoCube and its design is essential to creating a robust data warehousing solution. This chapter gets you started on this path.

5 InfoCubes

As a data warehouse, SAP NetWeaver BW stores data from different sources, predominantly the OLTP (online transaction processing) systems and other data warehousing solutions (if required), the way this data is stored affects the ease with which reporting and analysis is possible. There are a number of multidimensional models that support better OLAP (online analytical processing); SAP NetWeaver BW uses the *extended star schema model*. The *InfoCube* is based on this model and is one of the data targets (objects that physically store data) in SAP NetWeaver BW; in fact, it's the central object of SAP NetWeaver BW. Because it's based on the extended star schema, the InfoCube can perform OLAP requests more quickly than other objects, such as the DSO, so they play an integral role in addressing a majority of OLAP requirements in SAP NetWeaver BW.

In this chapter, we explain the conversion of analysis requirements from common business language to the technical requirements that are essential for modeling *InfoCubes.* We cover the types of InfoCubes and the process of creating them in the system as well as the finer aspect of their design.

5.1 Modeling InfoCubes

It's essential to understand the way analytical requirements are expressed in business language. These requirements are analyzed and translated into a multidimensional model that can then be used in modeling and designing an InfoCube. We therefore explain the process to translate the business requirements into a technical model to build an InfoCube.

A clear understanding of the business requirements and the source data is an essential precondition to ensure a scalable and maintainable design. We've described a stepped approach, of starting with a high-level business model involving key entities evolving into a logical data model. Then with the requirements in hand, determine the scope of the business process and drill down the processes to build a detailed logical data model. This is a best practice and benefits in two ways. First, it starts with a high-level business model; while building the detail logical model, a consistency check is automatically done with the bigger picture involving business functions. Second, over a period, if the solution scope expands, scaling it up will be a lot easier with minimum rework required.

The business intelligence (BI) requirements discussed in Chapter 1, The Business Scenario: ABCD Corp., were expressed in nontechnical terms. We now need to translate them into technical terms that will help us design a multidimensional model that meets the analysis requirements. This process begins by evaluating each aspect of a business process and its representation in the technical model of a BI information system. We can then use this information to generate reports in the form of tables, dashboards, charts, and so on, thereby providing the information needed to make intelligent business decisions.

The process begins with analysis of the scenario for our example company, ABCD Corp., and its sales processes. Then the key technical terms and their relation to the business entities are identified. The process then develops a bubble model leading to modeling the requirements into an InfoCube.

5.1.1 Key Terms

Before we begin our explanation of how to model an InfoCube, there are a number of important terms that you should understand.

- Characteristic: A characteristic defines a business entity that is being evaluated or measured by a key figure in SAP NetWeaver BW. Customers and companies, for example, are both characteristics.
- Key figure: Key figures are numeric values or quantities, such as Per Unit Sales Price, Quantity Sold, and Sales Revenue in SAP. Billing quantity and volume, for example, are both key figures.
- Fact: A fact represents data in the form of key figures or measures.
- Dimension: A dimension is a logical grouping of characteristics that belong together, for example, a product and product category or a customer and customer segment.
- Attributes: Attributes are features that define a specific aspect of a characteristic. For example, with the color of a product, the color is an attribute of the characteristics; the product.
- Granularity: Granularity is the level of detailing; for example, the data available at a day level is more granular than that at month level. Similarly, the more the num-

ber of characteristics that define a key combination for identifying a fact record, the higher is the granularity.

5.1.2 Assignment Tables for Characteristics and Key Figures

In a business process, all types of entities are related to each other. To visualize and understand their relationships, you draw an assignment table, which is a visual representation of these relationships (Figure 5.1).

❶

Characteristics → / Key Figures ↓	Customer	Company	Sales Office	Sales Group	Division	Plant	Sales Organization	Distribution Channel	Controlling Area	Region	Sales District	Product	Product Group	Customer Group 1	Customer Group	Value Type	Assignment Group	Billing Type	Billing Category	Item Category
Billing Quantity	✔		✔	✔ ❷		✔	✔	✔				✔								
Net Weight												✔								
Gross Weight												✔								
Volume ❸												✔								
Cost in Document Currency			✔				❹													
Net Value of Item in DC	✔		✔				✔	✔				✔								
Subtotal 1	✔		✔				✔	✔				✔								
Tax	✔		✔				✔	✔				✔								
Amount in Local Currency			✔																	

Figure 5.1 Assignment Table for Characteristics and Key Figures

As you can see, the assignment table has columns (❷ of Figure 5.1) that list the characteristics, and rows (❸) that list the key figures. The relationships of all of the characteristics and key figures are established by marking the cell where there is an association, markings which should be based on your individual business model. For example, if a billing document for a customer has a billing quantity, the cell at the intersection of these two entities should be checked (❹).

For the ABCD Corp. case study, let's study its billing process and key figures in a billing document. All key figures are related to all of the characteristics, so all cells in the assignment table should be checked. This is, of course, unique to this particular case study; the assignment tables will change depending on the individual business scenarios.

5.1.3 Create Bubble Models

After the assignment table is developed, you can develop a *bubble model* that articulates the relationships of entities in visual form. To do this, you must group characteristics based on their relationship with each other. There are two types of possible relationships:

- M:N Relationship: Relationship between two characteristics is many to many; for example, a customers can buy any of the products being sold, and the products can be sold to any customer.

- 1:N Relationship: Relationship between two characteristics is one to many; for example, a customers can belong to only one sales office, but each sales office can have multiple customers.

To simplify the model, characteristics that have M:N relationships are kept in different groups, whereas those that have 1:N relationships are grouped together. In our scenario, customers and products have an M:N relationship and are grouped separately. However, each material (earlier called a product) can have only one material group (earlier called a product group) and therefore has a 1:N relationship; so materials and material groups are grouped together.

Figure 5.2 shows a bubble model with all key figures in the center, surrounded by bubbles that represent grouped characteristics (i.e., characteristics with 1:N relationships).

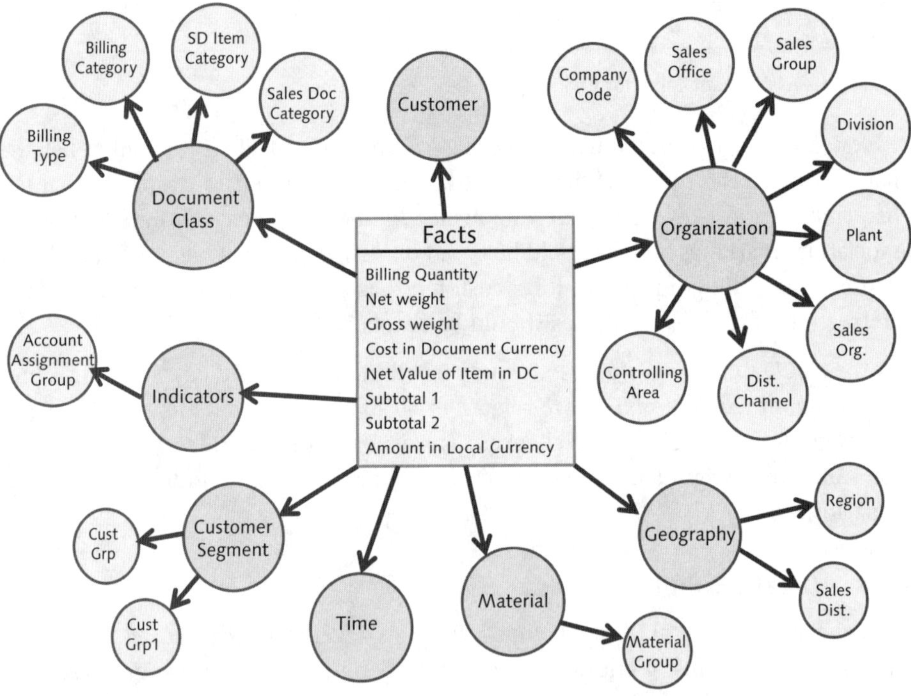

Figure 5.2 Bubble Model

Bubble models are the basis for extended star schema architectures, on which InfoCubes are based.

5.1.4 Dimensions

The bubble model in Figure 5.3 has *facts* (i.e., the key figures in the center) surrounded by bubbles, which represent characteristics. As shown by the circles in Figure 5.3, these characteristics are separated into groups, which are identified as dimensions.

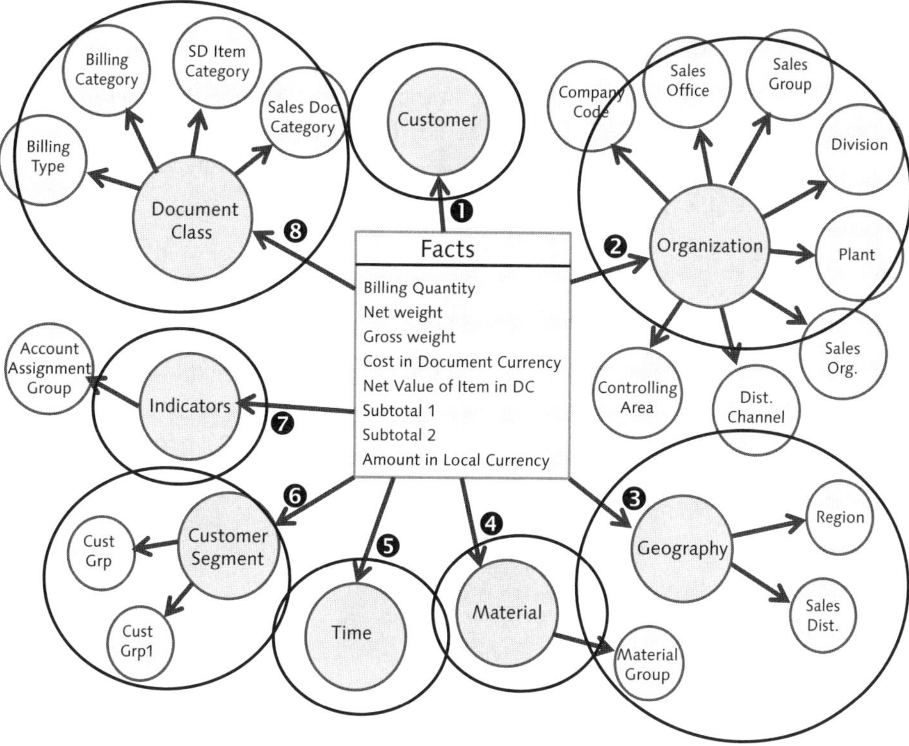

Figure 5.3 Identify Dimensions from Bubble Model

For the bubble model in Figure 5.3, the dimensions are shown as follows:

- Customer (❶)
- Organization (❷)
- Geography (❸)
- Material(❹)
- Time (❺)
- Customer Segment (❻)
- Indicators(❼)
- Document Class(❽)

5.1.5 Classic Star Schema

In this section, we explain how to convert a bubble model to a classic star schema model. The characteristics and their groups are identified from the bubble model, and the characteristics belonging to an identified group are assigned to that dimension in the InfoCube design. So, for example, it can be interpreted from Figure 5.3 that the Material and Material Group characteristics (0MATERIAL and 0MATL_GROUP, respectively) are assigned to the Material dimension.

In technical terms, a dimension is a table in the database, referred to as a dimension table. Each dimension table has a unique key (i.e., a character string) to identify a unique record from the table. For example, the key for the Material dimension is MATERIAL_DIM_ID.

Similarly, the key figures are part of the fact table and are linked to different dimensions using dimension IDss (DIM_IDs). The combination of DIM_IDs from all dimensions forms a unique key for the fact table.

Following these principles, the technical model is generated in Figure 5.4.

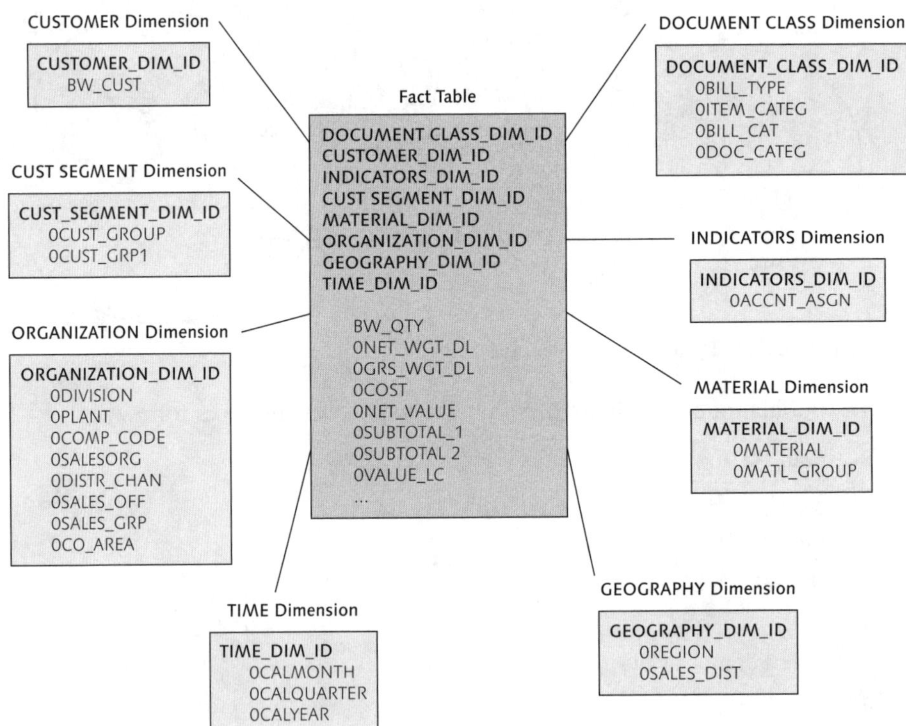

Figure 5.4 Technical Design Based on Bubble Model

This *classic star schema* model has the actual value of Material, and Material Group from the transaction data is stored in the Material dimension table.

5.1.6 The Extended Star Schema

SAP NetWeaver BW's technical architecture is based on an improved version of the classic star schema, known as the extended star schema. The extended star schema stores a generated value known as the surrogate ID (SID) in the dimension table, instead of storing the actual values of the characteristics. SIDs are system-generated numeric values that are stored in the SID table of a characteristic InfoObject. The SID table is created for each InfoObject when the InfoObject definition is activated.

For example, the Material dimension stores an SID for the Material (SID_0MATERIAL) and Material Group (SID_0MATL_GROUP) characteristics. InfoObject 0MATERIAL has its own SID values, which are stored separately in the SID table associated with InfoObject 0MATERIAL. In the same way, InfoObject 0MATL_GROUP has its own SID values, which are stored separately in an SID table associated with InfoObject 0MATL_GROUP (Figure 5.5).

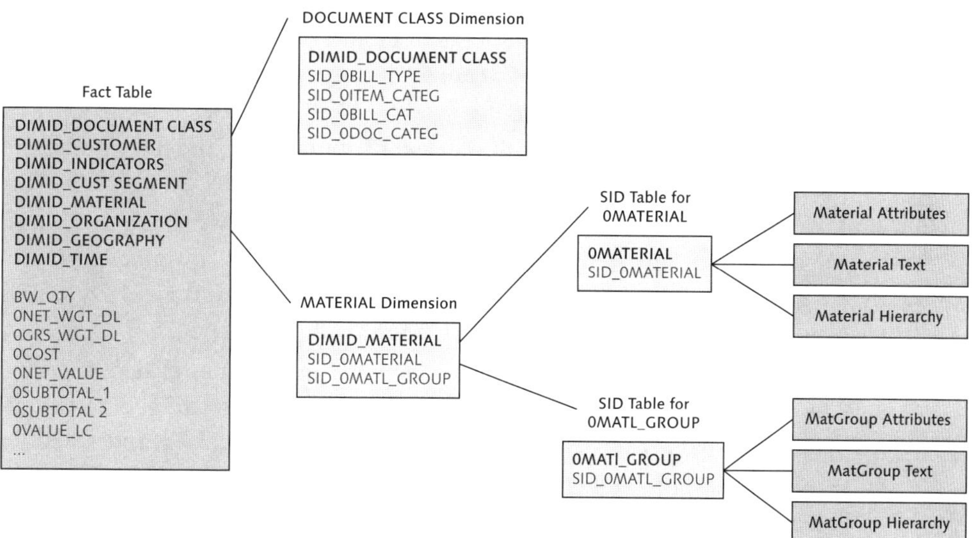

Figure 5.5 The Extended Star Schema

In the extended star schema, the dimension ID (DIM_ID) is also a system-generated numerical value, which is generated for each unique combination of SIDs in the dimension table. So, for the Material dimension, SAP NetWeaver BW generates a unique DIM_ID for each unique combination of 0MATERIAL and 0MATL_GROUP (Figure 5.5).

The DIM_IDs generated for all different dimensions in this manner are combined to form the key of the fact table. The key figure values stored in the fact table are linked to the values in the dimension table through DIM_IDs.

To explain the way data is stored in the extended star schema, let's consider an example of a simple model that includes only three dimensions in an InfoCube:

- Customer dimension (Cust Dimension): Has the customer (CUST) characteristic assigned to it.
- Material dimension (Mat Dimension): Has the Material (MAT) and Material Group (MGR) characteristics assigned to it.
- Time dimension: Has the Month (MONTH) characteristic assigned to it.

For the purpose of this example, make the following assumptions for the SIDs:

- The customer master data is loaded to the customer InfoObject, and the SIDs for the three customers (C1, C2, and C3) are 1, 2, and 3, respectively. This is shown in the SID table for CUST in Figure 5.6.
- The material master data is loaded to the material InfoObject, and the SIDs for the five materials (M1, M2, M3, M4, and M5) are 1, 2, 3, 4, and 5, respectively. This is shown in the SID table for MAT in Figure 5.6.
- The material group master data is loaded to the material group InfoObject, and the SIDs for the three material groups (MG1, MG2, and MG3) are 1, 2, and 3, respectively. This is shown in the SID table for MGR in Figure 5.6.
- The time granularity for this InfoCube is *month*. The time master data is generated by the system, and SIDs for all of the MONTH values are generated and available. The SIDs for the three month values (08.2009, 09.2009, and 10.2009) are 11, 12, and 13, respectively. This is shown in the SID table for MONTH in Figure 5.6. (For high-level analysis, you can also assign the quarter and year characteristics to the Time dimension. These are derived directly from the Month characteristic.)

Now let's assume that two transaction records, shown in Table 5.1, are to be loaded into this InfoCube.

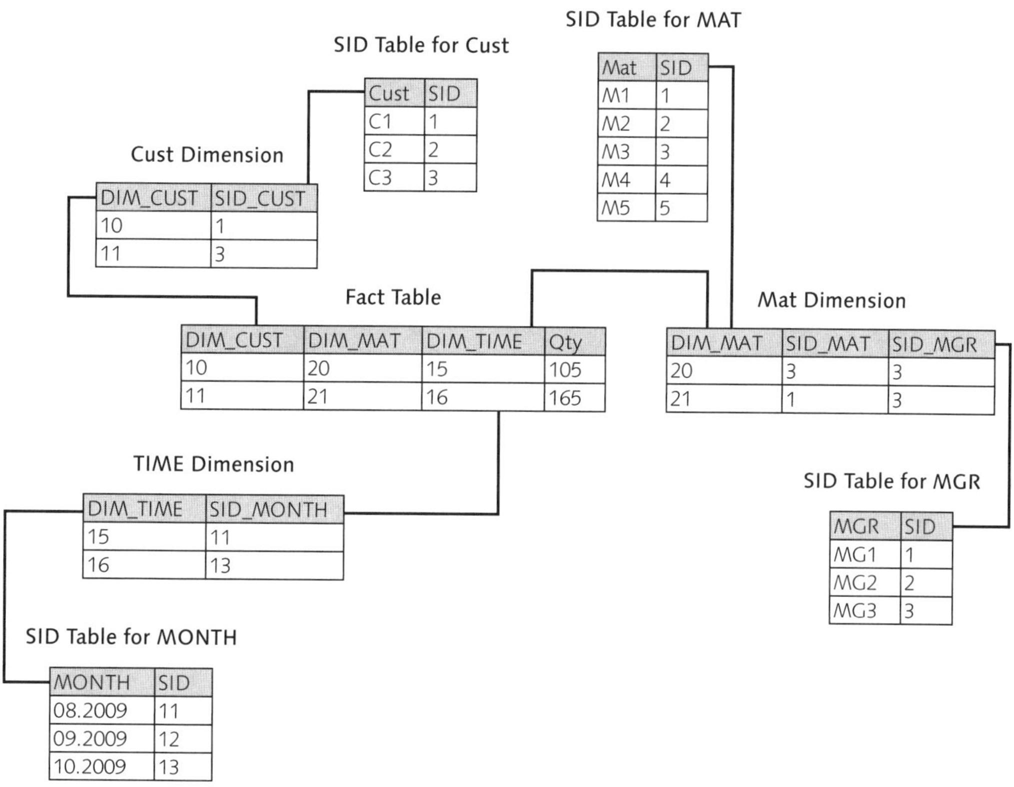

Figure 5.6 Extended Star Schema: Relation Between DIMs and SIDs

Customer	Material	Material Group	Month	Quantity
C1	M3	MG3	08.2009	105
C3	M1	MG3	10.2009	165

Table 5.1 Sample Data for Illustrating DIM/SID Relationship

When this data is loaded, it's stored in the InfoCube model as shown in Figure 5.6. Again, dimension tables save the data of the characteristics values shown in Table 5.1, but instead of storing the actual characteristic values, it stores the SID values. For example, the first record in the transaction data has the customer value listed as C1, but the dimension table stores the SID. Because only one characteristic is assigned to the CUST dimension, for each unique value of the customer SID, the system creates a DIM ID for it in the dimension table. In Figure 5.6, DIM_ID 10 is generated for SID_CUST = 1. The key of the Customer dimension table is DIM_CUST.

In a similar fashion, the Material dimension with two characteristics assigned to it forms a unique record from the combination of the material and material group SID values. A DIM_ID is generated for each unique combination of SIDs of the characteristics included in the dimension. The key of the Material dimension table is DIM_MAT.

Finally, the fact table stores key figures associated with the InfoCube. For this example, the values for the Quantity key figure (Qty in Figure 5.6) is stored in the fact table, along with the DIM_IDs from all of the dimensions.

In Summary

- The InfoCube design is based on the extended star schema.
- The key figure values are linked to different dimensions using DIM_IDs.
- The dimensions are linked to the actual values of characteristics through the SIDs stored in the dimension table.

5.1.7 InfoCube Considerations

To conclude our discussion about modeling an InfoCube, we should review a few requirements that must be considered when designing an InfoCube in SAP NetWeaver BW:

- You can include a maximum of 233 key figures in an InfoCube. All InfoCubes must have at least 1 key figure.
- You can attach a maximum of 248 characteristics to one dimension.
- You can include a maximum of 16 dimensions in an InfoCube. The minimum is 4, with 3 system defined and at least 1 customer defined.
- Out of these 16 dimensions, 3 are system-defined: time, unit, and data package.
- The Time dimension is mandatory, and you must assign at least one time characteristic to it.
- The Unit dimension stores units/currencies associated with the key figures within an InfoCube.
- The Data Package dimension is a technical requirement that SAP NetWeaver BW uses internally.

5.2 Types of InfoCubes

In this section, we explain the different types of InfoCubes that capitalize on the technical architecture of the extended star schema in different and unique ways.

5.2.1 Standard InfoCube

A *standard* InfoCube is the most commonly used InfoCube in SAP NetWeaver BW. This InfoCube physically stores data (using the extended star schema) and is classified as a data target. Data can be loaded to a standard InfoCube using the data staging process. This type of InfoCube is optimized for reading data from the cube; in other words, it's used for reporting.

5.2.2 Real-Time InfoCube

A *real-time* InfoCube is an InfoCube with the ability to write data. Real-time InfoCubes are the basis for any planning application in SAP NetWeaver BW. The data stored in a real-time InfoCube is also available for reporting.

While a standard InfoCube is optimized for reading data (i.e., reporting), a real-time InfoCube is optimized for writing data. Data generated or modified in a planning application is written to these types of cubes using an API interface.

A real-time InfoCube can't be used for data loads using standard SAP NetWeaver BW data flow. However, the real-time behavior of a real-time InfoCube can be changed to enable data loads to it. In other words, a real-time InfoCube can switch between the real-time mode and data load mode. A real-time InfoCube is also classified as a data target. (More about this type of InfoCube is discussed in Chapter 12, Integrated Planning.)

5.2.3 VirtualProvider InfoCube

In a VirtualProvider InfoCube, data doesn't physically reside in the cube; instead, the InfoObjects in this InfoCube are linked to source fields. So when a query is executed on it, the data is read from the source system during runtime. This type of InfoCube isn't a data target because it doesn't store the data physically; however, it *is* an InfoProvider because queries can be built on it.

Because data is read directly from a source system when queries are executed, this type of InfoCube is useful for real-time reporting (i.e., reporting where the latest data from the source system should be visible in the reports). However, because it must request data from the source system, the performance of queries on virtual InfoProvider InfoCubes can be poor (especially when large sets of data are requested). This type of InfoCube should be used sparingly, mostly for real-time reporting that requires only a small amount of data.

5.3 Creating a Standard InfoCube

Requirements for ABCD Corp. point to a standard InfoCube, so this section explains the procedure for creating one. The procedure to create all types of InfoCubes is the same, so the following applies to creating the other types too.

5.3.1 Initial Setup

InfoCubes are created in the Data Warehousing Workbench (DWW), which is started using Transaction RSA1. Select the InfoProvider under Modeling from the navigator section, as shown in ❶ of Figure 5.7.

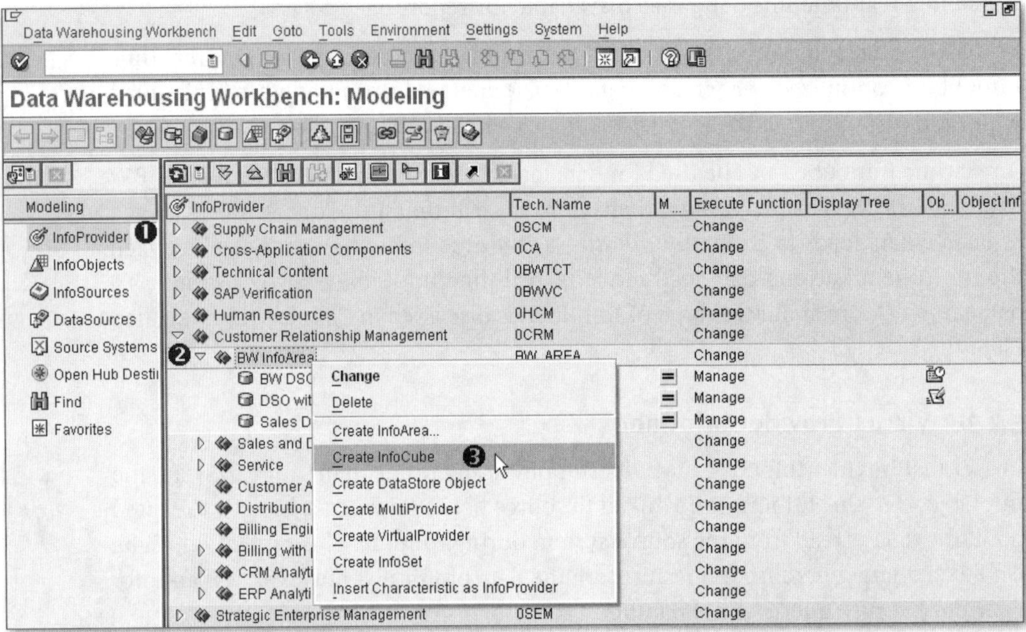

Figure 5.7 Create an InfoCube

InfoCubes are created under an InfoArea. Select the InfoArea under which you want to create your InfoCube (❷). From the context menu, select CREATE INFOCUBE (❸). The Edit InfoCube screen appears as shown in Figure 5.8.

Enter the technical name and description of the InfoCube (❶ of Figure 5.8). In our example, the InfoCube's technical name is BWSD_C01, and its description is Sales InfoCube. You can also use an existing InfoCube as a template to create a new InfoCube by entering the technical name of the existing InfoCube in the Copy From field, as shown in ❸ of Figure 5.8.

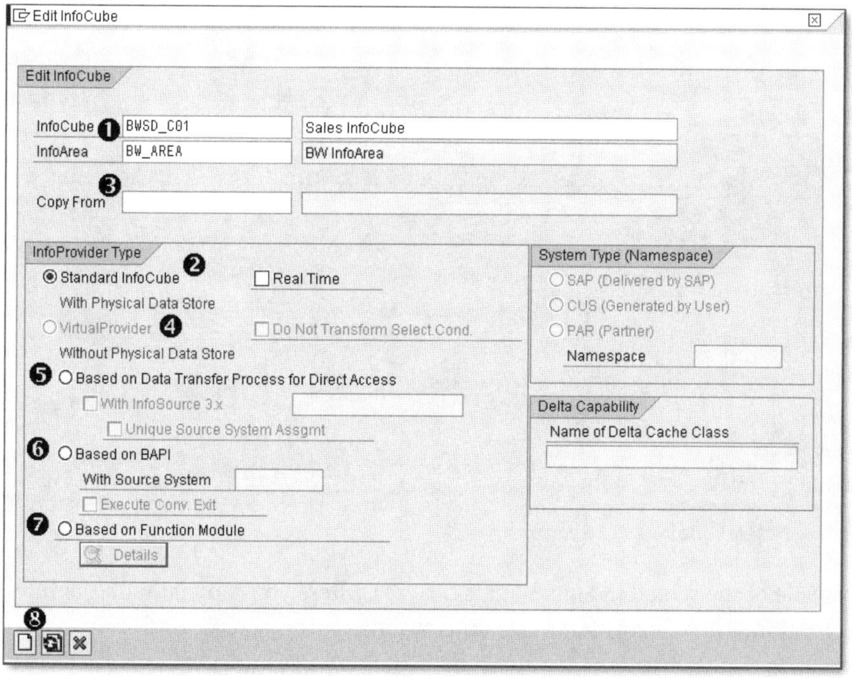

Figure 5.8 Edit InfoCube

As previously explained, there are three types of InfoCubes available in SAP NetWeaver BW. The type of InfoCube you want to create is defined in the InfoProvider Type area of the screen. Select the appropriate radio button or checkbox to define the type of InfoCube.

VirtualProvider InfoCubes

Although we won't discuss this here, it's worth noting that a VirtualProvider InfoCube offers three different options based on how data is accessed:

- Based on Data Transfer Process for Direct Access (❺)
- Based on BAPI (❻)
- Based on Function Module (❼)

For our example scenario, select Standard InfoCube, and click on the Create icon, as shown in ❽ of Figure 5.8. This takes you to the screen where you define the InfoCube (Figure 5.9).

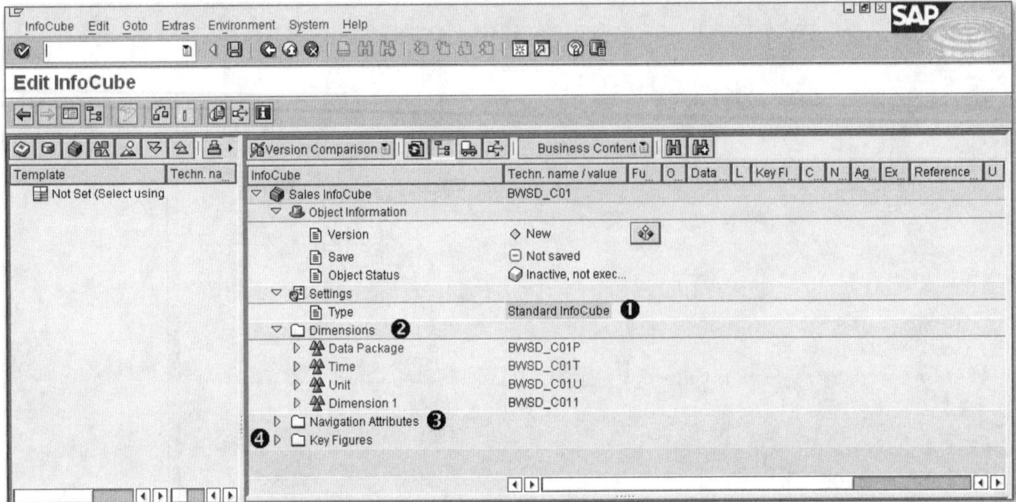

Figure 5.9 Edit InfoCube: Initial Screen

The right side of the screen in Figure 5.9 is the area where you can maintain the InfoCube definition. There are different sections visible on this screen, as follows:

- Object Information: This section shows you general information about the InfoCube, such as Version and Object Status.
- Settings: This section shows the type of InfoCube (refer to ❶ of Figure 5.9).
- Dimensions: You can maintain the dimensions of the InfoCube in this section (❷). By default, it shows four dimensions; three of them (Data Package, Time, and Unit) are system-defined dimensions, and the fourth dimension (Dimension 1) is a placeholder for the user-defined dimension. As we've explained, it's mandatory to create at least one custom dimension; you can change the name of this dimension and attach characteristics to it.
- Navigation Attributes: This section lists all of the navigation attributes of the master data InfoObjects included in the InfoCube definition (❸).
- Key Figures: The key figures of an InfoCube are included in the key figures section (❹). (Remember, all InfoCubes must have at least one key figure.)

5.3.2 Using Templates for InfoObject Selection

As shown in Figure 5.10, the left side of the screen allows you to select InfoObjects (characteristics, key figures, and time characteristics) to be included in the InfoCube definition.

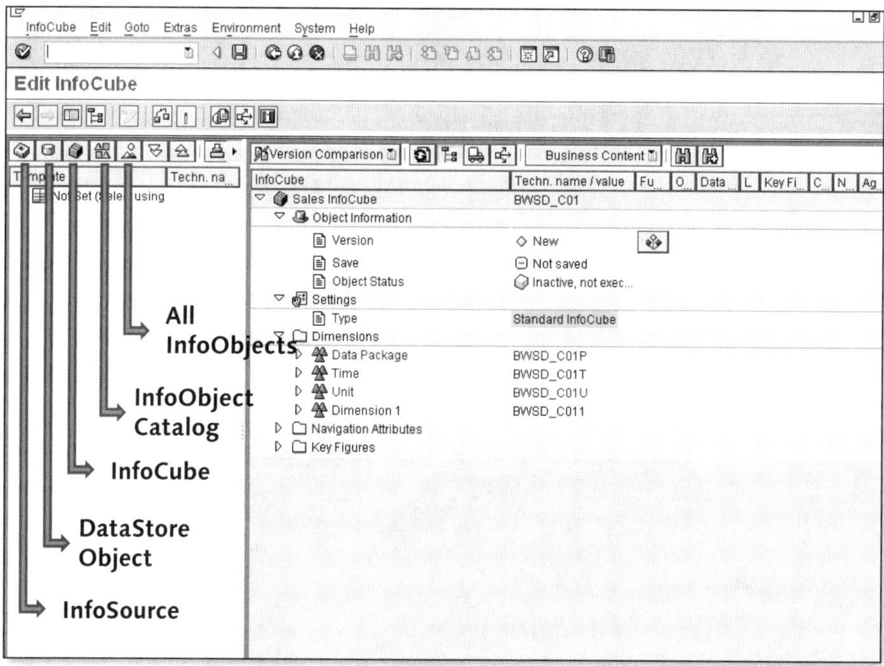

Figure 5.10 Adding InfoObjects to InfoCube

There are several different templates available that you can use to select the InfoObject. These templates are shown in Figure 5.10, and explained here:

- All InfoObjects: You can select InfoObjects for the InfoCube from the list of all available InfoObjects in the system.
- InfoObject Catalog: You can select InfoObjects for the InfoCube from a selected InfoObject catalog.
- InfoCube: You can use any of the existing InfoCubes as a template for selecting InfoObjects.
- DataStore Object: You can use any of the existing DSOs as a template for selecting InfoObjects.
- InfoSource: You can use any of the existing InfoSources as a template for selecting InfoObjects.

In the example shown in Figure 5.11, we explain the process of adding InfoObjects by using a DSO as a template. Select the DSO icon from the left side of the screen (refer to ❶ of Figure 5.11), and then select the DSO either by using the Search option or by directly double-clicking from the list shown after clicking on the InfoArea icon (❷). Select the BWSD_O01 DSO from the list (❸).

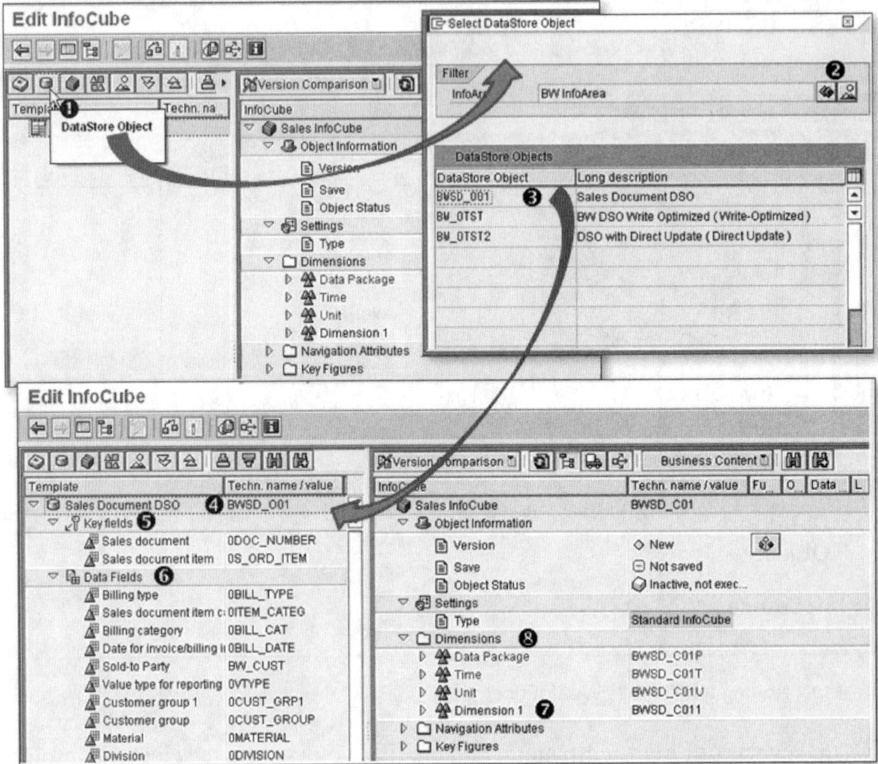

Figure 5.11 Using a DSO as a Template

Double-click on BWSD_O01. As shown in ❹ of Figure 5.11, SAP NetWeaver BW shows all of the InfoObjects reading the definition of BWSD_O01. It also classifies InfoObjects as key fields (❺) and data fields (❻).

The selection of a template doesn't add InfoObjects to dimensions. As shown in ❼ and ❽ of Figure 5.11, there are still four dimensions in the InfoCube, and no characteristics are yet assigned to them.

5.3.3 Editing Dimensions

Before we explain how to add new dimensions, let's explain the process of changing the description of Dimension 1, the placeholder name for the customer-defined dimension. (A dimension's description is visible in BEx Query Designer while designing a query based on an InfoCube and is a great help when working with queries.) As shown in ❷ of Figure 5.12, select the PROPERTIES option from the context menu of Dimension 1, under Dimensions (refer to ❶ of Figure 5.12).

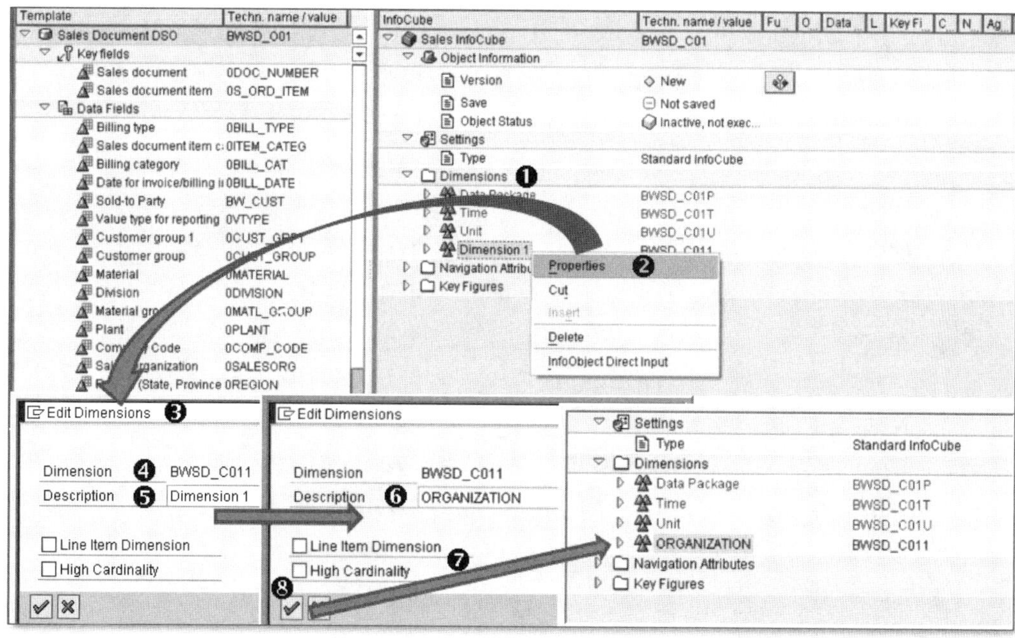

Figure 5.12 Change Dimension Description

A screen titled Edit Dimensions appears, as shown in ❸ of Figure 5.12. By default, the technical name BWSD_C011 is assigned to Dimension 1 (❹). The description of this dimension also appears as Dimension 1 (❺).

The technical names of dimensions follow a standard pattern, and you aren't allowed to edit them. Customer-defined and system-defined dimensions are treated in two different ways. For customer-defined dimensions, the technical name is <Technical Name of InfoCube>x, where x represents the dimension number. So, for the first dimension, the technical name is <Technical Name of InfoCube>1; for the second dimension, it's <Technical Name of InfoCube>2; and so on.

The three system-defined dimensions are treated slightly differently:

- Data Package: <Technical Name of InfoCube>P
- Time: <Technical Name of InfoCube>T
- Unit: <Technical Name of InfoCube>U

As an example, let's consider an InfoCube with the technical name BWSD_C01. The technical names of the customer-defined dimensions for this InfoCube are shown in Table 5.2.

Customer-Defined Dimension Number	Technical Name
First	BWSD_C011
Second	BWSD_C012
Third	BWSD_C013
Fourth	BWSD_C014
Fifth	BWSD_C015
Sixth	BWSD_C016
Seventh	BWSD_C017
Eighth	BWSD_C018
Ninth	BWSD_C019
Tenth	BWSD_C01A
Eleventh	BWSD_C01B
Twelfth	BWSD_C01C
Thirteenth	BWSD_C01D

Table 5.2 Technical Names for InfoCube Dimensions

Going back to our earlier example, edit the description of the first customer-defined dimension so it reads "ORGANIZATION" (❻ of Figure 5.12). Immediately beneath this, there are two check boxes (❼), which are explained next.

Line Item Dimension

In a business scenario, if you have a characteristic that can have a large number of distinct values, it's likely that the dimension table in which this characteristic is included contains an equally large number of records. In this case, the path from key figures in fact tables to DIM_IDs and then to SIDs can become critical for performance. The Line Item Dimension setting simplifies this path.

When a dimension is set as a line item dimension, SAP NetWeaver BW doesn't create a dimension table for it. Instead, it directly connects the fact table with the SID table of that characteristic. For example, if the Customer dimension is configured as a line item dimension, the fact table is directly connected to the SID table of the BW_CUST InfoObject, as shown in Figure 5.13.

Note
For a line item dimension, the SIDs of the characteristic become the fact table key instead of the DIM_IDs in non-line item dimension.

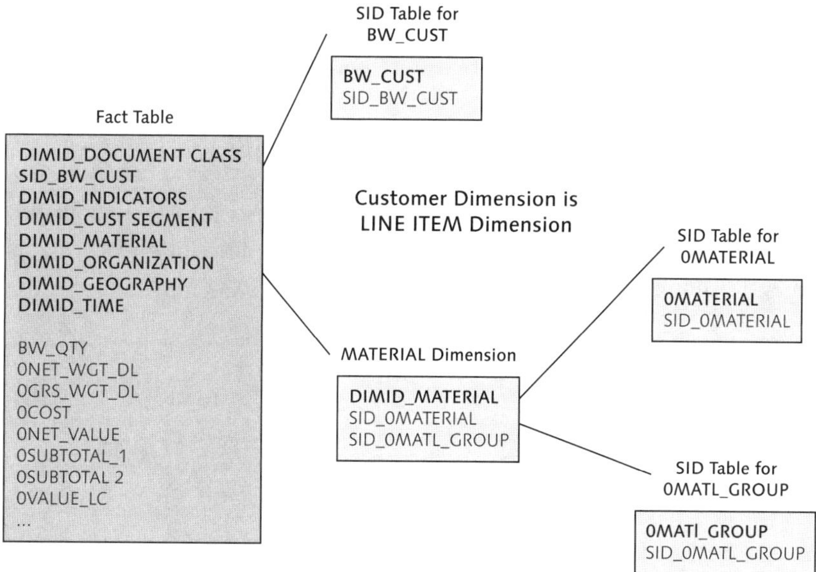

Figure 5.13 Line Item Dimension

High Cardinality

When data volume stored in a table is huge, it's difficult to retrieve particular records or set of records. Indexes are created on various columns of table to improve the retrieval of the required record.

By default, SAP NetWeaver BW creates a bitmap index on each dimension column of a fact table, which is useful when the number of distinct values in a dimension isn't very high. However, in cases where distinct values *are* high, and the dimension table is at least 20% of the size of the fact table, SAP recommends checking the High Cardinality flag for the dimension. This setting changes the index type on the dimension to B-Tree.

This setting is more applicable if the SAP NetWeaver BW system uses the Oracle database. For non-Oracle systems, setting the High Cardinality flag has no impact on the index type. The bitmap index is only used with Oracle, but there are some internal checks during the data load that determine different internal loading strategies.

When finished in the Edit Dimension screen, click on the CONTINUE icon (refer back to ❽ of Figure 5.12), or press ENTER to return to the InfoCube definition screen.

5.3.4 Adding New Dimensions

In this section, we explain the process of adding new customer-defined dimensions to the InfoCube. To add a new dimension, call the context menu for the Dimensions folder (❶ of Figure 5.14), and select the CREATE NEW DIMENSIONS option from the context menu (❷).

This action displays the Create Dimensions screen, which lists a system-generated technical name for the new dimension (❸). By default, the description is listed as "Dimension 2," as shown in ❹ of Figure 5.14.

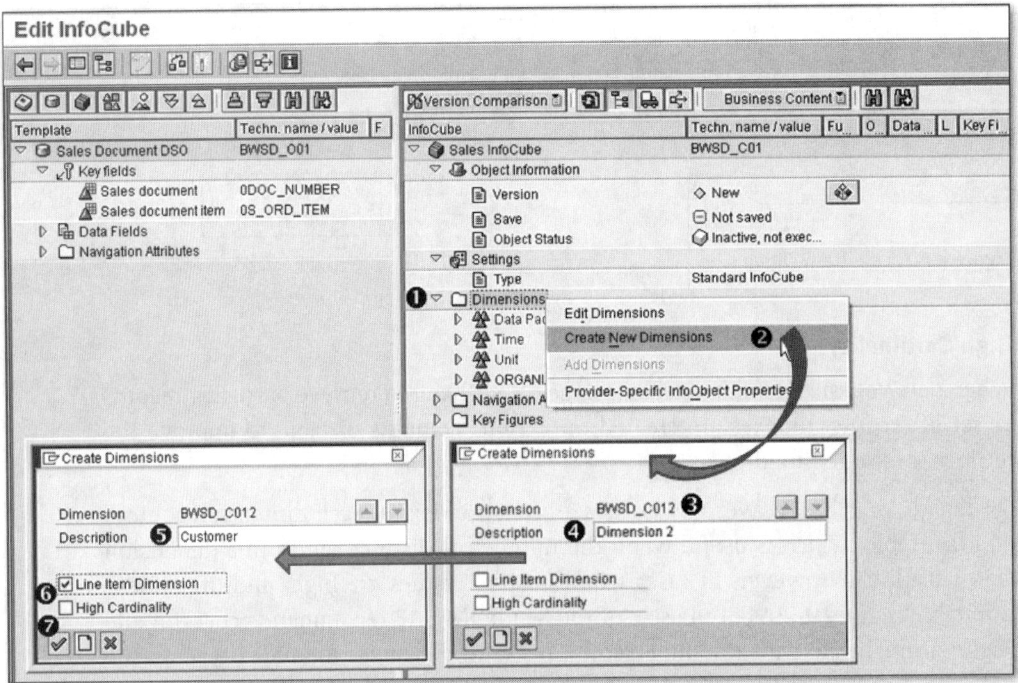

Figure 5.14 Adding New Dimensions

Enter the description as "Customer" (❺). Now, because there are a large number of customers in ABCD Corp., this Customer dimension should be a line item dimension. Select the Line Item Dimension checkbox (❻), and click on Continue (❼) to return to the InfoCube definition screen.

The new Customer dimension is now available as part of InfoCube BWSD_C01. Following this procedure, create the rest of the dimensions shown in Table 5.3, which were identified while developing the model based on requirements of ABCD Corp.

Dimension Number	Description	Line Item	High Cardinality	Technical Name
DIMENSION 1	Organization	NO	NO	BWSD_C011
DIMENSION 2	Customer	YES	NO	BWSD_C012
DIMENSION 3	Material	NO	NO	BWSD_C013
DIMENSION 4	Indicators	NO	NO	BWSD_C014
DIMENSION 5	Customer Segment	NO	NO	BWSD_C015
DIMENSION 6	Geography	NO	NO	BWSD_C016
DIMENSION 7	Document Class	NO	NO	BWSD_C017

Table 5.3 Customer-Defined Dimensions for InfoCube BWSD_C01

After all of the dimensions are created, the InfoCube definition will look like the one shown in Figure 5.15.

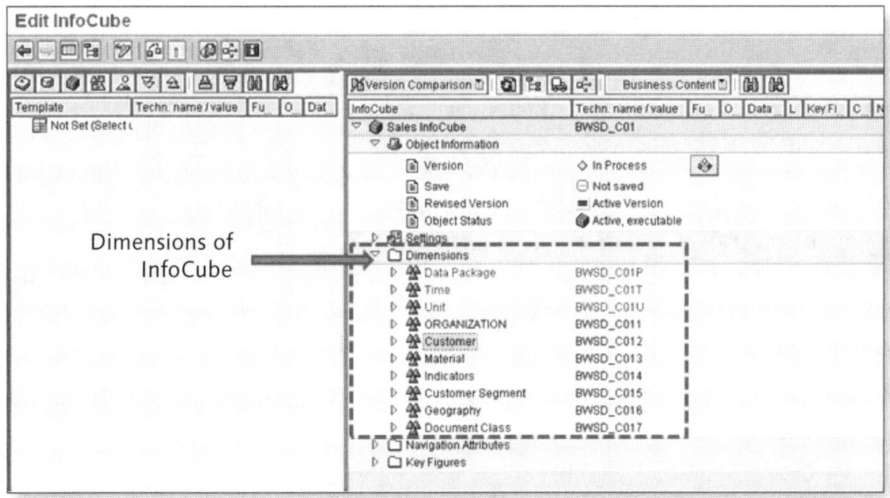

Figure 5.15 Custom-Defined Dimensions

5.3.5 Adding Characteristics to Dimensions

After the dimensions are created, you must assign characteristics to each dimension, per the extended star schema model created earlier. You can perform this task by using a template or by direct input.

As shown in Figure 5.16, using the DSO BWSD_O01 template gives you an already-populated list of InfoObjects.

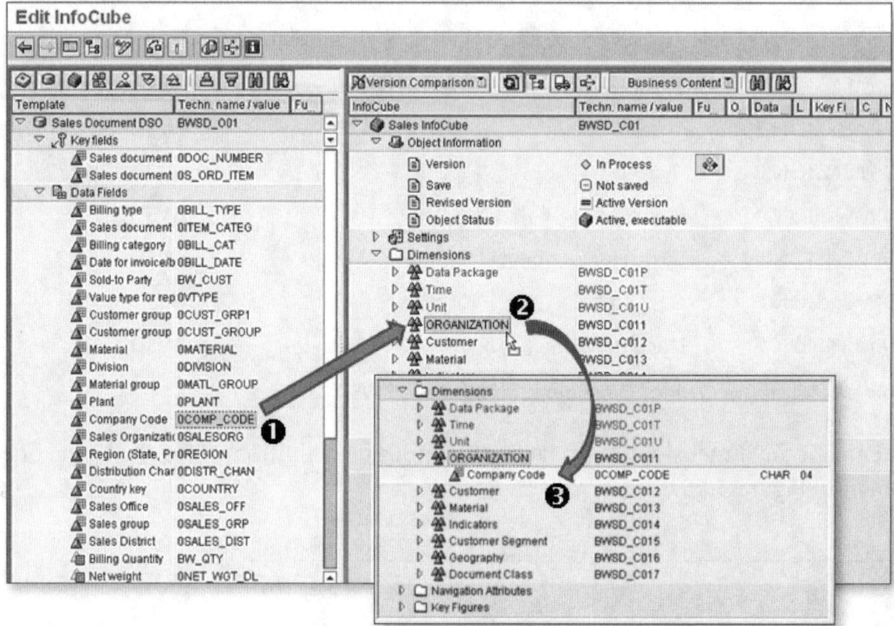

Figure 5.16 Attaching Characteristics Using a Template

Let's assign a few InfoObjects from this list as characteristics to the dimensions of the InfoCube. Select the InfoObject —0COMP_CODE (❶ of Figure 5.16) — and drag and drop it over the dimension, ORGANIZATION (❷). With this action, you assign the selected characteristic to the desired dimension (❸). To state this in SAP NetWeaver BW terminology, characteristic 0COMP_CODE is assigned to the Organization dimension.

Another way to assign characteristics is by using the direct input method. Using this method, you can directly assign multiple characteristics to a dimension by entering their technical names. All of the dimensions of an InfoCube are visible under the Dimensions folder (❶ of Figure 5.17). Select the dimension to which you want to assign characteristics (❷), and select the option INFOOBJECT DIRECT INPUT, (❸).

This action displays the Insert InfoObjects screen (❹). Enter the technical names of the InfoObjects you want to assign as characteristics to the selected dimension (❺). Finally, click on the CONTINUE icon (❻) to return to the InfoCube definition screen. As you can see in Figure 5.18, all of the characteristics are now assigned to the Organization dimension in the InfoCube definition.

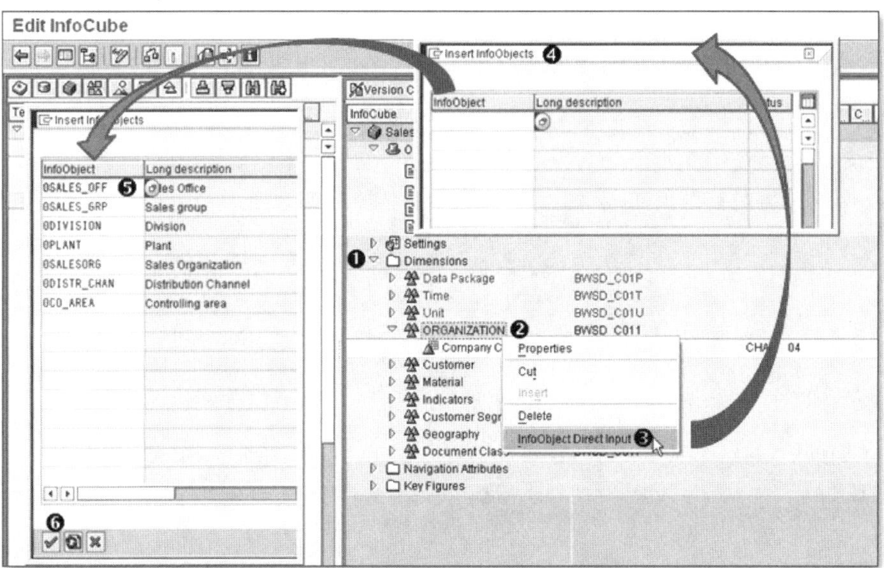

Figure 5.17 Add Characteristics to Dimensions with Direct Input

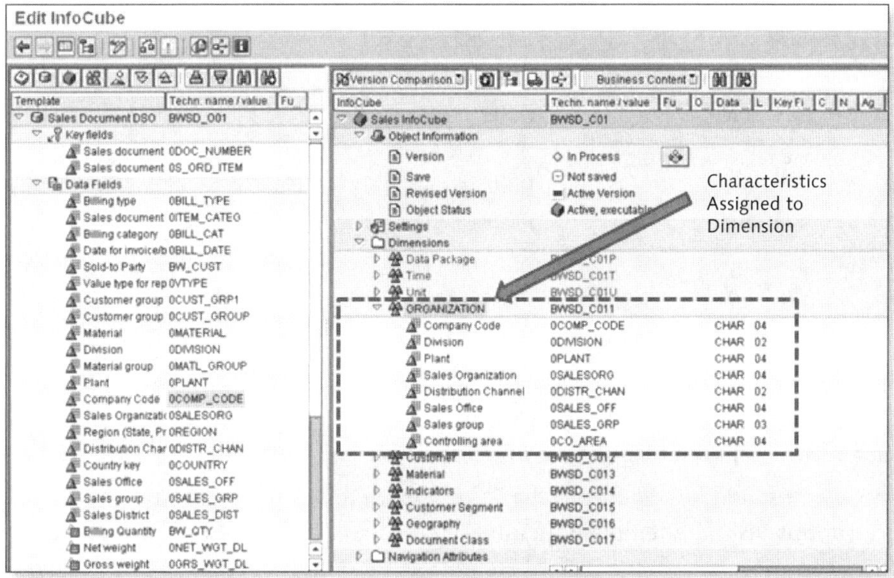

Figure 5.18 Characteristics Assigned to a Dimension

Using either the template procedure or the direct input procedure, assign characteristics to all of the dimensions of InfoCube BWSD_C01, as shown in Table 5.4.

Dimension	Characteristics
ORGANIZATION	0COMP_CODE 0DIVISION 0PLANT 0SALESORG 0DISTR_CHAN 0SALES_OFF 0SALES_GRP 0CO_AREA
CUSTOMER	BW_CUST
MATERIAL	0MATERIAL 0MATL_GROUP
INDICATORS	0ACCNT_ASGN
CUSTOMER SEGMENT	0CUST_GROUP 0CUST_GRP1
GEOGRAPHY	0REGION 0SALES_DIST
DOCUMENT CLASS	0BILL_TYPE 0ITEM_CATEG 0BILL_CAT 0DOC_CATEG
TIME	0CALMONTH 0CALQUARTER 0CALYEAR

Table 5.4 Characteristics to Dimension Relationship for InfoCube BWSD_C01

5.3.6 Adding Key Figures to an InfoCube

Now we must add key figures to the InfoCube. Here again we have two options to perform this task: the template method or the direct input method. Select the key figures context menu shown in ❶ of Figure 5.19, and then select INFOOBJECT DIRECT INPUT (❷).

In the Insert InfoObjects screen(❸), enter the technical names of the key figures that should be added to the InfoCube (❹) See Table 5.5. Select CONTINUE (❺) to return to the definition screen.

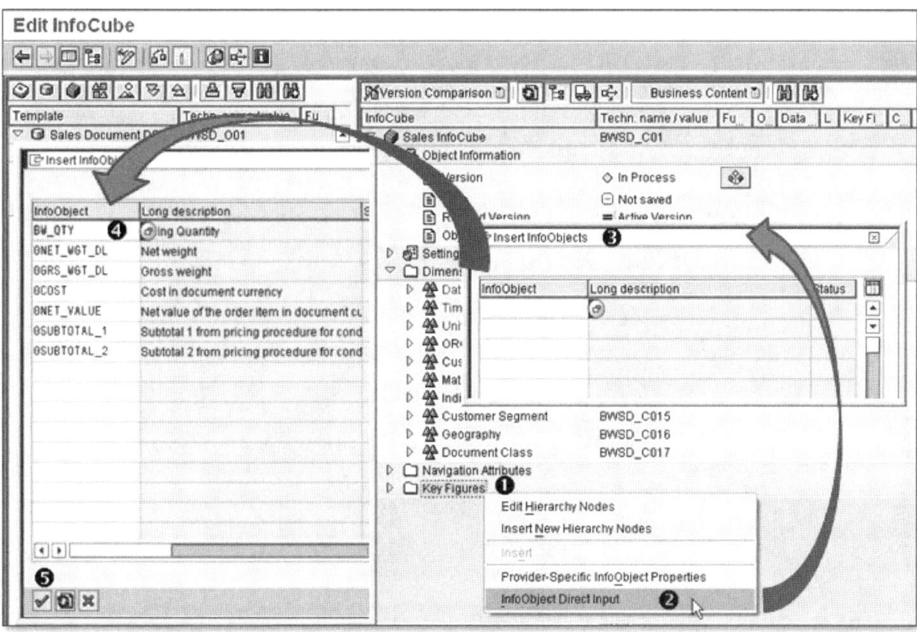

Figure 5.19 Adding Key Figures to an InfoCube

Key Figure	Description
BW_QTY	Billing quantity
0NET_WGT_DL	Net weight
0GRS_WGT_DL	Gross weight
0COST	Cost in document currency
0NET_VALUE	Net value of the order item in document currency
0SUBTOTAL_1	Subtotal 1 from pricing procedure for condition
0SUBTOTAL_2	Subtotal 2 from pricing procedure for condition
0VALUE_LC	Amount in local currency
BW_PRICE	Price of Item in document currency

Table 5.5 Key Figures

After all of the key figures are assigned, you can see them under the Key Figures section in the InfoCube definition (Figure 5.20).

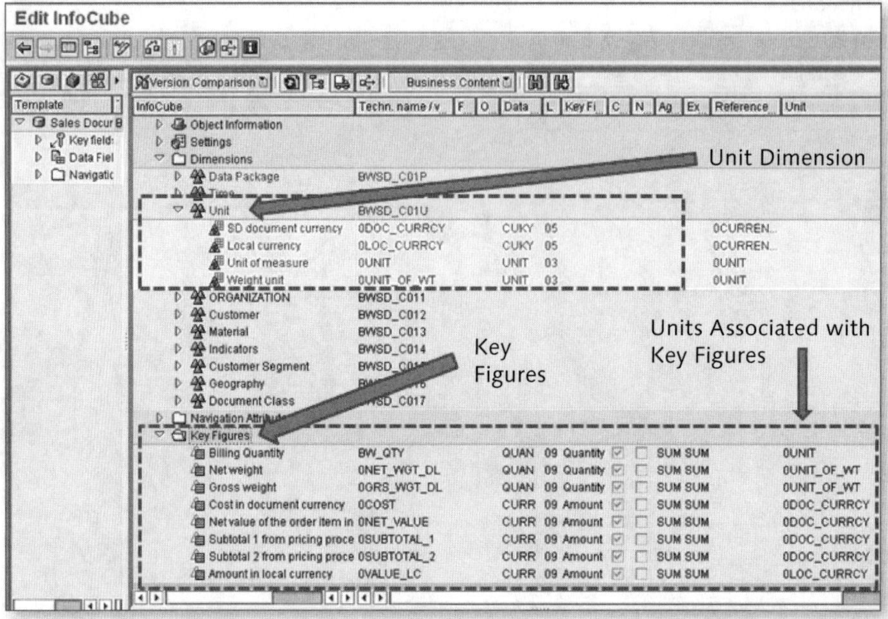

Figure 5.20 Key Figures and Units Assigned to the InfoCube

When you add a key figure to an InfoCube, the corresponding unit characteristic for that key figure automatically gets added to the Unit dimension (Figure 5.20). You can see the units associated with each key figure on the right side of the key figure in the InfoCube definition. For example, the unit associated with key figure BW_QTY is 0UNIT and is added to the Unit dimension.

5.3.7 Selecting Navigation Attributes

Some of the characteristics assigned to different dimensions of an InfoCube can be master data characteristics, which means they can have their own attributes. Some of these attributes may be configured as navigation attributes. All navigation attributes from all master data characteristics included in the InfoCube are available under the Navigation Attributes section of the InfoCube definition (refer to ❶ of Figure 5.21).

These navigation attributes aren't available for navigation by default. If you want to use any of the available navigation attributes in the InfoCube, you must explicitly select them using the check box in the On/Off column (❷). For our BWSD_C01 Info-Cube example, we want to switch on navigation for the Sales Office (0SALES_OFF) attribute of Customer (BW_CUST) master data (❸).

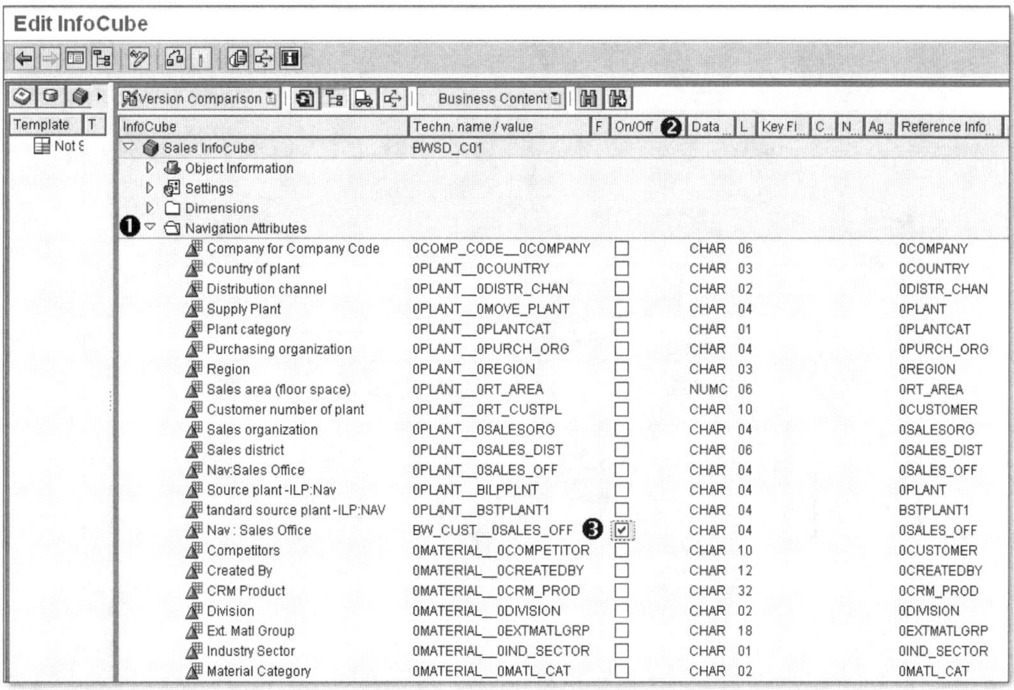

Figure 5.21 Selecting Navigation Attributes

5.3.8 Activating the InfoCube

The InfoCube design is now ready, and you can check its definition using the Check icon on the dynamic menu bar. If no inconsistencies are found, the system gives a message that reads "InfoCube BWSD_C01 is consistent," which appears on the status bar. This means that you can activate the InfoCube definition using the Activate icon (refer to ❶ of Figure 5.22).

> **Note**
>
> All of the relevant tables (dimension tables, fact tables, etc.) associated with an InfoCube are created when the InfoCube is activated.

The activated BWSD_C01 InfoCube can be seen under the BW_AREA InfoArea, as shown in ❸ of Figure 5.22.

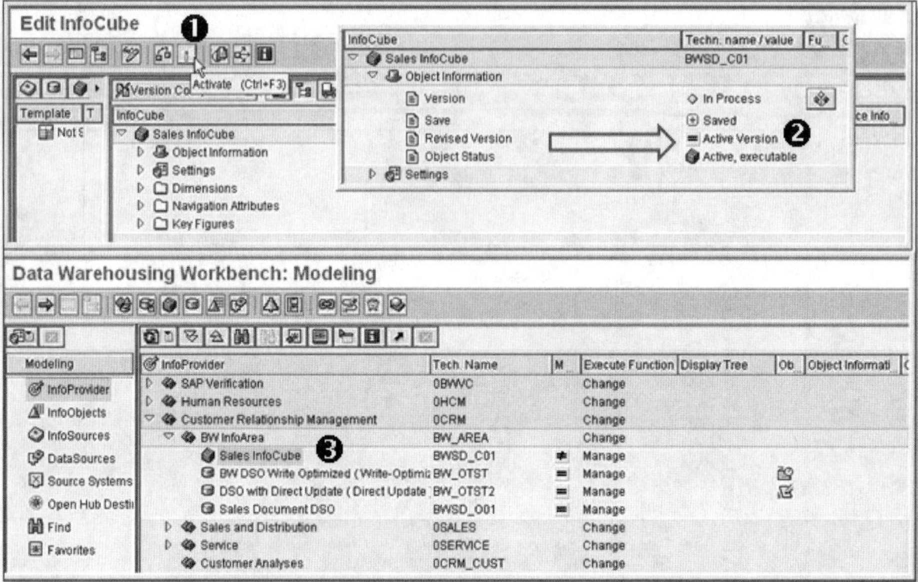

Figure 5.22 Activating the InfoCube

Having explained the design and creation of a standard InfoCube, let's now discuss some finer aspects of its design.

5.4 Provider-Specific Properties

The properties corresponding to different InfoObjects included in the InfoCube definition can be altered to suit specific requirements for an InfoCube. You can take advantage of this design aspect to meet some typical business requirements. For instance, assume that our example scenario requires that the 0MATERIAL characteristic be displayed with Medium Text and Key when used in queries, and that the input help (F4 search) should use the setting Values in Master Data Table. These settings are available when creating/configuring the 0MATERIAL InfoObject. The settings configured at the InfoObject level apply to all of the InfoCubes in which they're used. So, if the 0MATERIAL InfoObject has other settings than the required ones, the InfoCube where it's used will apply them by default. However, it's possible to change these settings for an InfoCube. In this section, we discuss this process for both single InfoObjects and multiple InfoObjects

5.4.1 Setting Provider-Specific Properties for a Single InfoObject

As the InfoCube is already activated, go to the edit mode of the InfoCube. From DWW, call the context menu for InfoCube BWSD_C01, and select CHANGE (Figure 5.23).

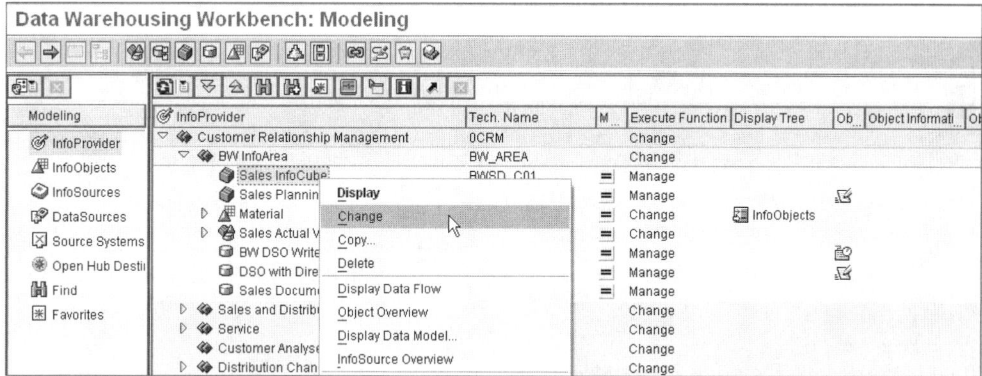

Figure 5.23 Editing an Existing InfoCube

This opens the InfoCube definition in edit mode. Call the context menu for the 0MATERIAL InfoObject, and select Provider-Specific Properties, as shown in Figure 5.24.

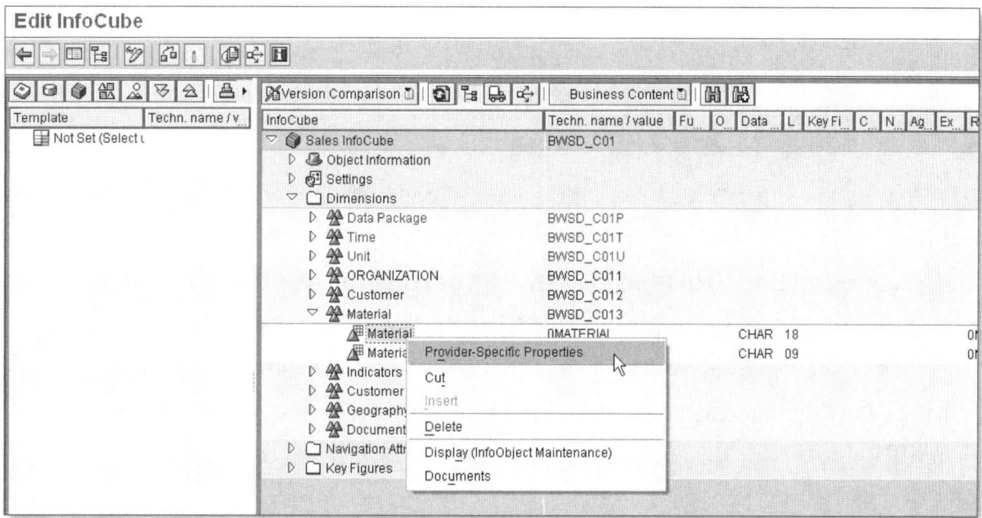

Figure 5.24 Selecting Provider-Specific Properties for an InfoObject

This action displays the Provider-Specific Properties of the InfoObject screen shown in ❶ of Figure 5.25. Different object-specific properties are visible (❷). To set the required properties of the 0MATERIAL InfoObject, select the drop-down menu next to Display (❸), and select Text and Key as Medium Text (❹). This setting influences the display for 0MATERIAL only in this specific InfoCube (❺). Click on the CONTINUE icon (❻) to return to the definition screen.

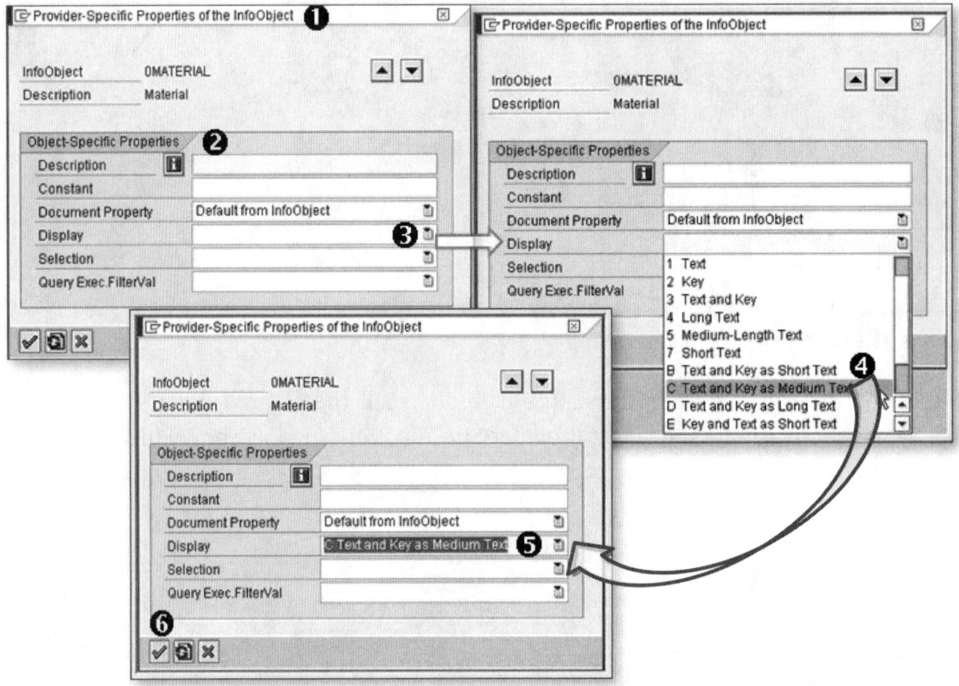

Figure 5.25 Setting Provider-Specific Properties of the InfoObject

5.4.2 Setting Provider-Specific Properties for Multiple InfoObjects

Open the context menu for the Dimensions folder in the InfoCube definition (Figure 5.26), and select PROVIDER-SPECIFIC INFOOBJECT PROPERTIES.

The Provider-Specific Properties of the InfoObject screen is visible, as shown in Figure 5.27.

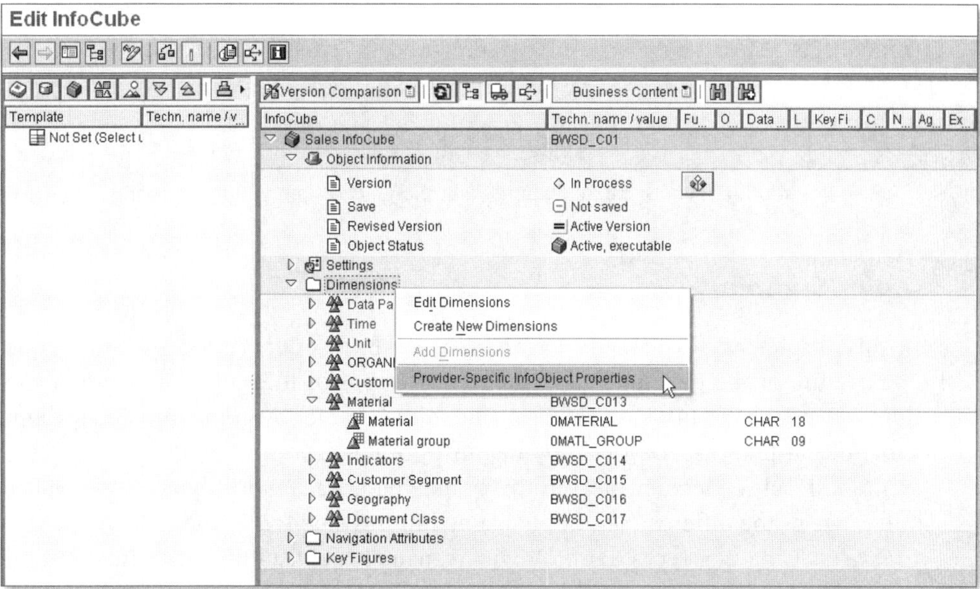

Figure 5.26 Provider-Specific Settings for Multiple InfoObjects

Provider-Specific Properties of the InfoObject

Object-Spec.Characteristic Properties

InfoObject	Long description	Specific Description	Constant	Document ...	D
0CALMONTH	Calendar year/month			Default 1	
0CALQUARTER	Calendar year/quarter			Default 1	
0CALYEAR	Calendar year			Default 1	
0DOC_CURRCY	SD document currency			Default 1	
0LOC_CURRCY	Local currency			Default 1	
0UNIT	Unit of measure			Default 1	
0UNIT_OF_WT	Weight unit			Default 1	
0COMP_CODE	Company Code			Default 1	
0DIVISION	Division			Default 1	
0PLANT	Plant			Default 1	
0SALESORG	Sales Organization			Default 1	
0DISTR_CHAN	Distribution Channel			Default 1	
0SALES_OFF	Sales Office			Default 1	
0SALES_GRP	Sales group			Default 1	
0CO_AREA	Controlling area			Default 1	

Figure 5.27 Maintain Provider-Specific Properties for Multiple InfoObjects

Using this screen, you can maintain the provider-specific properties of multiple InfoObjects. After you've completed the process, check, save, and activate the InfoCube.

Note

To use the InfoCube, you must activate its definition every time you make changes to it.

5.5 Summary

In this chapter, we explained the modeling of an InfoCube based on the unique architecture of the extended star schema, the types of InfoCubes, and the procedure for creating an InfoCube. We concluded the chapter by going into detail about some of the finer aspects of designing an InfoCube, specifically, provider-specific settings. In subsequent chapters of this book, you'll learn more about the relevance and usage of the different settings explained in this chapter. In the following chapter, we explain other types of InfoProviders, namely the MultiProvider, InfoSet, and VirtualProvider.

Understanding MultiProviders, InfoSets, and their design is essential for making use of the flexibility these objects provide. This chapter introduces you to important aspects of MultiProvider and InfoSet objects along with mention of VirtualProviders.

6 InfoProviders

MultiProviders, InfoSets, and VirtualProviders are InfoProviders that don't store data but rather are logical definitions based on a combination of two or more data targets such as InfoObject (characteristics with master data), DataStore Object (DSO) and InfoCube. These InfoProviders answer many business queries and save on efforts to extract and store the data. They provide flexibility in managing a data warehouse and offer scalability and efficiency. Queries can be created on MultiProviders, InfoSets, or VirtualProviders using standard query tools supplied by SAP NetWeaver BW.

6.1 Introduction to MultiProvider

Normally, the design of a data target such as an InfoCube or DSO is based on one business process, for example, an InfoCube for sales billing processing and another for sales order processing. In this way, SAP NetWeaver BW may have multiple InfoCubes, each supporting an individual business process. Business information requirements may invite a situation where data from two different InfoCubes needs to be joined.

SAP NetWeaver BW supports queries based on a single InfoProvider. To support reporting requirements across multiple data providers, you need not load data from the individual data providers to the new data provider. The system provides a better way to handle this situation, by way of a MultiProvider.

A MultiProvider is a logical definition that doesn't physically store data. The data lies in the underlying data provider on which the MultiProvider is based. You can create a MultiProvider based on the following objects. This is also shown in Figure 6.1.

- InfoCube
- DataStore Object

- InfoObject
- InfoSet
- Aggregation Level

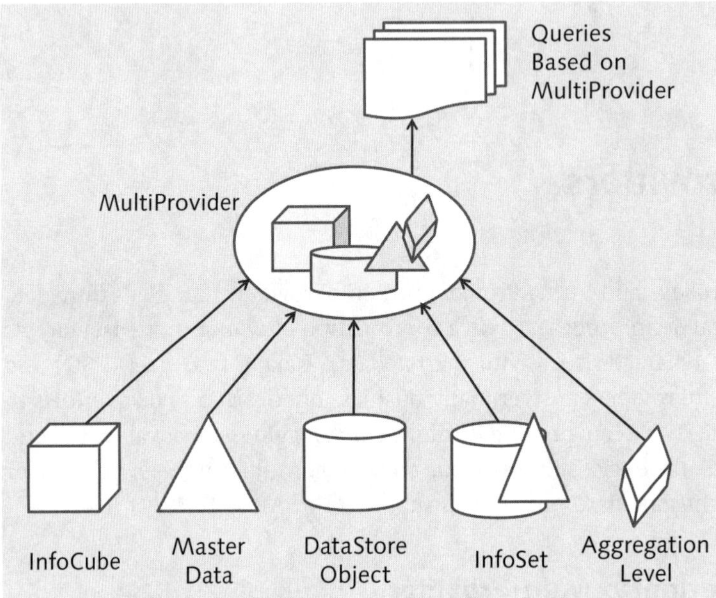

Figure 6.1 MultiProvider: A Logical Definition

MultiProviders can be created based on any combination of objects shown in Figure 6.1, for example, InfoCube to InfoCube (not limiting to two InfoCubes) or InfoCube to InfoObject or DSO to InfoCube. Again, the number of objects included in the definition of a MultiProvider isn't limited to two. And you create queries based on a MultiProvider.

Figure 6.2 shows an example of including two InfoCubes in a MultiProvider: InfoCubes on planning data and the other on actual sales. While the Actuals InfoCube stores the data from actual sales, the Plan InfoCube stores the data on planning. Another example of creating a MultiProvider based on InfoCube and InfoObject is having a sales InfoCube and the InfoObject 0MATERIAL. The queries on this MultiProvider might be for identifying the slow-moving material.

You can also use a MultiProvider when the InfoCube you're creating becomes very large. In this case, you can split the InfoCube into identical smaller InfoCubes and store the data based on the year. For reporting purposes, it's recommended to create MultiProviders based on these InfoCubes and create queries on the MultiProvider.

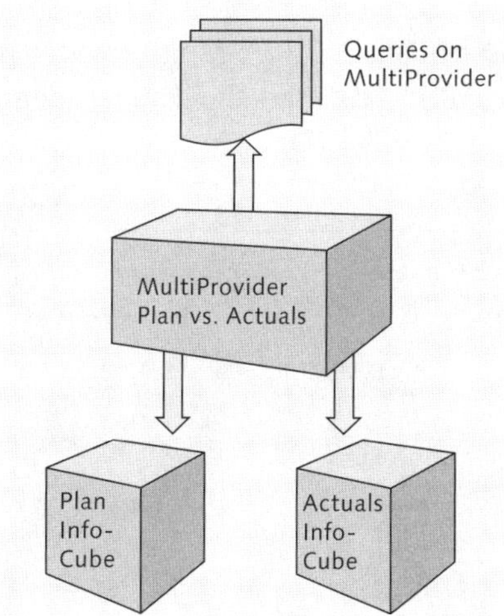

Figure 6.2 MultiProvider Example: Plan Versus Actual

MultiProvider advantages include the following:

- Designing InfoCubes based on individual business processes is much simpler and allows for the combination of various InfoCubes at a later stage. So, a MultiProvider allows you to keep your design of the InfoCubes simple and small.
- Small InfoCubes are easy to maintain.
- The system uses parallel processing when queries on a MultiProvider are executed. As shown in Figure 6.2, when a query is executed on MultiProvider plan versus actuals, the system internally starts multiple subqueries in parallel. After the results of these queries are available, they are combined using the union operation and presented to the user. The union operation combines result data sets from subqueries.

6.2 Designing a MultiProvider

Having explained MultiProviders and their advantages, we'll now explain how to create a MultiProvider in SAP NetWeaver BW using a step-by-step process.

In the example scenario, we have a requirement where the planning head from the ABCD Corp. requires the BI solution to report the status of actual sales compared to the planned sales forecast to ascertain whether company sales are on target or action is needed to address the variance between projected sales versus actual sales. Our reference scenario has the Sales InfoCube, which stores actual sales data. It also has the Planning InfoCube, which stores the plan data. (Planning is covered in Chapter 12, Integrated Planning.) We discuss creating a MultiProvider based on plan versus actual sales.

From your Data Warehousing Workbench (Transaction RSA1), select the InfoProvider from the Modeling section as shown in ❶ of Figure 6.3. A MultiProvider is created under InfoArea. Select the InfoArea BW_AREA (❷). Start the context menu of the InfoArea BW_AREA, and select Create MultiProvider (❸).

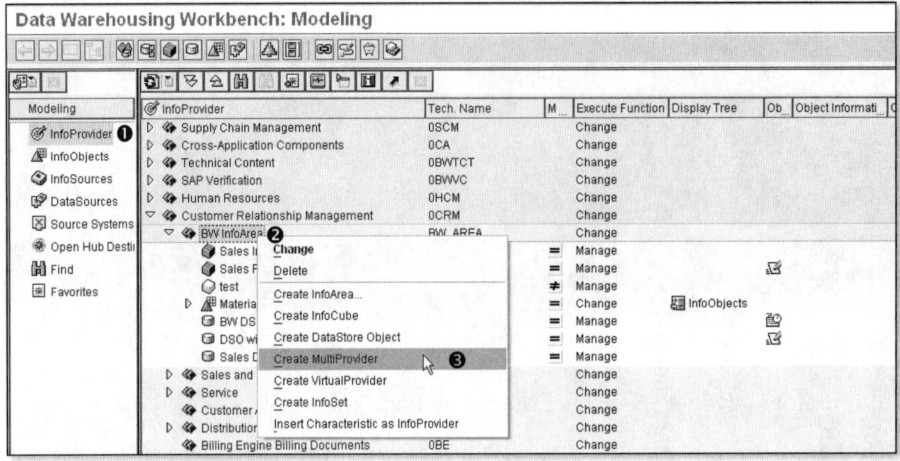

Figure 6.3 Creating a MultiProvider

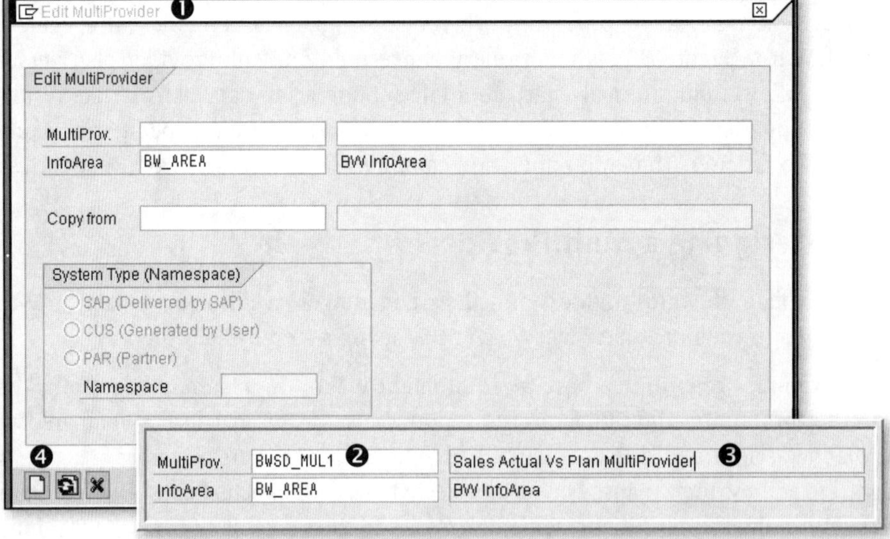

Figure 6.4 Create a MultiProvider: Adding Name and Description to a MultiProvider

The Edit MultiProvider pop-up box appears as shown in ❶ of Figure 6.4. You need to provide the unique technical name and description of the MultiProvider. Enter technical name "BWSD_MUL1" (❷). Provide the description "Sales Actuals Vs Plan MultiProvider" (❸). Click on the Create icon (❹).

The next screen is MultiProvider: Relevant InfoProvider as shown in Figure 6.5. Because a MultiProvider is based on different data targets/InfoProviders (as shown earlier in Figure 6.1), this screen offers you selections based on the data targets/InfoProviders you want to include in the definition of the MultiProvider.

There are five different tabs available as shown in ❶,❷,❸,❹ and ❺ of Figure 6.5. These tabs allow you to select InfoCubes, DataStore Object, InfoObjects, InfoSets, and Aggregation Levels, respectively. As shown in ❻ of Figure 6.5, nothing is selected.

There may be a large number of data targets/InfoProviders available in the system. There are three different display options available to list them (❼). By default, the system uses the option Display All InfoProviders for listing. The Search option is available by clicking (❽).

Select InfoCubes BWSD_C01 (Sales InfoCube) and BW_PLAN (Sales Planning Cube) (❾). Click on the Continue icon (❿) to move ahead.

The system takes you to the Edit MultiProvider screen, as shown in Figure 6.6. The initial definition of MultiProvider BWSD_MUL1 is shown with included InfoCubes (BWSD_C01 and BW_PLAN) as shown in ❶ of Figure 6.6. Four default dimensions are shown in ❷ of Figure 6.6, they are: Data Package, Time, Unit, and Dimension 1. This screen also offers a section to include navigation attributes (❸) and key figures (❹).

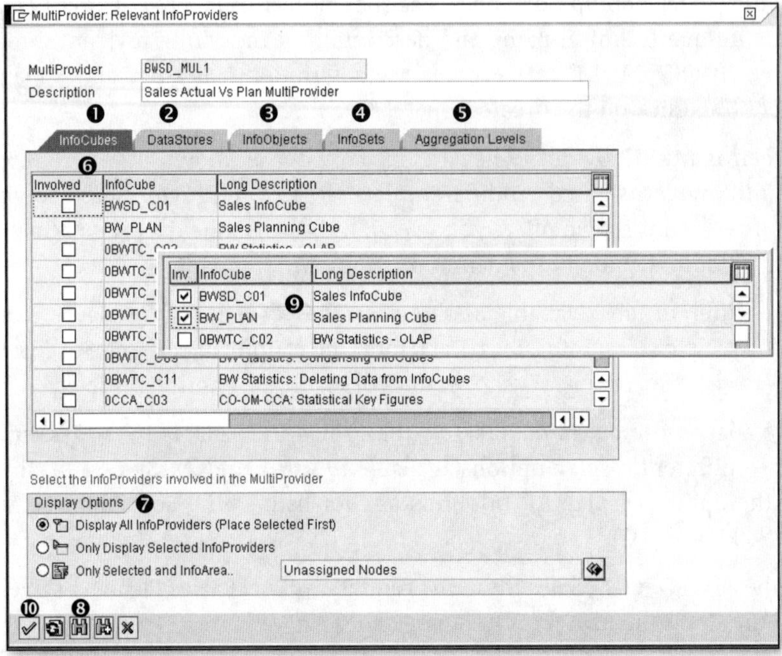

Figure 6.5 Creating MultiProvider: Selecting InfoProviders

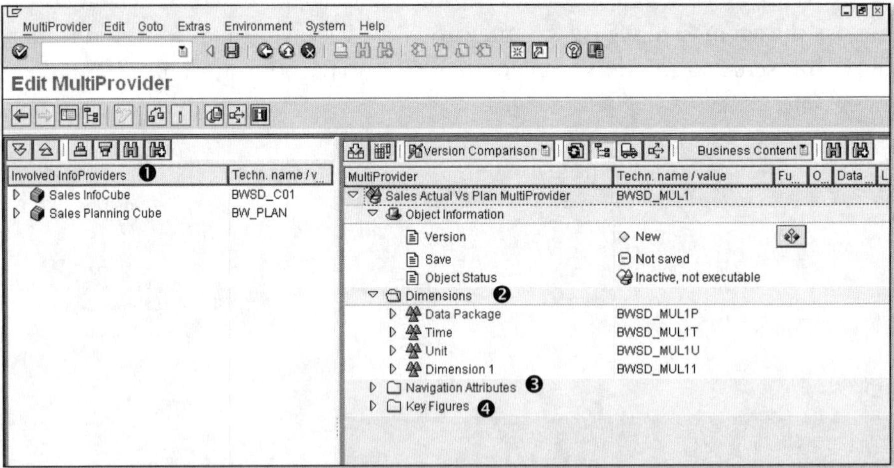

Figure 6.6 Edit MultiProvider Initial Screen

Because both InfoCubes are supporting a different business process, their definitions ought to be different. However, a few characteristics and key figures may be common between the two. Table 6.1 provides a list of characteristics and key Figures from both of the InfoCubes:

Type	Technical Name in BWSD_C01	Technical Name in BW_PLAN
Characteristics	0COMP_CODE	Not Available
	0DIVISION	0DIVISION
	0PLANT	Not Available
	0SALESORG	0SALESORG
	0DISTR_CHAN	Not Available
	0SALES_OFF	Not Available
	0SALES_GRP	Not Available
	0CO_AREA	Not Available
	BW_CUST	Not Available
	0MATERIAL	Not Available
	0MATL_GROUP	0MATL_GROUP
	0ACCNT_ASGN	Not Available
	0CUST_GROUP	Not Available
	0CUST_GRP1	Not Available
	0REGION	Not Available
	0SALES_DIST	Not Available
	0COUNTRY	Not Available
	0BILL_TYPE	Not Available
	0ITEM_CATEG	Not Available
	0BILL_CAT	Not Available
	0DOC_CATEG	Not Available
	Not Available	BW_PROD
Time Characteristics	0CALMONTH	Not Available
	0CALQUARTER	0CALQUARTER
	0CALYEAR	0CALYEAR
Key Figures	BW_QTY	Not Available
	0NET_WGT_DL	Not Available
	0GRS_WGT_DL	Not Available
	0COST	Not Available
	0NET_VALUE	Not Available

Table 6.1 Comparison of Definitions for Designing MultiProviders

Type	Technical Name in BWSD_C01	Technical Name in BW_PLAN
Key Figures	0SUBTOTAL_1	Not Available
	0SUBTOTAL_2	Not Available
	0VALUE_LC	Not Available
	BW_PRICE	Not Available
	Not Available	BW_VAL

Table 6.1 Comparison of Definitions for Designing MultiProviders (Cont.)

We can see that only a few characteristics of InfoCube BWSD_C01 are available in the BW_PLAN InfoCube. One of the basic conditions in designing a MultiProvider is to have the identical technical name of the characteristics across InfoCubes (or other included data targets).

All of the characteristics InfoObjects included in InfoCube BW_PLAN have the same InfoObject in InfoCube BWSD_C01, except BW_PROD. BW_PROD is used for relating to product or material in a reference scenario for ABCD Corp., which is similar to the use of InfoObject 0MATERIAL of InfoCube BWSD_C01. The two InfoObjects, BW_PROD and 0MATERIAL, can't be matched while designing a MultiProvider. Including such nonmatching InfoObjects is possible in a MultiProvider definition, but queries using them don't produce the proper results. We'll explain with an example.

This is applicable to time characteristics and key figures.

When defining the MultiProvider, we'll include the following characteristics and key figures:

- 0SALESORG
- 0DIVISION
- 0MATL_GROUP
- BW_PROD
- 0CALQUARTER
- 0CALYEAR
- 0NET_VALUE (Actual Value)
- BW_VAL (Planning Value)

The dimensions of InfoCube BWSD_C01 and BW_PLAN are shown in ❶,❷, and ❸ of Figure 6.7. In this figure, characteristics within dimension Organization for Sales Planning cube are shown in detail. Because a MultiProvider is a logical definition and doesn't physically store data, the design of various dimensions isn't as vital as it is during the design of a standard InfoCube. Even then, attaching characteristics in logical grouping in various dimensions helps the query designer. So, it's recommended to design dimensions even for a MultiProvider.

First, let's delete "Dimension 1," which is created by default by SAP NetWeaver BW. Select Dimension 1 as shown in ❹ of Figure 6.7, and open the context menu. Next, select Delete (❺).

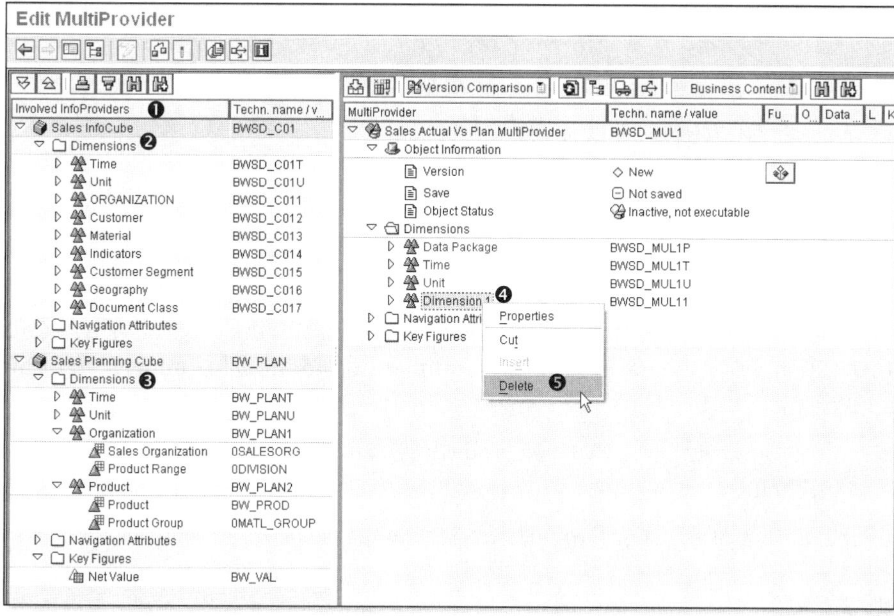

Figure 6.7 Edit MultiProvider: Deleting Dimension 1

Dimension design while creating a standard InfoCube is a very crucial step because standard InfoCubes store data physically. A small error in dimension design can seriously and negatively affect the performance of queries.

This doesn't apply to creating a MultiProvider, however, because it's an InfoProvider and doesn't store physical data. You can either create new dimensions or directly drag and drop dimensions from any of the InfoCube as shown in Figure 6.8. As shown in ❶ of Figure 6.8, select dimension Organization and drop it over Dimension (❷). The outcome of this activity is Dimension Organization, which is available in MultiProvider BWSD_MUL1 with both the characteristics (Sales Organization and Product Range) of Base InfoCube (BW_PLAN) (❸).

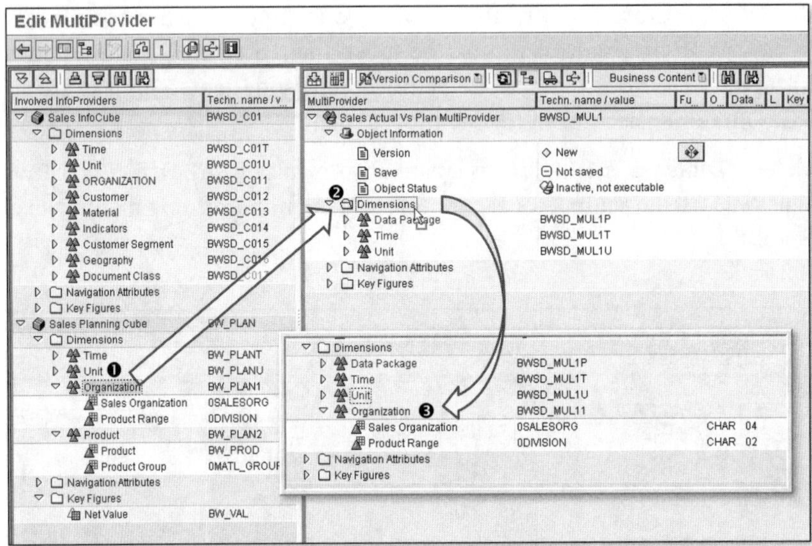

Figure 6.8 Edit MultiProvider: Drag and Drop Dimension

In a similar way, drag and drop the Product dimension and the characteristics 0CALQUARTER and 0CALYEAR from the Time dimension to the Time dimension of the MultiProvider.

Drag and drop key figures BW_VAL and 0NET_VALUE from the base InfoCube to the MultiProvider.

The final design of the MultiProvider BWSD_MUL1 is shown in Figure 6.9.

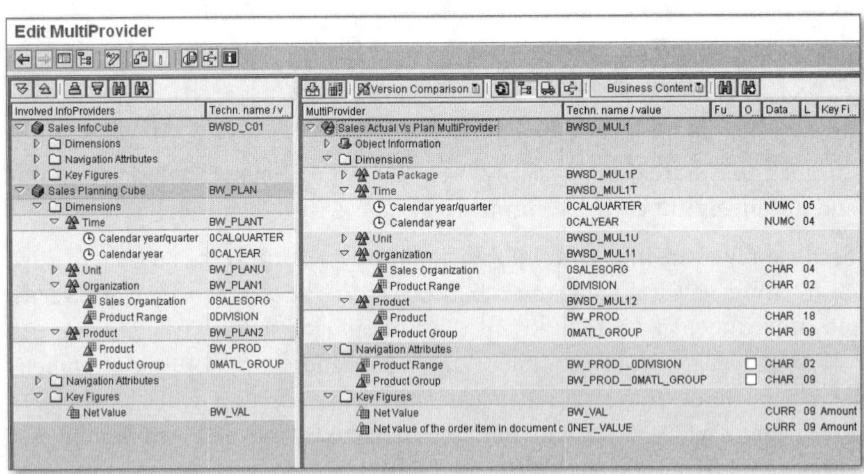

Figure 6.9 Edit MultiProvider: Dimensions and Key Figures

Now you need to identify each of the characteristics included in the MultiProvider and match them to the characteristics or navigation attributes of the base InfoCube. We'll now explain the process to identify and match the characteristics or navigational attributes.

Click on the Identify Characteristics icon as shown in ❶ of Figure 6.10. The Identification of Participating Characteristics/Nav. Attr. box appears (❷). It shows each characteristic included in the MultiProvider and offers the matching characteristics or navigational attributes available from the included InfoCube.

As shown in ❸ of Figure 6.10, it shows the characteristic 0CALQUARTER from the MultiProvider and offers matching characteristics 0CALQUARTER from the Sales InfoCube (BWSD_C01) (❹). It also offers the characteristic 0CALQUARTER from the Sales Planning Cube (BW_PLAN) (❺). You need to confirm this matching by clicking on the checkbox (❻).

You can select the next characteristics from the MultiProvider using the Next icon (❼). This process needs to be completed for all of the characteristics included in the MultiProvider.

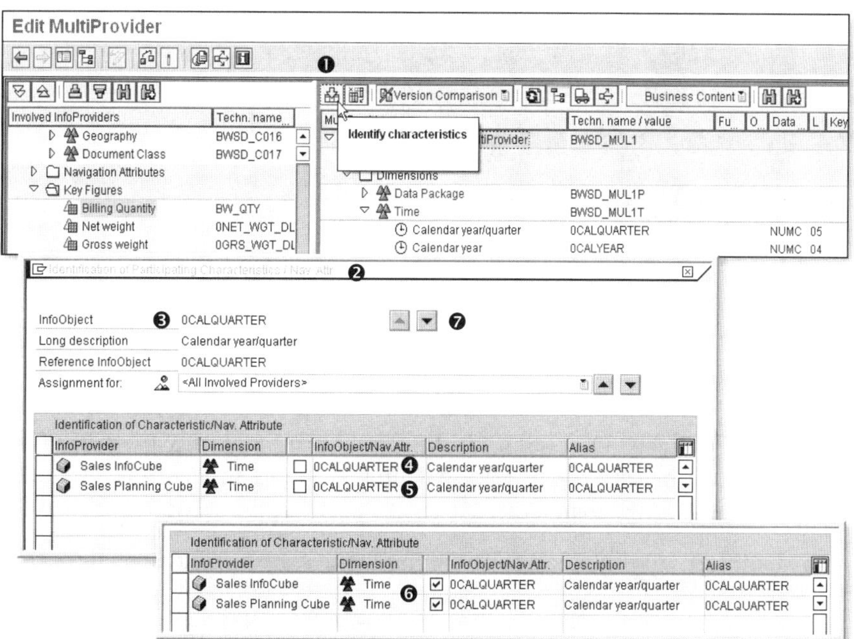

Figure 6.10 Edit MultiProvider: Identify Characteristics

Let's discuss the options for including characteristics in a MultiProvider, for instance, including characteristic 0DIVISION (see ❶ of Figure 6.11). SAP NetWeaver BW offers 0DIVISION from the Sales InfoCube to be matched with 0DIVISION and BW_PROD_0DIVISION (0DIVISION is the navigation attribute of BW_PROD) from the Sales Planning InfoCube (❷). You need to decide whether you want to match the 0DIVISION characteristics of InfoCube BWSD_C01 with the 0DIVISION characteristics of InfoCube BW_PLAN or with the 0DIVISION navigation attribute of BW_PROD. Select 0DIVISION characteristics from both the InfoCubes (❸).

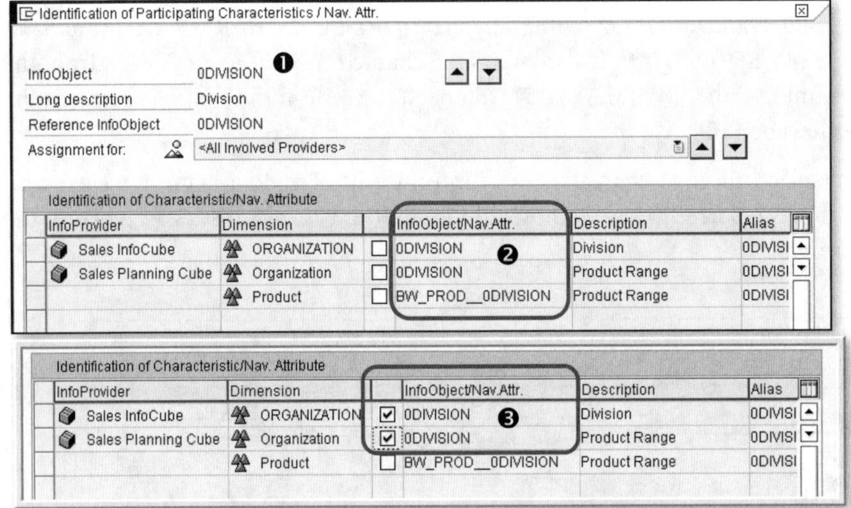

Figure 6.11 Edit MultiProvider: Identify Characteristics, Multiple Offered

You might also have a scenario while identifying the characteristics across InfoCubes within a MultiProvider where the characteristics can't be matched to a characteristics or navigation attribute in another InfoCube or data target included in the definition of MultiProvider. For example, characteristic BW_PROD is included in the MultiProvider definition (❶ of Figure 6.12), and BW_PROD is offered only from InfoCube Sales Planning Cube because there's no matching available in Sales InfoCube (❷). Select as shown in ❸ of Figure 6.12.

Your final identification of characteristics should be as shown in Table 6.2.

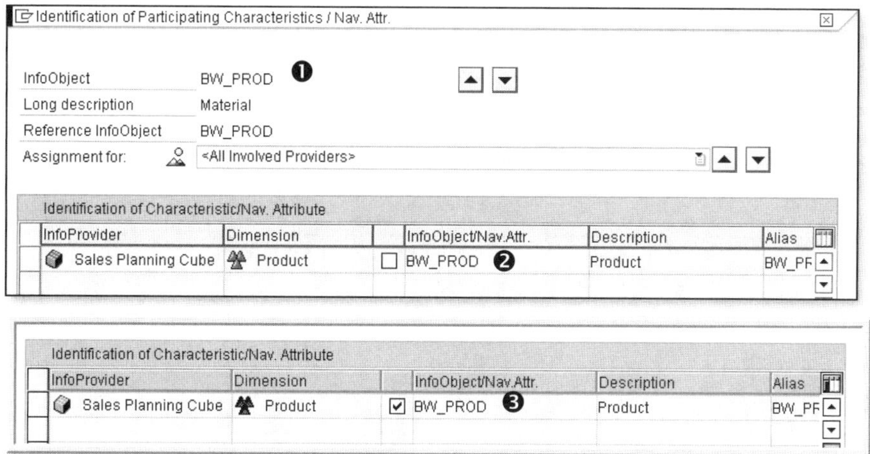

Figure 6.12 Edit MultiProvider: Identify Characteristics Only from One InfoCube

MultiProvider Characteristics	Offer from InfoCube BWSD_C01	Offer from InfoCube BW_PLAN	Selected from InfoCube BWSD_C01	Selected from InfoCube BW_PLAN
0CALQUARTER	0CALQUARTER	0CALQUARTER	0CALQUARTER	0CALQUARTER
0CALYEAR	0CALYEAR	0CALYEAR	0CALYEAR	0CALYEAR
0SALESORG	0SALESORG	0SALESORG	0SALESORG	0SALESORG
0DIVISION	0DIVISION	0DIVISION BW_PROD__0DIVISION	0DIVISION	0DIVISION
BW_PROD		BW_PROD		BW_PROD
0MATL_GROUP	0MATL_GROUP	0MATL_GROUP BW_PROD__0MATL_GROUP	0MATL_GROUP	0MATL_GROUP

Table 6.2 Identification of Characteristics in MultiProvider

After all of the characteristics included in a MultiProvider are matched, you also need to match the key figures. You need to select the Select Key Figures icon as shown in ❶ of Figure 6.13. The Selection of Key Figures Involved box appears (❷). The system lists each key figure involved in the MultiProvider one-by-one. Key figure BW_VAL is shown (❸). The system offers key figure BW_VAL from the Sales Planning InfoCube (❹). Because there's no matching key figure available in the Sales InfoCube, the system doesn't show any second key figures. Select the key figure BW_VAL (❺). You can go to the next key figure by clicking on the Next Object icon (❻).

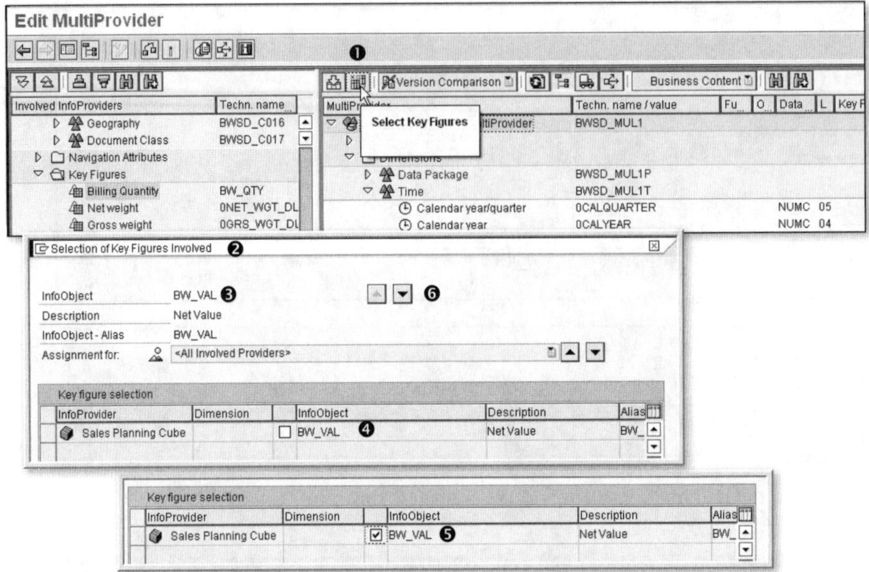

Figure 6.13 Edit MultiProvider: Selection of Key Figure Involved

The final identification of key figures is shown in Table 6.3.

MultiProvider Key Figure	Offer from InfoCube BWSD_C01	Offer from InfoCube BW_PLAN	Selected from InfoCube BWSD_C01	Selected from InfoCube BW_PLAN
BW_VAL		BW_VAL		BW_VAL
0NET_VALUE	0NET_VALUE		0NET_VALUE	

Table 6.3 Identification of Key Figures

There may be scenarios where you're planning to create a single InfoCube for one business process. At the time of configuring your InfoCube, you realize that this InfoCube is going to get a very large amount of records in the fact table. Query requirements by business require you to store the data for up to a couple of years. In this case, you can decide to use the MultiProvider. Basically, you're splitting a single InfoCube into multiple InfoCubes and storing the data by year. All of the base InfoCubes included in the definition on the MultiProvider have the identical set of characteristics and key figures.

Here you can select the key figure from both the base InfoCubes (while including it in MultiProvider). Selecting the key figure in both the InfoCubes results in the addition of key figure data for the same values of characteristics.

Now use the Check icon as shown in ❶ of Figure 6.14 to check the definition of the MultiProvider. If everything is okay, the system reports a message (❷). You can see that the MultiProvider is still not in Active status (❸). Click on the Activate icon (❹). After it's successfully activated, the system changes the status of the MultiProvider to Active (❺).

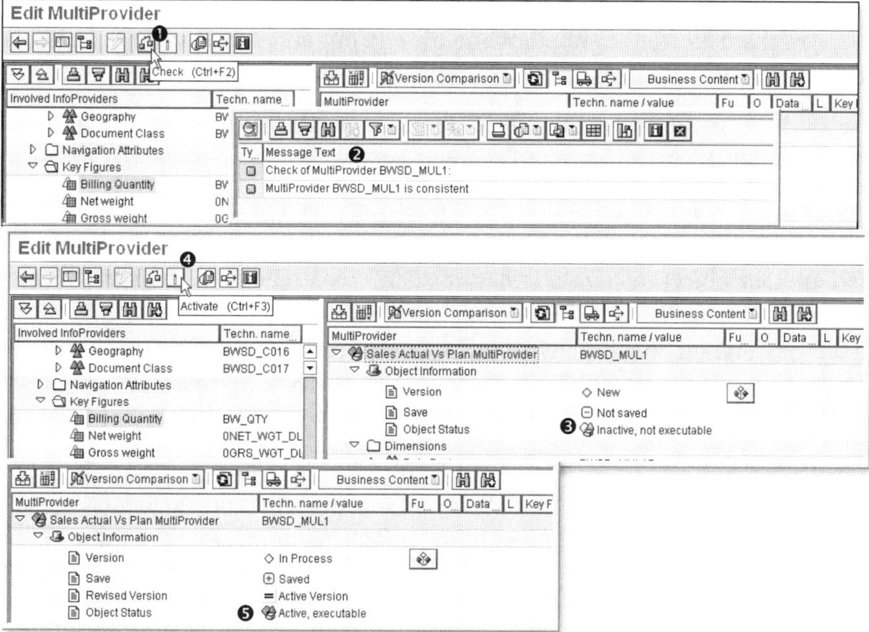

Figure 6.14 Checking and Activating the MultiProvider

After successful activation of the MultiProvider BWSD_MUL1, it's available under the InfoArea as shown in Figure 6.15.

Data Warehousing Workbench: Modeling

Modeling: InfoProvider, InfoObjects, InfoSources, DataSources, Source Systems, Open Hub Desti, Find, Favorites

InfoProvider	Tech. Name	M...	Execute Function	Display Tree	Ob...
Human Resources	0HCM		Change		
Customer Relationship Management	0CRM		Change		
BW InfoArea	BW_AREA		Change		
Sales InfoCube	BWSD_C01	=	Manage		
Sales Planning Cube	BW_PLAN	=	Manage		
Material	BW_PROD	=	Change	InfoObjects	
Sales Actual Vs Plan MultiProvider	BWSD_MUL1	=	Change		
BW DSO Write Optimized (Write-Optimized)	BW_OTST	=	Manage		
DSO with Direct Update (Direct Update)	BW_OTST2	=	Manage		
Sales Document DSO	BWSD_O01	=	Manage		
Sales and Distribution	0SALES		Change		

Figure 6.15 Activated MultiProvider BWSD_MUL1 Available Under InfoArea BW_AREA

Now that we've covered the MultiProvider, let's move on to another InfoProvider: the InfoSet.

6.3 InfoSets

An InfoSet is only a logical definition and doesn't physically store data. Queries can be created on an InfoSet using standard query tools supplied by SAP NetWeaver BW. Queries get the data from the underlying objects or sources. These sources can be InfoObjects (characteristics with master data), DSOs, or InfoCubes.

MultiProviders can include objects such as InfoCubes, DSOs, InfoObjects (characteristic with master data), InfoSets, and aggregation levels.

In this section, we'll explain and address questions such as the following: Can we state that an InfoSet is a subset of a MultiProvider, or why has SAP NetWeaver BW offered another object of the same nature? Can't we accomplish the same task by using a MultiProvider? The fundamental difference between the two is that MultiProviders use a union operator, while InfoSet uses a join operator. Depending on the requirement, you may need to choose a MultiProvider or an InfoSet.

6.3.1 Usage

InfoSets offer results from different underlying sources using the join operator, making it a more predictable kind of result. By default, an InfoSet uses the inner join operation. Inner join checks the data in all underlying sources for the joining condition, and if it's available in all, it's passed for the result set. InfoSet also offers outer join, which can be used in some typical scenarios, such as for products that aren't moving. In this case, you can create an InfoSet based on the InfoObject 0MATERIAL and the DSO (in which material-wise actual sales data is stored). This difference between inner and left outer join is explained with the following example.

An InfoObject on the Customer (e.g., T1 in short) has Sales Office as an attribute. The sample data is shown in the Table 6.4.

Customer Number	Sales Office
C1	SO1
C2	SO2
C3	SO3
C4	SO1
C6	SO2

Table 6.4 Example Data Customer InfoObject with Attribute Sales Office

Sales DSO (e.g., T2 in short) contains customer-wise, month-wise billing quantity in number as shown in Table 6.5.

Month	Customer Number	Billing Qty (in Nos)
10.2009	C1	100
10.2009	C2	120
10.2009	C3	150
10.2009	C5	140
10.2009	C6	110

Table 6.5 Example Data Sales DSO: Customer Month-Wise Billing Quantity

When the InfoSet on T1 and T2 is created with inner join on the customer number, the result looks similar to Table 6.6.

Customer Number	Sales Office	Month	Billing Qty (in Nos)
C1	SO1	10.2009	100
C2	SO2	10.2009	120
C3	SO3	10.2009	150
C6	SO2	10.2009	110

Table 6.6 Result of Making InfoSet on T1 and T2 with Inner Join

The record for customers C4 and C5 isn't included in the result set because the data isn't available for these customers in both the sources included in the InfoSet definition.

When the InfoSet on T1 and T2 is created with left outer join on the customer number while keeping the customer InfoObject on the left of outer join, the result looks similar to Table 6.7.

Customer Number	Sales Office	Month	Billing Qty (in Nos)
C1	SO1	10.2009	100
C2	SO2	10.2009	120
C3	SO3	10.2009	150
C4	SO1		
C6	SO2	10.2009	110

Table 6.7 Result of Making InfoSet on T1 and T2 with Left Outer Join

Transitive attribute reporting is also possible using an InfoSet. Let's first explain the meaning of a transitive attribute. As shown in Figure 6.16, you have the InfoObject BW_CUST, which has several attributes, one of which is 0SALESEMPLY. InfoObject 0SALESEMPLY has its own attributes. One of the attributes is 0CITY. Here, 0CITY is known as a transitive attribute of BW_CUST. Now you want a report that gives you a list of customers in each city.

While designing an InfoCube, you can switch on the navigation attribute. You can switch on 0SALESEMPLY as the navigation attribute of BW_CUST and use 0SALESEMPLY in the query design wherever BW_CUST is part of the InfoCube. But you can't use the attributes of 0SALESEMPLY in the query design when BW_CUST is part of the InfoCube.

In this scenario, you can use the InfoSet to get the information related to the transitive attribute.

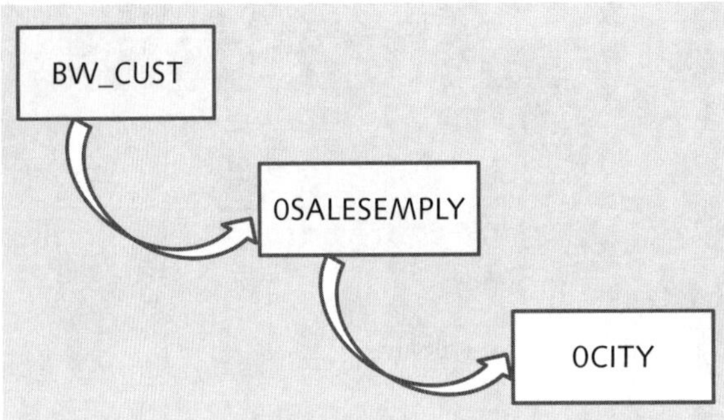

Figure 6.16 0CITY Is the Transitive Attribute of BW_CUST

InfoSets offer a unique facility called temporal join. When you have an InfoSet based on one of the sources with an InfoObject (with master data), and this InfoObject has time-dependent attributes, the join performed in this case is known as a time-dependent or temporal join. The scenario on temporal join is explained with an example in this chapter.

You can do most recent reporting using queries on InfoSet. When you load master data into an InfoObject, the latest data loaded isn't immediately available for reporting because it's stored in the M (modified) version in the underlying tables associated with the InfoObjects. There is a process of activating master data, which turns an M version into an A (active) version. By default, only active version data is read to query. Only the InfoSet allows you to query on data that isn't active. The setting is shown in Section 6.6.2, Most Recent Reporting for InfoObjects.

Usage Restriction

The following are restrictions in using an InfoSet:

- You can't define an InfoSet when the InfoCube is a right operand of a left outer join.
- SAP doesn't support InfoSets containing more than two InfoCubes.

6.4 Creating an InfoSet

In the reference scenario, we have a requirement for analyzing which products of ABCD Corp. aren't getting sold in specific markets. This analysis requires an InfoSet, which we'll now explain the step-by-step process of creating in SAP NetWeaver BW.

To begin, start Data Warehousing Workbench (DWW) using Transaction RSA1. Under Modeling in the Navigation section, select InfoProvider, as shown in ❶ of Figure 6.17. InfoSets are created under InfoArea. From the tree section of the screen, select the InfoArea you want to attach your InfoSet to (❷). In this example, InfoArea BW_AREA is selected.

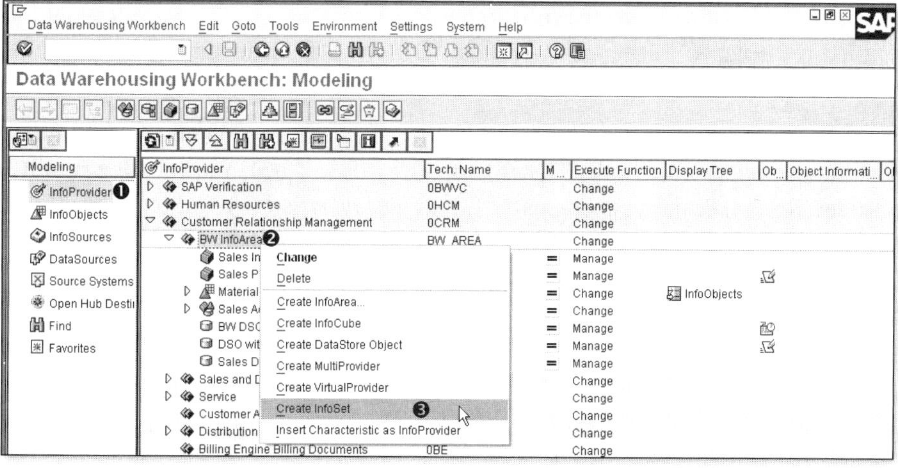

Figure 6.17 Creating the InfoSet

Using the context menu of InfoArea BW_AREA, click on the Create InfoSet option (❸). The Create InfoSet box appears as shown in Figure 6.18.

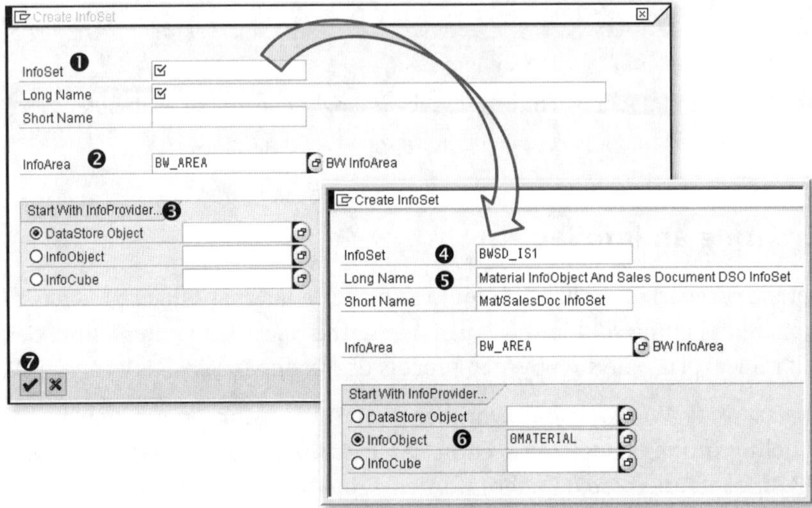

Figure 6.18 Create InfoSet: Initial Screen

InfoSets require a unique technical name and description as shown in ❶ of Figure 6.18. The technical name of the InfoArea BW_AREA in which the InfoSet would be grouped is displayed in the InfoArea field (❷). The Start with InfoProvider section (❸) offers three choices: DataStore Object, InfoObject, and InfoCube.

In this example, we'll use the technical name "BWSD_IS1" (❹) and the description "Material InfoObject and Sales Document DSO InfoSet" (❺). You can also supply a short description. Entering a long name is mandatory, whereas entering a short name is optional. We'll use "Mat/SalesDoc InfoSet" in our Short Name field.

The Start With InfoProvider area allows you to supply the technical name of the first source you want to include in the definition of your InfoSet BWSD_IS1. In our example, we want to include an InfoSet based on an InfoObject 0MATERIAL and DSO object BWSD_O01. Select the InfoObject radio button, and enter the name of the InfoObject 0MATERIAL (❻). Now click on the continue ✔ icon (❼). The resulting screen is shown in Figure 6.19.

InfoObject 0MATERIAL is included as part of InfoSet BWSD_IS1. SAP NetWeaver BW internally allocates the number T00001 to the first object that is included in this definition (see ❶ of Figure 6.19). For the subsequent objects you include, it gives the number T00002, and so on.

All attributes of the InfoObject 0MATERIAL are shown in the vertical box format. The technical name of the attribute is shown in the Technical Name column (❺).

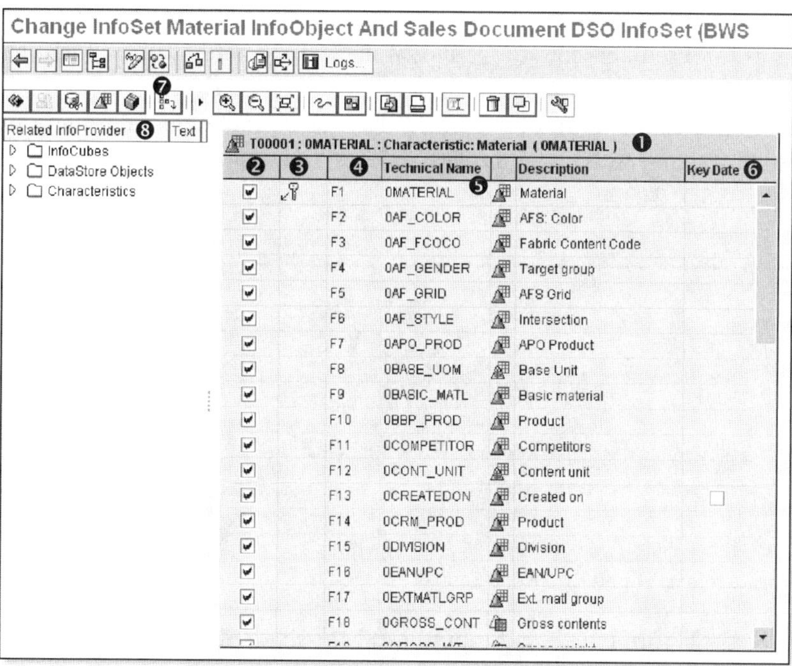

Figure 6.19 Create InfoSet: Understanding the Initial Screen

Not all columns have titles, so we've numbered them to explain their significance.

Column ❷ of Figure 6.19 allows you to decide whether you want to include the particular attribute of 0MATERIAL InfoObject in the final definition of the InfoSet. By default, SAP NetWeaver BW includes all of the attributes.

Column ❸ indicates when the particular InfoObject is a key. For example, the InfoObject 0MATERIAL key is the key for InfoObject 0MATERIAL; for a DSO, all of the key fields are indicated as key and the row has a key icon ( ).

Column ❹ indicates the internal number given to each field in the object. The number starts from F1 and goes in sequence to F2, F3, and so on.

Column ❻ indicates whether the field is included or excluded while defining the result for a temporal join. The checkbox is only shown where the field is of type date; for example, for field F13, the checkbox is shown because this field is 0CREATEDON, which is of type date.

The related InfoProvider section (❽) gives the list of InfoObjects, DSOs, and InfoCubes that can be used to join 0MATERIAL, that is, all of the objects that 0MATERIAL is part of and available for making InfoSet join with InfoObject 0MATERIAL.

Now you're ready to include your next source in the definition of InfoSet BWSD_IS1. Select the Insert InfoProvider icon [icon] as shown in ❼ of Figure 6.19. A pop-up box titled Insert InfoObject appears as shown in ❶ of Figure 6.20. Three choices (DataStore Object, InfoObject, and InfoCube) are available as InfoSet definitions and can include either of the objects. Our example InfoSet is based on InfoObject 0MATERIAL and DSO BWSD_O01.

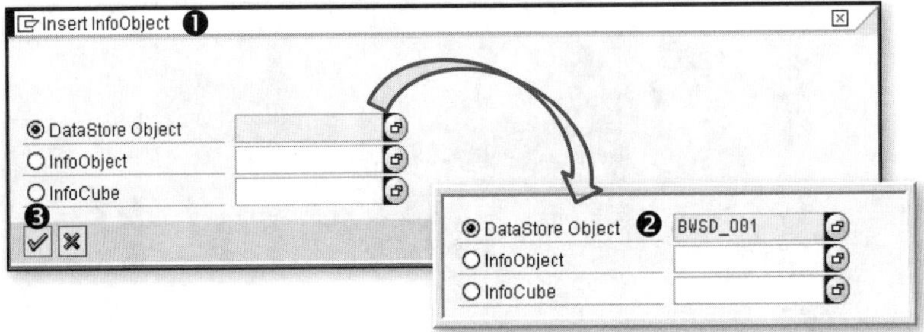

Figure 6.20 Create InfoSet: Inserting Second Source

Next, select the DataStore Object radio button (if not selected already), and enter the technical name "BWSD_O01" as shown in ❷ of Figure 6.20. Now click on the continue icon [icon] (❸).

The screen now changes as shown in Figure 6.21. DSO BWSD_O01 is displayed (❶). This time, the technical number attached to DSO BWSD_O01 is T00002. The column shown under ❷ shows 0DOC_NUMBER and 0S_ORD_ITEM. These two InfoObjects are configured as key fields of DSO BWSD_O01. The fields of DSO BWSD_O01 are numbered starting from F59 (❸). The fields F1 to F58 are used for InfoObject 0MATERIAL, so the DSO BWSD_O01 fields are numbered from the next running number.

Column ❹ shows the technical name of the InfoObjects of DSO BWSD_O01. Column ❺ shows the Key Date.

Now both sources are available in the screen. We need to decide which fields we want to include in the InfoSet definition and how to join it.

There are two ways you can select/deselect fields in the InfoSet definition. The first way is to click on the individual checkbox to exclude or include it in the definition of the InfoSet. By default, SAP NetWeaver BW includes all of the fields in the definition of the InfoSet, so you need to remove the tick in the checkbox in the first column. This may be cumbersome when you want to include only a few required fields in the definition of an InfoSet.

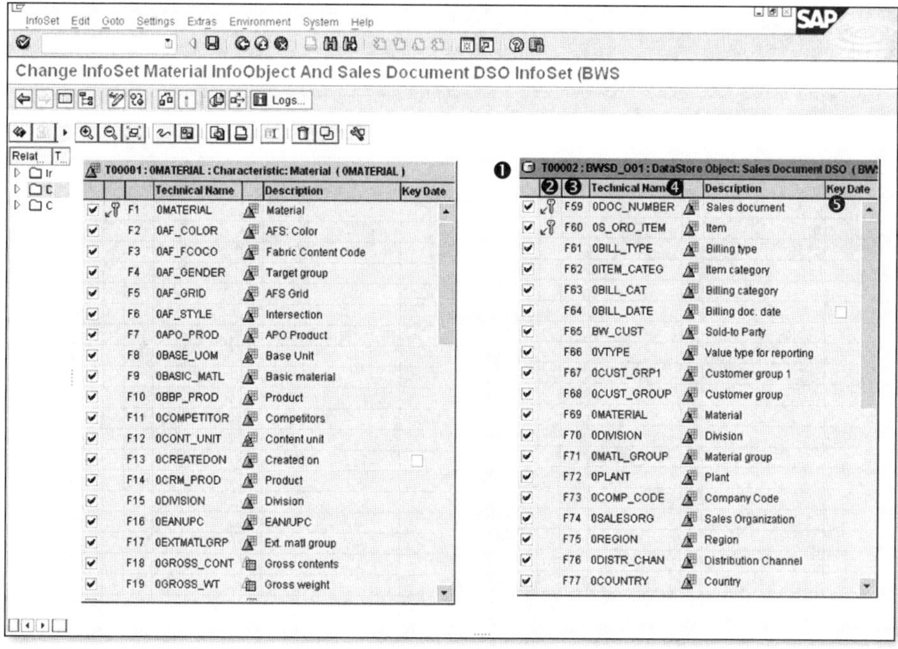

Figure 6.21 Creating InfoSet: Second Source Inserted

The second way is to deselect all of the checkboxes using one single click and include only those that are required. First, open the context menu by right-clicking anywhere on the source object for which you want to deselect all of the fields. For example, we want to deselect all of the fields for the source object 0MATERIAL. Start the context menu by right-clicking somewhere near the spot shown in ❶ of Figure 6.22, and then select Deselect All Fields (❷). You can perform similar steps on the source object BWSD_O01 and deselect all of the fields of DSO BWSD_O01.

All of the fields of both the source objects are now deselected. Now select only the required fields by clicking on the checkbox available in the first column. As shown in ❸, we've selected only fields 0MATERIAL (F1), 0MATL_CAT (F24), and 0MATL_TYPE (F26)) from source object T00001.

In a similar way, the fields 0MATERIAL (F69), 0DIVISION (F70), 0MATL_GROUP (F71), 0DISTR_CHAN (F76), 0SALES_OFF (F78), BW_QTY (F81), and 0UNIT (F85) are selected from source object BWSD_O01 (❹).

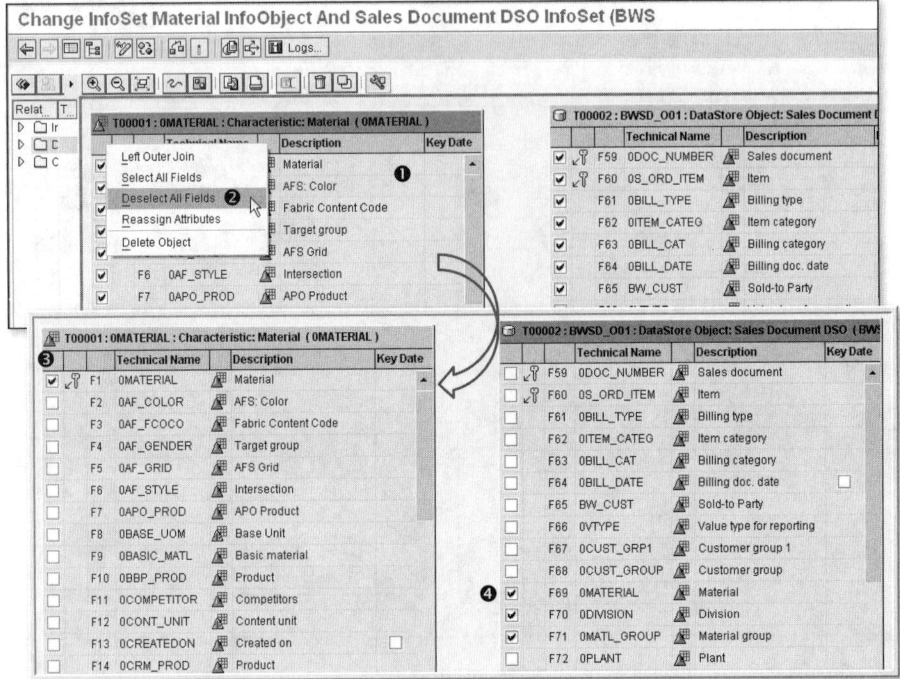

Figure 6.22 Selecting Required Fields

The next step after selecting the fields is to join the two source objects. You can join a field from one source object to the same field or a field with a similar data type and length of another source field. This process is very simple. In our example, we want to join field 0MATERIAL (F1) from source object T00001 to field 0MATERIAL (F69) of source object T00002. Select the field F1 of T00001, keep the left mouse button pressed, and drag the mouse over to the target field F69. The dragged mouse icon pointer changes from the normal pointer icon to a pencil icon. Drop it on the target field.

SAP NetWeaver BW now creates a join between field 0MATERIAL of source object T00001 and field 0MATERIAL of source object T00002. This is shown as a link from ❶ to ❷ in Figure 6.23.

Internally, SAP NetWeaver BW makes this as a join condition similar to T1.0MATERIAL = T2.0MATERIAL in technical terms.

If required, you can create another joining condition between the two fields T1 and T2. Our example scenario doesn't require another join condition. This completes the steps required to configure an InfoSet.

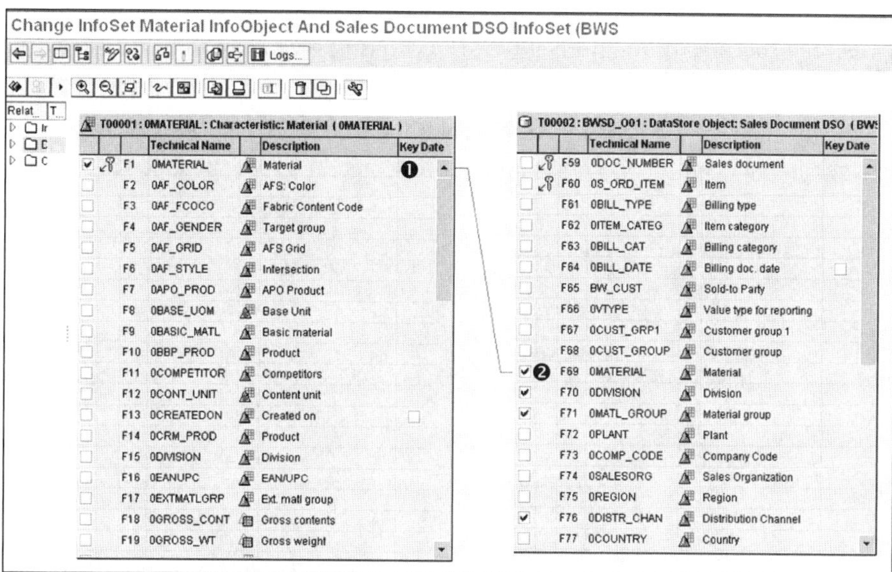

Figure 6.23 Joining Two Sources

Now check the definition using the check icon as shown in ❶ of Figure 6.24.

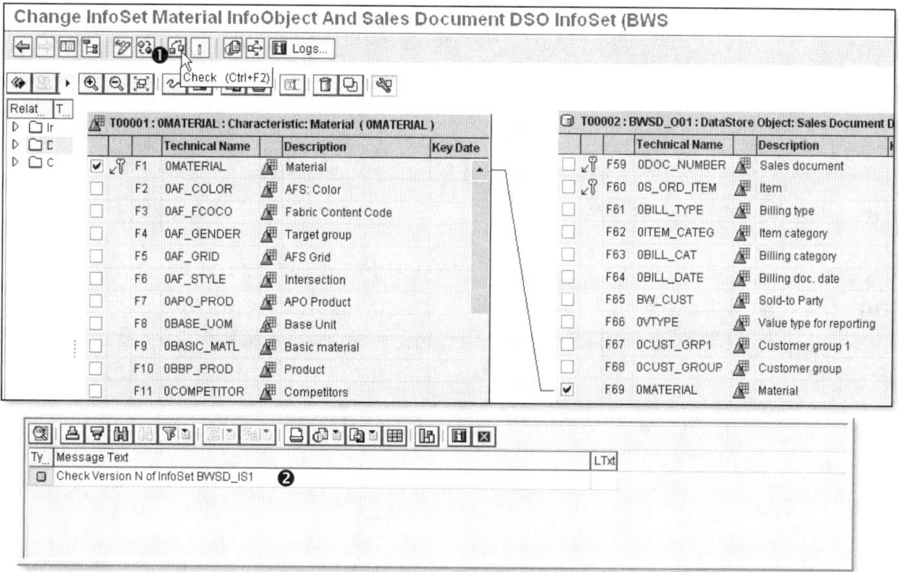

Figure 6.24 Checking the Definition of InfoSet

Checked messages are available at the bottom of the screen as shown in ❷ of Figure 6.24. As the checking of the InfoSet BWSD_IS1 hasn't given any error messages, we can now activate the InfoSet definition in the SAP NetWeaver BW system.

To activate, click on the activate icon [icon] as shown in ❶ of Figure 6.25. Activation messages are given at the lower section of the screen in a separate area (❷).

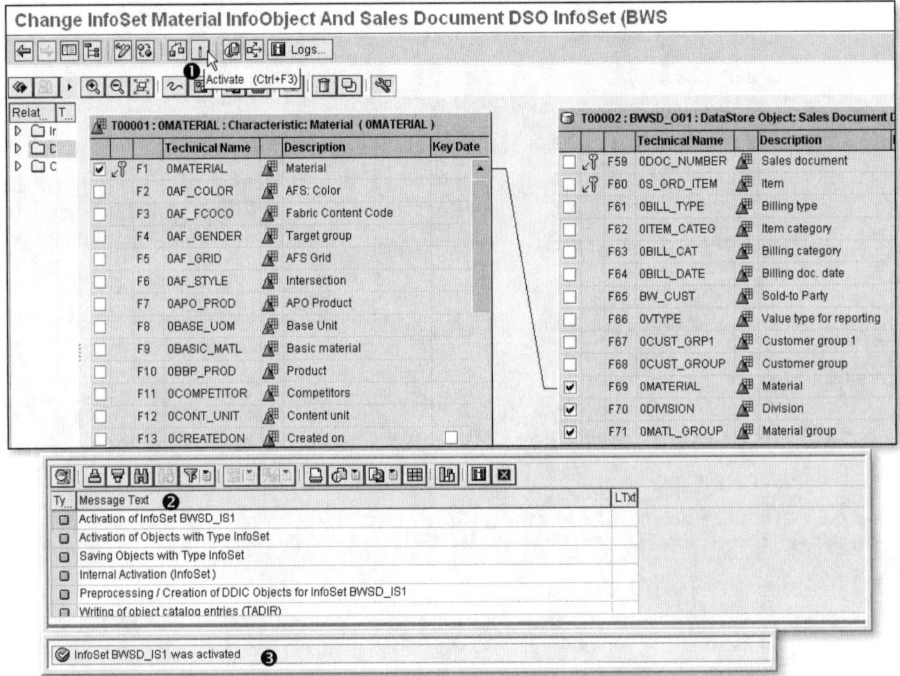

Figure 6.25 Activating the InfoSet

The final activation message is given at the bottom of the screen as shown in ❸ of Figure 6.25. Now the definition of the InfoSet is available for further use, including creating a query based on this InfoSet or creating a new MultiProvider that includes InfoSet BWSD_IS1.

As you can see in Figure 6.26, the newly created INFOSET BWSD_IS1 is available under InfoArea BW_AREA

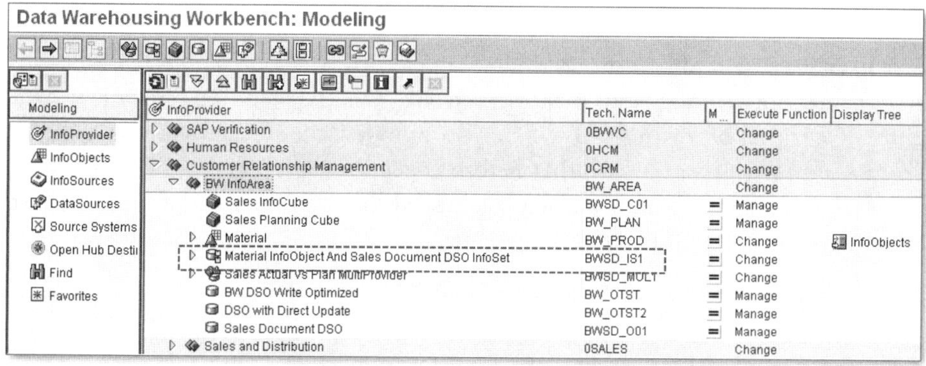

Figure 6.26 InfoSet Available in DWW

6.5 Additional Navigation Capabilities

There are a few facilities available for creating/editing an InfoSet. These facilities are typical for the InfoSet only, so they are explained in detail in this section. Start the InfoSet definition in change mode.

In DWW (Transaction RSA1), under Modeling in the Navigation section, select the InfoProvider, as shown in ❶ of Figure 6.27. Select InfoArea BW_AREA (❷). Using the context menu of InfoSet BWSD_IS1 (❸), select the Change option (❹).

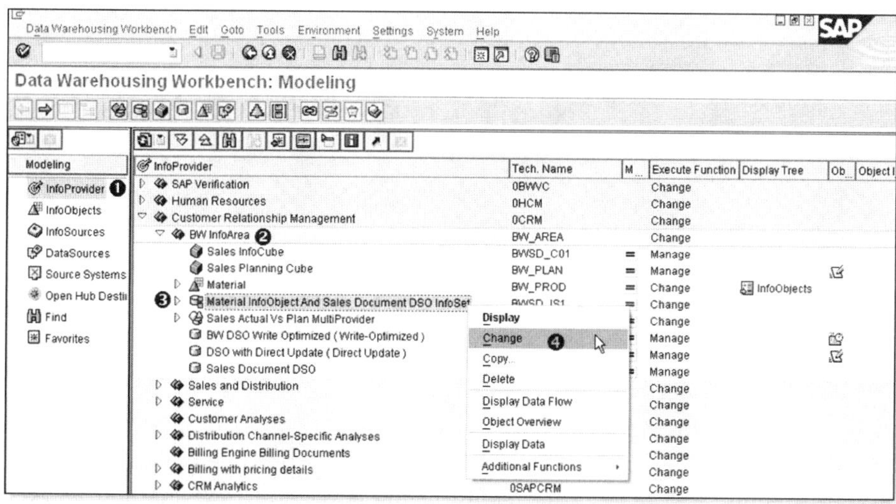

Figure 6.27 Editing the InfoSet

The Change InfoSet screen appears (Figure 6.28).

6.5.1 Auto Arrange

As you can see in ❶ of Figure 6.28, the join between two source objects isn't properly visible. Click on the Auto Arrange icon [icon] (❷). The resulting screen is shown in the lower part of Figure 6.28, where you can view the join properly (❸). In the process, you may also observe that before executing Auto Arrange, source object T00001 on the left side of the screen has moved to the right, and the source object T00002 has moved to the left of the screen.

This movement doesn't affect the functionality of the InfoSet.

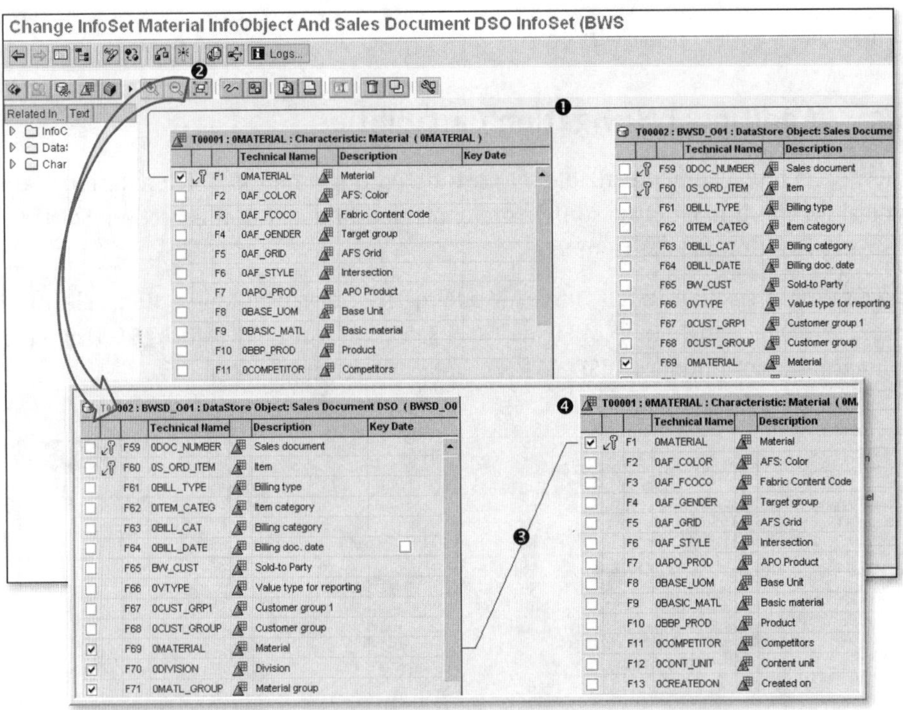

Figure 6.28 InfoSet Editing: Auto Arrange Facility

6.5.2 Navigator

When you're in the InfoSet change screen, sometimes all of the source objects aren't 100% visible because all may not fit within one screen. As shown in Figure 6.29, the rightmost column (e.g., Key Date) isn't visible in the screen. There are three ways in which you can adjust this viewing.

The first way is to use the standard horizontal scroll bar available on any SAP NetWeaver BW screen, and scroll to the right side.

The second way is to use the Zoom Out icon [icon], which reduces the size of the font to accommodate more visible area on the same screen. Note, there is a Zoom In icon [icon] that increases the size of the font to accommodate less visible areas on the same screen with more clarity.

The third way is to use the Navigator function. Click on the Show/Hide Navigator icon [icon] as shown in ❶ of Figure 6.29. The result is that SAP NetWeaver BW adds a small box titled Navigation (❷).

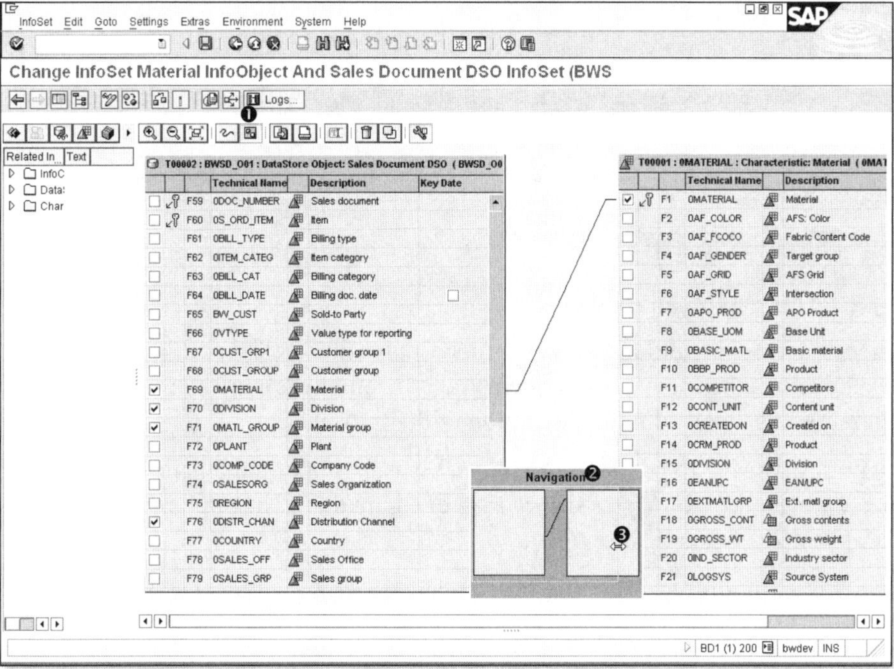

Figure 6.29 Using the Navigator Function

Use the icon [icon], as shown in ❸ of Figure 6.29, to drag the line and drop it at the rightmost side of the Navigation box. The resulting screen is shown in ❶ of Figure 6.30. The effect of this change in the Navigation box on the main screen is shown in ❷ of the Figure 6.30. All of the columns of source object T00001 are now visible properly.

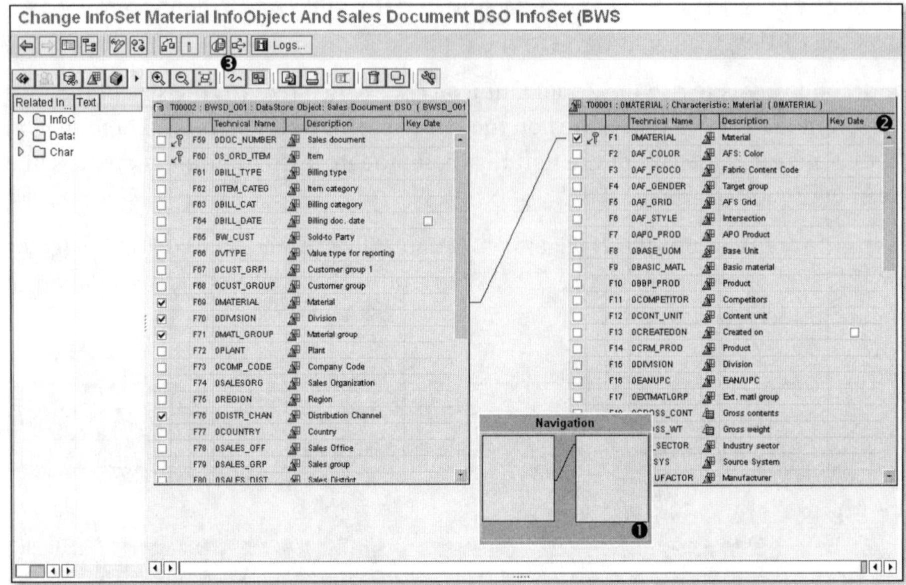

Figure 6.30 Result of Using the Navigator

6.5.3 Link Maintenance

When an InfoSet definition has two or more source objects and multiple joins, it may become difficult to move up and down and horizontally left or right to maintain the different joins involved in the definition of the InfoSet.

An alternative way to maintain the join is by using Link Maintenance. Click on the Link Maintenance icon as shown in ❸ of Figure 6.30. The pop-up box titled Link Maintenance appears (Figure 6.31).

A brief description regarding the functionality of link maintenance is shown in ❶ of Figure 6.31. A list of the included InfoProviders in the definition of the InfoSet is also given (❷). The right side panel is initially empty (❸).

Expand the definition of InfoProvider 0MATERIAL and double-click on the 0MATERIAL field (❹). The result of this action is shown on the right panel. The right panel now also shows field 0MATERIAL of DSO BWSD_O01 (❺). This is the join we've created in our InfoSet, and link maintenance shows it in this simple way.

Double-click on the 0AF_COLOR field of InfoProvider 0MATERIAL (❻). This time, there's no matching field available in DSO BWSD_O01; on the right side, it's displaying No Link Possible (❼).

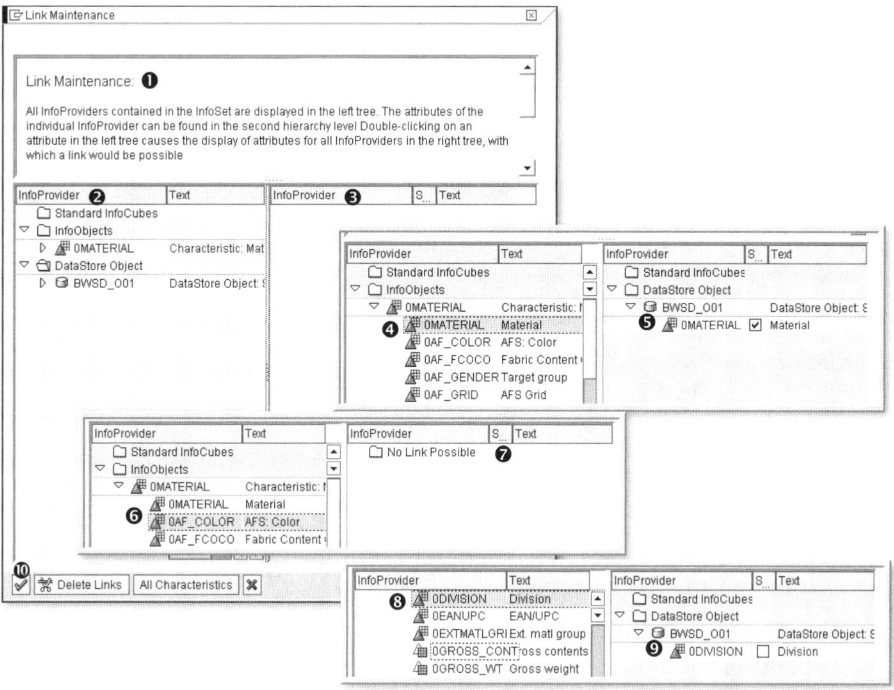

Figure 6.31 Link Maintenance

Double-click on the 0DIVISION field of InfoProvider 0MATERIAL (❽). On the right side panel, the 0DIVISION field of InfoProvider BWSD_O01 is displayed (❾). You can click on the checkbox to create a join between the 0DIVISION field of InfoProvider 0MATERIAL and the 0DIVISION field of InfoProvider BWSD_O01.

Because our example InfoSet doesn't require this join, we'll leave it untouched.

6.6 Global Properties

A few properties are known as global properties for an InfoSet. There are no icons available to access them. You need to use the menu path GOTO • GLOBAL PROPERTIES to access these global properties. The InfoSet BWSD_IS1: Global Properties box appears as shown in Figure 6.32.

The three available settings are explained in this section.

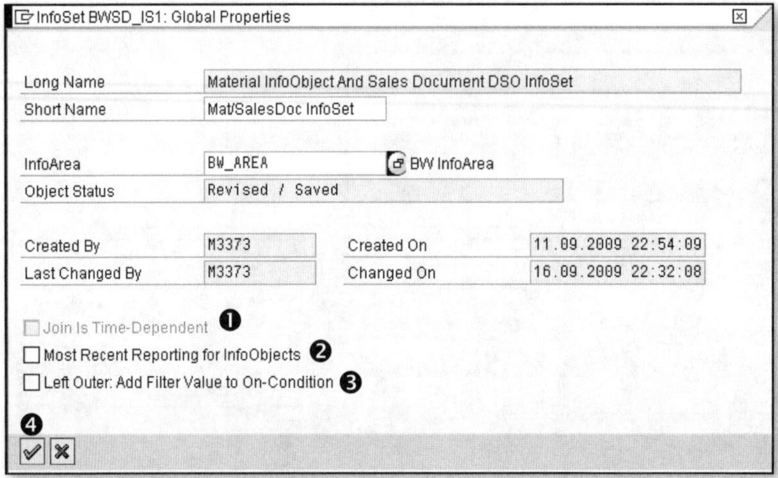

Figure 6.32 InfoSet Global Properties

6.6.1 Join Is Time-Dependent

This setting is display only (❶ of Figure 6.32). If any of the underlying InfoProviders included in the definition of the InfoSet is an InfoObject with a time-dependent attribute, this checkbox is checked, and the join created is known as a time-dependent join. In our example InfoSet, we've included InfoObject 0MATERIAL, but 0MATERIAL doesn't have any attributes that are time dependent, so this checkbox isn't available.

6.6.2 Most Recent Reporting for InfoObjects

An InfoSet can include an InfoObject as one of its underlying InfoProviders. In SAP NetWeaver BW, InfoObjects are used to store the master data. The newly created master data (along with updated master data) is regularly loaded into this InfoObject. SAP NetWeaver BW doesn't make this newly loaded master data available to the queries. Newly loaded master data is kept under M version (modified version) in the underlying tables associated with the InfoObject. The data is only available for query after it's moved into A (active) version.

You need to process the attribute hierarchy change run to make your newly loaded data active. This process may not get run very frequently because it's time consuming. Normally it's run as a part of process chain when regular data loading takes place.

When you have a scenario where master data is loaded a number of times in your SAP NetWeaver BW, but activation only happens once during the regular data loading, your user may not get the effect of the newly loaded master data until the activation of the master data process is completed. Using the settings available on the InfoSet, you can do reporting on the recently loaded master data (even if the data isn't activated). To make this happen, check the setting Most Recent Reporting for InfoObjects as shown in ❷ of Figure 6.32.

The first time the master data is loaded and activated, it's shown in Table 6.8. For the sake of simplicity, only a few columns are shown. Technically, SAP NetWeaver BW does have a few more columns to manage versions.

Customer Number	Version	City
C1	A	CITY-1
C2	A	CITY-2
C3	A	CITY-3

Table 6.8 Available Master Data

Now, the city of one customer has changed, and the newly loaded data (without the activation process) is shown in Table 6.9.

Customer Number	Version	City
C1	A	CITY-1
C2	A	CITY-2
C2	M	CITY-4
C3	A	CITY-3

Table 6.9 Data Loaded to Master: Activation Not Performed

The query on the InfoSet with configuration Most Recent Reporting for InfoObjects not switched will report the data as shown in Table 6.10.

Customer Number	City
C1	CITY-1
C2	CITY-2
C3	CITY-3

Table 6.10 Most Recent Reporting Not Configured

The query on the InfoSet with the configuration Most Recent Reporting for InfoObjects switched on will report the data as shown in Table 6.11.

Customer Number	City
C1	CITY-1
C2	CITY-4
C3	CITY-3

Table 6.11 Most Recent Reporting Configured

6.6.3 Left Outer Join: Add Filter Value to On-Condition

This indicator is useful when you've used *left outer join* while defining the join in the InfoSet. It's used to control how a condition on a field of the left outer table is converted in the *SQL statement* while the query based on this InfoSet is executed.

- When the indicator is set, the condition is evaluated before the join.
- When the indicator isn't set, the condition is evaluated after the join.

The query result is different in both the cases. You need to evaluate your reporting requirement and set the indicator accordingly.

6.6.4 Temporal Join

InfoSets offer a unique concept known as a temporal join, which is made available when an InfoSet is created with one of the InfoProviders that's included as an InfoObject with *time-dependent attributes*. In our example, the InfoObject BW_CUST has 0SALESEMPLY as a time-dependent attribute. When we include the InfoObject BW_CUST when creating the InfoSet, the temporal join can be used. We'll illustrate this with example data in Tables 6.12 and 6.13.

Customer Number	Sales Office	Sales Employee	Valid From	Valid To
C1	SO1	EMP1	01-JAN-1999	31-DEC-2005
C1	SO1	EMP2	01-JAN-2006	14-JUL-2009
C1	SO1	EMP3	15-JUL-2009	31-DEC-9999
C2	SO2	EMP4	01-APR-2006	14-JUL-2009
C2	SO2	EMP2	15-JUL-2009	31-DEC-9999
C3	SO1	EMP3	01-JAN-2006	31-DEC-9999

Table 6.12 Sample Master Data in InfoObject BW_CUST

Billing Document Number	Billing Date	Customer Number	Billing Quantity (In Nos.)
1234	10-JUL-2009	C1	100
1235	10-JUL-2009	C2	120
1236	10-JUL-2009	C3	150
2115	18-JUL-2009	C1	340
2116	18-JUL-2009	C2	200
2117	18-JUL-2009	C3	100

Table 6.13 Sample Data in DSO BWSD_O01

An InfoSet is created using InfoObject BW_CUST and DSO BWSD_O01 with the customer number as the join between the two. The Billing Date field is used as key date. To understand how to set the key date, see the checkbox shown earlier as ❺ of Figure 6.21.

The result of the query based on this InfoSet is shown in Table 6.14.

Billing Document Number	Billing Date	Customer Number	Sales Employee	Billing Quantity (In Nos.)
1234	10-JUL-2009	C1	EMP2	100
1235	10-JUL-2009	C2	EMP4	120
1236	10-JUL-2009	C3	EMP3	150
2115	18-JUL-2009	C1	EMP3	340
2116	18-JUL-2009	C2	EMP2	200
2117	18-JUL-2009	C3	EMP3	100

Table 6.14 Result of Query

As you can see, the value of the field Sales Employee is derived using the value of the billing date for each billing document number and its validity between valid from and valid to for the same customer in the BW_CUST.

6.6.5 Changing the InfoSet Visual Setting

The InfoSet creation screen offers two types of display:

- Network Display
- Tree Display

So far we've seen the network display in the earlier section. You can change between the two settings by using the menu path SETTINGS • DISPLAY. The Setting: InfoSet Maintenance box appears as shown in Figure 6.33. Select the Hierarchy Display (Tree Control) radio button (❶). Click on the continue icon ✔ (❷).

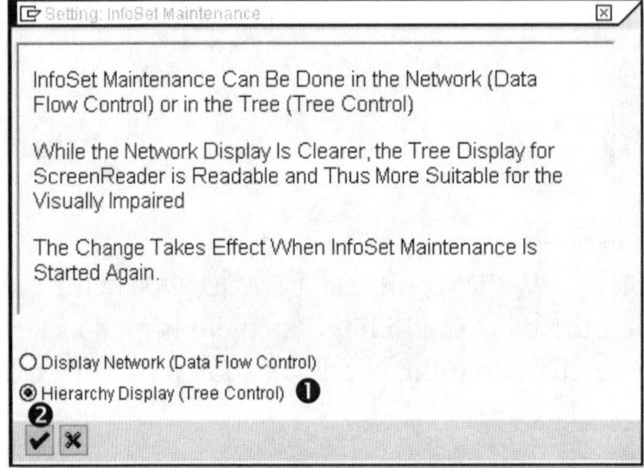

Figure 6.33 Changing the InfoSet Maintenance Screen Setting

The effect of this setting is visible the next time you open the InfoSet from DWW for editing. The screen should look like Figure 6.34.

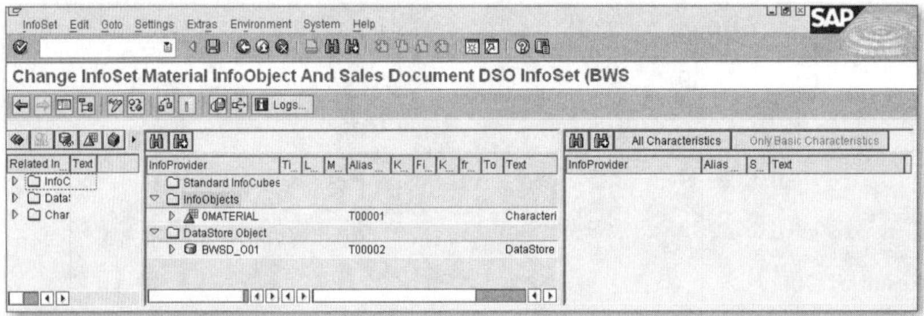

Figure 6.34 InfoSet Display in Tree Mode

The screen shown in Figure 6.34 is something similar to what is explained in the Link Maintenance screen. The rest of the functionality remains the same.

6.7 Left Outer Join in an InfoSet

By default, the join selected between two InfoProviders included in an InfoSet definition is an inner join. You can change that to left outer join if required. Select the

InfoProvider T00002, and open the context menu as shown in ❶ of Figure 6.35. Click on the Left Outer Join option (❷).

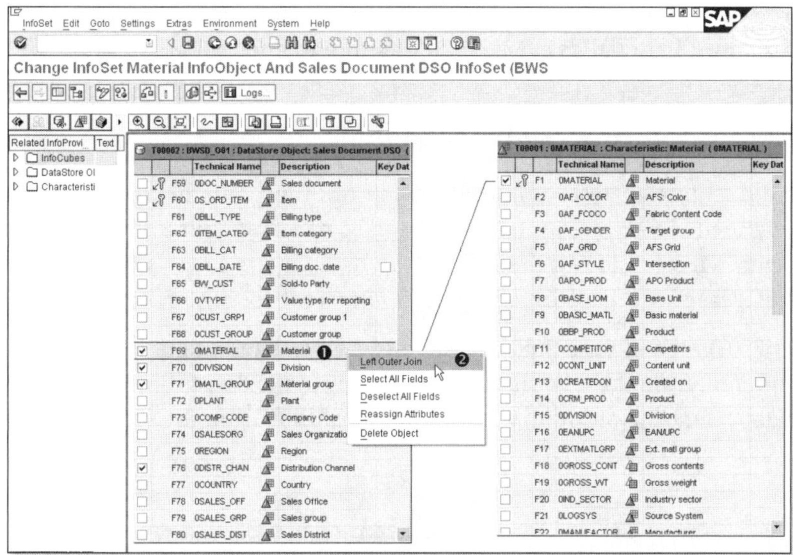

Figure 6.35 Selecting the Left Outer Join option

The screen changes as shown in Figure 6.36. Now the join shows the left outer join.

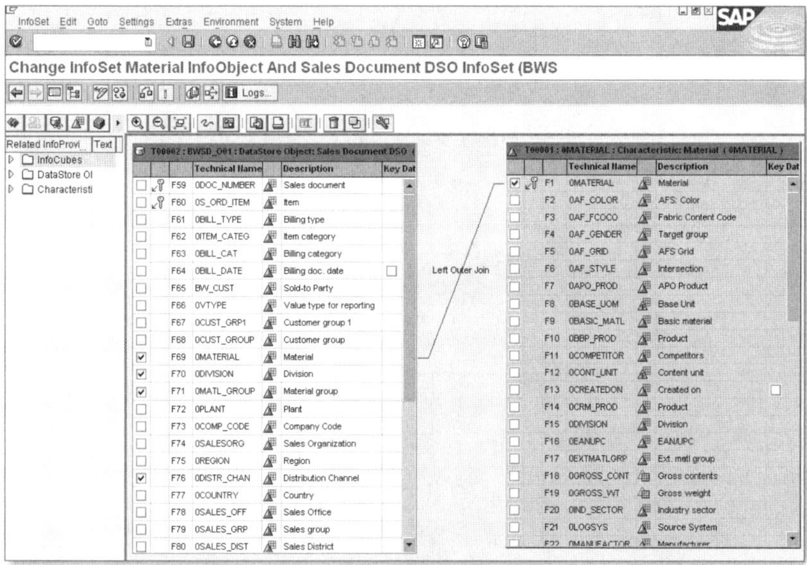

Figure 6.36 Left Outer Join in the InfoSet Definition

In this way, an inner join can be easily converted to a left outer join. Where you select *from* is important. The process you select keeps the InfoProvider T00001 to the left side of the join. The query on this left outer join brings all of the rows from InfoProvider T00001 irrespective of whether the matching value for the join condition (in our example, material) is available in the InfoProvider T00002 or not.

6.8 Introduction to VirtualProviders

Businesses often require analysis of information in real time, and the information is usually unstructured in nature. This leads to the need to online source the data from a source system, without storing the data in the data targets such as InfoCube or DSOs. SAP NetWeaver BW has VirtualProviders to meet these requirements.

Like the MultiProvider and the InfoSet, this is also a logical definition. However, it's completely different from them because it doesn't source the data from existing data within the data warehouse but sources the data in real time from the source system (see Figure 6.37).

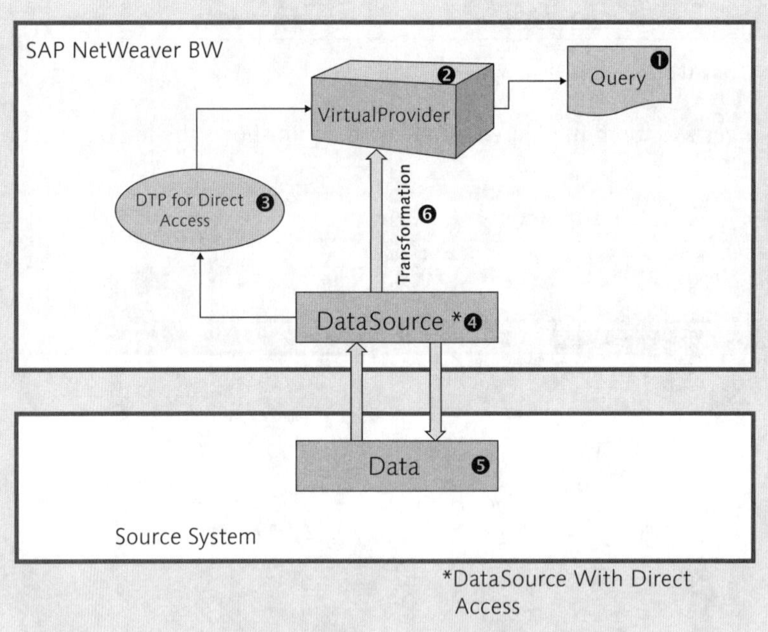

Figure 6.37 Illustration of VirtualProvider

We'll now explain the processes that enable reporting using a VirtualProvider. For instance, if we execute a query (see ❶ of Figure 6.37), the query is based on a VirtualProvider (❷). The data for this query is then sourced in real time from the source system, using the direct access type data source (❹). The data is read from the source system (❺) and passed back to the query using transformation (❻) and DTP for direct access (❸). Every navigation step in the query is a new process for reaching back to the source system for acquiring the relevant data set and relaying it to the query. The entire process of ETL happens in real time, and the data is converted to information and presented in the report. You can include the query variables to filter the data to be read from the source system. When a query is executed, the variable values are passed to the DataSource using inverse transformation.

The process of creating a VirtualProvider is very similar to creating a basic InfoCube (see ❹ of Figure 5.6 in Chapter 5, InfoCubes). You'll see there's a radio button available for defining a VirtualProvider. There are three options for creating a VirtualProvider:

- Based on the data transfer process for direct access
- Based on BAPI
- Based on the function module

Note that there are conditions that determine how applicable a VirtualProvider is. For instance, VirtualProviders should be used for scenarios that deal with a small data set, and the usage should be limited to a few users because the system has to execute the entire process from sourcing to presentation in real time.

6.9 Summary

In this chapter, we introduced you to MultiProviders, InfoSets, and VirtualProviders as InfoProviders. We addressed logical definitions and how the InfoProvider doesn't store data. We explained (in brief) the difference between MultiProviders and InfoSets and gave examples of their application scenarios. In this chapter, we also covered the step-by-step process for creating a MultiProvider and InfoSet in SAP NetWeaver BW. We also covered the various functions available with an InfoSet, such as temporal join and left outer join. We concluded this chapter with a brief introduction to VirtualProviders. In the next chapter, we explain the fundamental processes of data warehousing on extraction, transformation, and loading.

Extraction, transformation, and loading are essential to the management of data, and a thorough understanding of the ETL process is essential to making the most of your SAP NetWeaver BW system.

7 Extraction, Transformation, and Loading

In this chapter, we detail the ETL concepts, elements of the underlying processes, and their realization within SAP NetWeaver BW. We also explain the technical components and their functionalities that enable the efficient management of the ETL processes using the following the scenarios:

- Loading master data from a flat file source system to an InfoObject (to explain a basic ETL scenario).
- Loading transaction data from a flat file source system to a DSO (to cover a more specialized aspect of transformation).
- Loading data from a DSO to an InfoCube (to cover a complex transformation).

We also explain the details of the temporary storage areas and error stacks. In the concluding section, we introduce DB Connect and UD Connect, which enable the data extraction from non-SAP systems.

7.1 Introduction to ETL

We begin by explaining the concept of the ETL process, basic elements that comprise important processes in SAP NetWeaver BW, the interfaces that facilitate data acquisition, and the implementation of these processes. Three essential subprocesses comprise the ETL process: the processes that acquire data from heterogeneous sources, the processes that transform acquired data into the requisite format (e.g., consolidating data from different formats), and the processes that load data to the data targets.

7.1.1 Elements in the ETL Process

SAP NetWeaver BW has a variety of elements that comprise the ETL processes as illustrated in Figure 7.1.

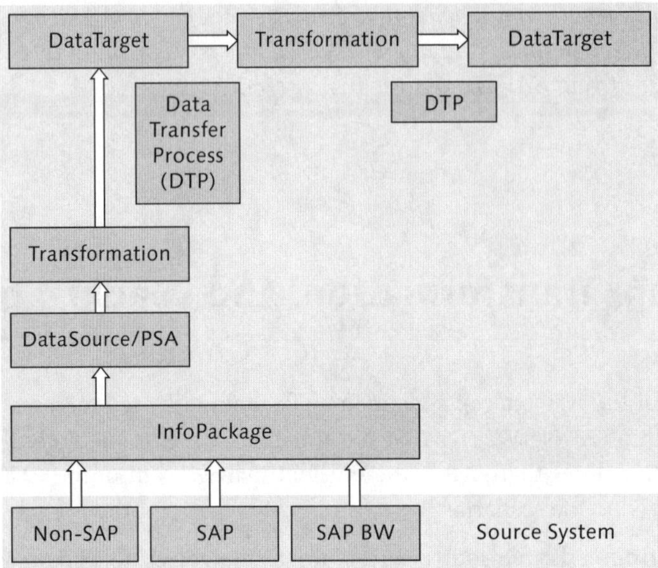

Figure 7.1 Overview of ETL Processes in SAP NetWeaver BW

The elements in the ETL processes are explained in the following list:

- **Source system**
  SAP NetWeaver BW is an online analytical processing (OLAP) system, so it doesn't generate any business transactions; business transactions are generated by online transaction processing (OLTP) systems. The source that supplies the data to SAP NetWeaver BW is known as the source system. SAP NetWeaver BW is capable of data acquisition from a wide variety of source systems, such as data from flat files in ASCII and CSV formats, database management systems (DBMS), relational database management systems (RDBMS), multidimensional data, and data from legacy systems. SAP NetWeaver BW offers predefined, customizable extractors for application data from the entire SAP Business Suite; you can also design extractors for customized SAP applications. The source system can store various kinds of data (master as well as transaction).
- **InfoPackage**
  An InfoPackage is the scheduler object defined for the combination of DataSources and source systems. You can supply various parameters while configuring InfoPackages, such as selection filters, parallel processing, the date of the extraction, and more. After the definition of all of the necessary objects to load the data from the source system to the data target is completed, you must execute the InfoPackage, which extracts data from the source system and saves the copy of the source sys-

tem data into a persistent staging area (PSA). (PSA is created when you activate your DataSource; it's a transparent table whose structure is the same as that of the associated DataSource. We explain more about PSAs later in this chapter.)

- **DataSource**
  When data is extracted into SAP NetWeaver BW, it's related to specific master data or business transactions. You can't simply extract all data at once; because different types of data are stored in different objects with different structures (e.g., in relational databases, data is stored in tables), you must design an object known as a DataSource to extract specific data in a specific format. For example, to extract customer master data into SAP NetWeaver BW, you must design a DataSource expressly for this purpose. Because different kinds of source systems are supported by SAP NetWeaver BW, there are various ways to create DataSources; when a source system is from SAP (e.g., SAP ERP or SAP CRM), there are special tools for just this task. SAP Business Content offers ready-made DataSources, the majority of which offer delta capability that helps you in extracting only newly created data or changed records. This reduces the volume of data extraction and results in quicker loads.
- **Transformation**
  A transformation converts the fields of the source into the format of the target. After the DataSource is created, you have data in the form of the source system, and heterogeneity of sources necessitates processing to consolidate and harmonize this data as each separate source system may use a different data organization/format. Transformation is the process of consolidating and harmonizing acquired data to the format in which it's stored in the data target in SAP NetWeaver BW.
- **Data transfer process (DTP)**
  DTP controls the distribution of data after it's available in SAP NetWeaver BW. It reads the data from PSA or another data target, transforms it, and supplies it to the appropriate data target. After the InfoPackage has extracted and saved the data into a PSA, you must execute DTP. In this case, DTP reads the data available in PSA, passes the source system data through transformation, and loads the cleansed data to the appropriate data target. To extract data from the source system and load it into a data target on a regular basis, SAP NetWeaver BW offers a tool called the process chain that automates this activity. We discuss the process chain in more detail in Chapter 14, Administration and Monitoring.
- **Data target**
  A data target is an object in which data is stored using a data staging mechanism; examples include InfoObjects with master data, DataStore objects (DSOs), and InfoCubes. In this chapter, we explain the process of how to load data into each of these data targets.

In the following section, we detail the technical components in SAP NetWeaver BW that enable acquisition of data from heterogeneous sources.

7.1.2 Data Acquisition Interfaces

As a leading BI solution, SAP NetWeaver BW is capable of acquiring data from a wide variety of sources; we detail the specific capabilities and technicalities of data acquisition interfaces in this section. SAP NetWeaver BW supports SAP as well as non-SAP systems, as shown in Figure 7.2. This figure also shows the data acquisition interfaces supported by the system.

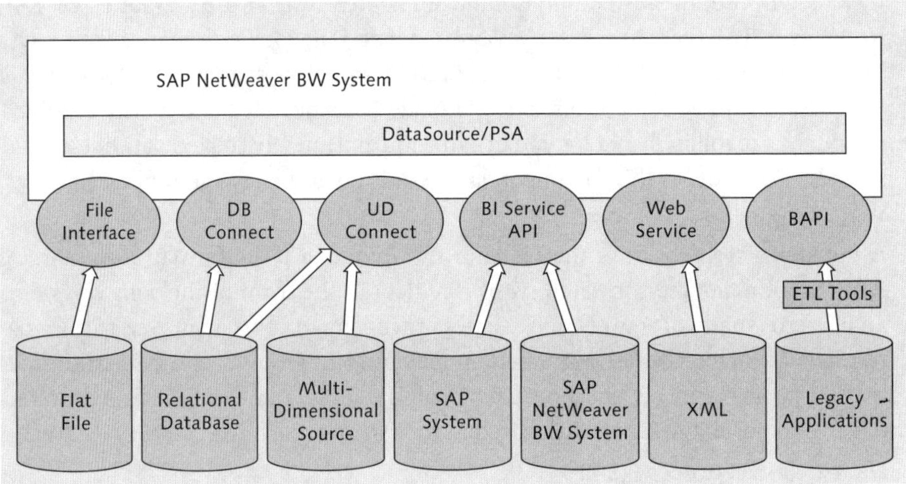

Figure 7.2 Supported Source Systems and Interfaces

- **File interface**
  Both CSV (comma-separated values) and ASCII (American Standard Code for Information Interchange) file types are supported by the file interface. CSV files can be easily created using Microsoft Excel, but ASCII files are a little more difficult.
- **DB Connect**
  With this interface, SAP NetWeaver BW supports extraction from a few popular relational database management systems (RDBMS), for example, Oracle, SQL Server, and IBM DB2. Check the SAP service market place to get the latest list of supported RDBMS.

- **UD Connect**
  Along with RDBMS, this interface supports extractions from multidimensional data sources such as Analysis Service, SAS, or Hyperion. UD Connect uses various JAVA Connectors available on the J2EE server, which is part of the SAP NetWeaver BW system. Installation of the J2EE server (JAVA stack) is essential to take advantage of UD Connect.
- **BI Service API**
  Using this interface, you can extract master and transaction data from various SAP systems (SAP ERP, SAP CRM, etc.). In addition, this allows one SAP NetWeaver BW system to supply data to another SAP NetWeaver BW system.
- **Web service**
  One of the most popular ways of exchanging data between different systems on the Internet is by defining data using XML; this can be used when you're required to extract data into SAP NetWeaver BW and the source application is Internet-based. SAP NetWeaver BW offers a tool to create a web service that reads the data from an XML format and stores it in a PSA. After the data is available in a PSA, you can use the normal data staging mechanism to send it to the required data target.
- **BAPI**
  SAP NetWeaver BW offers a number of Business Application Programming Interfaces (BAPIs) that use external tools to push data into SAP NetWeaver BW. These BAPIs should be used for legacy systems that aren't supported by the other interfaces. You can also use third-party ETL tools.

The preceding list should give you some perspective on the wide range of sources for data acquisition, which allows you to consolidate, cleanse, and integrate data from heterogeneous sources. In the following section, we briefly introduce the technical components in SAP NetWeaver BW that enable transformation of data from heterogeneous sources.

7.1.3 Transformation

SAP NetWeaver BW has multiple transformation options for the consolidation of data acquired from a wide variety of sources in different formats:

- **Direct assignment:** Also known as one-to-one transformations, this is used when source data is moved to a target without any changes.
- **Constant:** This is used when the source doesn't give a value for a specific field, and you want to supply a constant value for that field in all records in the target. For example, you may want to create a transformation where the company code for all records in the target is listed as 1000.

- **Formula:** This is used when the target value is derived using a formula, such as *value = price per unit × quantity.*
- **Initial:** This is used if you aren't interested in supplying values for a field; numerical fields will be populated with a zero, and character fields will be populated with a blank space.
- **Read master data:** This is best explained by example. Consider a target with two fields, Material and Color of Material. Assume that the source data has a value only for the Material field, and that the master data for Material InfoObjects within SAP NetWeaver BW has values for Color (an attribute of a material). In this scenario, you use the Read Master Data type of transformation, and the value for the Color field is read from the master data of the InfoObject.
- **Routine:** As the name suggests, this type of transformation is an ABAP code based transformation. It provides flexibility for handling complex requirements that aren't met by the other types.
- These options facilitate consolidation and harmonization of data from a very simple requirement to a highly complex one. In the following sections, we briefly introduce the technical components of the loading process in SAP NetWeaver BW.

7.1.4 Loading

SAP NetWeaver BW has several components that help in managing the loading process with ease and efficiency:

- **InfoPackage:** An InfoPackage extracts and loads data into the entry layer (i.e., PSA); it specifies when and how to load data from a given source system and also helps you decide filter conditions for the data request from a source system.
- **Data transfer process:** DTP determines how data transfers from one object to another within SAP NetWeaver BW, in accordance with transformations, filters, processing mode for optimizing and improving the performance of the transfer process, and separate delta processes for different targets. DTPs are used for standard data transfers, for real-time data acquisition, and for accessing data directly.
- **Error stack:** This is a transparent PSA table that stores erroneous data records being transferred from source to target using DTP.
- **Temporary storage:** This is a table that contains the data records processed with a request in a specific DTP processing step. The table contains correct records as well as erroneous records with a status display.

- **Monitor:** The monitor helps you track the entire ETL process in the various processing stages. DTPs and the InfoPackage loading processes are integrated into the monitor.
- **Process chain:** This component helps you automate the ETL process. We explain this in detail in Chapter 14.

In the following section, we detail the process of loading master data from a flat file DataSource system, as required by our ABCD Corp. case study. This will help you understand both the ETL process and its technical components in SAP NetWeaver BW.

7.2 Loading Master Data from a Flat File Source System to an InfoObject

In this section, we explain the entire process of loading master data from a flat file source system to an InfoObject. The section comprehensively covers the ETL process, from the source system and DataSource creation, to data transformation, to loading, to the monitoring process. The process involves seven basic steps:

1. Create a flat file source system.
2. Create a DataSource.
3. Create and activate a transformation.
4. Create a DTP for loading master data.
5. Create an InfoPackage and start data extraction.
6. Monitor data extraction to PSA.
7. Execute and monitor DTP.

7.2.1 Creating a Flat File Source System

In this section, we explain how to create a flat file source system, which is required to extract data from CSV and ASCII files. Source systems are created in the Data Warehousing Workbench (DWW), which is started using Transaction RSA1. Select the source system under Modeling, as shown in ❶ of Figure 7.3. A list of the different source system types supported by SAP NetWeaver BW is shown (❷).

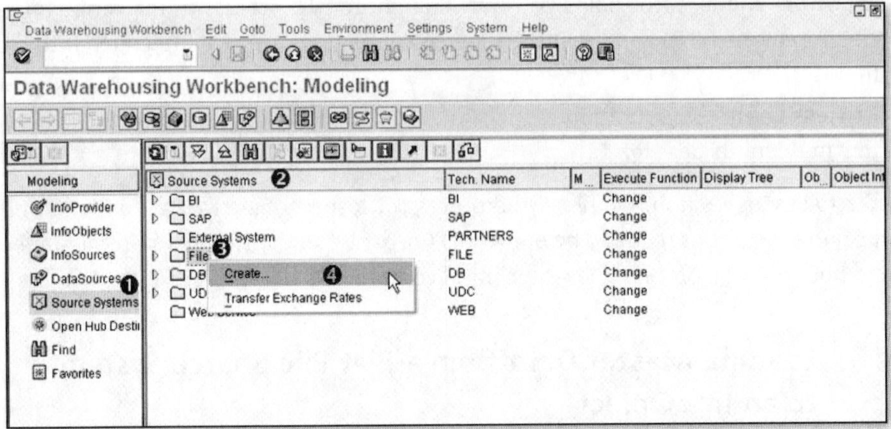

Figure 7.3 Creating Flat File Source System in DWW

For our example scenario, select File Source System (❸). From the context menu, select Create (❹). This action generates a screen titled Create Source System, as shown in ❶ of Figure 7.4.

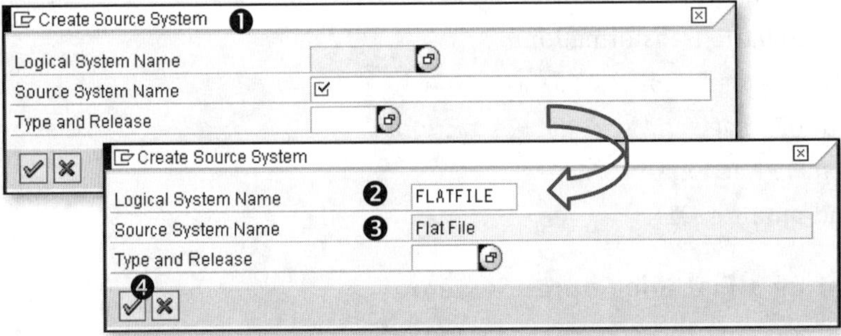

Figure 7.4 Create Source System

Enter the Logical System Name (❷) and the Source System Name (❸). Because there is no real flat file system, enter a description in the Source System Name field.

Click on the Continue icon (❹). The result of this action is shown in Figure 7.5, where Flat File is available under the Source Systems tree.

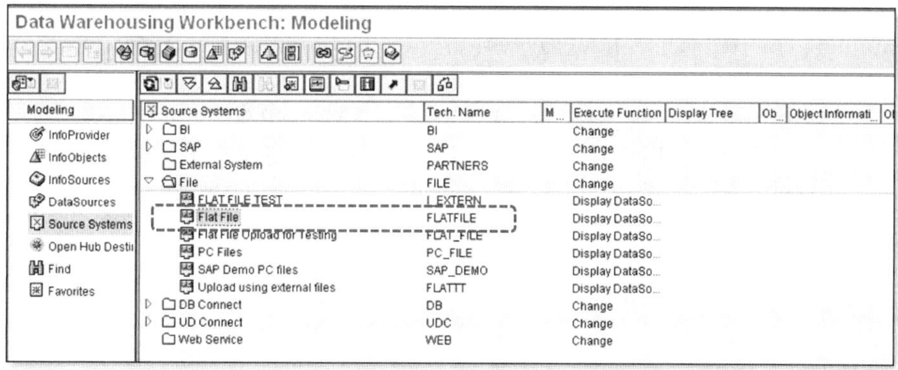

Figure 7.5 Source System Available in Source System Tree

7.2.2 Creating a DataSource

Now that we've created a source system, we can create a flat file DataSource. A DataSource defines the source of data, its structure, and the technical details of the fields. We'll create a DataSource pertaining to customer master data. In our example, customer master data is available in a flat file (a CSV file). We want to load the data available in this file to our BW_CUST InfoObject (which we created in Chapter 3, InfoObjects and Master Data).

To create a DataSource based on a flat file, select Source Systems under Modeling, as shown in ❶ of Figure 7.6. Select Flat File (❷). Open the context menu, and select Display DataSource Tree (❸).

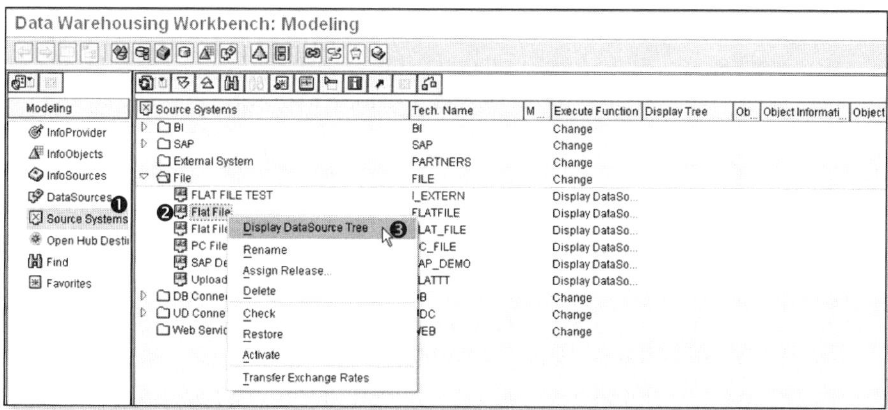

Figure 7.6 Displaying DataSource Tree

The result of this action is shown in Figure 7.7, which shows an application component hierarchy (❶); just as InfoProviders are attached to InfoAreas, DataSources are attached to application components (). These application components are used for organizing the DataSource. As shown in Figure 7.7, you can create application components within other application components, depending on your requirements.

SAP Source Systems

For SAP source systems, the application component hierarchy is delivered as part of SAP Business Content, and you simply need to replicate this hierarchy in the SAP NetWeaver BW system.

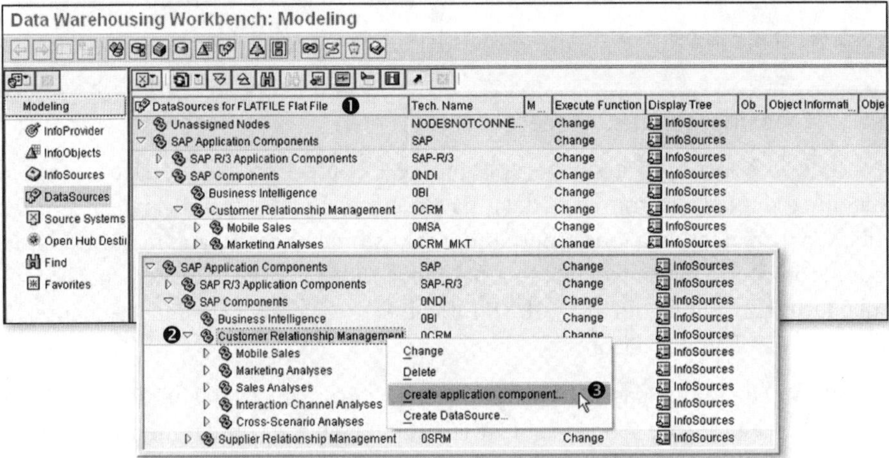

Figure 7.7 Creating Application Components

In our example, you'll create a new application component simply to learn the process (normally, you would use the application component hierarchy replicated from the SAP source system). Select 0CRM (Customer Relationship Management), as shown in ❷ of Figure 7.7, and select Create Application Component from the context menu (❸). The screen that appears next is shown in ❶ of Figure 7.8. Enter the technical name and description of the application component. In this example, we use technical name "BW_APP_COMP" (❷ of Figure 7.8) and the description "BW Application Component" (❸). Click on the Continue icon.

The result of this action is visible in ❺ of Figure 7.8. BW Application Component is now available under Customer Relationship Management, and the system has added the prefix "Z" to the technical name (❺), which indicates that it's a customer-defined application component.

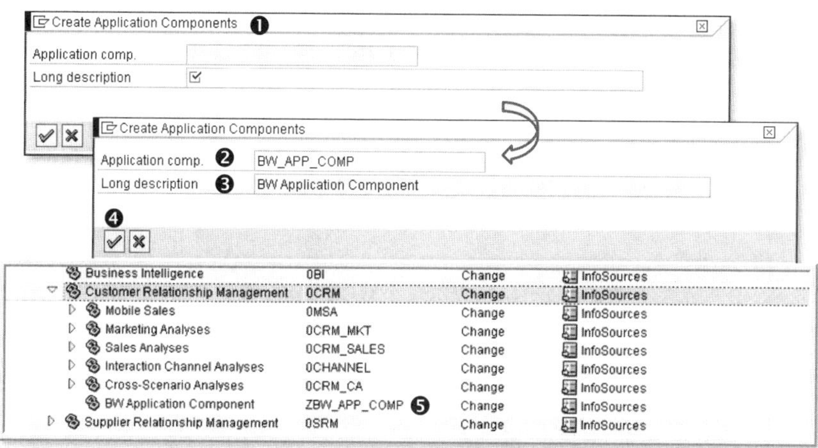

Figure 7.8 Creating Application Component ZBW_APP_COMP

You can now create a DataSource under the ZBW_APP_COMP application component. To do this, select the application component, open the context menu, and select Create DataSource (❷ of Figure 7.9). The screen that appears next is shown in ❸ of Figure 7.9.

Every DataSource requires a unique technical name. Use the technical name "BW_CUST_FF_DS_ATTR" (❹). It's a good practice to name the DataSource so that it easily indicates the DataSource and its contents. For example, in the current name, the first part (BW_CUST) indicates that this is for the BW_CUST InfoObject; the next part (FF_DS) indicates that it's a flat file DataSource; and the last part (ATTR) indicates that the DataSource represents the attributes.

You need to choose the type of DataSource you're creating; there are three different types in the Data Type DataSource list box (❺):

- **Transaction Data:** When data pertains to business transactions (such as sales order document data), you select this type of DataSource. The data target for this type of DataSource is either a DSO or an InfoCube.
- **Master Data Attributes:** When data pertains to master data attributes (such as customer attributes), you select this type of DataSource. The data target for this type of DataSource is either a characteristic InfoObject configured as master data, or a DSO.
- **Master Data Texts:** When data pertains to master data text (such as the name of a customer), you select this type of DataSource. The data target for this type of DataSource is a characteristic InfoObject configured with text.

In our example, we're loading customer attributes into InfoObject BW_CUST; thus, we select Master Data Attributes for our DataSource type (❺).

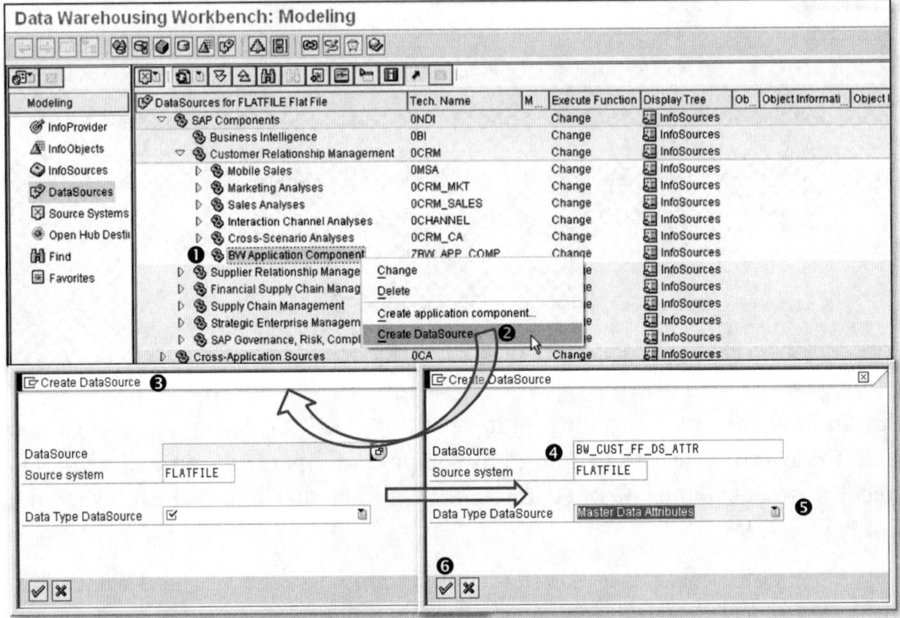

Figure 7.9 Creating DataSource BW_CUST_FF_DS_ATTR

Click on the Continue icon (❻). The resulting screen shown in Figure 7.10 has five different tabs (❶ through ❺), which change depending on the source system. We discuss each of these tabs in more detail next.

General Info Tab

In this tab (❶ of Figure 7.10), you define general information and properties about the DataSource (❻), including short, medium, and long descriptions (❼). For our example, we provide the following:

- Short Description: "Customer Master DS"
- Medium Description: "Customer Master DataSource Flat File"
- Long Description: "Customer Master DataSource Flat File"

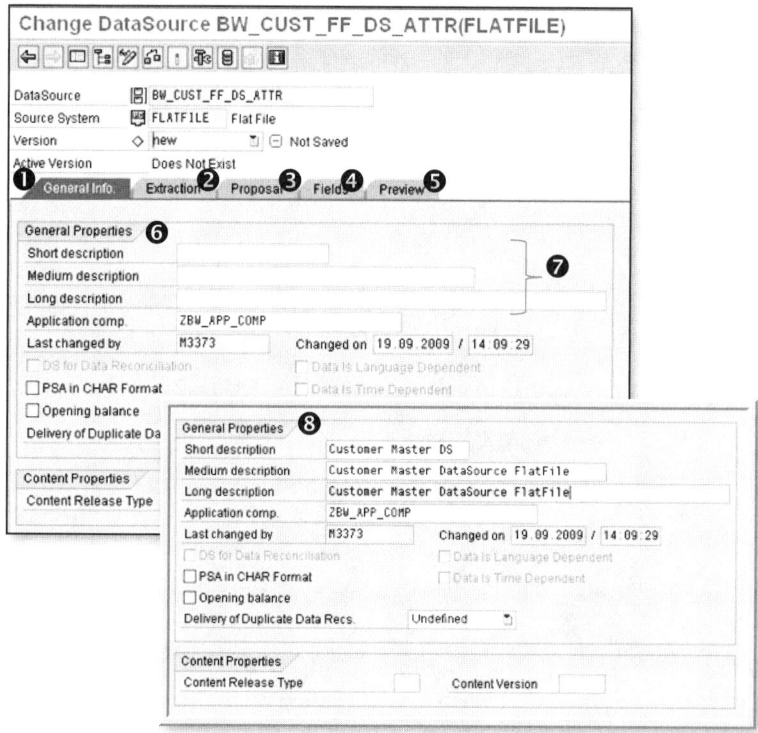

Figure 7.10 Create DataSource for Flat File: General Info

Other properties in this tab include the following:

- PSA in CHAR Format
- Opening Balance
- Delivery of Duplicate Data Recs

These fields aren't essential while creating a simple DataSource and aren't required for our scenario.

Extraction Tab

The Extraction tab (❷ of Figure 7.10) allows you to configure the delta process, type of access, and real-time access you want to set for your DataSource (❶, ❷, and ❸ of Figure 7.11). Provide the actual name of the file, its location, and its type in the Adapter and File Name fields (❹ and ❺). We explain all major configuration settings in this tab next.

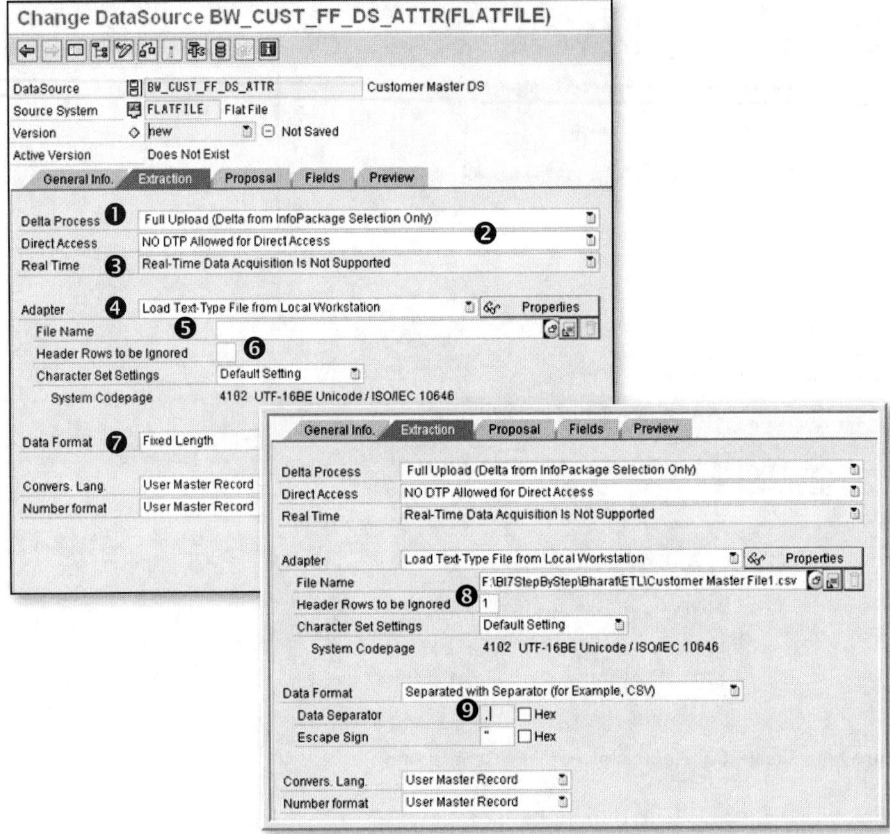

Figure 7.11 Create DataSource: Extraction Tab

Delta Process

This field describes all of the capabilities and restrictions of a DataSource. For flat file source systems, SAP NetWeaver BW offers three different types of delta processes: Full Upload (Delta from InfoPackage Selection Only), FILO (Delta Data with After Images), and FILE1 (Delta Data with Delta Images). Our example DataSource isn't supplying delta records, so choose Full Upload (❶ of Figure 7.11).

The following is a brief description of the other two delta processes offered by SAP NetWeaver BW:

- FILO (Delta Data with After Images): In this type, the DataSource only sends records that have new key figures or characteristics value. Data from this type of DataSource can't be loaded directly into an InfoCube; it must be loaded to a DSO first, and then the DSO will supply it to InfoCube.

- FILE1 (Delta Data with Delta Images): In this type, the DataSource only sends records with value changes for the key figures. Data from this type of DataSource can be directly loaded to a DSO and InfoCube.

Direct Access

There are two options for configuring the DataSources with direct access: NO DTP Allowed for Direct Access (the default option) and Allowed, which is relevant when you plan to configure a VirtualProvider based on this DataSource (see Chapter 6, InfoProviders, for more information about VirtualProviders). Most DataSources aren't capable of supporting direct access; also, the default setting for a DataSource for a flat file source system is NO DTP Allowed for Direct Access; choose this default option, as shown in ❷ of Figure 7.11.

Real Time

SAP NetWeaver BW allows you to access real-time data from the source system, a process handled by running a *daemon*. Because the DataSources based on flat files don't support real-time extraction, the field is uneditable (❸ of Figure 7.11).

Adapter

Adapters provide information about the type (text or binary) and location (local server or application server) of data. There are four options available when configuring flat files:

- Load Text-Type File from Local Workstation
- Load Text-Type File from Application Server
- Load Binary File from Local Workstation
- Load Binary File from Application Server

In our example, the file is available on a local workstation in CSV format, so we select Load Text-Type File from Local Workstation (❹ of Figure 7.11). When the file location is selected as a local workstation, you can't schedule the background job. To use background processing (and the process chain tool), the file must be located on the application server.

After you decide on the type of adapter, select the name and location of the physical file in which your data is available using the dropdown list (❺ of Figure 7.11). After you select a location, a full directory path is displayed (❽).

You may require that the file to be loaded be available with a new name (e.g., if you're loading customer master data every month, each new file created by the source system may have the month as part of its file name). In this scenario, you can create the ABAP routine to generate the file name instead of hard-coding it. To do this, click on the Create Routine for File Name icon (), which opens up the ABAP editor. Type "logic" in the ABAP editor to arrive at the file name dynamically. In our example, we hard-code the file name as shown in ❽ of Figure 7.11.

Figure 7.12 shows the sample data from the customer master file that we want to load into SAP NetWeaver BW. To eliminate confusion, it's always better to identify each column in the file using a column heading, as shown in Figure 7.12; however, these column headings don't become part of the customer master data, so you don't have to load the first row of this file. Indicate this by giving the number of the header rows to be ignored, as shown in ❽ of Figure 7.11.

	A	B	C	D	E	F	G	H	I
1	Customer	Customer GRP	Customer GRP1	Sales Group	Sales District	Sales Office	Sales Employee	Date From	Date To
2	100012	ST	WA	757	2717	3103	41	20000101	20081231
3	100012	ST	WA	757	2717	3103	42	20090101	99991231
4	100016	ST	UK	761	2402	3115	41	19990601	20001231
5	100016	ST	UK	761	2402	3115	43	20010101	99991231
6	100017	ST	UK	184	2218	1206	18	20020101	99991231
7	100018	RC	UK	821	1502	3407	44	20021201	99991231
8	100020	ST	WA	700	2140	3305	41	20000101	99991231
9	100022	RC	UK	762	2136	3114	41	20000101	99991231
10	100041	ST	UK	207	1908	1306	20	19900101	19911231

Figure 7.12 Sample Data Customer Master

As previously mentioned, text files can have two different formats, CSV and ASCII, and you must indicate the appropriate format in the Data Format field (refer to ❼ of Figure 7.11). By default, this field is filled with the Fixed Length (or ASCII) option. However, because our example data is stored in CSV format, we change this using the dropdown list (refer to ❾ of Figure 7.11).

CSV format allows you to select your own separator (commas, semicolons, etc.) when creating the CSV file, and you must indicate what you've chosen in the Data Separator field (refer to ❾ of Figure 7.11). In our example, we use the comma.

You can specify the language used to execute the conversion exit for the conversion language in the Convers. Lang. field. For our example, we use the default option (User Master Record). Finally, you can specify the number format to be used, which indicates whether the separator indicates thousands or decimal points. We use the default setting, User Master Record.

Proposal Tab

The Proposal tab (Figure 7.13) reads records from the file you specified in the Extraction tab and proposes the structure for the flat file and the technical specification of each field. The proposal given is solely based on the data available in the file and may not be 100% accurate.

As shown in ❶ and ❷ of Figure 7.13, the Proposal and Data areas of the screen are empty in the beginning. Click Load Example Data (❸). By default, SAP NetWeaver BW sets the number of data records to be read as 10,000. Reduce the number to 10 or 12 because that's all you need from the flat file to report anomalies in structure.

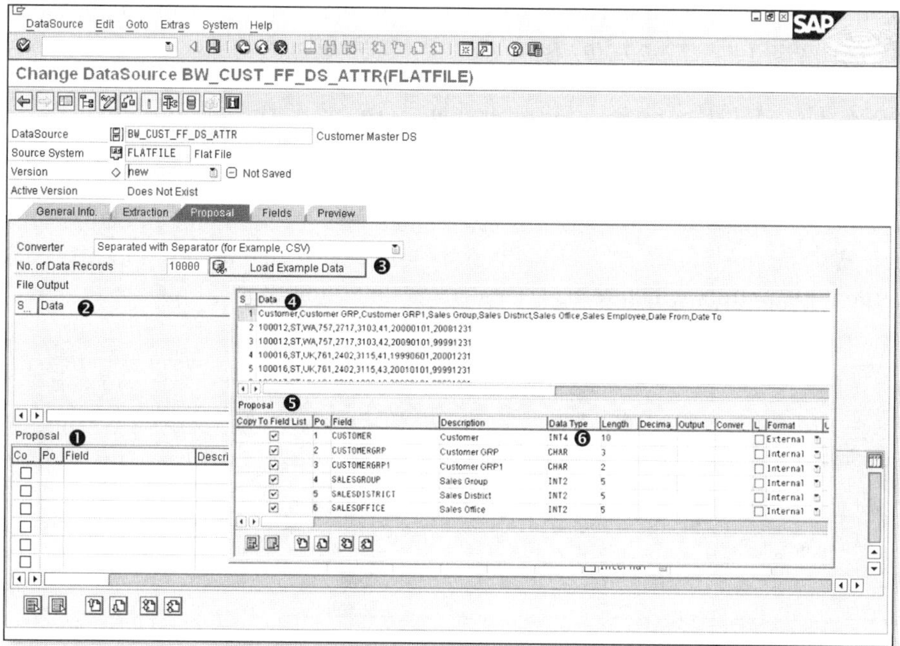

Figure 7.13 Create DataSource: Proposal Tab

When you click Load Example Data, the Data and Proposal areas are filled with information (❹ and ❺ of Figure 7.13). You can see from ❻ of Figure 7.13 that the first field's data type is INT4, and the length is 10. As you may recall, our definition of InfoObject BW_CUST listed the data type as CHAR = 10 (refer to Chapter 3), but the proposal given by the system is INT4 because the data available in the file is numerical. We'll describe how to change this incorrect information when we explain the Fields tab (next section). Even if some of the data is wrong, using the proposal function provides the list of fields in the correct sequence, so it's still useful.

For our example, we don't change anything on this tab, and move on to Fields. When moving to the Fields tab, a pop-up box displays a message asking if you want to copy your changes. Click Yes to continue.

Fields Tab

This is the tab where you finalize the structure of your DataSource. The data proposed by the system (in the Proposal tab) also appears here (❶ of Figure 7.14), and you can overwrite, if necessary. It's important to make sure that the sequence of fields given in this screen is the same as in the actual data file. Because we've used the proposal function, we don't have to worry about this; however, we do need to correct the technical specifications of the fields proposed. The best way to do this is to enter the technical name of the InfoObject in the InfoObject column. As we know from the data available in the actual data file, the first field pertains to the customer, which means InfoObject BW_CUST is used. Enter "BW_CUST" in the InfoObject column (❷), and press Enter. The Defaults from InfoObjects pop-up box appears. Click on the Copy button, which reads the metadata definition of the InfoObject.

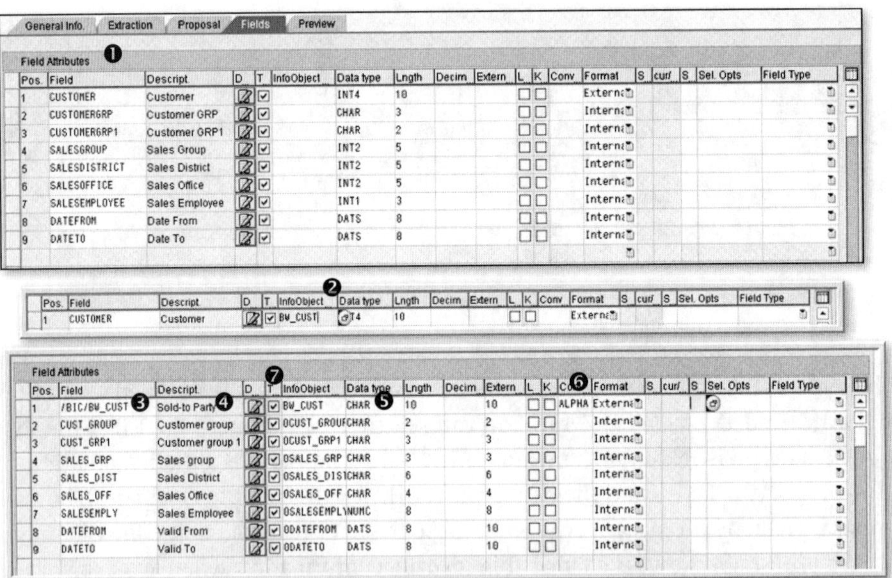

Figure 7.14 Create DataSource: Fields Tab

The result is shown in ❸, ❹, ❺, and ❻ of Figure 7.14. The system now reads the metadata from InfoObject BW_CUST, so the data type is changed from INT4 to CHAR. The conversion routine is also added as ALPHA, which was blank earlier.

Now enter the InfoObject for each row. Table 7.1 gives the technical name of each InfoObject to be entered in consecutive order. The Default from InfoObjects pop-up box appears after entering each InfoObject name; click on Copy every time.

Position	Technical Name of InfoObject
1	BW_CUST
2	0CUST_GROUP
3	0CUST_GRP1
4	0SALES_GRP
5	0SALES_DIST
6	0SALES_OFF
7	0SALESEMPLY
8	0DATEFROM
9	0DATETO

Table 7.1 Technical Names of InfoObjects

Another important setting in this tab is shown in the T column (❼ of Figure 7.14), which stands for "Transfer." A checkmark in this column indicates that you've chosen to include this field in the definition of DataSource. Our example requires that all of the fields be included, so we leave all fields checked.

Finally, the Sel. Opts. (stands for "selection options") column is also an important element of the Fields tab. Configuring this setting for a particular field makes it possible to be used as a selection filter in the InfoPackage, which helps in filtering and extracting only the relevant data from the source system. As shown in ❶ of Figure 7.15, enter "X" in the SALES_OFF column because we do want to filter the extraction based on Sales Office.

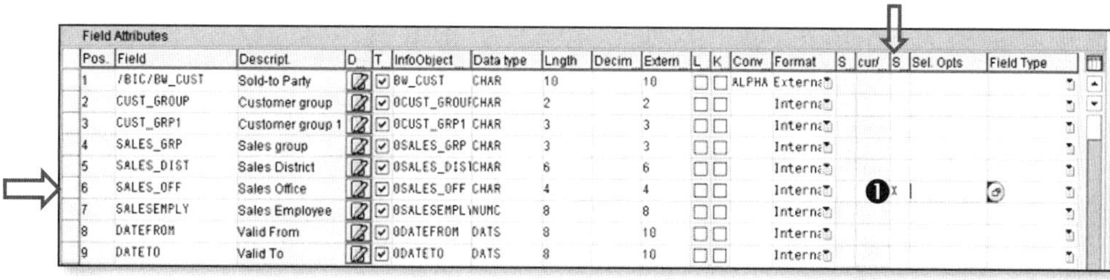

Field Attributes

Pos.	Field	Descript.	D	T	InfoObject	Data type	Lngth	Decim	Extern	L	K	Conv	Format	S	cur/	S	Sel. Opts	Field Type
1	/BIC/BW_CUST	Sold-to Party		☑	BW_CUST	CHAR	10		10	☐	☐	ALPHA	Externa					
2	CUST_GROUP	Customer group		☑	0CUST_GROUF	CHAR	2		2	☐	☐		Interna					
3	CUST_GRP1	Customer group 1		☑	0CUST_GRP1	CHAR	3		3	☐	☐		Interna					
4	SALES_GRP	Sales group		☑	0SALES_GRP	CHAR	3		3	☐	☐		Interna					
5	SALES_DIST	Sales District		☑	0SALES_DIS1	CHAR	6		6	☐	☐		Interna					
6	SALES_OFF	Sales Office		☑	0SALES_OFF	CHAR	4		4	☐	☐		Interna		❶	X		
7	SALESEMPLY	Sales Employee		☑	0SALESEMPL	NUMC	8		8	☐	☐		Interna					
8	DATEFROM	Valid From		☑	0DATEFROM	DATS	8		10	☐	☐		Interna					
9	DATETO	Valid To		☑	0DATETO	DATS	8		10	☐	☐		Interna					

Figure 7.15 Field Tab: Selection Options

You can now activate the DataSource using the Activate icon shown in ❶ of Figure 7.16. Activating the DataSource also creates the PSA associated with it (a PSA is technically a transparent table, and data is saved unchanged in it). There is no transformation between the source system and PSA. In SAP NetWeaver BW, storing data in PSAs is mandatory in almost all of the ETL scenarios.

At the time of activation, the system may show you some log messages (❷ of Figure 7.16). These messages appear because of discrepancies in the specified field length; in positions 8 and 9 of Figure 7.15, shown earlier, the internal length (Length column) is given as 8, and the external length (Extern column) is given as 10. The warning messages tell you that the system will use the internal length, ignoring the external length. As shown in ❸ of Figure 7.16, the symbol in front of both messages is yellow (which indicates a warning message); you can click on the Continue icon (❹).

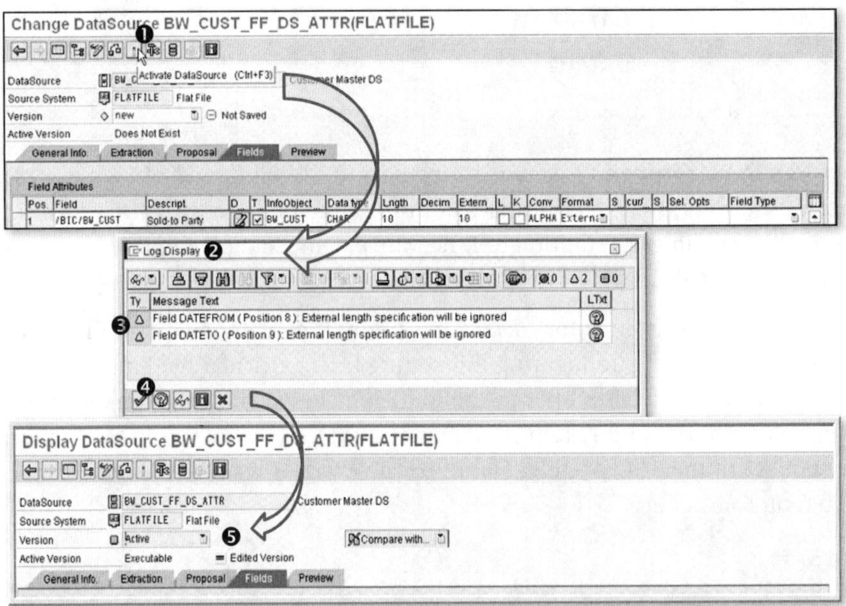

Figure 7.16 Activating DataSource

Once successfully activated, the version of the DataSource is changed from New to Active, as shown in ❺ of Figure 7.16.

Preview Tab

In the Preview tab, you can check whether your definition of the DataSource matches the actual data file definition; the tab allows you to see the data in the DataSource format before loading it to the SAP NetWeaver BW system (this can only be done, however, if the DataSource is active). As shown in ❶ of Figure 7.17, no data is shown initially. Select the number of records you want to view (5 records, for our example), and click Read Preview Data (❸). The result of this action is shown in ❹ of Figure 7.17. SAP NetWeaver BW reads the actual data and displays the requested number of records, allowing you to make sure your DataSource is correct.

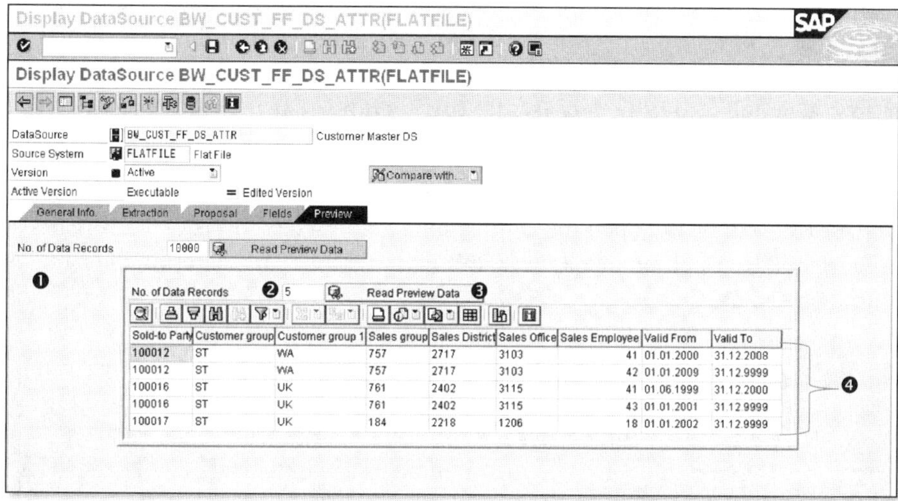

Figure 7.17 DataSource Creation: Preview Tab

The DataSource BW_CUST_FF_DS_ATTR is now ready to be used. Return to the DWW main screen by clicking the Back icon. As you can see from Figure 7.18, the DataSource BW_CUST_FF_DS_ATTR is available under application component ZBW_APP_COMP.

Data Warehousing Workbench: Modeling

DataSources for FLATFILE Flat File	Tech. Name	M..	Execute	Display Tree	Ob	Object Inform..
Business Intelligence	0BI		Change	InfoSources		
Customer Relationship Management	0CRM		Change	InfoSources		
Mobile Sales	0MSA		Change	InfoSources		
Marketing Analyses	0CRM_MKT		Change	InfoSources		
Sales Analyses	0CRM_SALES		Change	InfoSources		
Interaction Channel Analyses	0CHANNEL		Change	InfoSources		
Cross-Scenario Analyses	0CRM_CA		Change	InfoSources		
BW Application Component	ZBW_APP_COMP		Change	InfoSources		
Customer Master DataSource FlatFile	BW_CUST_FF_DS_ATTR	=	Change			FLATFILE
Supplier Relationship Management	0SRM		Change	InfoSources		
Financial Supply Chain Management	0FSCM		Change	InfoSources		

Modeling: InfoProvider, InfoObjects, InfoSources, DataSources, Source Systems, Open Hub Desti.., Find, Favorites

Figure 7.18 Newly Created DataSource Available in DWW

7.2.3 Creating and Activating a Transformation

In this section, we describe the basic steps that a user must take to create a transformation, and we then go into the technical details of what the transformation process entails.

Basic Steps for Creating and Activating a Transformation

At this point in the process, your data target is the InfoObject BW_CUST, and your DataSource is BW_CUST_FF_DS_ATTR. Now you must create the transformation between the data target and DataSource, to convert the data format from source to the format required by the data target. This requires that the InfoObject must be under an InfoProvider tree.

First, select the InfoProvider under Modeling, as shown in ❶ of Figure 7.19. Select InfoArea BW_AREA (❷), open the context menu, and select Insert Characteristics as *InfoProvider* (❸). A pop-up box appears (❹) with input box for entering the name of the InfoObject (❺)

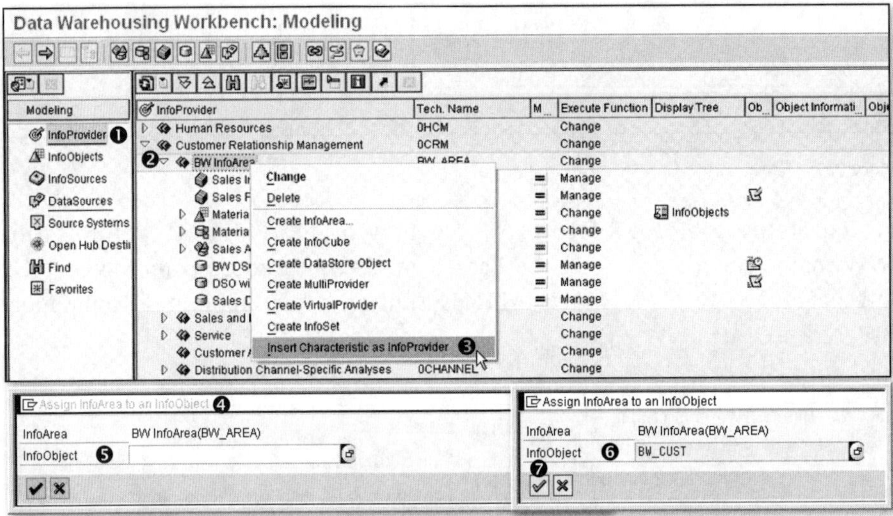

Figure 7.19 Inserting InfoObject as InfoProvider

Enter the technical name of the InfoObject, BW_CUST (❻ of Figure 7.19), and click the Continue icon. The result of this action is shown in Figure 7.20; the InfoObject is available under the InfoProvider tree in InfoArea BW_AREA (❶ of Figure 7.20). Expand the BW_CUST (text description: Sold-To Party) tree. This action shows three InfoProviders for BW_CUST: one is for hierarchies (❷), second one for attributes (❸), and the third for texts (❹). Recall that while configuring the InfoObject BW_CUST (in Chapter 3), we configured it to have exactly these InfoProviders.

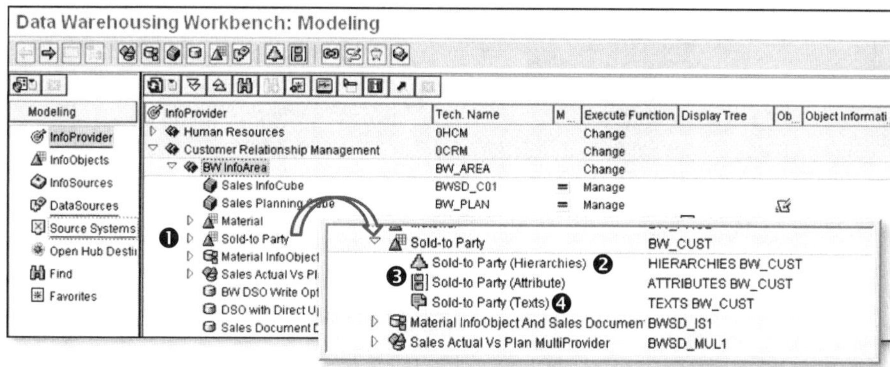

Figure 7.20 InfoObjects Available in InfoProvider Tree

Now that the InfoObject BW_CUST is available in the InfoProvider tree, a transformation can be created. In our example, we want to create a transformation between the InfoObject BW_CUST and DataSource BW_CUST_FF_DS_ATTR. Select Sold-To Party (Attribute), as shown in ❶ of Figure 7.21. Open the context menu, and select Create Transformation (❷), which results in ❸ of Figure 7.21. Because we've started the creation of the transformation from the InfoObject BW_CUST (attribute), the target of the transformation is set to Object Type = InfoObject (❹), Subtype of Object = Attribute (❺), and Name = BW_CUST (❻).

Next, supply the necessary information in the Source of the Transformation area (❼, ❽, and ❾ of Figure 7.21). Source can be any of the following:

- DataSource
- InfoSource
- DataStore Object
- InfoCube
- InfoObject
- InfoSet

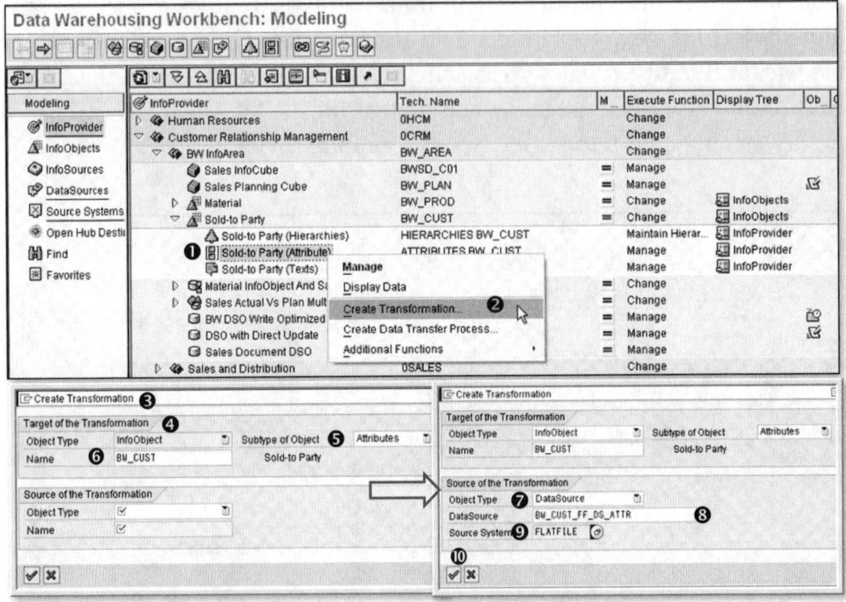

Figure 7.21 Creating a Transformation

InfoSources

The only object in this list we haven't previously discussed is *InfoSource*, which is a non-persistent structure consisting of InfoObjects that helps you to join two transformations. It doesn't store data, and you can't create queries based on it. In this way, it's neither an InfoProvider nor a data target.

Click on the Continue icon, which brings you to the Transformation screen (Figure 7.22). On the left side of the screen is the source object of the transformation; on the right is the target object of the transformation. SAP NetWeaver BW is able to find the matching InfoObject for all of the fields from the DataSource, with the exception of the InfoObject BW_CUST; this is because all of the other InfoObjects are from SAP Business Content. For InfoObject BW_CUST, you must instruct the system that the /BIC/BW_CUST field should be connected to InfoObject BW_CUST.

To accomplish this task, drag and drop /BIC/BW_CUST over InfoObject BW_CUST (❻ of Figure 7.22). This action completes the transformation and is known as a *direct assignment* transformation, which means that the data received by the DataSource field /BIC/BW_CUST is passed to InfoObject BW_CUST in as-is format (without any change). The other types of transformation are discussed in Section 7.3.2, Step 3: Creating a Transformation. The completed transformation is shown in ❼ of Figure 7.22.

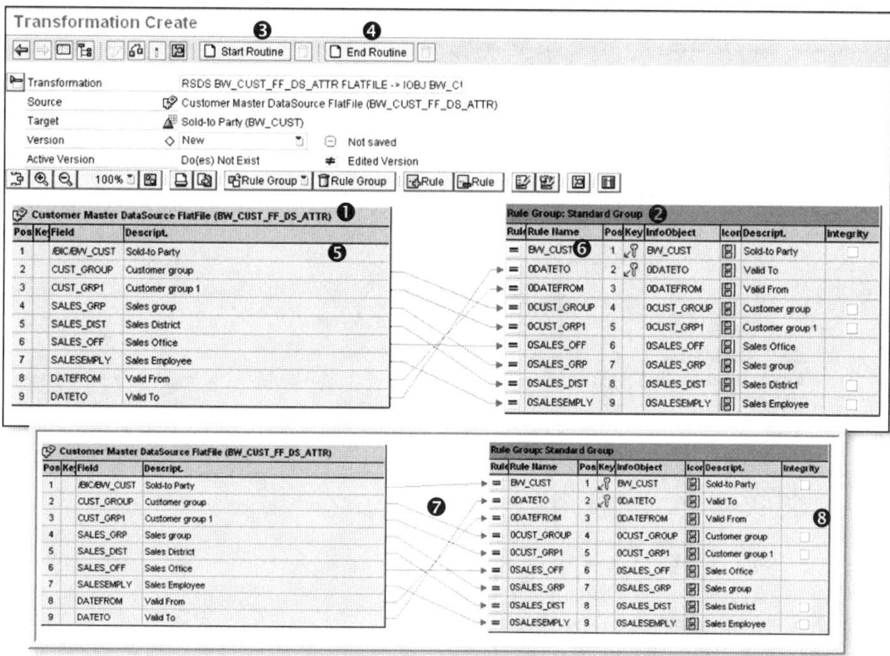

Figure 7.22 Making a Transformation

The Technical Process of Creating and Activating a Transformation

Here we explain the technical process that occurs as a result of the user-performed steps discussed immediately before this (Section 7.2.3, Creating and Activating a Transformation). At this stage, we simply introduce the basic concepts of transformation, keeping it simple. We'll introduce more complex transformation scenarios when we discuss the transformation between DSOs and InfoCubes, in Section 7.4, Loading Data from a DSO to an InfoCube.

Start Routine

Before being transformed, each record passes through a *start routine*, as shown in ❸ of Figure 7.23. The start routine is a place where a developer can write ABAP code that transforms the data within a record, according to requirements. The developer can work on a complete data package, defining variables, internal tables, and the values of both. The technique of filling internal tables in the start routine and then accessing them for individual transformation is a standard way to improve performance. The start routine is optional when defining transformation.

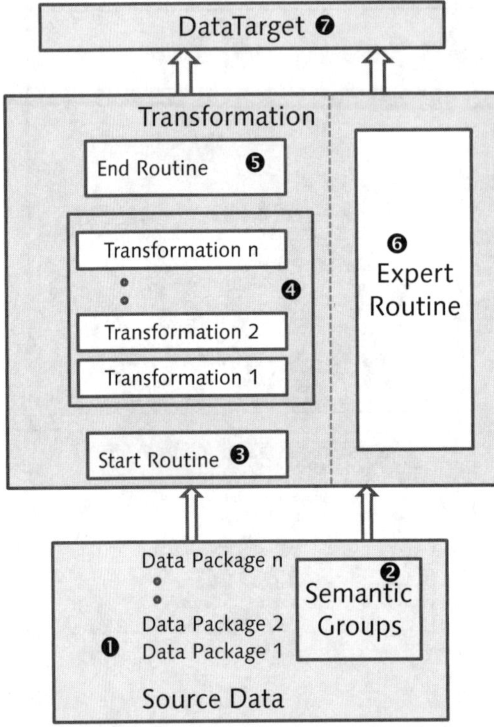

Figure 7.23 Overview of Transformation Process

Semantic Groups

It's sometimes necessary, from a coding perspective, to have a group of records in one data package (❶); in this situation, you must define a *semantic group* (❷). Semantic groups also define the key of *error stacks*. (Error stacks are covered in Section 7.5, Temporary Storage Areas and Error Stacks.)

Transformation Types

After the start routine is completed, individual data records pass through a transformation (❹). The *transformation type* defines the treatment on the data. The direct assignment, constant, formula, initial, read master data, and routine types of transformation were defined in Section 7.1.3, Transformations.

End Routine

Data packages pass though start routines before passing through individual transformations, and through *end routines* (in ❺ of Figure 7.23) after all transformations are completed. The end routine is the place where all of the transformations are completed, and transformed values for all records are available. The end routine allows a developer to write an ABAP code, if required; for example, you may require the deletion of a specific value in a record that is only available, only *after* the record has passed through transformation. You can use the end routine to perform a final quality check on a data record before it gets written to a data target (❼). Records that fail to meet quality checks can be deleted and aren't written to the data target. Like the start routine, the end routine is optional.

Expert Routine

In the expert routine (❻), you don't use the rule types offered by SAP NetWeaver BW, and you code the transformation program yourself, including monitor messages.

Activate a transformation by clicking on the Activate. Before activation, a version of the transformation is "New." Successful activation changes the version to "Active." Only active versions are used when loading data into a data target. Activating transformations actually generates an ABAP program that gets executed when a DTP is executed for loading data into a data target.

7.2.4 Creating a DTP for Loading Master Data

After activating a transformation, you must create the Data Transfer Process (DTP). When you activate a transformation and return to the main screen (❶), an icon for DTP is available, as shown in ❷ of 7.24.

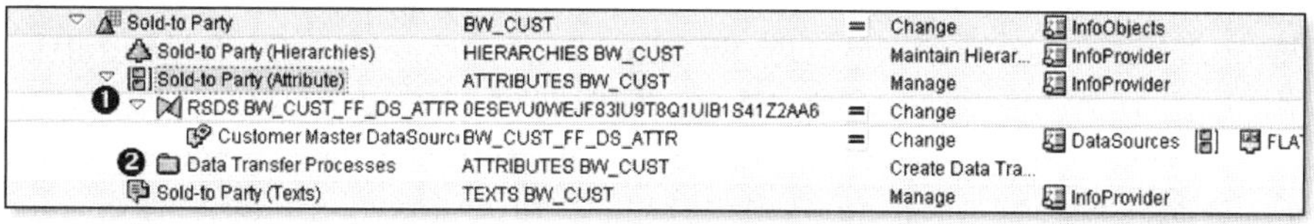

Sold-to Party	BW_CUST	=	Change	InfoObjects
Sold-to Party (Hierarchies)	HIERARCHIES BW_CUST		Maintain Hierar...	InfoProvider
Sold-to Party (Attribute)	ATTRIBUTES BW_CUST		Manage	InfoProvider
❶ RSDS BW_CUST_FF_DS_ATTR	0ESEVU0WEJF83IU9T8Q1UIB1S41Z2AA6	=	Change	
Customer Master DataSourc	BW_CUST_FF_DS_ATTR	=	Change	DataSources FLA
❷ Data Transfer Processes	ATTRIBUTES BW_CUST		Create Data Tra...	
Sold-to Party (Texts)	TEXTS BW_CUST		Manage	InfoProvider

Figure 7.24 DTP Icon

Select Data Transfer Processes, and then, from the context menu, select Create Data Transfer Process (❷ of Figure 7.25). The Creation of Data Transfer Process box appears (❸). Because you've started the creation of the DTP from the associated transformation, all of the required information is automatically supplied (❹ and ❺). Click the Continue icon (❻).

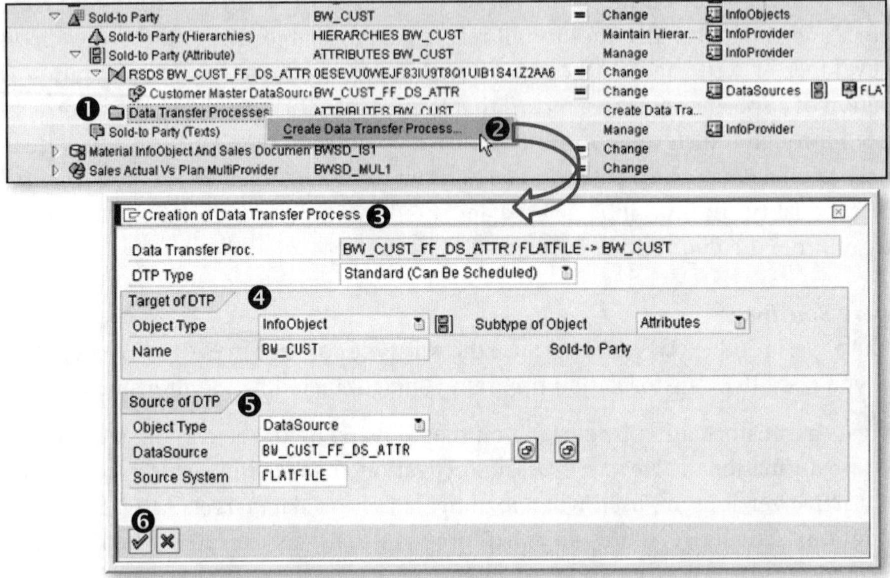

Figure 7.25 Creating Data Transfer Process

The result of this action is the Change Data Transfer Process screen shown in Figure 7.26. Three different tabs (❶, ❷, and ❸), are available, each of which we discuss next.

Extraction Tab

The Extraction tab provides details about the DataSource of the DTP, which is shown in ❹ of Figure 7.26. There are two different extraction modes (❺): full and delta. In the *full extraction mode*, all requests available in the associated PSA for the DataSource are loaded. In the *delta extraction* mode, the system loads only those requests from the associated PSA for the DataSource that are yet to be loaded to the data target. For our example, we use the delta mode.

> **Note**
>
> The delta mode for a DTP is linked to the requests in PSA and isn't the same as the delta mode of the DataSource. Associated DataSources in the data flow before DTP may or may not have delta capability.

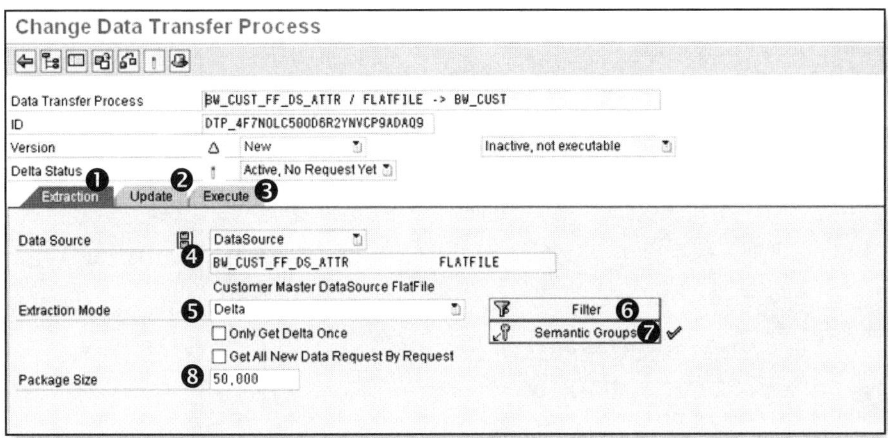

Figure 7.26 Change Data Transfer Process: Extraction Tab

There are several key elements of this screen:

- **Filter:** The Filter button (❻) allows you to select records based on selection conditions (e.g., you can decide to load data only for a specific month or sales office).
- **Semantic Groups: The Semantic Groups button** (❼) allows you to define keys for the extraction; data records with the same key are extracted in the same data package. Semantic keys also create a key for error stacks, which keeps track of erroneous records. These erroneous records can be corrected and loaded to a data target using an error DTP (we discuss this process in Section 7.5, Temporary Storage Areas and Error Stacks).
- **Package Size:** This field (❽) helps you change the parameters that control the bulk of extraction. Records from DataSources are extracted in a set, and the number of records in this set is called the *package size*. Determining the package size helps you control the extraction process and relate to the available processing capacity in the system; after a data set equal to the package size is extracted, the system starts loading it to a data target using another process. For our example, we don't change any default settings, and we keep the screen as shown in Figure 7.26.

Update Tab

Now click on the Update tab, where the BW_CUST data target is shown in ❶ of Figure 7.27.

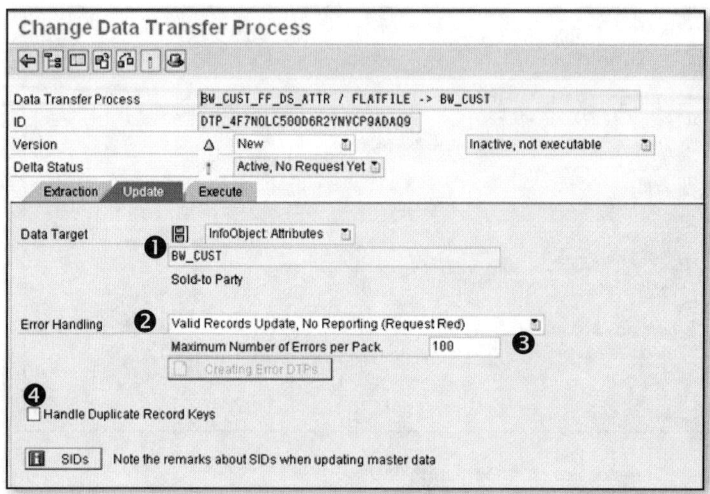

Figure 7.27 Change Data Transfer: Update Tab

DTP offers various options for error handling, as shown in ❷ of Figure 7.27 and described here:

- **Valid Records Update, No Reporting (Request Red)**
  Using this option, you tell the system to isolate erroneous records in a data packet from the data load and to load only valid records into the data target. The entire set of data uploaded from the request remains unavailable for reporting, and the request has a red status. An administrator can check the error records and then manually turn the uploaded request to green, making the data available for reporting. Erroneous records are written to an error stack that can be manually edited and loaded to a data target using error DTP.
- **Valid Records Update, Reporting Possible (Request Green)**
  When you select this option, you instruct the system to make the valid data immediately available for reporting in the data target. Erroneous records are written to an error stack that can be manually edited and loaded to a data target using error DTP.
- **No Update, No Reporting**
  When you select this option, you tell the system to suspend data processing to the data targets if it encounters an erroneous record, preventing further data from loading into the data target. The system keeps scanning the remaining data packages for erroneous records. The erroneous records aren't written to an error stack.
- **Deactivated**
  Erroneous records aren't written to an error stack. The request is terminated and needs to be updated fully.

We discuss the handling of errors more thoroughly in Section 7.5, Temporary Storage Areas and Error Stacks.

Maximum Number of Errors per Pack

The number of erroneous records that can be tolerated is entered in the Maximum Number of Errors per Pack field, as shown in ❸ of Figure 7.27. The system terminates the DTP if the number of erroneous records exceeds the number entered here.

The other important setting on the Update tab is the Handle Duplicate Record Keys checkbox (❹ of Figure 7.27). When set, this indicates that duplicate records should be handled in the order in which they occur in the data package.

Our example doesn't require changing any settings on the Update tab.

Execute Tab

Now click on the Execute tab. This tab offers various processing modes, as shown in ❶ of Figure 7.28.

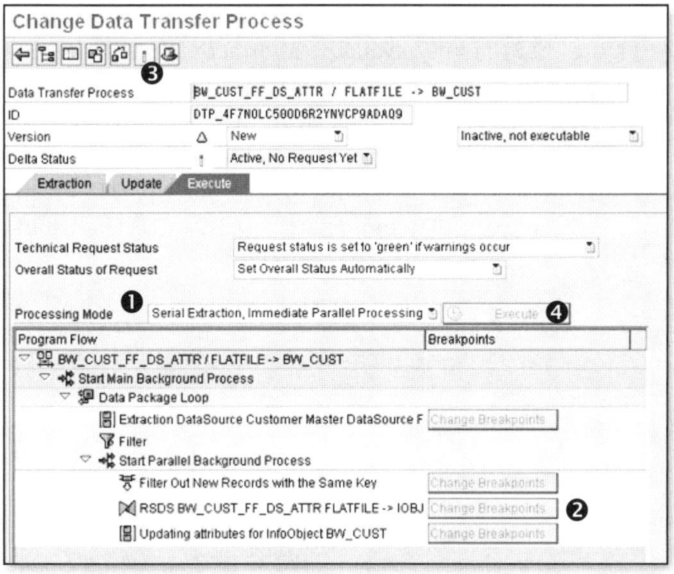

Figure 7.28 Change Data Transfer Process: Execute Tab

The *processing mode* describes in what order the processing of different steps occurs and also instructs the system whether the processing of these steps should happen in synchronous or asynchronous mode; that is, it controls the degree of *parallel processing*.

Synchronous Mode Versus Asynchronous Mode

In synchronous mode, the first process waits to invoke the second process until it receives a response from the second process. In asynchronous mode, the first process invokes the second process without waiting for a response from the second process.

Various processing modes are available in the system (although all of the processing modes may not be available at all times):

- **Serial Extraction, Immediate Parallel Processing:** In this case, data is processed asynchronously in a background process when a DTP is executed.
- **Serial in Dialog Process (For Debugging):** This kind of processing is used by developers to debug transformations. As shown in ❷ of Figure 7.28, different breakpoints are available. You can select them based on your requirements and select particular records for debugging.
- **No Data Transfer; Delta Status in Source: Fetched:** This is used when you want to transfer subsequent delta requests to the data target but *not* the existing data.

For our example, use the default settings shown in Figure 7.28. Activate your DTP using the Activate icon.

The Execute icon (❹ of Figure 7.28) is only available after activation of the DTP. At this point, however, we don't want to execute the DTP because we haven't yet extracted the data from the source system. (To do this, we must create an InfoPackage for our BW_CUST_FF_DS_ATTR DataSource; we discuss this process next.) Using the Back icon, return to the DWW main screen. You can now see that the DTP created between DataSource BW_CUST_FF_DS_ATTR and data target BW_CUST (attribute) is available (❶ of Figure 7.29).

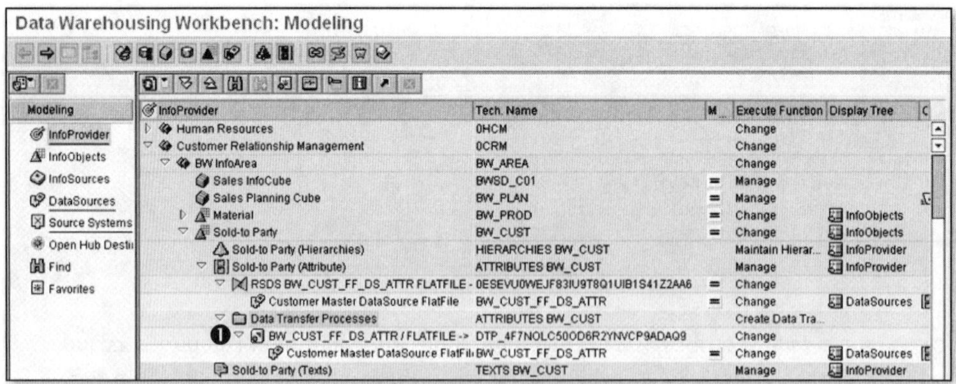

Figure 7.29 Newly Created DTP

7.2.5 Creating an InfoPackage and Starting Data Extraction

An InfoPackage is a scheduler object that, when executed, instructs SAP NetWeaver BW to extract data from a source system. It stores the extracted data in the first layer of SAP NetWeaver BW, which is the persistence staging area (PSA). To create an InfoPackage, select the DataSource from the source system under which you want to create it. For our example, select DataSource BW_CUST_FF_DS_ATTR, which is attached to the FLATFILE source system, as shown in ❶ of Figure 7.30.

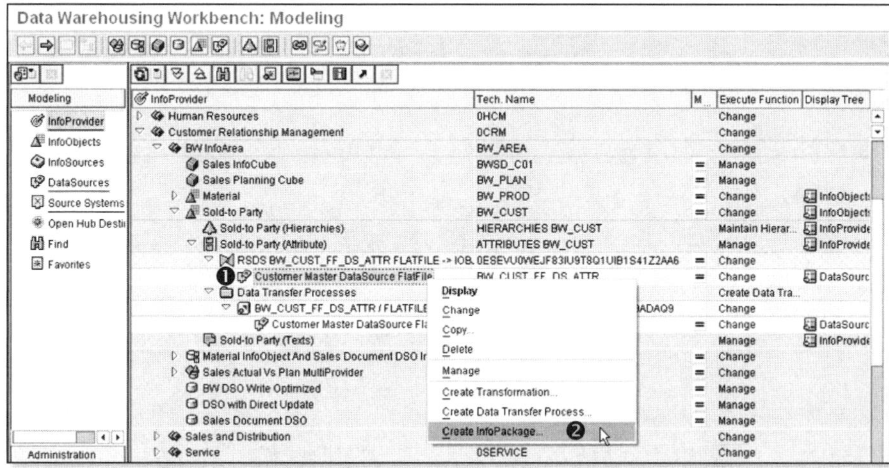

Figure 7.30 Creating an InfoPackage

Open the context menu, and select Create InfoPackage (❷). This action results in the Create InfoPackage screen (❶ of Figure 7.31), which also displays the source system (❷) and DataSource (❸) under which the InfoPackage is created. Enter the description (❹), and click on the Save icon (❺).

This action opens up the InfoPackage maintenance screen shown in Figure 7.32. The five different tabs here are explained next.

Data Selection Tab

The Data Selection tab (❶ of Figure 7.32) is displayed by default. This screen also shows details such as the DataSource, data type, and source system for which the InfoPackage is created (❷). Each InfoPackage is given a unique technical name by the SAP NetWeaver BW system, which always starts with ZPAK_*.

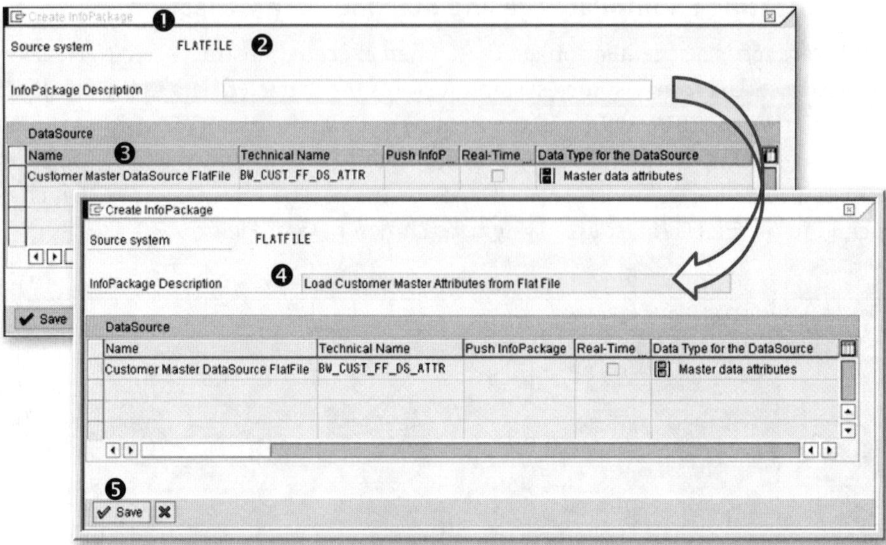

Figure 7.31 Entering an InfoPackage Description

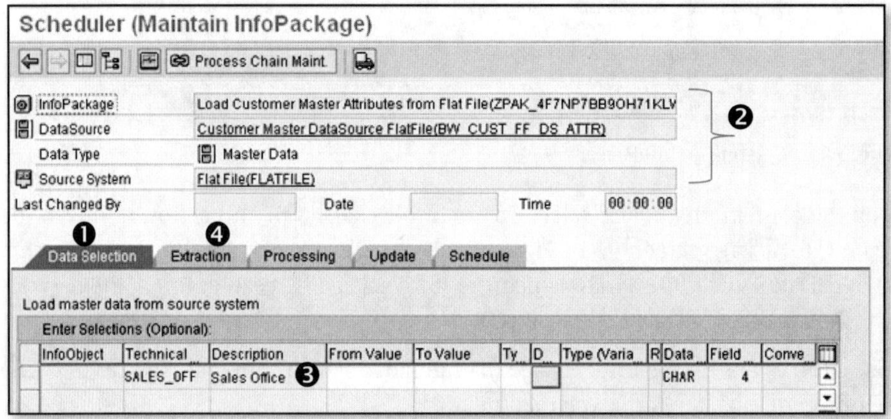

Figure 7.32 Creating an InfoPackage: Data Selection Tab

As shown in ❸ of Figure 7.32, this is the only field offered for filtering records based on value for SALES_OFF. This was configured when creating DataSource BW_CUST_FF_DS_ATTR, under the Field tab (refer to Figure 7.15). You can enter the value of a sales office as either a single value (e.g., 1768) or an interval (e.g., 1700 to 1799). The DataSource extracts data from the source system only for the entered values. Filling this field is optional; leaving it blank means that the system will extract all records from the source system. For our example, we keep the selection value blank.

Extraction Tab

Click on the Extraction tab (❹ of Figure 7.32). The details of the Extraction tab are shown in Figure 7.33.

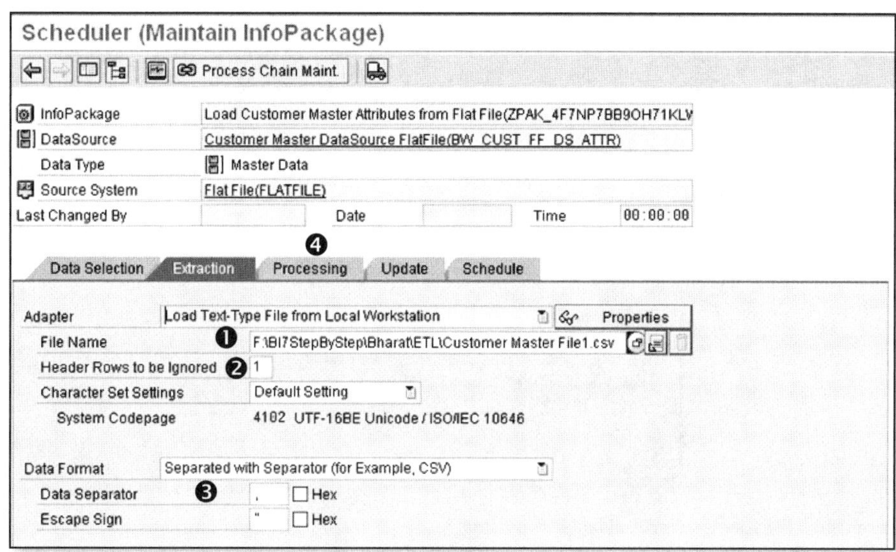

Figure 7.33 Creating an InfoPackage: Extraction Tab

This tab details information such as location, actual file name, type of file, and so on; the details are automatically provided based on the Extraction tab of the DataSource definition (refer to Figure 7.11). You can change details such as file name, header rows to be ignored, data separator, and so on (❶, ❷, and ❸ of Figure 7.33). Most of the settings available on this tab page are editable, but nothing needs to be changed for our example.

Processing Tab

Now click on the Processing tab, which allows you to determine how the extraction is processed by the SAP NetWeaver BW system and where it's stored. As shown in ❶ of Figure 7.34, the data extracted is stored in a PSA. If required, data in a PSA can be manually modified before it's loaded into any data target.

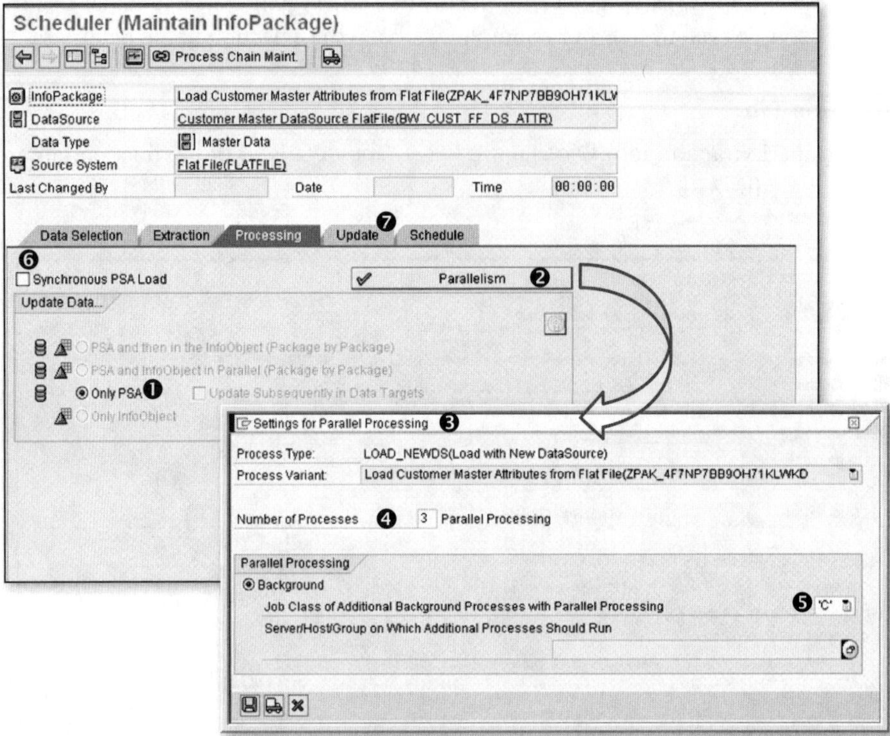

Figure 7.34 Creating an InfoPackage: Processing Tab

Parallel processing can be configured using this tab; click on Parallelism (❷), which takes you to the Setting for Parallel Processing screen (❸). You can set the number of processes to be used for parallel processing (❹). By default, this number is set to 3. If you change this to 1, the extraction is processed serially. You can also process extractions serially by setting the Synchronous PSA Load flag (❻).

During parallel processing, additional work processes are split off from the main work process. The parallel processes are usually executed in the background, and the job class for these background processes is set to C (low priority) by default (❺). B and A indicate a medium priority and a high priority, respectively.

Our example doesn't require any changes in the default settings.

Update Tab

Click on the Update tab. This tab only has one setting, Update Mode (❶ of Figure 7.35). The setting is determined by the delta capability of the DataSource associated with the InfoPackage. When the only update mode displayed is Full Update, you know that the associated DataSource isn't delta capable, and will provide full data every time you extract. Now click on the schedule tab (refer ❷ of figure 7.35).

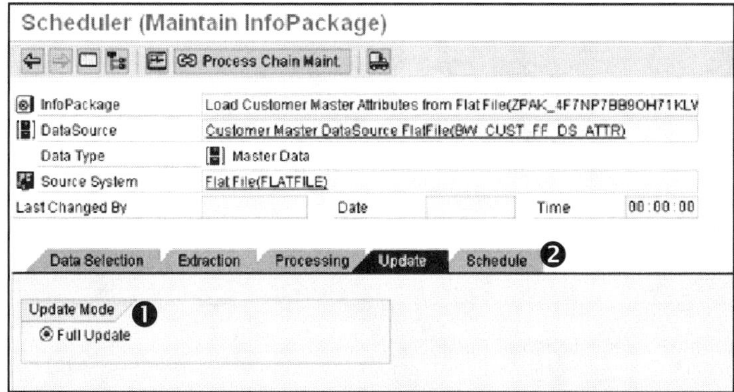

Figure 7.35 Creating an InfoPackage: Update Tab

Schedule Tab

Finally, the last tab is the Schedule tab, which allows you to start the extraction by selecting the Start Data Load Immediately radio button (❶ of Figure 7.36) and clicking Start (❻). Immediate extraction is done only once; if you want to extract data on a regular basis, select the Start Later in Background radio button (❷), and click Scheduling Options (❸). This results in the Start Time box shown in Figure 7.36.

Various options are available here. You can start the job in the background by clicking Immediate (❹); or, for extracting data on a regular basis, click on Date/Time (❺). This action allows you to set the start date, time, and periodicity of extraction, which can be hourly, daily, weekly, monthly, and so on. After this is set, click Start (❻).

For our example, we want to extract the data immediately and only once, so we select Start Data Load Immediately and click Start.

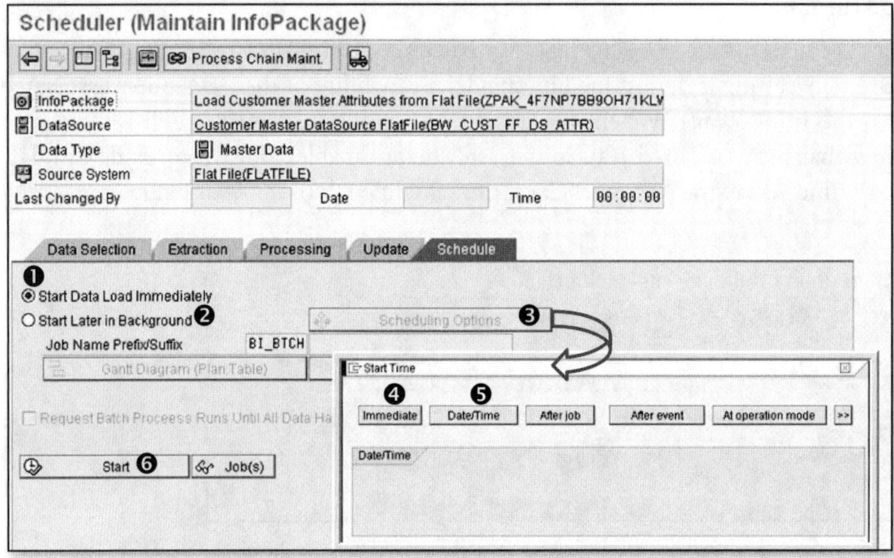

Figure 7.36 Creating an InfoPackage: Schedule Tab

7.2.6 Monitoring Data Extraction to the PSA

After the data extraction begins, you can click on the Monitor icon (▣) shown in ❶ of Figure 7.37 to check the status of the data extraction.

Figure 7.37 Monitor

The monitor shows a variety of information, such as the status of extraction, how many records have been extracted, the time taken by various steps involved in extraction, and so on. This detail is managed using three different tabs, each of which we discuss next. After explaining the tabs, we discuss the PSA Maintenance icon, which is another important feature of the monitor.

Status Tab

The monitor automatically opens with the Status tab, which is shown in ❶ of Figure 7.38.

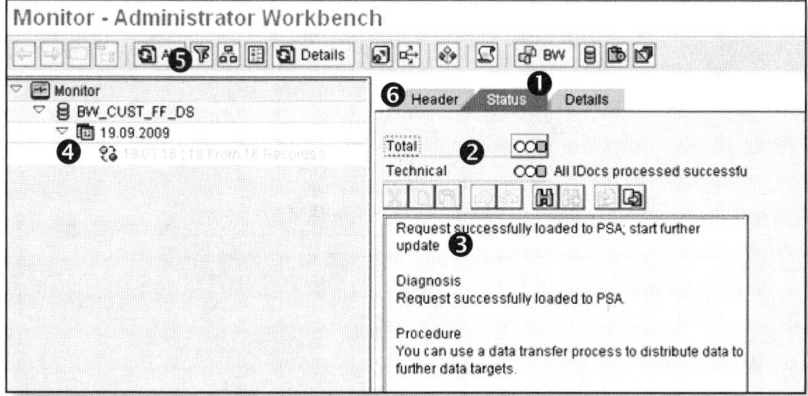

Figure 7.38 Monitor: Status Tab

This screen shows both the Total status and the Technical status (❷), and the progress of each is indicated by a traffic light:

- Technical Status
  - A yellow light means processing isn't completed or is completed with a warning.
  - A red light means that processing has encountered some error or the maximum wait time has been exceeded.
  - A green light means that processing has completed successfully.
- Total Status
  - The total status of a request is determined based on the technical status (based on all technical parameters in the system) and the QM Status (configurable and based on quality processes). Using the QM status, the total status of the request can be changed.

The extracted data is stored in a PSA, and the number of records extracted is displayed in ❹ of Figure 7.38. By default, the monitor shows the details of the current extraction (❸), but this display can be configured using the Filter icon (❺).

Header Tab

Click the Header tab to see the details of all of the objects involved in the extraction, as shown in Figure 7.39.

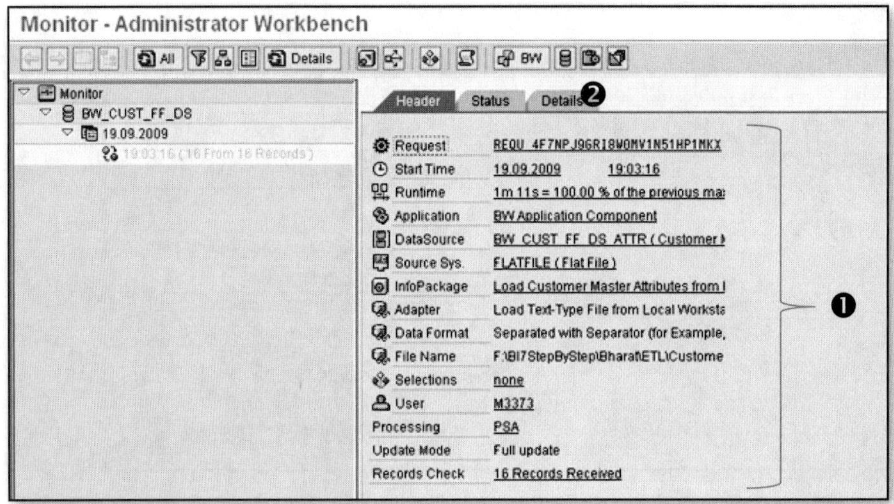

Figure 7.39 Monitor: Header Tab

The Header tab shows you information such as DataSource, source system, InfoPackage, update mode, selections, processing mode, user, date/time of the extraction, and runtime of the extraction (❶). Each extraction is assigned a unique request number, which you can use to identify each one. By default, this number starts with REQU_*.

Details Tab

The Details tab (❷ of Figure 7.39) shows extraction details broken into various steps, as shown in Figure 7.40. When extraction is started by executing an InfoPackage, the request for extraction is sent to the source system. Messages during *this phase* (❶ of Figure 7.40), extraction messages (❷), the transfer of extracted records in the form of data packets (❸), and the processing of each data packet (❹) are all shown in Figure 7.40.

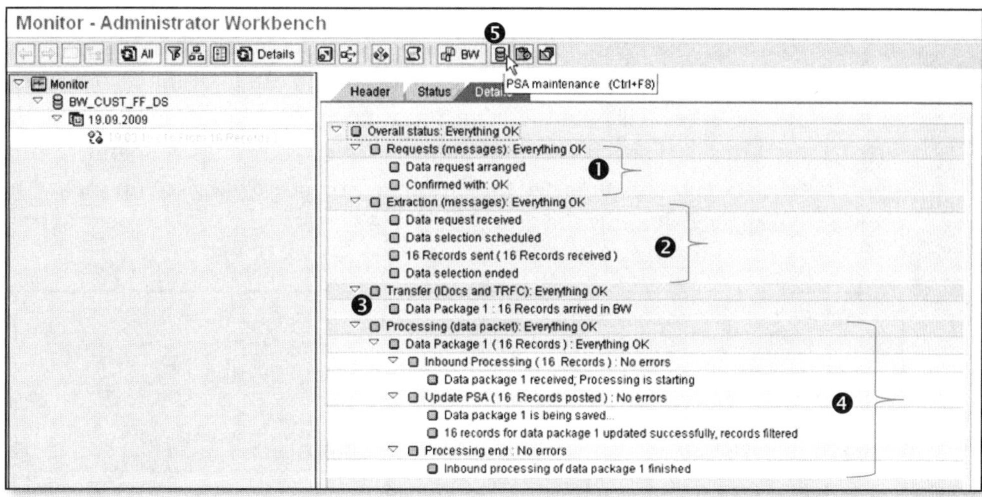

Figure 7.40 Monitor: Details Tab

PSA Maintenance

Another feature of the monitor is the ability to check the data stored in the PSA; to do this, click on the PSA Maintenance icon shown in ❺ of Figure 7.40. This results in the PSA Maintenance screen shown in Figure 7.41.

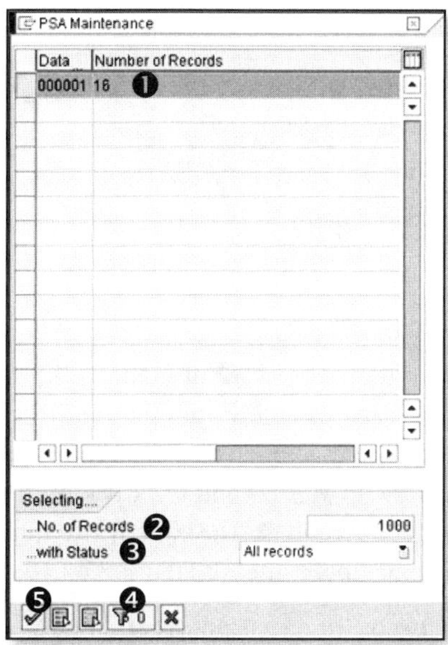

Figure 7.41 PSA Maintenance

The PSA Maintenance screen displays all data packets with the number of records in each one. Our example has only 1 data packet with 16 records (❶ of Figure 7.41), but, in practice, you'll probably have more than this. You can filter the records using the No. of Records field (❷) and the With Status field (❸). You can also click on the Filter icon (❹) to select specific record numbers. After you've filtered your records appropriately, select them, and click the Continue icon (❺)to view or edit them. The records are displayed as shown in ❶ of Figure 7.42.

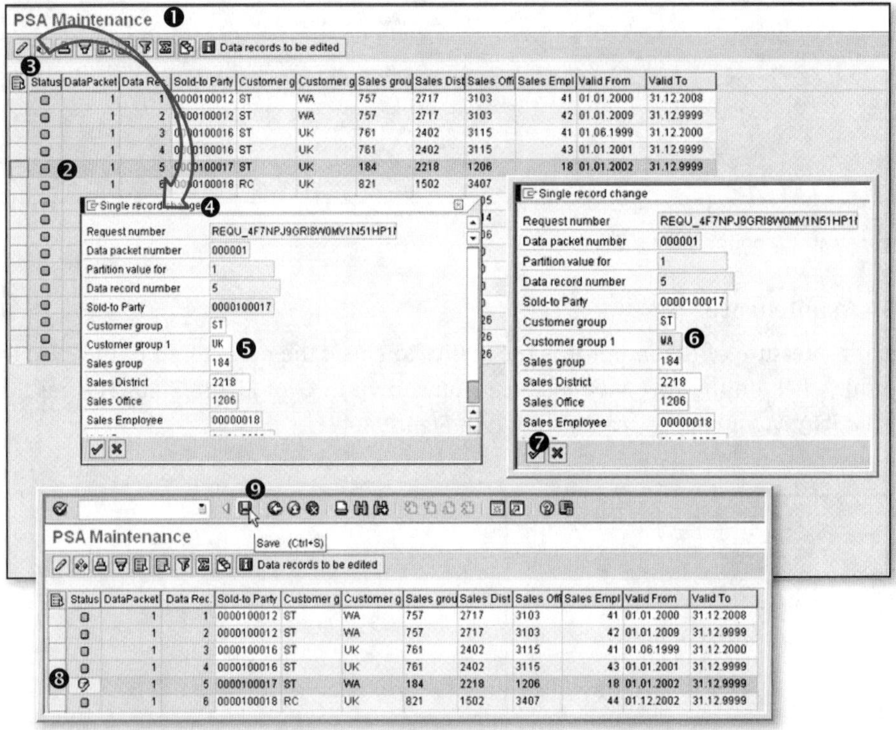

Figure 7.42 Editing Records in PSA Maintenance

In our example, we want to edit data record 5 of data packet 1 (❷ of Figure 7.42) to change the value of the Customer Group1 field. Select this record number, and click the Change icon (❸). This displays the Single Record Change box (❹). Select the value of the Customer Group1 field, and change it from UK to WA (❺ and ❻). Click on the Continue icon (❼); the changed value can be seen as shown in ❽. The system also indicates that the record has been changed with the icon shown in ❽ of Figure 7.42.

Save your changes, and use the Back icon to return to the monitor screen.

7.2.7 Monitoring the Data Transfer Process (DTP)

At this point, you have executed the InfoPackage and loaded the master data from the flat file to the PSA. Now you need to execute the DTP. The job of DTP is to read the data from PSA and pass it to the data target (InfoObject BW_CUST), transforming it in the process. You can directly jump to the associated DTP from the monitor screen by clicking the Display DTP icon shown in ❶ of Figure 7.43.

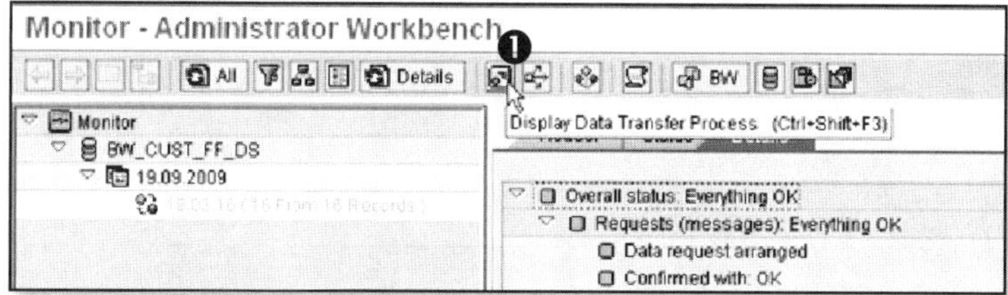

Figure 7.43 Starting DTP

This displays the Change Data Transfer Process screen shown in Figure 7.44. Click the Execute tab (❶) (recall our discussion of this tab from Section 7.2.4, Creating a DTP for Loading Master Data), and click the Execute icon (❷). This results in the Request Status box (❸).

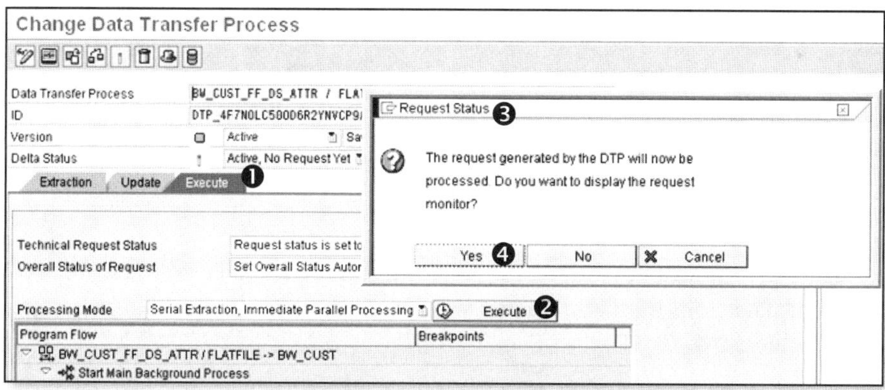

Figure 7.44 Executing DTP

Click Yes, and the DTP Monitor is displayed (Figure 7.45). The DTP Monitor has two different tabs, Details and Header. We describe both of these next, and then discuss the InfoProvider Administration screen.

Details Tab

By default you're shown the Details tab, which displays the unique request number of this DTP (❶ of Figure 7.45). More details about the DTP (❷) are organized by data packet. Different steps carried out during the DTP – extraction, filter, transformation, and updating – are shown here. The technical and overall status set for the request is shown in ❸ of Figure 7.45, and the duration of each step is shown in ❹ of Figure 7.45.

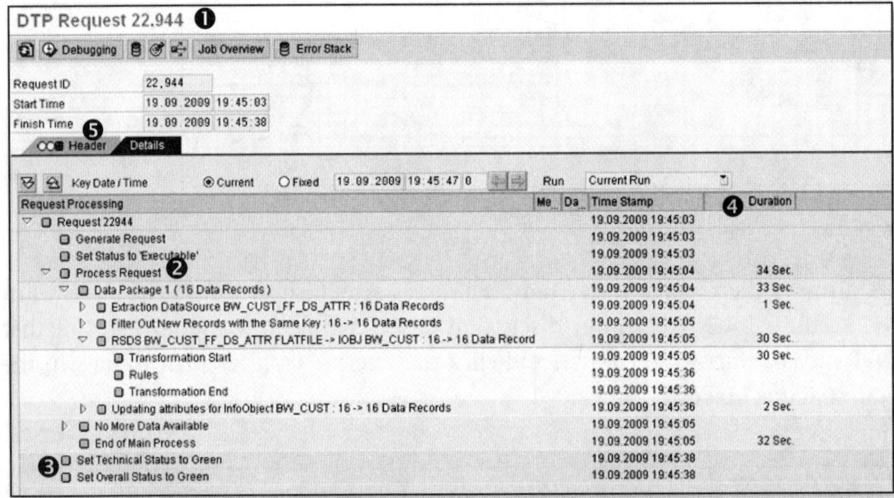

Figure 7.45 DTP Monitor: Details Tab

Header Tab

Click on the Header tab (❺ of Figure 7.45), and the screen shown in Figure 7.46 is displayed.

The Header tab shows all of the settings used for running this DTP (❶ of Figure 7.46). The master data from the flat file is now successfully loaded into tables associated with InfoObject BW_CUST.

InfoProvider Administration Screen

To view the loaded master data, click on the Administer Data Target icon shown in ❷ of Figure 7.46. The InfoProvider Administration screen appears (Figure 7.47).

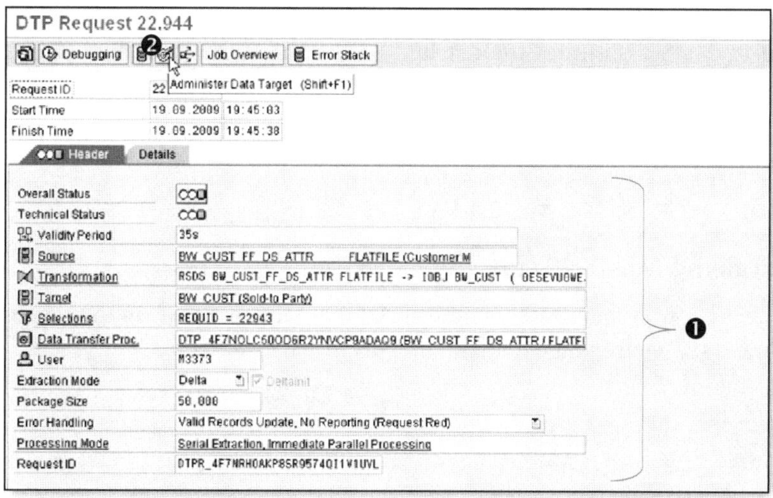

Figure 7.46 DTP Monitor: Header Tab

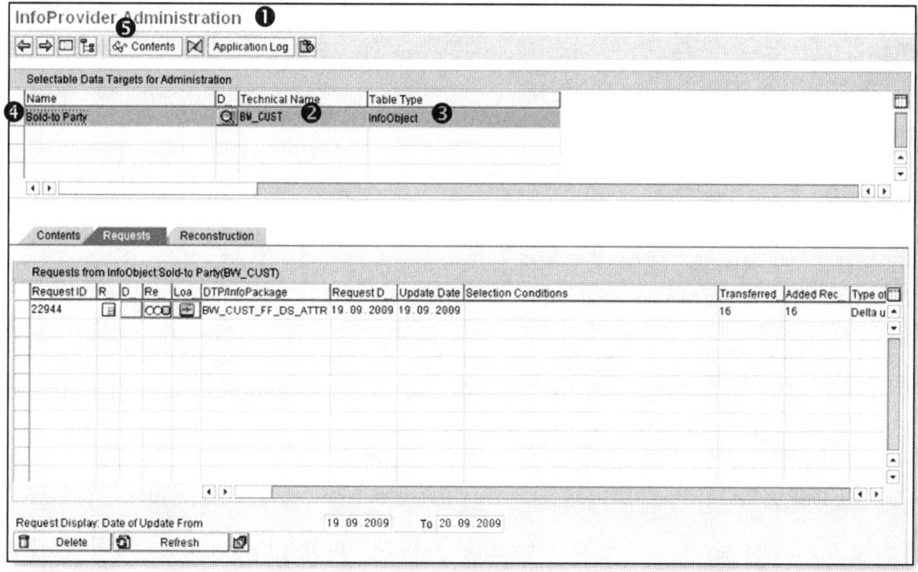

Figure 7.47 InfoProvider Administration Screen

As you can see, the InfoProvider is listed as InfoObject BW_CUST (❷ and ❸ of Figure 7.47). You can select the InfoProvider by clicking the start of the line (❹). A number of administrative tasks can be performed using the functionalities available in the lower part of Figure 7.47, but the details of this go beyond the scope of this chapter. Instead, these topics are addressed in Chapter 14, Administration and Maintenance.

7.2.8 Maintaining Master Data

From Figure 7.47, click on the Contents button (❺). This action results in the screen shown in Figure 7.48, where you can maintain master data.

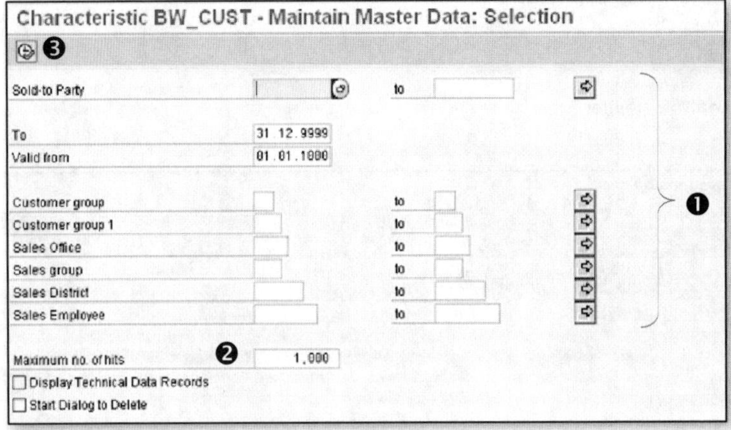

Figure 7.48 Maintain Master Data: Selection Screen

As shown in ❶ of Figure 7.48, the master data selection screen displays all of the attributes of InfoObject BW_CUST for making selections. You enter selection values for filtering master data records. Recall that when we defined the attributes of InfoObject BW_CUST (Chapter 3), we defined the sales employee attribute as time-dependent. The To and Valid From fields are available for selection as a result of this.

You can restrict the number of output records by setting the number in the Maximum No. of Hits field (❷). This is set to 1000 by default, and we won't change this for our example. Now click the Execute icon (❸). This shows you the master data records from the InfoObject BW_CUST (Figure 7.49).

Characteristic BW_CUST - maintain master data: List

Data Records to be Edited

Sold-to	To	Valid from	Customer g	Customer g	Sales Offi	Sales grou	Sales Dist	Sales Empl	Descript	Descript
100012	31.12.1999	01.01.1000	ST	WA	3103	757	2717			
100012	31.12.2008	01.01.2000	ST	WA	3103	757	2717	41		
100012	31.12.9999	01.01.2009	ST	WA	3103	757	2717	42		
100016	31.05.1999	01.01.1000	ST	UK	3115	761	2402			
100016	31.12.2000	01.06.1999	ST	UK	3115	761	2402	41		
100016	31.12.9999	01.01.2001	ST	UK	3115	761	2402	43		
100017	31.12.2001	01.01.1000	ST	WA	1206	184	2218			
100017	31.12.9999	01.01.2002	ST	WA	1206	184	2218	18		
100018	30.11.2002	01.01.1000	RC	UK	3407	821	1502			
100018	31.12.9999	01.12.2002	RC	UK	3407	821	1502	44		
100020	31.12.1999	01.01.1000	ST	WA	3305	700	2140			
100020	31.12.9999	01.01.2000	ST	WA	3305	700	2140	41		
100022	31.12.1999	01.01.1000	RC	UK	3114	762	2136			
100022	31.12.9999	01.01.2000	RC	UK	3114	762	2136	41		

Figure 7.49 Master Data from InfoObject BW_CUST

As you can see from ❶ of Figure 7.49, there are multiple records for one sold-to party (100016). This is due to the time-dependent sales employee attribute; a separate record is created for each time period assigned to a sales employee. Thus, 100016 has one record from January 1, 1000 (a standard date used by the system to indicate the past) to May 30, 1999; another record from June 1, 1999 to December 31, 2000; and a third record from January 1, 2001 until the present (which is indicated using the date December 31, 9999). The three different time periods coincide with the assignment of different sales employees; no employee was assigned during the first period, employee 41 was assigned during the second period, and employee 43 is currently assigned.

The preceding data in InfoObject BW_CUST is due to the input records shown in Figure 7.50. As shown, there are two different sales employees assigned to the sold-to-party (100016) during two different time periods.

Customer	Customer GRP	Customer GRP1	Sales Group	Sales District	Sales Office	Sales Employee	Date From	Date To
100016	ST	UK	761	2402	3115	41	19990601	20001231
100016	ST	UK	761	2402	3115	43	20010101	99991231

Figure 7.50 Sample Master Data for Customer 100016

We've now completed the loading of master data attributes into InfoObject BW_CUST from the flat file source system, but we still need to load the master data text. To do this, simply replicate these activities we performed for the master data attributes:

1. Create a DataSource for loading text.
2. Create a transformation between this DataSource and InfoObject BW_CUST (text).
3. Create a new DTP between this DataSource and the InfoObject.
4. Create an InfoPackage for the newly created DataSource.
5. Execute the InfoPackage.
6. Execute the DTP.

Now you'll be able to perform a one-time load of master data from a flat file into an InfoObject. In reality, you'll need to load master data periodically, and the process for this uses the process chain. (see Chapter 14, Administration and Monitoring).

In the following section, we've detailed the process of loading transaction data from a flat file DataSource into DSO to help you learn the difference in the ETL process from the master data that we just explained.

7.3 Loading Transaction Data from a Source System to a DSO

In this section, we discuss the steps involved in loading transaction data from a flat file into a DSO. Because many of these steps are similar to the steps involved in loading master data, we won't go into much detail here; we'll mostly use this example to explain the different types of transformations in more detail. The transformation types dealt with in this section are related to requirements of ABCD Corp., including using a fixed company code as a single company, creating an indicator for a value type that isn't captured in the OLTP system, and using the value of customer groups stored in customer master records but not being supplied in the flat file transaction DataSource.

DSOs generally store transaction data at the granular level. It can also store master data if required. Our example scenario requires transaction data in SAP NetWeaver BW. We use DSO BWSD_O01 for storing transaction data. Our transaction data is available in a flat file, so we load it to the DSO from the flat file.

Recall from Chapter 4, that we created a BWSD_O01 DSO. To load transaction data in the BWSD_O01 DSO, follow these steps:

1. Create a flat file source system. This process was explained in Section 7.2.1, Creating a Flat File Source System. We'll use this same source system in this example.
2. Create an application component and transaction DataSource. We created an application component and DataSource in Section 7.2.2, Creating a DataSource. We'll reuse the application component, but the DataSource for the DSO needs to be created. This process is described in more detail later in this section.
3. Create and activate the transformation between the DataSource and the DSO. The basic process of creating a transformation remains the same, but this time, we use a more complex example. This is described in more detail later in this section.
4. Create and activate the DTP between the DataSource and the DSO. The process of creating a DTP remains the same.
5. Create and execute the InfoPackage. The process of creating an InfoPackage remains the same.
6. Execute the DTP to load the data into the DSO. The process of executing the DTP remains the same.

Again, Steps 1, 4, and 5 in this process are similar to what we've already discussed, so we won't revisit them. Instead, we focus on Steps 2 and 3.

7.3.1 Step 2: Creating a Transaction DataSource

Referring to Figure 7.9 earlier in this chapter, ensure that FLATFILE is selected as your source system. Select application component ZBW_APP_COMP (❶ of Figure 7.9) and, from the context menu, select Create DataSource. In the Create DataSource box, enter the input parameters given in Table 7.2. Click the Continue icon.

Input Parameter	Input Given
DataSource	BWSD_O01_FF_DS_TRAN
Data Type DataSource	Transaction Data

Table 7.2 Input Parameters for Creating a Transaction DataSource

General Info Tab

In the General Info tab (❶ of Figure 7.51) of the Change DataSource screen, enter the short/medium/long description (❷).

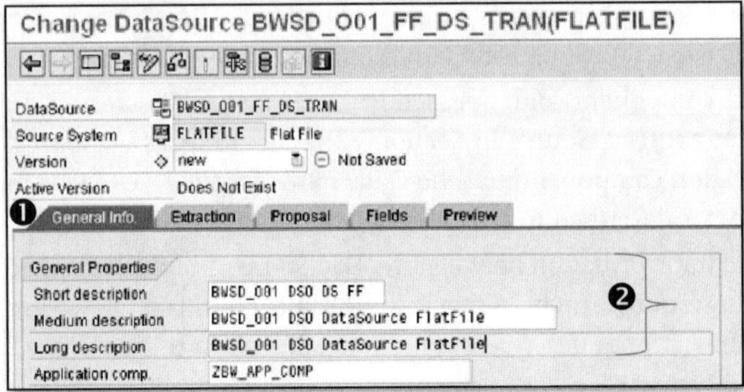

Figure 7.51 Transaction DataSource Creation: General Tab

Extraction Tab

In the Extraction tab, enter the parameters shown in Table 7.3.

Input Parameter	Input Given
Delta Process	FILO Delta Data (After Images)
Direct Access	NO DTP Allowed for Direct Access
Adapter	Load Text-Type File from Local WorkStation
File Name	F:\ETL\Billing Transaction Data File1.CSV* *Make sure that file path matches the location where you save this file.
Header Rows to be ignored	3
Data Format	Separated with Separator (e.g., CSV)
Data Separator	,

Table 7.3 Input Parameters for the Extraction Tab

There's usually a large volume of transaction data; as such, loading the full file may not be practical. With this in mind, we select FILO Delta Data (After Images). When a DataSource is created with this setting, you get the option of initialization, and subsequently delta, when extracting using an InfoPackage.

Our example scenario gets the data in a flat file for newly created and changed records. The fields of the changed record contain the latest information, so it's appropriate to select type FILO. In addition, because the DSO update type is set to overwrite, the data sent from the DSO to the InfoCube is loaded with the correct values. By default, DSO is set to overwrite mode. Section 1.4, Business Intelligence Requirements, in Chapter 1, The Business Scenario: ABCD Corp., explains the process of loading data from a DSO to an InfoCube.

Proposal Tab

Now click on the Proposal tab. Clicking the Load Example Data button (refer to ❸ of Figure 7.13) provides information from the system; recall, though, that the system simply reads your file to get the data type and may not always be 100% accurate. As such, we rely on the InfoObject definition in the Fields tab.

Fields Tab

In the Fields tab, the system has proposed fields and listed them in sequence. As shown in ❶ of Figure 7.52, field VBELN is listed in position 1. The definition of this field comes from the InfoObject; we type the associated InfoObject in ❷. Type "0DOC_NUMBER," and press the Enter key. Select Yes in the resulting pop-up box, and the change is shown in ❸. The mapping of field to InfoObject (i.e. field VBELN to InfoObject 0DOC_NUMBER) is based on analysis of business content and metadata repository.

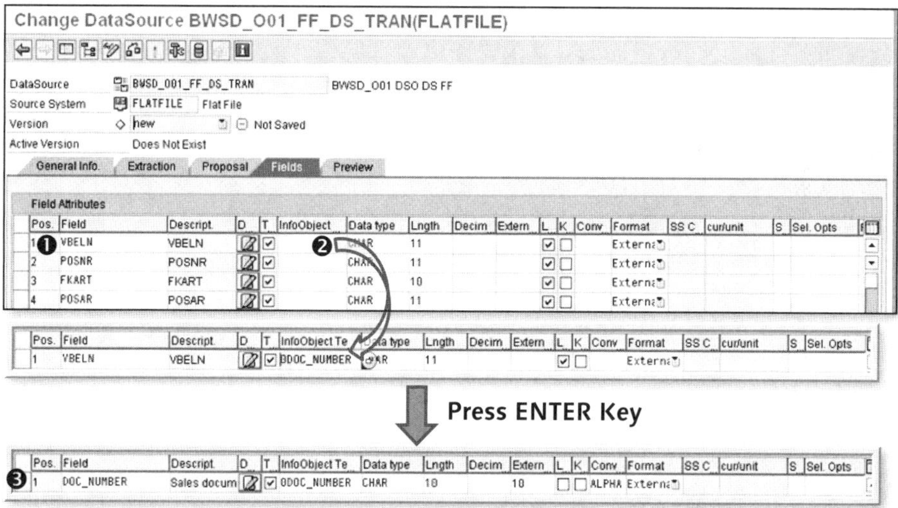

Figure 7.52 Create Transaction DataSource: Fields Tab

You must follow this same process — that is, typing the InfoObject name, pressing Enter, and selecting Yes — for each position in Figure 7.52. Enter the names show in Table 7.4.

Position	InfoObject
1	0DOC_NUMBER
2	0S_ORD_ITEM
3	0BILL_TYPE
4	0ITEM_CATEG
5	0BILL_CAT
6	0BILL_DATE
7	BW_CUST
8	0CUST_GROUP
9	0MATERIAL
10	0DIVISION
11	0MATL_GROUP
12	0PLANT
13	0COMP_CODE
14	0SALESORG
15	0REGION
16	0DISTR_CHAN
17	0SALES_OFF
18	0SALES_GRP
19	0SALES_DIST
20	BW_QTY
21	0NET_WGT_DL
22	0GRS_WGT_DL
23	0UNIT_OF_WT
24	0UNIT
25	0DOC_CATEG
26	0COST
27	0LOC_CURRCY
28	0DOC_CURRCY
29	0ACCNT_ASGN

Table 7.4 InfoObjects to be Entered in the Fields Tab

Position	InfoObject
30	0CO_AREA
31	0NET_VALUE
32	0SUBTOTAL_1
33	0SUBTOTAL_2
34	0VALUE_LC
35	0COUNTRY

Table 7.4 InfoObjects to be Entered in the Fields Tab (Cont.)

After this is completed, you can activate the DataSource by clicking the Activate icon (❶ of Figure 7.53). The activated DataSource (BWSD_O01_FF_DS_TRAN) is now available under the application component ZBW_APP_COMP (❸).

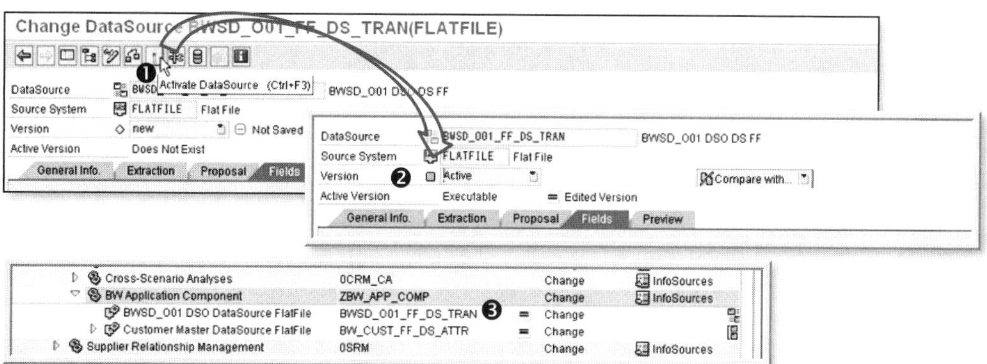

Figure 7.53 Activating DataSource

Preview Tab

After the DataSource is activated, you can use the Preview tab to see whether your configuration is correct. You should always confirm the configuration before using the DataSource in a transformation.

7.3.2 Step 3: Creating a Transformation

Here we again address the process of creating a transformation; however, in this section, we focus on the creation of a transformation between a DataSource and a DSO. In addition, we expand our discussion from Section 7.2.3, Creating and Activating a Transformation, to focus on four specific types of transformation: a direct assignment transformation from a DataSource, a constant transformation, a read master data transformation, and a formula transformation. We conclude our discussion with a brief explanation of the difference between key figure transformations and characteristic transformations.

Creating a Direct Assignment Transformation from a DataSource

Now that you have configured your DataSource, you can create the transformation between DataSource BWSD_O01_FF_DS_TRAN and DSO BWSD_O01. You can begin creating a transformation from the context menu of the data target or the context menu of the DataSource; earlier in the chapter, we started from the context menu of the data target (in this case, an InfoOject), so this time we start from the DataSource.

From the DWW, select DataSource (❶ of Figure 7.54). Make sure that your DataSource tree is shown for the FLATFILE source system (❷); if it isn't, refer to Figure 7.6 to fix this. Select DataSource BWSD_O01_FF_DS_TRAN (❸), and, from the context menu, select Create Transformation (❹). This action results in the Create Transformation screen (❺). The target of the transformation is blank (❻) because we started the process from the DataSource. Input the target of the transformation as shown in ❼, and click the Continue icon (❽).

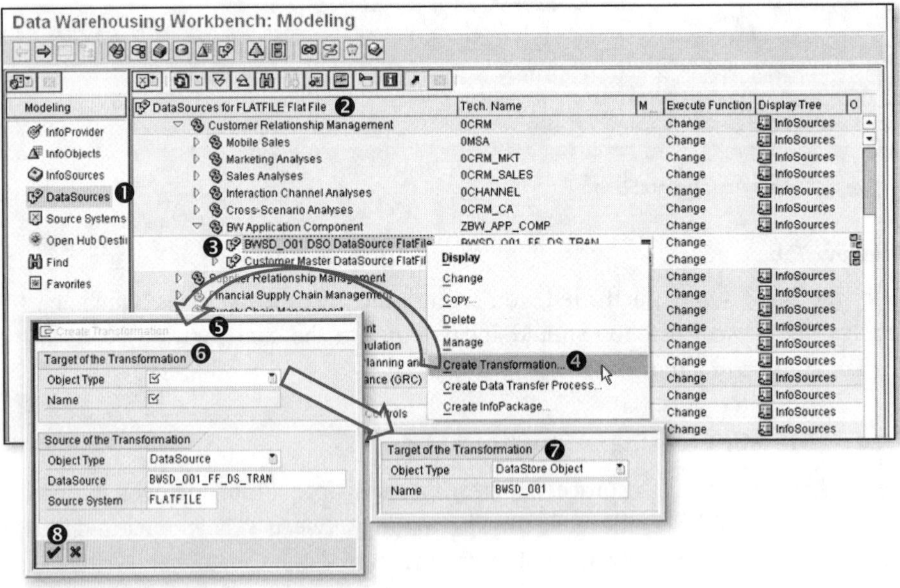

Figure 7.54 Creating a Transformation Between a DataSource and a DSO

This results in the Transformation Create screen shown in Figure 7.55, which allows you to create a transformation using drag and drop. As shown in ❶ of Figure 7.55, the source and target object are shown on the left and right, respectively. SAP NetWeaver BW automatically matches the field of the DataSource to the InfoObject and proposes the transformation based on metadata available in the system. This is a direct assignment transformation, meaning that the data from the DataSource is passed to the target InfoObject without any modification of values. If required, you can change this proposed transformation.

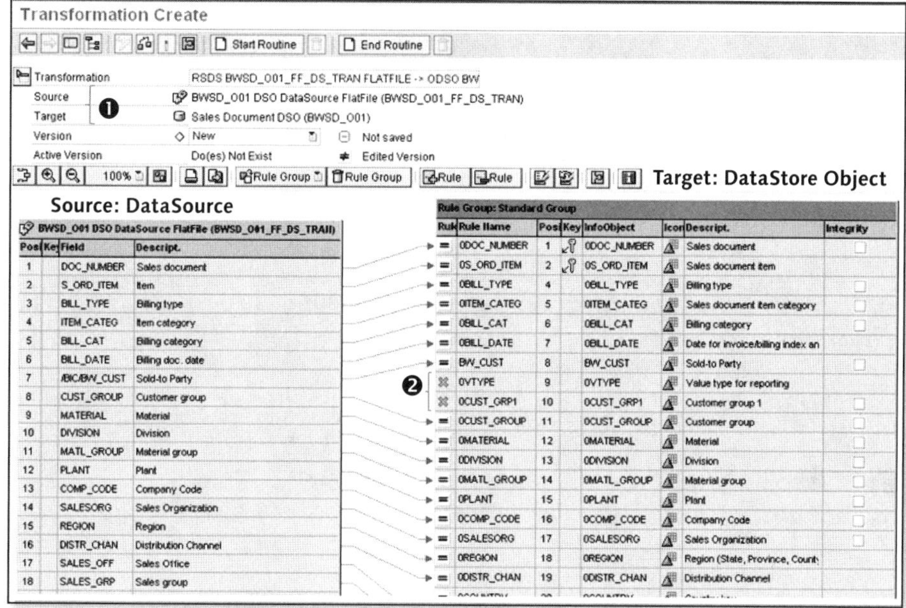

Figure 7.55 Creating a Direct Assignment Transformation

For our example, there are a few other direct assignment transformations from DataSource to DSO; the detail mapping from field to InfoObject is given in Table 7.5.

Field	InfoObject
DOC_NUMBER	0DOC_NUMBER
S_ORD_ITEM	0S_ORD_ITEM
BILL_TYPE	0BILL_TYPE
ITEM_CATEG	0ITEM_CATEG

Table 7.5 Transformation: Field to InfoObject Direct Assignment

Field	InfoObject
BILL_CAT	0BILL_CAT
BILL_DATE	0BILL_DATE
/BIC/BW_CUST	BW_CUST
CUST_GROUP	0CUST_GROUP
MATERIAL	0MATERIAL
DIVISION	0DIVISION
MATL_GROUP	0MATL_GROUP
PLANT	0PLANT
SALESORG	0SALESORG
REGION	0REGION
DISTR_CHAN	0DIST_CHAN
COUNTRY	0COUNTRY
SALES_OFF	0SALES_OFF
SALES_GRP	0SALES_GRP
SALES_DIST	0SALES_DIST
/BIC/BW_QTY	BW_QTY
NET_WGT_DL	0NET_WGT_DL
GRS_WGT_DL	0GRS_WGT_DL
UNIT_OF_WT	0UNIT_OF_WT
UNIT	0UNIT
DOC_CATEG	0DOC_CATEG
COST	0COST
LOC_CURRCY	0LOC_CURRCY
DOC_CURRCY	0DOC_CURRCY
ACCNT_ASGN	0ACCNT_ASGN
CO_AREA	0CO_AREA
NET_VALUE	0NET_VALUE
SUBTOTAL_1	0SUBTOTAL_1
SUBTOTAL_2	0SUBTOTAL_2
VALUE_LC	0VALUE_LC

Table 7.5 Transformation: Field to InfoObject Direct Assignment (Cont.)

Constant Transformation

There are two InfoObjects, 0VTYPE and 0CUST_GRP1, which have not had any transformation proposed by the system (❷ of Figure 7.55). The reason for this is that there are no fields in the DataSource that map to these two InfoObjects (as shown earlier in Table 7.4). As such, we must derive the value for these two InfoObjects using the formula and read master data transfer types (recall our discussion of the different types of transformation in Section 7.1.3, Transformations).

As shown in ❶ of Figure 7.56, the COMP_CODE field is mapped to InfoObject 0COMP_CODE using a direct assignment transformation. We want to change the transformation type to *constant*, so our first step is to delete the proposed rule. Select InfoObject 0COMP_CODE as shown in ❶ of Figure 7.56, open the context menu, and select Delete Rule (❷). Click Yes in the resulting pop-up box (❸). The X in ❹ of Figure 7.56 indicates that no rule is assigned to InfoObject 0COMP_CODE.

To create a new transformation, select 0COMP_CODE (❺), open the context menu, and select Rule Details (❻).

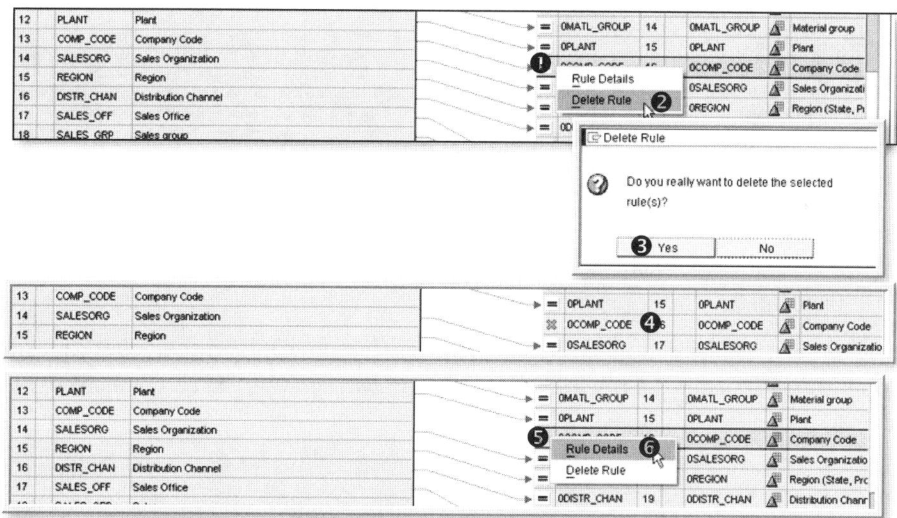

Figure 7.56 Deleting the Transformation Rule

This action results in the Rule Details screen shown in Figure 7.57. As you can see, the target InfoObject is shown as 0COMP_CODE. Because we've deleted the transformation rule in the previous step, the Rule Type field lists No Transformation (❷).

Target Fields

Normally, transformations have only one target field (as shown in ❸ of Figure 7.57). There may, however, be a situation where you can have more than one, such as when doing unit or currency translations for key figures.

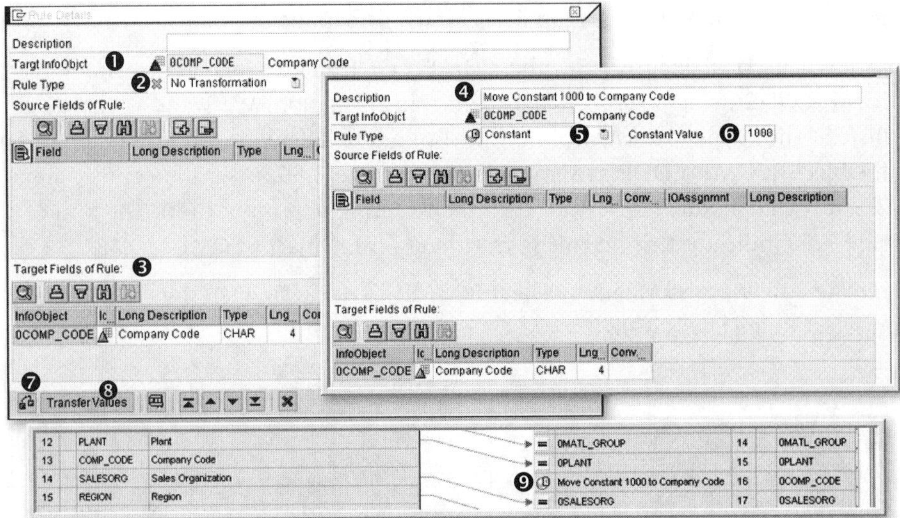

Figure 7.57 Creating a Constant Transformation

Give a proper description for the transformation type, as shown in ❹ Figure 7.57. Use the dropdown available for the rule type, and select Constant (❺). You can now enter the value for the company code (❻).

Check your transformation by clicking the Check icon (❼), and then click Transfer Values (❽) to transfer the rule change to your transformation. As shown in ❾ of Figure 7.57, a new rule is now available ( ).

Read Master Data Transformation

Now we must configure the transformation for InfoObject 0CUST_GRP1 because the transaction data file doesn't contain the value of this field (again, refer to Table 7.4). Recall that Customer GRP1 is an attribute of InfoObject BW_CUST; that is, for each customer, the value of Customer GRP1 is available as part of the customer master data. As such, tables associated with InfoObject BW_CUST contain these values for each customer. In this kind of scenario, the *read master data* transformation type should be used. There is no need to write a single line of code to get this value. We'll explain this with an example first, and then show you the step-by-step configuration.

Figure 7.58 shows the document data from the input file that is relevant for our example. It's composed of four fields: VBELN (document number), POSNR (item number), KUNAG (customer number), and KDGRP (customer group 1). The data target has five InfoObjects, and four of them are associated with fields from the input data. The other InfoObject, 0CUST_GRP1, doesn't have a corresponding field in the input file.

Again, recall that the customer master data (InfoObject BW_CUST) has a value for InfoObject 0CUST_GRP1 for each customer. Using the read master data transformation type, the system searches the customer number of each input record, and, if one is found, updates InfoObject 0CUST_GRP1 with the corresponding value.

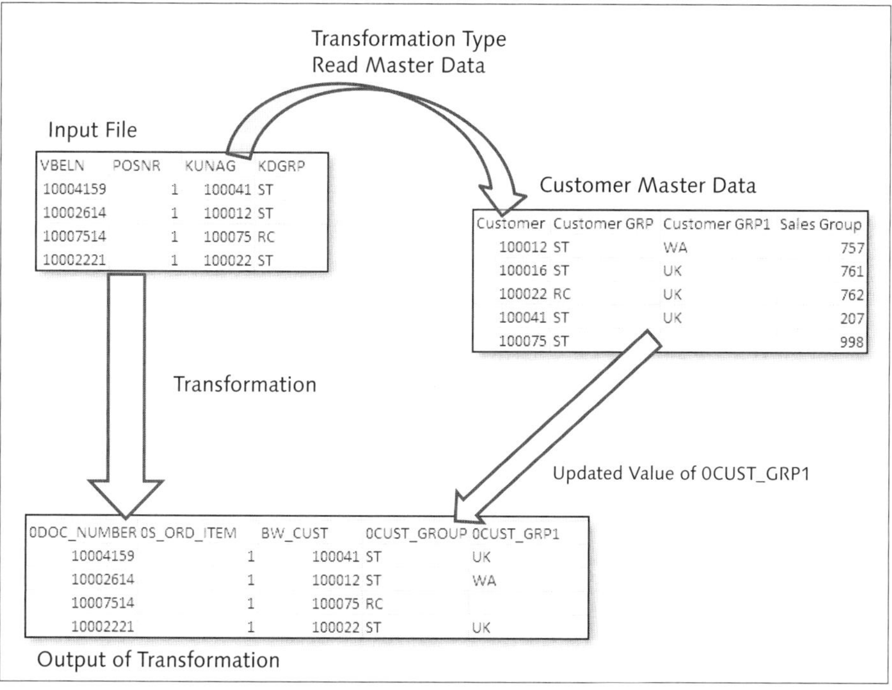

Figure 7.58 Read Master Data Transformation Type

To configure this, select InfoObject 0CUST_GRP1 (❶ of Figure 7.59), and, from the context menu, select Rule Details (❷), a pop-up box for Rule Details appears that shows the details of the target InfoObject (❸) give description for the rule (❹). Now select Read Master Data from the Rule Type dropdown list (❺), and instruct the transformation to read the attribute of InfoObject BW_CUST by clicking the icon shown in ❻.

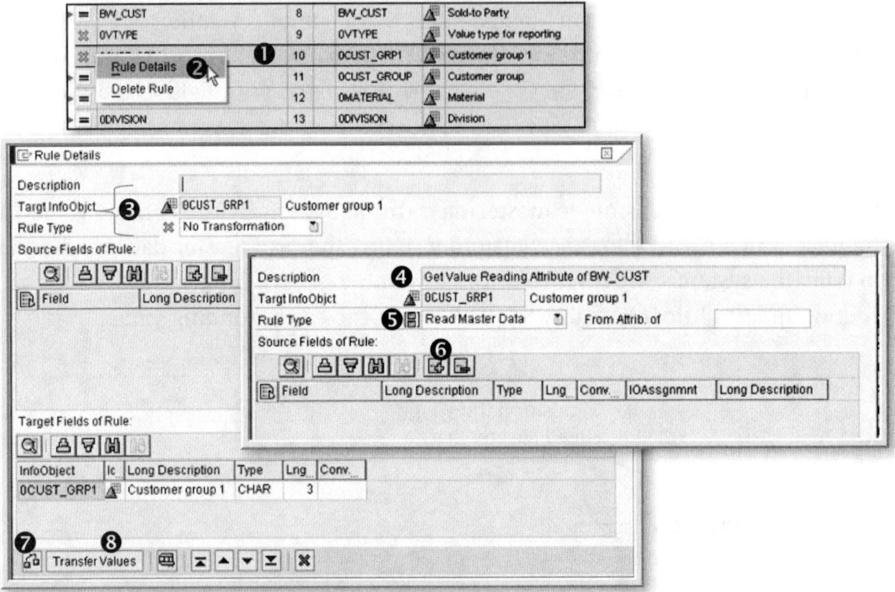

Figure 7.59 Read Master Data Transformation (Part I)

This results in the list shown in ❶ of Figure 7.60, which lists all of the fields from the source object. Select /BIC/BW_CUST (❷), which is available under Source Fields of Rule (❸). Because we need to read the master data from the InfoObject, you must type "BW_CUST" in IOAssgnmnt (InfoObject Assignment) (❹). Press Enter, and select From Attrib. Of (❺). Now press F4, which brings the InfoObject BW_CUST value in this field (❺).

You can check your transformation by clicking on the icon shown earlier in ❼ of Figure 7.59, and then click Transfer Values (❽ of Figure 7.59, shown earlier) to transfer the rule changes for target InfoObject 0CUST_GRP1 to your transformation.

As shown in ❶ of Figure 7.61, the new rule is now available for target InfoObject 0CUST_GRP1 (indicated by ▤).

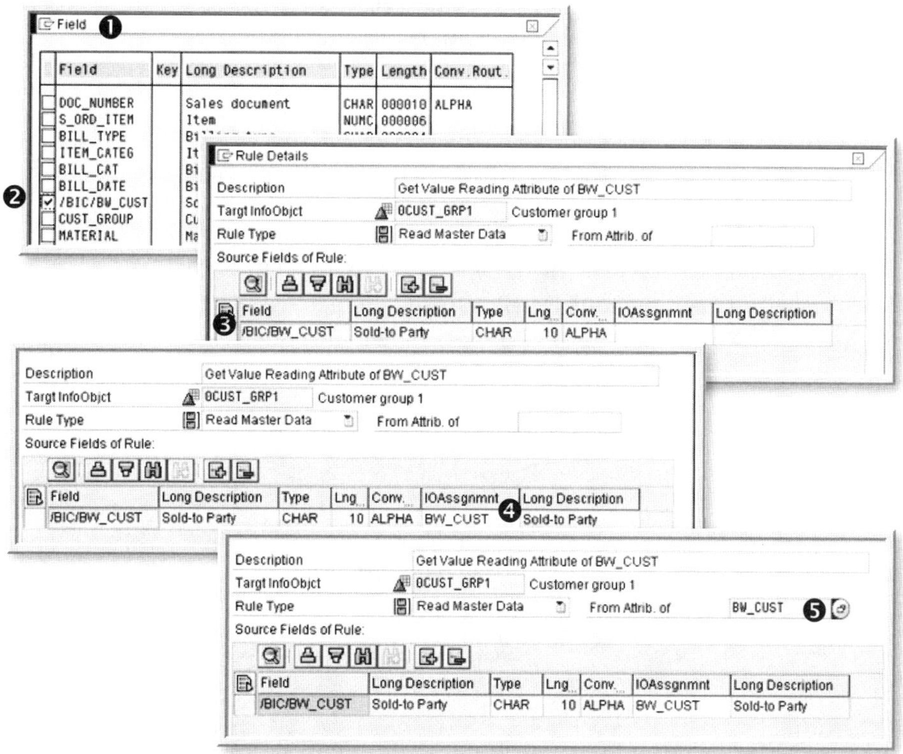

Figure 7.60 Read Master Data Transformation (Part II)

	Source Field	Description			Target		InfoObject
3	BILL_TYPE	Billing type	=	0BILL_CAT		6	0BILL_CAT
4	ITEM_CATEG	Item category	=	0BILL_DATE		7	0BILL_DATE
5	BILL_CAT	Billing category	=	BW_CUST		8	BW_CUST
6	BILL_DATE	Billing doc. date		0VTYPE		9	0VTYPE
7	/BIC/BW_CUST	Sold-to Party	❶	Get Value Reading Attribute of BW_CUST		10	0CUST_GRP1
8	CUST_GROUP	Customer group	=	0CUST_GROUP		11	0CUST_GROUP

Figure 7.61 Read Master Data Transformation Configured

Formula Transformation

Referring to a specific requirement by ABCD Corp. in Chapter 1, whenever the value of a record in the billing document goes above $10,000 USD, the transaction is identified as a high-value transaction, and the billing document is marked with an indicator to differentiate it from those with lower transaction values. We've used the InfoObject 0VTYPE for identifying the record as high value or low value. When using transformations, we need to derive the value for InfoObject 0VTYPE because the data for this is also not available from the DataSource; we perform this derivation using the Net Value field and the *formula* transformation type.

Assume the following:

- If the net value is equal to 0, Value Type = 000.
- If the absolute net value is greater than or equal to 10000, Value Type = 001.
- In all other cases, Value Type = 002.

Select the target object 0VTYPE (❶ of Figure 7.61) in the transformation screen, and double-click it to open the Rule Details screen (alternatively, you can open the context menu). The rule details for 0VTYPE are shown in Figure 7.62.

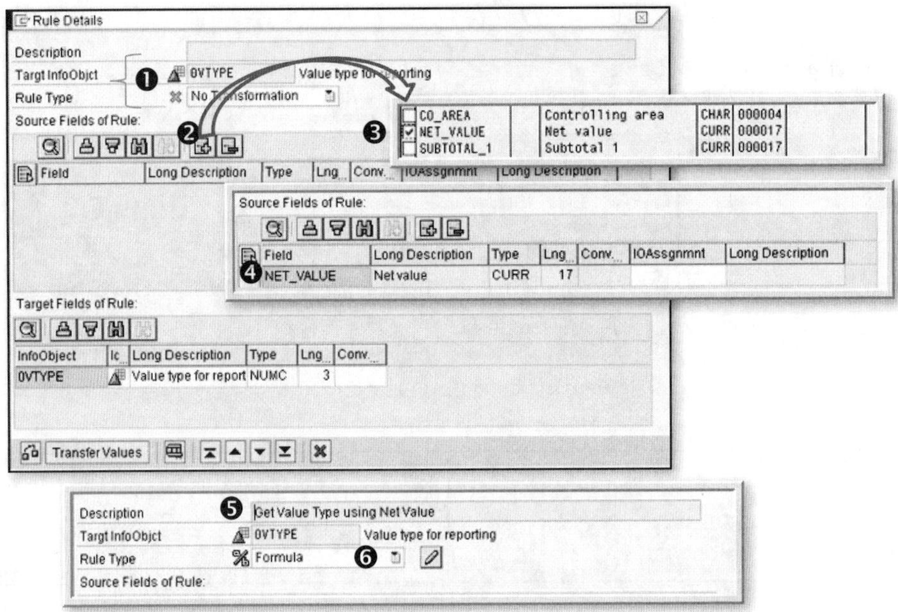

Figure 7.62 Selecting the Formula Transformation Type

To use the Net Value field to derive the value of 0VTYPE, you must add the field under Source Fields of Rule. To do this, click on the icon shown in ❷ of Figure 7.62. This results in ❸. Select NET_VALUE, and click on the Continue icon. NET_VALUE is now available under Source Fields of Rule (❹).

Enter a description for this transformation rule (❺), and then select Formula from the Rule Type dropdown list (❻). This action results in the Formula Builder screen shown in Figure 7.63.

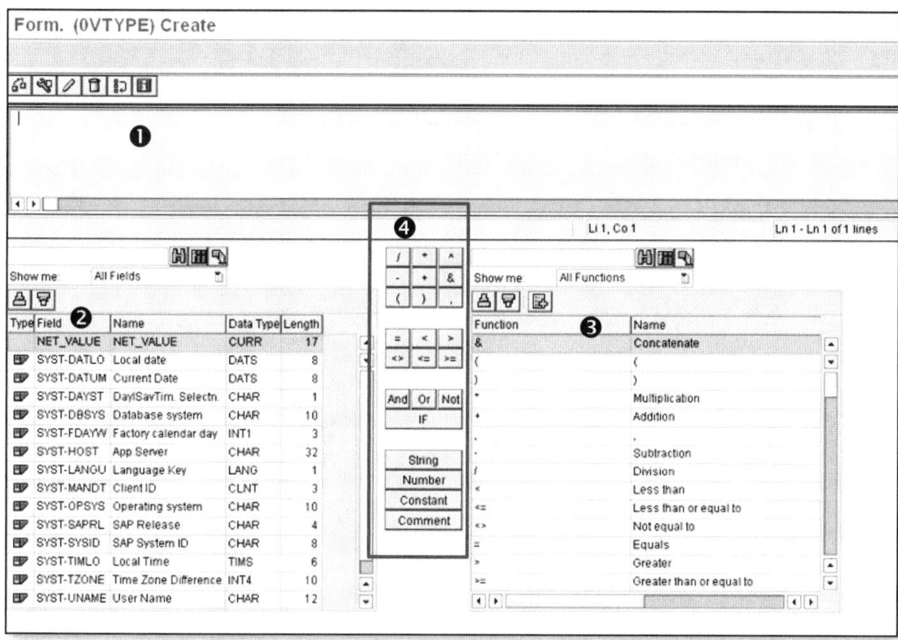

Figure 7.63 Formula Builder

The Formula Builder is a simple but powerful tool that allows nonprogrammers to create simple or complex formulas. It's divided into four different areas: an area to define your formula (❶ of Figure 7.63), an area where you can select the fields for the transformation (❷), standard functions (❸), and various operators used to define formulas (❹).

To derive values of 0VTYPE using NET_VALUE, click on operators (❹), fields (❷), and functions (❸) to include it in the formula definition area. You may need to enter a value with the use of the keyboard. When selecting the field and function (❷ and ❸), you need to double click.

The formula we want to create using Formula Builder is

```
IF( NET_VALUE >= 10,000 OR NET_VALUE <= 10,000-, '001', IF( NET_VALUE =
0, '000', '002' ) )
```

The building of the formula is shown step by step in Figure 7.64 and continued in Figure 7.65:

1. Click on IF; the formula definition area shows you IF(,).
2. Double-click NET_VALUE; the formula definition area changes to IF(NET_VALUE ,)

3. Click Number, and enter "10000"; the definition area now changes to IF(NET_VALUE >= 10,000|,).

The cursor position is very important when defining a formula. Moving the cursor one position to its right must be done explicitly, before any other click; this is also shown under the Enter Manual Value column in Figure 7.64.

Button to Click on Formula Builder	Enter Manual Value	How Formula Looks
IF		IF(|,)
NET_VALUE		IF(NET_VALUE|,)
Number	10000	IF(NET_VALUE >= 10,000|,)
>=		IF(NET_VALUE >=|,)
Or		IF(NET_VALUE >= 10,000 OR|,)
NET_VALUE		IF(NET_VALUE >= 10,000 OR NET_VALUE|,)
<=		IF(NET_VALUE >= 10,000 OR NET_VALUE <=|,)
Number	-10000	IF(NET_VALUE >= 10,000 OR NET_VALUE <= 10,000-|,)
	Move the cursor to 1 place right	IF(NET_VALUE >= 10,000 OR NET_VALUE <= 10,000-,|)
String	001	IF(NET_VALUE >= 10,000 OR NET_VALUE <= 10,000-, '001|)
	Move the cursor to 1 place right	IF(NET_VALUE >= 10,000 OR NET_VALUE <= 10,000-, '001'|)
		Cont...

Figure 7.64 Building a Formula Using Formula Builder (Part I)

Button to Click on Formula Builder	Enter Manual Value/Action	How Formula Looks
IF		IF(NET_VALUE >= 10,000 OR NET_VALUE <= 10,000-, '001', IF(|,))
NET_VALUE		IF(NET_VALUE >= 10,000 OR NET_VALUE <= 10,000-, '001', IF(NET_VALUE|,))
=		IF(NET_VALUE >= 10,000 OR NET_VALUE <= 10,000-, '001', IF(NET_VALUE =,))
Number	0	IF(NET_VALUE >= 10,000 OR NET_VALUE <= 10,000-, '001', IF(NET_VALUE = 0|,))
	Move the cursor to 1 place right	IF(NET_VALUE >= 10,000 OR NET_VALUE <= 10,000-, '001', IF(NET_VALUE = 0,|))
String	000	IF(NET_VALUE >= 10,000 OR NET_VALUE <= 10,000-, '001', IF(NET_VALUE = 0, '000|))
	Move the cursor to 1 place right	IF(NET_VALUE >= 10,000 OR NET_VALUE <= 10,000-, '001', IF(NET_VALUE = 0, '000'|))
String	002	IF(NET_VALUE >= 10,000 OR NET_VALUE <= 10,000-, '001', IF(NET_VALUE = 0, '000', '002'))

Figure 7.65 Building a Formula Using Formula Builder (Part II)

The final formula is shown in the formula definition area of Figure 7.66. You can use the Check icon (❶) to check for any syntax errors. In addition, the Formula Builder offers an expert mode, which you can access by clicking the icon shown in ❷. The expert mode allows you to create formulas using the keyboard.

Click the Back icon (❸) to exit the formula builder and revert to Rule Details (❹), and click Transfer Values (❺) to transfer the formula to the transformation between the DataSource and DSO. You're now back to the main transformation screen.

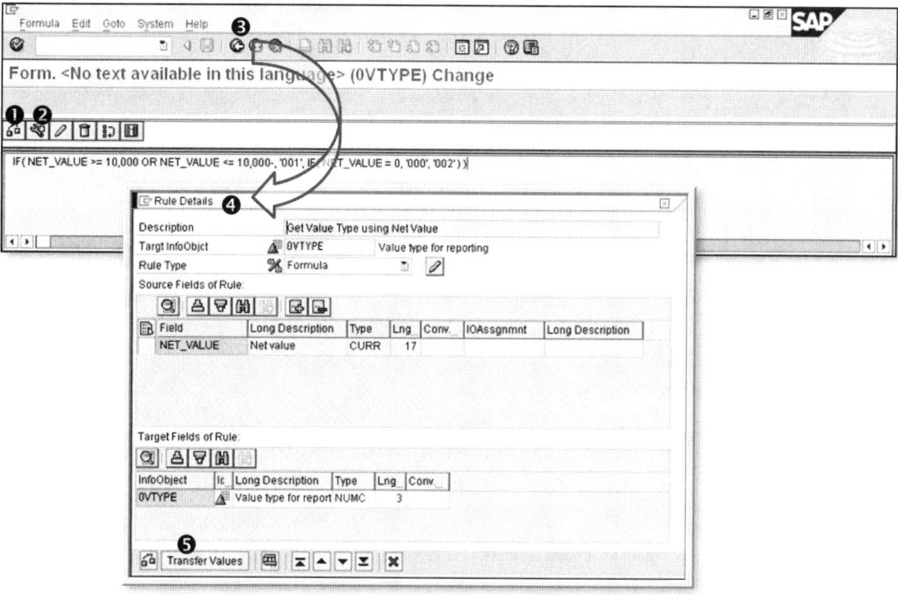

Figure 7.66 Exiting Formula Builder after Checking Formula

The transformation type formula is indicated with the icon shown in ❶ of Figure 7.67.

3	BILL_TYPE	Billing type
4	ITEM_CATEG	Item category
5	BILL_CAT	Billing category
6	BILL_DATE	Billing doc. date
7	/BIC/BW_CUST	Sold-to Party
8	CUST_GROUP	Customer group

0BILL_CAT	6	0BILL_CAT
0BILL_DATE	7	0BILL_DATE
BW_CUST	8	BW_CUST
❶ Get Value Type using Net Value	9	0VTYPE
Get Value Reading Attribute of BW_CUST	10	0CUST_GRP1
0CUST_GROUP	11	0CUST_GROUP

Figure 7.67 Formula Transformation Type Icon

Now you're ready to activate your transformation. Click on the Activate icon (❶). On successful activation, the version of the transformation changes to Active (❷), Now return to the main DWW screen. You can view the transformation between DataSource BWSD_O01_FF_DS_TRAN and DSO BWSD_O01 as shown in ❸ of Figure 7.68.

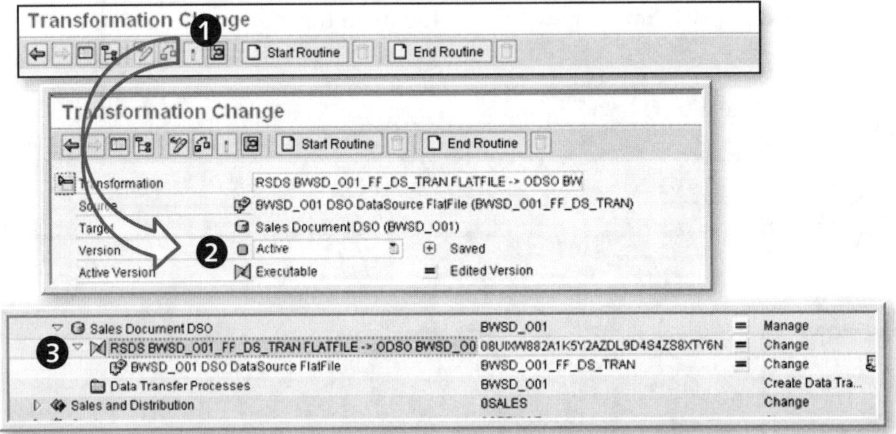

Figure 7.68 Activating the Transformation

You need to create InfoPackages for extracting data, and these InfoPackage will have Initialization set in the Update tab, which needs to be changed to Delta Mode after the successful initialization. You execute DTP for transfer or data from PSA to DSO. You need to activate the loaded request into the DSO and then load it into the InfoCube.

Characteristics Versus Key Figure Transformations

Data targets can have characteristics as well as key figures, and the rule details we've discussed in this section have been specifically for characteristics. Rule details for key figures are similar but offer the additional option of aggregation, as shown in ❸ of Figure 7.69. The Aggregation option specifies how key figures should be stored when the key fields (DSO) and characteristics (InfoCube) have the same value. There are two options available for a key figure InfoObjects in the data field of a DSO: Overwrite and Summation (we also discussed this in Chapter 4, DataStore Object). By default, the aggregation option for key figures of a DSO is set to Overwrite. Because our DataSource delta process is set to After Image, all key figures of the DSO must be set to Overwrite. Rule details for the key figure displays target InfoObject (❶ of figure 7.69) and Rule type (❷ of figure 7.69)

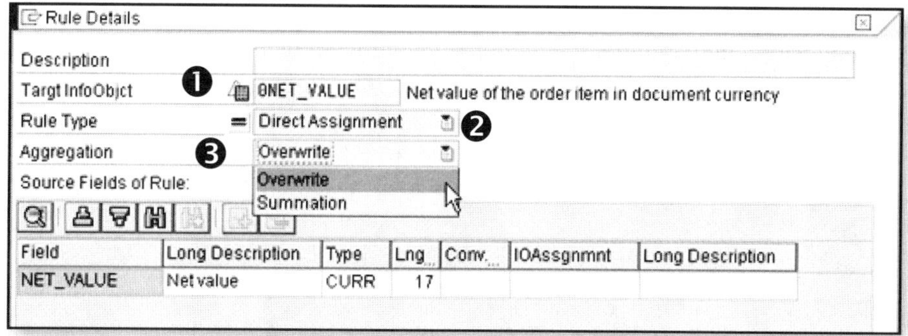

Figure 7.69 Aggregation for Key Figure in Rules Detail

7.4 Loading Data from a DSO to an InfoCube

In the previous section, we discussed the process of loading data to a DSO. Now we want to understand the process of loading a DSO (in our example, DSO BWSD_O01) to an InfoCube (in our example, BWSD_C01). The main difference between these two types of objects is that DSOs store data at the document level, and InfoCubes store data at an aggregated level. As a result, some of the details (document number, item number, date) are removed from the InfoCube definition. In this section, we've used the routine transformation type for meeting another analysis requirement of ABCD Corp. for analyzing the price of a material. This needed a transformation because it isn't being supplied by source.

In this case, the DSO becomes the source of data, so we can say that the source system is the SAP NetWeaver BW system. There are two steps required to complete the task at hand:

1. Create and activate the transformation between the DSO and InfoCube. The process of creating s transformation remains the same as discussed previously; however, we cover additional functionality in this section.
2. Create and execute the DTP between the DSO and the InfoCube. The process of creating the DTP remains the same.

As you can see, this process doesn't have a step involving the creation of a source system because the source system is the SAP NetWeaver BW system (i.e., the *myself* system), and this connection is automatically created. There is also no step required to create a DataSource because the data is already available in the DSO, which acts as the DataSource. As such, the only step we need to address is the creation of a transformation between the DSO and the InfoCube.

In DWW, select the InfoProvider section shown in ❶ of Figure 7.70; then select InfoCube BWSD_C01 from the InfoProvider tree (❷). From the context menu, select Create Transformation (❸), which results in the Create Transformation box (❹). The target object and name are displayed (❺), and the source object and name are blank (❻). Select Data Store Object from the Object Type dropdown list, and enter "BWSD_O01" (❼).

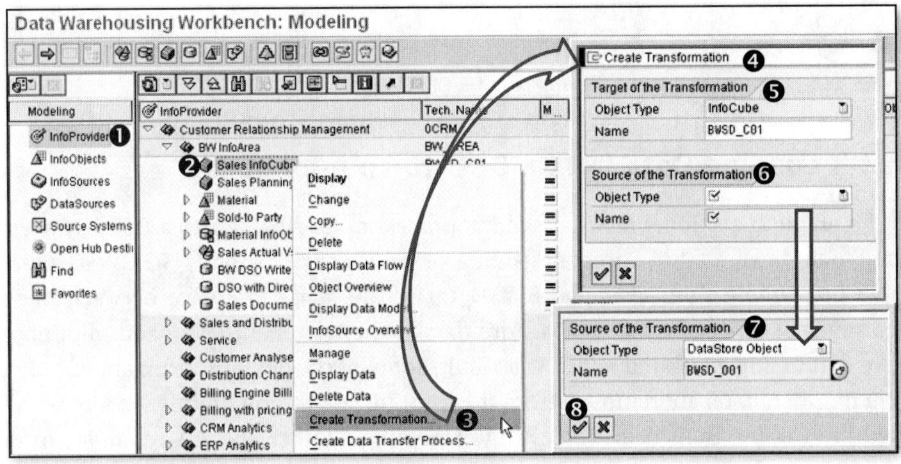

Figure 7.70 Creating Transformation for InfoCube

Click on the Continue icon (❽), which displays the Transformation Create screen in Figure 7.71. The source (Sales Document DSO BWSD_O01) and target (Sales InfoCube BWSD_C01) objects are displayed as shown in ❶ of Figure 7.71. Because the source is a DSO, the left side of the screen displays the names of InfoObjects instead of fields. The system offers direct assignment transformation whenever the name of the InfoObject in the source and target matches.

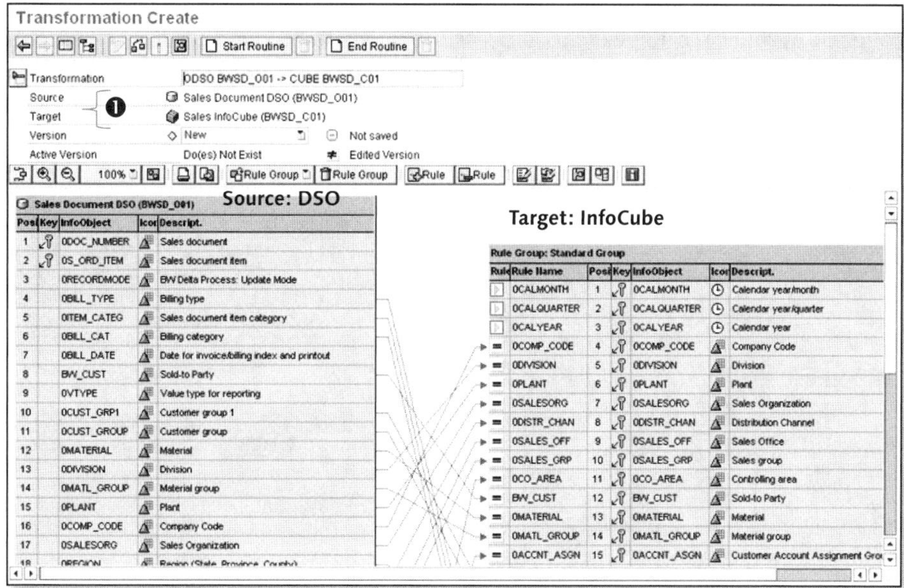

Figure 7.71 Transformation Screen

Per the requirement scenario for ABCD Corp., while loading the data from DSO to InfoCube, we apply two types of transformation, one using the time conversion transformation and the other using the routine transformation.

> **Note**
>
> Time conversion applies only to InfoCube transformations, which is why we didn't discuss it earlier in the chapter.

7.4.1 Time Conversion Transformation

The DSO contains a Billing Date InfoObject (0BILL_DATE), whereas in the InfoCube we've decided not to store the data at the date level because it's granular and not required in most analyses; instead, we store it at the month, quarter, and year levels. So, we must match the source InfoObject 0BILL_DATE to target InfoObjects 0CALMONTH, 0CALQUARTER, and 0CALYEAR. This type of transformation is known as a *time conversion*.

As shown in ❶ of Figure 7.72, the system doesn't propose any transformations for the target InfoObjects because there are no matching source InfoObjects available; to fix this, you must associate 0BILL_DATE with the three target InfoObjects

(0CALMONTH, 0CALQUARTER, and 0CALYEAR). Select 0BILL_DATE (❷), and drop it over 0CALMONTH. Repeat this process for 0CALQUARTER and 0CALYEAR. The result of these activities is shown in ❸ of Figure 7.72.

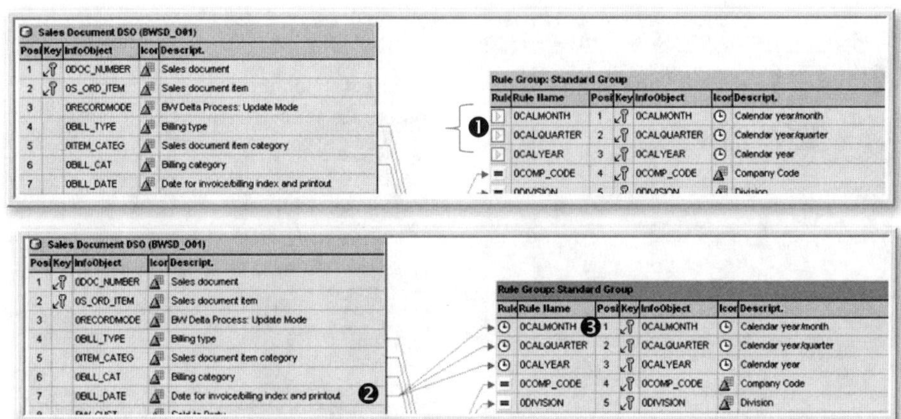

Figure 7.72 Time Conversion Transformation

7.4.2 Routine

Our example InfoCube has a BW_PRICE key figure (indicating the price of an item in the document currency), as shown in ❶ of Figure 7.73. The DSO that acts as a DataSource doesn't have any key figures that match BW_PRICE, so we must derive the value of this key figure using values from 0NET_VALUE and BW_QTY by an ABAP code program. This type of transformation is known as *routine*. We could alternatively meet the same requirement using a formula transformation type.

Open the Rule Details pop-up box by double-clicking BW_PRICE, as shown in ❶ of Figure 7.73. The InfoObject and rule type are displayed (❷). (Unlike DSOs, InfoCubes don't allow overwriting; aggregation only offers summation.) Enter an appropriate description (❸). Because this key figure has a currency associated with it, we use the *routine with unit* transformation type (❹); this results in the display of currency information (❺). The target currency is 0DOC_CURRCY, as this is associated with BW_PRICE (❻).

Routine Versus Routine with Unit

The routine transformation type allows you to return only one value. When you have a key figure associated with a unit or currency, you must use the routine with unit type for the system to return both values.

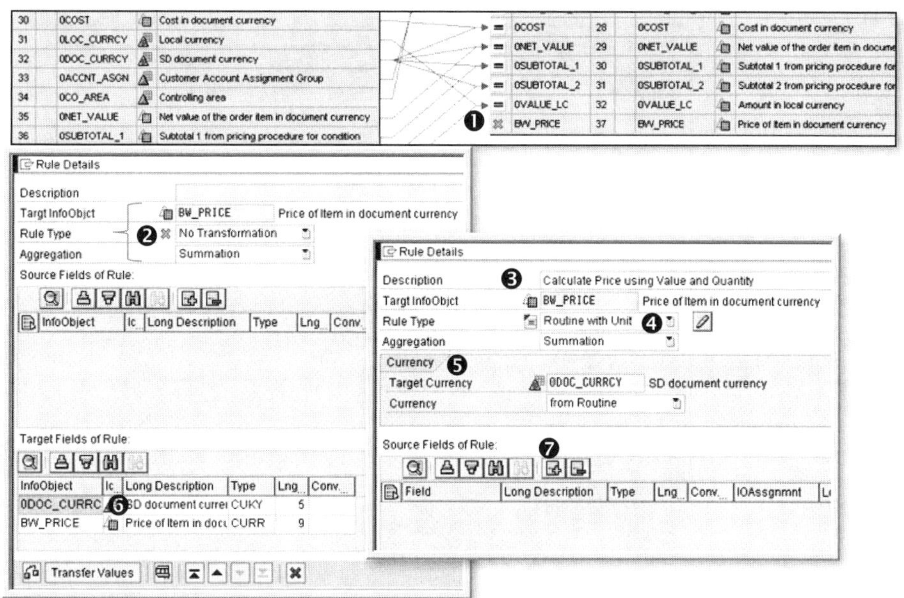

Figure 7.73 ABAP Routine Transformation Type (Part I)

Because we need to use the values of 0NET_VALUE, BW_QTY, and 0DOC_CURRCY in the ABAP routine, click on the icon shown in ❼ of Figure 7.73. This action results in the pop-up box shown in ❶ of Figure 7.74. Select InfoObjects BW_QTY, 0UNIT, 0DOC_CURRCY, and 0NET_VALUE, as shown in ❶ of Figure 7.74. Click on the Continue icon (❷), and you can see that the selected fields are available under Source Fields of Rule (❸), making them available for use in an ABAP routine for any calculation.

Click on the Change icon (❹) to invoke the ABAP editor (Figure 7.75). In the ABAP routine, we calculate the value of BW_QTY by using the following formula:

```
BW_PRICE = NET_VALUE / BW_QTY.
```

ABAP routines follow certain naming conventions. The input values are available in the ABAP routine with the prefix source_fields_rule or source_fields and the internal name of the InfoObject; for example, InfoObject 0NET_VALUE is referred to as source_fields_rule-net_value. There's normally one return value of an ABAP routine, which is available in the RESULT field. Whenever you use the ABAP routine with the unit transformation type, you get one more return value for the unit or currency value.

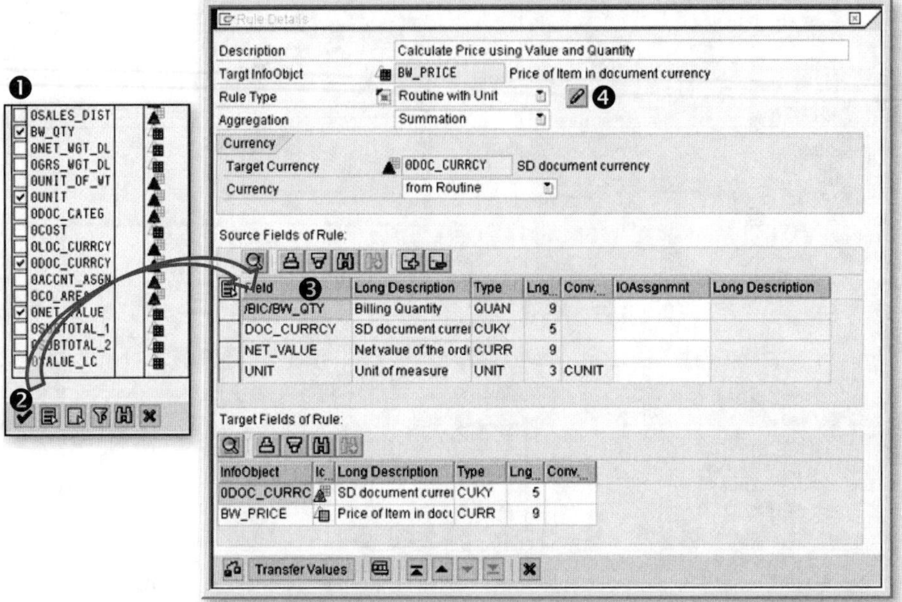

Figure 7.74 ABAP Routine Transformation Type (Part II)

Replace the lines shown in ❶ of Figure 7.75 with the lines shown in ❷ of Figure 7.75. Check your ABAP routine using the Check icon (❸ of Figure 7.75), and save the ABAP routine (❹).

Return to the Rule Details box using the Back icon, and click on Transfer Values to return to the main transformation screen (Figure 7.76). The ABAP routine transformation type is attached to BW_PRICE, as shown in ❶ of Figure 7.76, and indicated by [icon]. Activate the transformation by clicking the Activate icon (❷). Upon successfully activation, the version is displayed as Active (❸).

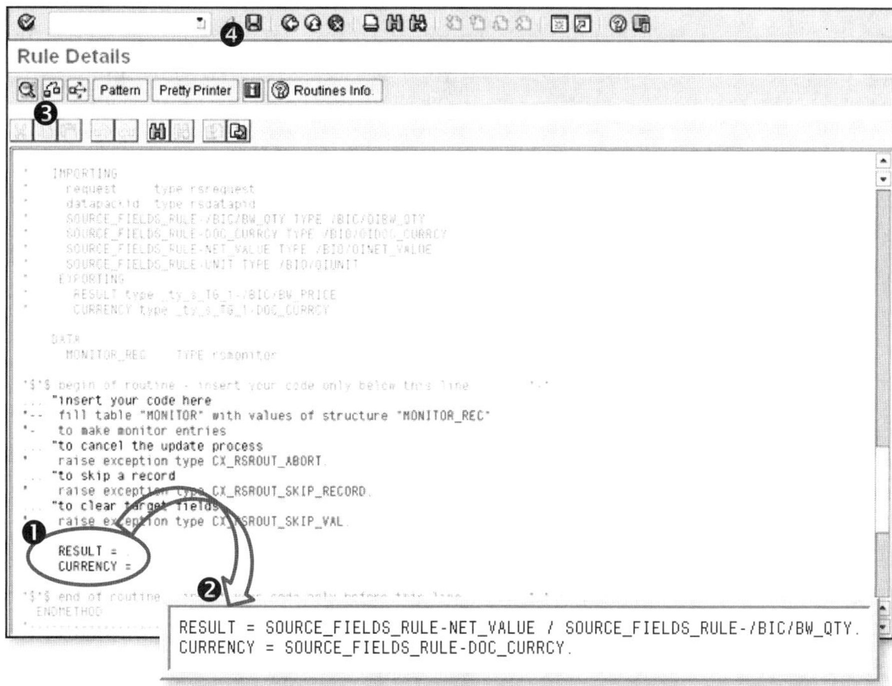

Figure 7.75 ABAP Routine

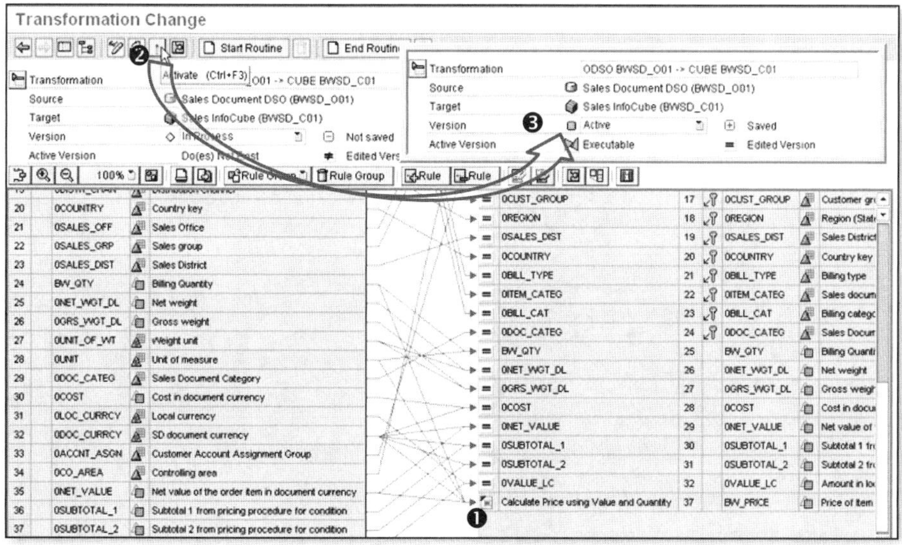

Figure 7.76 Activating the Transformation

Use the Back icon to return to DWW, and the newly created transformation is displayed. To extract data from the DSO, you must create a DTP between the DSO and InfoCube; we've already discussed this earlier in the chapter, so we won't cover it again here.

Execute DTP. After the DTP execution is complete, the data is successfully loaded to our example InfoCube BWSD_C01. We can now create BEx queries and evaluate billing data. (The creation of queries is covered in subsequent chapters.) A number of administrative tasks can also be performed on this InfoCube, which are covered in Chapter 14, Administration and Monitoring.

Now that you understand the basic ETL process using a flat file source system, we'll explain the two technical components of the loading process: temporary storage areas and error stacks.

7.5 Temporary Storage Areas and Error Stacks

When loading data into a data target, the system includes a number of standard checks to make sure everything is going smoothly; you can also customize checks based on your requirements. If any of these checks result in the identification of errors, SAP NetWeaver BW stores the erroneous records in a separate container called the *error stack*. After these records are corrected, they are again loaded into the data target using a special DTP called the *error DTP*. The overall position of the error stack during the loading process is shown in Figure 7.77.

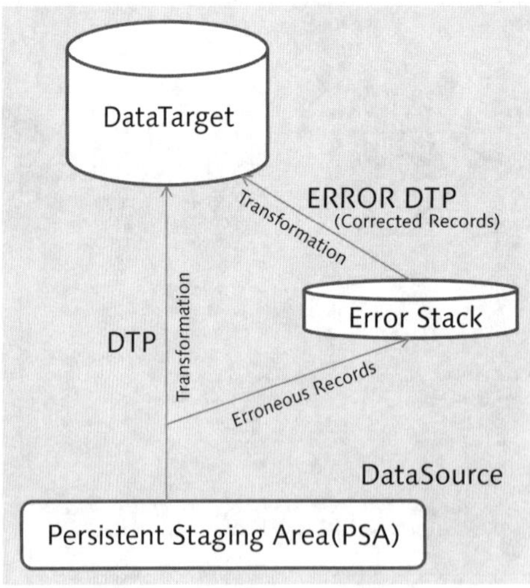

Figure 7.77 Position of Error Stack

In this section, we explain the temporary storage area (which is an important part of correcting erroneous records), the process of configuring standard integrity checks and viewing the errors that result from these checks, and the process of loading corrected records via the error DTP.

Temporary Storage

At this point, we should introduce another function offered by SAP NetWeaver BW: *temporary storage*. Once configured, this function stores data in various stages of transformation in a separate area known as the temporary storage area, which contains both correct and erroneous records and displays their current status. During complex transformations, this informs you of the exact processing step in which problems are encountered.

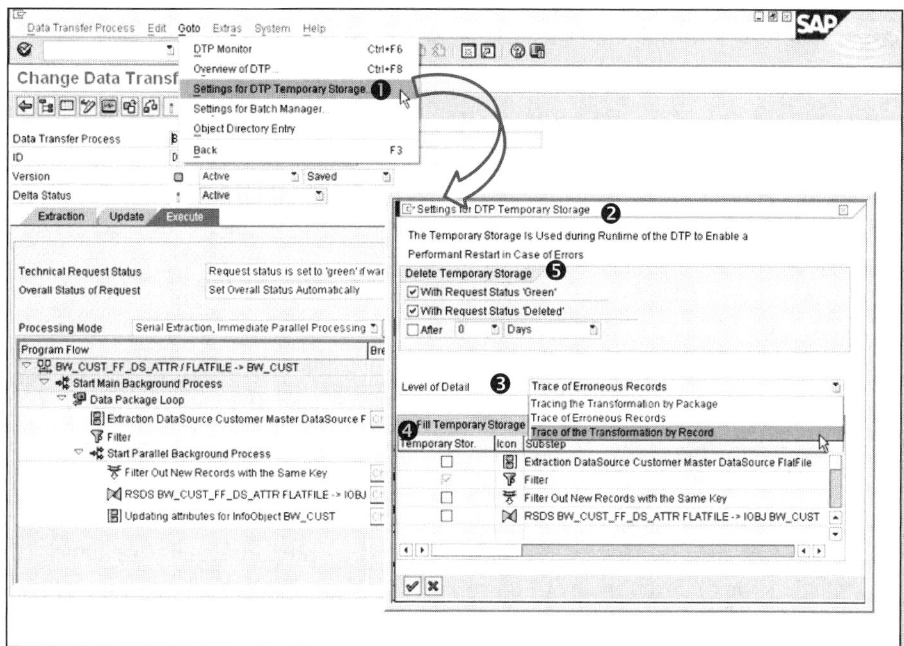

Figure 7.78 Configuring Temporary Storage

You can configure temporary storage from the DTP configuration screen, as shown in Figure 7.78. Use the menu path GOTO • SETTINGS FOR DTP TEMPORARY STORAGE (❶). This action results in the Settings for DTP Temporary Storage screen (❷), which allows you to trace records to various levels of detail (❸). You can define the step in the sequence of processing substeps to fill the temporary storage (❹). Standard processing substeps are available here, and you can select multiple steps, if required. As shown in ❺, you can instruct the system when to delete data stored in the temporary storage area.

Note

Configuring the temporary storage functionality is optional.

Configuring Integrity Checks and Viewing Errors in Temporary Storage

InfoObject BW_CUST has one attribute, 0CUST_GRP1. When loading master data for BW_CUST, the flat file has a value for the 0CUST_GRP1 attribute for each value contained in BW_CUST. We want the system to check the value of 0CUST_GRP1 for each customer; this check is performed in the master data table of InfoObject 0CUST_GRP1. If the value isn't found in the table associated with 0CUST_GRP1, the master data record of BW_CUST should be stored in the error stack.

Let's explore this concept more thoroughly by using an example. Figure 7.79 shows a new data file to be loaded into InfoObject BW_CUST. There are three customers, each with a different value for Customer GRP1. Assume that, at this moment, Customer GRP1 value WA is already loaded as master data (in tables associated with the Customer GRP1 InfoObject), but values BK and AP aren't loaded as Customer GRP1 master data.

Customer	Customer GRP	Customer GRP1	Sales Group	Sales District	Sales Office	Sales Employee	Date From	Date To
100095	ST	WA	757	2717	3103	41	20000101	20081231
100096	ST	BK	757	2717	3103	42	20090101	99991231
100097	ST	AP	757	2717	3103	40	20090101	99991231

Figure 7.79 Sample Data for Error Stack

As we said, we must configure an integrity check so that the system checks the value of 0CUST_GRP1 for each respective value of the customer. You therefore check the Integrity checkbox shown in ❶ of Figure 7.80.

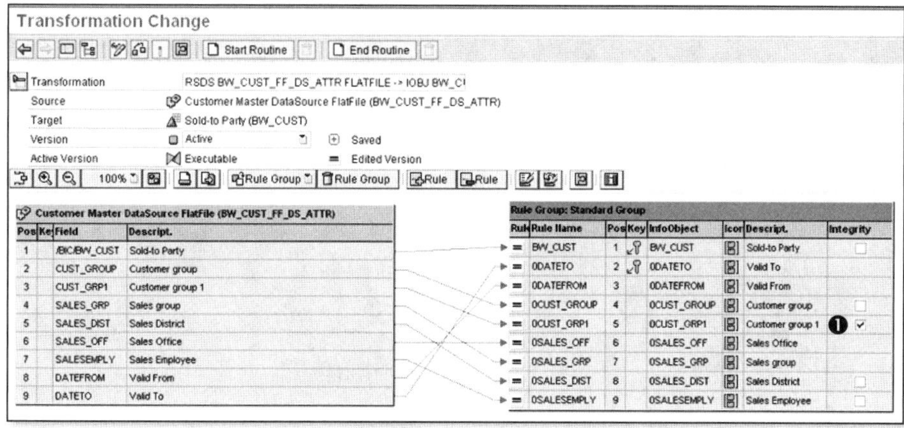

Figure 7.80 Setting an Integrity Check

Now that the check is set, we can load the data from the sample file to PSA. The data in PSA is shown in Figure 7.81. There is no error yet; transformations aren't executed while moving data to PSA.

PSA Maintenance

Data records to be edited

Status	DataPacket	Data Rec.	Sold-to Party	Customer g	Customer g	Sales grou	Sales Dist	Sales Offi	Sales Empl	Valid From	Valid To
▢	1	1	0000100095	ST	WA	757	2717	3103	41	01.01.2000	31.12.2008
▢	1	2	0000100096	ST	BK	757	2717	3103	42	01.01.2009	31.12.9999
▢	1	3	0000100097	ST	AP	757	2717	3103	40	01.01.2009	31.12.9999

Figure 7.81 Data Loaded into PSA Without Error

Now execute DTP and start the DTP monitor. This time, DTP is unsuccessful, which is indicated by the red status in ❶ of Figure 7.82 (the load failed because the BK and AP values aren't loaded as part of the Customer GRP1 master data). As shown in ❷, the displayed message indicates that loading has encountered an error. (You can see the detailed message by clicking on the icon shown in ❸.)

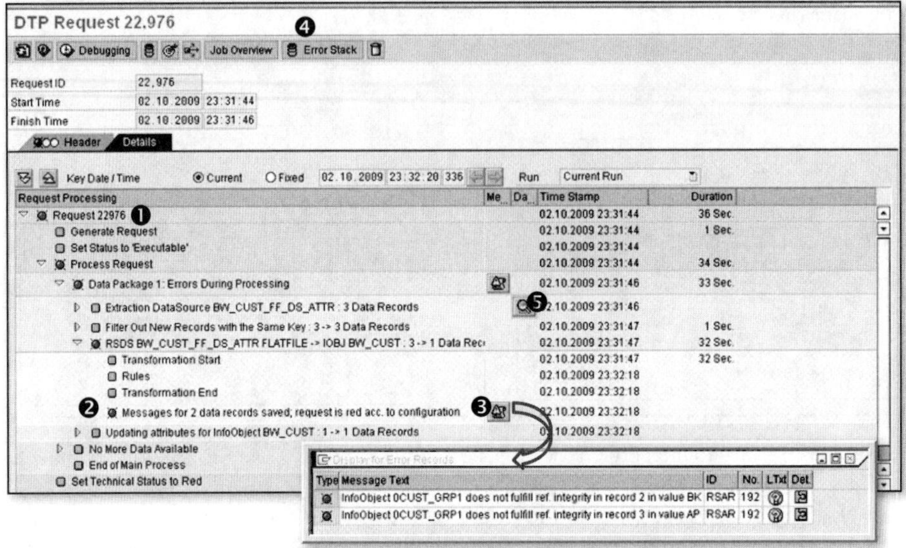

Figure 7.82 Error During Loading

Viewing the records in the error stack is the same as viewing the data in PSA; to do so, click the Error Stack button (❹). This displays the Error Stack box shown in ❶ of Figure 7.83. Each data packet and its number of records are listed (❷ of Figure 7.83). Select the data packet, and click the Continue icon (❸), which opens the box shown in ❹. All of the erroneous records from the selected data packet are listed in this screen. To view the error details for a particular record, select the record and double-click the icon shown in ❺. The error detail for the selected record is shown in another pop-up box (❻). To correct value errors, select the record, and click the Change icon ( ).

To view records in temporary storage, click on the icon shown in ❺ Figure 7.82. The result of this action is the Display Temporary Storage screen shown in Figure 7.84. Each record has a status (❶); indicates that the record has no errors, and indicates that the record is erroneous and stored in the error stack.

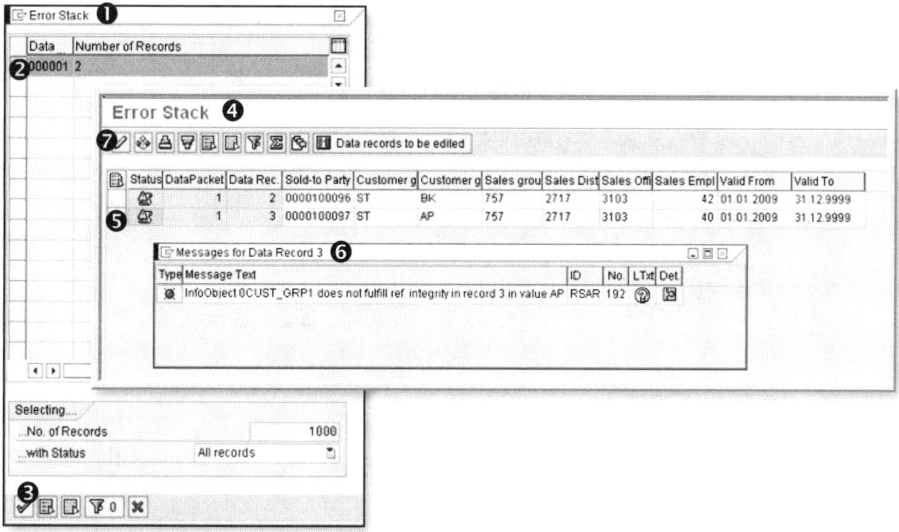

Figure 7.83 Data in the Error Stack

Display Temporary Storage

Segment 0001

RE	Status	/BIC/BW_CUST	CU	CUST	SALES	SALES_DIST	SALES_	SALESEMPLY	DATEFROM	DATETO
1		100095	ST	WA	757	2717	3103	41	01.01.2000	31.12.2008
2		100096	ST	BK	757	2717	3103	42	01.01.2009	31.12.9999
3		100097	ST	AP	757	2717	3103	40	01.01.2009	31.12.9999

Figure 7.84 Records in Temporary Storage

Creating and Monitoring the Error DTP

To fix the errors in this example, you must load the BK and AP values as master data for InfoObject 0CUST_GRP1; assume that this has now been done. After the errors have been corrected, you can create the error DTP. In the DTP maintenance screen, select the Update tab shown in ❶ of Figure 7.85. Click on the Creating Error DTP button (❷), and the error DTP is created (❸). (You can switch to a standard DTP by clicking on the Associated Standard DTP button (❹).

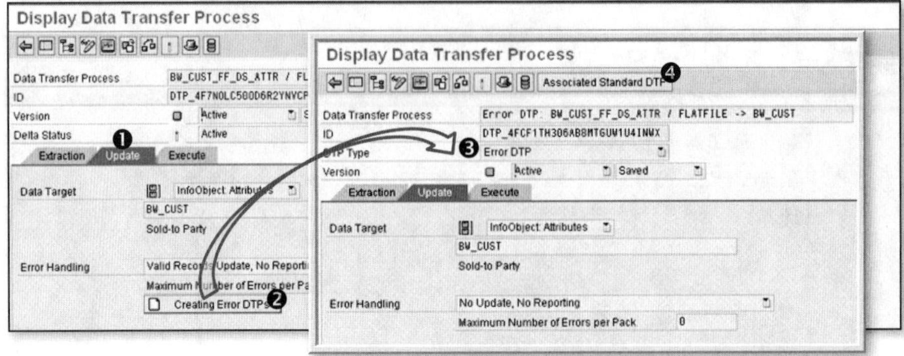

Figure 7.85 Creating an Error DTP

Refer ❶ of figure 7.86 showing the DTP Type as Error DTP, now select the Execute tab (❷ of Figure 7.86), and start the execution of the error DTP by clicking the Execute button (❸).

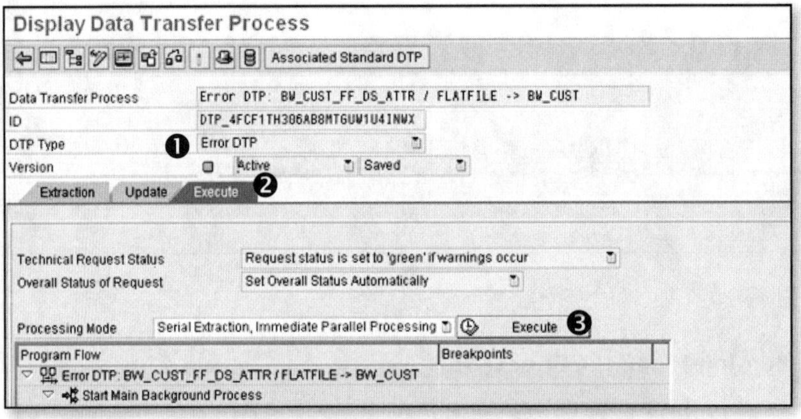

Figure 7.86 Executing Error DTP

This brings you to the monitor screen of the error DTP, as shown in Figure 7.87. This time, instead of extracting records from a DataSource, the system is extracting them from the error stack (❶). Because the error has been addressed, the request status is successful (green) (❷), and the system deletes the record from the error stack.

The error DTP can be seen in the DWW under data target BW_CUST, as shown in ❶ Figure 7.88. The same error DTP can be used every time the standard DTP encounters errors (after taking corrective action, of course).

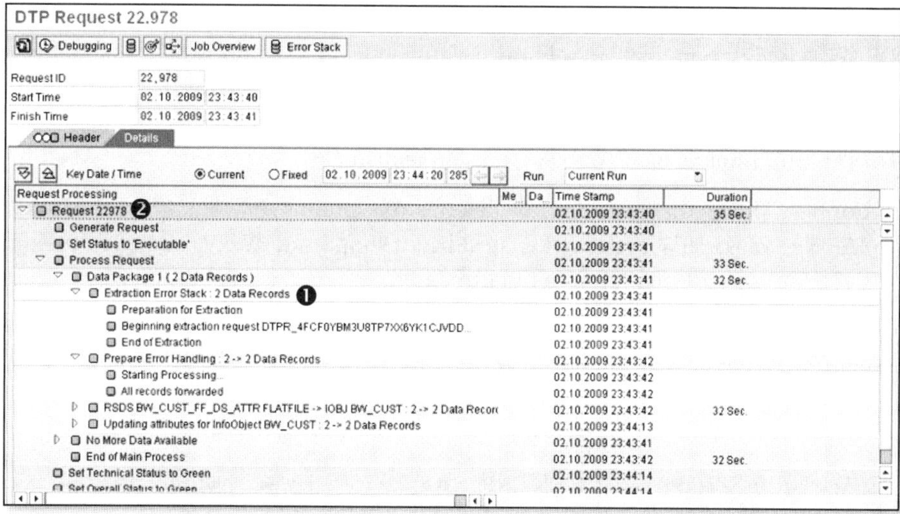

Figure 7.87 Monitoring Error DTP

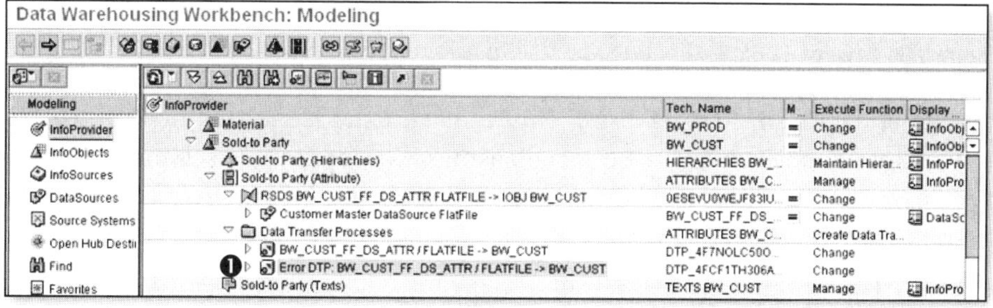

Figure 7.88 Error DTP in DWW

In this section, we explained the ETL process using a flat file source system. In the following section, we introduce other extraction interfaces for extraction from non-SAP systems, specifically DB Connect and UD Connect.

7.6 Data Extraction from Non-SAP systems

The open architecture of SAP NetWeaver BW gives it the flexibility to extract data from a large variety of sources. In this section, we provide a brief introduction to the extraction of data from relational database management systems (RDBMS) using DB Connect, and multidimensional sources using UD Connect.

7.6.1 DB Connect

RDBMS is a very popular way of storing business application data. To extract data from RDBMS, SAP NetWeaver BW offers two different mechanisms, DB Connect and UD Connect. Here we focus on DB Connect specifically; UD Connect, which is also used for multidimensional sources, is discussed later.

DB Connect allows the extraction of data from a number of popular RDBMSs into the SAP NetWeaver BW system; the latest list of supported RDBMSs can be obtained from the SAP service marketplace (Figure 7.89).

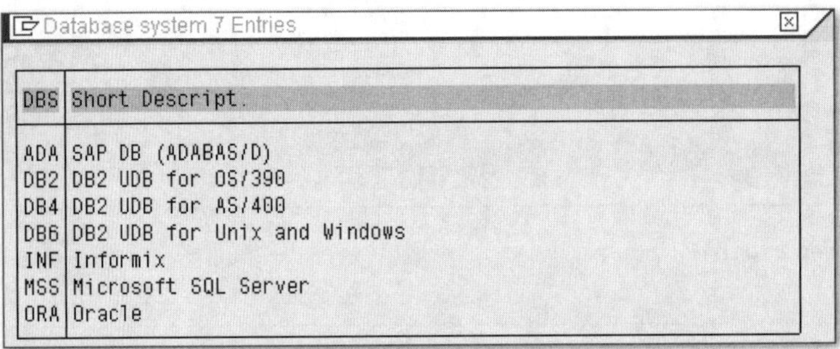

Database system 7 Entries

DBS	Short Descript.
ADA	SAP DB (ADABAS/D)
DB2	DB2 UDB for OS/390
DB4	DB2 UDB for AS/400
DB6	DB2 UDB for Unix and Windows
INF	Informix
MSS	Microsoft SQL Server
ORA	Oracle

Figure 7.89 List of RDBMSs supported by DB Connect

To extract data from RDBMS using DB Connect, database shared libraries (DBSL) of the source database must be installed on each application server in the SAP NetWeaver BW landscape. This is illustrated in Figure 7.90, where two different scenarios are displayed.

Scenario 1 has both source application data and SAP NetWeaver BW data stored on an Oracle RDBMS; as such, there is no need to install DBSL on SAP NetWeaver BW system's application server. In the second scenario, the source application data is stored using an Informix RDBMS, but the SAP NetWeaver BW server stores data in an Oracle RDBMS. In this case, Informix's DBSL must be installed on the SAP NetWeaver BW application server.

You also require a database-specific DB client with the database manufacturer in both the scenarios. Execute the steps as follows:

1. Create a source system for the external database using DB Connect.
2. Create a DB Connect source system from the Source System section of Modeling in the DWW. Different kinds of RDBMSs expect various parameters for source system connections; OSS notes are available for connecting to each supported RDBMS (see *http://service.sap.com/notes*)

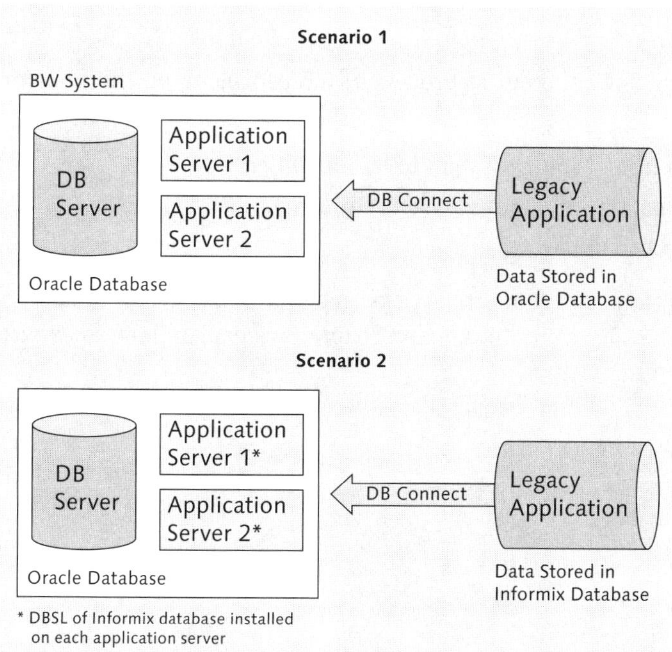

Figure 7.90 DB Connect Overview

3. Create a DataSource by selecting a view or table from the source RDBMS.
4. Create a transformation between the DataSource and the data target.
5. Create a DTP between the DataSource and the data target.
6. Create an InfoPackage for the DataSource (connected to the DB Connect source system).
7. Execute the InfoPackage.
8. Execute the DTP.

These steps load the data into the SAP NetWeaver BW data target, which can be a master data InfoObject, DSO, or InfoCube.

7.6.2 UD Connect

UD Connect allows the extraction of data stored in multidimensional structures (such as those created by Hyperion or Cognos). It also allows data extraction from RDBMSs. The prerequisite for using UD Connect is the installation of the J2EE engine in the SAP NetWeaver BW system. The steps for extracting data using UD Connect are the same as those of DB Connect.

7.7 Summary

In this chapter, we explained the entire process of ETL, focusing on three major processes:

- Loading master data from a source system to an InfoObject.
- Loading transaction data from a source system to a DSO.
- Loading a DSO to an InfoCube.

We concluded with an explanation of error stacks, and a brief discussion of how to extract data from a non-SAP system. In the next chapter, we explain how to extract data from an SAP ERP system.

In this chapter, we describe the process of data extraction from SAP source systems. We briefly explain the SAP Business Content DataSource for billing data, extracting data from an SAP system using a generic extractor, and checking the extraction process by using the extractor checker tool.

8 Extraction from an SAP Source System

In the previous chapter, we described the ETL process in SAP NetWeaver BW. In this chapter, we discuss the extraction from SAP source systems in more detail and the process of configuring the SAP ERP source system to support data extraction.

DataSource

A DataSource is a structure where source system fields are logically grouped together and contain ETL-related information. Four types of DataSources exist: for transaction data, for master data attributes, for master data texts, and for master data hierarchies. If the source system is R/3, replicating DataSources creates identical DataSource structures in the SAP NetWeaver BW system.

Having SAP ERP (and other SAP systems such as CRM, SCM, etc.) as a source system is the best way to gain the most from SAP Business Content, which offers an extremely large number of DataSources that support a wide range of analysis requirements. For those requirements that aren't met by using SAP Business Content, you can create a DataSource based on your own logic. Such a custom DataSource is called a *generic DataSource.*

In this chapter, we begin our discussion by describing the settings that must be configured in SAP ERP for it to act as a source system. We then move on to the topic of activating SAP Business Content DataSources, which needs to be done to use them, and explain how you can extract data from DataSources by using the Logistics Cockpit. If you want to use a custom DataSource, you must create and configure a generic DataSource, which is the topic of the next section. If you want this generic DataSource to be delta-capable, you must perform another set of steps, which is discussed in the section after that. Finally, we conclude with a brief description of the Extractor Checker tool.

8.1 Settings in SAP ERP

Specific settings have to be configured in the SAP ERP source system, including the activation of the DataSources in SAP Business Content and the performance tuning of the extraction process. We'll now explain some of the important settings and their relevance.

Select Transaction SBIW in the source system. The screen that appears is shown in Figure 8.1. This displays various settings and configuration options related to data extraction from SAP ERP to SAP NetWeaver BW. As shown in the figure, some of these settings can be directly called using a transaction code (e.g., Transaction RSA7 for Check Delta Queue), while other settings can only be invoked using the menu path (e.g., Maintain Control Parameters for Data Transfer).

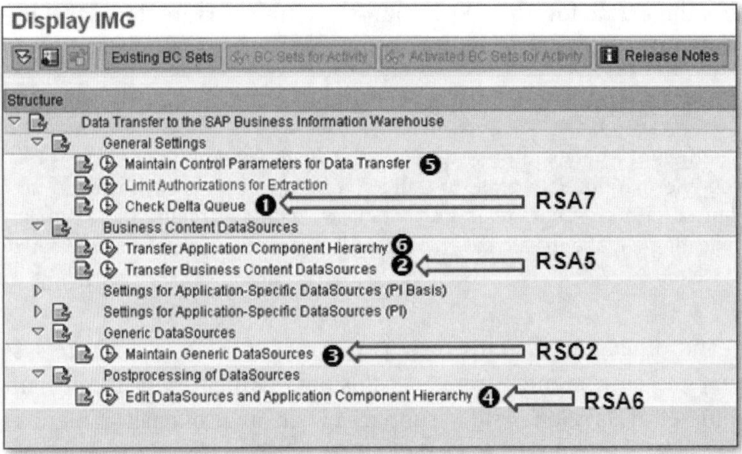

Figure 8.1 Settings in the SAP ERP Source System

8.2 Activating Business Content DataSources

For our case study, we need to use the DataSource that extracts the billing transaction data; the SAP Business Content DataSource for billing transaction data (with item level information) is 2LIS_13_VDITM. To use this DataSource, you must first activate it. In this section, we explain that process.

To activate a DataSource, use Transaction RSA5 in the SAP ERP source system. All of the SAP Business Content DataSources (transaction as well as master data) are listed in a hierarchical manner (❶ of Figure 8.2) and grouped together based on the functional area or business process. These groups are called application components (❶).

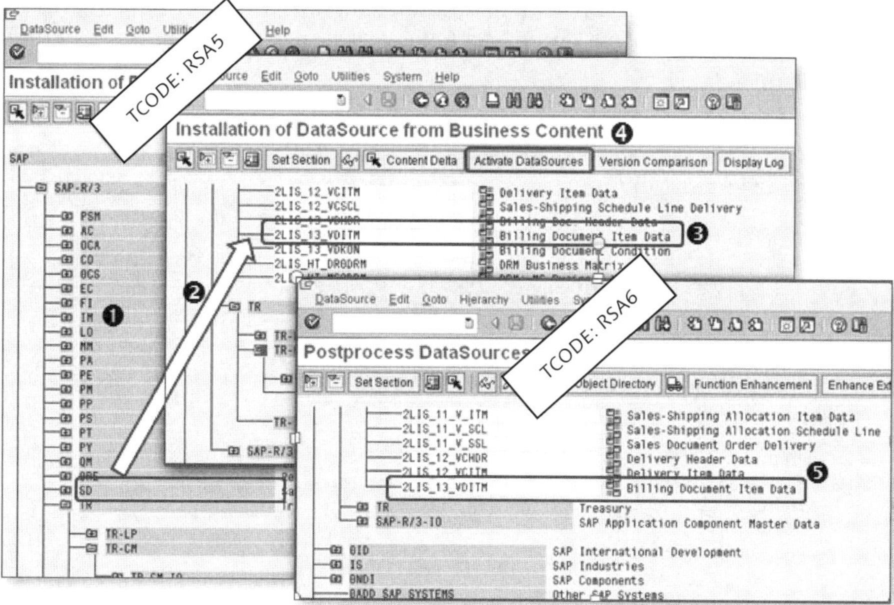

Figure 8.2 Activating SAP Business Content DataSource

The DataSource for billing item information (❷) falls under the SD (Sales and Distribution) application component. Place the cursor on the required DataSource (❸), and then click Activate DataSources (❹) to activate the selected DataSource. You can view all active DataSources by using Transaction RSA6 (Postprocess DataSources) (❺).

Transfer Application Component Hierarchy

SAP delivers a standard application component hierarchy, which can be activated by clicking on Transfer Application Component Hierarchy (refer to ❻ of Figure 8.1).

8.3 Data Extraction Using the Logistic Cockpit

SAP ERP has a number of Logistics (LO) applications, so SAP provides a number of DataSources that are related to Logistics. These DataSources require special attention because their extraction follows a well-defined process that uses a special framework: the *Logistics Cockpit*. Figure 8.3 gives an overview of the Logistics Cockpit.

The reference scenario for ABCD Corp. has an analysis requirement based on a billing application that is part of the Logistics Cockpit. The standard billing application allows you to create, change, or delete billing documents, as shown in ❶ of Figure

8.3. Each of these activities results in addition, modification, or reduction to the multiple billing documents stored in the billing application tables (VBRK and VBRP in ❷ of Figure 8.3).

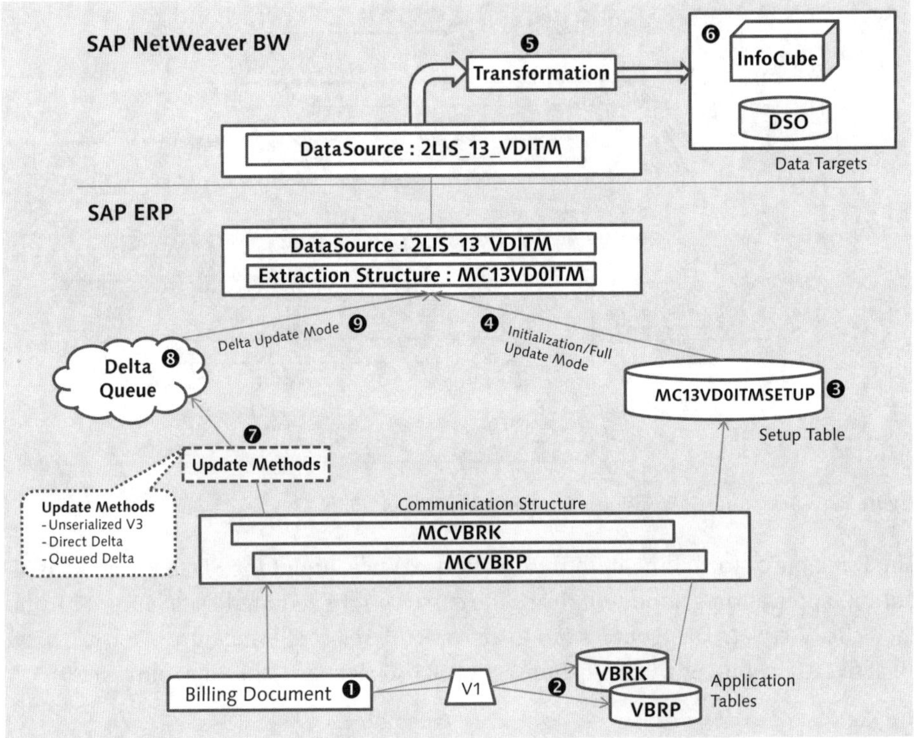

Figure 8.3 Logistics Cockpit Overview

Next we discuss several topics relevant to data extraction using the Logistics Cockpit, as well as the concepts and specific customization of initialization, full upload, and delta upload.

8.3.1 Initialization/Full Upload

The SAP ERP system usually exists prior to the SAP NetWeaver BW system and therefore has historical data for applications. To carry out a trend analysis, SAP NetWeaver BW requires this historical data.

Almost all of the logistics-related applications offer delta-capable DataSources. To identify the new data (or changes to the existing data from history) from the historical data, the two sets of data are distinguished using a process called *initialization*, which sets a point of reference for the historical data and also gives the option to load this historical data to SAP NetWeaver BW. To use the delta capability of the DataSource, this process of initialization (❹ of Figure 8.3) must be carried out. Any new data generated after an initialization is identified as *delta data*. Next we discuss the steps involved in this process.

Filling Setup Tables

To move historical data from the SAP ERP system to the SAP NetWeaver BW system, you must fill up the setup tables (i.e., copy the historical data based on the selection condition from the application tables, and replicate it in the setup tables) in the SAP ERP system (❸ of Figure 8.3). The data in the setup tables is read either during the initialization process or during the full update mode. The setup tables are filled for the entire application component, not for individual DataSources; you use selection conditions to filter the relevant data from underlying application tables.

Executing an InfoPackage with the Initialize with Data Transfer option reads the data from the setup table and passes it to data targets (❻) in SAP NetWeaver BW after applying transformations (❺). The setup table is also used to extract the data in full update mode.

Deleting Data from Setup Tables

After initialization is completed successfully, you no longer need the data in the setup table. It can be deleted using Transaction LBWG. Depending on the volume of data in the underlying tables and the selection criteria entered while filling up the setup table, the time it takes to complete this activity varies.

When the setup tables for an application are being filled, it's possible for transactions occurring in SAP ERP to change the transaction data, which could cause an inconsistency between the data in SAP ERP and the data in SAP NetWeaver BW. To avoid this situation, it's best to lock transactions that can interfere with the data being extracted in a setup table while the setup tables are being filled.

8.3.2 Delta Loads

After the successful initialization, delta records get captured and passed to an area known as the delta queue, which stores records that are ready to be extracted by SAP

NetWeaver BW, after the InfoPackage is executed in delta mode (❽ of Figure 8.3). There are three different update methods for processing this data (❼, ❽, and ❾):

- **Unserialized V3**
  This method stores posted document data in an update table using the V3 collective run, which happens before the data is written to the delta queue. Another V3 collective run than reads the data from the update table without considering the sequence, and transfers the data to the delta queue (❼). Because this method doesn't retain the sequence in which records were generated, you shouldn't load data with this update type directly into a DSO. This is used when serialization of data isn't required.
- **Direct Delta**
  This method stores the posted documents in the delta queue using V1 update. VI update accords the highest priority to this process over other others and is generally used only for most critical updates. This method is recommended only when a small number of documents are being posted. SAP recommends using this method when the maximum number of document changes (creation, modification, or deletion) are less than 10,000 per day for the application.
- **Queued Delta**
  This method stores posted document data in an extraction queue using the V1 update. A collective run is required to read the data from the extraction queue and transfer it to the delta queue. Unlike the unserialized V3 method, this method guarantees the sequence of records because the V1 update is used to store data in the extraction queue. This method can be used when the number of documents posted are large, and serialization is also required.

8.3.3 Data Extraction

Start the Logistics Customizing Cockpit using Transaction LBWE. As shown in ❶ of Figure 8.4, all of the logistics applications available in the SAP ERP system are listed here. Each application is identified with a unique number, for example, 02 for Purchasing, 03 for Inventory Controlling, and so on.

SAP delivers an extraction structure for each DataSource. If SAP ERP has active Logistics Information System (LIS), you can use additional fields from the LIS communication structure to the extraction structure of the DataSource by clicking on the Maintenance link (❷ of Figure 8.4) of the DataSource.

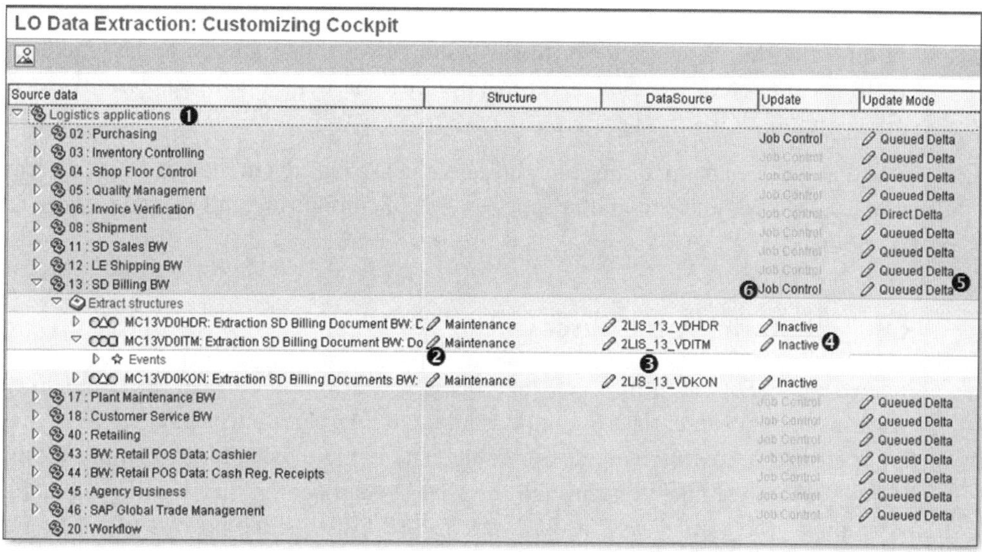

Figure 8.4 Logistics Data Extraction: Customizing Cockpit

You can customize a DataSource by clicking its technical name (❸ of Figure 8.4). Customization options include selecting fields, hiding fields, configuring for inversion, and allowing fields to be used in SAP exits (e.g., for calculation) (Figure 8.4). This is discussed in more detail in Section 8.4.2, Creating a Generic DataSource.

You activate the DataSource by clicking the Inactive link shown in ❹ of Figure 8.4. By setting this to Active, the data is written into extraction structures online and also in setup or restructure tables. Only active state DataSources can be used for filling up a setup table or capturing deltas.

You set the update mode for the application by clicking the Update Mode (Queued Delta, in our example) as shown in ❺ of Figure 8.4. Depending on the update mode set, you may need to schedule the job for application by clicking on Job Control (❻). This moves the delta records from the update table/extraction queue to the delta queue. (The direct delta update method doesn't require this job.) When the InfoPackage with delta update mode is executed from SAP NetWeaver BW for this DataSource, the delta records available in the delta queue are passed to SAP NetWeaver BW.

These steps complete the configuration for this screen. When you activate the DataSource 2LIS_13_VDITM and successfully complete the initialization, the system starts writing all creations/modifications/deletions of billing documents into the extraction queue. When the collective run job is executed, all of the records from the extraction queue are moved to the delta queue. In general, the collective run job is scheduled to move data regularly. In our example, the job is scheduled with the Immediate option. After the maintenance of the DataSource with the required update mode in LBWE is completed, the data starts to flow into the delta queue via various paths corresponding to the mode selected.

Now that we've explained the configuration of a DataSource in the Logistics Customizing Cockpit, we let's move on to the process of configuring and creating a generic DataSource.

8.4 Generic DataSources

A generic DataSource must be created when SAP Business Content doesn't deliver an extractor that can extract the required data to SAP NetWeaver BW (e.g., if a customer created his own tables and stored the data in them using his own application). In this section, we take you through the step-by-step process for creating a generic DataSource. The source system used here is SAP ERP, but the process of creating a generic DataSource is similar for all SAP source systems.

You start Transaction RSO2 in SAP ERP to open up the Maintain Generic DataSource screen shown in Figure 8.5. This transaction allows you to create the following three types of DataSources:

- **Transaction DataSource**
  This type of DataSource is used for transaction data. The extracted data is loaded to a DSO or an InfoCube in SAP NetWeaver BW.
- **Master Data Attributes**
  This type of DataSource is used for master data attributes. The extracted data is loaded to an InfoObject (configured with master data attributes in SAP NetWeaver BW).
- **Texts**
  This type of DataSource is used for master data in a textual format (as opposed to master data attributes), such as a customer name or the description of a material code. Extracted data is loaded to InfoObjects (configured with master data text in SAP NetWeaver BW).

In Chapter 7, Extraction, Transformation, and Loading, we created a master data and transaction DataSource. This time, we'll select a text DataSource (❸ of Figure 8.5). Enter the technical name of the DataSource, and click on the Create button (❹). This action opens the screen shown in Figure 8.6.

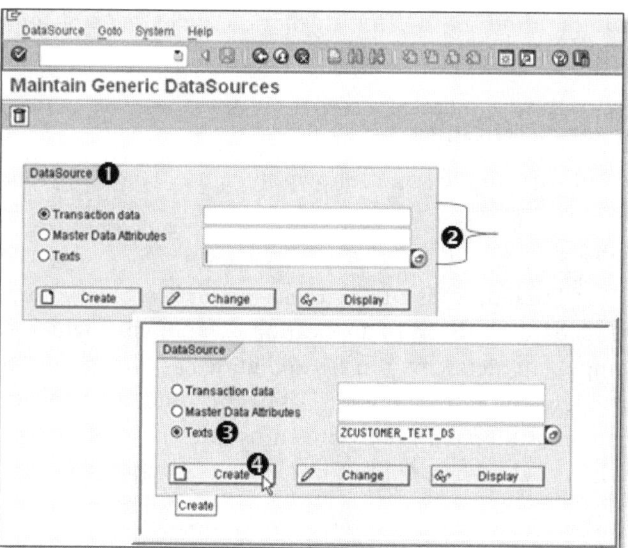

Figure 8.5 Create Generic DataSource

Create DataSource for Texts: ZCUSTOMER_TEXT_DS
Generic Delta 8
DataSource ZCUSTOMER_TEXT_DS
Applic. Component 1
Reconciliation
Obj. status New
Extraction from View
Extraction from Query
Extraction by FM
Extraction fr.Domain
3
Texts
Short description
Medium description
Long description
2
Extraction from DB View 4
View/Table
ExtractStruct.
Extraction frm SAP Query 5
InfoSet
Extraction by Function Module 6
Function Module
Extract.Struct.
Extraction from Domain Fixed Values 7
Domain

Figure 8.6 Create DataSource Initial Screen

Next we explain how to configure the settings for a generic DataSource and then discuss the steps required to actually create the DataSource.

8.4.1 Settings for a Generic DataSource

We'll now explain the different parts of the screen shown in Figure 8.6.

Application Component Field

Just as in SAP NetWeaver BW, a DataSource is attached to an application component in SAP ERP. SAP delivers a standard structure of application components, which is known as the application component hierarchy. You can add more nodes to the delivered application component hierarchy or create your DataSource under a standard node. The application component hierarchy can be seen by clicking on the drop down icon on the extreme right as shown in ❶ of Figure 8.6.

Reconciliation Field

SAP offers a number of standard DataSources in SAP Business Content that help reconcile the data in an SAP NetWeaver BW data target with the live data available in the SAP ERP system. DataSources configured with the reconcile setting pass the data to a VirtualProvider in SAP NetWeaver BW, and a MultiProvider is created on the original data target and VirtualProvider. A query is created on the MultiProvider to compare key figures from the original data target and the virtual InfoCube. Generic DataSources can also be used for this kind of scenario.

Texts Area

A DataSource is described using text. You can attach a short, medium, and/or long description to a DataSource (❷ of Figure 8.6).

Extraction Options

As shown in ❸ of Figure 8.6, there are four different options available to create a DataSource, selected based on how your data is stored:

- **Extraction from View**
  If data is stored in a single table or set of tables that are related via a common key, you can select this option. Then enter the details in the area shown in ❹ of Figure 8.6. (Note: This option is selected by default.)

- **Extraction from Query**
  SAP queries allow users to define and execute custom evaluations of data in the SAP system; they are easy to use and don't require knowledge of ABAP coding. When the data required is available upon execution of a SAP query, you can create a DataSource based on this query. Selecting this option allows you to enter the details of the SAP query name in the area shown in ❺ of Figure 8.6.
- **Extraction by FM (Function Module)**
  Use this method when data to be extracted is available in multiple tables, and the relationship between them is complex. ABAP programming knowledge is required because this method requires the creation of a function module. Selecting this option allows you to enter the details of a function module in the area shown in ❻ of Figure 8.6.

  A function module has only a few input parameters (all optional) and returns output to the calling program or object. The sample function module delivered by SAP, RSAX_BIW_GET_DATA_SIMPLE, will give you an idea about what import and export parameters are required, as well as some hints about how logic should be written. A function module can be developed using Transaction SE37.
- **Extraction Fr.Domain**
  This option is only available when you're creating a text DataSource. Domains store a fixed set of values for text; for example, to record someone's marital status, you can use a domain that stores fixed values like the ones shown in Table 8.1.

M	Married
U	Unmarried
W	Widower
D	Divorcee

Table 8.1 Fixed Values for Domain

You create a DataSource based on a domain to load master data text into an InfoObject in SAP NetWeaver BW. Selecting this option allows you to enter the details of the domain in the area shown in ❼ of Figure 8.6.

Generic Delta Button

By default, generic DataSources aren't delta-capable; they always provide a full data set based on selection criteria. To change this, click the Generic Delta button shown in ❽ of Figure 8.6. We describe more about this button in Section 8.5, Making Generic DataSources Delta Capable.

8.4.2 Creating a Generic DataSource

Now that we've reviewed the screen details, let's create a generic text DataSource based on Table ZCUST_TEXT in SAP ERP. Select the appropriate application component from the dropdown list; in our example, we select SAP-R/3-IO, as shown in ❶ of Figure 8.7.

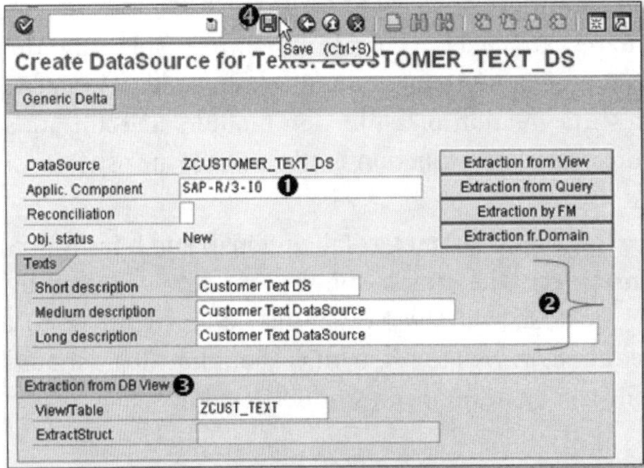

Figure 8.7 Create DataSource Initial Screen

Enter the short, medium, and long text in the entry box (❷). Enter the name of Table ZCUST_TEXT in the entry box (❸). The extraction structure is created by the system by reading the definition of the table entered. Now click Save. The resulting screen is shown in Figure 8.8.

The DataSource can be customized based on the settings shown next.

ExtractStruct. Field

The extraction structure of the DataSource is created and given a unique name by the SAP ERP system, as shown in ❶ of Figure 8.8. The extraction structure contains fields included in the definition of the DataSource.

Direct Access Field

A DataSource with direct access can be used in configuring a VirtualProvider. By default, a generic DataSource is configured for direct access. Values 1 and 2 in this field allow direct access; value D in this field doesn't allow direct access. For our example scenario, no change is required (❷ of Figure 8.8).

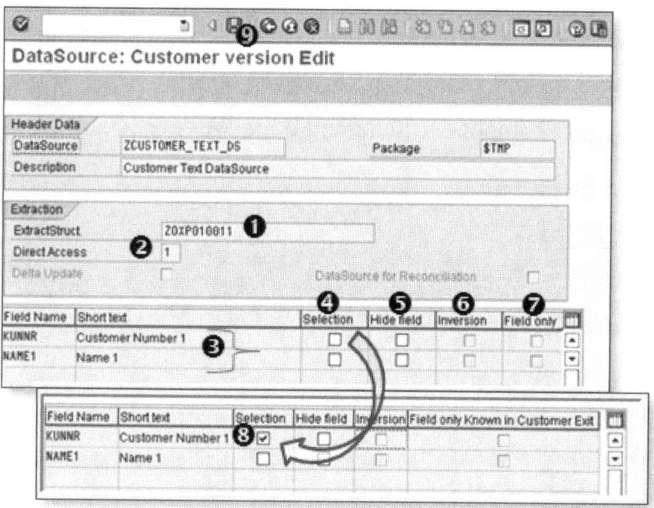

Figure 8.8 Configuring DataSource Fields

Customizing DataSource Fields

Fields included in the DataSource definition of Table ZCUST_TEXT are shown in ❸ of Figure 8.8: KUNNR (Customer Number 1) and NAME1 (Name 1). Four different settings are available for each field; the significance of each is explained next.

- **Selection**
  Checking this checkbox allows you to enter selection values for this field in the InfoPackage created for this DataSource in SAP NetWeaver BW. For our example scenario, we flag this for the KUNNR field, as shown in ❽ of Figure 8.8.
- **Hide Field**
  If you don't want to pass a specific field value to SAP NetWeaver BW, you can select this indicator (❺ Figure 8.8).
- **Inversion**
  The Inversion setting is only valid for transaction DataSources and is applicable to fields that are numeric in nature and that allow reverse postings in the SAP ERP application.
- **Field Only Known in Customer Exit**
  This setting is used specifically when you include additional fields in the already-available DataSource. Using this setting, you can define whether the value of that specific field should be passed on to SAP NetWeaver BW or should just be available in the customer exit.

After these settings are configured, click Save. Click the Back icon twice, which brings you back to the main screen for DataSource creation (refer to Figure 8.5).

The creation of a generic DataSource is now complete. The created DataSource is now available in the application component hierarchy node SAP-R/3-IO, as shown in Figure 8.9.

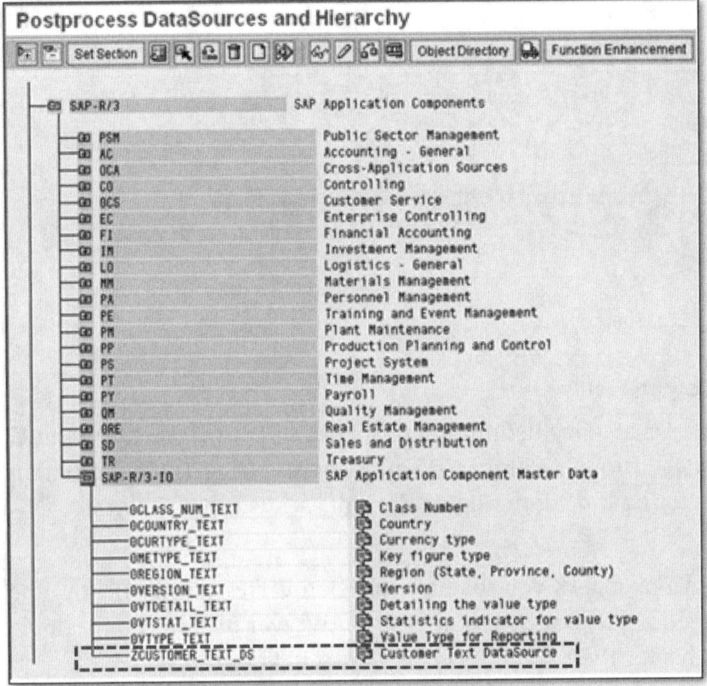

Figure 8.9 Generic DataSource Available in Application Component Hierarchy

The generic DataSource ZCUSTOMER_TEXT_DS can be accessed using Transaction RSA6.

To use this DataSource in SAP NetWeaver BW, you must replicate it. The process of replication can be started from SAP NetWeaver BW as explained briefly next.

1. Start Transaction RSA1.
2. From Modeling, select Source Systems.
3. From the right panel, select the SAP ERP system in which the DataSource has been created.
4. Using the context menu, select Display DataSource Tree. The application component hierarchy tree is displayed.

5. Select the application component under which you have created the DataSource in the SAP ERP system (e.g., SAP-R/3-IO).
6. Use the context menu to select Replicate DataSource.

8.5 Making Generic DataSources Delta Capable

As mentioned earlier, a generic DataSource doesn't offer delta capability. Every time you extract the data using a generic DataSource, it extracts the full set of data, which may not be practical when the data volume is large. Generic DataSources can be converted into delta-capable DataSources using the Generic Delta button (❽ of Figure 8.10).

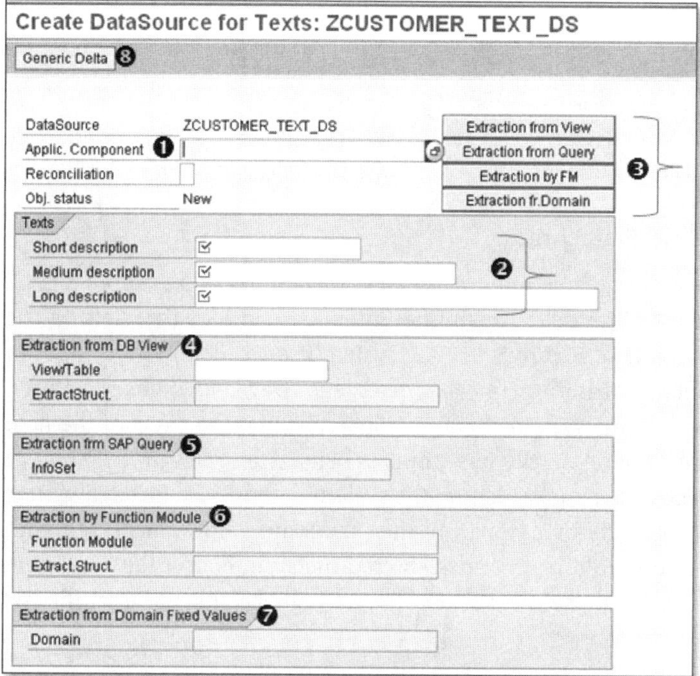

Figure 8.10 Create DataSource Initial Screen

When you click the Generic Delta button, a pop-up box appears, as shown in Figure 8.11. Next we divide our discussion of the fields on the screen based on the screen's two main areas: Delta-Specific Field, and Settings.

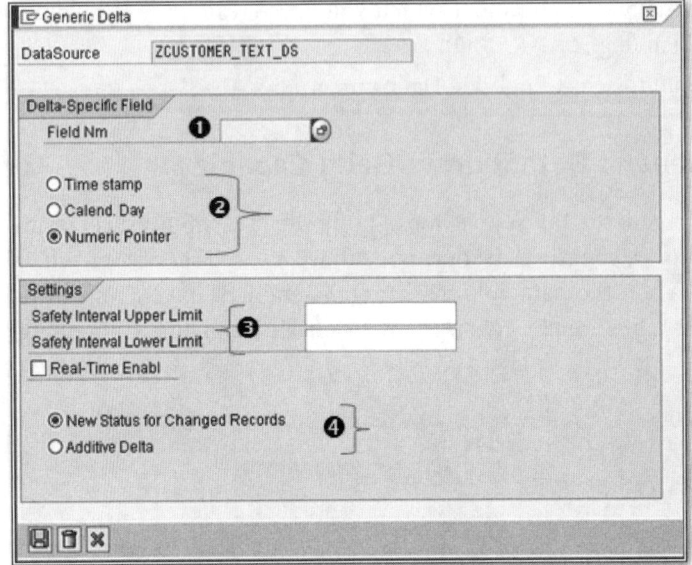

Figure 8.11 Setting Available for Creating Delta-Capable Generic DataSources

8.5.1 Delta-Specific Field Area

Making a DataSource delta capable requires a delta-relevant field that supports delta identification and enables the delta capability. Enter the name of that field in the Field Nm field shown in ❶ of Figure 8.11. The system uses three different types of fields to recognize delta records (❷): Time Stamp, Calend. Day, and Numeric Pointer. The assumption regarding the generic delta DataSource is that the value of the field declared here increases monotonically over time. When a delta-relevant field (e.g., a timestamp) exists in the extraction structure, the system determines the data volume transferred in the delta mode by comparing the maximum value transferred with the last load, to the amount of data that has entered the system after the maximum value of the last load. Only those records that have a higher value are identified as delta records.

8.5.2 Settings Area

In ❸ of Figure 8.11, you can see the fields for setting a safety interval. The purpose of a safety interval is to make the system extract records (with the next extraction) that appear during the extraction process but aren't extracted (perhaps because they haven't been saved at the time of extraction).

Safety Interval Upper Limit defines the safety pointer value for the lower limit. For example, assume that the delta-relevant field is a numeric pointer whose last read numeric pointer was 1000. Also, assume that when the next delta extraction begins, the current numeric pointer is 1100. If the safety interval for the lower limit is set to 10, the selection interval is set by the system for delta, 990 to 1100 (subtracting the safety interval value of 10 from the lower limit of 1000 makes the lower value of the selection interval 990). The selection interval is used as a filter to extract the records using the DataSource. When the extraction is successfully completed, the pointer is set to 1100.

Setting this safety interval results in duplicate records in the subsequent delta extraction (due to the overlapping selection interval). As such, you should not load data extracted from this DataSource directly into an InfoCube; you must load the data to a DSO and then to an InfoCube.

Safety Interval Lower Limit defines the safety pointer value for the upper limit. Let's now assume that the delta-relevant field is a numeric pointer whose last read numeric pointer was 1000. Also assume that when the next delta extraction begins, the current numeric pointer is 1100. If the safety interval for the upper limit is set to 10, the selection interval set by the system for delta is 1000 to 1090 (subtracting the safety interval value of 10 from the upper limit of 1100 makes the upper value 1090). The selection interval is used as a filter to extract the records using the DataSource. When the extraction is successfully completed, the pointer is set to 1090.

Setting this safety interval doesn't result in duplicate records in the subsequent delta because there's no overlapping in the selection interval. You can directly load the data extracted by this DataSource into an InfoCube.

There are two remaining fields in the Settings area:

- **New Status for Changed Records**
  A DataSource with this setting indicates that a record to be loaded returns the latest value for all characteristics and key figures. The data from this type of DataSource can be loaded to a DSO and InfoObject with master data in SAP NetWeaver BW (❹ of Figure 8.11).
- **Additive Delta**
  The DataSource with this setting indicates that records to be loaded only return changes to key figures that can be aggregated. The data from this type of DataSource can be loaded to a DSO and InfoCube in SAP NetWeaver BW.

8.6 Extractor Checker

After a DataSource is created in the source system, you may want to check its accuracy. For this, SAP has provided a tool called the Extractor Checker. Start Transaction RSA3 in SAP ERP to bring up the Extractor Checker S-API screen shown in Figure 8.12.

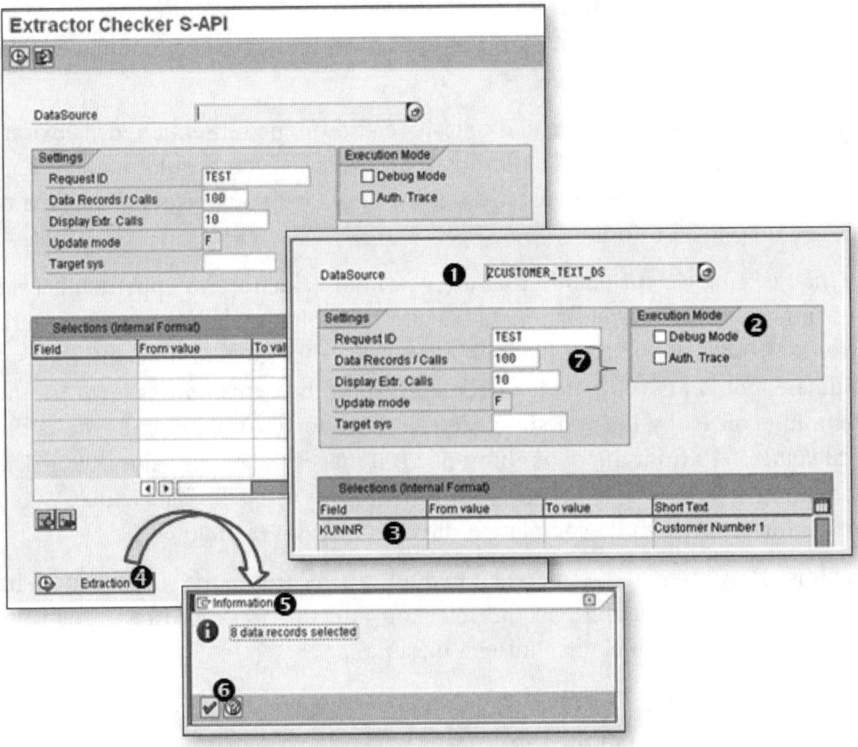

Figure 8.12 Extractor Checker Initial Screen

Enter the name of the DataSource you want to test in the DataSource field, as shown in ❶ of Figure 8.12. You have two options (❷) for the execution mode: Debug Mode, which helps in starting the debugger and takes you through step-by-step execution of the underlying DataSource program; and Auth. Trace, which is used for tracing authorization while accessing various tables and objects used by the underlying DataSource program.

The selection fields flagged when you created the DataSource are also available here. As shown in ❸ of Figure 8.12, KUNNR is available for selection.

You can restrict the number of records to be extracted by configuring the parameters Data Records/Calls and Display Extr. Calls. By default, 1000 records are extracted.

Click the Extraction button (❹) to simulate the execution of the DataSource. The system extracts the records and displays them in the pop-up box that appears with details on the number of records extracted (❺). Now click the Continue icon, which results in the screen shown in Figure 8.13.

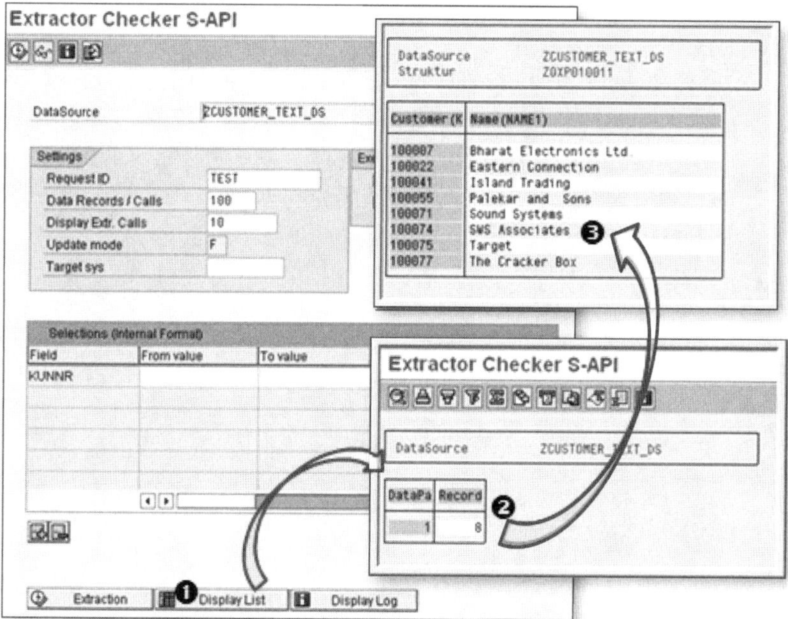

Figure 8.13 Result of Extractor Checker

The DataSource has extracted the records based on the selection criteria. If you want to see the records extracted, click the Display List button (❶ of Figure 8.13). This brings you the screen shown in ❷ of Figure 8.13, which shows the number of extracted records for each data package. Our example table, ZCUST_TEXT, on which the DataSource is defined, has only eight records extracted in a single data package. Double-click on the data package to view the details of the extracted records (❸ of Figure 8.13).

8.7 Summary

In this chapter, we described the details of data extraction from SAP source systems. You should now understand how to configure SAP ERP for this process, activate SAP Business Content DataSources, create generic DataSources that are delta capable, and check your work by using the Extractor Checker tool. In the next chapter, we explain the query designing tool and its functionalities.

Reporting and analysis is an integral part of a BI Solution. SAP NetWeaver BW offers a set of Business Explorer (BEx) tools that are used to create queries and to present the data to the users for analysis. The data can be presented in Excel or in a web environment.

9 BEx Query Designer

Companies employ BI solutions to have visibility and control across their entities, functions, and business processes by providing the decision makers with correct information in the right format. In the previous chapters of this book, you've learned about the data warehousing capabilities of SAP NetWeaver BW. We now explain the process of transforming data into information by presenting the data in reports that generate useful insights and help users make informed decision at the right time. Making an informed decision often involves analysis of the data from multiple perspectives and in an easily understandable format. SAP NetWeaver offers a flexible set of tools that can be used to create queries and reports and present the data to users along with extensive analysis options. These tools collectively form the Business Explorer (BEX) component of SAP NetWeaver BW. After the queries are created using *BEx query designer*, the reporting and analysis in SAP NetWeaver BW can be performed using either Microsoft Excel (*BEx analyzer*) or a web browser (*web application designer*).

In this chapter, we explain creating queries in SAP NetWeaver BW using BEx Query Designer and different functions that can be built on a query for effective analysis.

9.1 BEx Tools Landscape

As mentioned earlier, BEx is a set of tools that can be used to query, report and analyze the data available through different SAP NetWeaver BW InfoProviders. Figure 9.1 shows how the BEx component is structured.

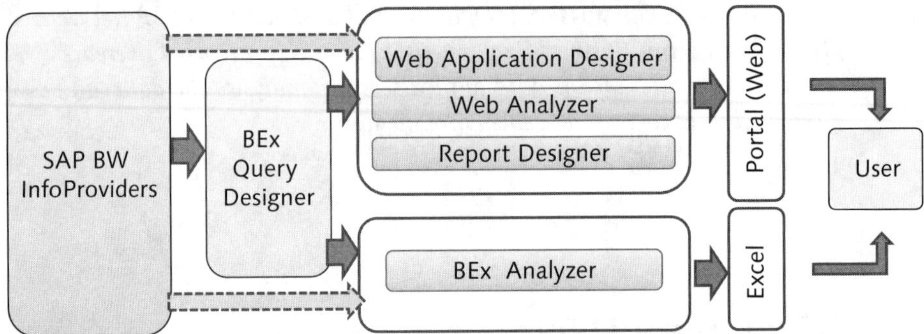

Figure 9.1 SAP Business Explorer Components

In SAP NetWeaver BW, the data is made available for reporting through InfoProviders. An InfoProvider can store the data physically (standard InfoCubes, Real-time InfoCubes, master data InfoObjects, DataStore Objects) or can be only a logical InfoProvider, which doesn't store any data physically (Virtual InfoProviders, MultiProviders, InfoSets, Aggregation Levels).

The BEx tool that is used to create queries on InfoProviders is *BEx query designer*. This is a user friendly development tool that enables you to create the queries using simple drag and drop on the characteristics and key figures from the InfoProvider. BEx query designer also allows you to create different reusable query elements, which can be used across different queries.

The queries created in BEx Query Designer are used to present the data to the users for reporting and analysis by different means.

- **BEx analyzer**
  Using BEx analyzer, you can create an Excel-based reporting and analysis application based on one or multiple queries built in BEx query designer. Also, it supports ad-hoc analysis directly on the InfoProvider. The application created using BEx analyzer is saved as a workbook, which can be made available to multiple users for use.
- **BEx web application designer**
  The BEx web application designer tool is used to create the web-based reporting and analysis application. These applications are built using a variety of subcomponents called web items. This includes items to present the data in different formats, such as tables and charts, or the items to facilitate analysis of data such as filters, dropdowns, navigation blocks, and so on. The web application created using the web application designer is saved as a web template and is made available to users through the portal or web browser.

- **BEx web analyzer**
  The BEx web analyzer is a powerful web based application that can access the data from a query built in BEx query designer or can even access the data directly from the InfoProvider for ad-hoc analysis. Users can access the BEx web analyzer tool through the portal or directly through the web browser.
- **BEx report designer**
  The BEx report designer is an intuitive tool with a lot of features that can be used to generate formatted reports from SAP NetWeaver BW data. We haven't discussed BEx report designer in this book.

In SAP NetWeaver BW 7.0, BEx query designer, web application designer, and analyzer are available in both 7.x as well as 3.x version for development. These tools are separate components and can be used independently of each other. The queries, reports, and web applications created using the BEx components from older versions of SAP NetWeaver BW (SAP NetWeaver BW 3.x) are executed on the ABAP stack of SAP NetWeaver BW. On the other hand, the BEx reports and applications created using SAP NetWeaver BW 7.x BEx components use the Java stack of SAP NetWeaver BW.

The BEx tools in the 7.x version contain additional features and are more advanced than the 3.x set of tools. In this book, we've covered only the BEx tools from the 7.x version.

9.2 Example Scenario

Our example company ABCD Corp. wants to support its sales process with the reporting and analysis from SAP NetWeaver BW. To make the right decision, the company needs to find answers to the following questions(among others):

- What products are selling in different sales organizations?
- Which product lines or specific products are selling highest or lowest?
- How are ABCD Corp.'s current year sales as compared to the previous year?
- What are top 10 best-selling products?

Also, the auditors of ABCD Corp. require the solution to provide traceability to the specific billing documents for a customer, and, when necessary, to analyze instances of variances. This sales document level investigation needs to be addressed in SAP NetWeaver BW rather than going into the transactional system for the detailed information.

We'll refer to these requirements for ABCD Corp. while explaining the use of different tools and features discussed in this chapter.

9.3 BEx Query Designer

Queries built on data provided by different InfoProviders enable structured analysis of data. BEx query designer is the tool to create such queries in SAP NetWeaver BW. This tool has evolved into a user-friendly development tool, providing enriched features to support business analytical needs in different forms.

BEx query designer is a standalone application, so you don't need to log in to the SAP NetWeaver BW frontend applications to use BEx query designer. It can be launched directly from the Start menu of your computer using the path: START • PROGRAMS • BUSINESS EXPLORER • QUERY DESIGNER (❶ of Figure 9.2). Select the SAP NetWeaver BW system and login using the user id and password (❷).

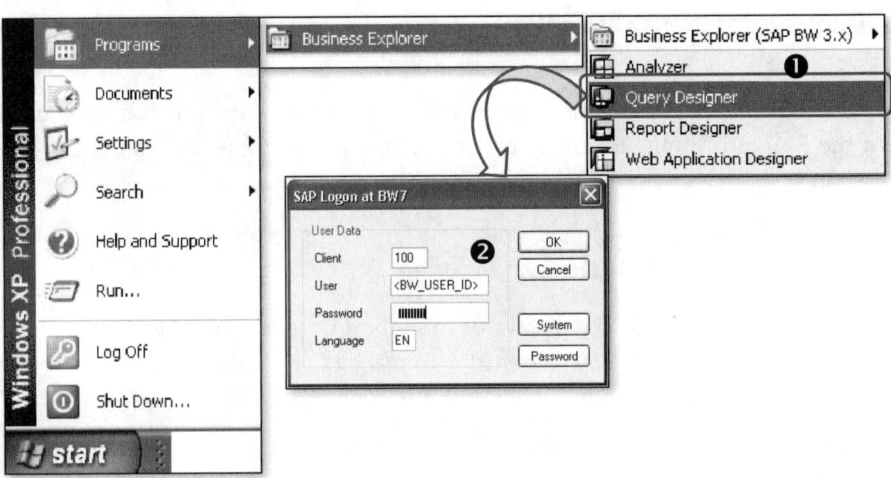

Figure 9.2 Start BEx Query Designer

Now we'll explain the different components of BEx query designer and the menu functions.

9.3.1 BEx Query Designer Screen Layout

When you log in to the BEx query designer, the default screen appears as shown in Figure 9.3.

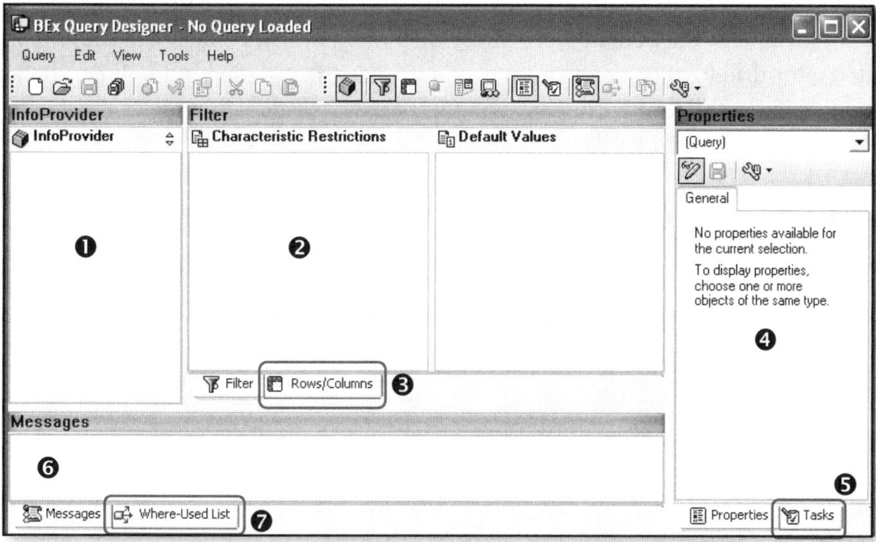

Figure 9.3 BEx query designer Screen Layout

The screen layout sections include InfoProvider, Messages, Filter, and so on. These screen areas and their uses are explained next.

InfoProvider

A query has to be built on an InfoProvider. The InfoProvider definition upon which the query is built is displayed in the InfoProvider area of the query designer (❶ of Figure 9.3). This becomes the base for the query because you can drag the necessary elements (characteristics, key figures, attributes, etc.) from the InfoProvider area into the query definition.

Filter

If the query has to be restricted to certain characteristic values, then those filter restrictions are defined in the Filter area of the query designer (❷ of Figure 9.3). The static filters are defined in the Characteristic Restrictions sections. The default values for which the query should be first executed are defined in the Default Values area.

Rows/Columns

The layout of the query is defined on the Rows/Columns tab of the query designer (❸ of Figure 9.3). This screen area is displayed in Figure 9.4. The characteristics and key figures to be included as rows or columns in the report layout are specified in the Rows and Columns area, respectively. If there are characteristics that you don't want to include in the default view of the query, but you want to make those fields available for drilldown if needed, such characteristics are added to the Free Characteristics area on the Row/Columns tab. The preview section provides a preview of the query structure and layout.

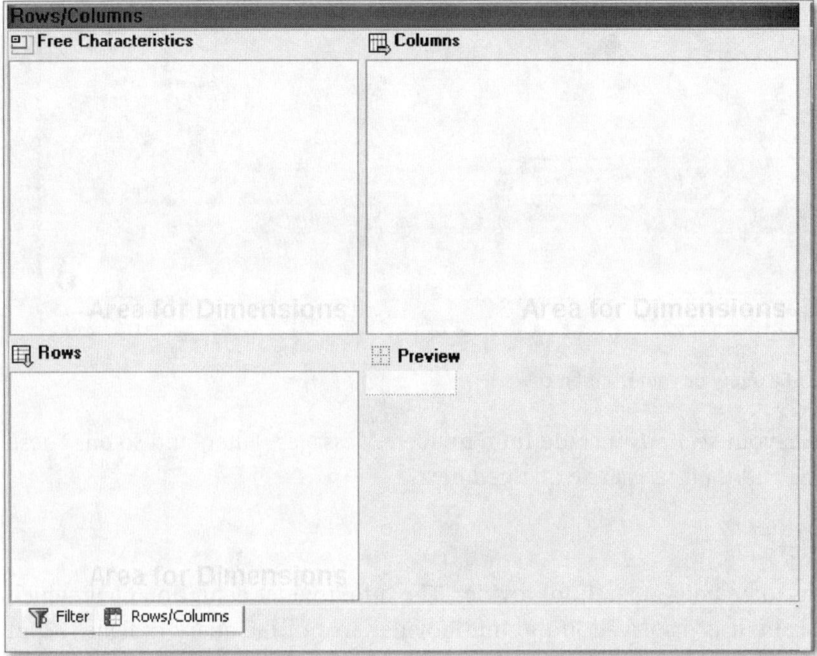

Figure 9.4 Rows/Columns Screen Area

Properties

All components of the query (including the query itself) have their own sets of properties, descriptions, display settings, and so on, which determine the behavior of that element. The properties for the selected query element are visible in the Properties screen area of the query designer (refer to ❹ of Figure 9.3).

Tasks

For different components of a query, there are different tasks or actions that can be performed. These tasks vary based on the element that is selected. Different tasks related to the selected item are listed in the Tasks area, so you can find all relevant actions for an object listed under tasks. In case of errors, the possible corrective actions and error help are also visible in the Task area (refer to ❺ of Figure 9.3).

Messages

Different messages, such as errors, warnings or other information related to the query, are displayed in the Messages screen area (refer to ❻ of Figure 9.3).

Where-Used List

A query or the reusable components can be used in multiple other objects such as workbooks, web templates, and so on. When you use the where-used list for the query or a reusable component, the list of all of the objects where the component or query is used is displayed in the Where-Used List screen area of the Query Designer (refer to ❼ of Figure 9.3).

9.3.2 BEx Query Designer Menu Bar

Having reviewed the basic screen sections, let's now look at the different functions available under the BEx query designer menu bar (see Figure 9.5).

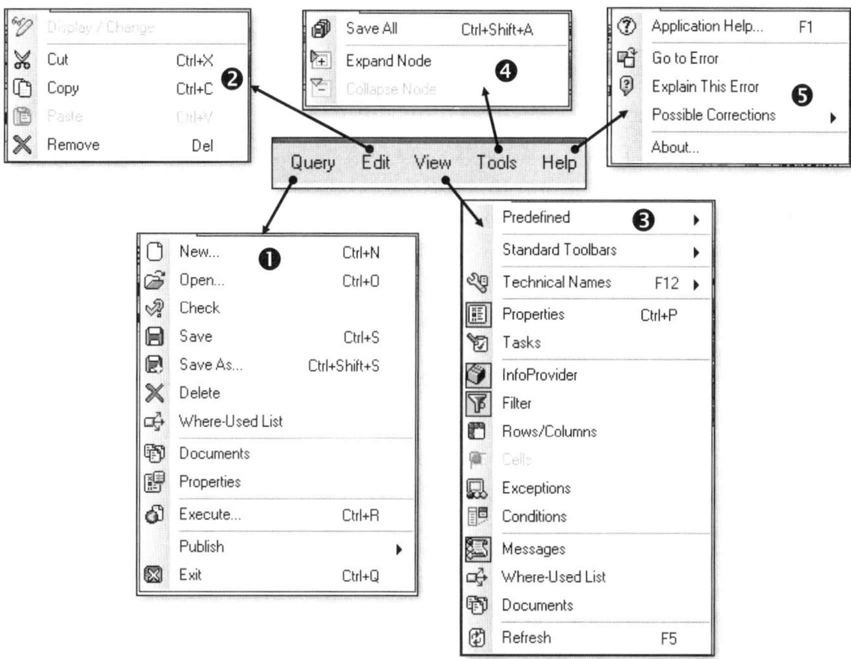

Figure 9.5 BEx Query Designer Menu Bar

Following are the five menu options available in the menu bar:

- **Query (❶):** The functions under this menu options allow you to create, save, open, check, execute, and delete a query.
- **Edit (❷):** You can perform different edit functions using this menu option. Also, you can toggle between the display only and edit mode of the query.
- **View (❸):** The functions under this menu option allow you to display different screen areas as well as toolbars. You can also toggle between different options to display the technical name and description of query elements.
- **Tools (❹):** The Save All function under this menu option saves the query definition as well all other reusable components that are created while working on the query.
- **Help (❺):** Functions under this menu option provide error help and also provide access to SAP online documentation.

In the subsequent sections of this chapter, we explain the procedure to create the queries and understand different features offered by BEx Query Designer.

9.4 Create a Simple BEx Query

Let's begin creating a simple query based on the sales InfoCube (BWSD_C01) that we created earlier in Chapter 5, InfoCubes. When you log in to BEx Query Designer, you see a default screen as shown in earlier in Figure 9.3. To create a new query, you can either use the menu QUERY • NEW OR click on the toolbar icon shown in Figure 9.6.

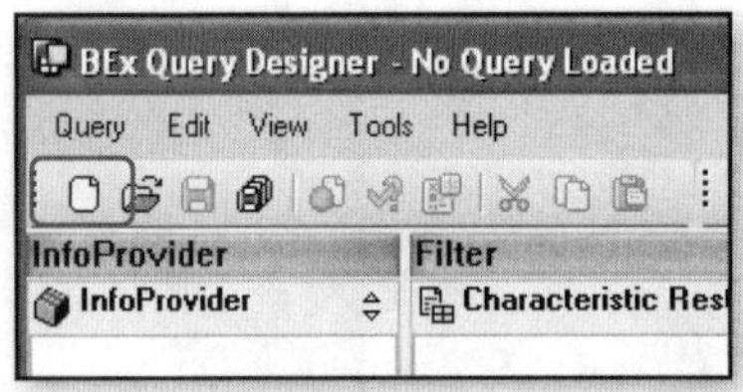

Figure 9.6 Create New Query

As mentioned earlier, a query in SAP NetWeaver BW has to be based on an InfoProvider. When you create a query, a window pops up asking you to select an InfoProvider (see Figure 9.7). On this screen, you can navigate through the InfoAreas to select the InfoProvider on which you want to create the query (❶) and then click on the Open button (❷) to return to the query designer screen.

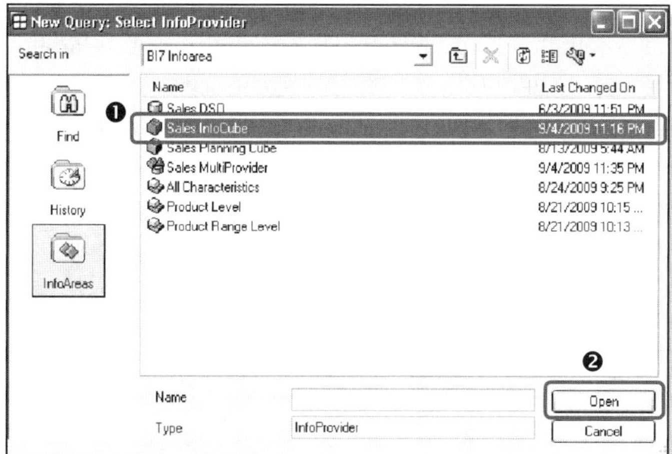

Figure 9.7 Select an InfoProvider

The definition of the selected InfoProvider becomes visible in the InfoProvider screen area of the query designer (see Figure 9.8).

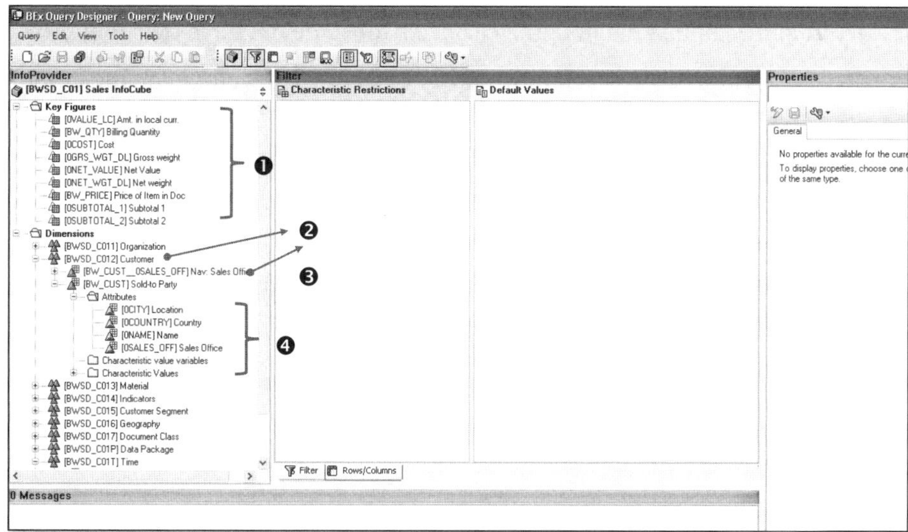

Figure 9.8 InfoProvider Definition in Query Designer

You can see all of the key figures (❶ of Figure 9.8) and characteristics grouped within respective dimensions (❷) in the query designer. The master data navigation attributes, which are selected in the InfoCube definition, appear in the query designer, grouped with the master data characteristic in the same dimension (❸). You can also see additional information about the characteristics of the InfoCube, such as the attributes (if the characteristic is a master data), variables, and values (❹).

Let's now create a query to answer the following analysis requirements for ABCD Corp. business analysts:

- What were the yearly net sales for all products sold in the year 2009 for Sales Organization 3000 (AMERICA)? (Show the data by division, material group, and product.)
- Can the values be seen by calendar quarter, if needed?
- Can the same data be viewed by division, customer group, and product (if needed)?

9.4.1 Define Filter

From these requirements, it's clear that the query needs to be *restricted* to year 2009 and Sales Organization 3000. These restrictions can be applied on the Filter screen area and under Characteristic Restrictions section. So if you want to restrict the query results for calendar year, drag and drop the characteristic calendar year from the InfoProvider area to the Characteristic Restrictions area (❶ of Figure 9.9). Then, select Restrict from the context menu of the characteristic to define the restrictions (❷).

After you select Restrict, a selection window pops up where you can define the values with which you want to restrict the characteristic (see Figure 9.10).

You can restrict the characteristic either with a single value or with a range, or you can choose to use a variable to restrict the characteristic. Select the appropriate option from the drop-down (❶ of Figure 9.10).

Highlight the desired value from the list (❷), and add it to the selections by clicking on the arrow button (❸). You can also make a selection by directly entering the value in the Direct Input box (❹) and then clicking on the arrow button.

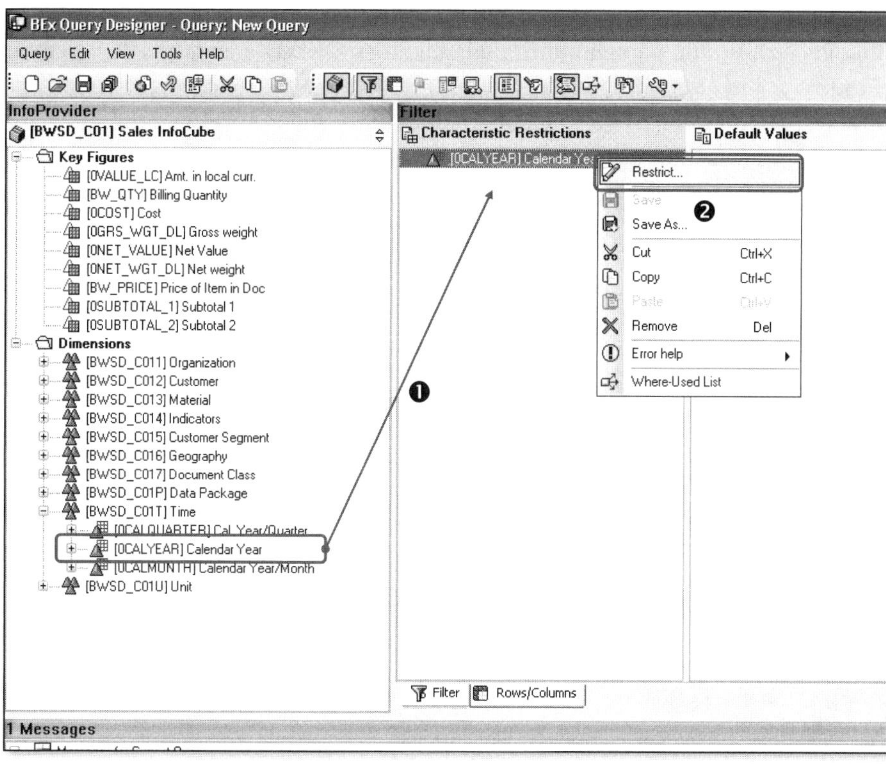

Figure 9.9 Add Characteristic for Query Restrictions

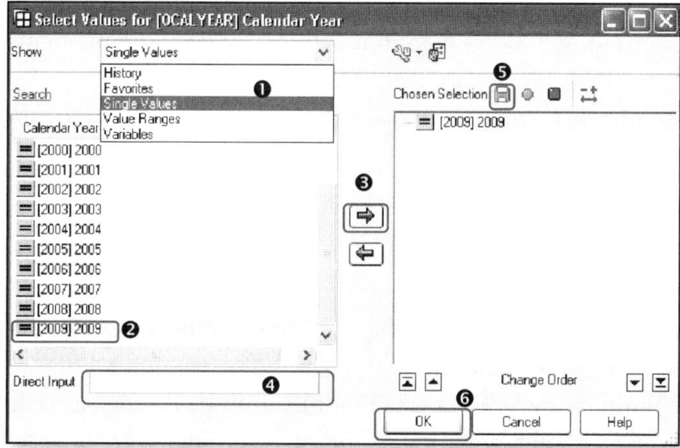

Figure 9.10 Select Filter Values for a Characteristic

Using the save button (❺), you can save this selection as a variant in your favorites so that you can use the same in future. Finally, click OK (❻) to confirm the selection and return to the query definition. You can see that the characteristic calendar year is now restricted for year 2009 (see Figure 9.11).

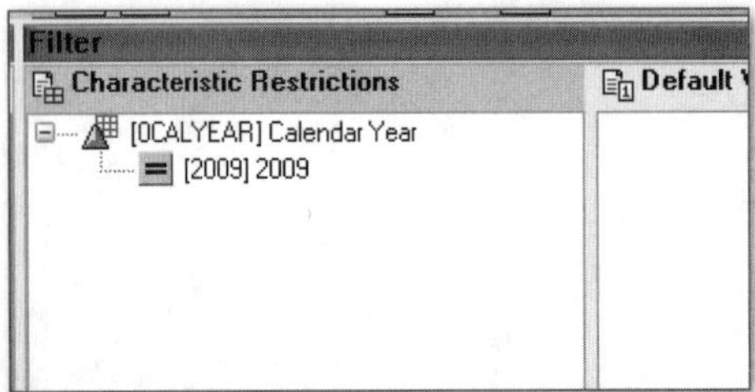

Figure 9.11 Calendar Year Restriction

Similarly, you can restrict the query for characteristic Sales Organization = 3000 (AMERICA) as shown in Figure 9.12.

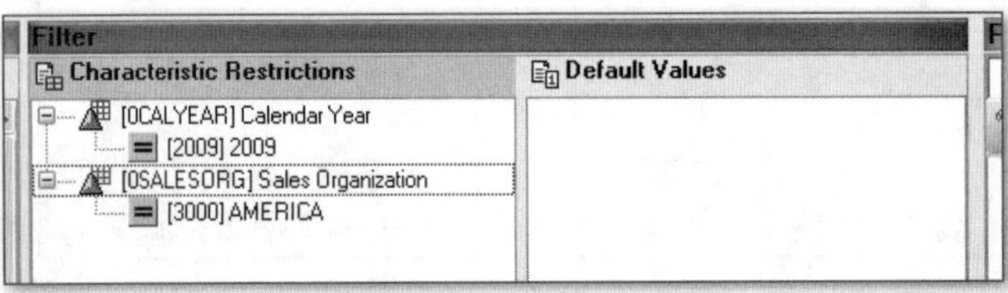

Figure 9.12 Add Sales Organization Restriction

Having defined these filters, we've now restricted the result data set of the query to year 2009 and Sales Organization 3000 as mentioned in the example requirements.

9.4.2 Define Rows/Columns

The layout of the query is defined in the Row/Columns screen area of the query designer. The four sections under the Row/Columns area are explained next:

- Rows: All those characteristics that need to appear as rows in the query display should be dragged and dropped into this area.
- Columns: The characteristics or key figures that form the columns of the query display should be dragged and dropped into this area.
- Free Characteristics: Those characteristics that don't need to be displayed in the default query result when the query is executed but can be brought into the result display as needed should be dragged and dropped into the Free Characteristics

area. Free characteristics can be added to the rows (drilldown) or to the columns (drill-across) per the analysis needs after the query is initially executed.

- Preview: A preview of the query layout is displayed in this section based on the rows and columns of the query definition.

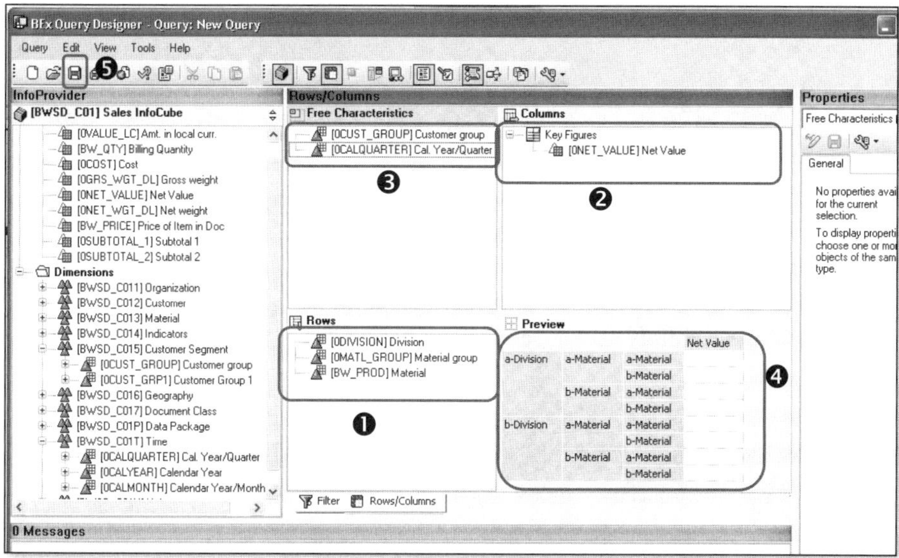

Figure 9.13 Define Rows, Columns, and Free Characteristics

Based on our example requirements, the report (the query output) should show the data by division, material group, and material, so these characteristics should be dragged into the rows section (❶ of Figure 9.13). The sales value should be displayed as a column, so drag the key figure Net Value (0NET_VALUE) to the Columns area (❷).

The requirements also mention that the analysts want to see the data by customer group or calendar quarter if needed. This means you have to place these two characteristics as free characteristics (❸). The preview of the layout can be seen under the Preview section (❹).

The query is ready. To save this query definition, click on the save button (❺). You can also use menu function QUERY • SAVE to save the query. You have to specify the technical name and the description of the query in the pop-up box and click on the Save button to save the query (see Figure 9.14).

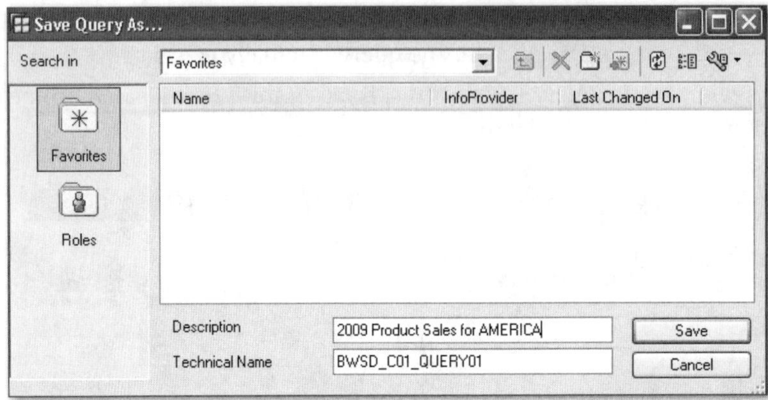

Figure 9.14 Save Query Definition

The Messages screen area in the query designer displays a message indicating that the query was successfully saved (see Figure 9.15).

Figure 9.15 Success Message After Query Save

In the next subsection, we'll see how to execute this query and perform analysis on the data.

9.4.3 Execute the Query and Analyze Data

After the query is defined and saved, it can be executed by clicking on the button shown in Figure 9.16. You can also follow the menu path QUERY • EXECUTE to execute the query.

Figure 9.16 Execute Query

The query is executed in the web browser, so when you execute a query, a new web browser window opens up and displays the result of the query. The result from the execution of the query is displayed as shown in Figure 9.17. It uses the ad-hoc analysis template from *BEx web analyzer* to display the query result. We discuss the *BEx web analyzer* in detail in the next chapter of the book.

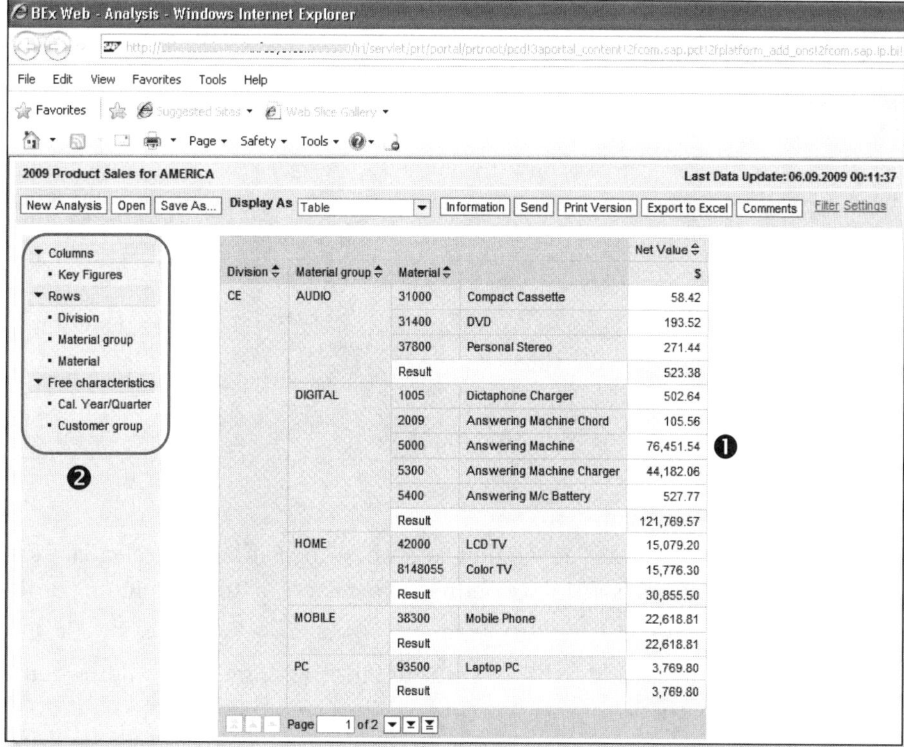

Figure 9.17 Query Output

You can see that the query output is displayed per the example requirements. The query displays the net sales value (Year 2009 and Sales Organization 3000) for all of the products by division and material group (❶ of Figure 9.17).

The query elements included in the rows, columns, and free characteristics of the query definition are visible on the left side of the screen (❷). These elements can be used to further analyze the data displayed in the query.

For example, if an analyst wants to see the net sales data by calendar quarter, he can simply drag the Calendar Quarter from the Free Characteristics and drop it in the Columns as shown in ❶ of Figure 9.18.

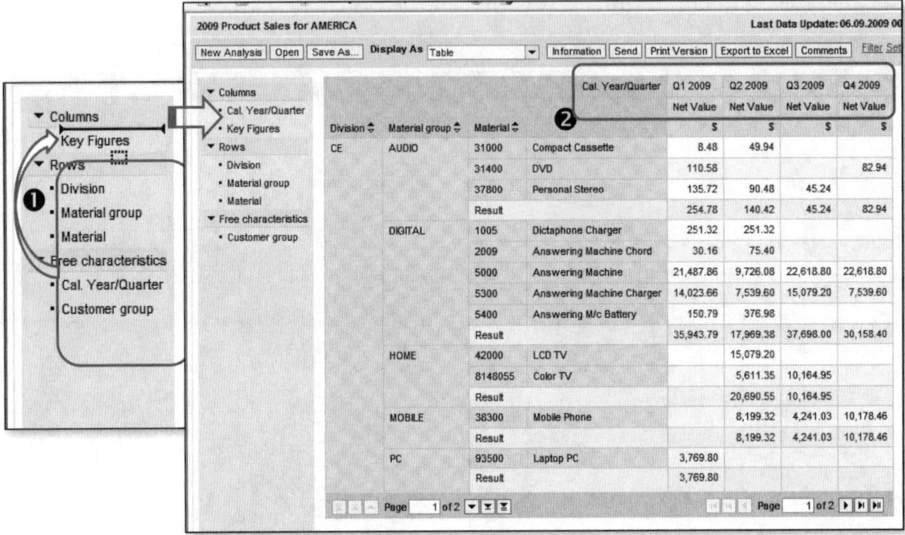

Figure 9.18 Drill-Across by Calendar Quarter

As a result, the query output is now modified to show the net sales by calendar quarter (❷ of Figure 9.18). This action of adding a characteristic to the columns of the query is called *horizontal drilldown*.

On the other hand, if you add a characteristic to the rows of the query, this action is called *vertical drilldown*.

For example, if an analyst now wants to see the data by customer group instead of material group in the query, this navigation can be performed in two steps. First, remove the material group from the layout and then drill down by customer group. You can also directly swap the display of characteristic material group with customer group as shown in ❶ of Figure 9.19.

As a result of this navigation, the query output is refreshed to display Customer Group in the result area and characteristic Material Group is added to Free Characteristics (❷ of Figure 9.19).

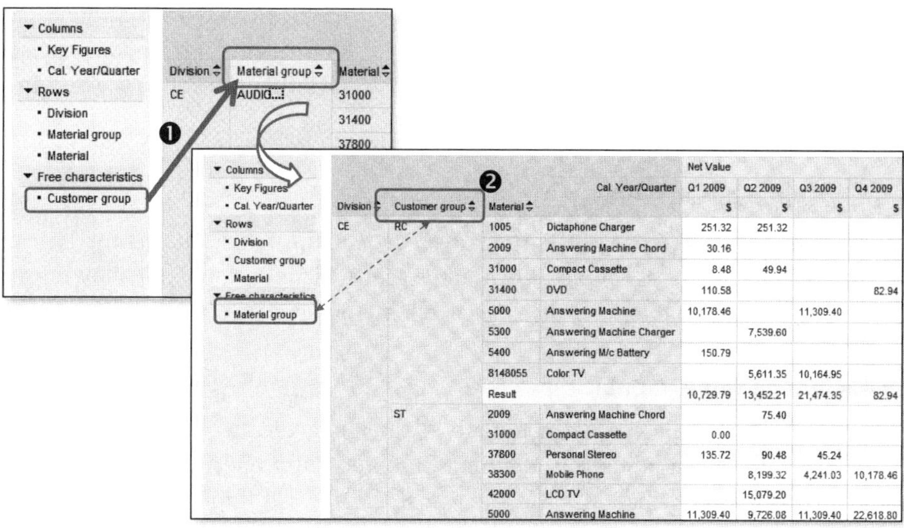

Figure 9.19 Swap Characteristics

9.5 OLAP Variables

The simple query that was discussed in the previous section determined material sales for year 2009. As such, we designed the query to restrict the characteristics for all calendar years to value 2009. What if a user now modifies the requirement as follows?

- Show sales for all of the material that belongs to the material group selected by the user.
- Don't fix the query to year 2009; instead, the user should be able to select the year for which the query should be executed. However, the user entry should default to the previous year value; that is, if the current the year is 2010, then the default value should be 2009, and when the year changes to 2011, the default value should be 2010.

These and other similar requirements are addressed using OLAP variables in SAP NetWeaver BW. Variables can be used for characteristics, texts, hierarchies, and so on, and using them in a query makes it more flexible. The most common use of variables in a query is to provide users with a prompt (or selection screen) where users can decide the parameters for which the query should be executed. There are also many other types of variables available in SAP NetWeaver BW.

The OLAP variables are reusable objects, so the variables created for a query can also be used in all of the InfoProviders in the system. In this section, we explain different types OLAP variables and the different ways they can be processed in a BEx query.

9.5.1 Types of Variables

Variables in SAP NetWeaver BW are context dependent, which means the type of variable actually depends on the type of object for which it's defined. Following are different types of variables and the objects where they can be used.

Characteristic Value Variables

These types of variables are used to restrict the characteristic values. Characteristic value variables can be used in defining the filters for a query. The characteristic variables created on a characteristic are available across all InfoProviders wherever that characteristic is used. For example, a characteristic value variable can be used on characteristic calendar year if the user wants to select the year while executing the query.

Text Variables

The text variables provide flexibility in displaying the text description of the query and different query elements. This type of variable can be used where you define the text or description of a query or another query component. For example, a text variable can be used to dynamically generate the key figure column name based on the year value; that is, if the query is executed for year = 2010 then the key figure column name should be displayed as Net Sales 2010, and when the same query is executed for year 2011, the key figure name should be Net Sales 2011.

Hierarchy Variables

Hierarchies are used in a query either to restrict a characteristic or to display query results using a hierarchy. Hierarchy variables are used to select a hierarchy in the query.

Hierarchy Node Variables

Hierarchy node variables can be used wherever a characteristic is restricted using a specific node of a hierarchy. For example, if a customer characteristic has a hierarchy based on region, then by using a hierarchy variable, the user can select a specific region node, and the query is executed for all of the customers belonging to the selected region node.

Formula Variables

These variables can be used wherever there is a numeric input in the query definition, for example, in formulas, calculated key figures (CKFs), exceptions, and/or conditions. Let's take an example where you have a query that should display average sales per day for a month, selected by the user. For this requirement, you have to define a formula where the total sales value for the selected month has to be divided by the number of days in that month. In this scenario, you can use a formula variable that represents the number of days in the selected month and divide the monthly total sales with the variable value.

The procedure to create different types of variables is discussed in later sections of this chapter.

9.5.2 Processing Types of Variables

We've seen different types of variables in the previous subsection. All of these variables are passed with a value (depending on the type of variable) when the query is executed. There are different ways the values can be passed to these variables. The way in which a variable gets its value depends on the *processing type* of the variable. The processing type governs the process that fills the variable with a value when the query is executed.

SAP NetWeaver BW offers the following five different ways to process variables:

- Manual entry/default value
- Replacement path
- Authorizations
- Customer exit
- SAP exit

These processing types are explained next.

Manual Entry/Default Value

The variable created with the manual entry/default value processing type allows the variable value to be entered manually in the beginning of the query execution. You can also define the default values for the variable so that when the query is executed, the variable is prepopulated with the default value, or if the variable isn't enabled for user entry, the query is executed for the default values mentioned in the variable.

In Figure 9.20, the characteristic variables for characteristics year and sales organization are enabled for user input, and users can manually enter the values for these to variables and execute the query for these values (by clicking OK).

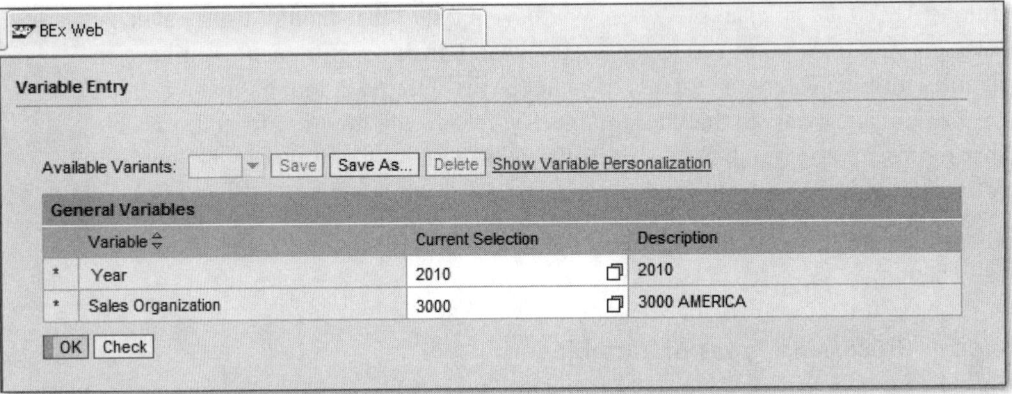

Figure 9.20 Manual Entry/Default Value Variables

This processing type is available for all of the types of variables mentioned earlier.

Replacement Path

Variables defined using the replacement path processing type are replaced automatically with the value(s) defined in the variable when the query is executed. A variable with replacement path processing can be replaced using one of the following options:

- Replace with a characteristic/attribute value.
- Replace with the values returned by another query.
- Replace with value of other variable.

Take an example of a formula variable that represents the number of days in the month (selected by the user) and then divide the key figure monthly total sales by the value of the formula variable. In this case, you can define a formula variable with the replacement path processing type. And in the definition, you specify that the value of the formula variable should be replaced with the value of the attribute number of days of characteristic calendar month.

Another example of the replacement path variable is illustrated in Figure 9.21.

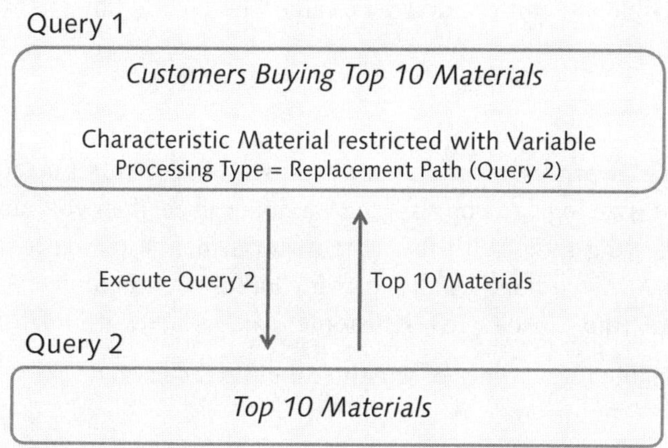

Figure 9.21 Example for Replacement Path Processing Type

Query 1 shows a list of all customers who bought the top 10 selling materials. Query 1 needs to be executed with characteristic material restricted to the top 10 materials. There's another query (Query 2) that shows the top 10 materials when executed. To address the given requirement, you can restrict the characteristic material in Query 1 with a characteristic value variable using the replacement path processing type. The definition of this variable will include Query 2 as a source of material values. So whenever Query 1 is executed, Query 2 will also be executed in the background to determine top 10 material values for this variable.

This processing type isn't available for hierarchy node variables.

Authorizations

The variables with authorizations processing type are automatically populated from the authorizations of the user. This type of processing is useful if you want to provide restricted access to the query. When a user executes the query with the authorization variable in it, he can see only the data that he's authorized to see.

For example, you want plant managers to see the data only for their plants. In the query definition, you can define a characteristic value variable on the characteristic for plant with the processing type set as authorizations. When the U.S. plant manager executes the query, the plant characteristic is automatically restricted for value = US.

This processing type is available only for characteristic value variables and hierarchy node variables.

Customer Exit

If the preceding SAP-delivered processing types don't satisfy your requirements, and you want to create your own logic to populate the variable values, then you can use the customer exit processing type. With this type, you can define the custom logic for the variable using ABAP coding. SAP has provided a function module exit EXIT_SAPLRRS0_001 to write the ABAP logic for customer exit variables.

This processing type is available for all types of variables mentioned earlier.

SAP Exit

This processing type is used in variables that are readily delivered by SAP as a part of standard SAP NetWeaver BW Business Content. This type of variable is for use only. You can't create variables with processing type SAP exit.

Table 9.1 consolidates different types of variables and the applicable processing types.

	User Entry/ Default Value	Replacement Path	Authorizations	Customer Exit
Characteristic Value	✓	✓	✓	✓
Text	✓	✓	✗	✓
Hierarchy	✓	✓	✓	✓
Hierarchy Node	✓	✗	✗	✓
Formula	✓	✓	✗	✓

Table 9.1 Variable Types and Applicable Processing Types

In the next section, we explain the procedure for creating different types of variables as discussed in this section.

9.6 Variable Editor

To create variables, SAP NetWeaver BW provides a context-dependent variable editor. Using the variable editor, you can create, change and delete variables. Context dependent means that it provides you the options to create variables based on the object from which you called the editor. For example, when you call the editor from a characteristic restrictions screen, it automatically selects the variable type as a characteristic value. When you call the editor from the formula screen, it automatically selects the variable type as a formula variable and removes the option for processing type authorizations (because it isn't allowed for formula variables).

In this section, we explain the use of the variable editor to create some of the important and most commonly used variables.

9.6.1 Characteristic Variables (Manual Entry/Default Value)

For creating a characteristic variable, you can access the variable editor from the InfoProvider screen area as shown in Figure 9.22.

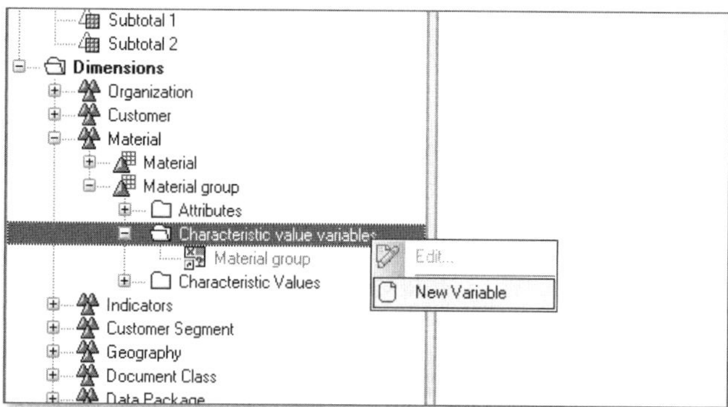

Figure 9.22 Access the Variable Editor from the InfoProvider Area

Expand the characteristic on which you want to create the variable, and select the option New Variable from the context menu of the Characteristic Value Variables folder.

Alternatively, you can create a variable directly from the Characteristic Restrictions screen. Choose Variables from the dropdown option (see Figure 9.23) on the selection screen for the selected characteristic.

For our example scenario, let's create a variable based on the characteristic material group. After you select Variables from the dropdown, the list is refreshed to the variable values available for the selected characteristic (❶ of Figure 9.24).

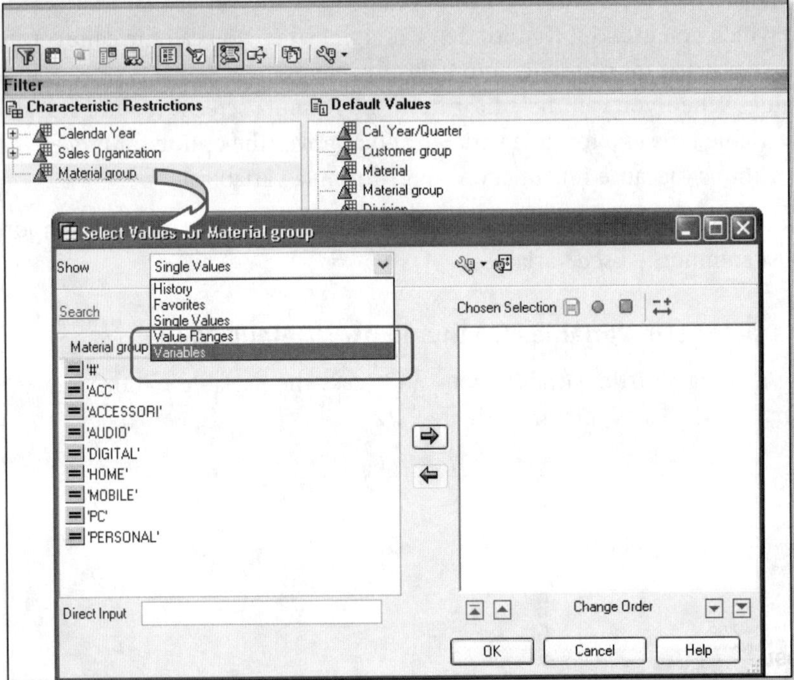

Figure 9.23 Access the Variable Editor from Characteristic Restrictions

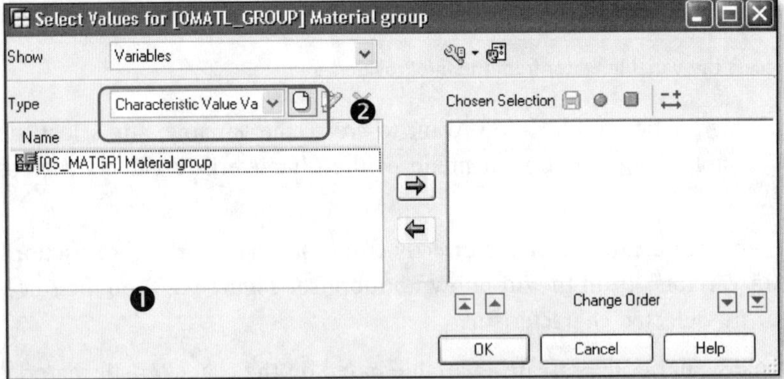

Figure 9.24 Create a New Characteristic Variable

To create a new characteristic variable, select the characteristic value variable from the Type dropdown, and then click on the create icon (❷ of Figure 9.24). This action takes you to the variable editor screen (see Figure 9.25).

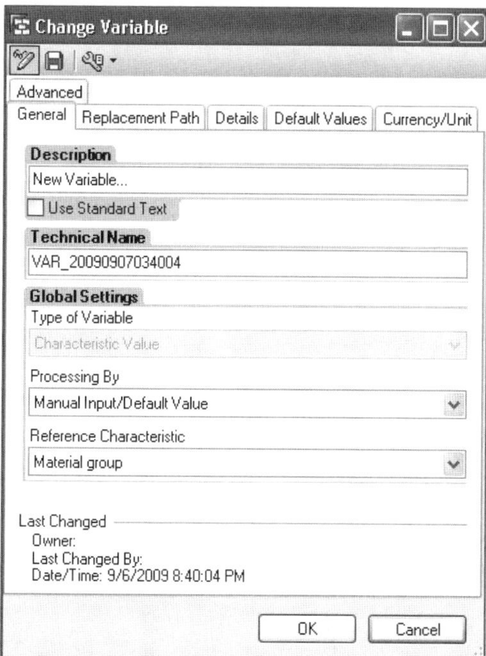

Figure 9.25 Variable Editor Screen

The different tabs visible in the variable editor are described here:

- **General:** Provides basic information about the variable, such as name and description, processing type, and so on.
- **Replacement Path:** On this tab, you define the replacement settings for a variable with a replacement path processing type. For all other processing types, this tab is grayed out.
- **Details:** This tab is used to define additional settings for a variable. The Details tab is applicable for all processing types except replacement path.
- **Default Values:** This tab is used to define the default values for a variable and is applicable only for those variables with processing type manual entry/default value.
- **Currency/Unit:** This tab is applicable only for formula variables and is used to define the dimension for the variable value, that is, whether the numeric value is an amount, price, date, time, and so on.
- **Advanced:** This is a display tab only and displays the internal system ID of the variable.

Maintain the Description and Technical Name of the variable as shown in ❶ and ❷ of Figure 9.26.

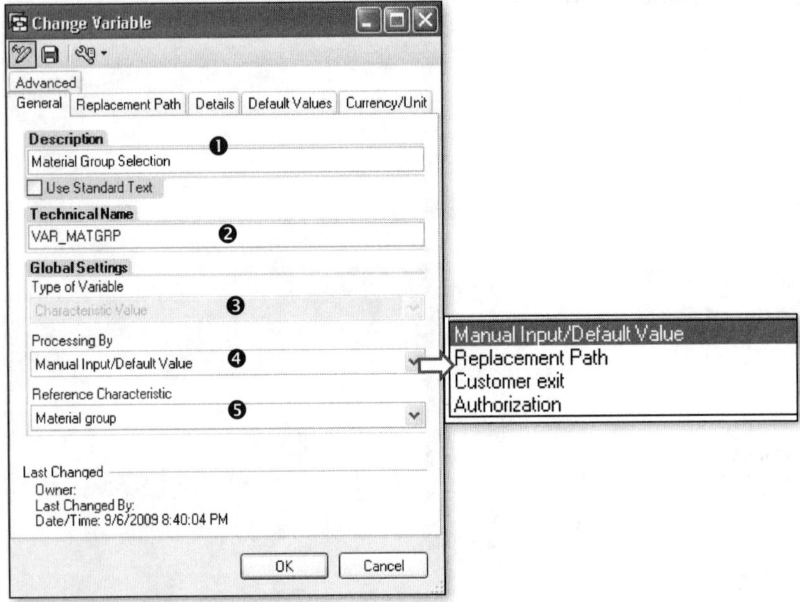

Figure 9.26 Maintain the General Tab for VAR_MATGRP

The Type of Variable (❸ of Figure 9.26) is already determined by the editor based on the element from which the variable editor is called. In this case, the editor is called from a characteristic; so the variable type is prepopulated as a characteristic value.

Select the processing type of the variable from the Processing By dropdown menu (❹). The characteristic visible in the field Reference Characteristic (❺) is the base for the variable.

The remaining definition for this variable is defined on the Details tab as shown in Figure 9.27.

On the Details tab, you decide what the variable represents from the available options (❶ of Figure 9.27). You can also define if the variable should be made as an optional variable (the user can run the query without entering a value for this variable), a mandatory variable (the user must enter a value for this variable), or a mandatory variable where the initial value isn't allowed (# isn't accepted as an input for the variable) (❷).

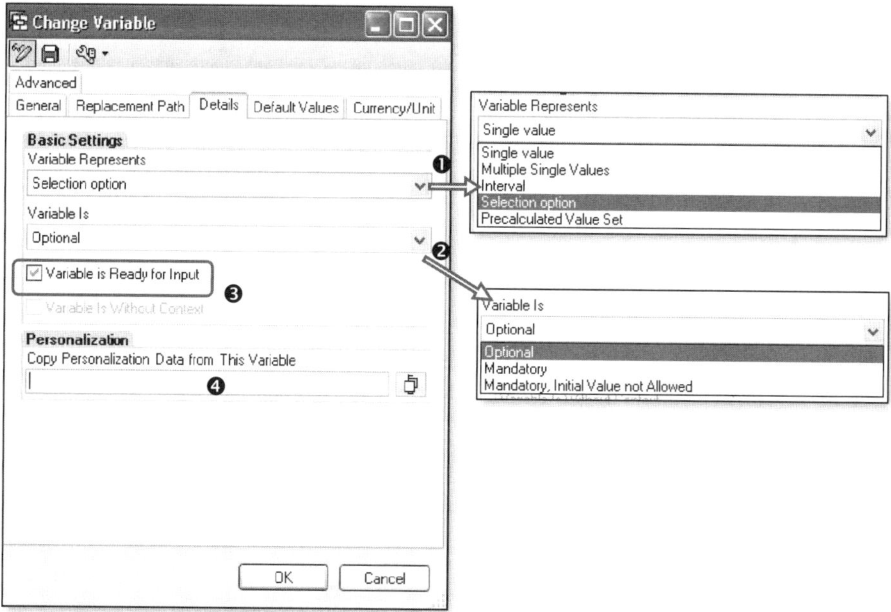

Figure 9.27 Details Tab for VAR_MATGRP

Note

If a query containing a characteristic value variable with optional entry is executed, and a user leaves the variable blank, then the query is executed for all values of that characteristic.

The checkbox setting Variable Is Ready for Input is an important setting for a variable (❸ of Figure 9.27). If this setting is checked, then the variable appears on the selection screen when the query is executed, and the user can input the values for the variable. If the box is unchecked, the user can't input the value for the variable, so the query is executed using the default values of the variable. For our example variable, we need the user to select the material group, so Variable Is Ready for Input is checked.

If you want to copy the personalization setting of an existing variable to this new variable, you can do so by including the existing variable under the Personalization section of the Details tab.

Finally, if you want to maintain the default values for the variable, those can be maintained on the Default Values tab (see Figure 9.28).

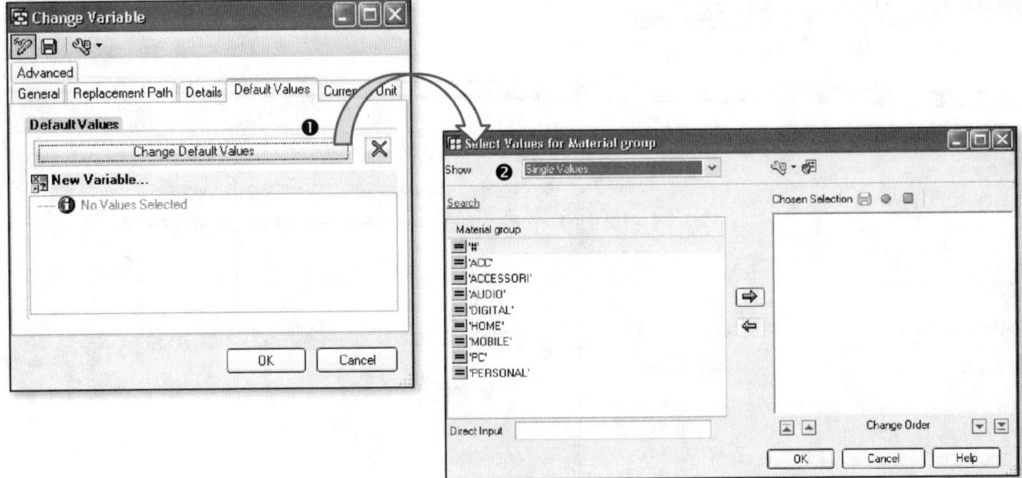

Figure 9.28 Default Values Tab for VAR_MATGRP

Click on the button Change Default Values (❶ of Figure 9.28) so you can assign the default values to the variable using the selection screen, similar to the one shown in ❷ of Figure 9.28.

Finally, save the definition by clicking the Save button as shown in ❶ of Figure 9.29.

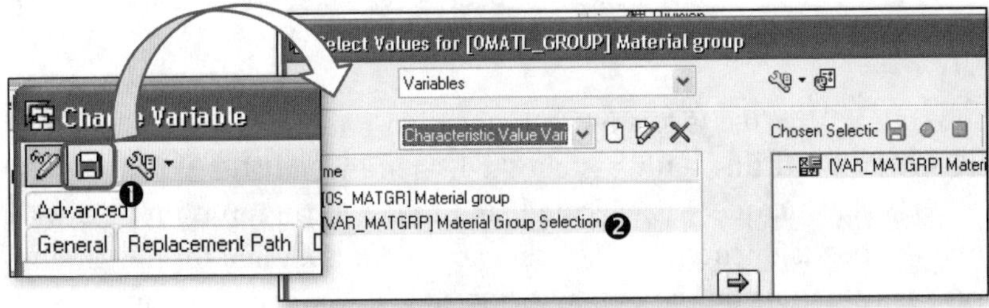

Figure 9.29 Save Variable VAR_MATGRP

The newly created variable VAR_MATGRP is now displayed in the variables list of the characteristic material group (❷ of Figure 9.29) and can be used to restrict the characteristic in the query.

9.6.2 Characteristic Variables (Replacement Path)

To define a replacement path variable, select Replacement Path as the processing type from the Processing By dropdown (❶ of Figure 9.30) on the General tab of the variable editor.

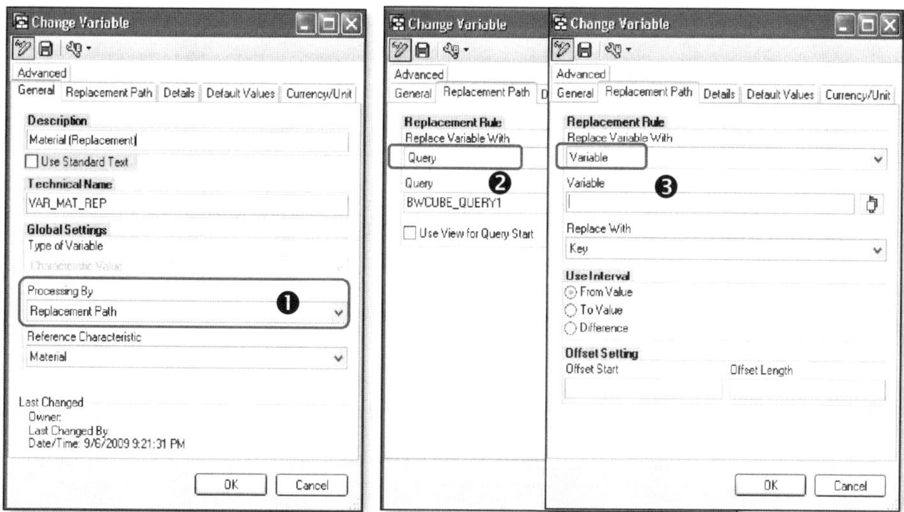

Figure 9.30 Creating Characteristic Value Replacement Path Variable

For the selected processing type, the Replacement Path tab is now enabled. On this tab, you can specify if the variable should be replaced with the value from a query (❷ of Figure 9.30) or if it should be replaced with a value from another variable (❸). The corresponding settings for the selected option can be done on the same tab.

9.6.3 Characteristic Variables (Customer Exit)

The customer exit processing type is commonly used for characteristic variables. We explain the procedure to create this type of variable with an example where the user wants to select the year for which the query should be executed. However, the user entry should, by default, be populated for the previous year value; that is if the current year is 2010, then the default value should be 2009, and when the year changes to 2011, the default value should be 2010.

To address this requirement, you can create a variable based on the characteristic year with the customer exit processing type (❶ of Figure 9.31). A customer exit variable can be built in two steps. The first step is to define the variable using the variable editor, and the second step is to write the ABAP logic in a customer exit.

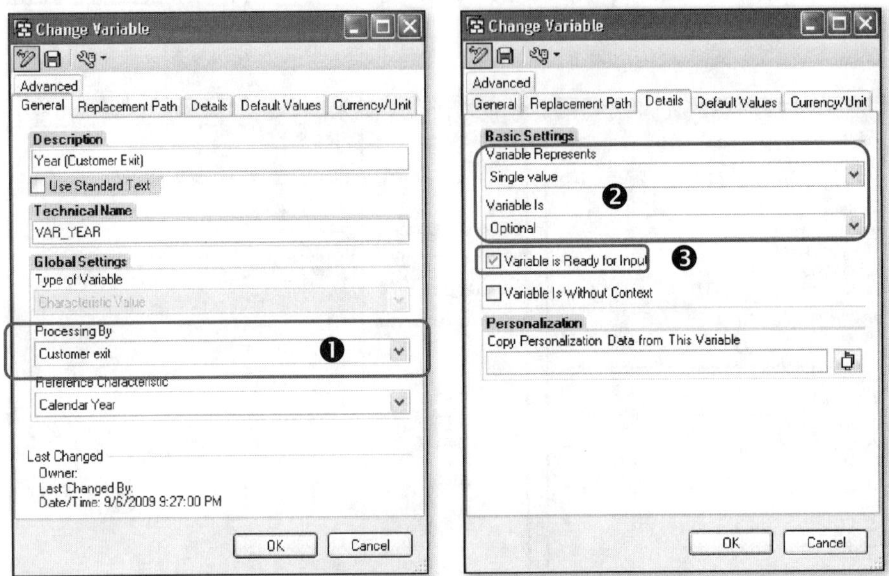

Figure 9.31 Define Variable with Customer Exit Processing Type

Define the variable as shown in Figure 9.31. The query has to be run for one year only, so the variable should represent a single value (❷). Note that because a user wants to decide on the year value for which the query should be executed, you have to select the Variable Is Ready for Input checkbox (❸).

Finally, save the variable definition.

To write the ABAP logic for customer exit variables, SAP has provided a function module exit EXIT_SAPLRRSO_001 in SAP NetWeaver BW. This exit can be accessed only through a project for SAP enhancement. The project can be created using Transaction CMOD in SAP NetWeaver BW (❶ of Figure 9.32).

The project used for customer exit query variables should contain the enhancement RSR00001 (❷ of Figure 9.32), which makes the function exit EXIT_SAPLRRSO_001 available under components of the project (❸). Double-click on the function exit to enter the code. The function builder screen for the exit is displayed as shown in Figure 9.33.

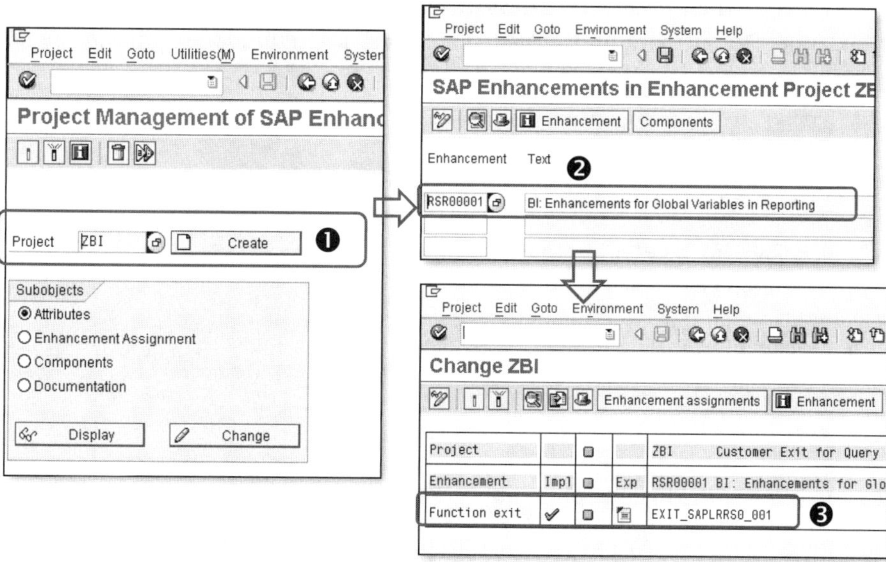

Figure 9.32 Define a Project Using the Function Module for Customer Exit

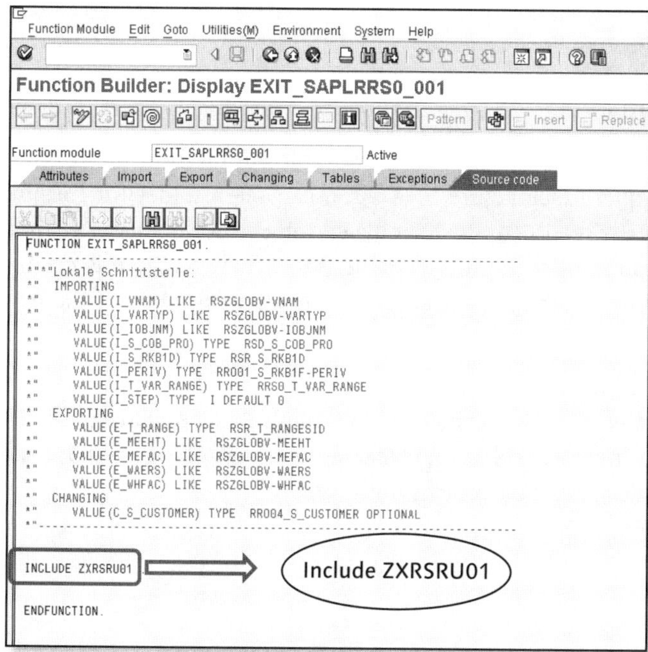

Figure 9.33 Include to Write Custom Logic

SAP has provided an INCLUDE ZXRSRU01 as a separate placeholder for all of the custom code. Double-click on this include to enter it in edit mode, and add the following code to the include:

```
when 'VAR_YEAR'.
DATA YEAR(4).    " Data Declaration
IF i_step = 1. " For default value
YEAR = sy-datum+0(4). " Get Year from system date
YEAR = YEAR - 1. " Get Previous Year
  l_s_range-low =  YEAR.
  l_s_range-sign = 'I'.
  l_s_range-opt  = 'EQ'.
  append l_s_range to e_t_range.
  exit.
endif.
```

Save and activate the Include program.

A customer exit variable can be defined in this manner. When the query using this variable is executed, this logic is executed first, and the previous year is derived based on the system data. Also, because the variable is marked as ready for input, a user can see the default value of this variable as previous year and can change it to some different value is needed.

9.6.4 Formula Variables

To create a formula variable, you can access the variable editor from the formula screen while defining a query (see Figure 9.34). You can see a folder for formula variables under the operands section of the formula editor. Select New Variable from the context menu to create a new formula variable (❶). A new variable is created in the folder. To define this variable, select Edit from the context menu of the new variable (❷).

For example, you want to create a formula variable that should return the total number of days for the selected calendar month. To achieve this, you have to set the processing type of the formula variable as replacement path (❶ of Figure 9.35) and the reference characteristic as calendar year/month (❷).

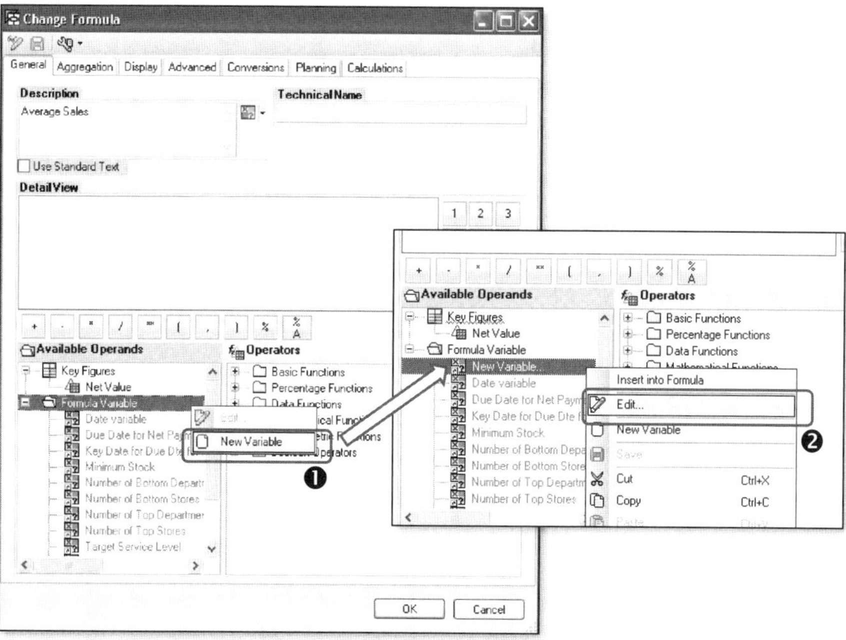

Figure 9.34 Accessing the Variable Editor from the Formula Dialog

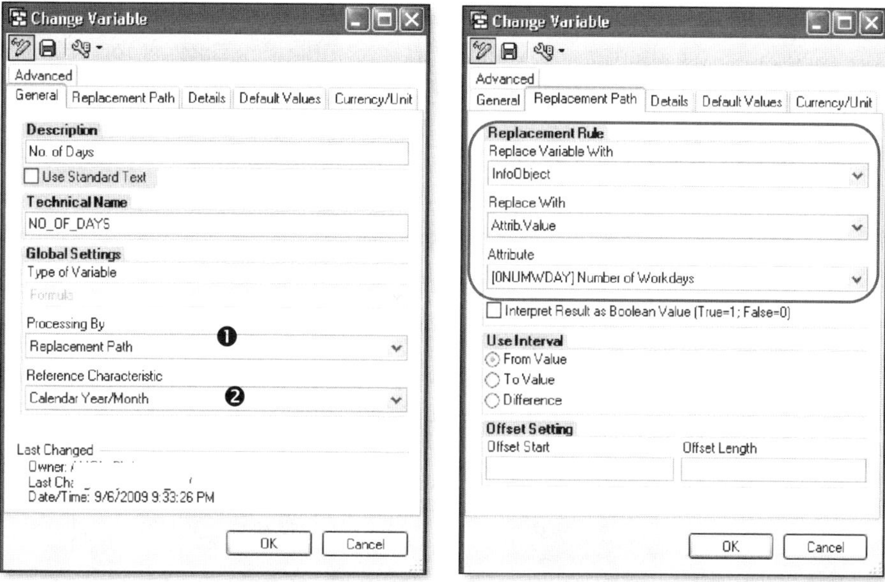

Figure 9.35 Define the Formula Variable

The details for this variable are maintained on the Replacement Path tab. Maintain the settings as shown in Figure 9.35.

Also, the Currency/Unit tab becomes applicable for the formula variable. On this tab, you can define the dimension for the numeric value stored in the variable (see Figure 9.36). Because the numeric value stored in the formula variable we've defined (number of days in a month) is purely a number, the dimension can be set as Number.

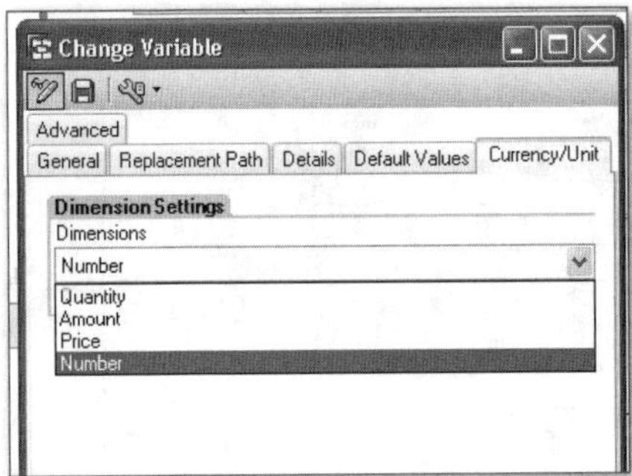

Figure 9.36 Currency/Unit Tab

Save the variable, and it's available to be used in the query definition.

9.6.5 Text Variables

Text variables can be used if you want to have flexible descriptions for different query elements. You can use a variable in the description wherever there is a variable icon available. To call the variable editor, click on this icon (❶ of Figure 9.37), and then click on New Variable (❷).

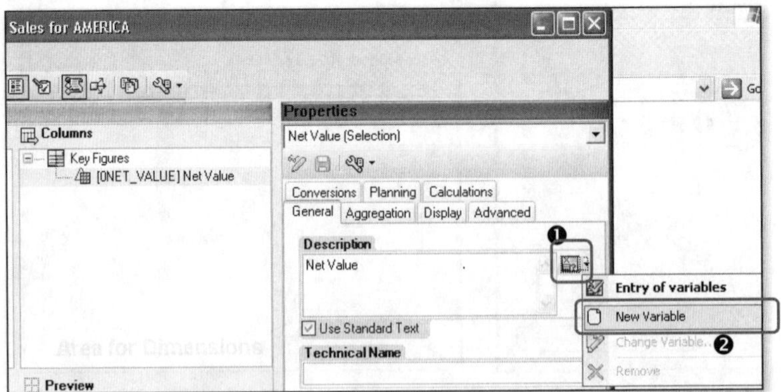

Figure 9.37 Calling the Variable Editor for a Text Variable

Let's take an example where you want the column description for key figure net value to be dynamically populated with the year for which the query is executed. To achieve this, you have to set the processing type of the text variable as replacement path and the reference characteristic as calendar year (see ❶ of Figure 9.38).

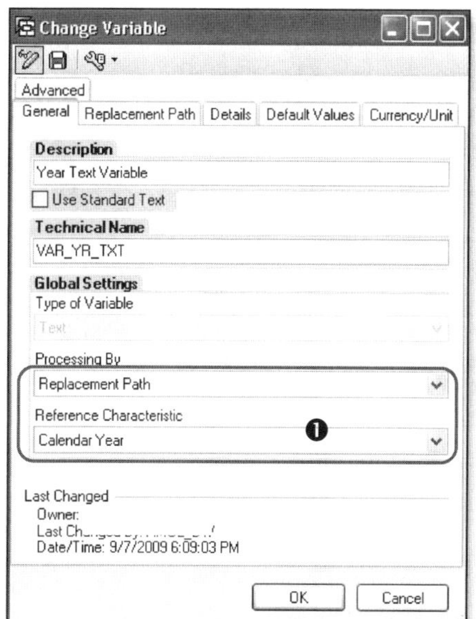

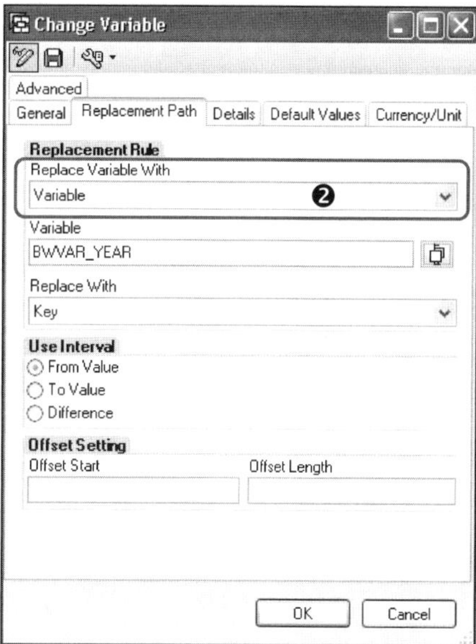

Figure 9.38 Define Text Variable

The details for this variable are maintained on the Replacement Path tab. Maintain the settings as shown in Figure 9.38. Note that in this example we're replacing the text variable with the value of calendar year entered in another characteristic variable (❷).

9.7 Filters — Selection Objects

Filters are used to restrict the query execution to a specific data set. These restrictions can be applied on a set of characteristics together. You can also save the filter defined in one query as a reusable object that is available for all other queries built on that InfoProvider.

Let's take an example where users want to see the sales data with the following restrictions:

- **Year:** Users should select the value for the year. However, the selection screen should show the previous year as the default value.

- **Division:** Users should be able select the division for which they want to see the data.
- **Country:** Users should be able to run the query only for selected entries.
- **Sales Document Category:** The values displayed in the report should not include the sales from sales documents with document category as N.

To create these restrictions in a query, first drag the relevant characteristic into the Characteristic Restrictions area of the query, and then call the restrictions window from the context menu of the characteristic (❶ of Figure 9.39).

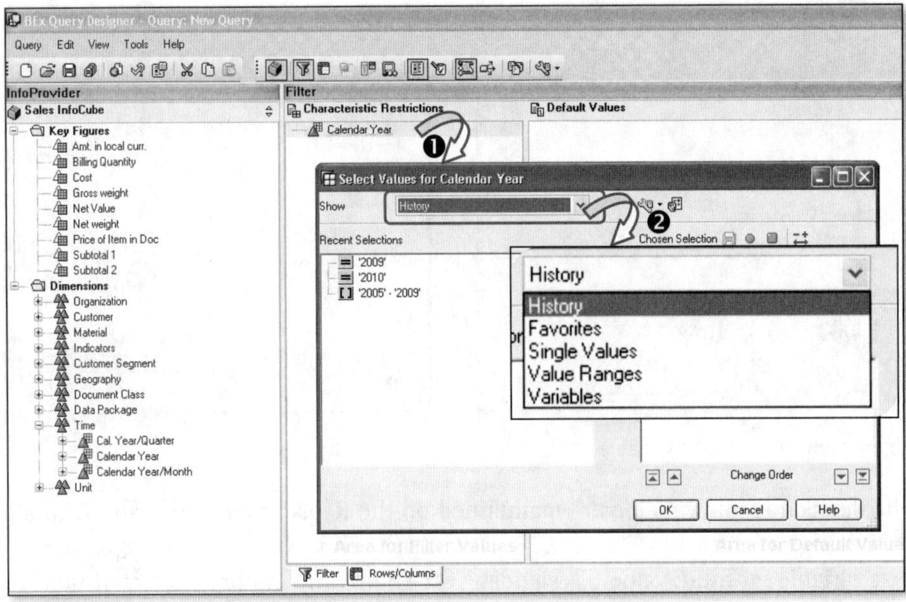

Figure 9.39 Restricting a Characteristic

There are different options available on this screen to restrict a characteristic (❷):

- **History:** The restrictions you've recently used are saved here.
- **Favorites:** This view shows you all of the selections you've saved earlier as your favorites.
- **Single Values:** Use this option if you want to restrict the characteristic with a single value or multiple single values.
- **Values Ranges:** Select this option for restrictions involving a value range or multiple value ranges.

- **Variables:** You can restrict the characteristic with different variables available for the selected characteristic.

Using the example mentioned earlier, select the customer exit variable for calendar year as shown in ❶ of Figure 9.40.

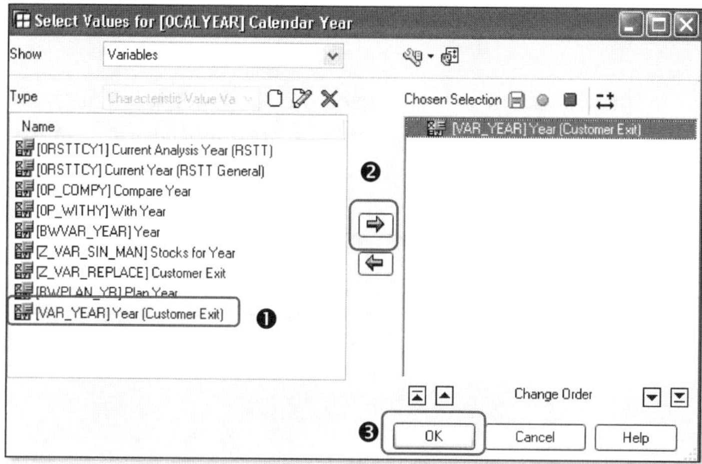

Figure 9.40 Restrict with Variable

Use the arrow button (❷) to include it in the selection. Finally, click the OK button (❸) to return to the query design.

Some additional functions are available on the selection screen with respect to the values selected for the characteristic. These functions are shown in Figure 9.41.

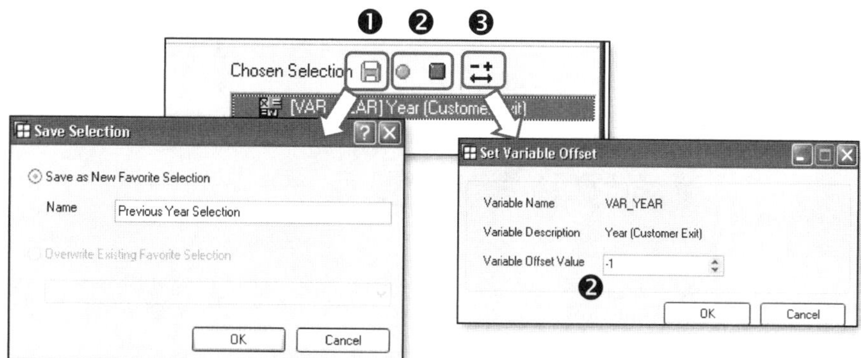

Figure 9.41 Additional Functions on the Selection Screen

If you want to use the selected values frequently, then you can save those values under your favorites list by clicking on the save button (❶).

The red and green buttons (❷) are used to exclude or include the values form the selection.

If you want to define an offset on the selection value, you can use the offset option for the selection. Click the button (❸), and maintain the desired offset for the selected value.

Restrictions can be maintained for different characteristics together in a query. For the given example, you can drag the other characteristics, such as division, country, or document category, and restrict it per the logic (see Figure 9.42).

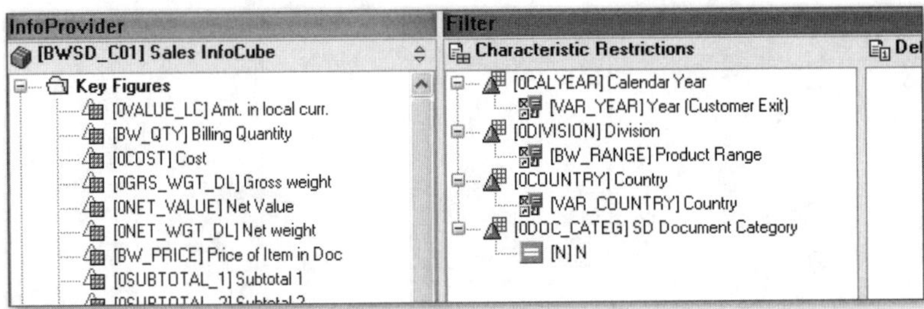

Figure 9.42 Filter Defined for Multiple Characteristics

Note that in Figure 9.42, the characteristic SD Document Category is excluded for the value N. After this filter is defined for a query, it can be saved as a reusable component to be used in other queries built on the same InfoProvider (Figure 9.43).

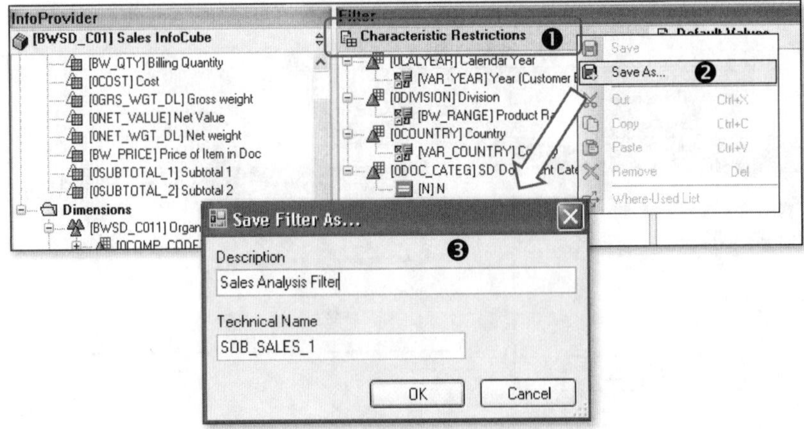

Figure 9.43 Saving the Filter as a Reusable Component

To save this filter, open the context menu (right-click) from the Characteristic Restrictions bar (❶ of Figure 9.43), and select Save As (❷). Maintain the description and technical name for the filter, and save it as a reusable component (❸).

Note

The saved filters are available as selection objects (SOB) in the SAP NetWeaver BW metadata.

Now, if you create a new query on the same InfoProvider, the saved filters are visible under the Filter folder in the InfoProvider screen area of the designer (❶ of Figure 9.44).

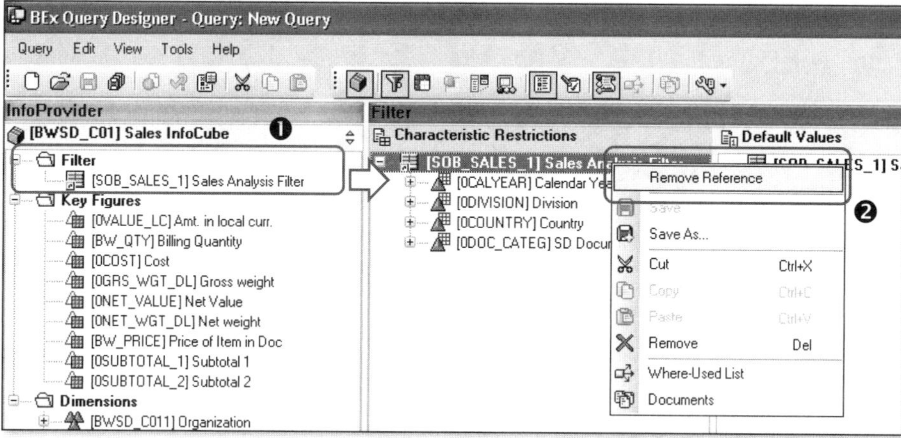

Figure 9.44 Reusing Saved Filters

To reuse the already existing filters, you have to select, drag, and drop the filter into the Characteristic Restrictions area. If you make any changes to this filter in this query, those changes will be reflected in all of the queries that are using the same filter. So if you want to make any changes that are specific only for that query, you must remove the reference for the filter used in the query. For this, open context menu for the filter and select Remove Reference to detach the filter (❷ of figure 9.44).

9.8 Structures

Structures (identified with) are basic structural components of a BEx query that are used to define the layout of the query for a row or column. There are two types of structures based on the type of components contained in a structure:

- Key figure structures
- Characteristic structures

9.8.1 Key Figure Structures

Key figure structures include the components that are based on a key figure such as basic, formula, restricted, and calculated key figures. A key figure structure is automatically created in the query when you drag and drop key figures from the InfoProvider screen to the query rows/columns. This structure is by default named Key Figures (see Figure 9.45).

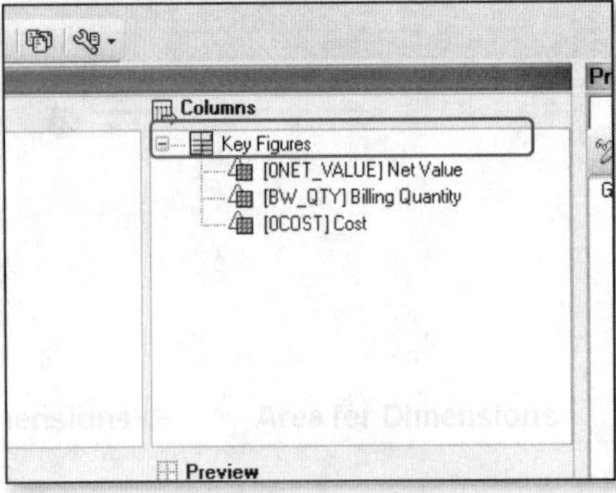

Figure 9.45 Key Figure Structure

Each component included in a key figure structure should include a key figure. This means you can include key figures, formula key figures, selection with key figures, restricted key figures (RKFs), and calculated key figures (CKFs) in a key figure structure. But a characteristic or a selection without a key figure can't be included in the key figure structure.

Note

A maximum of two structures are allowed in a query definition, and only one of those can be a key figure structure.

9.8.2 Characteristic Structures

Characteristic structures are optional in query definition and are used if you want to display a specific number of characteristic values in a specific sequence. To create a new structure, select Create New Structure from the context menu of the Rows area (see Figure 9.46).

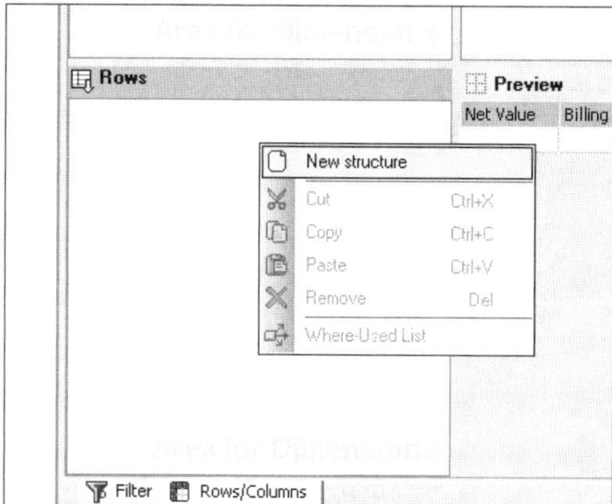

Figure 9.46 Create New Structure

You can add the structural components to the structure by selecting an option from the context menu (see Figure 9.47).

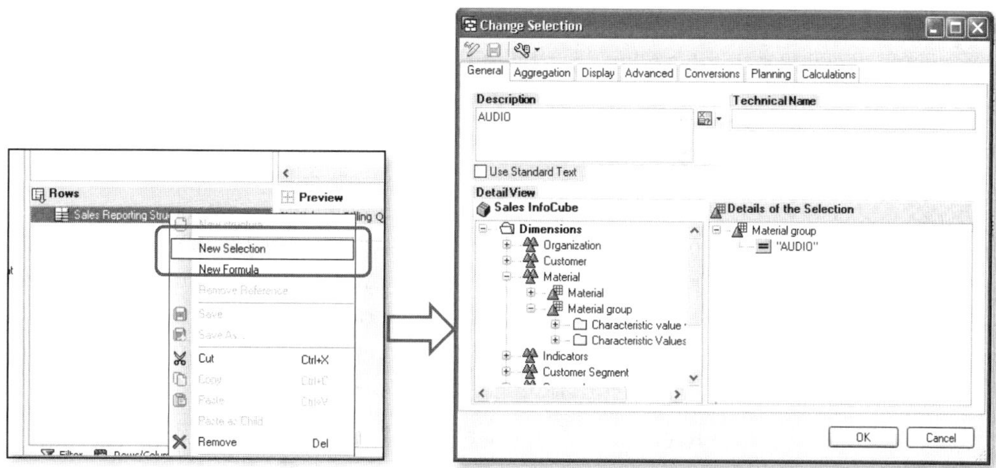

Figure 9.47 Add Structural Components to a Structure

When you use two structures in a query, you can additionally define a separate logic (selections or formula) for each cell formed due to the intersection of the two structures. This logic will override the cell values generated implicitly from the intersection of structures. Click on the cell definition button (❶ of Figure 9.48) or use menu path VIEW • CELLS. This option is activated only when there are two structures in the query.

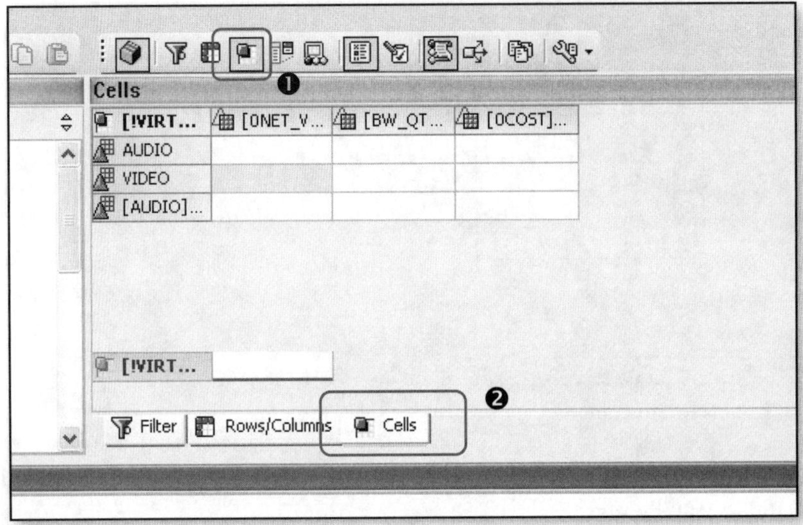

Figure 9.48 Cell Definition

When cell definition is enabled, an additional Cells tab area is visible on the query designer layout (❷ of Figure 9.48).

9.8.3 Reusing Structures

Take the example where ABCD Corp. uses the following three key figures most commonly in all of the queries: value, qty, and cost. You've used these key figures in a query, and they are part of the KF structure. You can save this structure as a reusable component, which can be included in other queries on the same InfoProvider. To save the structure, select Save As from the context menu, and save it after providing the appropriate technical name and description (see Figure 9.49).

When you create a new query on the same InfoProvider, this saved structure is visible under the Structures folder in the InfoProvider tab (❶ of Figure 9.50).

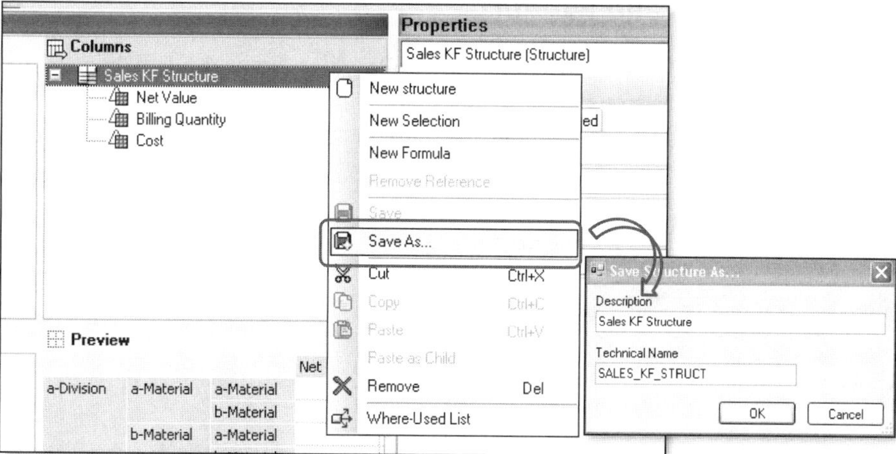

Figure 9.49 Save the Structure for Reuse

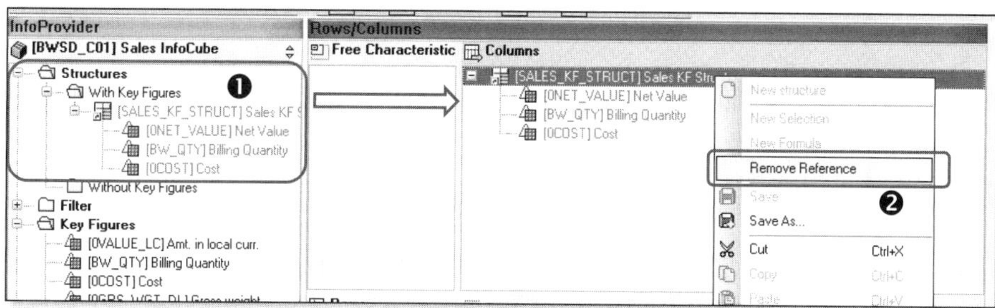

Figure 9.50 Reusing Structures

This can be directly pulled into the Rows/Columns area to use in the new query. However, if you make changes to this structure, those will be reflected in all queries that use it. So if you want to make some changes to this structure that are specific to only one query, you should detach the definition in the query by selecting Remove Reference from the context menu (❷).

Reusable structures built for commonly used collections of key figures or characteristics can make query development easier and faster due to its reuse in multiple queries (e.g., a plan/actual variance set of key figures or a year-on-year comparison scenario).

9.9 Selections and Formulas

The characteristics and key figures from the InfoProvider can be directly dragged into the Rows/Columns area to define the query. But sometimes using the elements just as available in the InfoProvider isn't enough. Take the example of a report as shown in Figure 9.51.

KF Net Value for Year = 2009 KF Net Value for Year = 2008

Division	Material Group	Sales 2009	Sales 2008
CE	AUDIO	$6,831.67	$5,504.44
CE	DIGITAL	$638,493.30	$260,472.99
CE	HOME	$30,855.50	$14,072.42
CE	MOBILE	$22,618.81	$28,826.48
CE	PC	$18,974.66	$21,661.73
CL	PERSONAL	$46,393.59	$3,910.54
DA	HOME	$124,251.23	$0.00

Figure 9.51 Columns Restricted with Year Values

In this case, the key figure net value is used in both columns, but each column is restricted by a specific characteristic value (year = 2009 and 2008, respectively). This kind of requirement can be addressed using selections in the query key figure structure.

Let's add one more field to the query shown in Figure 9.51. Per the requirements, the analysts now want to compare the 2009 sales with respect to sales values from year 2008 (see Figure 9.52). This additional column involves a calculation logic that needs to be defined in the query. This and similar requirements that involve calculations can be addressed using formulas in the query key figure structure.

{(Sales 2009 – Sales 2008)/Sales 2008}*100

Division	Material Group	Sales 2009	Sales 2008	YoY Comparison (%)
CE	AUDIO	$6,831.67	$5,504.44	24.11
CE	DIGITAL	$638,493.30	$260,472.99	145.13
CE	HOME	$30,855.50	$14,072.42	119.26
CE	MOBILE	$22,618.81	$28,826.48	-21.53
CE	PC	$18,974.66	$21,661.73	-12.40
CL	PERSONAL	$46,393.59	$3,910.54	1,086.37
DA	HOME	$124,251.23	$0.00	0.00

Figure 9.52 Column Based on a Formula

In this section, we explain you the process to create selections and formula for the query using the same example mentioned above.

9.9.1 Selection

To begin with, get all of the characteristics needed to define the query in the Rows section (❶ of Figure 9.53), and also drag the key figure Net Value, which is needed to define the query. When you add the first key figure to the columns, the key figure structure is automatically created (❷).

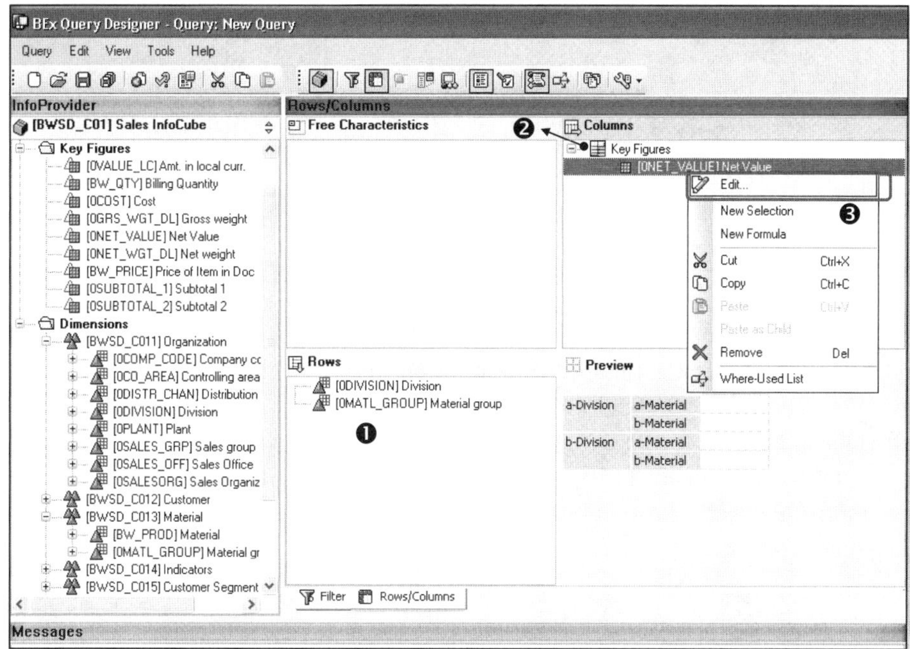

Figure 9.53 Edit Key Figure

You can restrict this key figure by applying selections to it. Double-click on the key figure, or select Edit from the context menu for the key figure (❸ of Figure 9.53). This action will open a selection screen for the key figure (Figure 9.54).

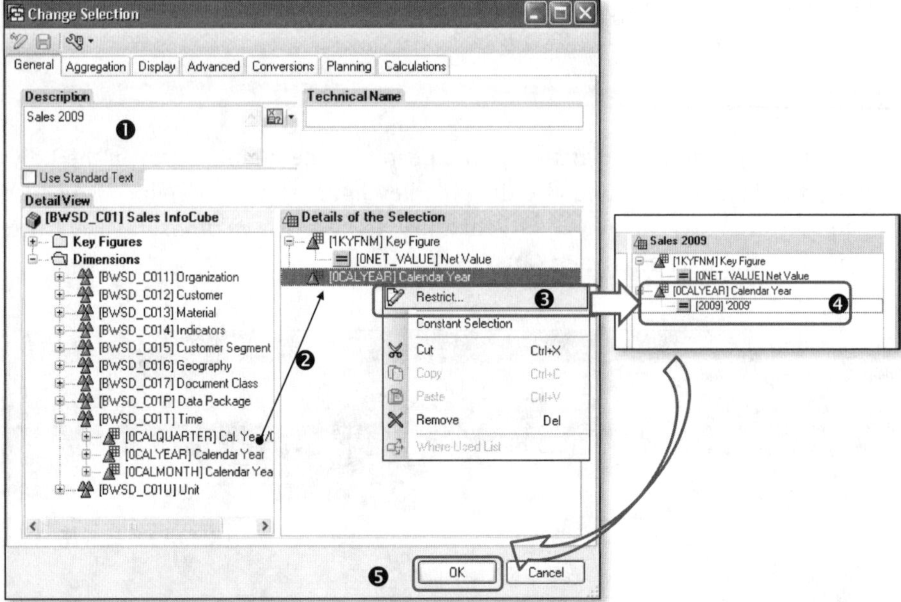

Figure 9.54 Define Selection

In this screen, you can maintain the description for the structure element (❶ of Figure 9.54). Then, select Calendar Year from the InfoProvider definition visible on the left side, and drag it to the Details of the Selection area on the right side (❷). Here you can restrict the characteristic to the desired value using the Restrict option from the context menu (❸). Restrict the characteristic calendar year to value 2009 (❹), and click on OK (❺) to return to the query definition.

Note

You can also use characteristic variables in the selection.

To create a new selection, use the New Selection option from the context menu (❶ of Figure 9.55). This will create a new selection component in the key figures structure (❷). Double-click or select Edit from the context menu to define this selection.

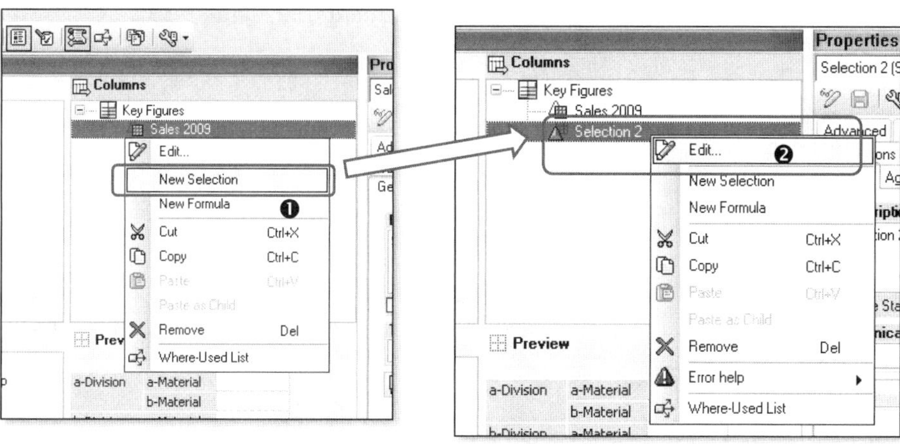

Figure 9.55 Create New Selection

As explained earlier, define this selection for Sales 2008 as shown in Figure 9.56.

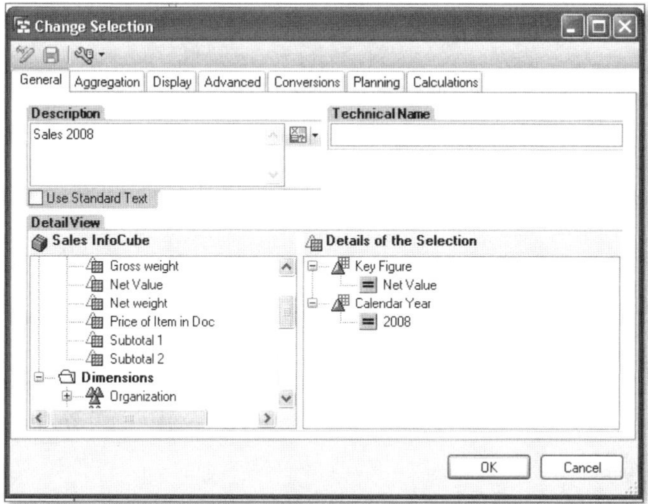

Figure 9.56 Define New Selection

When you create a new selection like this, you also have to specify the key figure in the selection.

Note

You can add only one key figure for a selection element, and because it's part of a key figure structure, you must have a key figure in all selections under this structure.

Both the columns are now ready per the requirement (see Figure 9.57).

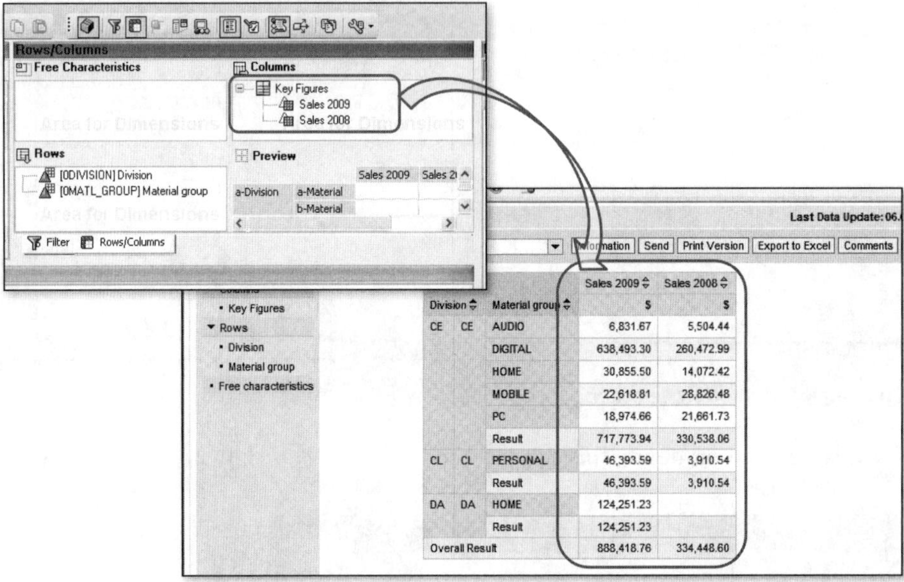

Figure 9.57 Query Output with Selections

You can address more complex requirements using selections involving multiple characteristics and variables, and by using include/exclude and offset features.

9.9.2 Formula

Let's now move on to the next requirement, which is to add a column that compares the 2009 and 2008 values in the column Comparison YoY (%) (refer to Figure 9.52 earlier in this chapter). This type of calculation is addressed using the formula component in the structure. To create a formula, select the option New Formula from the context menu as shown in ❶ of Figure 9.58.

This action creates a new formula component in the key figure structure. To define the calculation for this formula, double-click or select Edit from the context menu (❷). The formula editor screen appears in the pop-up where you can define the logic (see Figure 9.59).

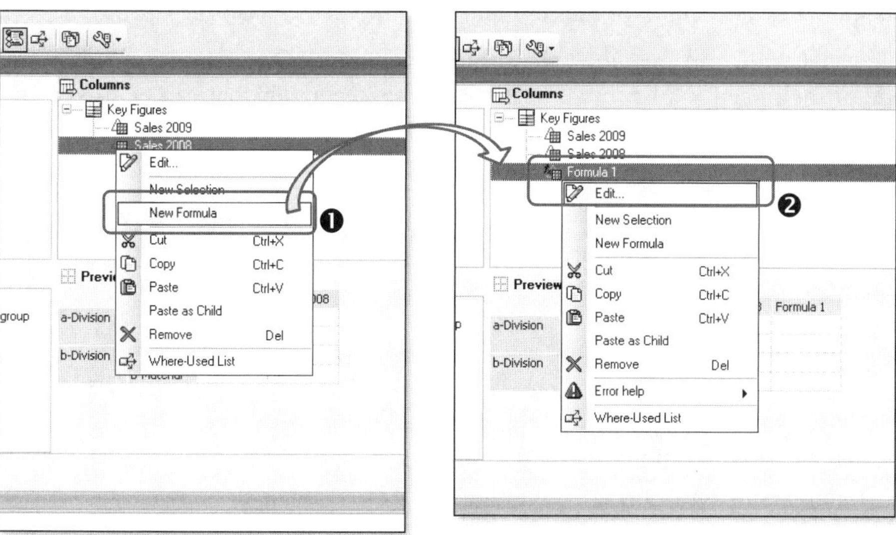

Figure 9.58 Create New Formula

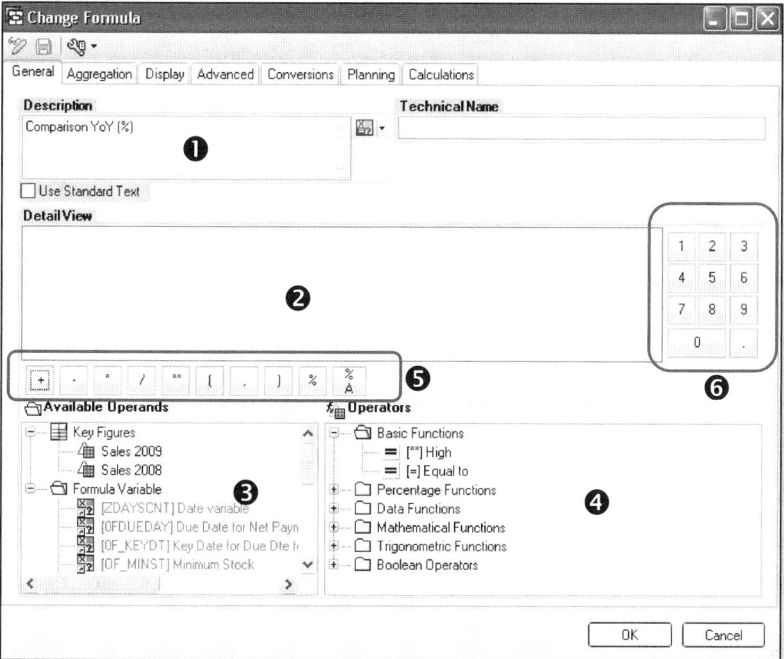

Figure 9.59 Formula Editor

Maintain the description of the component on this screen (❶ of Figure 9.59).

The Detail View section shows the formula definition (❷), and on the bottom-left side of the screen is a list of all of the Available Operands that can be used in the formula (❸). The operands can be any available key figures for the InfoProvider or any formula variables.

On the bottom-right side of the screen, there is a list of operators that could be used to define the formula (❹). These functions are grouped together into the following categories:

- Basic Functions
- Percentage Functions
- Data Functions
- Mathematical Functions
- Trigonometric Functions
- Boolean Operators

You have to select any operator and operand from the bottom part of the screen and double-click to add it to the formula. You can also use the basic operators (❺) and the number pad (❻) to define a formula.

Let's create a formula for the comparison column mentioned in our example. The logic is

```
((2009 Value - 2008 Value) / (2008 Value))*100
```

This logic can be built for the formula as shown in Figure 9.60.

Note the use of the NDIVO(x) function. This is used to handle the scenario when the denominator is zero. In this case, the formula will return value 0 instead of x. The result of the query is shown in Figure 9.61.

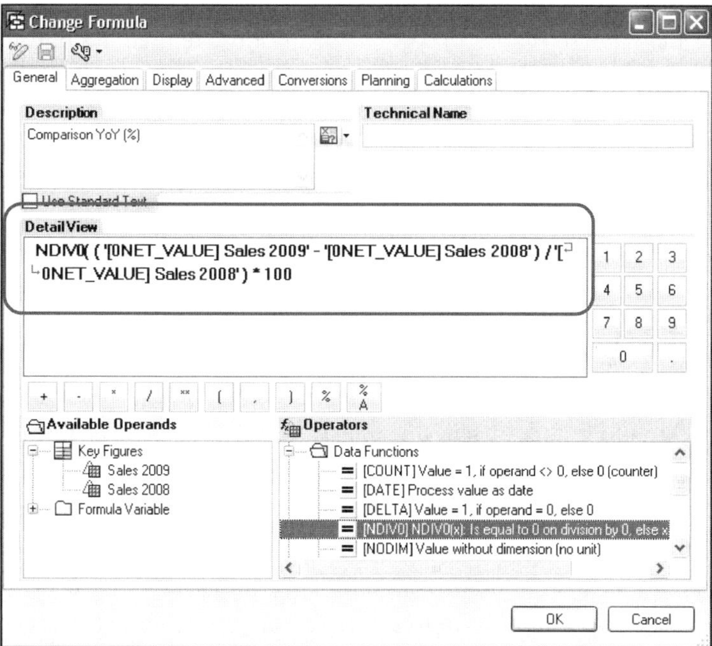

Figure 9.60 Define the Formula

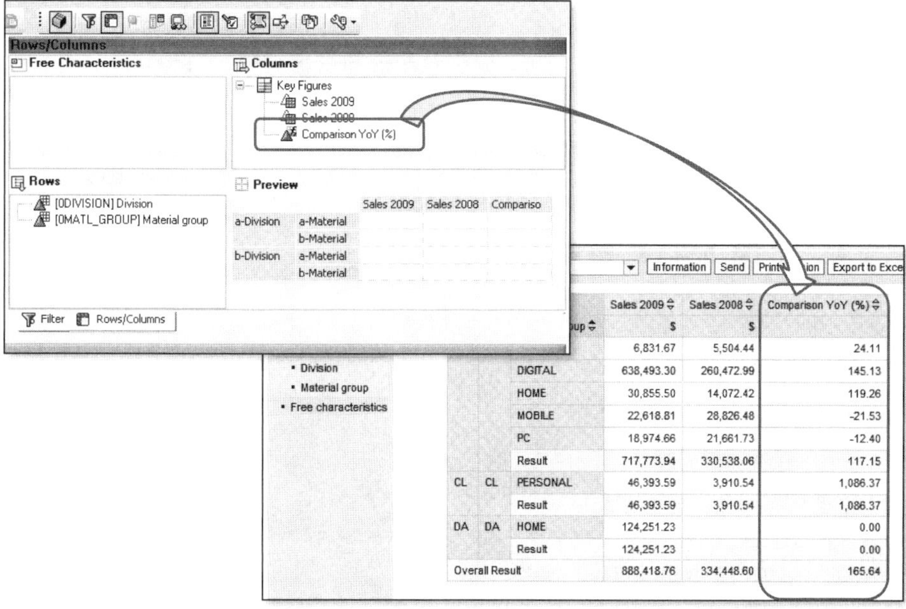

			Sales 2009 $	Sales 2008 $	Comparison YoY (%)
			6,831.67	5,504.44	24.11
		DIGITAL	638,493.30	260,472.99	145.13
		HOME	30,855.50	14,072.42	119.26
		MOBILE	22,618.81	28,826.48	-21.53
		PC	18,974.66	21,661.73	-12.40
		Result	717,773.94	330,538.06	117.15
CL	CL	PERSONAL	46,393.59	3,910.54	1,086.37
		Result	46,393.59	3,910.54	1,086.37
DA	DA	HOME	124,251.23		0.00
		Result	124,251.23		0.00
Overall Result			888,418.76	334,448.60	165.64

Figure 9.61 Query Output with Formula

Now you know the procedure to create selections and formulas in a BEx query. There are situations where the same selections or formula definitions are used in multiple queries. In these situations, you can obviously create the selections and formulas separately for each query. However, there is a better option available in the form of restricted key figures (RKFs) and calculated key figures (CKFs), where you can create the reusable selections and formulas that can be used in multiple queries. In the subsequent sections, we'll explain to you the procedure for creating restricted key figures and calculated key figures.

9.10 Restricted Key Figures

Restricted key figures (RKFs) are reusable query elements where the selection definition can be built on the InfoProvider itself, thus making the definition available for all of the queries on that InfoProvider.

For illustration, let's take the example of a selection called Mexico Sales, which displays the key figure value for net sales where Country = Mexico. This particular definition is used in multiple queries on the Sales InfoCube. It makes sense to create a RKF for the same so that you don't have to create the same key figure again and again for each query.

RKFs are created directly on the InfoProvider definition visible in the InfoProvider area (see Figure 9.62).

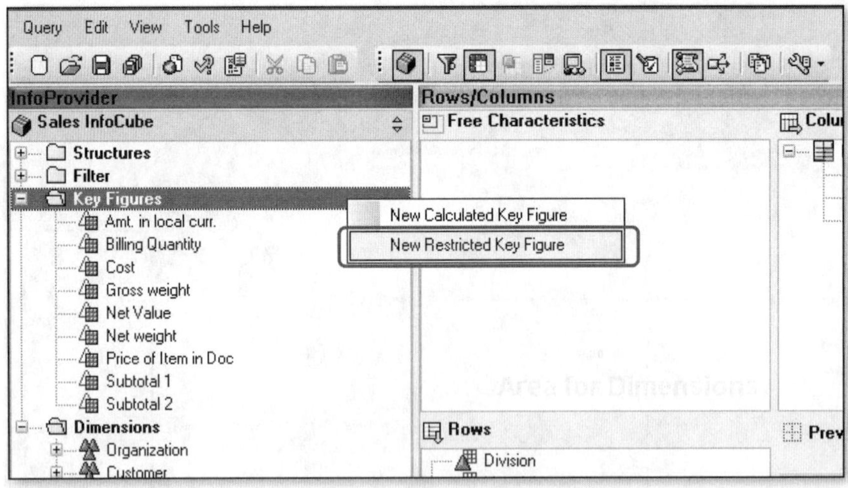

Figure 9.62 Create a Restricted Key Figure

Open the context menu for the Key Figures folder in the InfoProvider area, and select New Restricted Key Figure from the context menu (see Figure 9.62).

You have to provide the RKF a suitable Description (❶ of Figure 9.63) and also a Technical Name (❷) in the definition screen.

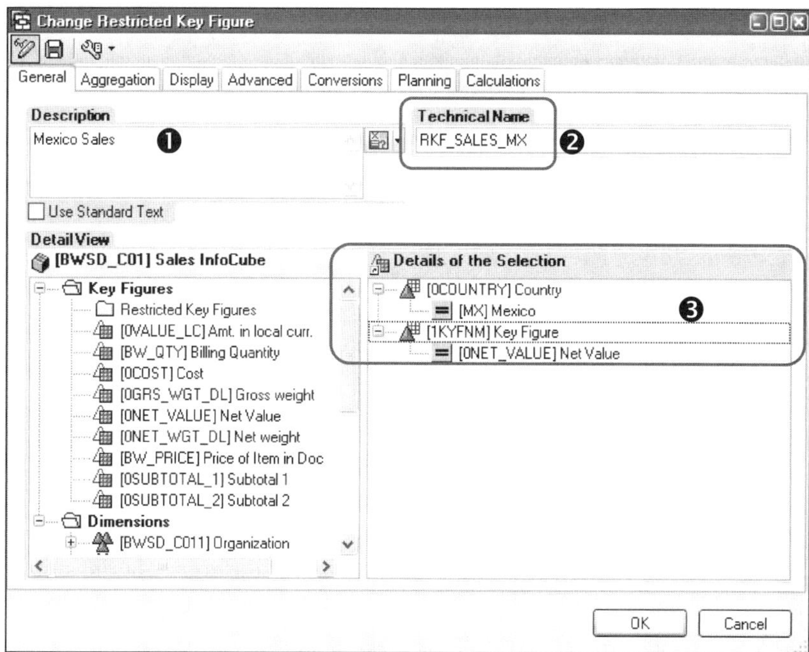

Figure 9.63 Define Restricted Key Figure

Define the selections for the RKF per the example requirement stated earlier where Key figure = Net Sales for Country = Mexico (❸).

Save the RKF by using the Save button from the toolbar.

The saved RKF is now visible under the Restricted Key Figures folder on the InfoProvider screen area (see Figure 9.64).

This RKF is defined at the InfoProvider level and is available for all of the queries that are defined on this InfoCube. To reuse the RKF in a query definition, you simple have to drag and drop the RKF to the desired location in the query definition (Rows or Columns area).

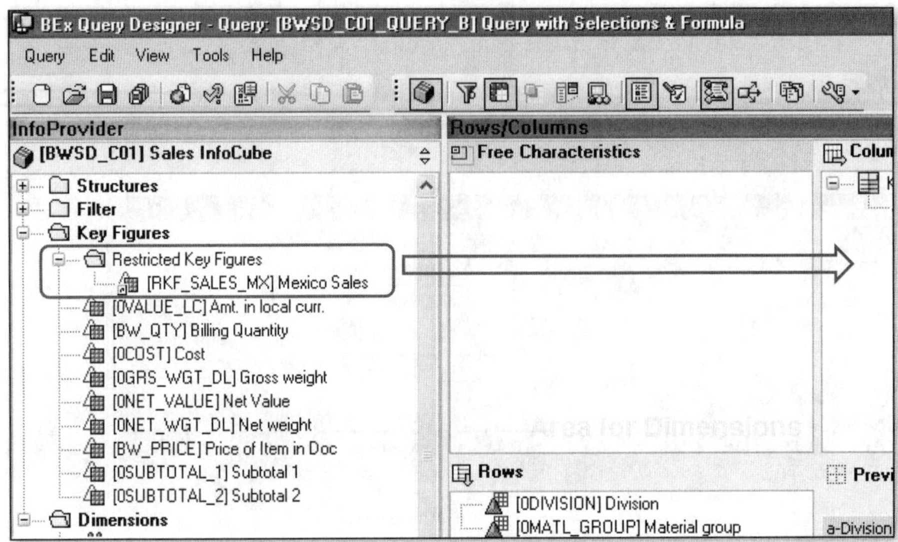

Figure 9.64 Reuse Restricted Key Figure

9.11 Calculated Key Figures

Similar to RKFs, calculated key figures (CKF) are defined at the InfoProvider level. The CKF facilitates the reuse of a formula definition across different queries on the InfoProvider.

CKFs can be created using the New Calculated Key Figure option from the context menu of the Key Figures folder in the InfoProvider screen area (refer to Figure 9.62 earlier in this chapter).

Define the CKF in the pop-up box as shown in Figure 9.65. You have to maintain the Description and the Technical Name for the CKF (❶).

Further, define the formula logic in the Detail View section for the CKF (❷). After the definition is complete, click the Save button on the toolbar.

The newly defined CKF is available in the InfoProvider screen area under the folder Calculated Key Figures (see Figure 9.66).

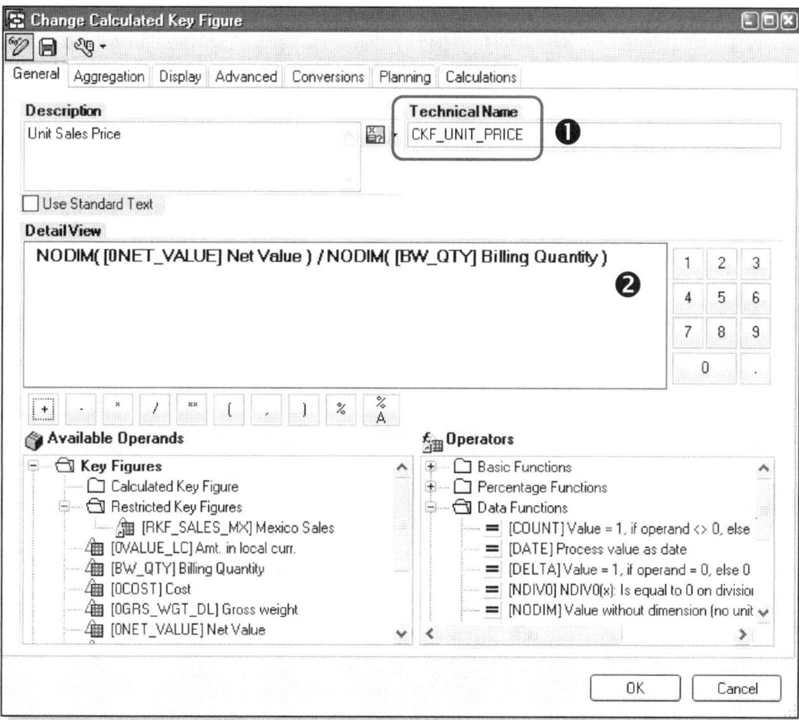

Figure 9.65 Define the Calculated Key Figure

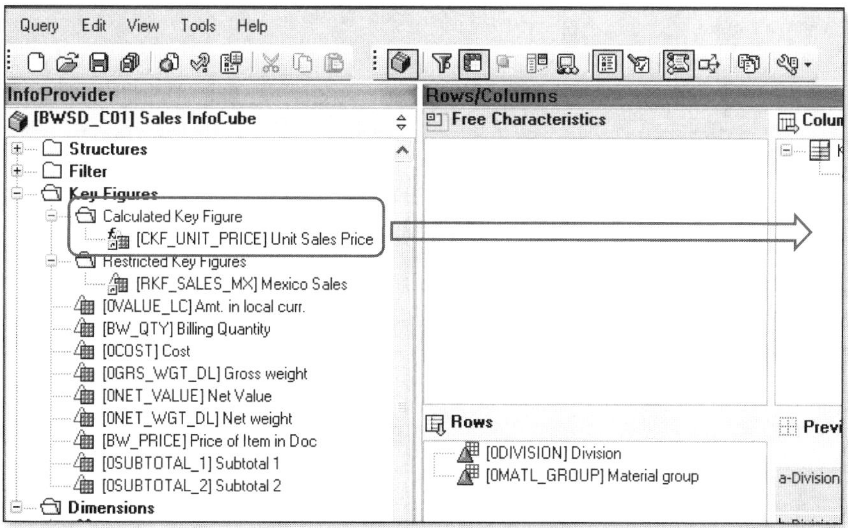

Figure 9.66 Reuse Calculated Key Figure

The definition in the CKF is available for reuse in all of the queries that are built on that InfoProvider. To use the CKF during query designing, you simply have to drag and drop the selected CKF into the desired query area (Rows or Columns area).

9.12 Properties of Query Elements

All components of the query (including the query itself) have their own set of properties, which include settings for description, display, data access, calculation, and so on. These properties determine the behavior of that element. The properties for the selected query element are visible in the Properties screen area of the BEx Query Designer. Also, you can select a query element for which you have to define the properties from the dropdown available in the Properties screen area (see Figure 9.67).

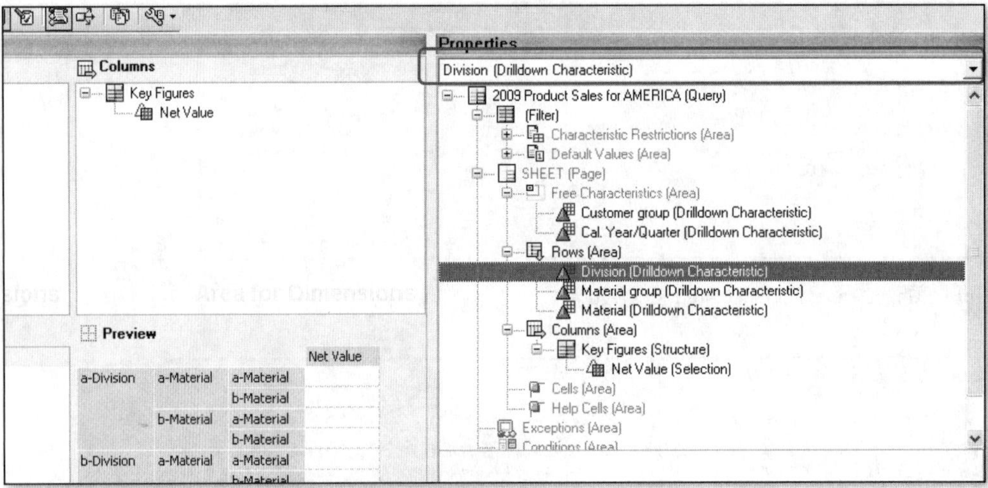

Figure 9.67 Access Properties of Query Elements

9.12.1 Set Properties of Characteristic Query Elements

In this section, we explain the different properties that correspond to a characteristic query element. Select the characteristic for which you want to define the properties as shown in Figure 9.67.

The properties for the selected characteristic element will appear in the Properties screen area as shown in Figure 9.68. There are five different tabs available. Let's discuss each of these tabs one by one.

Characteristic Properties: General Tab

In the General tab (see Figure 9.68), you maintain the description of the characteristic of that query. The same description (❶) will be visible in the query output when the query is executed. If you select the Use Standard Text checkbox, the description as mentioned in the InfoObject definition is selected.

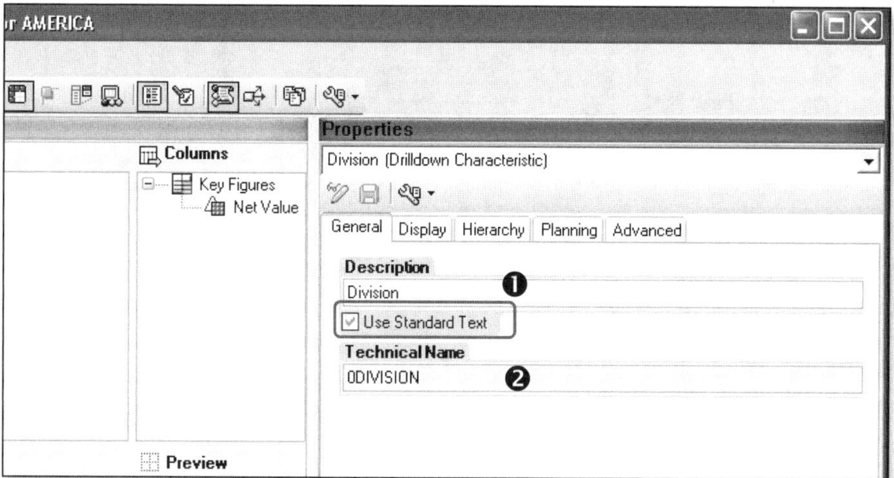

Figure 9.68 Characteristic Properties – General Tab

You also see the Technical Name of the characteristic on this Properties tab (❷).

Characteristic Properties: Display Tab

You control the display-related settings of the characteristic in the query on this tab (see Figure 9.69). There are three sections available on this screen.

In the Value Display section, you can select the way characteristic values should be displayed (❶ of Figure 9.69). Also, in the Text View field, you can specify which text (short, medium, or long) should be displayed.

> **Note**
>
> For a characteristic that doesn't have any texts maintained, the key value of the characteristic is displayed as text in the query output.

In the Sorting section (❷), you define how the characteristic should be sorted (ascending or descending) in the query output.

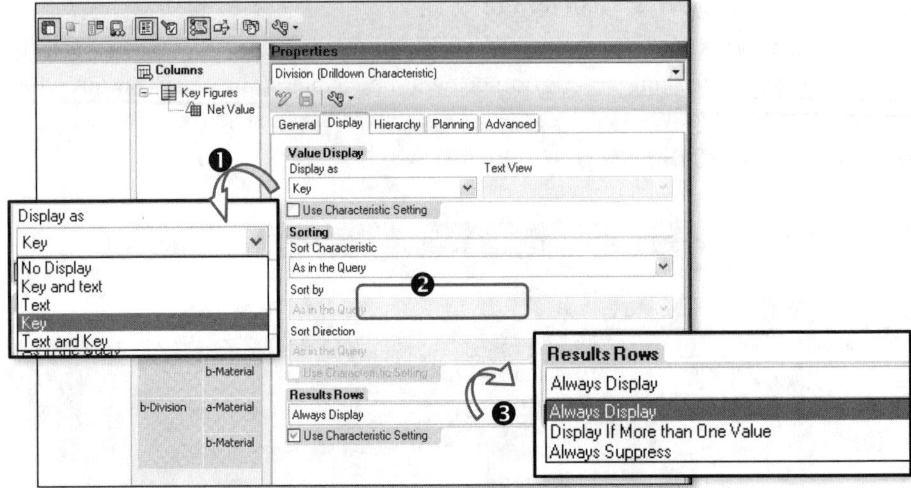

Figure 9.69 Characteristic Properties – Display Tab

The Result Rows section allows you to set the display options of the totals (result rows) in the query output (❸).

Characteristic Properties: Hierarchy Tab

If the characteristic, for which properties are being maintained, contains hierarchies built on it, then you can set different properties on the Hierarchy tab. On this tab, you can select the hierarchy to used in the query, and you can define the display and sorting settings for the selected hierarchy.

Characteristic Properties: Planning Tab

The options specific to planning on hierarchy nodes are available on the Planning tab of characteristic properties. This setting is relevant for input-ready queries only. Input-ready queries in planning are explained in Chapter 12, Integrated Planning.

Characteristic Properties: Advanced Tab

The properties related to data access and data selection are maintained on the Advanced tab of the characteristic properties (see Figure 9.70).

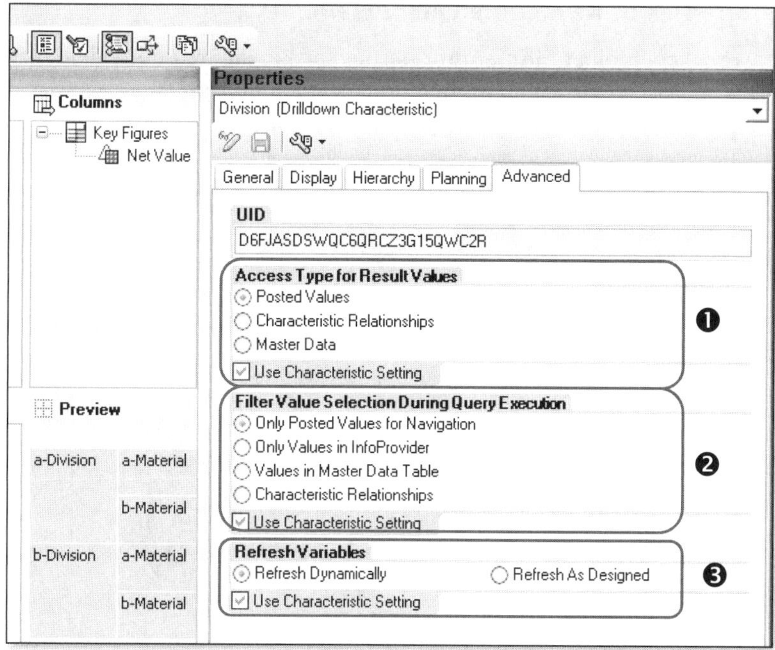

Figure 9.70 Characteristic Properties – Advanced Tab

Under the Access Type for Result Values section (❶ of Figure 9.70), you can define what values of the characteristic should be displayed in the query output. These options are explained here:

- If you use the Posted Values option, only posted values of the characteristics (per the query definition) are displayed in the query output.
- If you want to display the data per the characteristic relationships, then choose the Characteristic Relationships option as the access type. Characteristic relationships are discussed in detail in Chapter 12, Integrated Planning.
- The Master Data option displays all of the characteristic values from the master data, whether transaction data exists for those values or not.

Similarly, in the Filter Value Selection During Query Execution (❷ of Figure 9.70), the setting determines the list of values you would get while selecting a filter value during query execution. You can also make variable refresh settings under the section shown in ❸ of Figure 9.70.

9.12.2 Set Properties of Key Figure Query Elements

In this section, we take a look at different properties for key figure query elements. The Properties screen for a query element involving a key figure shows seven different tabs (see Figure 9.71). These tabs and important properties are explained next.

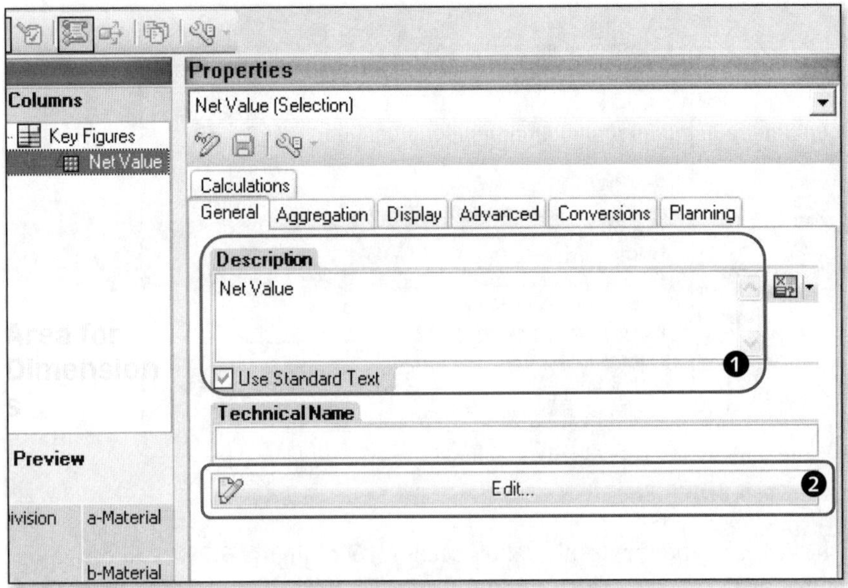

Figure 9.71 Key Figure Properties – General Tab

Key Figure Properties — General Tab

You maintain the description and technical name for the query element on this tab (❶ of Figure 9.71). The description maintained here is visible in the query output. If you want to keep the default description from the key figure InfoObject description, select the Use Standard Text checkbox. Additionally, you can edit the definition of the element by clicking on the Edit button (❷).

Key Figure Properties — Aggregation

On this tab page, you can specify how the aggregation should take place for the key figure when the query is executed. This tab is enabled only for query elements of type formula or CKFs (see Figure 9.72).

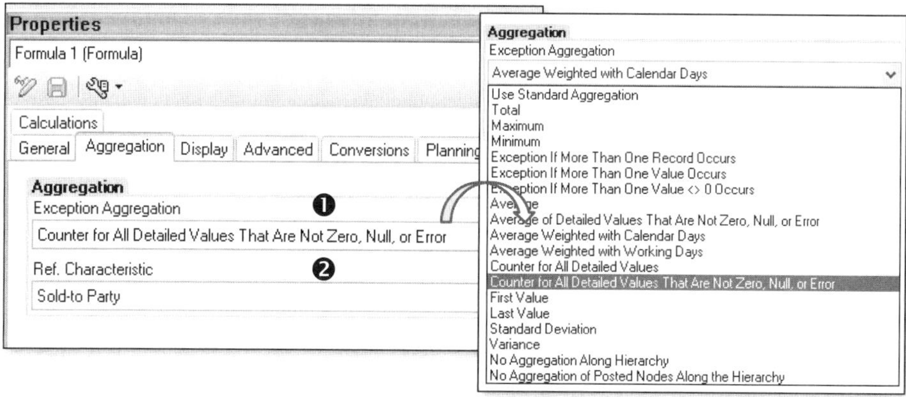

Figure 9.72 Key Figure Properties - Aggregation

By default, the key figures are aggregated using standard aggregation. In a standard aggregation, the data read from the InfoProvider is first aggregated by the characteristics included in the rows/columns of the query. Then the formula is applied to the data after this aggregation. The Exception Aggregation option (❶) allows you to define if you want to aggregate the data in a certain specific manner and with respect to the reference characteristic. The different options of Exception Aggregation are available under the dropdown shown in Figure 9.72.

If you choose to use an exception aggregation, then you have to specify one of the characteristics from the InfoProvider as the reference characteristic against which the formula will be calculated (❷).

For example, if you want to calculate the number of customers who are buying a particular material, you create a formula with key figure net value. Then, in the properties of the formula, you select Exception Aggregation as Count <> 0 and Customer as the Reference Characteristic.

Key Figure Properties — Display Tab

On the Display tab of the properties, you have different options available to control the display of the key figure value in the query output (see Figure 9.73).

Use the settings under the Hide section (❶ of Figure 9.73), if you want to hide the key figure in the output. There is also an option available to highlight the key figure value under the Highlight section (❷). Additional settings related to the number of decimal places, scaling factor, and so on, can also be set on this Display tab.

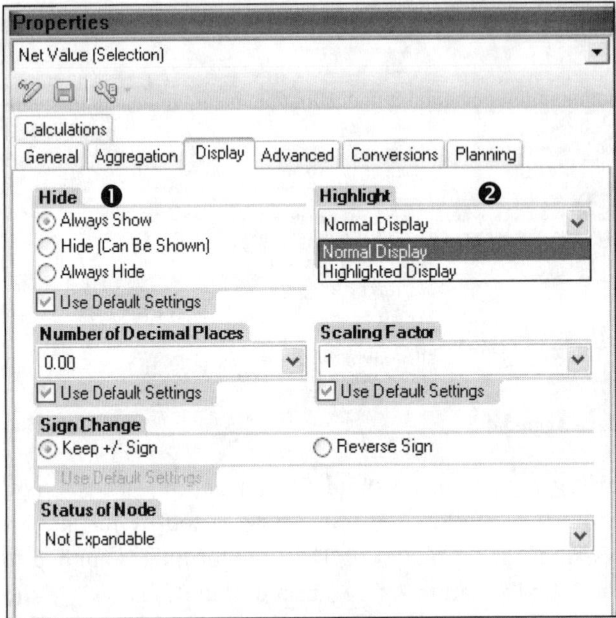

Figure 9.73 Key Figure Properties – Display Tab

Key Figure Properties — Advanced Tab

The Constant Selection setting on the Advanced tab of a key figure query element (❸ of Figure 9.74) is available only for elements of type selections/RKFs.

This setting of constant selection is used if you want to keep the characteristic selections mentioned in the definition of the selection/RKF as constant. It means that during the query execution and navigation, the restrictions applied on the key figure do not change.

This setting is particularly important if you want to use a key figure value as a fixed reference for comparison with other key figures. Take an example where the business analysts at ABCD Corp. want to compare the sales for different material groups with respect to the sales for Material Group = DIGITAL. The report would look as shown in Figure 9.74.

You can see in Figure 9.74, that the Digital Sales column has a constant value for all of the rows (❶ of Figure 9.74), and this value is nothing but the sales value where Material Group = DIGITAL (❷). As a result, the comparison can now easily be achieved using a simple formula.

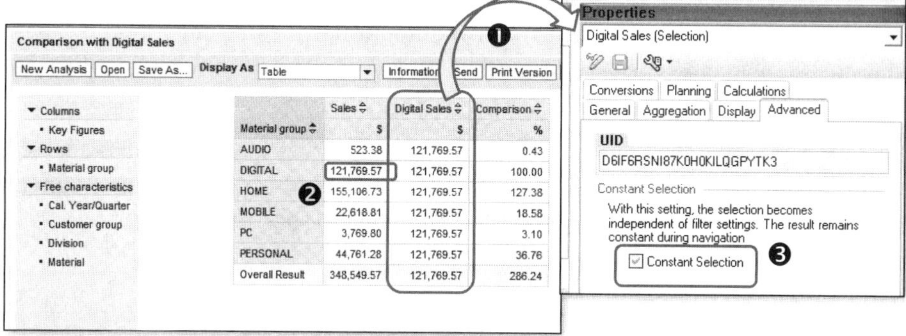

Figure 9.74 Constant Selection

In this case, the setting Constant Selection was used on the Digital Sales (Selection) (❸).

Key Figure Properties — Conversions Tab

The settings on the Conversions tab (see Figure 9.75) are useful if there is a key figure of type amount or quantity included in the query element definition, and you need to convert the amount or quantity in a uniform currency/unit.

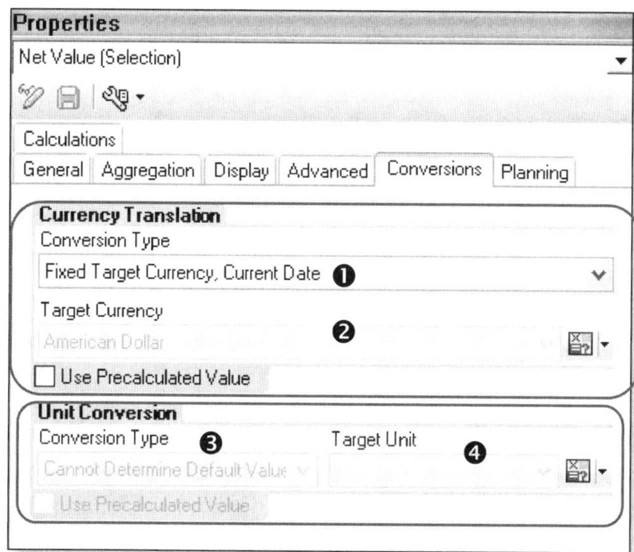

Figure 9.75 Key Figure Properties – Conversions

The Currency Translation section of this tab is available for key figures of type amount. Here, you can define the way the amount needs to be converted by specifying the Conversion Type (❶ of Figure 9.75) and the Target Currency to which the key figure value is translated (❷).

If the key figure is of type quantity, the Unit Conversion section of this tab is enabled. Similar to the settings for currency translation, here you have to define the Conversion Type (❸) and the Target Unit (❹) as parameters for unit conversion.

Key Figure Properties – Planning Tab

The Planning tab allows you to set the properties for a key figure included in an *input-ready query*. The Planning tab and the significance of all of the available settings are explained in Chapter 12, Integrated Planning.

Key Figure Properties – Calculations Tab

The Calculations tab allows you to define the way you want the results and the single values to be calculated for the report output (see Figure 9.76).

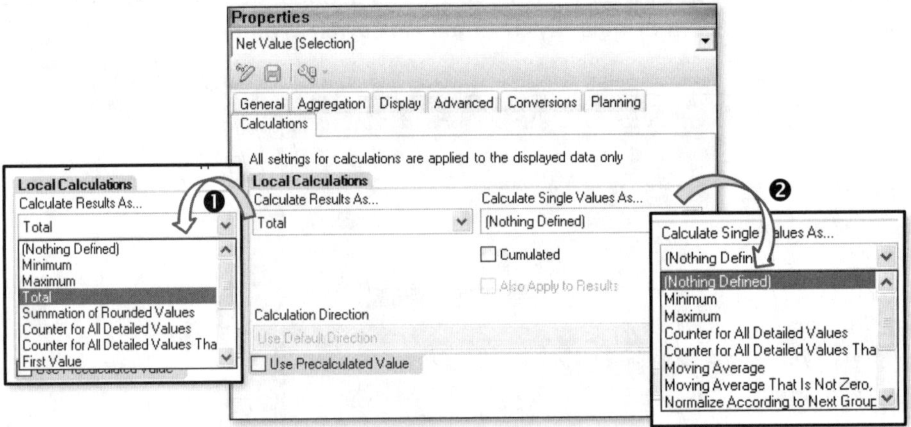

Figure 9.76 Key Figure Properties – Calculations Tab

The option you choose in the Calculate Result As area (❶ of Figure 9.76) will actually recalculate the result per the selected option. Similarly, the option you select under Calculate Single Value As (❷) will influence the way single values are recalculated for the query output display.

9.12.3 Query Properties

Different properties that are defined at the query level are discussed in this section. To display the query properties, select the query node from the dropdown available in the Properties screen area (❶ of Figure 9.77).

There are seven different tabs where you can set the query properties. These tabs are explained next.

Query Properties — General Tab

The General tab of query properties displays the technical name and allows you to maintain the description of the query (❷ of Figure 9.77). This description is visible to the report user when the query is executed. You can also use text variables for flexible query description.

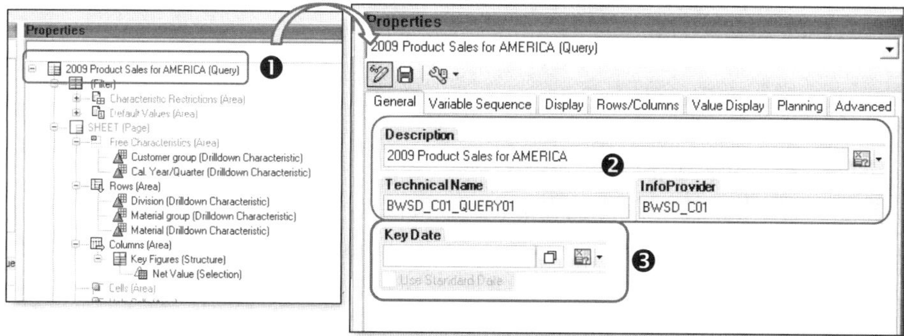

Figure 9.77 Query Properties – General Tab

If the query involves any time-dependent master data, then the date specified in the Key Date field is used to derive the values from the time-dependent data (❸ of Figure 9.77). You can maintain any specific date as a key date in the query, or you can use a characteristic variable on the date as a more flexible option. If nothing is included in the Key Date settings for a query, then the date of query execution is considered as the key date for that query.

Query Properties — Variable Sequence Tab

The Variable Sequence tab displays a list of all of the variables that are enabled for user entry. You can change the order in which the variables should appear on the selection screen when the query is executed.

Query Properties — Display Tab

The display-related settings for the query are maintained on the Display tab (see Figure 9.78).

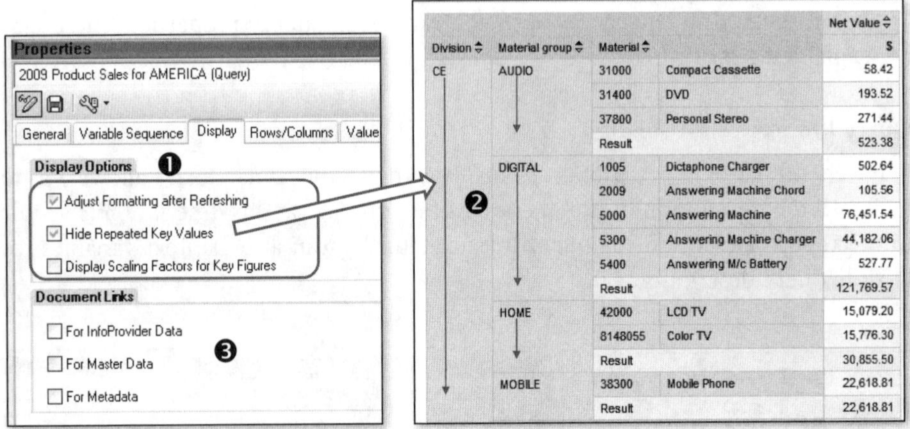

Figure 9.78 Query Properties – Display Tab

The formatting, display of key values, and display of scaling factors settings are done in the Display Options section (❶ of Figure 9.78). Hide Repeated Key Values is typically the most frequently used display setting for a query. When you select this setting, the key values (characteristic values in the query) that are repeated in successive records are hidden, and only the first record displays the characteristic value, which is repeated. As shown in ❷ of Figure 9.78, the values for Division and Material Group are repeated for multiple records, so only the first record shows the value and hides the repeated values in the query display.

You can also select if you want to provide document links in the query by selecting the options shown in ❸ of Figure 9.78.

Query Properties — Rows/Columns Tab

As the name suggests, this tab allows you to maintain settings related to rows and columns displayed in the query result (see Figure 9.79).

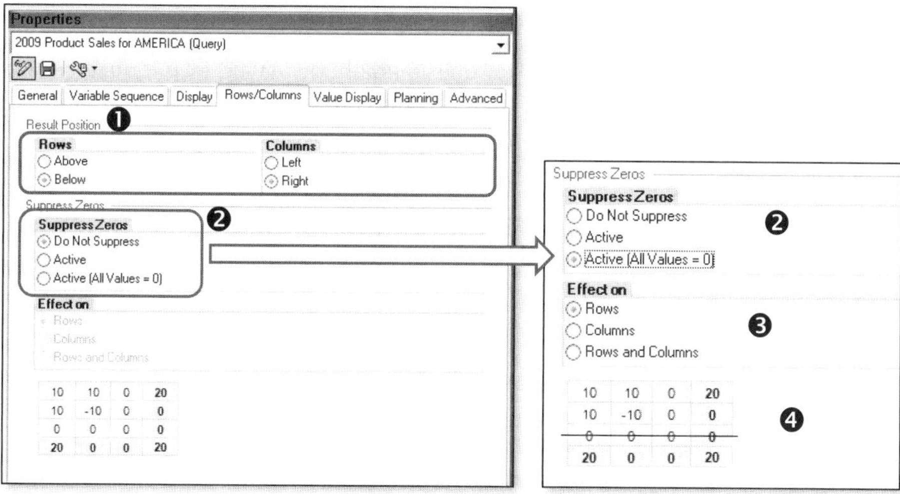

Figure 9.79 Query Properties – Rows/Columns Tab

The position of the result rows and result columns in a query is determined based on the settings maintained under the Result Position section (❶ of Figure 9.79). You can also decide to suppress the zero values from the query output in the Suppress Zeros section (❷). Further, you can decide if you want to apply the suppression either to rows or columns or both rows and columns in the Effect On section (❸). This tab also displays a preview of the settings chosen on this tab (❹).

Query Properties — Value Display Tab

The settings related to key figure display, such as display of +/- signs or display of zero values, are maintained on the Value Display tab.

Query Properties — Planning Tab

The Planning tab is relevant only to the *input-ready* queries where you can make the setting to open the query in change mode. This means users can enter and change the key figure values that are enabled for input. Chapter 12 covers input-ready queries and this setting in more depth.

Query Properties — Advanced Tab

The Allow External Access to This Query setting on this tab determines if the query can be executed through OLE DB for OLAP. You'll learn about the significance for this setting, when you read Chapter 13, Reporting with SAP BusinessObjects.

9.13 Conditions

Conditions allow you to filter the data that is finally displayed in the query result, based on the parameters defined in the condition. This is an OLAP function provided by BEx to aid information analysis in SAP NetWeaver BW.

For example, the business analysts of ABCD Corp. want to see their top 10 best selling products. In this section, we'll see how a condition built in the query helps address this requirement. Following is the procedure to create a condition on a BEx query:

1. The conditions are maintained in the Conditions screen area of the query designer. To display this area, click on the conditions icon from the toolbar (❶ of Figure 9.80). The Conditions screen area appears (❷).

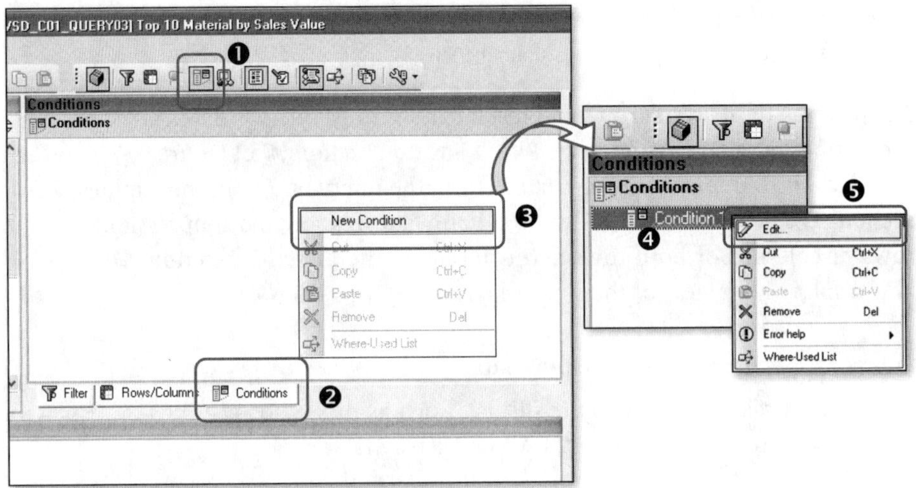

Figure 9.80 Create a New Condition

2. To create a new condition, open the context menu from the Conditions screen area, and select New Condition (❸). This creates a new condition with a system generated description (❹). To edit and define this condition, double-click on it or select Edit from the context menu (❺).
3. The Change Condition screen appears (see Figure 9.81). The condition defined is applied only if the Condition Is Active checkbox shown in Figure 9.81 is selected.

You can now maintain the Description for the condition (❶ of Figure 9.81). Click on the New button (❷) to create a new condition parameter; where you can define the logic for the condition.

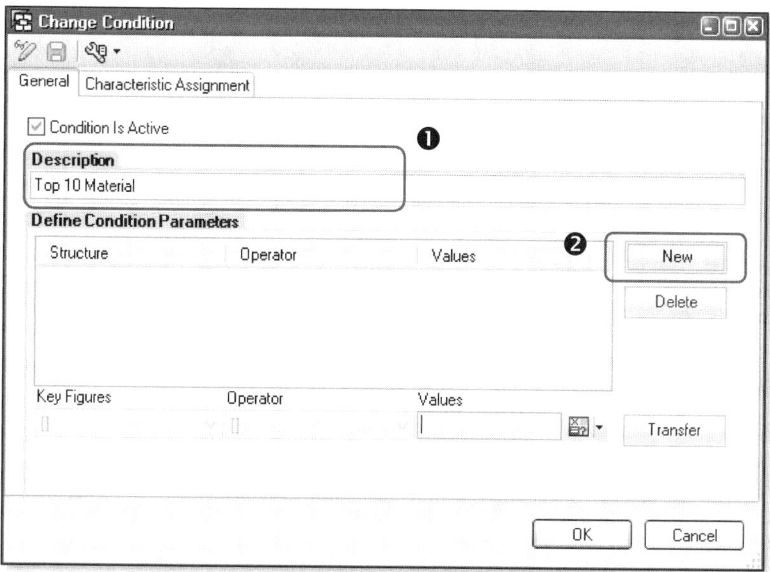

Figure 9.81 Change Condition

4. Define the condition parameter as shown in Figure 9.82. You have to specify three fields to define a condition parameter. First select the key figure on which this condition should be applied (❶ of Figure 9.82). Then select an operator from the list of available operators for a condition (❷). For our example, we're selecting the operator Top N. (Had the requirement been to show only those materials where total sales is more than 1000 USD, you could have chosen the operator Greater Than.) Then select the value for the condition (❸). In this case, we have to display the top 10 materials, so we enter the value 10. However, you can make this condition more flexible by using a variable for the value (❹).
5. Click on the Transfer button (❺ of Figure 9.82) after the parameter is defined. The defined condition is now visible as shown in ❶ of Figure 9.83. Click on the Characteristic Assignment tab (❷) to configure more settings for the condition.

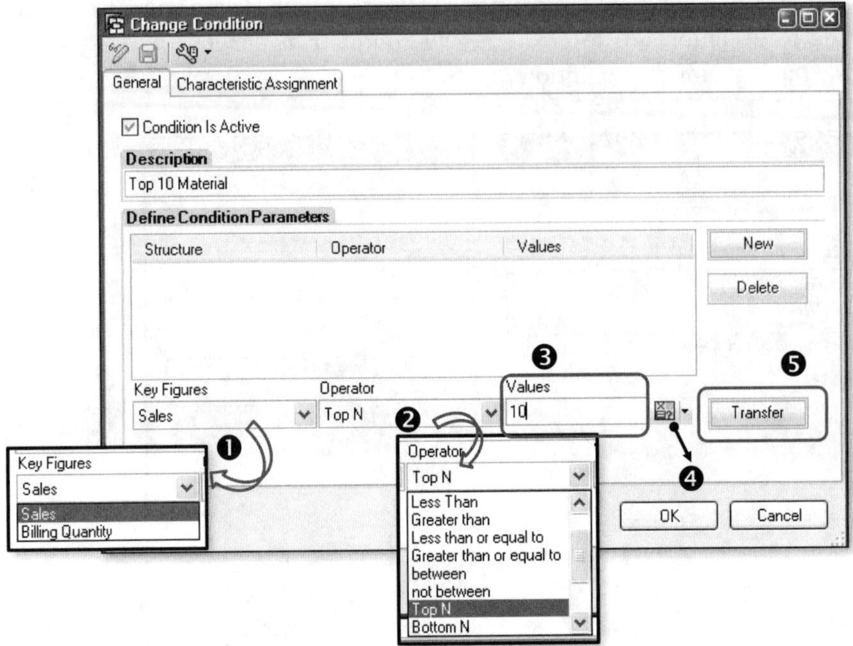

Figure 9.82 Define Condition Parameter

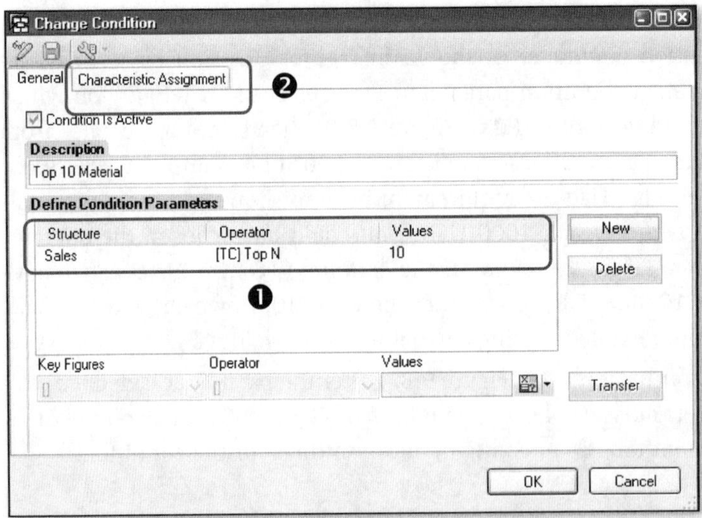

Figure 9.83 Go to Characteristic Assignment

6. On the Characteristic Assignment tab, you define how the condition should be applied to the query result (❶ of Figure 9.84). For the All Characteristics in the Drilldown Independently setting, the condition will be applied to the characteristics that are used in the drilldown of the query. You can also choose to apply the condition to the Most Detailed Characteristic Along the Rows or Columns. If you want that condition to be applied to some specific characteristics only, you select the Individual Chars. and Char. Combinations option. Here you can select the characteristics for which the condition should be evaluated (❷).

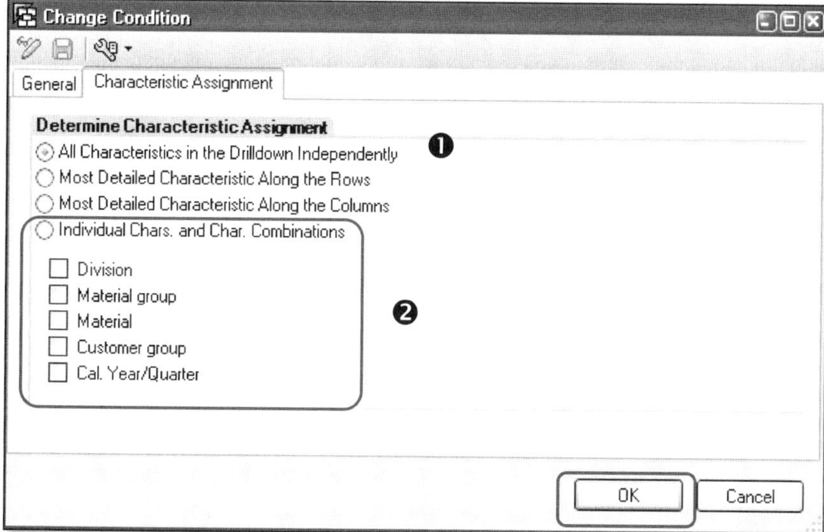

Figure 9.84 Maintain Characteristic Assignment for a Condition

7. Click OK to complete the Condition definition (see Figure 9.84).

When you execute the query with this definition and material in the query drilldown, the condition evaluates the result and displays the records that satisfy the condition. See Figure 9.85 where the condition has evaluated the top 10 records by sales value and filtered the query output for the same.

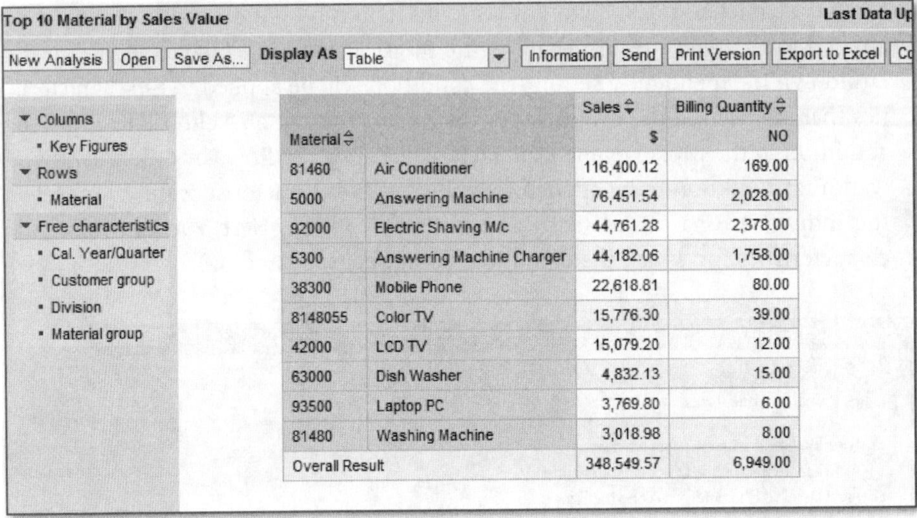

Figure 9.85 Query Output with Condition

9.14 Exceptions

Like conditions, the exception is another OLAP feature with which you can highlight the cells in the query output if the value is beyond the threshold mentioned in the exception definition.

For example, you want to create a report that will highlight the cells in the query output in green if the sales value is *more than 1000 USD*, and in red if the sales value is *less than 200 USD*. This visualization can be achieved using exceptions in the query.

Follow these steps to create an exception in the BEx Query Designer:

1. Display the exceptions screen area in the Query Designer by clicking on the Exceptions icon as shown in ❶ of Figure 9.86. The Exceptions area will be visible as shown in ❷. Create a new exception by selecting New Exception from the context menu in the Exceptions area.
2. An exception with a system-defined default description is created (❹). To edit and define this exception, select Edit from the context menu (❺).
3. Maintain the Description for the exception (❶ of Figure 9.87).

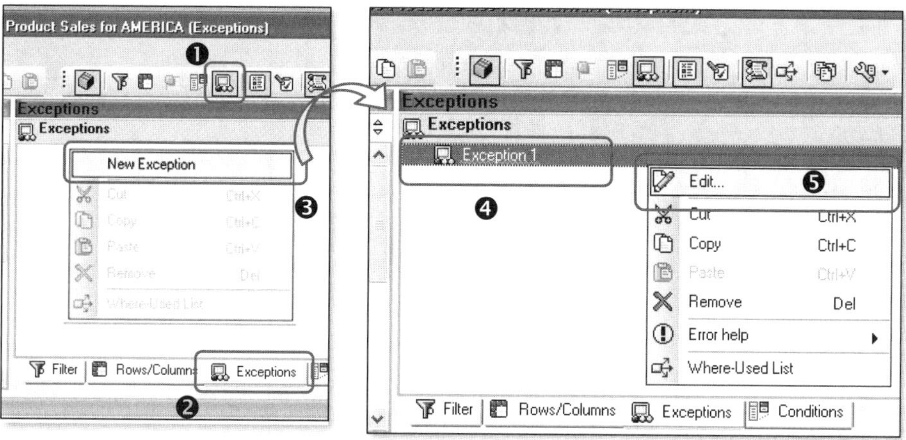

Figure 9.86 Create a New Exception

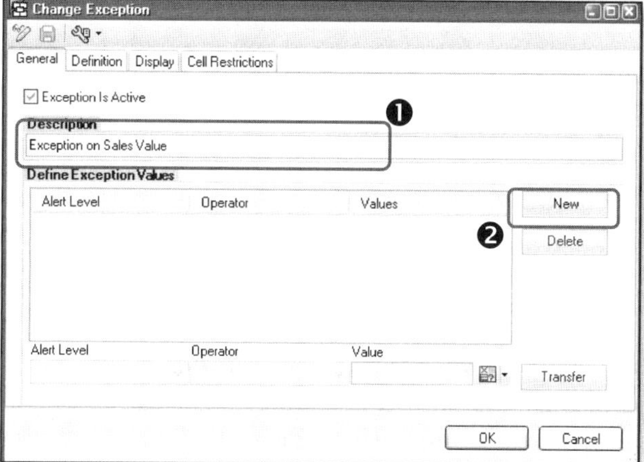

Figure 9.87 Change Exception

4. Click on the New button (❷ of 9.87) to define the threshold values for the exception.
5. Define the exception values by maintaining the fields as shown in Figure 9.88. Select the Alert Level (❶), for example, Good1 for Green or Bad 1 for Red. Then select the Operator from the dropdown (❷) to define the exception, and then specify the threshold value in the Value field (❸). You can also use a variable for the value to make the exception more flexible (❹). Finally, click on the Transfer button to transfer the defined exception (❺). All of the defined exceptions are visible (❻).

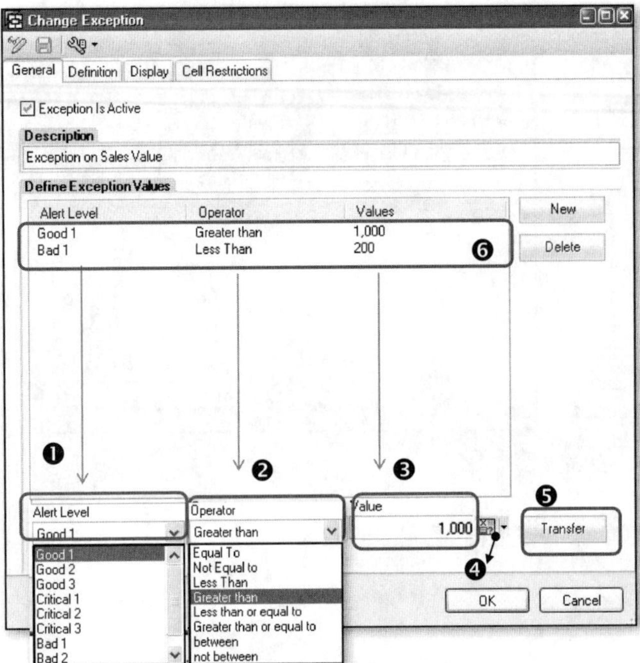

Figure 9.88 Define Exception Values

6. After the exceptions are defined, you then select the query element on which this exception should be defined on the Definition tab (see Figure 9.89). In our example, we want to highlight the exception on sales, so select Sales from the Key Figure dropdown. If you want all of the key figures to be evaluated for this, select All Structure Elements. You can also use the setting Before List Calculation if you want the exception to be determined before the local calculations are performed in the query.
7. The Display tab contains the settings where you can define the query elements that should be highlighted for the exception (see Figure 9.90). If you select the setting Exception Affects Data Cells (❶), then you can select which data elements should be highlighted for this exception (❷). Similarly, if you select the setting Exception Affects Characteristic Cells, you can specify if the rows or columns or both rows and columns should be highlighted if an exception occurs (❸).

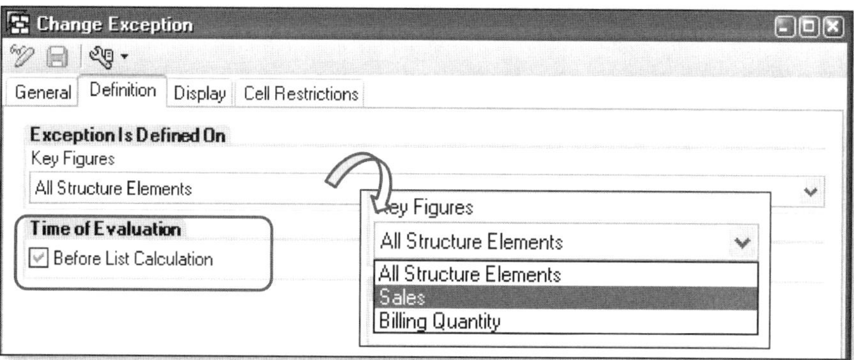

Figure 9.89 Change Exception – Definition

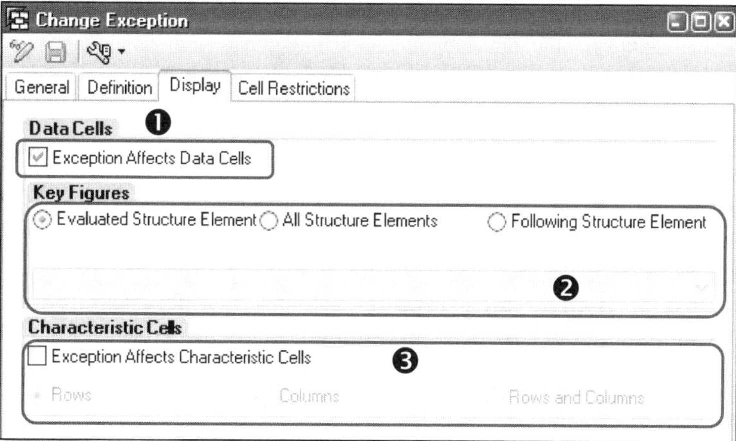

Figure 9.90 Exceptions – Display

8. On the Cell Restrictions tab, you define the data set that should be evaluated for the exception. The option Exception Affects Everything (❶ of Figure 9.91) will apply the exception to all of the records in the query output, whereas the setting Exception Only Affects Results will evaluate and hence highlight only the result rows of the query output. You can also define specific cell restrictions if you want the exception to be evaluated for only a specific set of data. To create this restriction, click on the New button (❷), and then define and transfer the restriction using the fields and the Transfer button (❸).

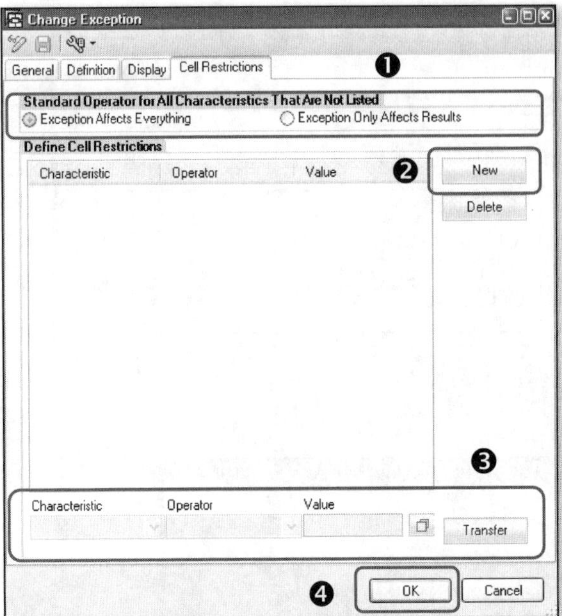

Figure 9.91 Exceptions – Cell Restrictions

9. Finally, click on the OK button to complete the exception definition.

When you save and run this query, the exception evaluates the query output based on the settings and highlights the fields as mentioned in the exception definition (see Figure 9.92).

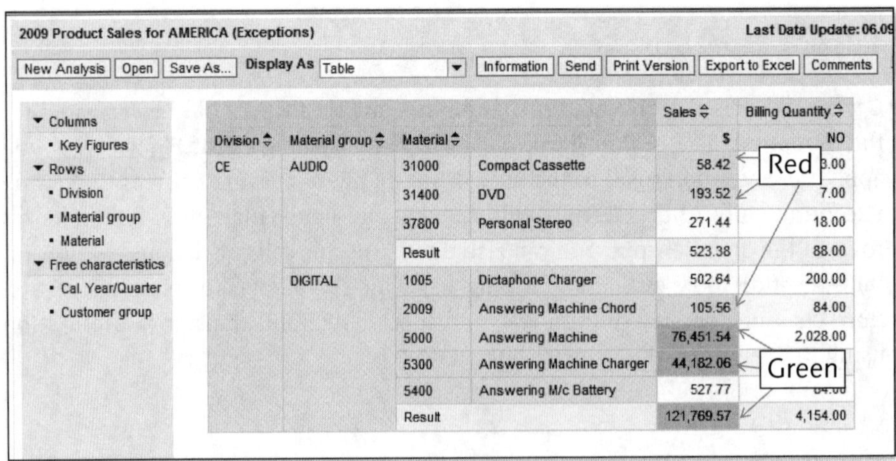

Figure 9.92 Query Output – Exceptions

Exceptions can be effectively used for analyzing a huge set of data. Using exceptions, the business analyst can quickly focus on the values that are highlighted in the query output, accelerating the analysis process.

9.15 Report-to-Report Interface

While explaining the example scenario in the beginning of the chapter, we mentioned a requirement where the auditors of ABCD Corp. needed a solution to provide traceability to the specific sales documents for a customer when needed to analyze instances of variances. This billing document level investigation needs to be addressed in SAP NetWeaver BW rather than going into the transactional system for the detailed information.

You have a report on the InfoCube that shows you the sales by customer, but the data is consolidated at the customer and material level, so there's no sales document level information available in the InfoCube.

However, there is a DSO in which the detailed information is stored separately in SAP NetWeaver BW. Per the requirement, you should be able to get a list of all sales documents for the selected customer when needed.

SAP NetWeaver BW offers report-to-report interface (RRI) to address such requirements, where the analysts need to jump into detailed information of the selected value in a report.

For the given example, say there is a customer sales query on the InfoCube, which shows sales for different customers (❶ of Figure 9.93), and there is another query built on the DSO with detailed information that shows sales document details (❷). Using RRI, you can pass a specific value of customer from the customer sales query to the sales document query, which will show the documents for that specific customer.

In this case, the query on the InfoCube sends the information to another query, so hence it's called as the *sender* in RRI. On the other hand, the query on the DSO is executed based on the information received from the sender, so the DSO query is called the *receiver* in RRI. The sender will send the value of selected customer (BW_CUST) to the receiver to display the sales documents for that customer (❸). This is also termed *a jump target*.

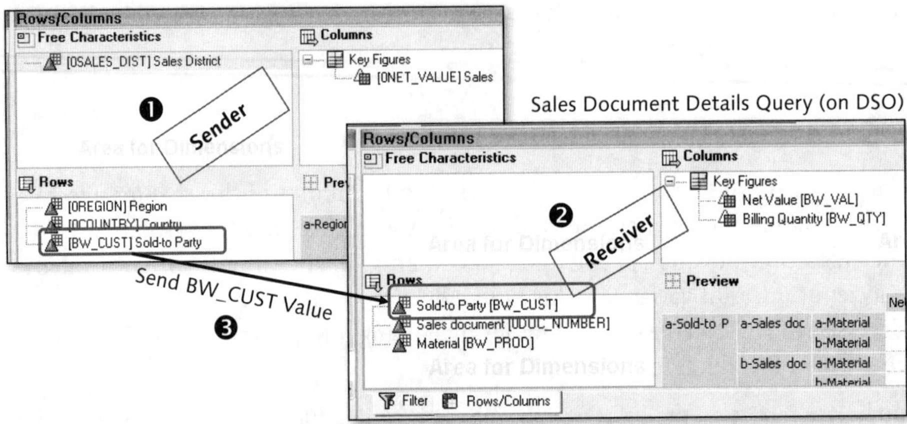

Figure 9.93 The Concept of Report-to-Report Interface (RRI)

Follow these steps to configure a RRI (sender/receiver assignment) in SAP NetWeaver BW:

1. Use transaction code RSBBS to call the transaction Maintain Sender/Receiver Assignment (see Figure 9.94).

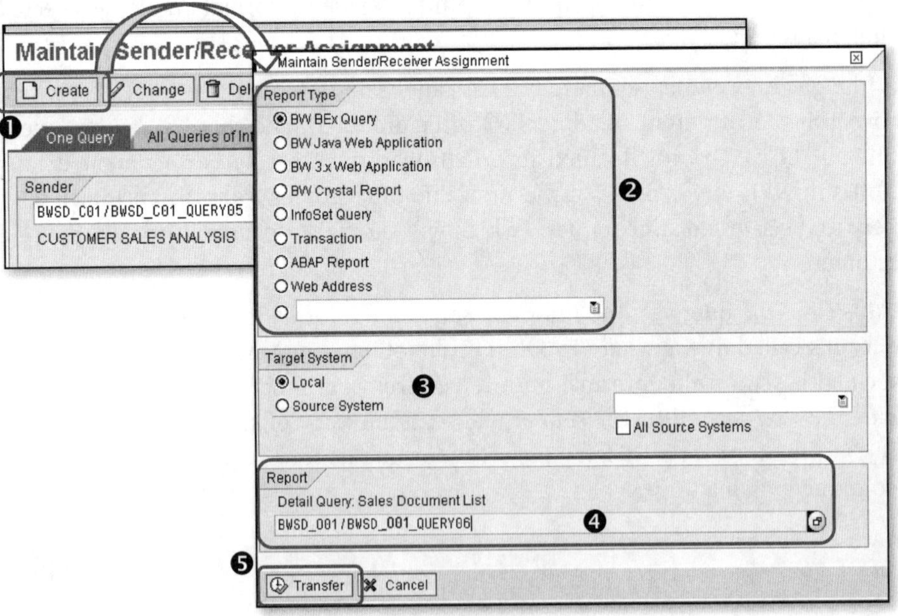

Figure 9.94 Create a New Assignment

2. The RRI settings can be maintained for a specific query as well as for all of the queries on an InfoProvider. Select the One Query tab, and then select the Sender query (see Figure 9.94).
3. After you select the sender query, click on the Create button (❶) to create a new sender/receiver assignment. A pop-up will appear where you can define the assignment.
4. In the pop-up box shown in Figure 9.94, define the receiver information. The receiver could be queries and web applications from BEx as well as from older versions of SAP NetWeaver BW (SAP NetWeaver BW 3.x). The receiver could also be a transaction or a report or a web address. Different options are shown in ❷ of Figure 9.94. For our example, select the option BW BEx query as the receiver.
5. Select whether the receiver is in the same system as that of the sender or in some different system (❸), and define the receiver query (❹). For our example, the Detail Query: Sales Document List is maintained as the receiver.
6. Click on the Transfer button (❺) to complete this configuration and return to the main screen. This newly created assignment is now visible in the Receiver section as shown in Figure 9.95.

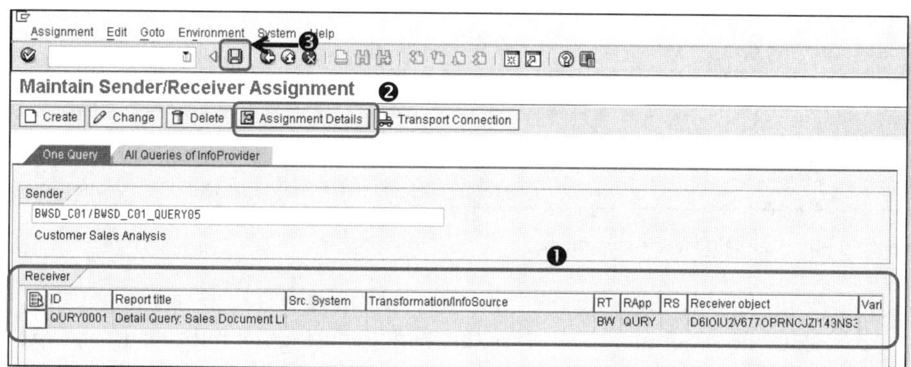

Figure 9.95 Go to Assignment Details

7. You have to now maintain the specific parameters of this assignment where you specify how the information will be exchanged between the sender and the receiver. Select the assignment (❶ of Figure 9.95), and click on the Assignment Details button (❷). This opens the Field Assignments pop-up box as shown in Figure 9.96.

8. On the Field Assignments screen, you actually define how the information will be passed from the Sender to the Receiver. Select the type of assignment (❶ of Figure 9.96), and specify the InfoObject name as the Field Name (❷). Maintain the Selection Type (❸), and select the checkbox in the column Required (❹), so that the receiver query is called and executed only if it's called for a customer value.

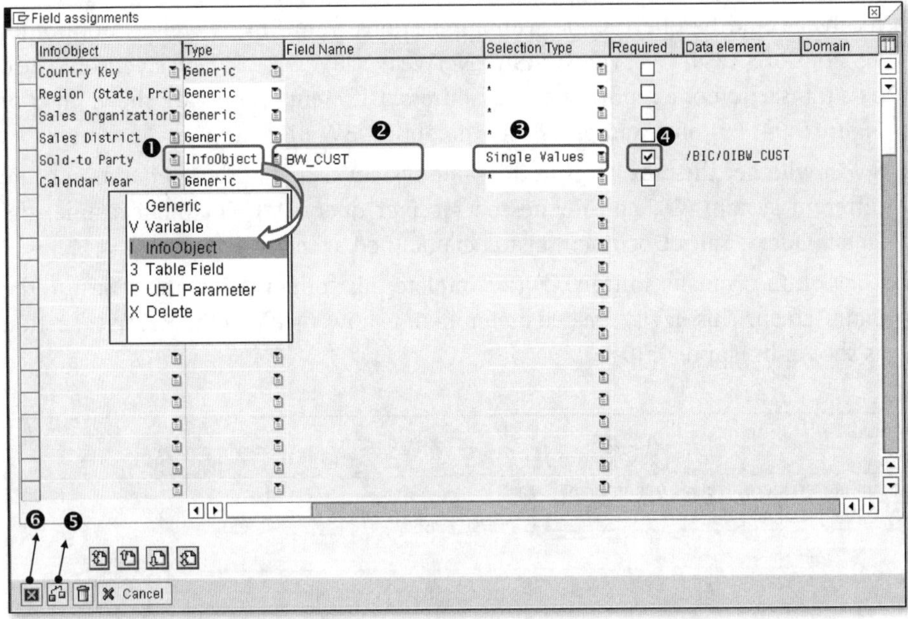

Figure 9.96 Maintain Field Assignments

9. Check the details by using the button shown in ❺ of Figure 9.96, and finally complete the assignment and close this window using the button shown in ❻.
10. The RRI definition is complete, and you can now save this definition using the save button shown earlier in ❸ of Figure 9.95.

Figure 9.97 shows the use of RRI, which has been just defined.

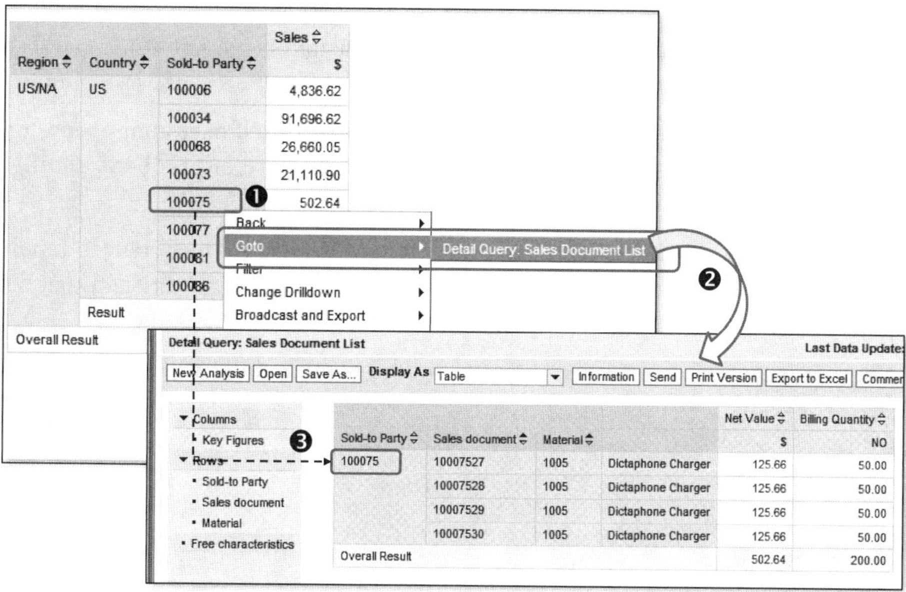

Figure 9.97 Using Report-to-Report Interface (RRI)

RRI is available for the characteristic value for which it's defined (❶ of Figure 9.97). For this example, you can see in Figure 9.97 that the Goto section in the context menu for customer value 100075 shows RRI for Detail Query: Sales Document List (❷). Select the RRI query, and it will call the receiver query and display the detailed list of all sales documents. As you can see from ❸ of Figure 9.97, the value 100075 for the customer is passed as a parameter from the sender to the receiver. This is based on the field assignments defined for RRI.

Using RRI, you can provide additional features to perform detailed analysis on the data. Different types of jump targets can be assigned to a BEx query to make the analysis more flexible.

9.16 Summary

In this chapter, we explained the different SAP Business Explorer (BEx) tools available in SAP NetWeaver BW and how they fit into the landscape. Focusing on creating queries in BEx query designer, we initially explained how a simple query can be created. The significance of OLAP variables in the query design was explained as well as the different types and processing types of variables that can be used in a query design. Some commonly used variable types were also discussed in detail.

As we explored additional features and query elements such as filters, selections, formulas, structures, restricted key figures (RKFs), calculated key figure (CKFs), and so on, we saw how different business requirements can be met using these elements.

The properties of different query elements and the query itself have an influence on the query output. We explained the significance of the different property settings with real-life business scenarios.

Finally, we looked at features such as conditions, exceptions, and the report-to-report interface (RRI), which can be built on a BEx query to make the reporting and analysis on SAP NetWeaver BW data more flexible and effective.

In the next chapter, we'll discuss different modes of analyzing the data using these BEx queries.

Reporting and analysis in SAP NetWeaver BW can be done in two ways: via an Excel interface (using BEx analyzer) or a web interface (using BEx web analyzer). In this chapter, we explain both methods of reporting.

10 Reporting and Analysis

In previous chapters, we explained the procedure of creating a query on InfoProviders, which can then be used to generate reports or perform data analysis. In SAP NetWeaver BW, you can perform analysis using a Microsoft Excel interface or a web interface; the SAP Business Explorer (BEx) application suite provides two tools for just this purpose:

- **BEx analyzer:** Using BEx analyzer, you can run queries and perform ad-hoc analysis in an Excel environment. BEx analyzer is integrated with Excel by using an Excel add-in. You can also design your own analysis or planning application using the design option in BEx analyzer.
- **BEx web analyzer:** This is a data reporting and analysis tool designed for a web environment. You can execute queries and perform ad-hoc analysis using BEx web analyzer.

In this chapter, you'll learn about both of these tools. First, we explain how analysis can be performed in BEx analyzer and the procedure used to build your own application. Then we discuss BEx web analyzer and the different analysis or ad-hoc analysis options available on the web. We conclude with a brief discussion about information broadcasting.

10.1 Running Queries in BEx analyzer

BEx analyzer allows you to perform reporting and analysis in the Excel environment. The BEx analyzer is a standalone application that can be started by following START MENU • PROGRAMS • BUSINESS EXPLORER • ANALYZER, as shown in Figure 10.1.

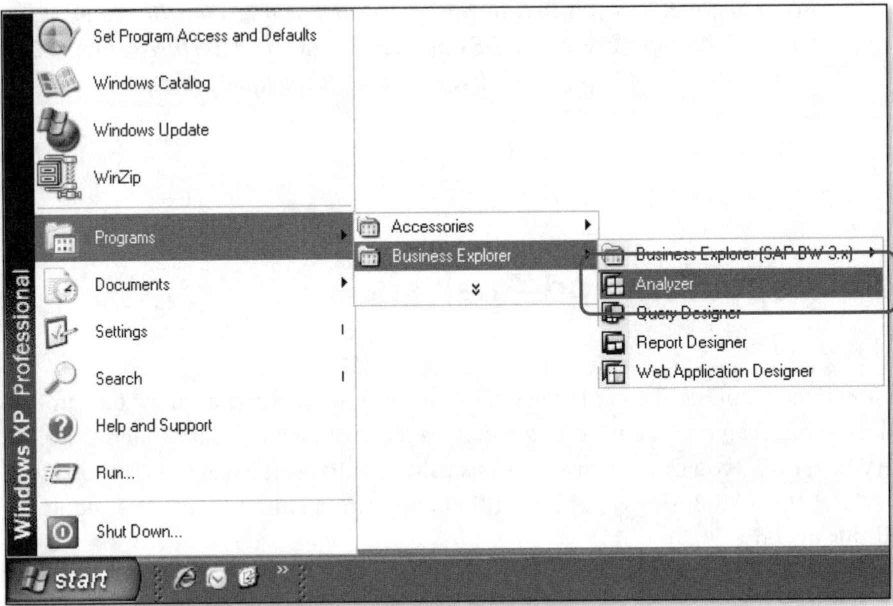

Figure 10.1 Open BEx analyzer

Starting BEx analyzer opens an Excel session on your computer. The BEx analyzer functions are available in Excel through the Excel add-in. These functions can be seen by clicking on the Add-Ins tab on the Excel toolbar, as shown in ❶ of Figure 10.2.

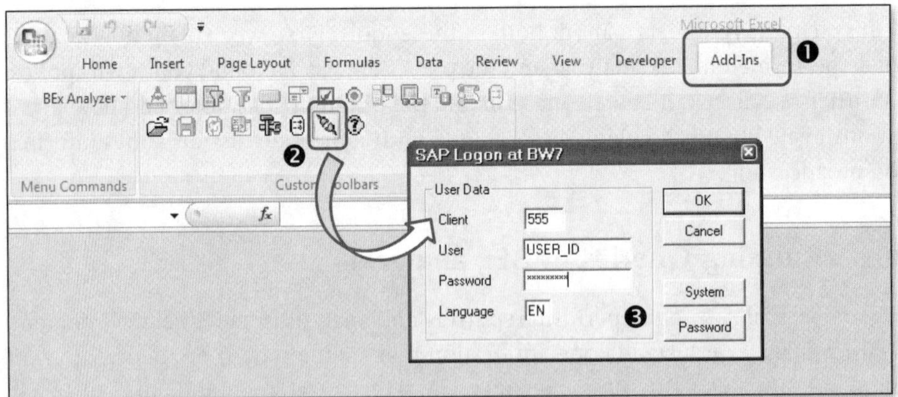

Figure 10.2 Connect to BEx analyzer

Figure 10.2 displays the BEx analyzer add-in in Microsoft Excel 2007. If you're using Microsoft Excel 2003, the BEx analyzer functions can be accessed as shown in Figure 10.3.

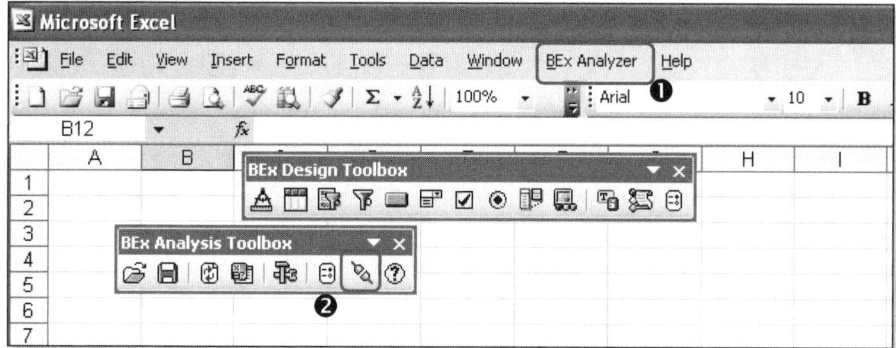

Figure 10.3 Connect to BEx analyzer (Excel 2003)

The BEx analysis Toolbox and BEx Design Toolbox are visible as two separate toolbars, and a new BEx analyzer menu is available in the Excel menu bar, as shown in ❶ of Figure 10.3. In this chapter, all of the figures and illustrations are made using Microsoft Excel 2007. The BEx functions remain the same in both versions of Excel.

To execute a query or to perform an analysis in BEx analyzer, you must first establish a connection with the SAP NetWeaver BW system. To make a connection, click on the Connection button (❷ of Figure 10.2; or ❷ of Figure 10.3). This opens the login screen for the SAP NetWeaver BW system; enter the login credentials to connect the BEx analyzer with SAP NetWeaver BW (❸ of Figure 10.2).

After the connection is established, all of the queries and InfoProviders from the connected SAP NetWeaver BW system are now available for reporting and analysis in BEx analyzer. With this accomplished, we can now explain how to execute a query in BEx analyzer, as well as the various functions of this application.

10.1.1 Execute a Query in BEx analyzer

To execute an existing query from the connected SAP NetWeaver BW system, you have to first open the query (Figure 10.4).

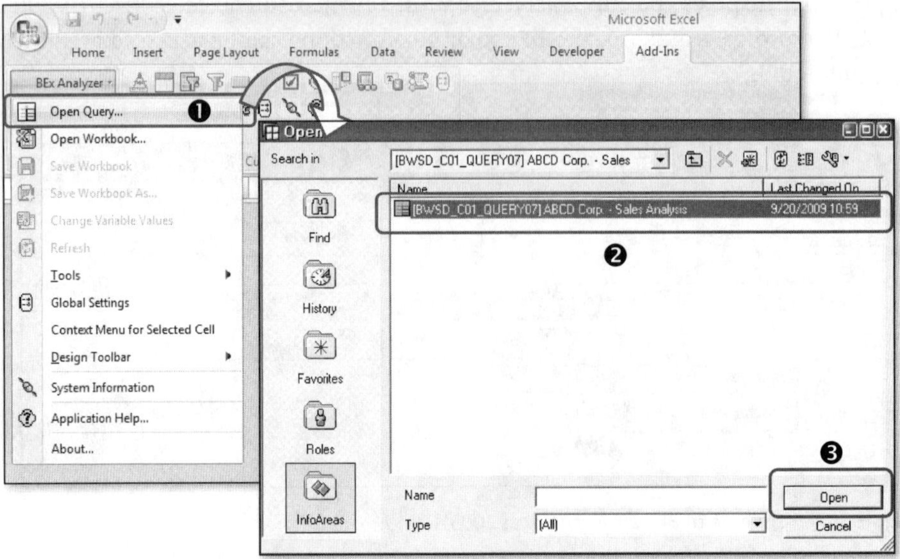

Figure 10.4 Open a Query in BEx analyzer

Click on the BEx ANALYZER menu and select OPEN QUERY (❶ of Figure 10.4), which opens a pop-up screen. Navigate through the InfoAreas to locate the required query (❷), and click on Open (❸).

This executes the selected query in BEx analyzer. If the selected query has user entry variables included in it, the variable screen Select Values for Variables appears, as shown in Figure 10.5.

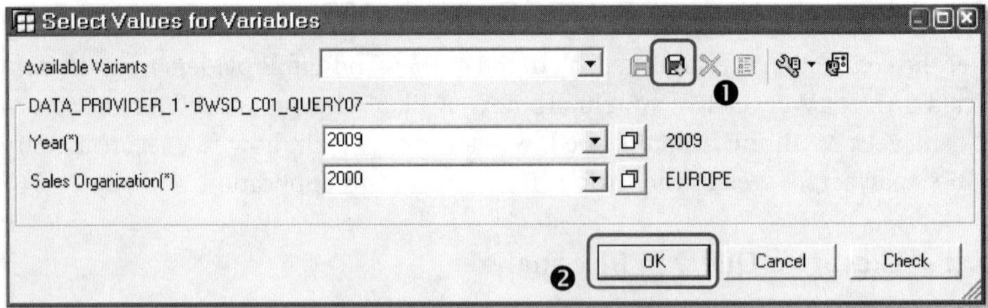

Figure 10.5 Select Values for Variables

Select the required values for the variables on this screen. If you want to save this selection for future use, you can save it as a variant using the button shown in ❶ of Figure 10.5. Finally, select OK (❷) to execute the query for the select variable values.

The query results are displayed in the Excel sheet, as shown in Figure 10.6.

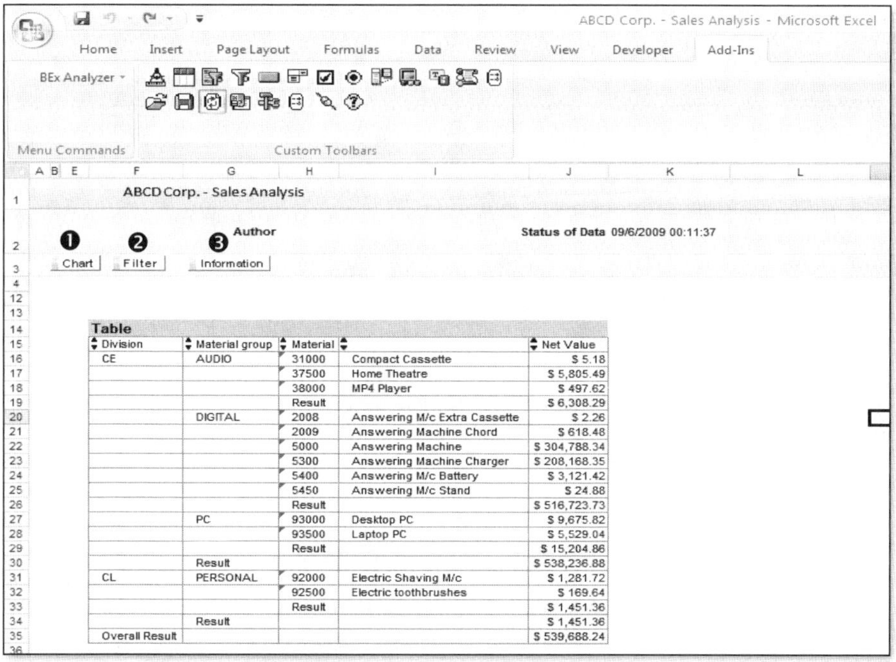

ABCD Corp. - Sales Analysis

Table

Division	Material group	Material		Net Value
CE	AUDIO	31000	Compact Cassette	$ 5.18
		37500	Home Theatre	$ 5,805.49
		38000	MP4 Player	$ 497.62
		Result		$ 6,308.29
	DIGITAL	2008	Answering M/c Extra Cassette	$ 2.26
		2009	Answering Machine Chord	$ 618.48
		5000	Answering Machine	$ 304,788.34
		5300	Answering Machine Charger	$ 208,168.35
		5400	Answering M/c Battery	$ 3,121.42
		5450	Answering M/c Stand	$ 24.88
		Result		$ 516,723.73
	PC	93000	Desktop PC	$ 9,675.82
		93500	Laptop PC	$ 5,529.04
		Result		$ 15,204.86
	Result			$ 538,236.88
CL	PERSONAL	92000	Electric Shaving M/c	$ 1,281.72
		92500	Electric toothbrushes	$ 169.64
		Result		$ 1,451.36
	Result			$ 1,451.36
Overall Result				$ 539,688.24

Figure 10.6 Query Result in BEx analyzer

Along with the query result, you can also see the query description, the author of the query, and the status of the data in the InfoProvider. There are three buttons – Chart, Filter, and Information – available in the display (❶, ❷, and ❸ of Figure 10.6). Usage of these buttons is explained next.

Using the Chart button, you can convert the tabular display of data into a graphical display. As shown in Figure 10.7, the graph is displayed for the tabular data we saw earlier.

You can now revert back to the tabular view by clicking on the Table button, as shown in Figure 10.7.

Clicking on the Filter button displays a Filter pane in the layout (Figure 10.8). Here, you can see a list of all of the query elements available in rows/columns/free characteristics of the query. These can be used to filter the query result or to perform different navigations on the query result. (The details about different navigation options in BEx analyzer are discussed in subsequent sections of this chapter.)

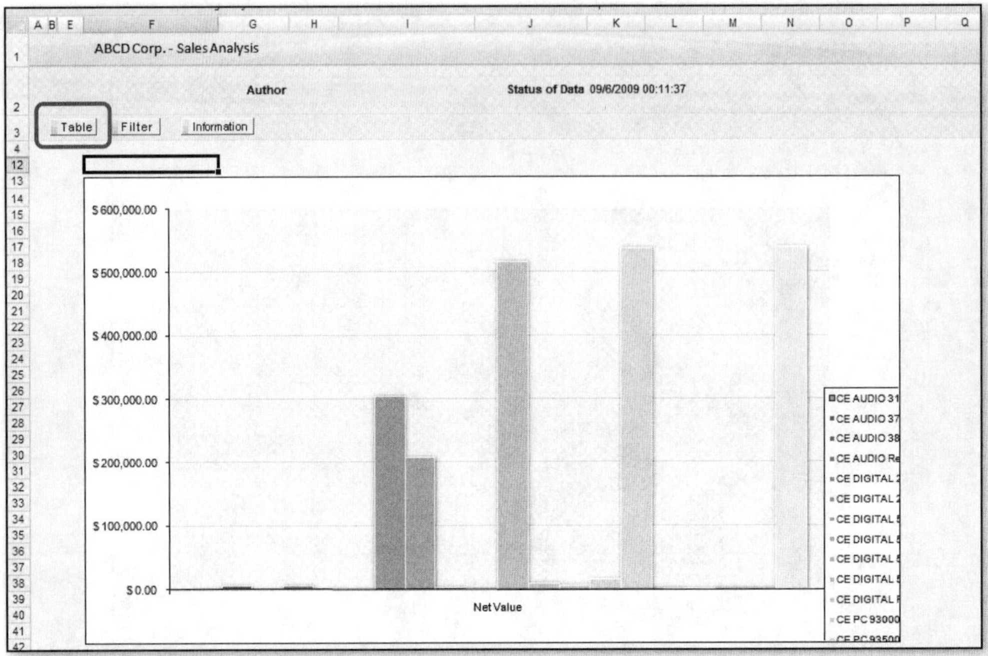

Figure 10.7 Graphical Display of Data

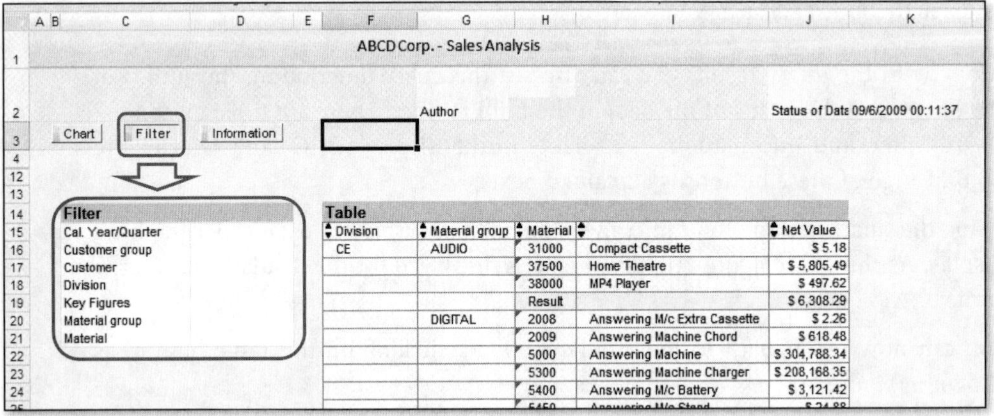

Division	Material group	Material		Net Value
CE	AUDIO	31000	Compact Cassette	$ 5.18
		37500	Home Theatre	$ 5,805.49
		38000	MP4 Player	$ 497.62
		Result		$ 6,308.29
	DIGITAL	2008	Answering M/c Extra Cassette	$ 2.26
		2009	Answering Machine Chord	$ 618.48
		5000	Answering Machine	$ 304,788.34
		5300	Answering Machine Charger	$ 208,168.35
		5400	Answering M/c Battery	$ 3,121.42

Figure 10.8 Filter Button in BEx analyzer

The Information button displays the technical information about the query that is executed (Figure 10.9). This information includes details such as the technical name of the query and InfoProvider, different timestamps, and so on.

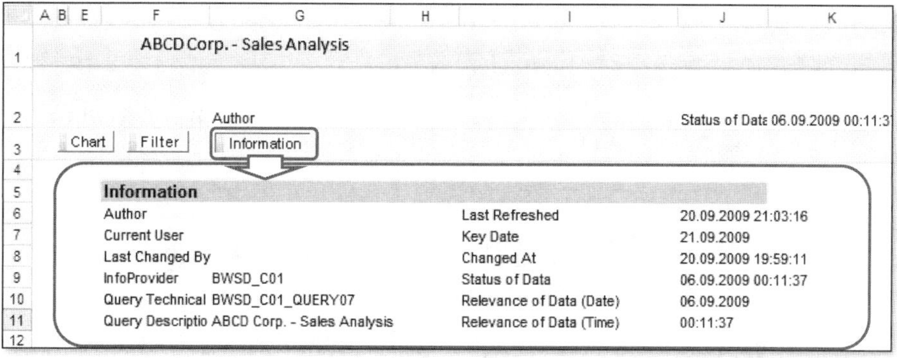

Figure 10.9 Information Button in BEx analyzer

The Excel sheet with query results is called a *workbook*. Having explained the default layout of the workbook in BEx analyzer, we now look into different analysis options available in the BEx analyzer.

10.1.2 BEx Analysis Functions

The BEx analyzer has two different sets of functions available in the form of two different toolbars: the Design toolbar and the Analysis toolbar. As shown in the boxed area of Figure 10.10, the top part of the BEx analyzer functions are design functions and constitute the Design toolbar. The lower part of the BEx analyzer functions constitute the Analysis toolbar (shown enlarged in Figure 10.10). The significance of each of these buttons on the Analysis toolbar is discussed next.

- Open: This button is used to open an existing query or workbook in BEx analyzer (❶ of Figure 10.10).
- Save: This button is used to save the workbook (❷) with the same name (Save Workbook) or as a different workbook (Save Workbook As). The Save View option stores the navigational state and the filter values for the selected query element.
- Refresh: This button refreshes the query results in the workbook (❸). When the workbook is refreshed using this button, you can use the same button to pause the automatic refresh of the data in the workbook.
- Change Variable Values: This button is used if you want to call the variable selection screen for the selected query in the workbook (❹).
- Tools: Use this button to open different BEx tools and applications (❺).
- Global Settings: Use this button (❻) to maintain different settings for BEx analyzer. There are four tabs available where you can maintain settings: Behavior, Default Workbook, Trace, and Statistics (Figure 10.11).

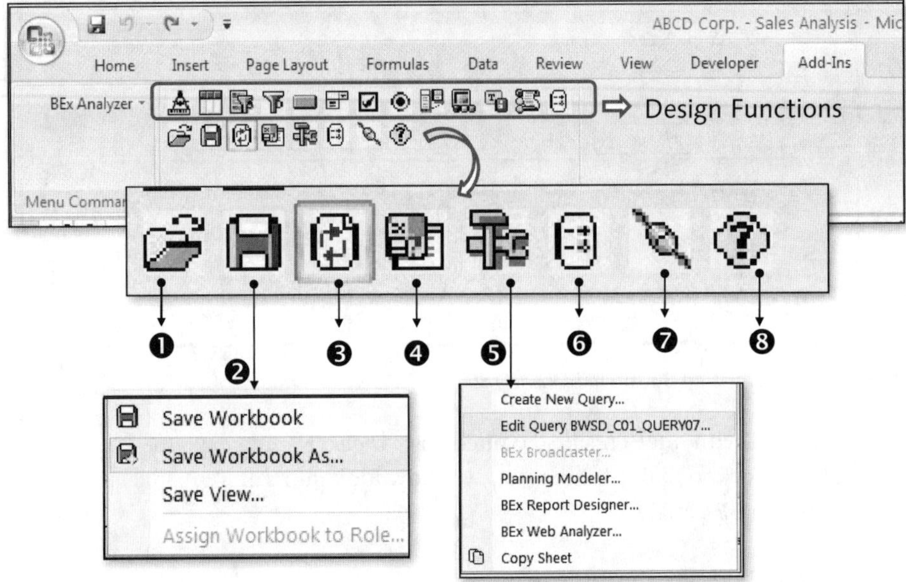

Figure 10.10 BEx analyzer Analysis Toolbar

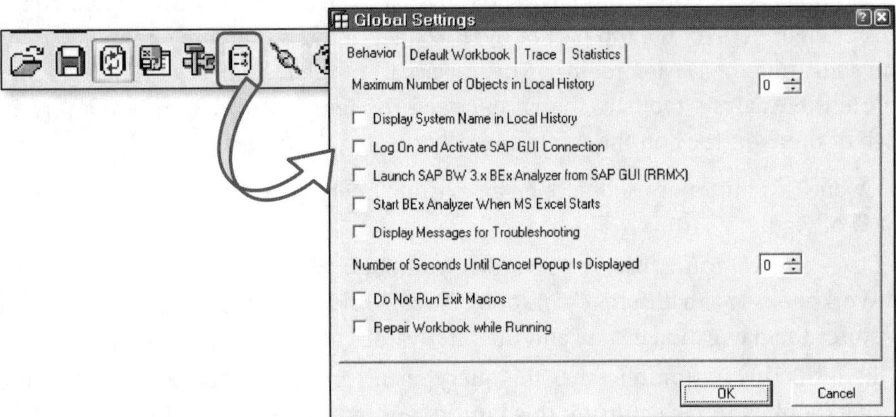

Figure 10.11 Global Settings for BEx analyzer

- System Information/Connect: Use this button (as you did earlier) to establish the connection between BEx analyzer and the SAP NetWeaver BW system. If you click on this button after the system is connected, it gives you information about which system is connected and provides you with an option to disconnect the system (❼).

- Application Help: Use this button to display standard SAP help documentation (❽).

10.2 Performing Information Analysis in BEx analyzer

As we mentioned earlier, you can perform analysis and navigate through information to build your own view in BEx analyzer. Two different options for analyzing data in BEx analyzer are discussed in this section: filters and navigation options.

10.2.1 Applying Filters

As we mentioned earlier, the Filter button is available in the workbook (❶ of Figure 10.12). Clicking on this button displays the filter pane with all of the characteristics and structures used in the query. You can use this pane to restrict the query result to the selected value(s) of the characteristic(s) or to the selected structure element. To apply the filter from the filter pane, select a characteristic or structure and choose SELECT FILTER VALUE from the context menu (❷).

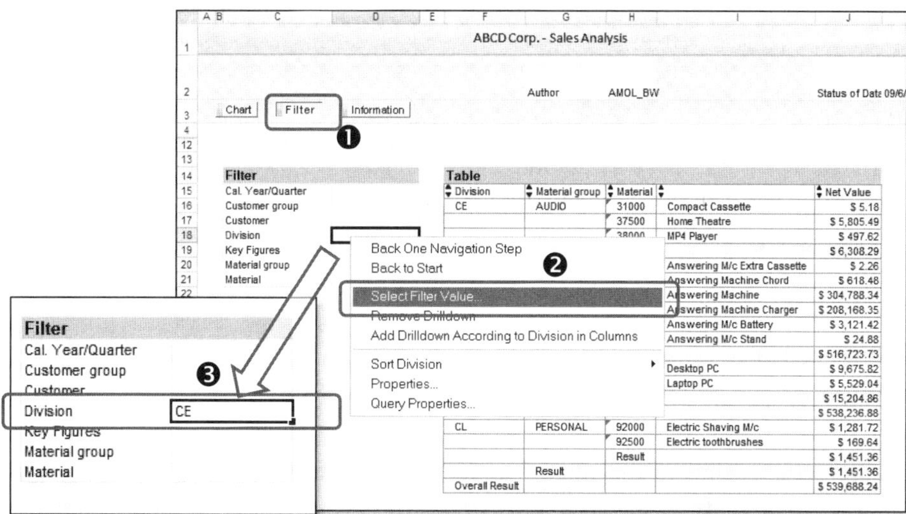

Figure 10.12 Applying Filters in a Workbook

You can also apply a filter by directly entering the value of the characteristic in the Excel cell (❸).

Similarly, you can restrict the key figures to be displayed by selecting a specific key figure value from the key figures structure.

10.2.2 Navigation Options

Apart from applying filters, many navigation options are available to perform intuitive analysis on the data displayed. These navigation options are discussed next.

Back One Navigation Step and Back to Start

Using the Back One Navigation Step option (Figure 10.13), you can undo the latest navigation and revert back to the previous navigation state. For example, if you drill down by a characteristic and then choose this option, the drilldown will be removed, taking you to the previous state of navigation.

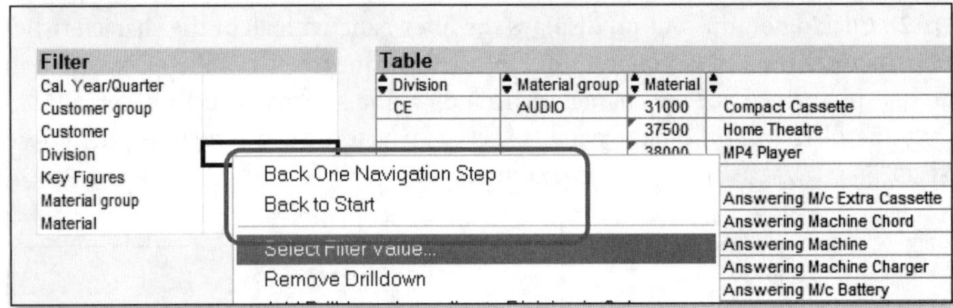

Figure 10.13 Navigating Backwards

Similarly, if you use the Back to Start option (Figure 10.13), the system reverts all navigations performed and takes the navigation state to the initial one, as it was when the query was first executed.

Drilldown

Drilldown (either in rows or columns) is one of the most heavily used navigation options in data analysis. By using this feature, analysts can actually view data from different perspectives, as well as at different levels of detail.

For the example shown in Figure 10.14, if you want to see the sales values split by Cal. Year/Quarter (❶), you can drill down by this characteristic in the columns. To perform this navigation, select Add Drilldown According to Cal. Year/Quarter in Columns from the context menu of the Cal. Year/Quarter characteristic (❷). As a result, the selected characteristic is added to the query, and the data is refreshed as the drilldown (❸).

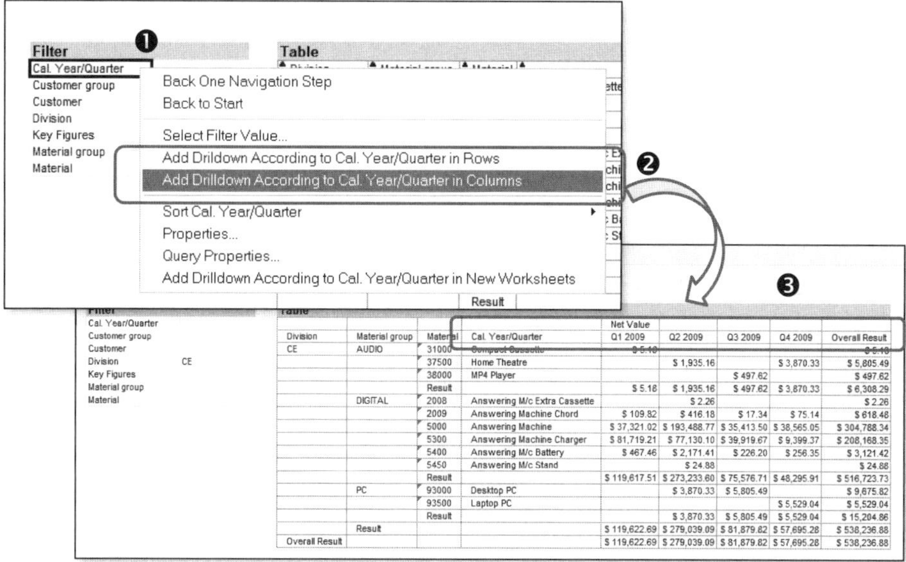

Figure 10.14 Drilldown Options

Similarly, Add Drilldown According to Cal. Year/Quarter in Rows is also an option in the context menu (❷) and can be used if you want to add the drilldown in the rows.

If you want to remove a drilldown from the query display, you can do so by selecting Remove Drilldown, available in the context menu of the characteristic in the report layout (Figure 10.15).

Swap

The Swap option is available to alter the position of a characteristic in the report by swapping it with another characteristic. For example, for the report shown in Figure 10.15, the net value is displayed with respect to the material group characteristic (❶ of Figure 10.15). If you want to display the net value by the customer group characteristic, you can swap *material group* with customer group.

To do this, select Swap Material Group With. The menu expands to show you a list of all of the characteristics used in the query, which can be selected for a swap. Select the Customer Group characteristic from the list (❷), and the result is refreshed accordingly (❸).

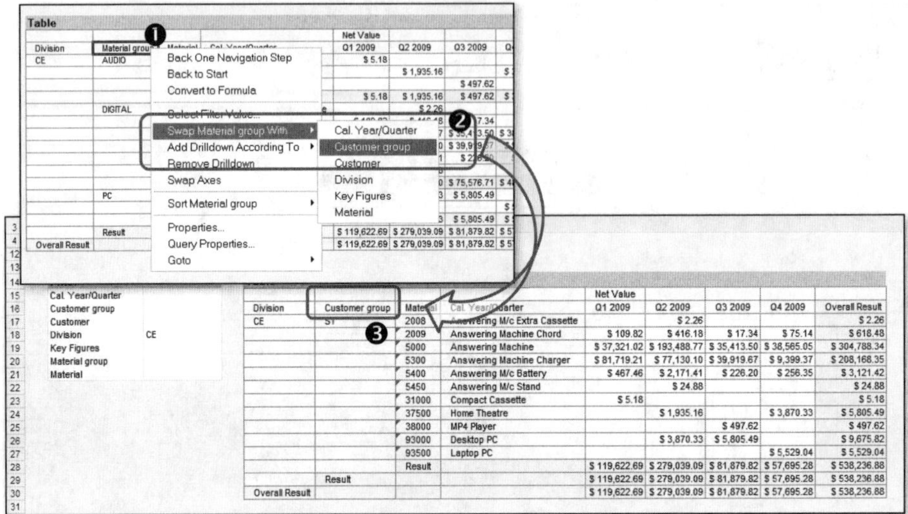

Figure 10.15 Swapping Characteristic Display

Using Drag and Drop

BEx analyzer also enables most of the navigations in the workbook using simple drag and drop actions. For example, if you want to add a characteristic to the drilldown, simply drag it from the filter pane and drop it to the position in the report where you want it. The user is guided with a small arrow symbol (pointing right [→] if it's a drilldown in columns, or pointing down (↓) if it's a drilldown in rows) to know the exact impact of the drop.

To remove a drilldown, simply drag the column header out of the layout and that characteristic will be removed from the display.

For swap characteristics, drag the column header for that characteristic, and drop it over the characteristic with which you want to swap.

Applying filters is also very easy using drag and drop options. If you don't want to see the values for Division = CE, simply drag the value CE out of the layout in an empty cell. With this, the filter on the division characteristic automatically excludes this value. On the other hand, if you drag the CE value and drop it on the division characteristic in the filter pane, the division characteristic is restricted by that value.

This intuitive drag and drop feature expedites the navigation and analysis of data in SAP NetWeaver BW.

Some additional navigation functions are available in the context menu of selected cells in query results:

- Convert to Formula: This function converts the result displayed in the report to a formula in Excel and is used when you want to preserve the local formatting even after you refresh the query. When the query is converted into a formula, it fetches only the value from the SAP NetWeaver BW system; the formula and local formatting are retained.
- Keep Filter Value: This function is available only for those cells with an actual characteristic value. Using this function, you can restrict the report result to that specific characteristic value for which the function is called. The report values are refreshed, and that characteristic is removed from the report display. For example, if you want to display only the values for Division = CE, select Keep Filter Value from the context menu of the cell containing CE. This restricts the report and removes Division from the report display.
- Swap Axes: Using this function, you can swap the query axes (rows and columns) with each other. Thus, query elements defined in the rows are sent to columns, and query elements from columns are sent to rows.
- Sort: This function allows you to sort the selected characteristic values in ascending or descending order in the report display.
- Goto: If there is any jump target defined on the query (report-to-report interface), the target is visible under the Goto option in the context menu.

10.3 Local Properties and Formulas in BEx analyzer

Apart from the filter and navigation options discussed in earlier sections, there are options available in the context menu to maintain the following:

- Local properties of a characteristic
- Local properties of a key figure
- Local query properties
- Local formulas

In this section, we discuss each of these concepts.

10.3.1 Local Properties of a Characteristic

To access the local properties of a characteristic, select Properties from the context menu of the characteristic (Figure 10.16).

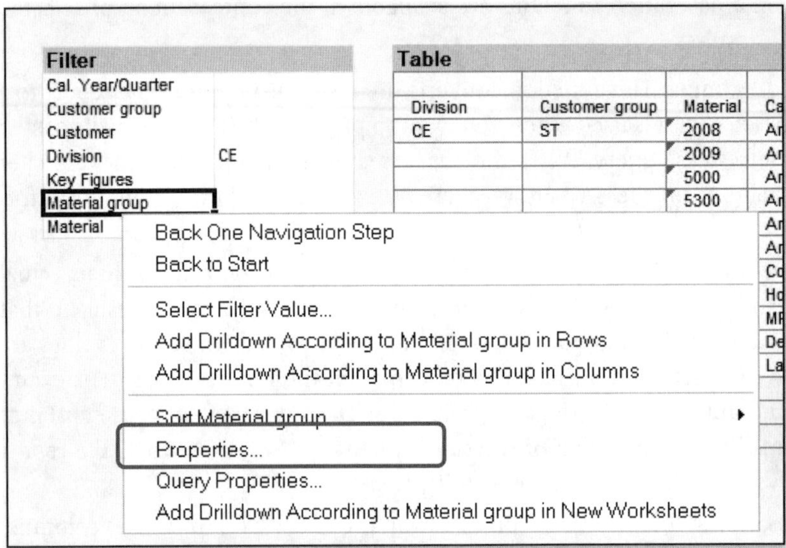

Figure 10.16 Local Properties for a Characteristic

This opens up a properties dialog box where you can maintain the properties (Figure 10.17).

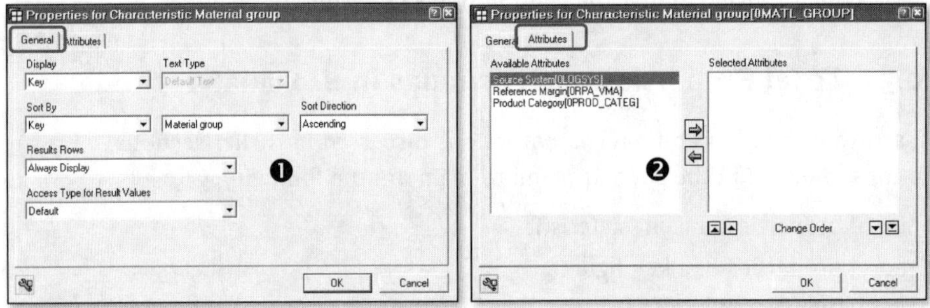

Figure 10.17 Maintaining Characteristic Properties

There are two tabs visible in Figure 10.17 for the material group characteristic: General and Attributes. However, if the selected characteristic has hierarchies defined for it, an additional Hierarchy tab is also displayed in the characteristic properties.

On the General tab page, you specify the properties related to display, sort order, result rows, or the access type for the values (❶ of Figure 10.17). The Attributes tab is applicable only for those characteristics that have some attributes defined for them. On this tab (❷), you see a list of all of the attributes for the selected characteristic. If you want to display any of these attributes in the report, select them and bring them to the right side of in the Selected Attributes box, using the arrow keys (❷).

The properties maintained here are applicable to all of the values of the selected characteristic. However, the settings are local to this specific workbook only.

10.3.2 Local Properties of a Key Figure

Similar to the characteristics, the properties for a key figure query element can also be maintained locally in the workbook. The key figure properties can be called from the context menu of the *data cell* (a cell displaying key figure values) for the key figure (Figure 10.18).

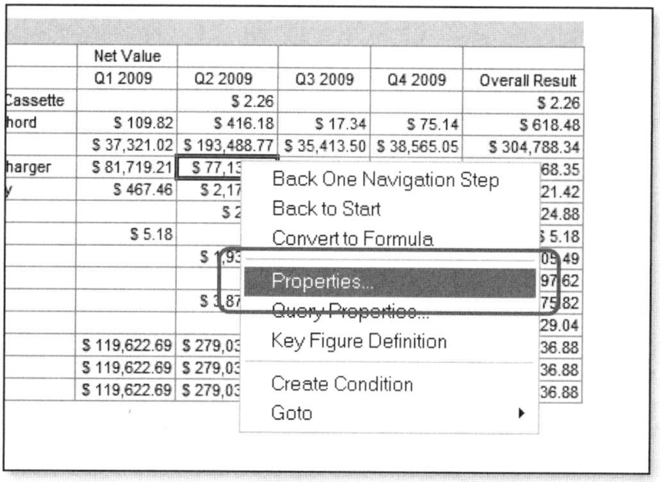

Figure 10.18 Local Properties for Key Figures

The properties dialog for a key figure consists of three different tabs: Number Format, Calculations, and Sorting (Figure 10.19).

The Number Format tab page contains the settings that correspond to the display behavior of the selected key figure (❶ of Figure 10.19). These settings include the scaling factor, decimal places, and highlighted display-related settings.

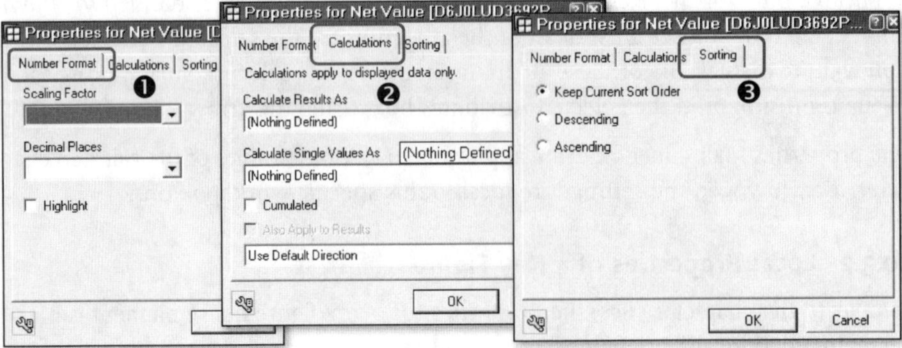

Figure 10.19 Maintaining Key Figure Properties

On the Calculations tab page, you can define the calculation behavior of the selected key figure. The key figure is locally recalculated based on the settings mentioned on this tab (❷). The significance of these key figure settings (Calculated Results As, Calculate Single Values As, etc.) is discussed in Chapter 9, BEx Query Designer.

The sort order for the selected key figure is defined in the Sorting tab of the properties (❸)

10.3.3 Local Query Properties

Apart from the local properties that are defined for an individual characteristic or a key figure, you can maintain the properties for the query as well. To access the query properties, select Query Properties from the context menu of a filter/characteristic/key figure (Figure 10.20) used in the query.

The query properties window displays eight tabs where you can set properties to control the query behavior locally in the workbook (Figure 10.21).

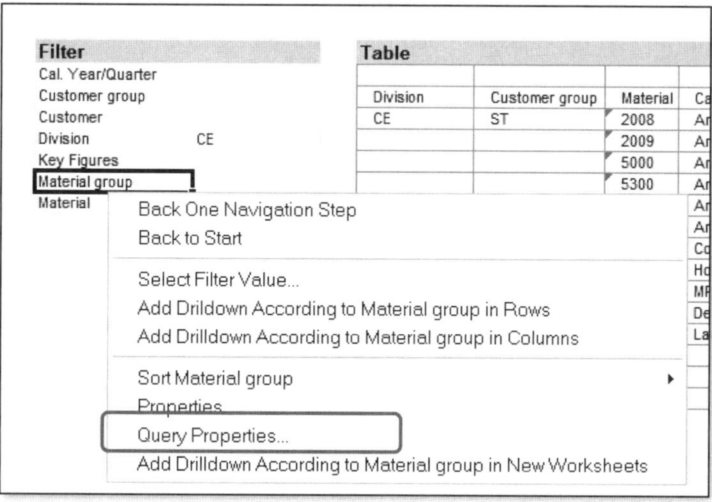

Figure 10.20 Local Query Properties

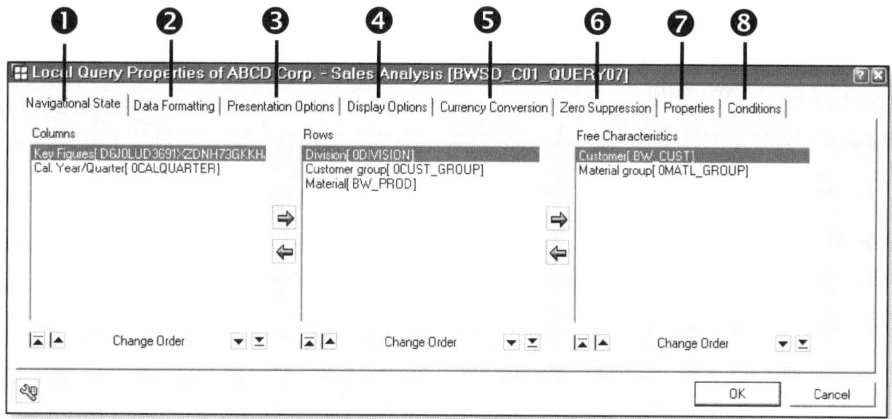

Figure 10.21 Maintaining Query Properties

The Navigational State tab page controls the layout of the query (❶ of Figure 10.21). Here you can redefine the rows/columns/free characteristics in the query by moving the query elements using the arrow buttons.

The Data Formatting tab (❷) allows you to define the way query results should be displayed in the workbook. You can specify if the query result should be displayed in a tabular format or in a multidimensional format on this tab page.

The presentation settings related to the display of results position in the report, represented by +/- signs and zero values, are determined on the Presentation Options tab page (❸).

You can maintain the scaling factors for key figure elements in the query on the Display Options tab page (❹). You can also maintain the setting to display the document links for objects such as data, metadata, and master data on this tab.

If you want to perform currency translation locally in the workbook, the related settings are maintained on the Currency Conversion tab page (❺).

The Zero Suppression tab page (❻) allows you to define settings to suppress rows/columns (or both) if all of the values in a particular row or column are zero.

General information about the query, such as the owner, is visible on the Properties tab page (❼). The setting to toggle between change mode and display mode for an input-ready query is also available on this tab page.

The Conditions tab page (❽) displays the list of conditions that are built on the query and also the state of the condition (active/inactive). You can also build a local condition on the query in a workbook.

10.3.4 Local Formula

When analyzing data in a workbook, you sometimes need to perform some additional calculations on the existing key figure values. For example, consider a situation where you have a report displayed in a workbook that shows the net value for different materials for the entire year. However, during analysis, you need to know the average monthly net value for different materials. In BEx analyzer, you can create a local formula to address such a requirement. In a local formula, you can define your own calculation, which remains local to the workbook.

The option to create a local formula in a workbook is available in the context menu for the key figure column header cell (Figure 10.22).

Select Add Local Formula from the context menu of the key figure header, as shown in ❶ of Figure 10.22. This opens the Local Formula pop-up window where you define the formula logic.

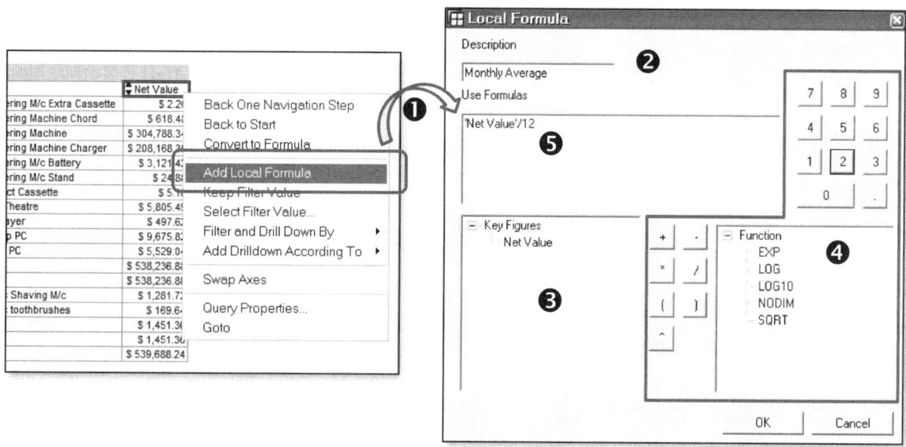

Figure 10.22 Add a Local Formula

Maintain the description for the new formula (❷). All of the key figure elements used in the query are listed under key figures to be used in the formula (❸). You can define the formula using these key figures and the numbers and basic mathematical/scientific operators available on this screen (❹). The defined formula definition is visible (❺). For the example mentioned here, the formula would be (Net Value/12). Click on OK to complete the definition of the formula and to return back to the workbook. As shown in Figure 10.23, an additional Monthly Average column is now visible in the report display.

Table

Division	Customer group	Material		Net Value	Monthly Average
CE	ST	2008	Answering M/c Extra Cassette	$ 2.2	$ 0.19
		2009	Answering Machine Chord	$ 618.4	$ 51.54
		5000	Answering Machine	$ 304,788.3	$ 25,399.03
		5300	Answering Machine Charger	$ 208,168.3	$ 17,347.36
		5400	Answering M/c Battery	$ 3,121.4	$ 260.12
		5450	Answering M/c Stand	$ 24.8	$ 2.07
		31000	Compact Cassette	$ 5.1	$ 0.43
		37500	Home Theatre	$ 5,805.4	$ 483.79
		38000	MP4 Player	$ 497.6	$ 41.47
		93000	Desktop PC	$ 9,675.8	$ 806.32
		93500	Laptop PC	$ 5,529.0	$ 460.75
		Result		$ 538,236.8	$ 44,853.07
	Result			$ 538,236.8	$ 44,853.07

Figure 10.23 Modified Layout with Local Formula

10.4 Saving and Reusing Workbooks in BEx Analyzer

After you've finished analysis in the workbook, you can save it on the SAP NetWeaver BW server so that you can later reuse the analysis or perform a new analysis. To save a workbook, click on the Save button, as shown in ❶ of Figure 10.24. Select Save Workbook to save this workbook on the server.

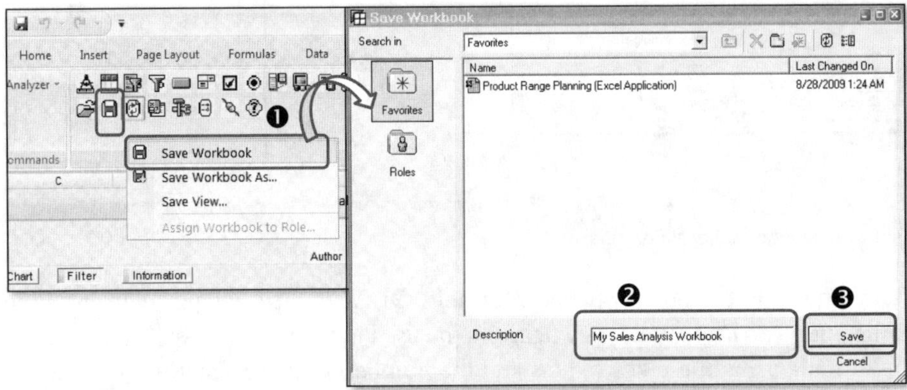

Figure 10.24 Save a New Workbook

Give a proper description to the workbook (❷), and click on Save (❸) to save the workbook in your favorites for future access.

If you want to make this workbook available to other users, you can save it under a specific role (Figure 10.24). All of the users under that role can then access the same workbook for their analysis.

To open an already saved workbook, click on the Open button, and select OPEN WORKBOOK from the menu (❶ of Figure 10.25).

Select the workbook in the pop-up window (❷)and click on Open (❸) to open the workbook for analysis.

To open an existing workbook, you must first connect to that SAP NetWeaver BW system. If you want to save the data locally so that you can refer to the data without connecting to the SAP NetWeaver BW system, you can do so by saving the Excel sheet using the normal Excel Save function (Figure 10.26).

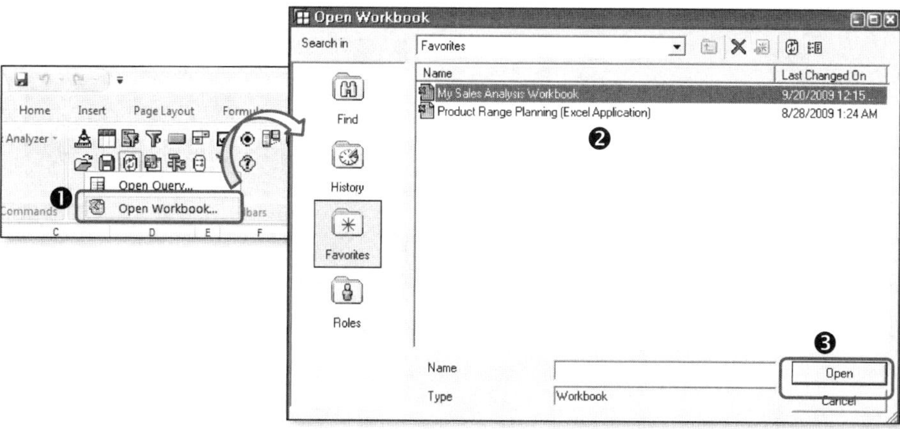

Figure 10.25 Open an Existing Workbook

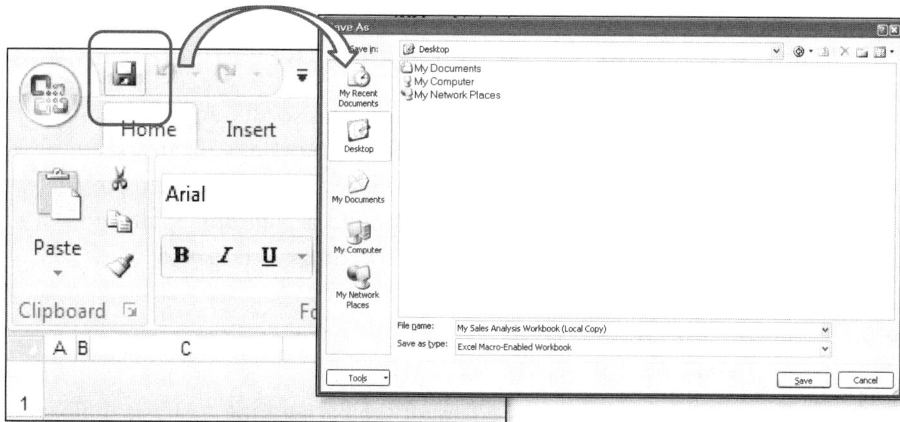

Figure 10.26 Save the Workbook as a Local Copy

You can also connect your local workbook back to the SAP NetWeaver BW system by opening that Excel workbook in a BEx analyzer session. The context menu on any of the query cells gives you the option to refresh the query (Figure 10.27). Selecting Refresh shows the login screen where you can enter the logic credentials and connect to the SAP NetWeaver BW system to perform online analysis of the data.

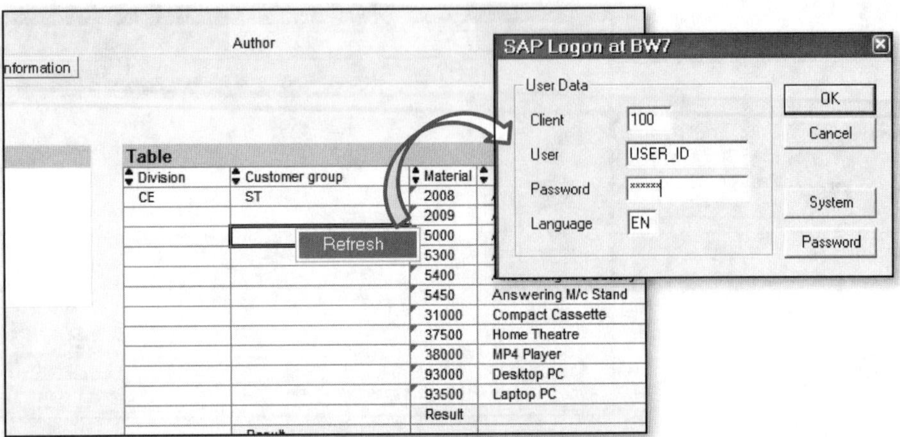

Figure 10.27 Reconnect the Local Copy to the SAP NetWeaver BW System

10.5 Building an Analysis Application in BEx analyzer

In addition to running existing queries, BEx analyzer also allows you to build your own analysis applications with custom layouts and functions. In this section, we explain the BEx design functions and the procedure for building a simple analysis application. (BEx analyzer can also be used to build a planning application in an Excel interface; this topic is covered in Chapter 12, Integrated Planning.)

10.5.1 BEx Design Functions

When you start BEx analyzer, you can see two different sets of functions available in the form of two different toolbars, the Design toolbar and the Analysis toolbar. As the name suggests, the Analysis toolbar is used to perform analysis. (We discussed the use of this toolbar in previous sections of this chapter.) The Design toolbar, shown in Figure 10.28, is comprised of different design functions that can be used to design and build an application in BEx analyzer.

Following are the different functions on the Design toolbar (Figure 10.28):

- Toggle Between Design Mode and Analysis Mode (❶): Using this button, you can switch the workbook to the design mode, and back to analysis mode from the design mode.
- Insert Analysis Grid (❷): This button inserts the *analysis grid* design item in the workbook. The analysis grid is an important design item for workbooks; query

results are displayed in the analysis grid, and it's where you perform different navigations on the data you're analyzing.

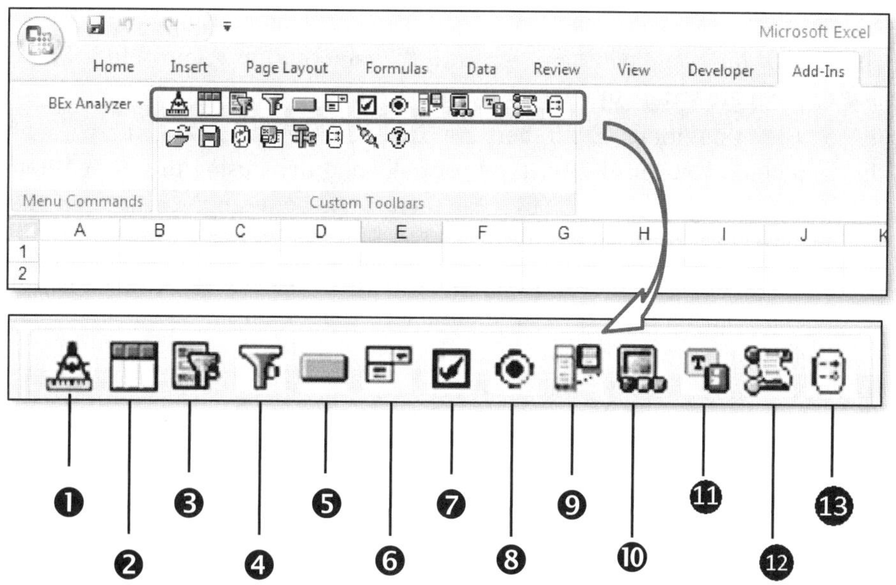

Figure 10.28 Design Functions in BEx analyzer

- Insert Navigation Pane (❸): This button is used to insert the *navigation pane* in the workbook. The navigation pane design item displays all of the characteristics, key figures, and structure elements that can be used to perform navigation on the data. You can add/remove drilldown, filter values for characteristics, and so on, in the navigation pane.
- Insert Filters (❹): This design item allows you to display the list of all of the filters applied to the query results. You can specifically select the query elements for which you want to display filters.
- Insert Button (❺): This design item adds a button to the application. You can configure a command that is assigned to this button so that it's executed when this button is clicked.
- Insert Dropdown Box (❻): With this design item, you can provide users with a dropdown box to make a selection in the workbook.
- Insert Checkbox Group (❼): This design item inserts a checkbox group in the workbook. You can assign a query element to this checkbox group so that a list of

values for that query element is displayed in the workbook. Users can then select multiple values for that element by using the checkbox option.

- Insert Radio Button Group (❽): With this design item, you can provide the user with an option to select a value for a specific query element using a radio button. The specific query element is assigned to the radio button group, and values of that element are visible to the user for selection.
- Insert List of Conditions (❾): If there are conditions defined on the query used in the workbook, you can display the list of all conditions using this design item. While performing analysis, the user can then toggle between the active and inactive states of each condition, if needed.
- Insert List of Exceptions (❿): Similar to the list of conditions, if there are any exceptions defined on the query used in the workbook, this design item displays a list of them. These exceptions can be set as active or inactive during the analysis.
- Insert Text (⓫): This design item allows you to display different text elements for a query in the workbook. You can select from a list of different text elements that can be displayed in the workbook.
- Insert Messages (⓬ of Figure 10.28): In the course of navigation and analysis, there are different messages generated either by BEx analyzer or by the SAP NetWeaver BW system. These messages can be error messages, warnings, or information. You can use this design item to display these messages in the workbook and make a selection about the type of messages to be displayed.
- Workbook Settings (⓭): This function calls the Workbook Settings dialog, where you can maintain different settings on general workbook properties, display, variables, and so on, for the workbook.

10.5.2 Build a Simple Analysis Application

Now that you are familiar with the basic design functions available in BEx analyzer, we can build a simple analysis application in BEx analyzer for ABCD Corp. sales analysis. The analysts need a dropdown to select the material group characteristic, and also an option to filter the results using a condition on high-value orders.

Follow these steps to create this custom analysis application:

1. Log in to BEx analyzer, and open a new Excel sheet from the Excel menu. This will enable all of the functions on the BEx Design toolbar.
2. Enter the heading "ABCD Corp. Sales Analysis" for the workbook, as shown in ❶ of Figure 10.29.

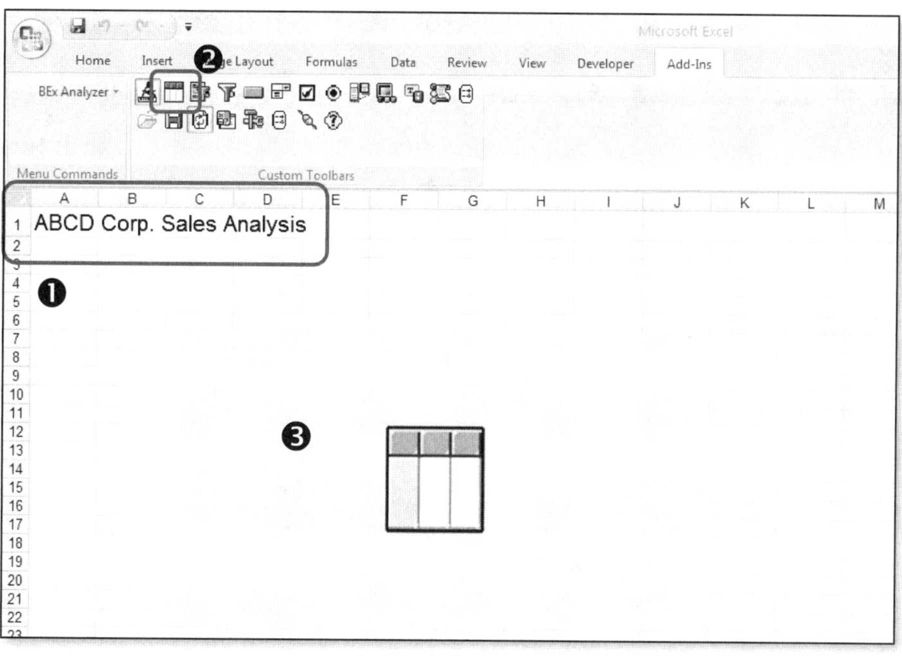

Figure 10.29 Insert Analysis Grid

3. To insert the analysis grid design item in the workbook, click on the button shown in ❷ of Figure 10.29. This adds the analysis grid to the workbook (❸).
4. Double-click on the design item to call the properties dialog as shown in Figure 10.30. You must assign a data provider to the analysis grid, which acts as a source of data to the design item. Create a new data provider by clicking the button shown in ❶ of Figure 10.30. When you click on the Create button, another pop-up appears. Based on our example scenario, we assign the Sales Analysis query to the data provider using button ❷ of Figure 10.30. Finally, give a name to the data provider (❸), and click OK (❹) to return to the properties screen. After the assignment of the data provider is complete, you can also define some additional settings for the analysis grid by selecting appropriate checkboxes, as shown in Figure 10.30. Finally, click on the OK button (❺) to return to the workbook.

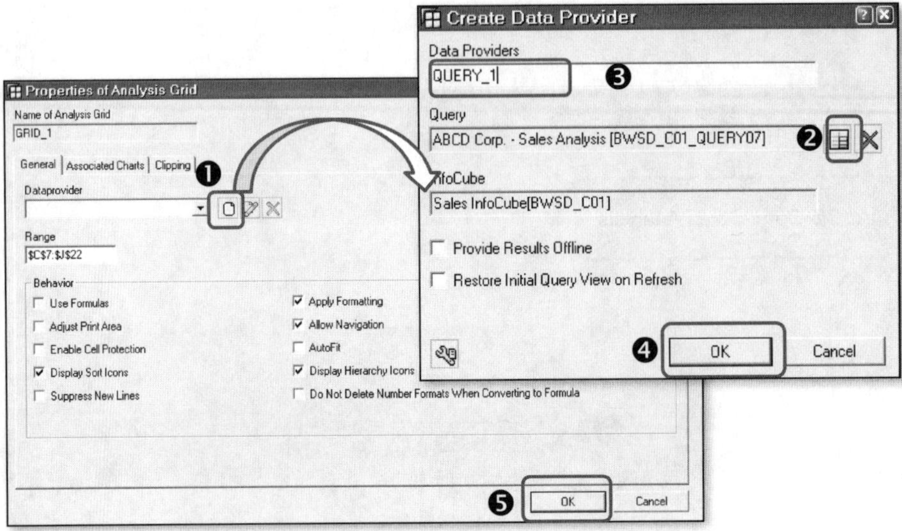

Figure 10.30 Set Properties of an Analysis Grid

Multiple Queries in a Workbook

You can add multiple analysis grid design items in a workbook, each of which can be assigned to a different data provider. In other words, you can actually perform analysis on data from multiple queries together in a single workbook.

5. If the query assigned to the data provider in the analysis grid (❶ of Figure 10.31) contains some user entry variables, you must maintain these variables. To do this, click on the Variables button (❷) on the Analysis toolbar. This shows you the screen where the values for those variables can be maintained.
6. Select the cell where you want to add the dropdown box in the workbook, and then click on the dropdown button in the Design toolbar (❶ of Figure 10.32). The dropdown box design item is added to the workbook (❷).

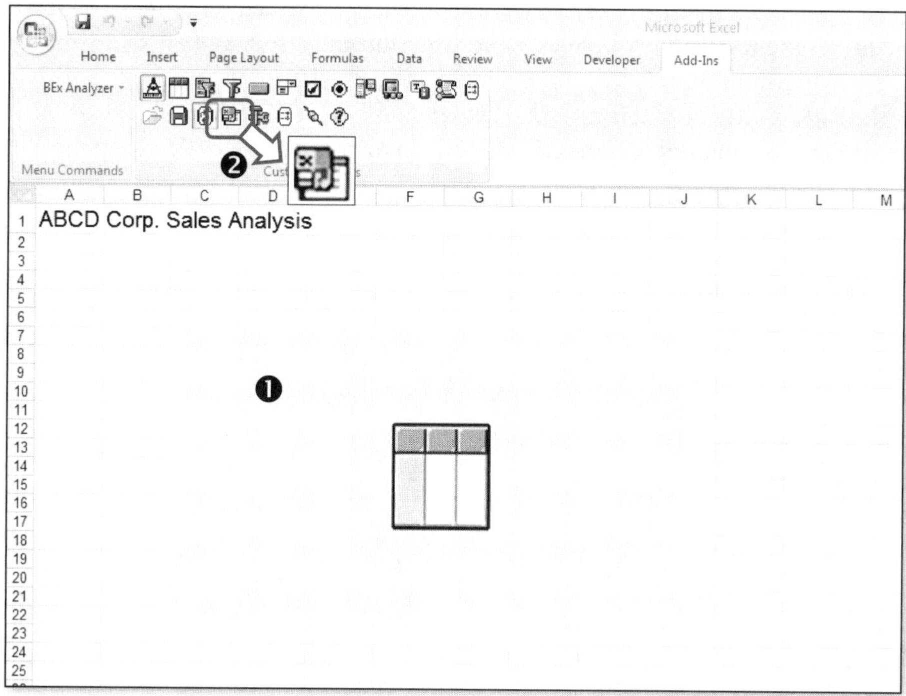

Figure 10.31 Maintain Variable Values

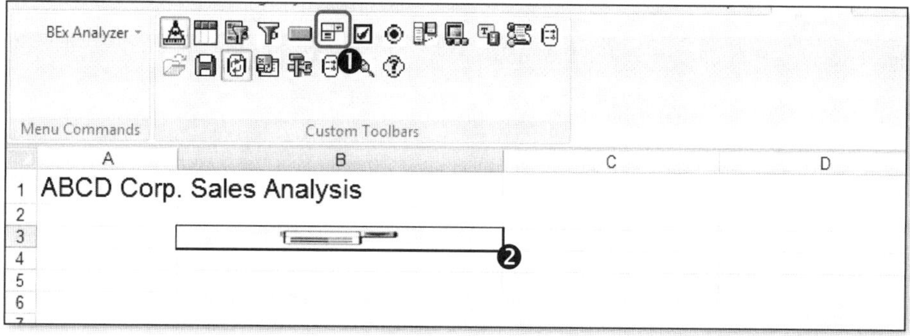

Figure 10.32 Insert Dropdown Box Design Item

7. Open the Properties of Dropdown Box dialog by double-clicking on the item. The Properties of a Dropdown Box dialog contains three tabs. On the General tab page (❶ of Figure 10.33), you assign the data provider to the dropdown and select the location of the dropdown in the workbook. On the Selection tab page (❷),

you assign the specific query element (characteristic/structure) to the dropdown, and set the read mode of the characteristic. You can also maintain some display-related settings on this tab. For example, you can choose if you want to display the label of the characteristic and whether an All Values entry should be visible in the dropdown or not. On the Affected Data Provider tab page (❸), select the data provider that will get impacted by the selection made using this dropdown box. Finally, click OK to return to the workbook.

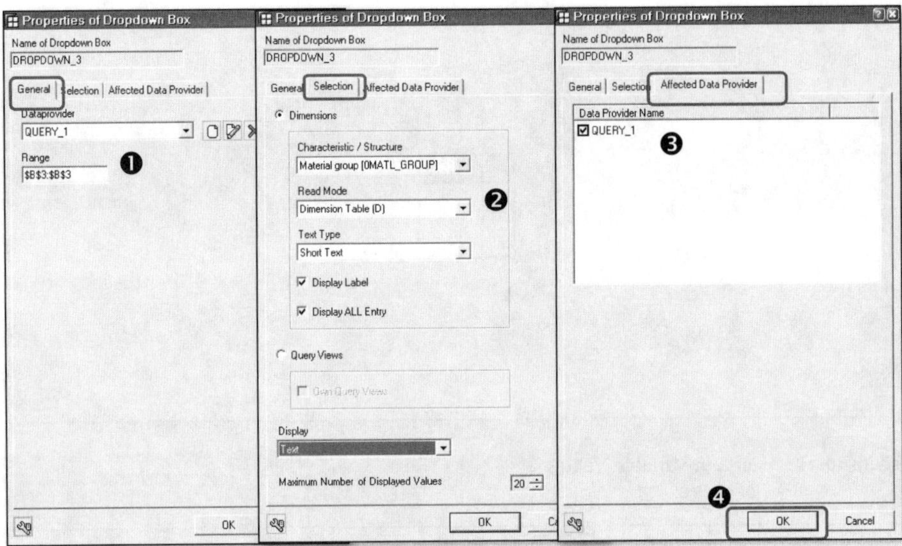

Figure 10.33 Set Properties for the Dropdown Box

Dropdown Box for Query Views

If multiple query views are defined on a selected data provider, you can provide a dropdown box in the workbook that will give you a list of views created on that query. The user can then select a specific query view from this dropdown, and the affected data provider gets refreshed accordingly. To achieve this, you have to select the Query Views option on the Selection tab of the Properties of Dropdown Box page (❷ of Figure 10.33).

8. Now, insert a button design item in the workbook using the function button from the Design toolbar (❶ of Figure 10.34). Double-click on the newly inserted button (❷) in the workbook to call the properties screen for it.

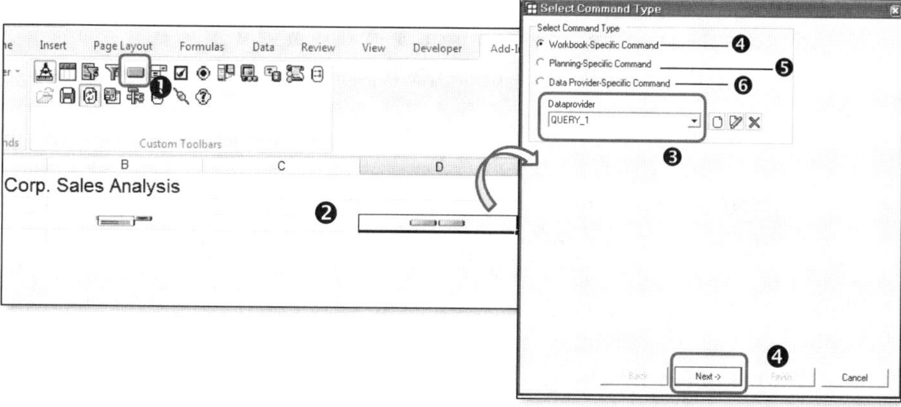

Figure 10.34 Insert Button Design Item

9. Assign the data provider to the design item (❸). For a button design item in a workbook, you can assign custom commands to be performed when this button is clicked. There are three types of commands that can be assigned to a button: Workbook-Specific Command, Planning-Specific Command, and Data Provider-Specific Command. The different commands available under each of these categories are listed here:
   - **Workbook-Specific Commands:**
     - Process Variables (with an option to enable Display of Personalized Variables; this command calls the variable screen)
     - Toggle Drag and Drop State
     - Disable Drag and Drop
     - Allow Drag and Drop
   - **Planning-Specific Commands:**
     - Save
     - Transfer Values
     - Execute Planning Function
     - Planning: Execute Sequence

Note

The planning-specific commands are explained in more detail in Chapter 12, Integrated Planning.

- **Data Provider-Specific Commands:**
  - Edit (sets the input-ready data provider in edit mode)
  - Display (sets the input-ready data provider in display mode)
  - Filter Command
  - Assign Query/Query View

10. For our example scenario, select Workbook-Specific Command (❶ of Figure 10.35) for the inserted design item, and click Next (❷). On the next screen, select Process Variables from the list of workbook-specific commands (❸), and click Next. The next screen displays the static parameters for the selected command. You can also maintain the button text and range for the button in the workbook (❺). Finally, click OK to return to the workbook.

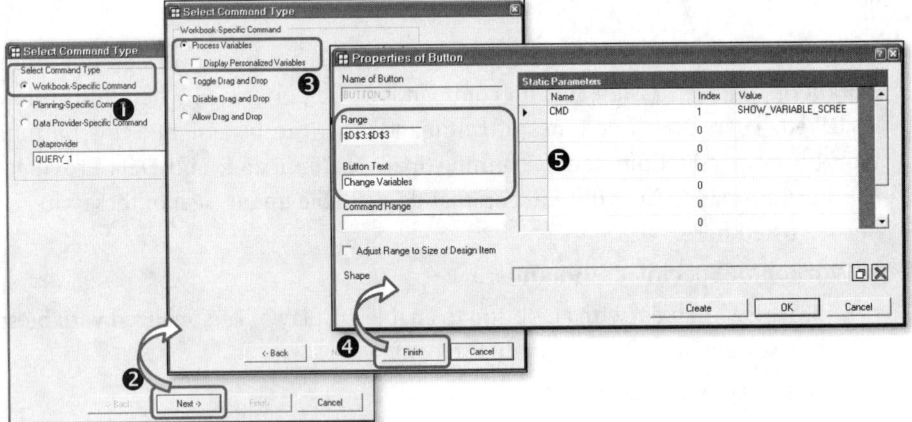

Figure 10.35 Set Properties for Button

11. Insert the *list of conditions* design item using the button shown in ❶ of Figure 10.36. Call the properties for the inserted design item by double-clicking on the inserted item, (❷) and assign the data provider to the item (❸). Finally, click OK to return to the workbook (❹).

The custom analysis application is now ready for use. To begin the analysis, click on the button shown in ❶ of Figure 10.37. This exits the design mode and switches to the analysis mode. After you switch to the analysis mode, the workbook is refreshed with data, as shown in Figure 10.37.

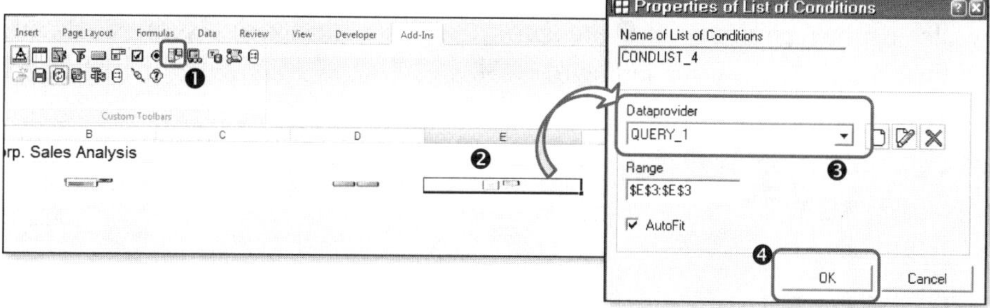

Figure 10.36 Insert List of Conditions

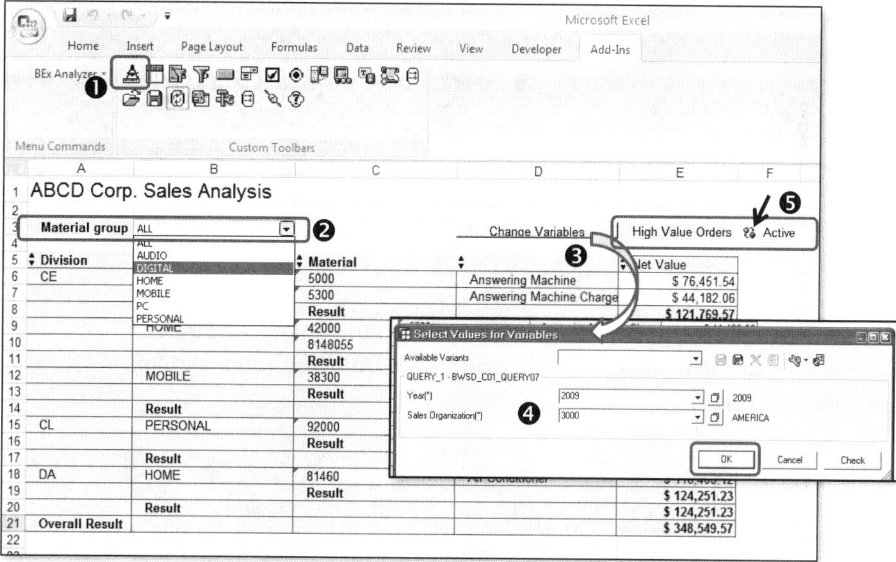

Figure 10.37 Working with Custom Analysis Application

You can see from ❷ of Figure 10.37 that there is a dropdown box option available for the material group characteristic, as well as a Change Variables button (❸). When clicked, this button calls the variable entry screen (❹). The user can change the values of the variables and then refresh the data in the workbook by clicking OK on the variable screen.

You can also see the list of conditions built on the query displayed in the workbook (❺).

For analysis, you can toggle between the active and inactive states of the condition by clicking the icon shown in ❶ of Figure 10.38. The query result is refreshed without the condition, as shown in Figure 10.38.

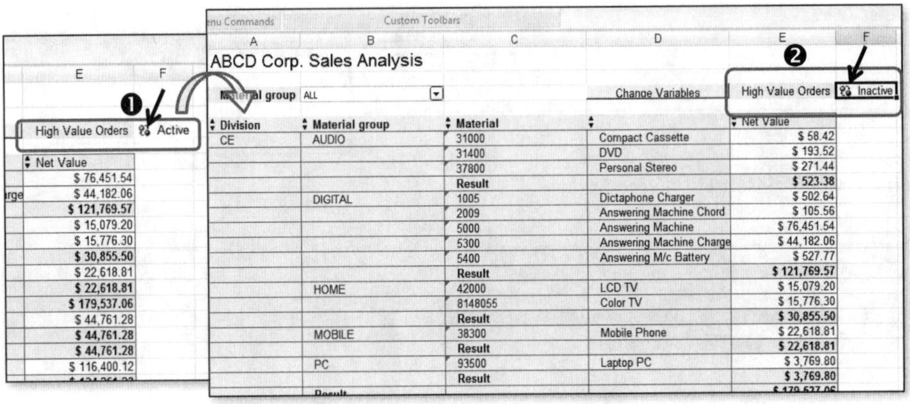

Figure 10.38 Toggle Between Condition States

You can revert the condition back to the active state by clicking once on the same icon (❷ of Figure 10.38).

This custom analysis application can be saved on the SAP NetWeaver BW server for future use. Use the Save Workbook command from the toolbar (Figure 10.39) to save this workbook.

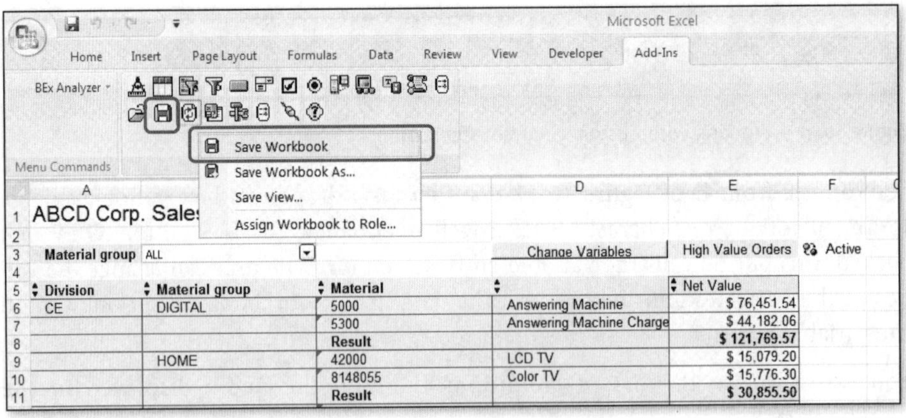

Figure 10.39 Save Workbook

As you've seen from this section, you can use different design items to build a custom application using BEx analyzer, thereby providing an interactive and flexible analysis interface for business users.

10.6 Running Queries in BEx Web Analyzer

In an organization, different users accessing a set of data might want to see the same data in different ways or analyze that data in an ad-hoc manner. The BEx web analyzer tool is available to fulfill these ad-hoc query and analysis requirements in a web environment. This is a powerful web-based application that can access data from a query built in BEx query designer or even from an InfoProvider for ad-hoc analysis.

You can access the BEx web analyzer tool either through a portal or directly through the web browser. The standard SAP Business Intelligence portal role (❶ of Figure 10.40) includes BEx web analyzer (❷). Click on the links to open the BEx web analyzer.

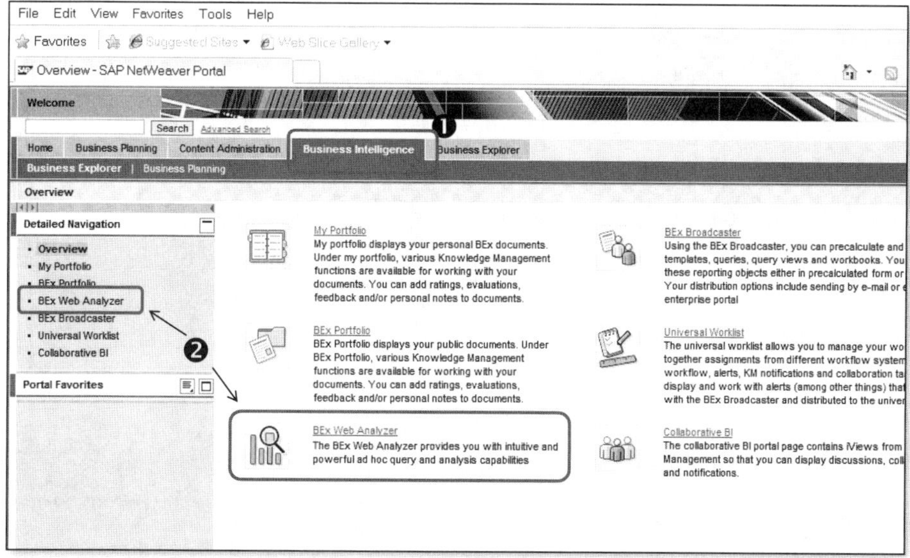

Figure 10.40 Accessing BEx Web Analyzer

Next we discuss how to create a new analysis with BEx web analyzer and then explain the different functions available.

10.6.1 Create a New Analysis with BEx Web Analyzer

The default layout of BEx web analyzer is shown in Figure 10.41. Using the buttons available on the top toolbar, you can create a new analysis or open an existing one (Figure 10.41). To open a new analysis, click on the New Analysis button (❶), and the Open window appears. Here you can select the data provider for your analysis from the available tab pages (❷). Ad-hoc analysis can be performed on different types of data providers; you can open an existing query or InfoProvider for one of the views based on your specific need. Select the type of object from the dropdown (❸).

Analysis on Data from External Systems

Using BEx web analyzer, you can also perform analysis on the data from external systems, which can be connected using XMLA or ODBO interfaces (❹ of Figure 10.41). For this, the external system must first be defined in the portal. Normally, portal administrators perform this task for you.

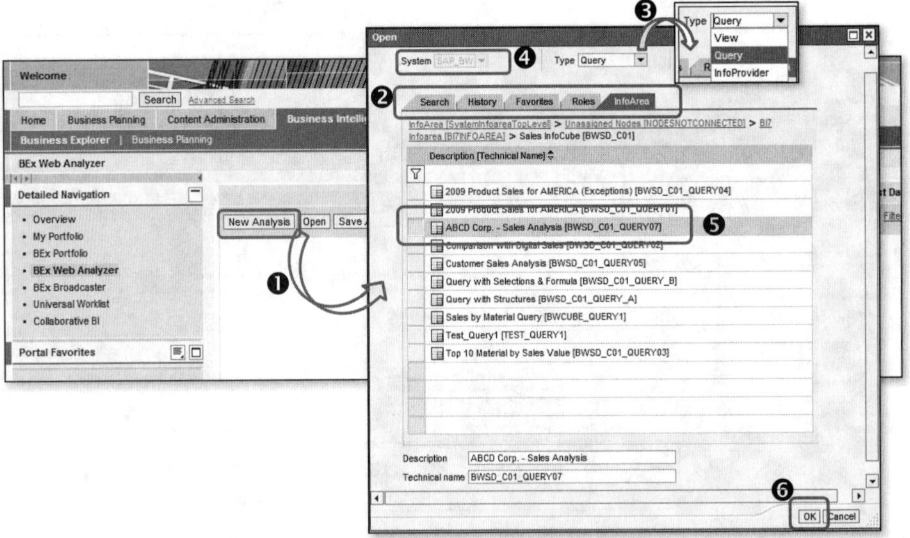

Figure 10.41 Create New Analysis

Navigate through the InfoProviders to locate the data provider (❺), and click OK to run the analysis (❻). If the data provider involves some user-entry variables, the variable entry screen is displayed where you can maintain the values of different variables (Figure 10.42). You can save this selection as a variant for future use by using the Save As button (❶ of Figure 10.42). Click on OK (❷) to run the analysis with selected variable values.

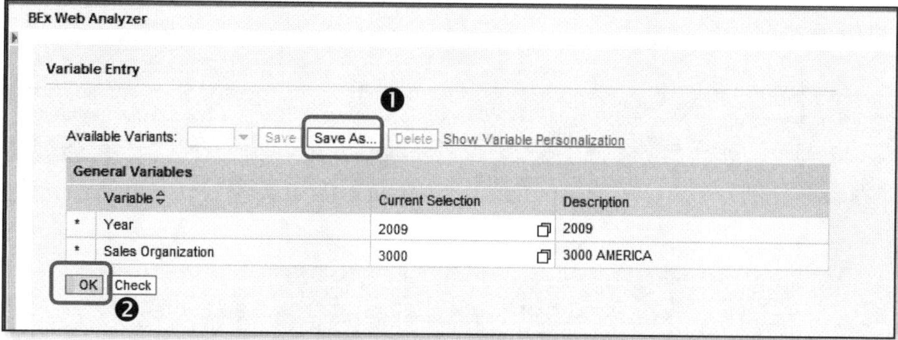

Figure 10.42 Enter Variable Values

Data from the InfoProvider is displayed in the tabular format on the right side of the screen (❶ of Figure 10.43). All query elements, such as characteristics in rows/columns and key figure structures, are visible in a navigation pane on the left side (❷).

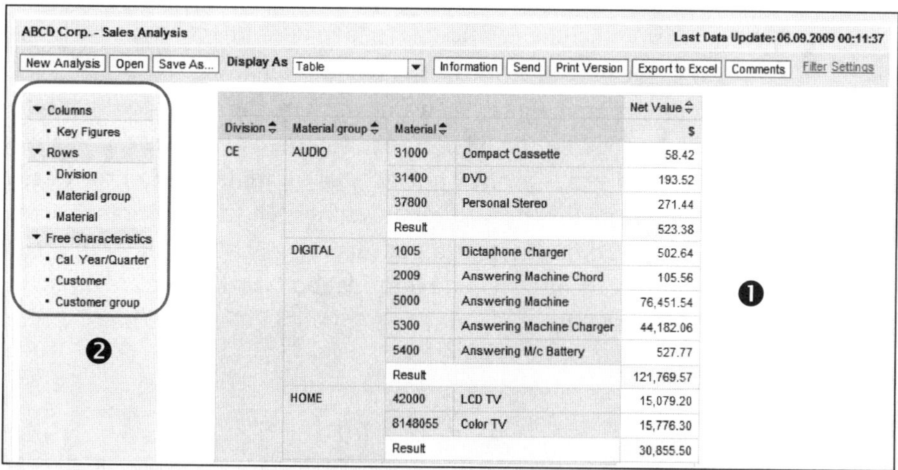

Figure 10.43 BEx Web Analyzer Layout

10.6.2 BEx Web Analyzer Functions

The buttons available on the top of the analysis provide some additional functions to assist with analysis:

- Display As: Selecting an option from the Display As dropdown, you can display the analysis result as a graphic, a table, or as both a table and graphic together (Figure 10.44).

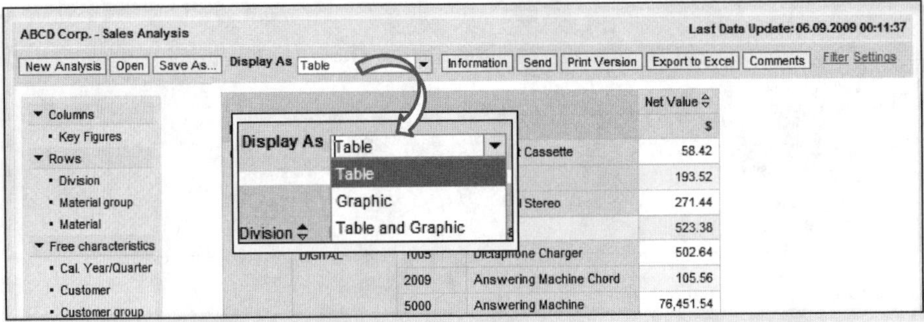

Figure 10.44 BEx Web Analyzer Function - Display Graphic

- Information: This button displays the information about the data provider used in the analysis. Apart from the metadata corresponding to the data provider (❶ of Figure 10.45), the information screen also displays the current state of filters on the data provider. This includes static filters, dynamic filters, and restrictions applied to the data provider using variables (❷).
- Send: If the person performing analysis wants to share the results with another person, he can use the Send button (❶ of Figure 10.46) to distribute this analysis. The Send function actually calls the BEx broadcaster wizard from BEx broadcaster, which allows you to create these distribution settings. The data from the current analysis can be distributed in different output formats, as shown in ❷ of Figure 10.46. Details about BEx broadcaster and information broadcasting are discussed in later sections of this chapter.

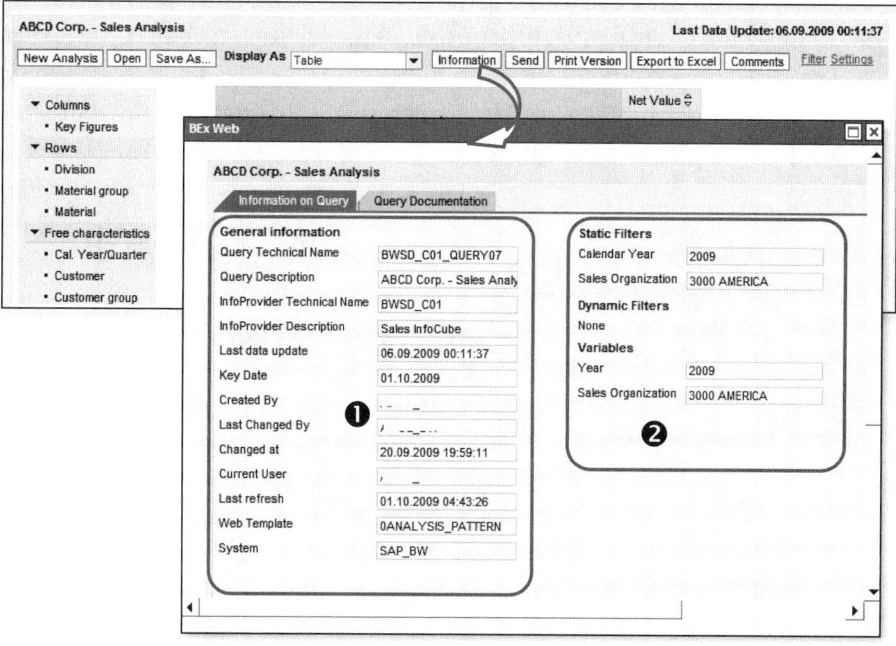

Figure 10.45 BEx Web Analyzer Function – Information

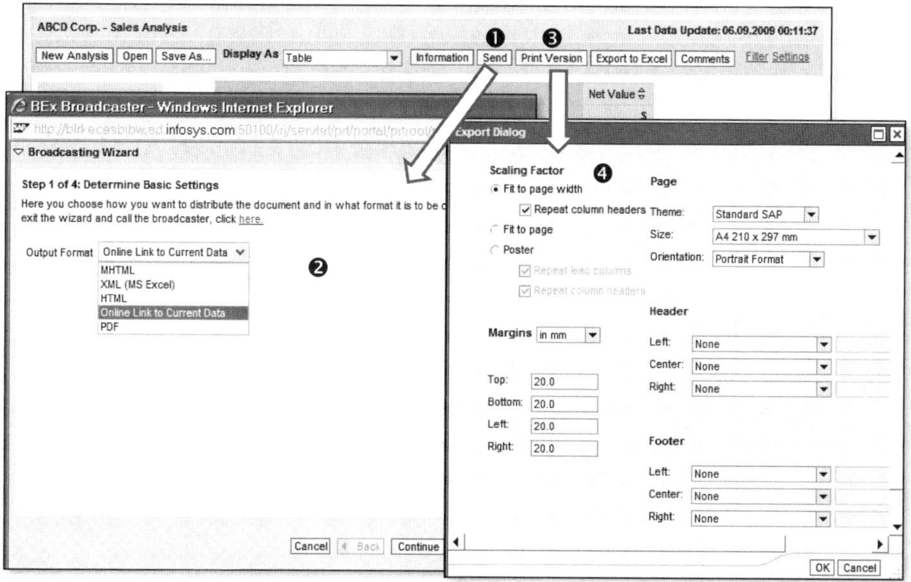

Figure 10.46 BEx Web Analyzer Function – Send and Print Version

- Print Version: This function (❸ of Figure 10.46) allows you to prepare the analysis for printing. You can make print-specific settings, add headers/footers, and generate a PDF that can be printed (❹).
- Export to Excel: Use this function (❶ of Figure 10.47) to download the analysis in Excel (❷).

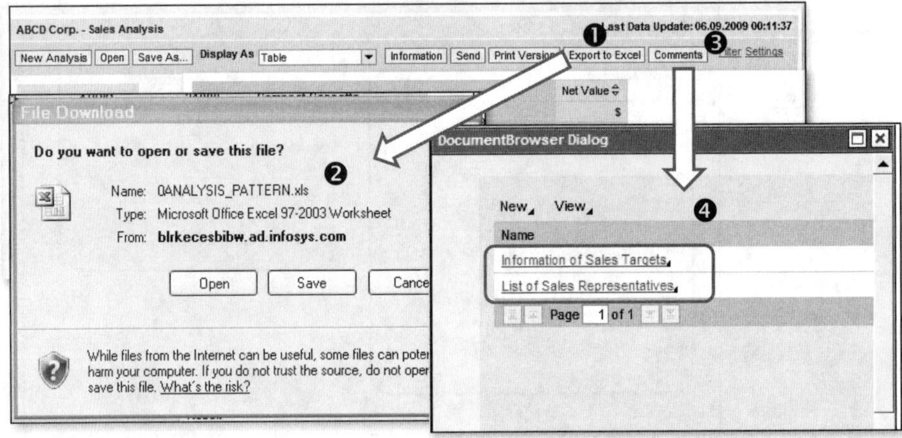

Figure 10.47 BEx Web Analyzer Function – Export to Excel and Comments

- Comments: You can create or maintain comments/documents for the data provider using the Comments function button (❸ of Figure 10.47). All of the existing documents created on the data provider are displayed for view and editing (❹).

10.7 Performing Information Analysis in BEx Web Analyzer

Using BEx web analyzer, you can navigate through data (using drilldown, filters, changing the layout, calculating key figures in a different way, etc.) to analyze it from various perspectives. These navigations can be performed via drag and drop or via context menu options. Similar to BEx analyzer, context menu functions are available for query elements in the navigation pane (❶ of Figure 10.48), characteristic column headers (❶), specific characteristic values (❶), key figure headers (❷), and specific key figure values (❸). Drag and drop can also be used to navigate through data, which makes analysis very easy (minimizing the number of mouse clicks) and very interactive.

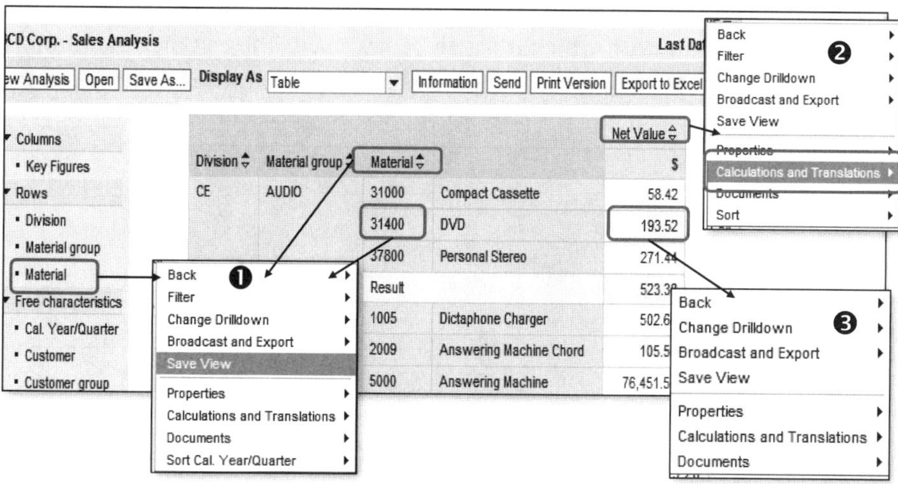

Figure 10.48 BEx Web Analyzer Context Menu Functions

Some of the commonly used navigations are described here:

▶ Add Drilldown: To add a drilldown to the analysis (in rows or columns), you have to drag the relevant characteristic from the navigation pane and then drop it in the layout, as shown in ❶ of Figure 10.49. The same navigation can be achieved by placing the characteristic in the required section on the navigation pane (❷). In the example shown in Figure 10.49, the Cal Year/Quarter characteristic is added to the columns (❸ and ❹).

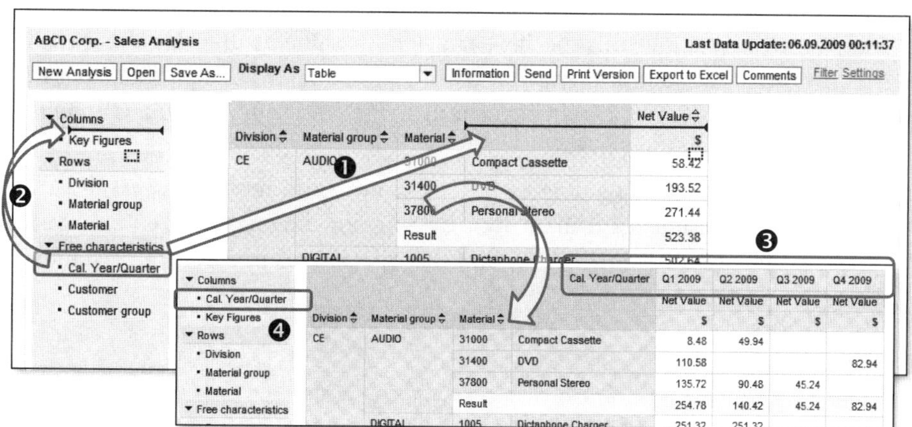

Figure 10.49 Navigation: Add Drilldown

▸ Swap characteristics: To swap characteristics, drag the characteristic and place it on the characteristic with which it has to be swapped. You can drag and drop in the analysis table (❶ of Figure 10.50) as well as in the navigation pane (❷). In the example shown in Figure 10.50, the customer group characteristic is swapped with the material group characteristic (❸).

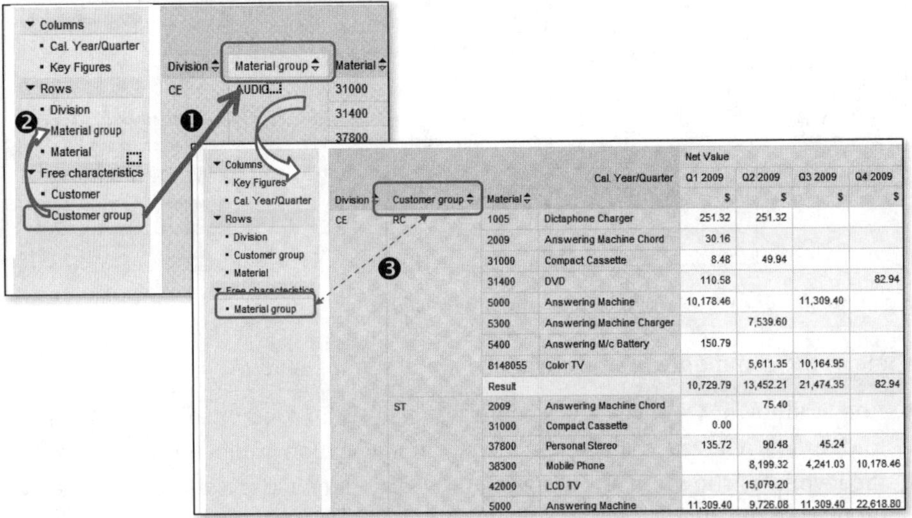

Figure 10.50 Navigation: Swap Characteristic

▸ Exclude characteristic value: In the example shown in Figure 10.51, if the analyst doesn't want the values for Cal. Year/Quarter = Q1 2009 to be displayed in the analysis, he can remove this specific characteristic value by dragging the Q1 2009 characteristic value out of the layout (❶ of Figure 10.51). This puts an exclusion filter on the Cal. Year/Quarter characteristic, and the query result is modified according to this exclusion (❷).

▸ Remove result rows: Using drag and drop, you can also remove the result values from the query result. This can be done by dragging the result row/column out of the result area (❶ of Figure 10.52) and that specific result row will be removed from the query result display (❷).

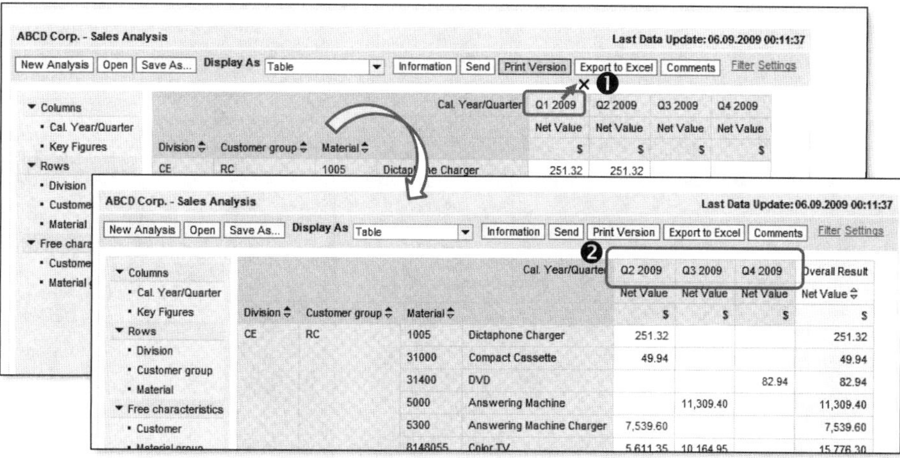

Figure 10.51 Navigation: Exclude Characteristic Value

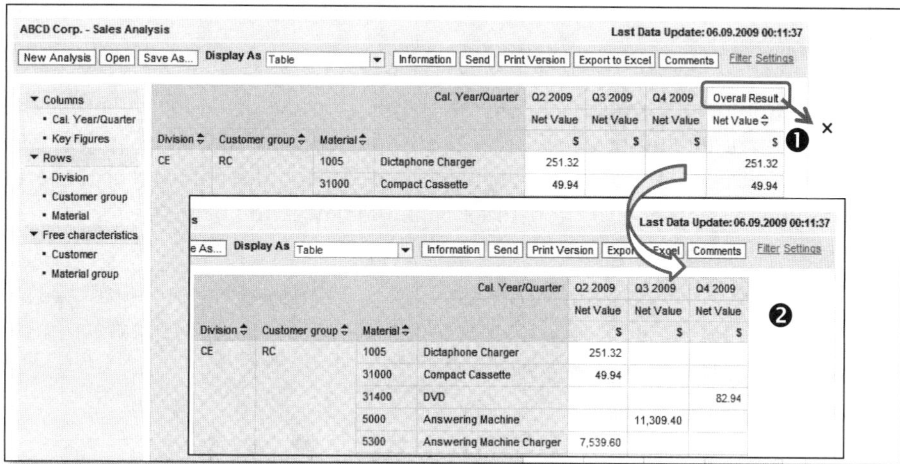

Figure 10.52 Navigation: Remove Result Rows

- Filter by characteristic value: Refer to the analysis shown in Figure 10.53. If you want to restrict the results for the Customer Group = RC characteristic value, simply drag the RC value and drop it over the customer group characteristic in the navigation pane (❶ of Figure 10.53). This navigation is equivalent to the Keep Filter Value context menu function. The customer group characteristic is restricted for RC value and is removed from the drilldown (❷ and ❸).

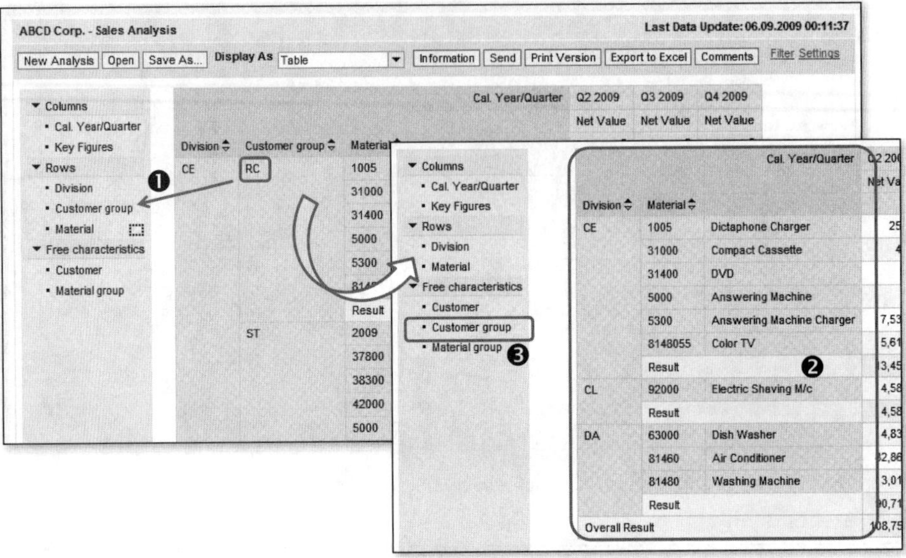

Figure 10.53 Navigation: Filter by a Characteristic Value

- Remove drilldown: To remove a characteristic from the drilldown, you have to drag the characteristic header out of the layout area (❶ of Figure 10.54). The analysis is refreshed without that characteristic (❷), and the removed characteristic is added to the free characteristics area in the navigation pane (❸).

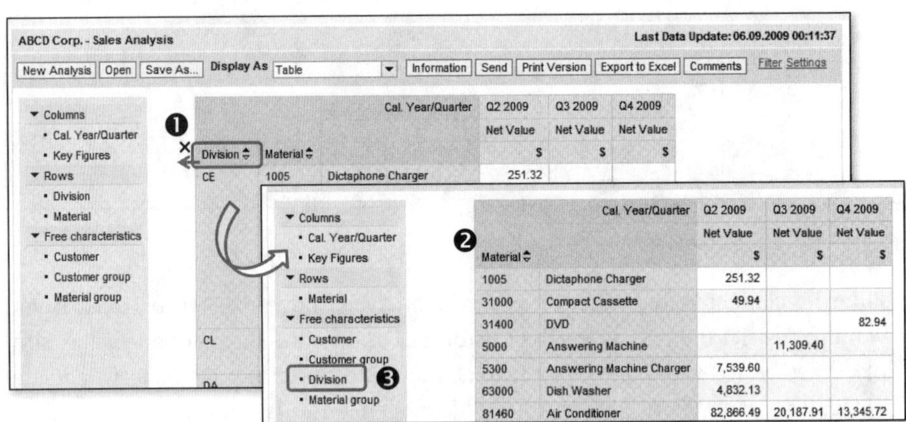

Figure 10.54 Navigation: Remove Drilldown

10.8 Analysis Filters and Settings in BEx Web Analyzer

Apart from all of the navigation options discussed previously, if you also want to work with the multiple filters applied to the data, a detailed filters view is available after you click on the Filter link (❶ of Figure 10.55). This action displays all of the characteristics and structures used in the query, and you can specify the filter on the displayed data. The Variable Screen button (❷) calls the variable selection screen and allows you to change the variable selection for the query.

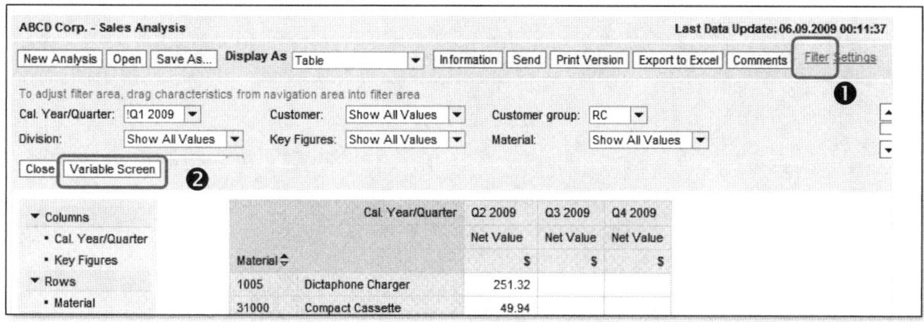

Figure 10.55 Analysis Filters

BEx web analyzer also allows you to maintain additional settings, which can be used to perform advanced analysis on the data. Click on the Settings link (Figure 10.56) to call the settings view.

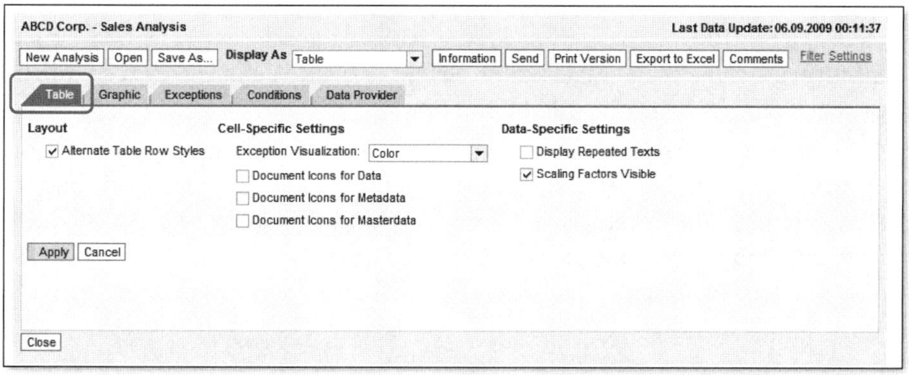

Figure 10.56 Analysis Settings: Table

There are five tabs where you can maintain different types of settings for the data displayed in BEx web analyzer:

- Table: You can maintain the display settings for the tabular display of the data on this tab page (Figure 10.56).
- Graphic: The settings related to the graphical display of the data in the analysis are maintained on this tab page (Figure 10.57). The details corresponding to the chart type, axis settings, legends, and so on are controlled here.

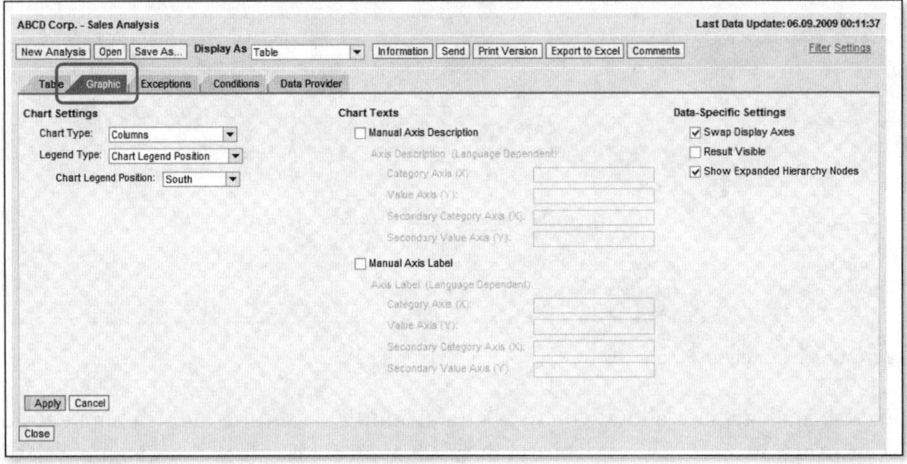

Figure 10.57 Analysis Settings: Graphs

- Exceptions: This tab page shows the list of all exceptions defined on this data provider (Figure 10.58). You can toggle the state of the selected exception (active/inactive) using the Toggle State button (❶). You can also define new exceptions on the data provider using the Add button (❷).
- Conditions: This tab lists all conditions defined on the data provider (Figure 10.59). You can add, delete, or edit the details for a condition using the buttons provided here. The Toggle State button is used to switch the selected condition from active to inactive, or vice versa.

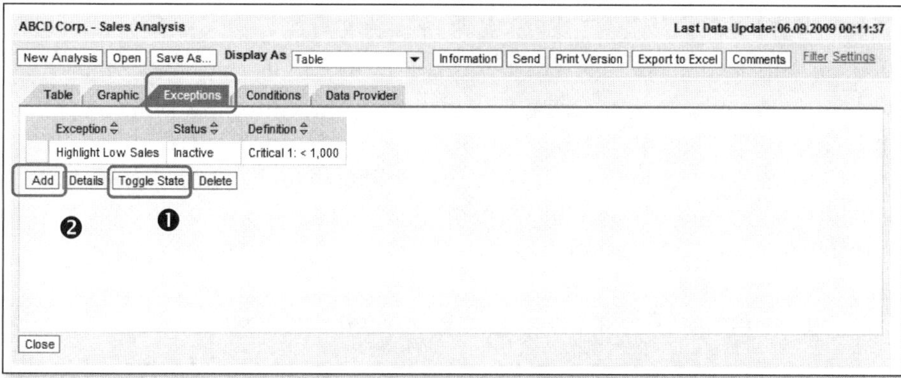

Figure 10.58 Analysis Settings: Exceptions

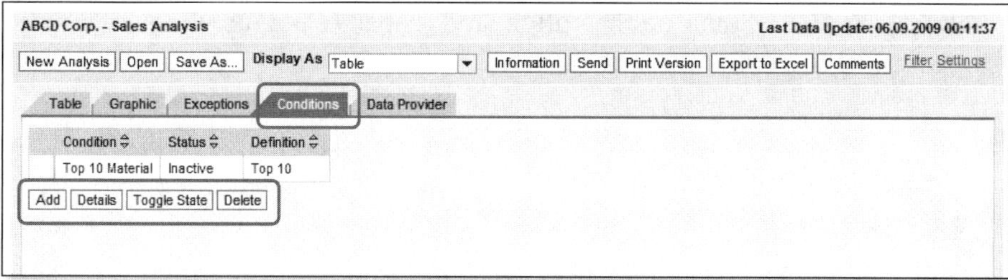

Figure 10.59 Analysis Settings: Conditions

- Data Provider: The settings related to the display of data elements from the data provider are maintained on this tab page (Figure 10.60). These include the settings for the position of the result rows, display settings for the result set, display settings for numbers, and settings related to the suppression of zero values in the analysis.

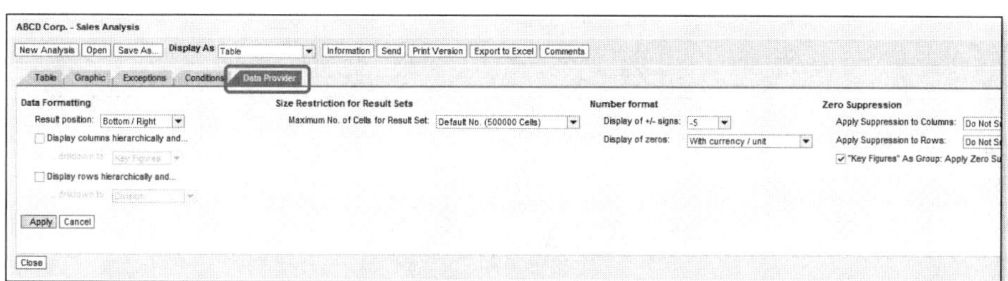

Figure 10.60 Analysis Settings: Data Provider

10.9 Information Broadcasting

The data, information, or analysis performed in BEx tools can be distributed (or *broadcasted*) to multiple users using information broadcasting. The BEx component that includes this function is called the BEx *broadcaster*. In this section, we discuss the process of information broadcasting using BEx web analyzer, explain how to maintain broadcasting settings for different BEx objects, and then illustrate how to create a new setting in BEx Broadcaster.

10.9.1 Information Broadcasting in BEx Web Analyzer

The following steps show how information broadcasting can be achieved in BEx web analyzer:

1. The analysis done on BEx web analyzer can be broadcasted using the Send button (❶ of Figure 10.61). Click on the button, and it opens a pop-up window from the Broadcasting Wizard.

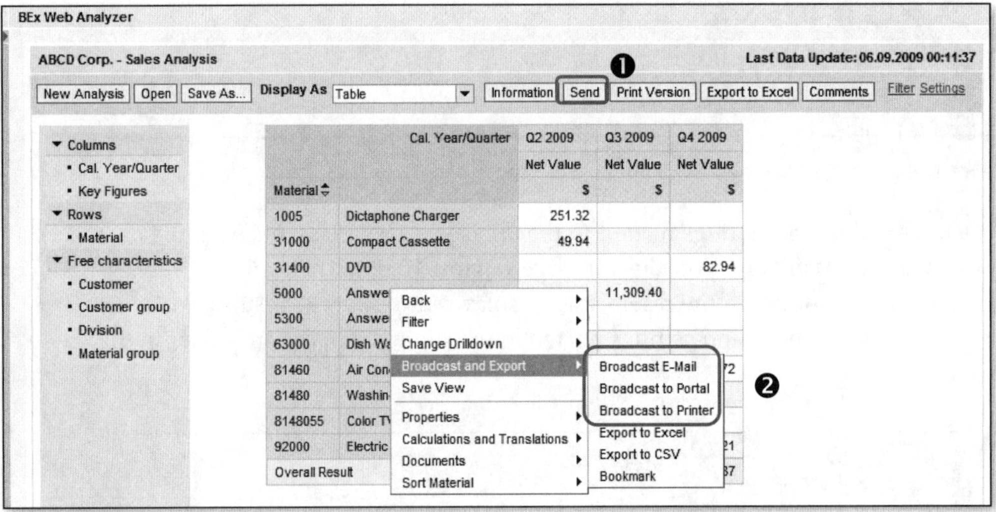

Figure 10.61 Calling BEx Broadcasting Wizard

The wizard can also be called from the Broadcast and Export context menu function, as shown in ❷ of Figure 10.61.

2. Select the output format for broadcasting from the options available in the dropdown (❶ of Figure 10.62), and click on the Continue button (❷) to proceed to the next screen.

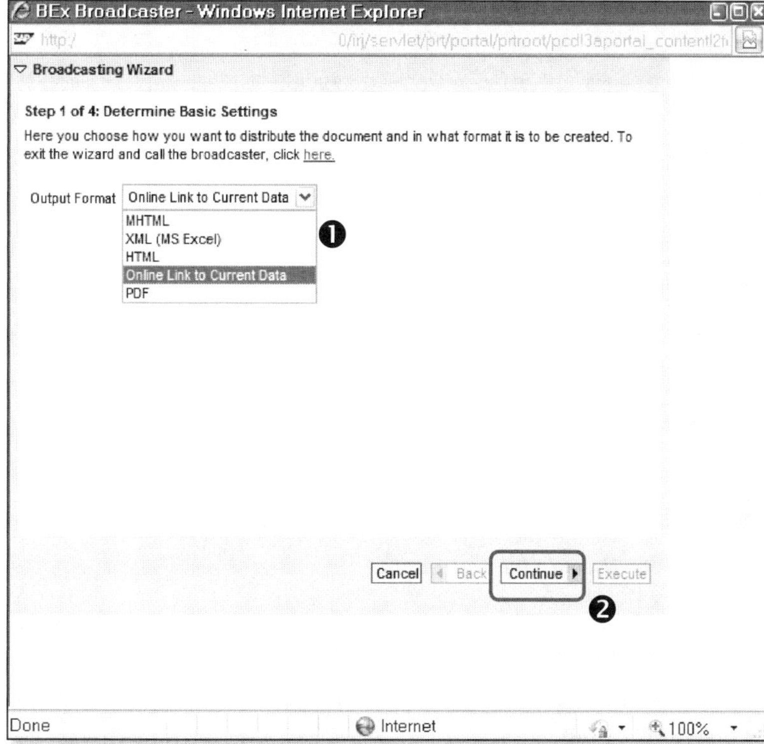

Figure 10.62 BEx Broadcaster: Determine Basic Settings

3. On the next screen, maintain the details of the broadcasting settings (Figure 10.63), which depend on the output format selected earlier. Include the email addresses of the intended recipients of this data (❶), and create your own message, which will be sent to the users along with the information.

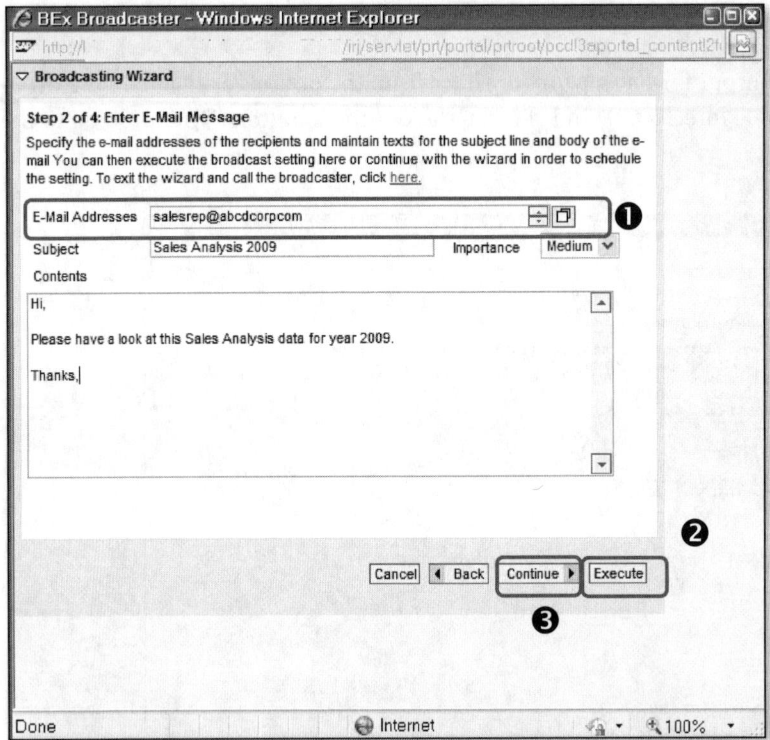

Figure 10.63 BEx Broadcaster: Maintain Message Settings

4. If this is a one-time broadcast, you can execute this setting directly from this screen using the Execute button (❷). Click on the Continue button (❸) if you want to save this setting for future use or want to schedule it to be executed automatically at some predefined time.
5. Save the broadcasting settings by proving a Technical Name and Description (❶ of Figure 10.64), and click on Continue to proceed to the next screen (❷).
6. On the next screen, you're provided with different options to schedule the broadcasting setting. Selecting the checkbox shown in ❶ of Figure 10.65 executes the setting every time there's a change of data in the selected InfoProvider. Selecting the checkbox shown in ❷ allows you to schedule the background processing of the setting at the predefined time. Click on the Schedule button to save the broadcasting and scheduling settings (❸).

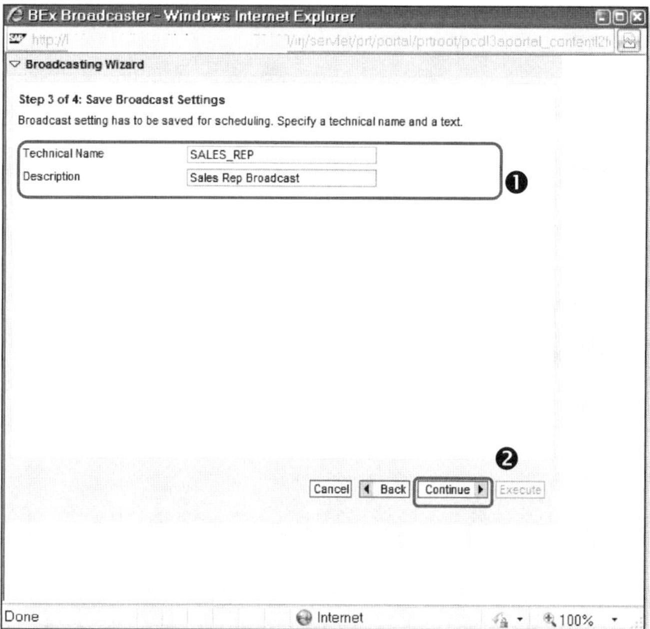

Figure 10.64 BEx Broadcaster: Save Broadcast Settings

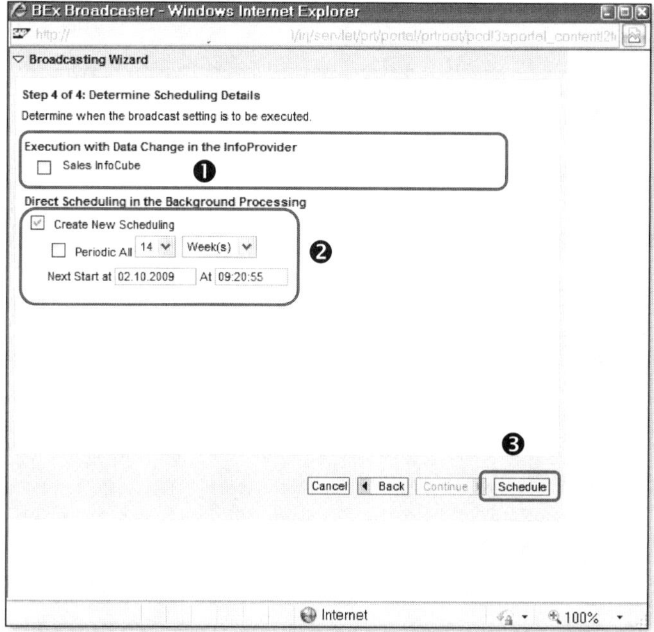

Figure 10.65 BEx Broadcaster: Determine Scheduling Details

The preceding procedure explains how you can broadcast information from BEx web analyzer.

10.9.2 Maintain Broadcasting Settings on Different BEx Objects

The broadcasting settings on different objects in BEx can be maintained in BEx Broadcaster, which can be accessed from all BEx tools, as well from the BEx iView in the portal (Figure 10.66).

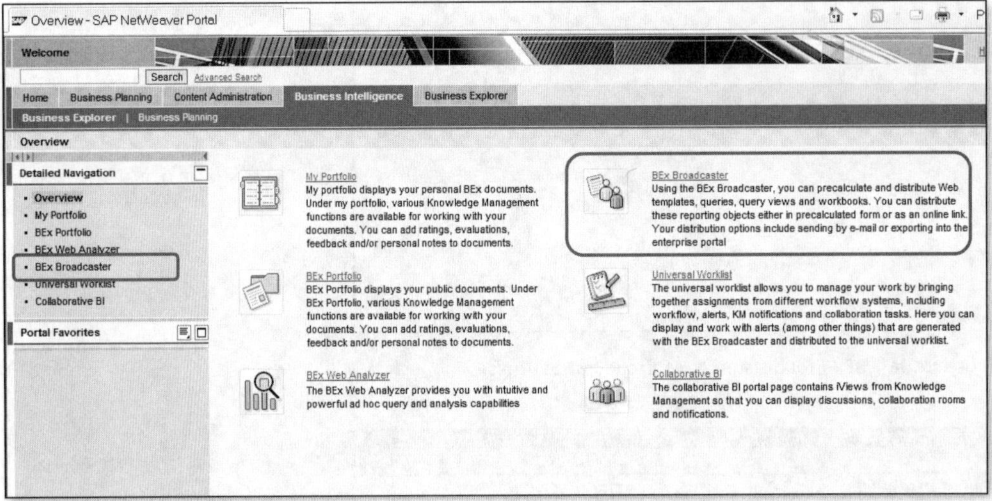

Figure 10.66 Access BEx Broadcaster from Portal

To maintain the broadcasting settings on any BEx object, first select the object type from the dropdown (❶ of Figure 10.67), and then click on the Open button (❷) to select the specific object. This displays a list of the broadcasting settings that are defined and scheduled on the selected object (❸).

To search and get an overview of all settings scheduled in the SAP NetWeaver BW system, click on the Overview of Scheduled Settings link (❹).

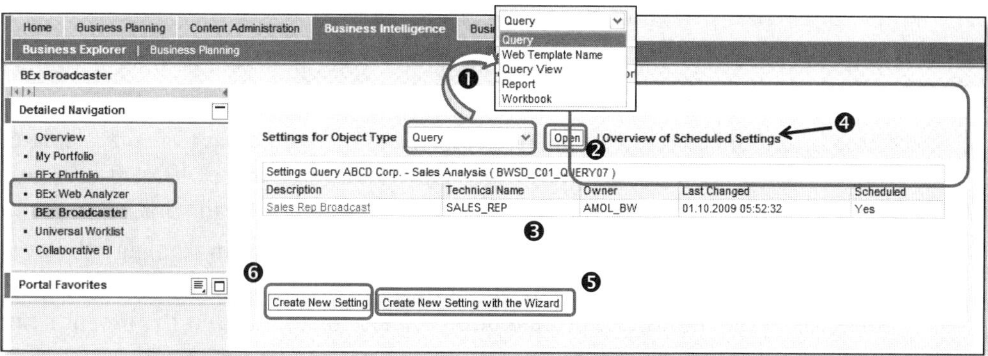

Figure 10.67 BEx Broadcaster Settings

10.9.3 Create a New Setting in BEx Broadcaster

To create a new setting, use the Create a New Setting with the Wizard button (❺ of Figure 10.67), which takes you to the same Broadcasting Wizard that is accessed from the Send button of BEx web analyzer. Create New Setting (❻) allows you to create the setting in BEx broadcaster.

Creating a setting in BEx broadcaster instead of the Broadcasting Wizard provides you with some additional distribution types for broadcasting (Figure 10.68).

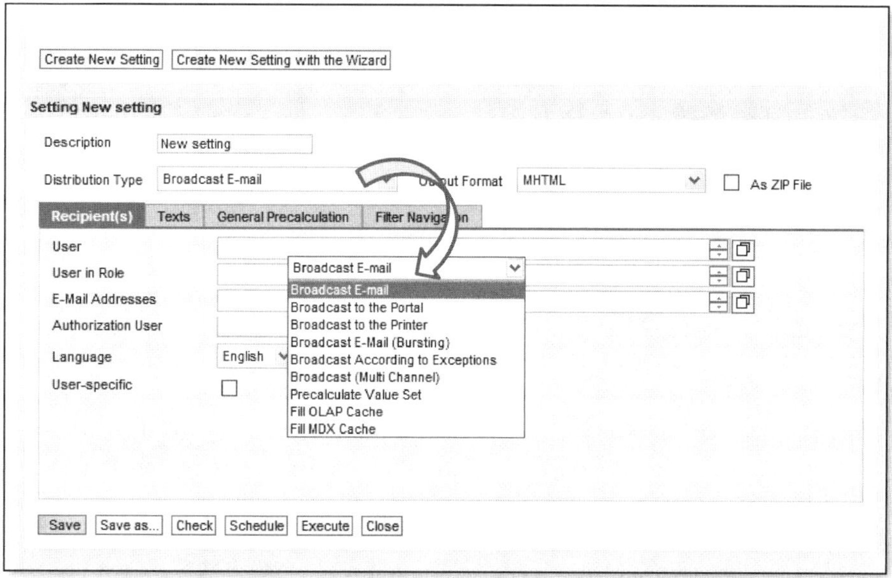

Figure 10.68 Distribution Types

These different distribution types are explained here:

- Broadcast E-Mail: Using this distribution type, you can broadcast information via email to multiple recipients.
- Broadcast to the Portal: This distribution type allows you to save the precalculated analysis or post an online link to the analysis on the portal. Different users can then access the information using this saved information or the link.
- Broadcast to the Printer: Using this distribution type, you can configure the print settings for the information contained in a select BEx object. BEx Broadcaster then sends the information to the output device maintained in the broadcasting settings at the scheduled time.
- Broadcast E-Mail (Bursting): If you want to distribute information to a specific set of users based on master data, you can use this distribution type. This type allows you to determine the recipients of the email based on the characteristic values (Figure 10.69).

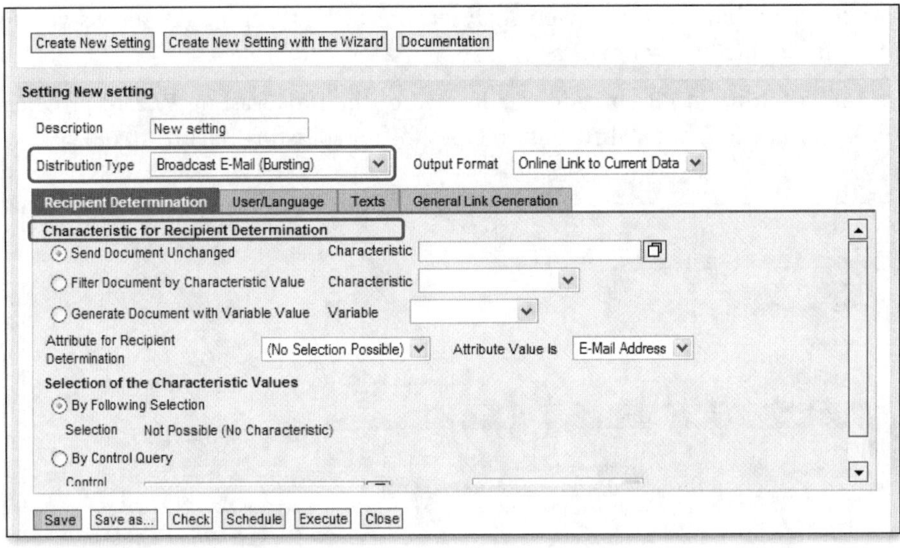

Figure 10.69 Broadcast E-Mail (Bursting)

- *Broadcast According to Exceptions*: This distribution type broadcasts the data based on the exceptions defined on the selected BEx object and is especially useful if you want to send alerts to a set of recipients based on the threshold value defined in the exception (Figure 10.70).

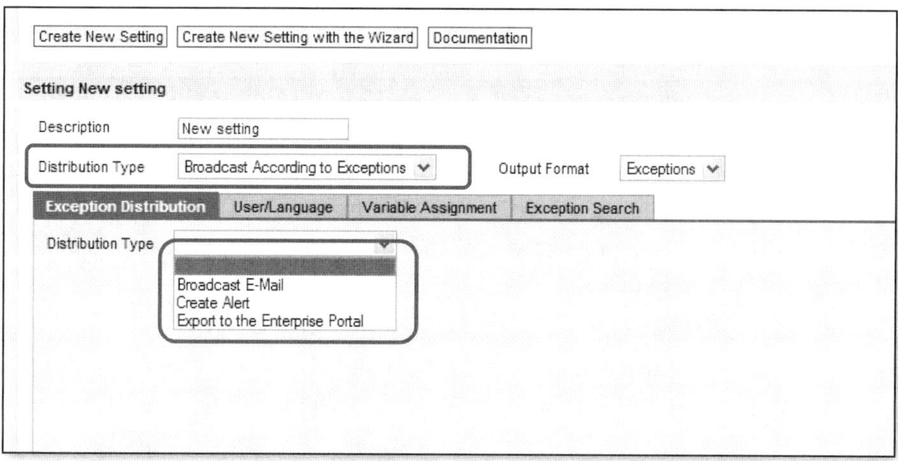

Figure 10.70 Broadcast According to Exceptions

- Broadcast (Multi Channel): If you want to configure a broadcasting setting combining multiple channels of broadcasting (portal, email, print), this distribution type allows you to do so.
- Precalculate Value Set: This distribution type is applicable for those OLAP characteristic variables that are filled using precalculated value sets. This broadcast setting determines the precalculated values that are then used to populate the variables with characteristic values.
- Fill OLAP Cache: When the queries are executed in BEx, the data fetched by the query from the InfoProvider is retained in the OLAP cache. As a result, when the same set of data (or a subset of data in the OLAP cache) is requested again, the data is fetched from the OLAP cache instead of the InfoProvider. The query execution is actually faster in the latter case because the data is readily available in the OLAP cache. The distribution type Fill OLAP Cache allows the specified query to run in the background to fill the OLAP cache, so the performance of that query can be improved.
- Fill MDX Cache: Similar to the Fill OLAP Cache type, this distribution type is used to provide better performance of the Crystal Reports that are executed on the selected query. Broadcast settings with this distribution type precalculate the query results and fill the MDX cache, which is used by Crystal Reports based on BEx queries.

10.10 Summary

BEx analyzer and BEx web analyzer provide reporting and analysis capabilities to business analysts in Excel and web environments, respectively, and this chapter has discussed the different analysis functions available in both tools. We have also explained the different design functions that can be used when creating a simple analysis application in BEx analyzer. Finally, we discussed the concept of information broadcasting and explained how a collaborative analysis can be performed using BEx Broadcaster functions.

The quality and ease of information access and data analysis are one of the major evaluation criteria for any BI tool. The components discussed in this chapter highlight the capabilities of SAP NetWeaver BW against these criteria.

In the next chapter, we discuss building web applications using the BEx web application designer.

The reporting and analysis features are important criteria to consider when evaluating a BI tool. SAP NetWeaver BW offers a wide range of features to perform reporting and analysis. The SAP Business Explorer (BEx) tools allow analysis in Excel as well as in a web/portal environment. This chapter deals with the BEx web application designer, which is used to create custom web applications in SAP NetWeaver BW for reporting and analysis.

11 Web Application Designer

In the previous chapters of this book, we explained the use of BEx query designer to create queries on different SAP NetWeaver BW InfoProviders. We also explained the different analysis options available in BEx, including the Excel analyzer and the web analyzer. Most importantly, the procedure to create a custom analysis application in Excel using BEx analyzer was also discussed. In this chapter, we take you through the BEx web application designer tool, which is used to create custom analysis applications for a web environment.

The objective behind this chapter is to make you familiar with the BEx web application designer and the different options available in it to create a web application.

11.1 Web Application Designer Overview

The BEx web application designer is a standalone tool that can be accessed through the desktop without logging on to a SAP GUI. The web applications built using the web application designer are based on HTML pages and can be based on data providers such as BEx queries, views, filters, or InfoProviders. The web applications created in this tool are saved as *XHTML documents*. These XHTML documents form the base for the web application and are called web templates. Placeholders for all of the objects included in the web application, their properties, settings, and so on are translated into the XHTML format in the web template.

XHTML

XHTML stands for Extensible Hypertext Markup Language, which is an extension of the HTML language and is based on XML rules.

11.1.1 Starting the Web Application Designer

Similar to other BEx tools such as the Query Designer or BEx analyzer, the web application designer is also a standalone tool that can be accessed through a desktop without actually logging into SAP GUI. Follow the path START • PROGRAMS • BUSINESS EXPLORER • WEB APPLICATION DESIGNER from the Start menu of your computer to open the tool (see Figure 11.1).

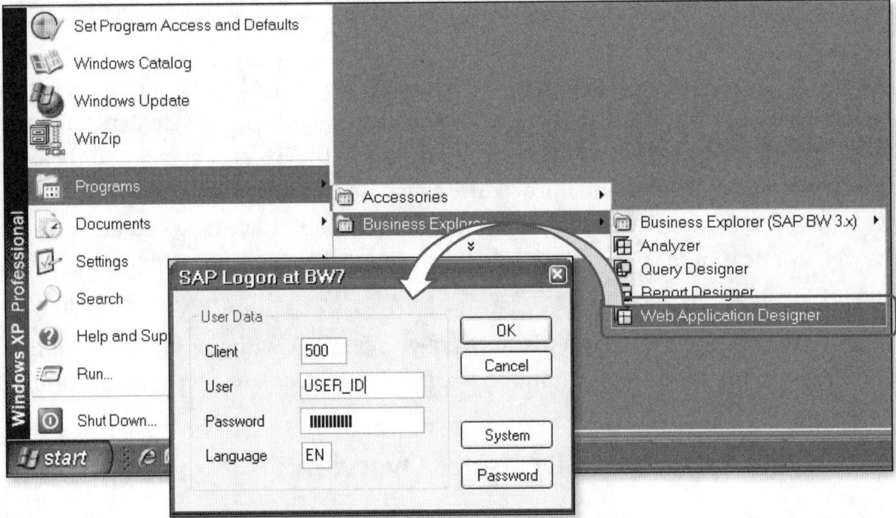

Figure 11.1 Open BEx Web Application Designer

The system will prompt you for the login credentials for the SAP BW system. Enter the user ID and password, and log on to the BEx web application designer (see Figure 11.1).

On the entry screen, you see options to Create New Web Template or to Open Existing Web Template. A list of recently accessed web templates is also displayed for quick access (see ❶ of Figure 11.2). To open a new web template, click on the link Create New Blank Web Template, or use the menu path WEB TEMPLATE •NEW (❷).

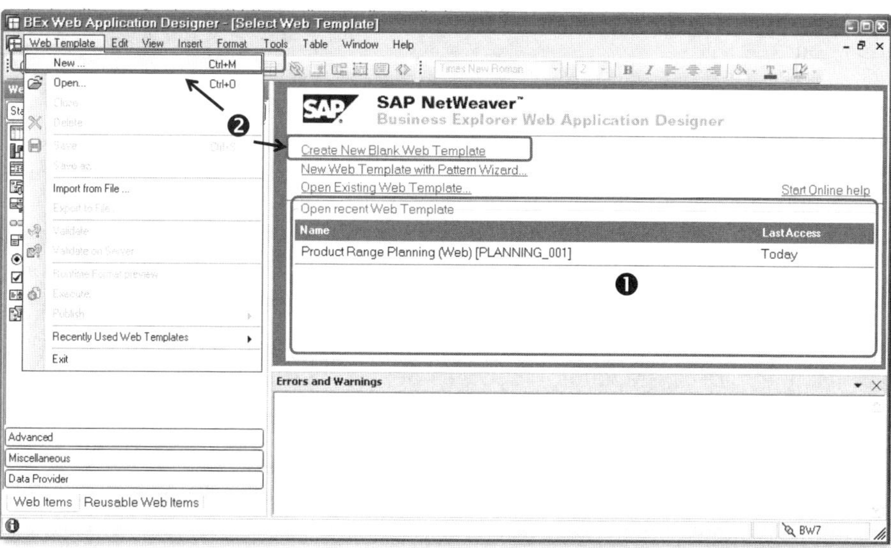

Figure 11.2 Create New Web Template

11.1.2 Different Screen Areas of Web Application Designer

The web template screen in the web application designer consists of different screen areas as shown in Figure 11.3.

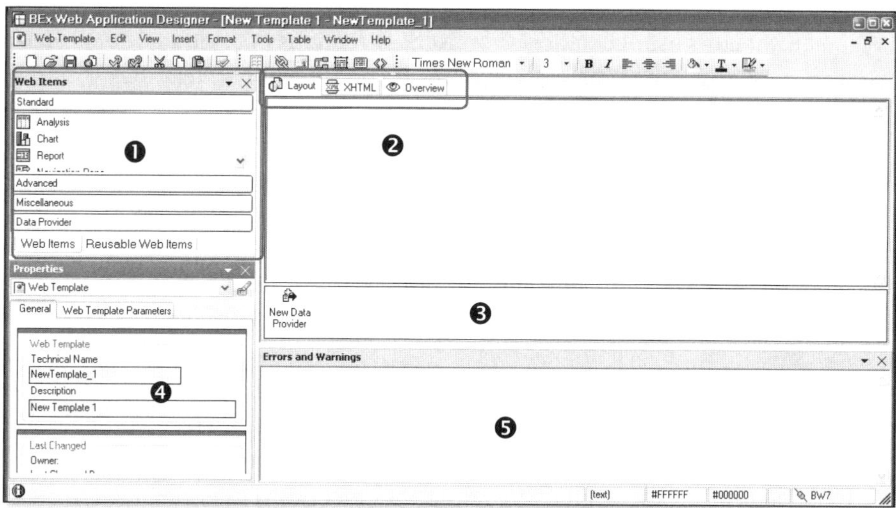

Figure 11.3 Web Application Designer Screen Layout

The significance of each area in a web template design is explained in the following subsections.

Web Items

To facilitate easy and faster development of web applications, the web application designer provides a bunch of prebuilt components called *web items*, which can be used directly in the web application. The web items are available in the Web Items screen area as shown in ❶ of Figure 11.3. Each web item performs some design function or is linked to a data provider to perform some data function, such as displaying the data in tabular format, displaying the data in graphical format, and so on. Available web items are classified into three web item groups:

- **Standard web items**
  This web item group contains the most commonly used web items for a web application, such as an analysis grid, chart, different filter and navigation components, and so on.
- **Advanced web items**
  These components can be used to create more complex web applications. Web items such as container, group, tab, and so on help you configure the web application in a sophisticated manner. You can also embed another web template, documents, information items, and so on in the web template.
- **Miscellaneous web items**
  Different web items are used to add additional features to the web application. Web items such as list of conditions or list of exceptions provide additional analysis options. On the other hand, web items such as menu bar, text, ticker, and so on, add additional features to the web application.

All of these web items are explained in later sections of the chapter.

Layout/XHTML/Overview

The layout of the web template is displayed under the Layout tab of this area (see ❷ of Figure 11.3). You can add a web item to the web template layout using simple drag and drop from the Web Items area. The XHTML tab page displays the XHTML document, which is generated based on the web items added to the web template. You can add your own XHTML code on this tab for additional features or logic. The Overview tab page provides an overview of all of the components used in the web template. You can edit the components from the Overview tab page directly.

Data Provider

The section shown in ❸ of Figure 11.3 is used to manage the data providers used in a web template. Data providers are those elements that act as a source of data for different web items. Queries defined in BEx query designer, query views, query filters, and SAP BW InfoProviders can be used as a data provider in a web template. You can define a new data provider or change an existing data provider in this area. This also corresponds to the Data Provider section that is visible in Web Items screen area.

Properties

All of the web items and the web template itself have properties that control their behavior in the web application. These properties are maintained in the Properties pane shown in ❹ of Figure 11.3. For the web items based on a data provider, the data provider assignment is also maintained in the General tab of the Properties pane.

Other parameters for a web item/web template, for example, Display, Behavior, and so on, are maintained on the Web Item Parameters tab of the Properties pane. Important properties of web items and web template are discussed in later sections of the chapter.

Errors and Warnings

This section on the screen displays error messages or warnings if there are any discrepancies in the definition of the web template (see ❺ of Figure 11.3).

11.2 Create a Simple Web Application

To begin with, we take a scenario from our example company ABCD Corp. and then address it by creating a web application using the BEx web application designer.

The analysts at ABCD Corp. want a *Sales Overview Dashboard* where they can see quarterly material sales for a selected sales organization and year. The representation of the data has to be in both *tabular* and *graphical* format. They also need an easy to use *dropdown* feature where they can select a material group, and the *table* and *graph* should be refreshed for the selected value. There also needs to be the flexibility to *change* the selected sales organization or year if needed.

11.2.1 Create a Data Provider

The base for the web items displaying data in a web template is a data provider. As a first step, create the data provider that should be used by different web items in a web template. To create a data provider in a web template, click on the New Data

Provider icon as shown in ❶ of Figure 11.4. A pop-up box titled Maintain Data Provider appears.

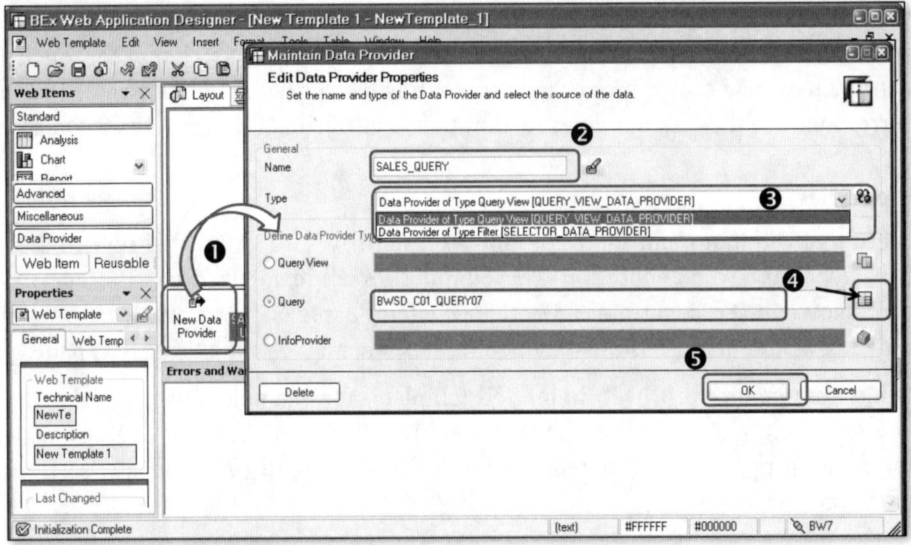

Figure 11.4 Create Data Provider

Give a name to the data provider (see ❷ of Figure 11.4). This data provider is referred to by different web items in the query using this name.

There can be different types of data providers. The queries defined in BEx query designer, query views, query filters, and SAP NetWeaver BW InfoProviders can be used as data providers in a web template. The dropdown shown in ❸ of Figure 11.4 allows you to select the data provider type. The Data Provider of Type Filter option is normally used while creating planning applications. The use of this type of data provider is discussed in Chapter 12, Integrated Planning.

If you select a data provider of type Query View, you can further select an option among a Query View, a Query, or an InfoProvider. For this example scenario, select the Query option, and select the query that should be used as a data provider using the input help button shown in ❹ of Figure 11.4.

Click OK (see ❺ of Figure 11.4) to complete the definition of the data provider and to return to the web template layout screen.

11.2.2 Using an Analysis Web Item

Before you begin adding different web items to the web template, first create a heading for the web application. You can enter the text directly into the template layout screen (see ❶ of Figure 11.5) and can control its display using the formatting toolbar shown in ❷ of Figure 11.5.

You can now start including required web items in the layout. The Analysis web item is used when you have to display data in a tabular format in the web application. To add this web item to the template, drag it from the Web Items area, and place it in the layout (see ❸ of Figure 11.5).

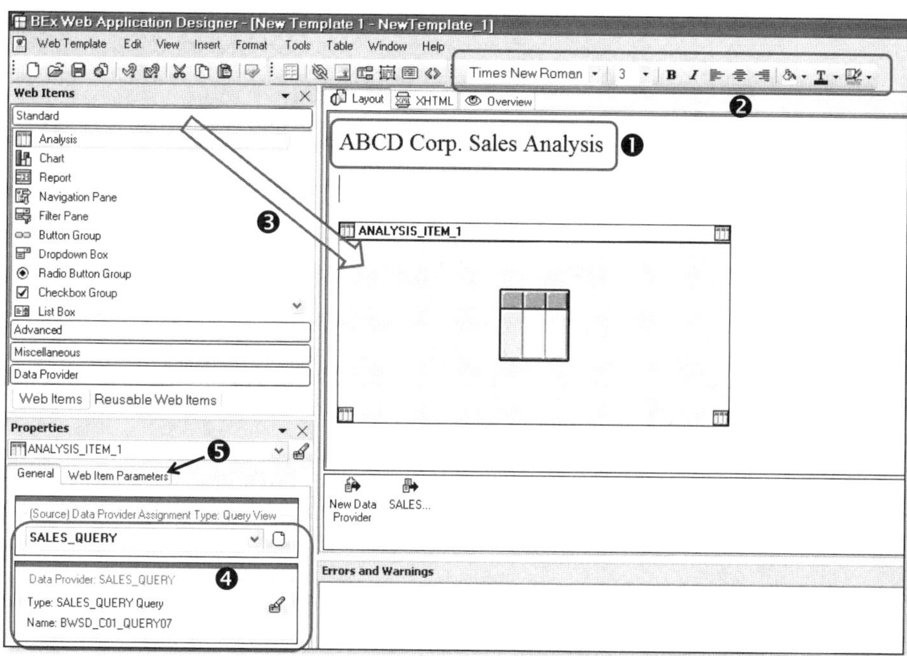

Figure 11.5 Add Heading and Insert Analysis Web Item

Because the Analysis web item displays data, it needs to be assigned to a data provider. The data provider assignment can be done on the General tab in properties area (see ❹ of Figure 11.5).

Click on the Web Item Parameters tab (see ❺ of Figure 11.5) to maintain settings for the selected Analysis web item. The Web Item Parameters tab for an Analysis web item is shown in Figure 11.6.

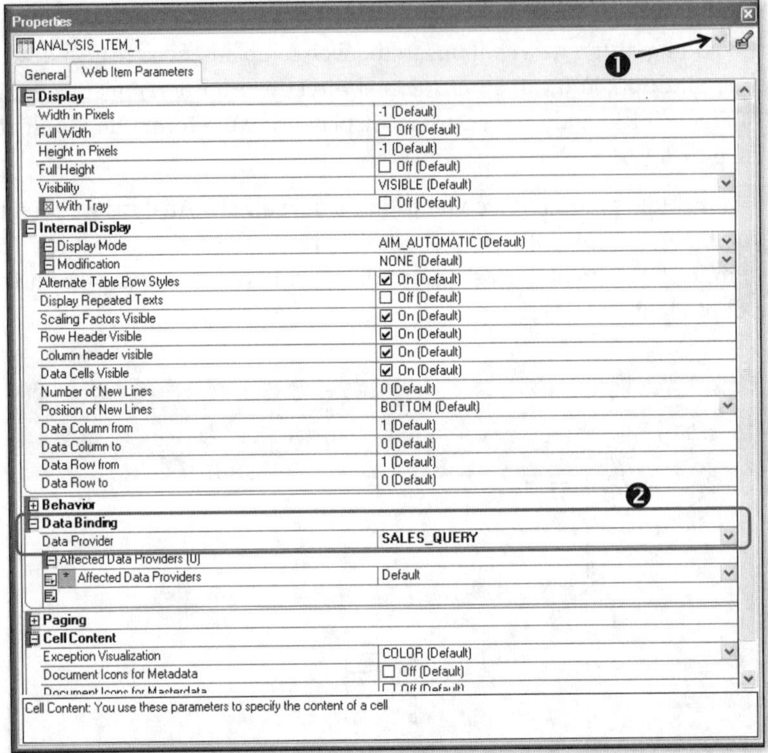

Figure 11.6 Maintain Properties of Analysis Web Item

You can change the name of the web item by clicking on the Edit icon shown in ❶ of Figure 11.6. You can control the display and behavior of the web item in the application by setting different parameters on this screen.

> **Data Binding**
>
> If the web item is based on a data provider or changes to this web item can impact other data providers (affected data providers), then these settings for the web item are maintained under the Data Binding section of the properties (see ❷ of Figure 11.6).

11.2.3 Using a Dropdown Box

The analysts at ABCD Corp. want an easy-to-use dropdown feature so that they can filter the data displayed by selecting a value from the dropdown. To add a dropdown to the web template, drag the Dropdown Box web item from the Web Items area, and drop it to the desired location in the web template (see ❶ of Figure 11.7).

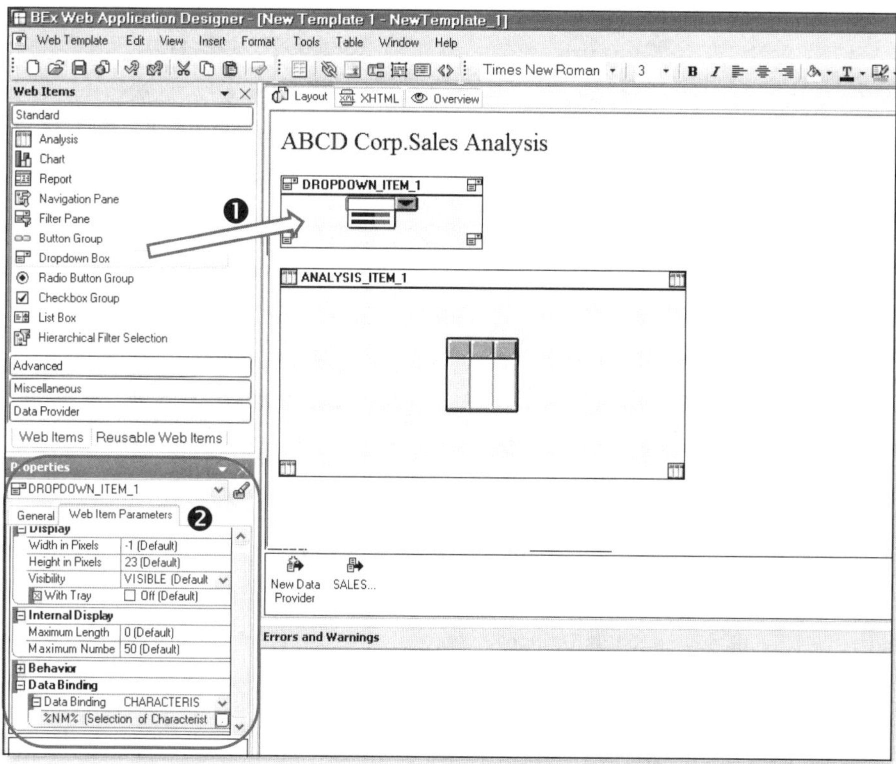

Figure 11.7 Add Dropdown Box

The parameters for this Dropdown box can be maintained in the Properties area (see ❷ of Figure 11.7). The properties for this web item are maintained as shown in Figure 11.8. A dropdown box actually reads the contents from the object to which it's tied. The assignment is maintained under the Data Binding section, where the property Data Binding Type provides you with multiple options that can be used as a source of data for the dropdown box (see ❶ of Figure 11.8). Per the requirements, the dropdown box must display the values of material group characteristic, so select the Char/Structure Member option as the data binding type.

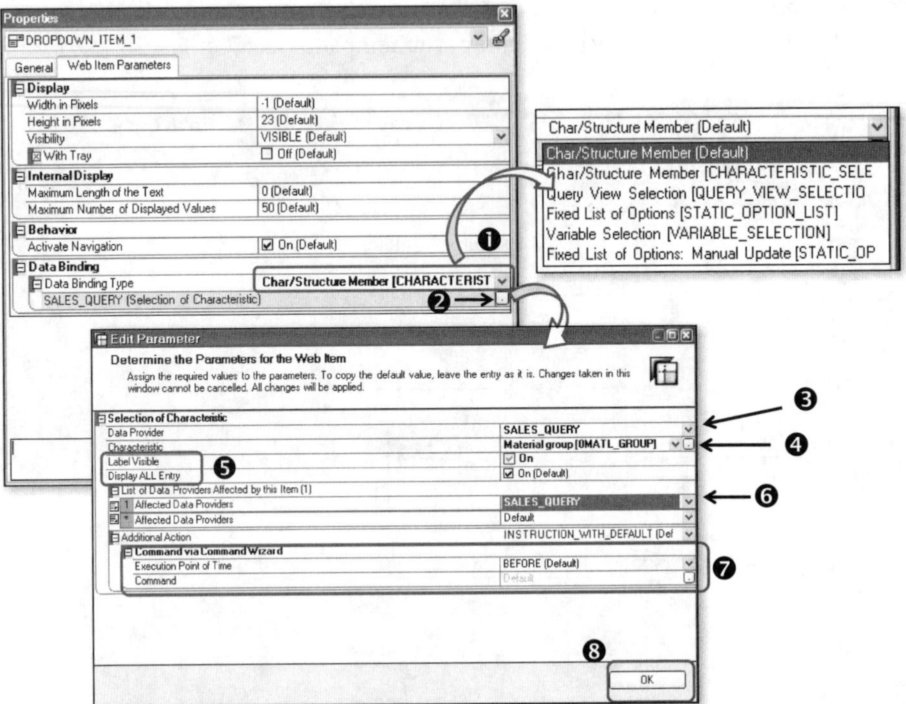

Figure 11.8 Maintain Properties of Dropdown Box

To define the Selection of Characteristic for the dropdown, click on the button shown in ❷ of Figure 11.8. The Edit Parameters box appears. You maintain the characteristic selection and set the following for Selected Characteristic:

- Data Provider (see ❸ of Figure 11.8): The data provider from where the dropdown box should read the characteristic value.
- Characteristic (❹): Select the specific characteristic that will be assigned to the dropdown. Input help is available for this parameter.
- Display parameters settings (❺): The display-related settings, such as whether the label of the characteristic should be visible or not, and whether to display the ALL entry, are maintained on this screen.
- Affected Data Providers (❻): This is one of the most important settings for the dropdown box because it determines which data providers within the web template should change per the specific value selected in the dropdown. If there are multiple data providers in the query, and you want more than one data provider to change due to the dropdown, you can maintain a list of different data providers under the Affected Data Providers section.

- Command via Command Wizard (❼): Command Wizard is one of the most powerful features available in the web application designer. It enlists many useful commands that can be used to assign a specific action to a web item. For example, set the exceptions to inactive state whenever a value is selected in the dropdown box. The details about the Command Wizard and the different available commands are discussed in later sections of this chapter.

Finally, click on OK (❽) to complete the Selection of Characteristic and return to the web template layout.

11.2.4 Creating Charts

The Chart web item displays data from the data provider in graphical format. To add a chart to the web template; drag the Chart web item from the Web Items area into the layout (see ❶ of Figure 11.9). Assign the data provider to this web item in the Properties box (❷). The detailed setting for the graphical display is done in the Web Item Parameters tab of the Properties box (❸).

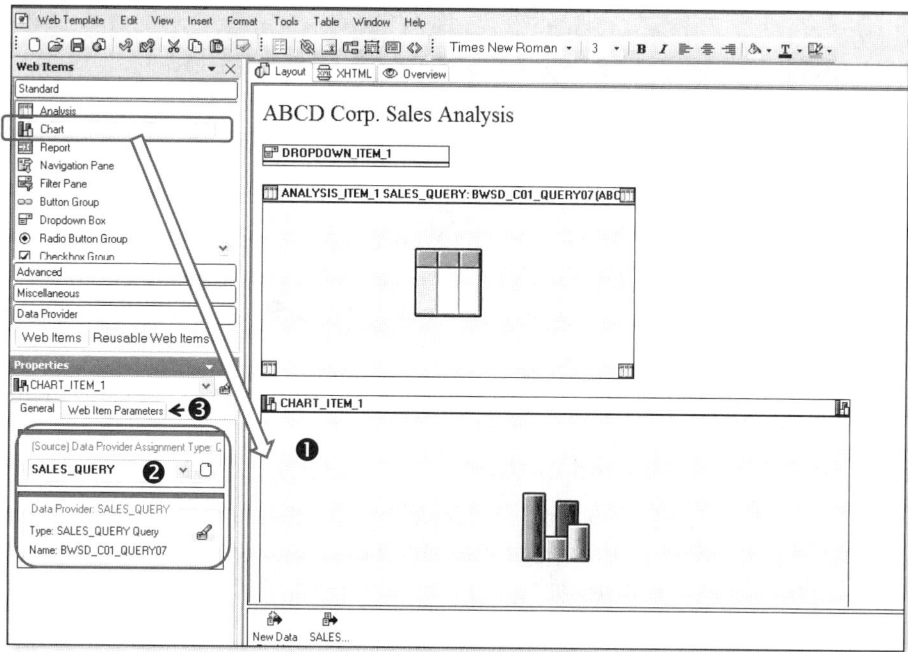

Figure 11.9 Add Chart Web Item

Different parameters that control the display, behavior, and other chart settings are maintained as a part of chart properties (see Figure 11.10).

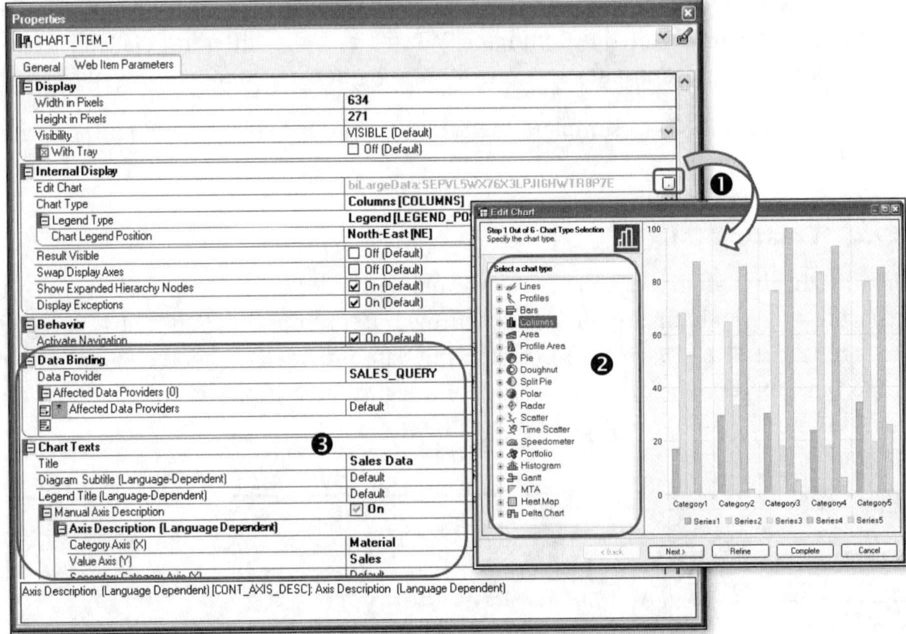

Figure 11.10 Maintain Chart Properties

The Edit Chart option (see ❶ of Figure 11.10) opens up an Edit Chart window, which is much like a chart wizard (similar to that of Excel). On this screen, you can select the type of chart from the numerous available chart types (❷) and configure the chart at a detailed level.

Maintain the data binding and chart-specific settings as shown in ❸ of Figure 11.10.

11.2.5 Adding a Command Button

We'll now draw your attention to the previously mentioned requirement of analysts needing flexibility to change the selected sales organization or year if needed. This requirement means there must be a provision to call the variable screen when needed. In this case, *calling the variable screen* is a command, and we'll use a button in the web application that will execute this command.

To add a button in the web template, drag the Button Group web item from the Web Items area into the layout as shown in ❶ Figure 11.11. Then go to the Web Item Parameters tab for the button group to configure the button group (❷).

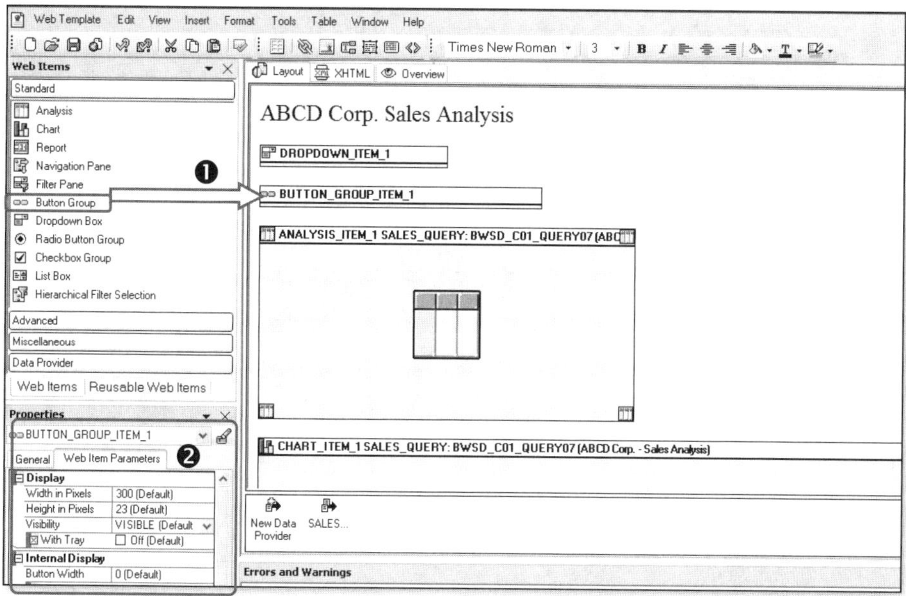

Figure 11.11 Add Button Web Item

Apart from maintaining the display settings for the button group (see ❶ of Figure 11.12), you must define a button (or multiple buttons) on this screen (❷).

To add a button, click on the button shown in ❸ of Figure 11.12. The Edit Parameter box appears, in which you define the button settings (❹). You also have to select one of the available button designs (❺).

Now that you've configured the button, the next step is to assign an action to it. You can either assign a command from the already available set of commands, or you can assign a custom *JavaScript* function to the button. We have to assign an action that will call the variable screen. This command is available in the Command Wizard, so select Command via Command Wizard as the Action as shown in ❻ of Figure 11.12. Click on the button shown by ❼ of Figure 11.12 to call the Command Wizard.

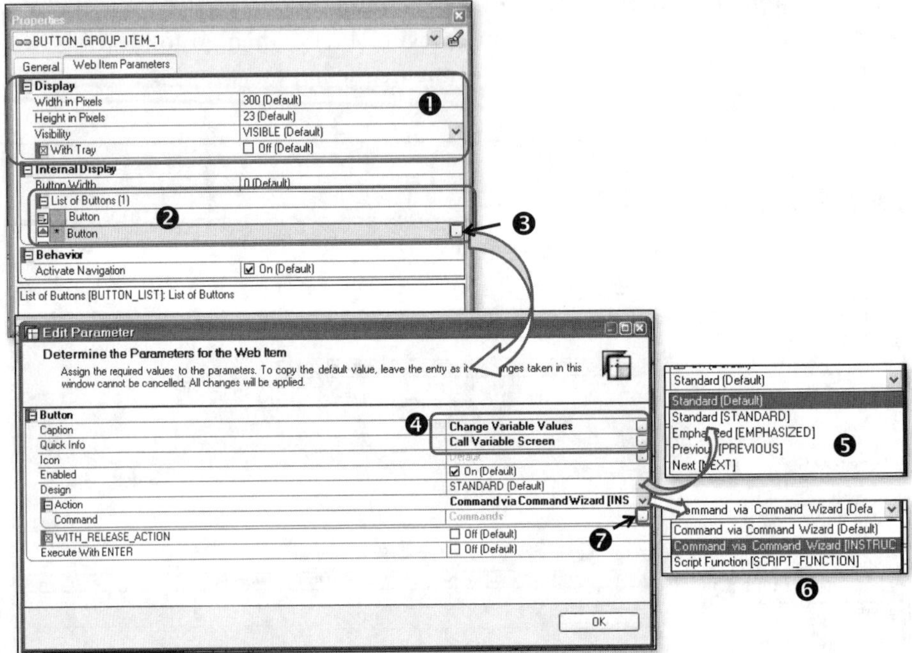

Figure 11.12 Maintain Button Group/Add a Button

The Command Wizard includes a variety of commands that can be used in the web template to create effective applications for analysis or planning (see Figure 11.13). Based on the usage and applicability, these commands are grouped in four different sections as shown in ❶ of Figure 11.13. These commands are discussed in a separate section later in this chapter.

For the example scenario, we need a command to call up the variable screen. This command is available under the Commands for Web Templates section (see ❶ of Figure 11.13). Select the command Open Variable Dialog (OPEN_VARIABLE_DIALOG) (❷), and click on the Next button to set the parameters for this command (❸). You can also maintain a list of frequently used commands as your favorites by selecting the checkbox in front of a command (❹). All commands where the checkbox is selected will appear on the Favorite Commands tab page (❹).

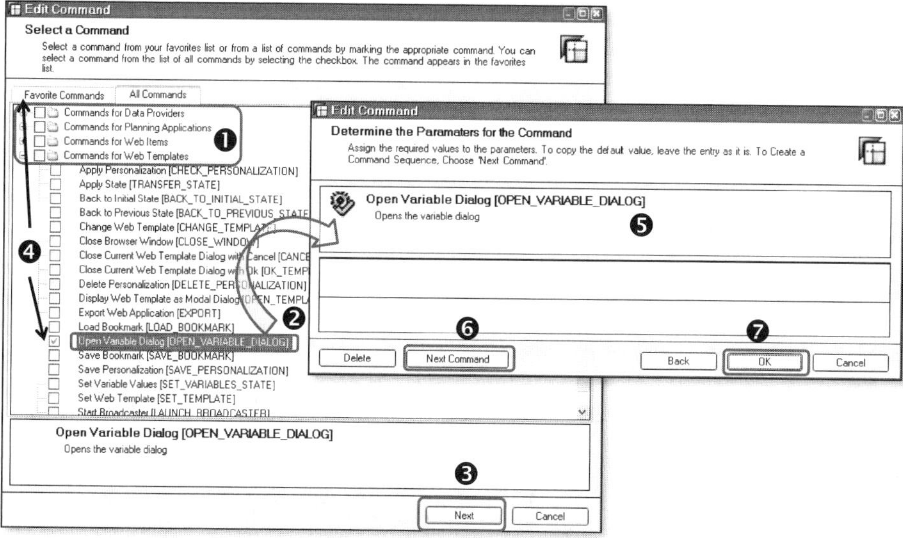

Figure 11.13 Assign a Command

When you click on the Next button, the next screen appears based on the command selected. Each command has a different set of parameters that should be maintained for that command in the next screen (❺). For example, for the command Set Web Template, you have to define the web template name as a parameter. On the other hand, the command Open Variable Dialog doesn't need any parameters, so the next screen doesn't show any configuration.

You can also add more than one command to the same button so that a sequence of commands is executed when the button is clicked. Click on the Next Command button (❻) to add new commands to the button. When finished, click on OK (❼), and return to the button definition screen (see Figure 11.14).

The selected command is now linked to a button (see ❶ of Figure 11.14). If you want a specific command to be executed when the user presses the Enter key, then check the setting Execute with ENTER in the button configuration (❷).

Finally, click OK (❸) to return to the web template design screen.

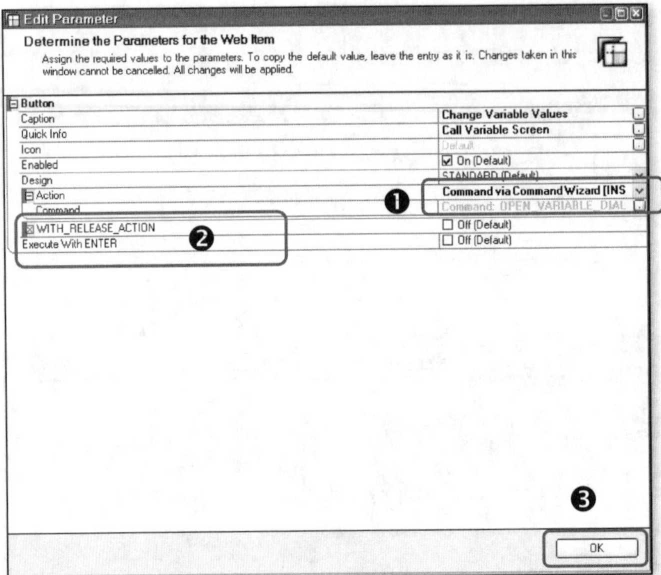

Figure 11.14 Complete Button Settings

11.2.6 Arrange Web Items

All of the web items needed in the web application are now included and are configured. You can now arrange the web items in the web template for a structured display. For example, you might want to display the dropdown and button next to each other, rather than displaying them in two separate rows.

For this and other similar purposes, the web application designer allows you to use some standard XHTML elements in the web template.

To insert a table in the web template, first position the cursor where you want to insert it, and then click on the Insert Table button on the toolbar as shown in ❶ of Figure 11.15.

The Edit HTML Element box appears, in which you can customize the element per the requirement (❷). Finally, click on OK to return to the web template design screen.

The table is inserted in the web template layout per the settings (see ❶ of Figure 11.16).

To arrange the web items, simply drag them into the different cells of the table (❷).

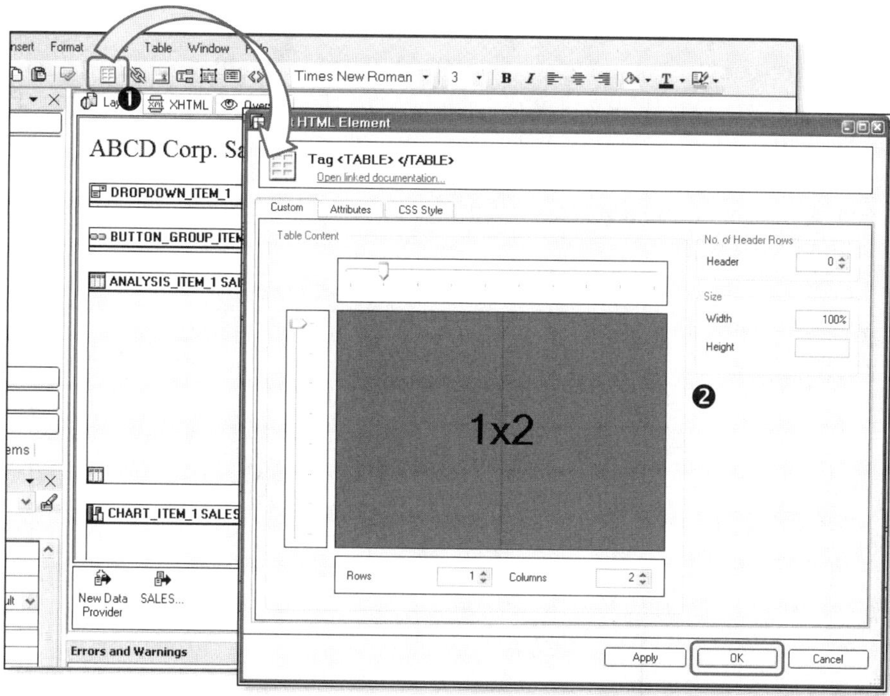

Figure 11.15 Insert Table

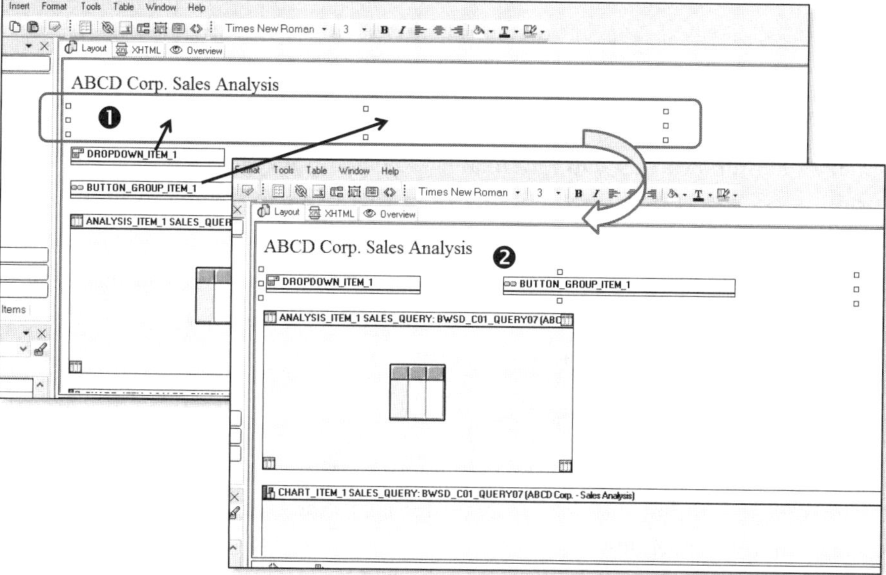

Figure 11.16 Arrange Web Items in a Table

11.2.7 Validate and Save the Web Template

After the web template is designed, you can validate the definition of the web template using the options shown in ❶ of Figure 11.17. Use the Validate option to validate the definition of the web template for consistency in the definition. The other option, Validate on Server, validates the web template definition as well as checks the consistency with respect to the data providers and other elements based on their definition on the server.

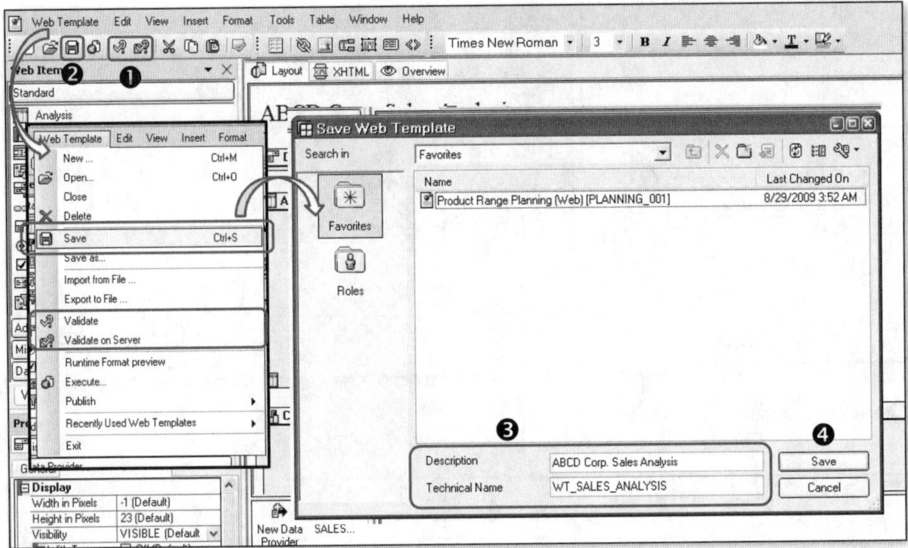

Figure 11.17 Validate and Save the Web Template

After the definition of the web template is validated, save the web template using the button shown in ❷ of Figure 11.17. You can also use the menu option WEB TEMPLATE • SAVE to save the template.

The Save Web Template box appears, in which you enter the description and technical name of the web template (❸). Click on the Save button (❹) to save the web template with the given name and description.

As you create the web template using different web items in the layout, the XHTML code for the same is updated for all of the settings and configurations made to the web items. The XHTML code can be seen on the XHTML tab page (see ❶ of Figure 11.18). You can jump to the code relevant for a specific web item by selecting that web item from the dropdown.

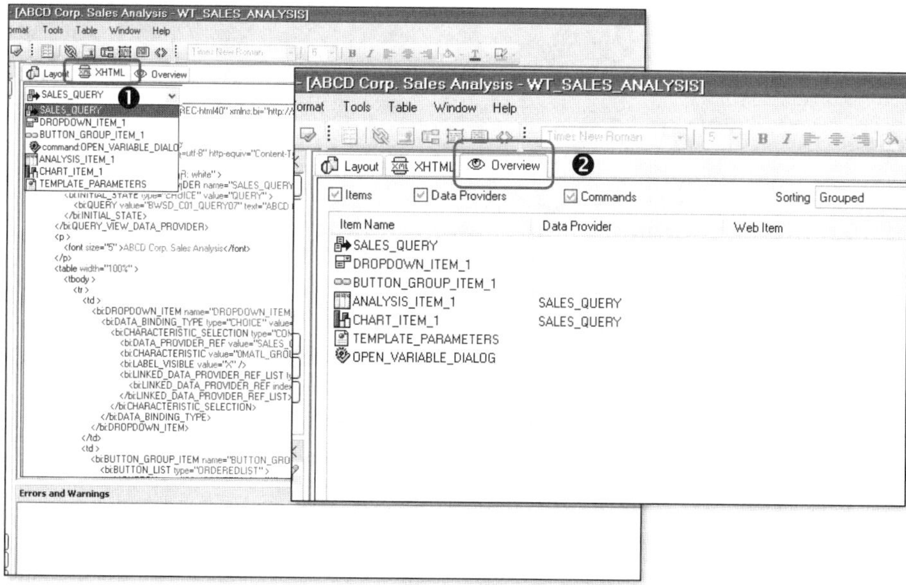

Figure 11.18 XHTML Tab and Overview Tab

The Overview tab page (❷) is more like a blueprint of the web template. This tab page lists all of the elements used in the web template. Any of these elements can be edited from this screen.

11.2.8 Execute Web Template

Follow the menu path WEB TEMPLATE • EXECUTE to execute the web template, or use the button shown in ❶ of Figure 11.19 to execute one. The web template is executed in a separate web browser window.

If any of the data providers in the web template include user entry variables, then the variable screen is displayed in the beginning, prompting users to make variable entries. Enter the variable selection as shown in ❷ of Figure 11.19, and then click on the OK button to execute the web template (❸).

The resulting web application is displayed in the web browser as shown in Figure 11.20.

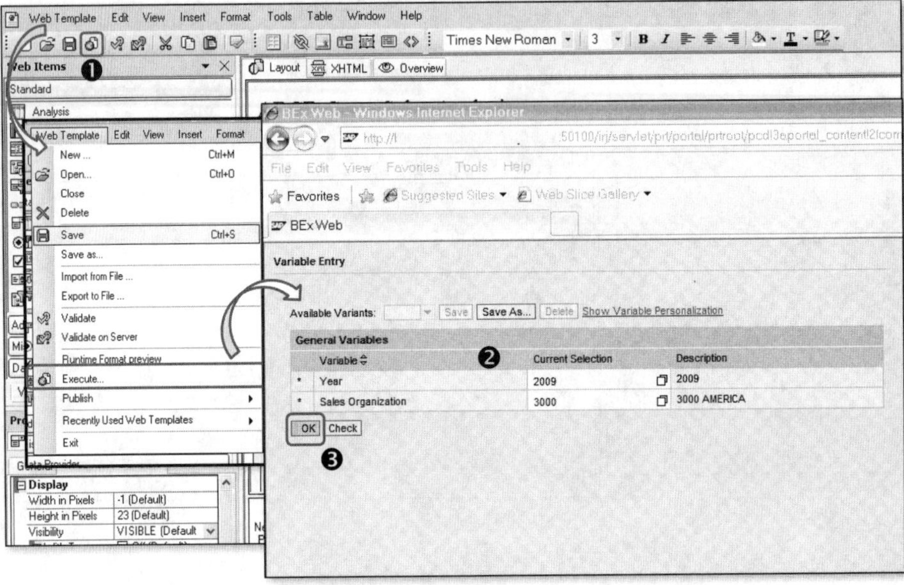

Figure 11.19 Execute the Web Template

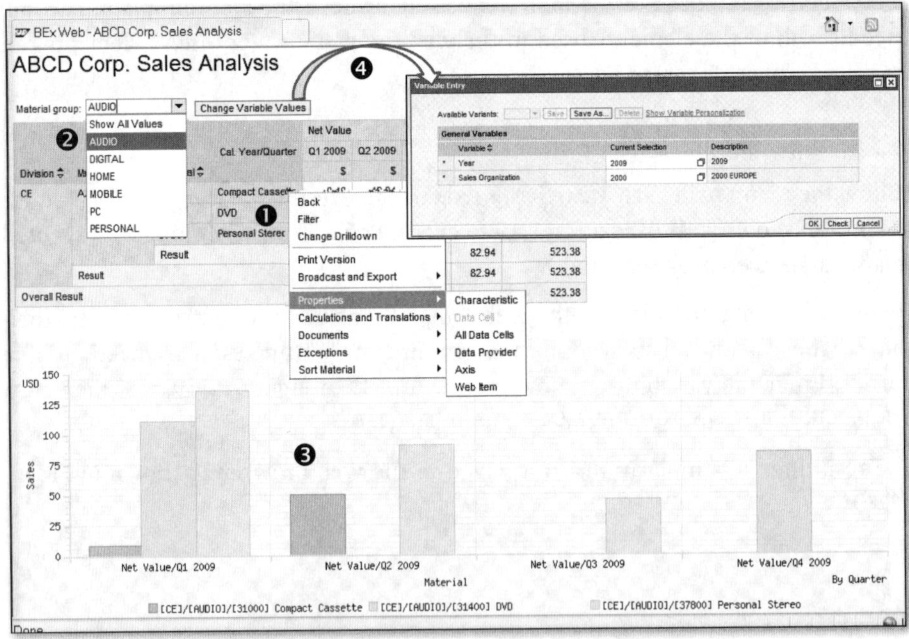

Figure 11.20 Perform Analysis in the Web Application

This web application, ABCD Corp. Sales Analysis, displays quarterly sales by material in a tabular format, and the different BEx navigation options are visible in the context menu for this web item (see ❶ of Figure 11.20).

A Material Group dropdown is available to filter the results of the web application (❷).

The data is displayed in the graphical format based on the selections made in the drilldown (❸). Finally, if you click on the Change Variable Values button (❹), the Variable Entry box appears in which you change the values for Sales Organization and Year.

11.3 Web Items

As we said earlier, Web items are the objects that can be readily used in the web template and thus eliminate the need to write the XHTML code to create a web application. As you'll recall, a web item carries out a design function or is linked to a data provider. Again, the available web items are classified into three web item groups:

- Standard web items
- Advanced web items
- Miscellaneous web items

In this section, we'll discuss the web items available in the web application designer and their use in creating a web application.

11.3.1 Standard Web Items

Standard web items are the most common and are discussed next.

Analysis

As we've seen while creating the web application in the previous section, the Analysis web item is used to display the data from the data provider in a tabular format. All of the navigation functions we explained in BEx Web Analyzer (i.e., drag and drop, filters, drilldown, etc.) are supported by this web item. However, you can control whether these options are available to the users by controlling the properties and context menu options for the web template.

This web item is based on a data provider, and the data provider is assigned to the web item on the General tab of the Properties pane (see ❶ of Figure 11.21). You can change the web item name by clicking on the button shown in ❷ of Figure 11.21.

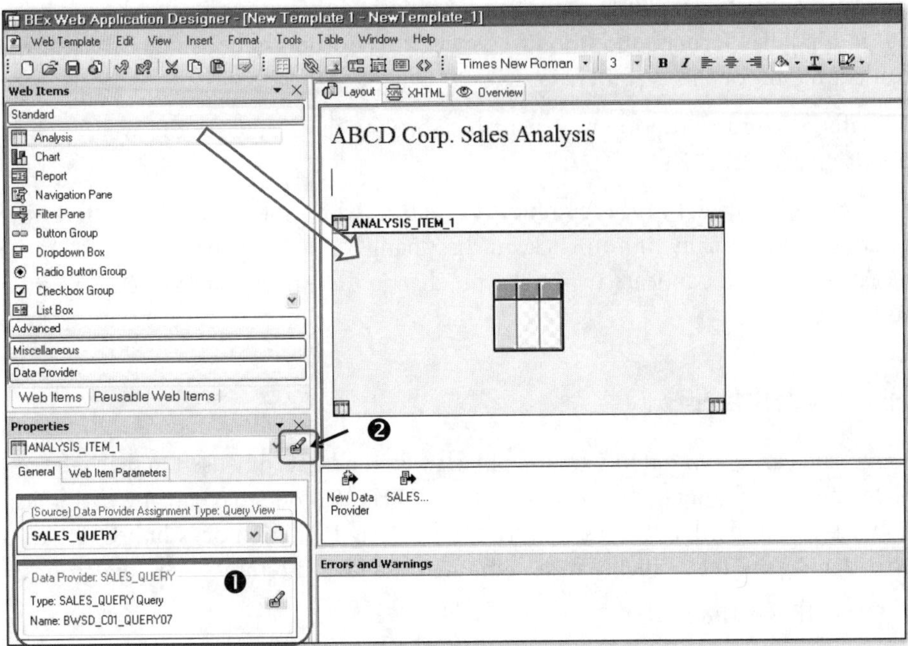

Figure 11.21 Analysis Web Item

Different parameters corresponding to the Analysis web item are maintained on the Web Item Parameters tab. The parameters are grouped by category as shown in Figure 11.22. You can maintain the display-related settings, such as length, width, and appearance of the Web item, using the parameters under the Display section (see ❶ of Figure 11.22). The parameters that control the display of data within the Analysis web item are available under Internal Display (❷).

Using the parameters under the Behavior section (❸), you can decide if the navigation and analysis can be allowed for the Analysis web item. Set the Active Navigation parameter to Off for fixed format and static reporting. Using the parameters Row Selection/Column Selection, you can select the rows or columns from the tabular display and then perform specific actions on the selected data.

Under the Data Binding section (❹), you maintain the reference data provider to the web item and a list of those data providers that are affected due to changes in this web item.

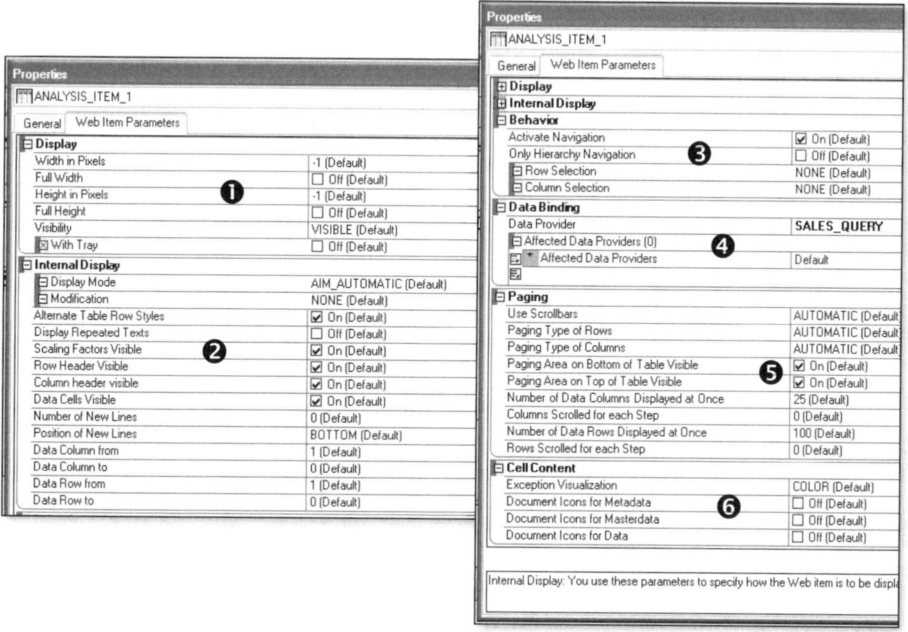

Figure 11.22 Analysis Web Item Parameters

The Paging settings for an Analysis web item define how the data should be displayed in the table format (❺), and the Cell Content section (❻) contains the parameters for the cells displayed in the Analysis web item. Here you can set the way exceptions should be displayed and control the display of document icons in the analysis display.

Chart

We discussed this web item while creating the web application in Section 11.2, Create a Simple Web Application. The Chart web item is used to display the data in a graphical format and is based on a data provider. The different parameters shown earlier in Figure 11.10 control the display, behavior, and so on for the chart. A wide variety of chart options is available in the web application designer. These charts/ graphs can be customized using the chart wizard, which can be called from the chart properties (refer to Figure 11.10).

Report

The preformatted reports created in the BEx report designer can be inserted in web application using the Report web item.

Navigation Pane

The Navigation Pane web item can be used in the web application to provide users with an option to perform slice and dice, filters, and other operations on the data. The navigation state of the data provider (e.g., characteristics in rows/columns/free characteristic area, and position of key figures) is displayed in the navigation pane. In the properties of this web item, you can control the query elements to be displayed in the navigation pane (see Figure 11.23).

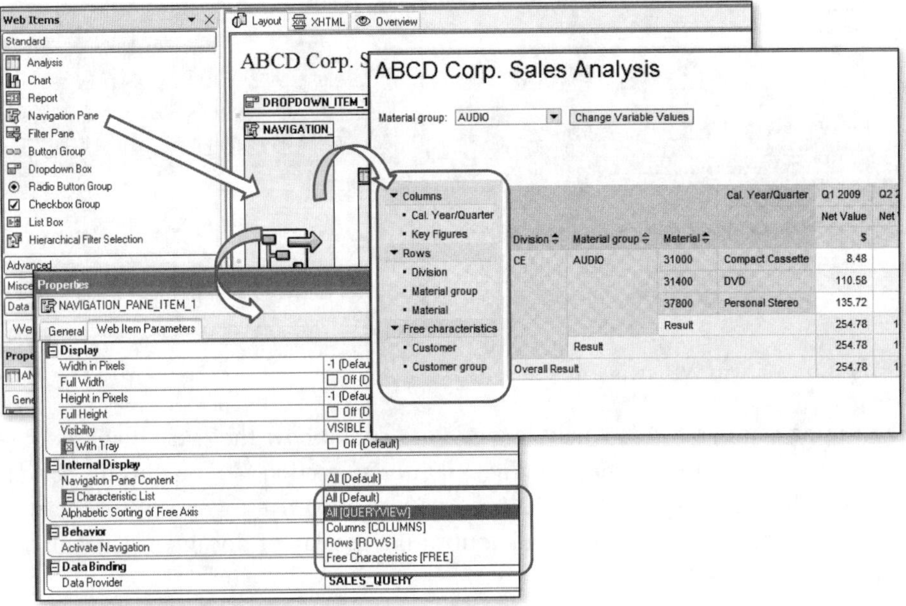

Figure 11.23 Navigation Pane Web Item

Filter Pane

The Filter Pane web item is used if you want to let the users select the values for selected characteristics or specific key figures from the key figure structure by applying a filter. The same web item can also be used to display the filter values for selected characteristics in the web application (see Figure 11.24).

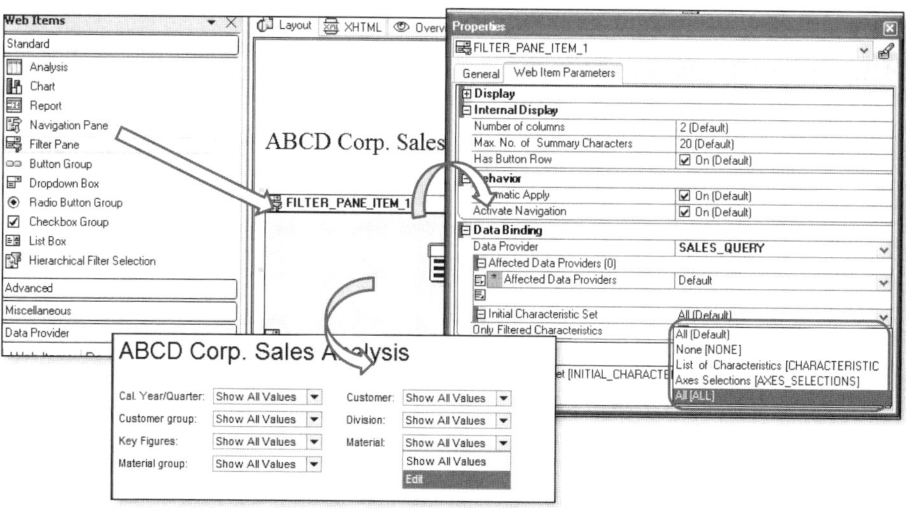

Figure 11.24 Filter Pane Web Item

Button Group

Earlier, we discussed the use of buttons while creating the web application for ABCD Corp. The main purpose of the Button Group web item is to provide actions to the web application. Different commands that are available in the Commands Wizard can be attached to a button. Multiple buttons can be included in a single button group, and each button in the button group can have a separate command/sequence of commands linked to it (see Figure 11.25). The Command Wizard and its different commands are discussed in later sections of this chapter.

Dropdown Box

The Dropdown Box web item is used to provide an easy option for user selections. The use of the dropdown box was discussed when we explained the creation of a web application (refer to Figure 11.8). The dropdown box that was created was based on a characteristic. However, a dropdown box can get populated from multiples sources:

- **Characteristic Values:** The dropdown list is populated from the selected characteristic of a data provider. The data provider display is controlled based on the value selected in the dropdown box.

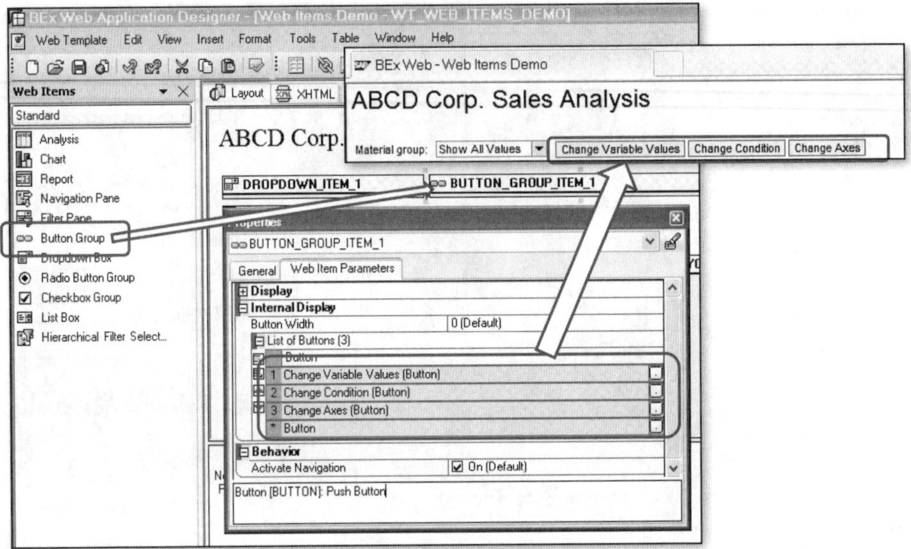

Figure 11.25 Button Group Web Item

- **Query View Selection:** If there are views built on the data provider, then the dropdown displays the list of all those views from a selected data provider. Using this option, the users can select different views of the data provider in the drop down.
- **Fixed List of Options:** Using this option you can define your own values which should appear in the dropdown list and then you can assign action (a command) to each of the values added to the dropdown.
- **Fixed List of Options: Manual Update:** This option is similar to the Fixed List of Options setting. The difference is this web item also allows users to trigger manual update.
- **Variable Selection:** This option populates the dropdown list with the values for the selected BEx variable.

Radio Button Group

The Radio Button Group web item allows you to filter selected characteristic values using a radio button. Characteristic values for the selected characteristic are displayed in a group in the web application. You can control the number of values to be displayed and whether to display an ALL entry or not, in the web item parameter settings. This option is typically used if characteristics need to be restricted with a single value (see Figure 11.26).

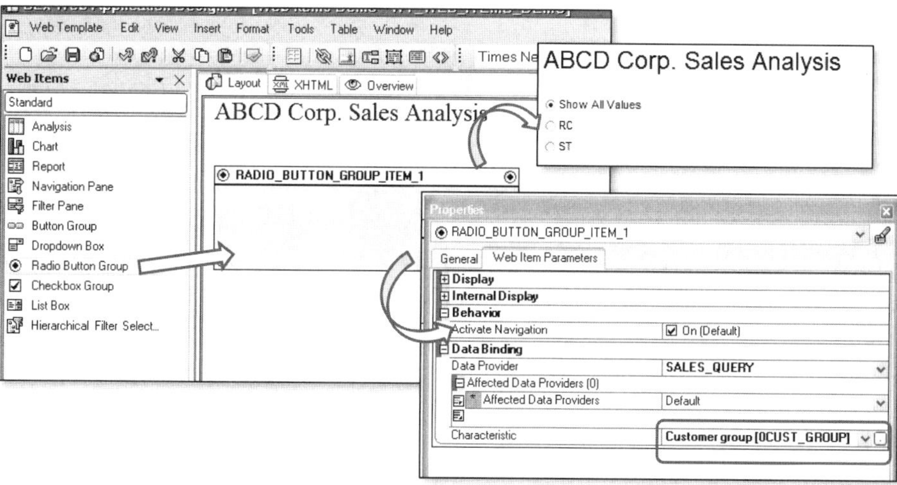

Figure 11.26 Radio Button Group Web Item

Checkbox Group

Using a Checkbox Group web item, you can display values for a selected characteristic that can be selected using checkboxes. This option is useful for selecting one or more values of characteristic for which the data providers are filtered (see Figure 11.27).

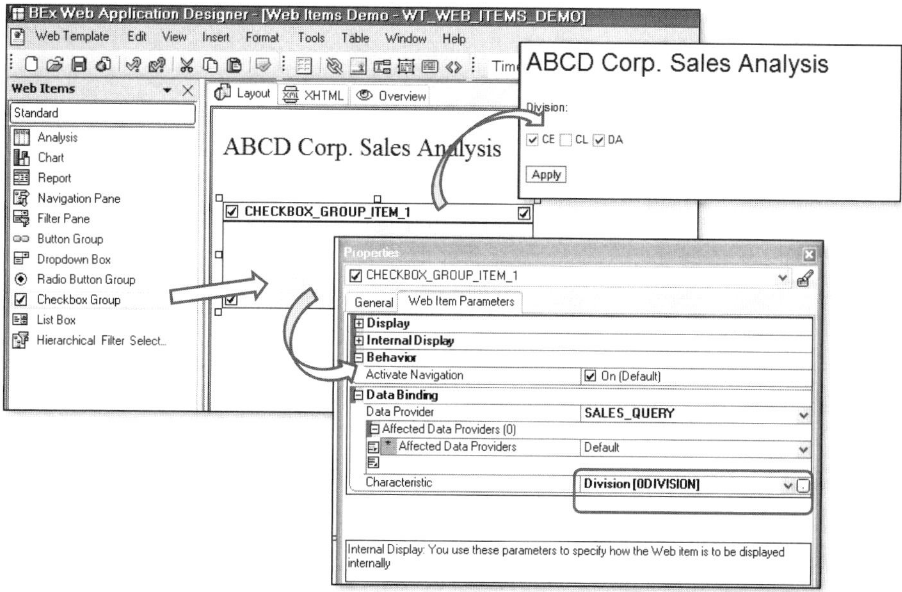

Figure 11.27 Checkbox Group Web Item

List Box

The List Box web item is used if you want to select filters for a characteristic using a list box. You can select one or multiple values at a time as a filter (see Figure 11.28).

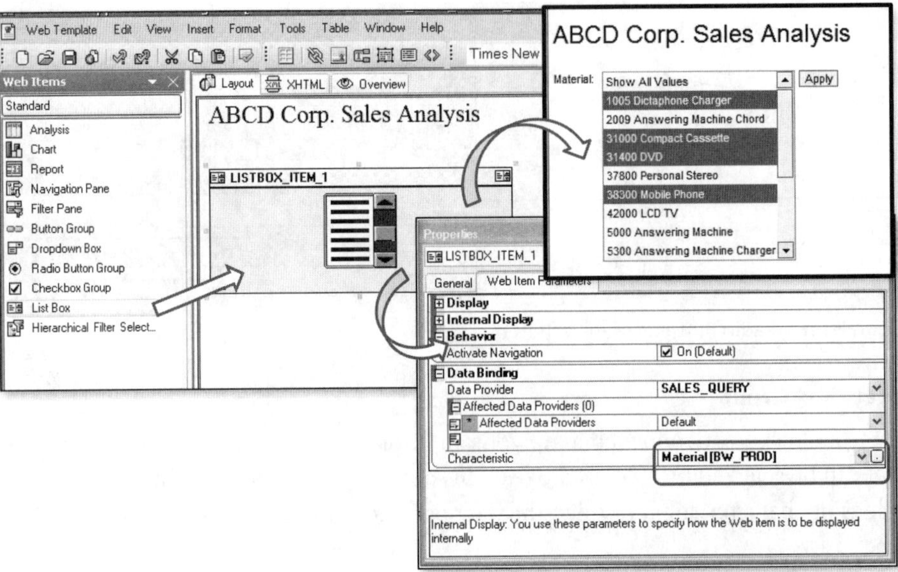

Figure 11.28 List Box Web Item

Hierarchical Filter Selection

The Hierarchical Filter Selection web item allows user to select the filter values based on the hierarchy built on the selected characteristic. The user can expand or collapse the hierarchy and can select a specific node (or leaf) that is used to filter the attached data provider (see Figure 11.29).

11.3.2 Advanced

Advanced web items are used for more complex applications such as a group or tab. The details are discussed next.

Web Template

The Web Template web item can be used to insert another web template into the web template definition (see Figure 11.30).

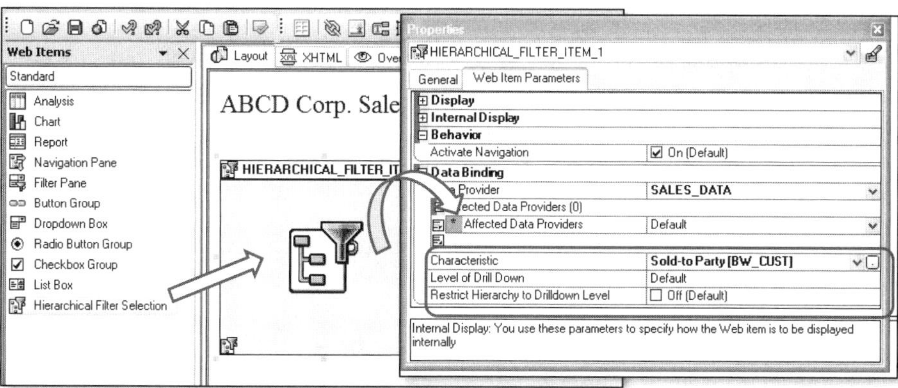

Figure 11.29 Hierarchical Filter Selection Web Item

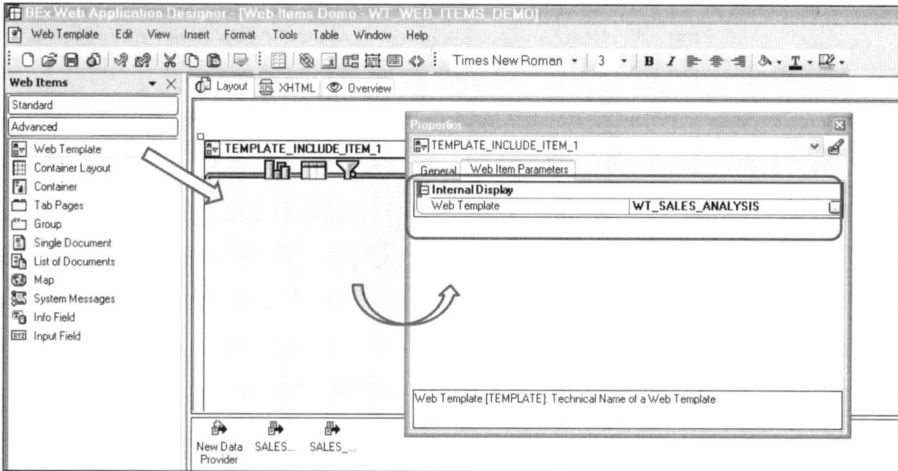

Figure 11.30 Web Template Web Item

Container Layout

You use the Container Layout web item to place and space the different web items included in the web template. A Container Layout is used to create an organized display for the web application. This web item offers you a grid to arrange the web items. Note that one cell in the grid accommodates only one web item.

Container

The Container web item is used to group contents from different web items together in the web template. For example, grouping items on different tab pages of the web application can be achieved using a container on each of the tabs.

Tab Pages

Use the Tab Pages web item to organize the web items included in the web template across different tab pages (see Figure 11.31).

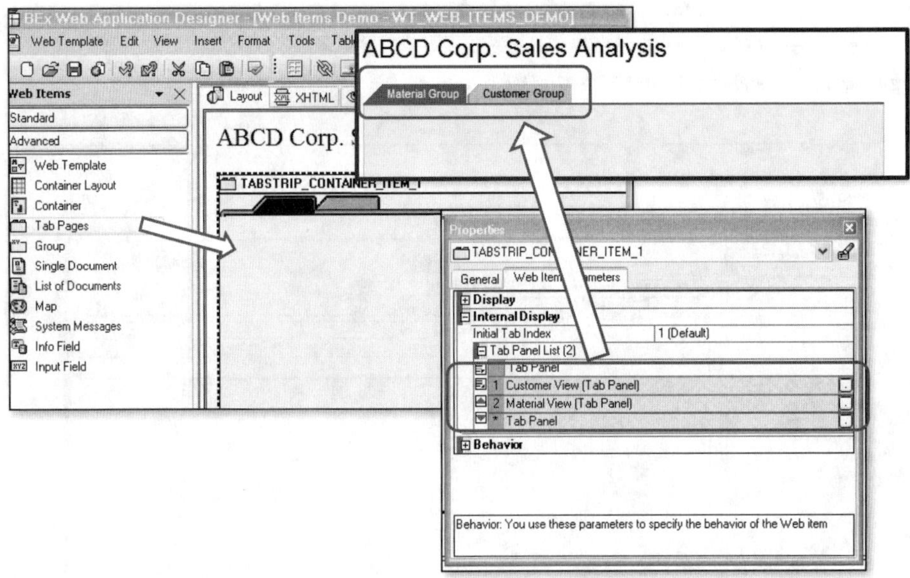

Figure 11.31 Tab Pages Web Item

Group

A Group web item is used to display the contents of the web application together as a group.

Single Document

Using the Single Document web item, you can embed a document in the web application that is maintained for the selected data provider. You can also specify the *document class* (i.e., InfoProvider, metadata, or master data) of the document, which should be displayed in the web application.

List of Documents

Use the List of Documents web item to display the list of documents corresponding to a data provider. This web item is context sensitive, so only those documents are shown in the list that are applicable to the current state of navigation for the data provider.

Map

You can use the Map web item to display the data provider information on a map with respect to the geographical characteristic such as country, region, state, and so on. Using this feature and web item is dependent on the geo-characteristics that form the base for maps in SAP NetWeaver BW.

System Messages

Different system messages, errors, warnings, and information messages can be displayed in the web application by inserting the System Messages web item.

Display/Suppress Messages

The setting to display or suppress messages/errors/warning/information is configured at the web template level.

Info Field

The information regarding the user, data provider, filters, status of data, and so on can be displayed using the Info Field web item. You can select the list of information parameters to be displayed in the web application in the web item properties.

Input Field

The Input Field web item provides you with a general user input field in the web application. Users can enter characteristic filter values, numeric values, and so on in this field, and this information can be read by other web items for processing in the web application.

11.3.3 Miscellaneous

Miscellaneous web items are used to add other features to the web application as discussed next.

Data Provider Information

The Data Provider web item is used to generate an XML for the query results or the navigation state of the data provider. This XML generation is not visible to the user because the code is generated at the source of the web application. To view the generated XML, view the source for the web application.

Text

The Text web item is used to display general text, characteristic descriptions, or other text elements, such as queries, data providers, and user information, in the web application.

Link

Using the Link web item, you can include a link in the web application and assign a command to it that is executed when the link is accessed.

List of Exceptions

The List of Exceptions web item displays the list of all exceptions defined on the data provider used in the web template. These exceptions can be set as active or inactive during the analysis.

List of Conditions

The List of Conditions web item displays a list of conditions defined on the data provider used in the web template. While performing analysis, the user can then toggle between the active and inactive states of each condition if needed.

Menu Bar

The Menu Bar web item is used in a web template to build a menu bar for the web application. Using this web item, you can create your own menu options and provide action to each of these menu options by assigning commands.

Ticker

Using the Ticker web item, you can display the data in the form of a ticker in the web application.

Properties Pane

Use the Properties Pane web item if you want to allow users to edit the properties of web items included in the web application during runtime.

Context Menu

While working in a web application, you can use different context menu options to perform analysis on the data displayed using an Analysis web item or the Navigation Block web item. Using the Context Menu web item, you can control different menu options that should be made available to the user using the web application. You have an option to hide/display each function of the context menu in the properties of this web item.

Script

Using the Script web item, you can integrate a JavaScript in the web template.

Custom Extension

The Custom Extension web item is used to address some of the complex requirements that can't be addressed using any of the readily available web items. You can integrate a custom ABAP code or an HTML code with the web template using this web item.

Reusable Web Items

Web items that are included and configured in a web template can be saved as a Reusable web item in the web application designer. These saved web items are available under the Reusable Web Items tab in the Web Items panel (see ❶ of Figure 11.32).

To save a web item for reuse, select Save as Reusable Web Item from the context menu of the web item (❷), and then save it after providing a technical name and description in the pop-up box (❸).

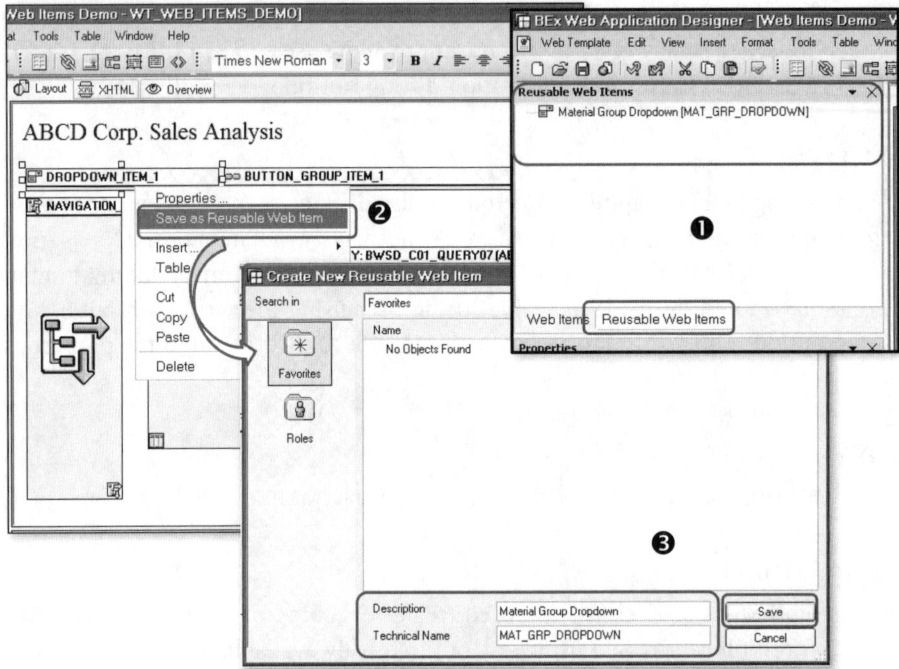

Figure 11.32 Reusable Web Items

11.4 Working with Commands

Assigning commands to different components and user actions is very important while creating a web application. You can assign commands to different web items included in the web template using a custom JavaScript. However, to eliminate coding and reduce the complexity of development, the web application designer comes up with a variety of ready-to-use commands. You can set your own parameters per the requirements for these commands. You can assign these commands to web items using the Command Wizard.

You call the Command Wizard from the Action section of the Web Item Parameters tab of the Properties box. Using of these available commands makes the web application design an easy and intuitive process.

There are two tab pages in the Command Wizard (see Figure 11.33):

- All Commands: All of the available commands in the command wizard are displayed on the All Commands tab page.

- Favorite Commands: You can select and add the frequently used commands for your ready access in the Favorite Commands tab page. Simply select the checkbox next to a command to add it to the Favorites tab (see Figure 11.33).

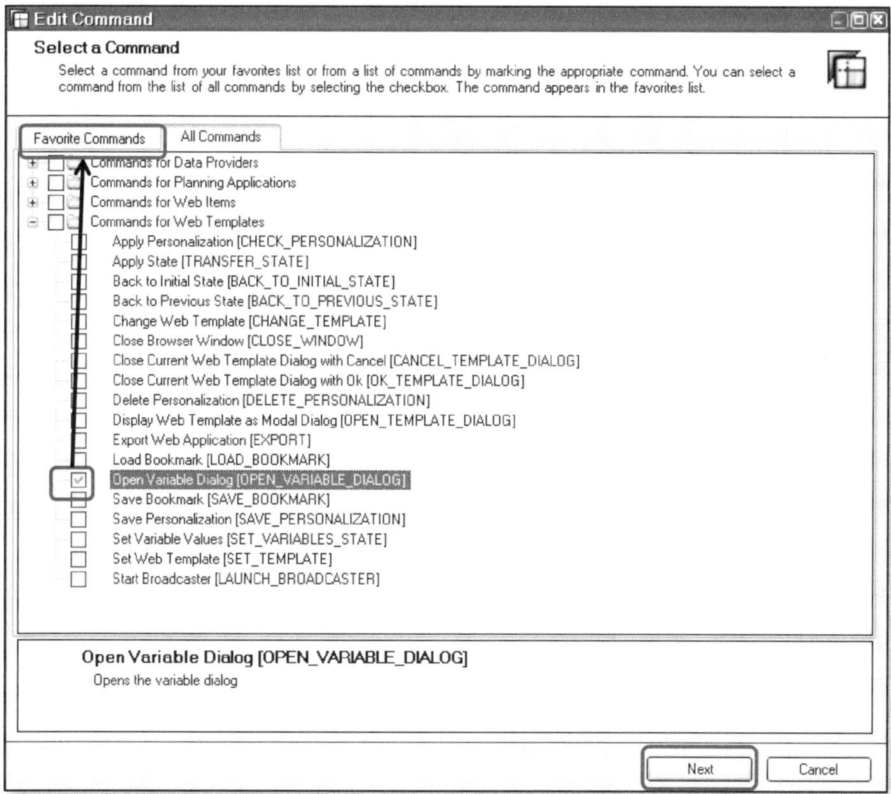

Figure 11.33 Command Wizard

Based on the usage and applicability, these commands are grouped into four different sections:

- Commands for Data Providers
- Commands for Planning Applications
- Commands for Web Items
- Commands for Web Templates

Each of the available commands has its own specific parameters to be defined. When you select a command and click on the Next button (see Figure 11.33), the next screen displays all of the parameters that can be set for the selected commands. The description of the commands and the parameters for that command are displayed in the Command Wizard to assist the development.

11.4.1 Commands for Data Providers

The commands that correspond to a data provider are grouped as Commands for Data Providers. Based on the application of the commands, they are further divided into subgroups. The list of all of the commands for data providers is given next.

Basic Data Provider Commands

The commands under Basic Data Provider are listed in Table 11.1.

Command	Technical Name
Report-Report Interface	RRI
Set Data Provider Parameters	SET_DATA_PROVIDER_PARAMETERS
Set Zero Value Display	SET_ZERO_PRESENTATION
Set Sign Display	SET_SIGN_PRESENTATION
Back to Initial State	BACK_TO_INITIAL_DP_STATE
Back to Previous State	BACK_TO_PREVIOUS_DP_STATE
Translate Currency	SET_CURRENCY_TRANSLATION
Export Data Provider as XML	EXPORT_XML

Table 11.1 Basic Data Provider Commands

Data Provider Commands for Axes

The commands related to the data provider axes, drilldowns, navigations, and so on are grouped as Data Provider Commands for Axes. The commands under this group are listed in Table 11.2.

Command	Technical Name
Set Hierarchical Display of Axis	SET_AXIS_HIERARCHY
Set Position of Results Row	SET_RESULT_ALIGNMENT
Swap Axes	SWAP_AXES
Remove Drilldown	REMOVE_DRILL_DOWN
Drill Down a Characteristic	DRILL_DOWN
Exchange Characteristics/Structures	EXCHANGE

Table 11.2 Data Provider Commands for Axes

Data Provider Commands for Characteristics

The commands that correspond to the display and presentation of characteristic values in the data provider are grouped as Data Provider Commands for Characteristics. Table 11.3 lists the different commands that belong to this group.

Command	Technical Name
Set Display Attributes	SET_ATTRIBUTES
Set Presentation	SET_PRESENTATION
Set Display of Results Row	SET_RESULT_VISIBILITY
Set Sorting	SET_SORTING

Table 11.3 Data Provider Commands for Characteristics

Data Provider Commands for Conditions/Exceptions

Commands related to exceptions and conditions, such as calling up the Conditions/Exceptions dialog box or toggling between the status, are grouped as Data Provider Commands for Conditions/Exceptions. Commands under this group are listed in Table 11.4.

Command	Technical Name
Set Condition	SET_CONDITION
Set Status of a Condition	SET_CONDITION_STATE
Set Exception	SET_EXCEPTION
Set Status of an Exception	SET_EXCEPTION_STATE
Call Conditions Dialog	OPEN_CONDITIONS_DIALOG
Call Exceptions Dialog	OPEN_EXCEPTIONS_DIALOG

Table 11.4 Data Provider Commands for Conditions/Exceptions

Data Provider Commands for Data Cells

The commands grouped as Commands for Data Cells (see Table 11.5) allow you to call the data cell properties or set local calculations for the data provider.

Command	Technical Name
Set Data Cell Properties	SET_DATA_CELL_PROPERTIES
Set Local Calculations	SET_LIST_CALCULATION

Table 11.5 Data Provider Commands for Data Cells

Data Provider Commands for Filter Values

Different commands that can be used to apply filters on the data providers or on a characteristic in the data provider are grouped together as Data Provider Commands for Filter Values. These commands are listed in Table 11.6.

Command	Technical Name
Remove All Filter Values	CLEAR_ALL_SELECTION_STATES
Call Input Help Dialog	OPEN_SELECTOR_DIALOG
Set Filter Value for a Characteristic	SET_SELECTION_STATE_SIMPLE
Set Filter Values	SET_SELECTION_STATE
Remove Filter Values for a Characteristic	CLEAR_SELECTION_STATE
Remove Filter Values for a List of Characteristics	CLEAR_SELECTION_STATES
Set Filter Values Using Different Sources	SET_SELECTION_STATE_BY_BINDING
Set Filter Values Using Filter	SET_SELECTION_STATE_BY_FILTER

Table 11.6 Data Provider Commands for Filter Values

Data Provider Commands for Hierarchies

Hierarchy-related commands are grouped as Data Provider Commands for Hierarchies (see Table 11.7).

Command	Technical Name
Expand/Collapse Hierarchy Nodes	SET_DRILL_STATE
Set Hierarchy	SET_HIERARCHY
Set Node Alignment	SET_NODE_ALIGNMENT

Table 11.7 Data Provider Commands for Hierarchies

Data Provider Commands for Open/Save Functions

The commands grouped under Open/Save Functions are listed in Table 11.8.

Command	Technical Name
Call Open Dialog	LOAD
Call Save Dialog	SAVE_AS
Save Query View	SAVE_VIEW

Table 11.8 Data Provider Commands for Open/Save Functions

Data Provider Commands for Documents

The commands for documents are grouped as Data Provider Commands for Documents and are listed in Table 11.9.

Command	Technical Name
Open Document Browser	OPEN_DIALOG_DLG_DOC_BROWSER
Open Dialog for New Document	OPEN_DIALOG_DLG_NEW_DOCUMENT

Table 11.9 Data Provider Commands for Documents

11.4.2 Commands for Planning Applications

The commands that are grouped under Commands for Planning Applications are used when creating a web-based planning application. This includes commands to save and refresh the data, commands to execute different planning functions, and so on. A list of all planning-related commands is given in Table 11.10.

Command	Technical Name
Refresh Data	REFRESH_DATA
Save Changed Data	SAVE_DATA
Reset Changed Data	RESET_DATA
Set Data Entry Mode	SET_DATA_ENTRY_MODE
Execute a Planning Function	EXEC_PLANNING_FUNCTION_SIMPLE
Execute a Planning Function	EXEC_PLANNING_FUNCTION
Execute a Planning Sequence	EXEC_PLANNING_SEQUENCE_SIMPLE

Table 11.10 Commands for Planning Applications

Using these commands for planning applications is explained in detail in Chapter 12, Integrated Planning.

11.4.3 Commands for Web Items

Different web items used in the web template can also be modified from the web application. The commands listed in Table 11.11 belong to the group Commands for Web Items.

Command	Technical Name
Call Chart Properties Dialog	OPEN_CHART_DIALOG
Call Properties Dialog	OPEN_DIALOG_PROPERTIES_PANE
Set Web Item Parameters	SET_ITEM_PARAMETERS
Restore Initial State	BACK_TO_INITIAL_ITEM_STATE
Back to Previous State	BACK_TO_PREVIOUS_ITEM_STATE
Set Status of Module	SET_MODULE_STATE

Table 11.11 Commands for Web Items

11.4.4 Commands for Web Templates

The Commands for Web Templates group includes all commands that are applicable for a web template. Table 11.12 lists the different commands under this group.

Command	Technical Name
Save Bookmark	SAVE_BOOKMARK
Load Bookmark	LOAD_BOOKMARK
Start Broadcaster	LAUNCH_BROADCASTER
Close Browser Window	CLOSE_WINDOW
Transfer State	TRANSFER_STATE
Set Variable Values	SET_VARIABLES_STATE
Open Variable Dialog	OPEN_VARIABLE_DIALOG
Export Web Application	EXPORT
Change Web Template	CHANGE_TEMPLATE
Display Web Template As Modal Dialog	OPEN_TEMPLATE_DIALOG
Close Current Web Template Dialog with Cancel	CANCEL_TEMPLATE_DIALOG
Close Current Web Template Dialog with OK	OK_TEMPLATE_DIALOG
Set Web Template	SET_TEMPLATE

Table 11.12 Commands for Web Templates

Command	Technical Name
Restore Initial State	BACK_TO_INITIAL_STATE
Restore Previous State	BACK_TO_PREVIOUS_STATE
Delete Personalization	DELETE_PERSONALIZATION
Save Personalization	SAVE_PERSONALIZATION

Table 11.12 Commands for Web Templates (Cont.)

11.5 Web Template Properties

Before we conclude this chapter, let's consider the different properties that can be set for a web template. Similar to all of the web items included in the web template, the web template itself has a set of parameters that can be set based on the requirement. The different parameters available for a web template are shown in Figure 11.34.

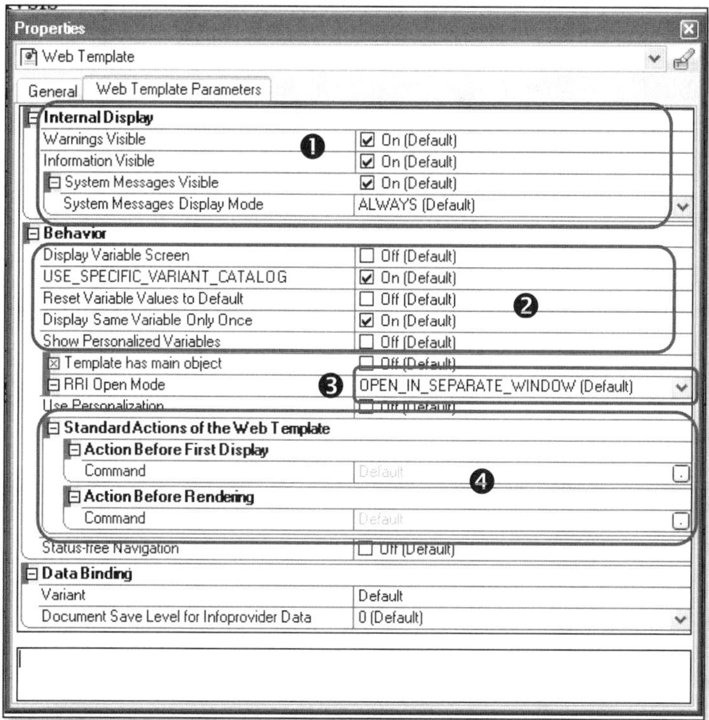

Figure 11.34 Web Template Properties

You can control the display of various system messages, information, warnings, and error messages in the web application. The Internal Display parameters (see ❶ of Figure 11.34) are set accordingly based on the need. The parameters that impact how the web template acts with respect to the variables included in its data providers are available under the Behavior section (❷).

The RRI Open Mode parameter (❸) decides how the jump targets or report-to-report interface on the data provider should open when they are called in the web application.

You can also assign commands to the web template that are executed before the first display or before the rendering of the web application (❹).

As you can see, you can define the properties of the web application by specifying the parameter values for the web template.

11.6 Summary

In this chapter, we explored how a web application can be created using the BEx web application designer. We discussed the functions and use of the different web items that are available for web templates. Another important feature available in the BEx web application designer is the Command Wizard, which enlists numerous commands to be readily used in the web application. These commands can be linked to different web items to provide actions in the web application. The variety of web items and rich collection of ready-to-use commands in the Command Wizard makes development of a web application an easy and intuitive task in BEx web application designer.

The Integrated Planning component in SAP NetWeaver BW provides a way to build planning applications to address business planning needs. In this chapter, we discuss the Integrated Planning component with the help of a typical Sales planning scenario.

12 Integrated Planning

Today's competitive global market makes most companies attempt to focus on their core business areas and synergize with trading partners in all possible forms of collaboration, information, and business process sharing. When doing this, it's important to create a business plan that is truly integrated because without integration, pitfalls often arise. In this chapter, we discuss the Integrated Planning component of SAP NetWeaver BW, which can be used to build integrated applications that support business planning.

The Integrated Planning component was introduced with the release of SAP NetWeaver 2004s version of BW. With Integrated Planning, you can build flexible planning applications that are integrated with typical SAP NetWeaver BW interfaces, ensuring homogeneity between reporting/analysis and planning. The key advantages of Integrated Planning are listed here:

- The Integrated Planning component is integrated with SAP NetWeaver BW's analytical features. This means you can use analysis features such as filters, slice-n-dice reporting, exception reporting, and so on while working on planning data.
- To build a planning application using Integrated Planning, you use the same design and development tools that are used to build analytical applications, such as web application designer, SAP Business Explorer (BEx), or BEx analyzer.
- The OLAP variables are shared and are available in Integrated Planning. This once again ensures consistency of information between planning and reporting within SAP NetWeaver BW.

Figure 12.1 illustrates how the Integrated Planning component relates to the other areas of SAP NetWeaver BW. Both the reporting and planning applications use the same OLAP engine for data processing, and they share InfoProviders, data models, transaction data, master data, OLAP variables, OLAP documents, and OLAP metadata.

Also, Integrated Planning uses the BEx query designer, web application designer, and BEx analyzer for designing the planning user interface.

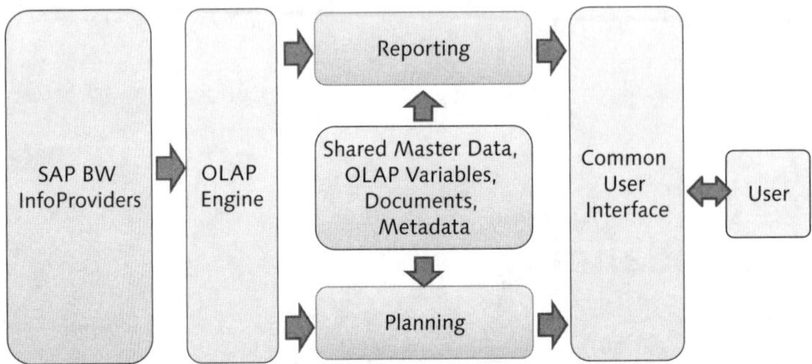

Figure 12.1 Integrated Planning as a Part of SAP NetWeaver BW

In this chapter, we cover the different components of Integrated Planning one by one, so that by the end of the chapter, you'll be able to start design and development on your own. However, note that there's no specific rule or a ready planning data model available for Integrated Planning; instead, the system provides you with the building blocks needed for a planning application, which can be flexibly used to build applications that address a variety of scenarios.

SAP NetWeaver BW Integrated Planning Prerequisite

The installation of the BI-Java component on your SAP NetWeaver BW portal is essential to use Integrated Planning because the modeling is done using a web-based application, which is installed on the J2EE engine. Installation of this component is an activity performed by the SAP Basis team.

To begin with, we first give you an overview of planning and explain some of the typical planning scenarios, including an example sales planning scenario for ABCD Corp. In the subsequent sections of the chapter, we explain the different parts of BW-IP using this sales planning example scenario. We'll also see how a simple planning application can be built using the web application designer as well as using BEx analyzer. Finally, we conclude with some technical aspects such as planning locks and behavior of real-time InfoCubes in SAP NetWeaver BW.

12.1 An Overview of Planning

In a general sense, *planning* is the process of creating a plan to achieve certain goals. For a business, planning provides focus to the organization and helps determine what exactly needs to be achieved to meet these goals.

Planning can be done at different levels within an organization. If the planning is done at a very high level, and the objective is to define business strategy and to define an organization's future direction, it's called *strategic planning*. A strategic plan often aims at a long-range time frame (e.g., 5 to 10 years). The planning for shorter time duration, say one or two years, is called *operational planning*. An operational plan can be by weeks, months, or quarters and is derived from the strategic plan. Planning at the operational level is specific to functional areas such as sales planning, financial planning, and so on. A plan addressing further details and focusing on the immediate future can be derived from the operational plan. This planning addresses execution-level details and is often the lowest level of planning in an organization.

Different organizations follow different approaches for planning. In some organizations, plan values for entire organizations are determined at the top-most level, and these high-level targets are then used to create targets for the lower levels of the organization. This approach is called *top-down planning*. A budget planning process typically follows the top-down approach. In another approach, the planning cycle begins at the lowest level of an organization, and then these goals at lower levels are aggregated as a basis in planning for the higher levels. This is called *bottom-up planning*. Finally, some organizations proceed with a hybrid approach for planning, which combines both top-down and bottom-up planning.

For a planning process to be more effective, it has to be integrated with business functions as a closed-loop process. This means that the plan has to be taken to the execution level, and then the outcome of the actions has to be measured against the plan values to evaluate the effectiveness of the plan. This enables a continuous improvement in the plan, leading to better execution. Figure 12.2 shows how SAP NetWeaver BW Integrated Planning fits into this overall closed-loop planning scenario.

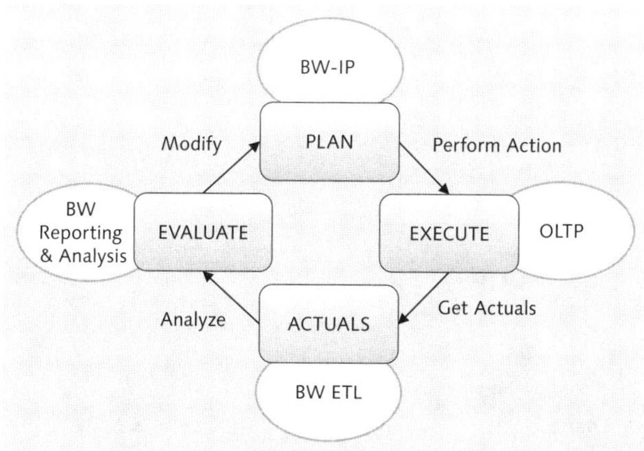

Figure 12.2 SAP NetWeaver BW and Closed-loop Planning

When put into action, the planning done in BW-IP forms the base for the execution that generates actual values. The execution happens in the transaction system (OLTP), and data is then extracted to SAP NetWeaver BW using its extraction, transformation, and loading (ETL) process. The plan values and actual values, now both available in SAP NetWeaver BW, provide a platform for analyzing plan and actual data together, and SAP NetWeaver BW's reporting and analysis tools can then measure the plan performance. Such an analysis further leads to optimizing the plan, making it a closed-loop process.

12.2 Planning Requirements in ABCD Corp.

We've used a simple sales planning scenario within ABCD Corp. to illustrate different features of SAP NetWeaver BW Integrated Planning. In this company, sales planning is an annual cycle for all of the three sales organizations: 1000 (APAC), 2000 (Europe), and 3000 (North America). Each sales organization plans for the sales figures of three different divisions or product ranges: Consumer Electronics (CE), Daily Appliances (DA), and Consumer Lifestyle Appliances (CL). This is a high-level plan for the organization, and the high-level values for each of the product ranges are transferred to different products belonging to them; each sales organization has a product range manager who is responsible for planning the sales of each product under his assigned product range. The plan for a year (January to December) is done by quarter; so there are four planning periods: quarter 1 (Q1), quarter 2 (Q2), quarter 3 (Q3), and quarter 4 (Q4). Figure 12.3 is a graphical representation of this scenario.

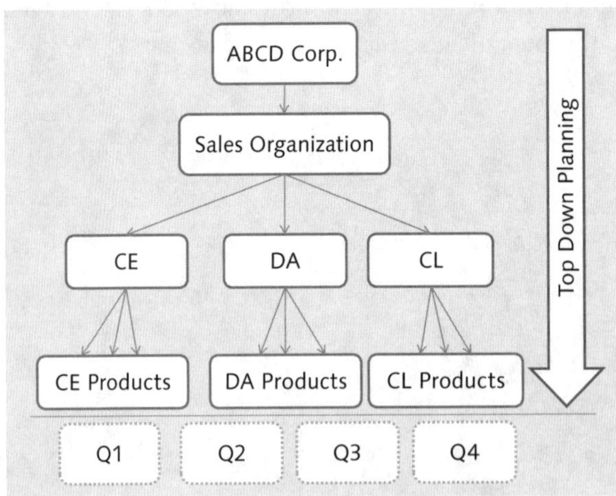

Figure 12.3 ABCD Corp. Planning Scenario

12.3 SAP NetWeaver BW Integrated Planning Components

SAP NetWeaver BW Integrated Planning includes different components, which are available to a developer as building blocks of any planning application. The relationship among these different components is depicted in Figure 12.4.

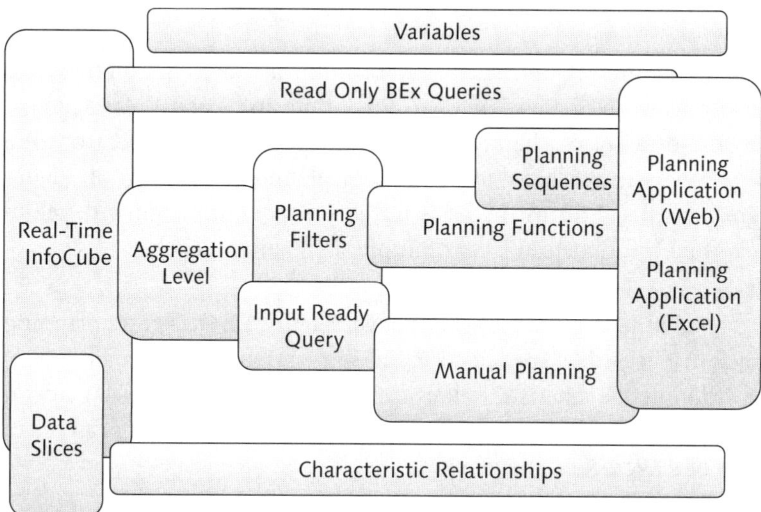

Figure 12.4 Planning Components and Their Dependencies

In the following list, we provide you with an overview of the different planning components and their relationship with each other.

- **Real-time InfoCube**
  A *real-time InfoCube* is an InfoCube with an ability to write data. As shown in Figure 12.4, a real-time InfoCube is the base for any planning application in SAP NetWeaver BW. The data entered by different planners is saved into a real-time InfoCube, and data stored there is also available for reporting.
- **Characteristic relationships**
  Characteristic relationships provide a means of maintaining data consistency in a planning application. Using characteristic relationships, you can build the logic to check, propose, or derive valid combinations of various characteristics values used in planning scenarios. As shown in Figure 12.4, characteristic relationships are defined at the InfoCube level.

- **Data slices**
  Data slices are used to lock a specific set of plan data based on the characteristic selections defined at the InfoCube level and can be used to protect a set of data stored in a real-time InfoCube from changes. The data selected under data slices can't be changed during planning. Data slices are defined on the real-time InfoCube.
- **Aggregation level**
  Aggregation levels are InfoProviders specific to planning and are built on real-time InfoCubes (also on MultiProviders involving real-time InfoCubes). An aggregation level consists of a set of characteristics and key figures selected from the underlying InfoProvider, which are to be used for planning. As shown in Figure 12.4, the aggregation level forms the basis for all subsequent planning development. One real-time InfoCube can have multiple aggregation Levels.
- **Planning filters**
  Planning filters are defined on an aggregation level (Figure 12.4). Using a planning filter, you can restrict the data contained in an aggregation level by maintaining selections for different characteristic values from the aggregation level. An aggregation level can have multiple planning filters, whereas a planning filter can relate to one and only one aggregation level.
- **Planning functions**
  Planning functions are used to automatically create/change/delete plan data based on the logic defined in the function. There are some predefined (standard) functions available in Integrated Planning, but you can define your own custom planning function if needed. A planning function is built on an aggregation level but is always executed on a planning filter, so a planning function can be used by multiple planning filters based on the same aggregation level.
- **Planning variables**
  Integrated Planning uses the same OLAP variables in building a planning application that are used in creating the queries. The variables are available for use in almost all of the planning components. Because the variables are dependent on the InfoObjects, after they are defined, they are available throughout for all planning components (Figure 12.4). OLAP variables are discussed in detail in Chapter 9.
- **Planning sequences**
  Planning sequences are used to define an execution sequence for multiple planning functions. As shown in Figure 12.4, planning sequences are based on planning functions.

- **Manual planning**
  Manual planning is a process where you manually create/change/delete the plan data in a planning application. The process to build applications with manual planning using the web application designer or BEx analyzer are discussed in later sections of this chapter. As shown in Figure 12.4, manual planning applications are based on input-ready queries (defined next).
- **Input-ready query**
  Input-ready queries form the base for manual planning. These are queries where you can manually enter data, which then gets written to the real-time InfoCube. Input-ready queries are built using the BEx query designer.
- **Planning application**
  A *planning application* is built by putting different planning components together so that users can perform manual planning as well as execute different planning functions. This can involve input-ready queries as well as read-only BEx queries (see Figure 12.4). Different planning functions and planning sequences can also be included in a planning application. An Excel-based planning application is built using BEx analyzer, and a web-based planning application is built using the web application designer.

There are two ways you can create, change, and administer the different planning components defined in this list: the Planning Modeler, and the Planning Wizard.

In the following sections, we begin by explaining how both these tools work. Then we move on to discuss each of the planning elements in more detail.

12.3.1 Planning Modeler and Planning Wizard

Both the Planning Modeler and Planning Wizard are web-based development applications that run on the SAP J2EE server and can be accessed directly through the portal. As such, they don't need SAP GUI to be installed on your computer. For a standard SAP-delivered BUSINESS PLANNING portal role, these two tools are available under the DETAILED NAVIGATION tab (Figure 12.5). The technical name of the portal role is `com.sap.ip.bi.business_planning_showcase`.

However, both the Planning Modeler and the Planning Wizard can also be accessed from the backend SAP NetWeaver BW system using Transaction RSPLAN (Figure 12.6).

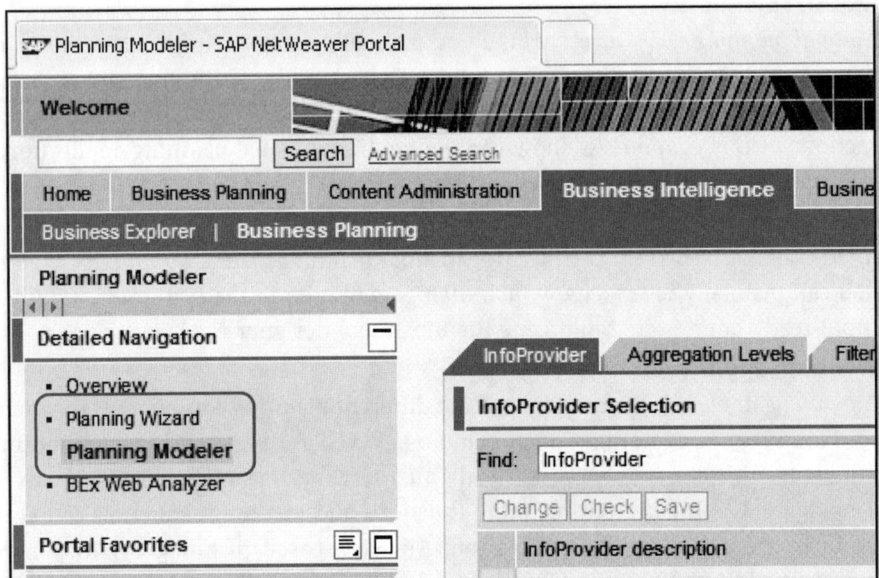

Figure 12.5 Accessing Planning Modeler/Planning Wizard from Portal

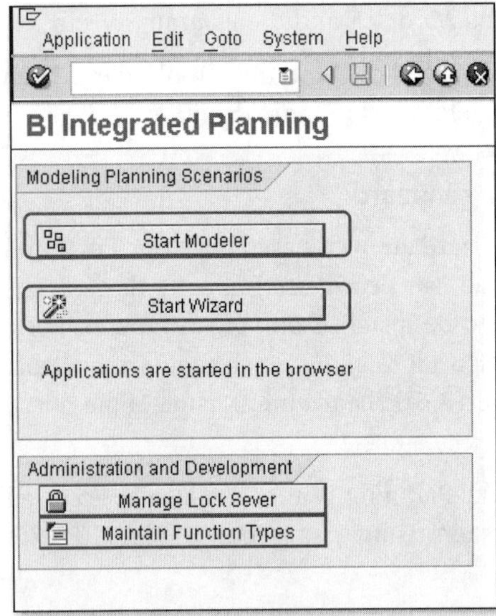

Figure 12.6 Accessing Planning Modeler/Planning Wizard from RSPLAN

Both the Planning Modeler and the Planning Wizard can be used to create a planning model, but the Planning Modeler provides a more comprehensive development interface than the Planning Wizard. On the other hand, the Planning Wizard guides you through the process of creating a planning model step by step.

The Planning Modeler, as shown in Figure 12.7, consists of five different tab pages. These tabs are explained here:

- InfoProvider: On this tab page, you can select the InfoProvider for the planning application. You can also define the characteristic relationships and data slices (❶ of Figure 12.7).
- Aggregation Level: This tab page allows you to define aggregation levels on selected InfoProviders (❷).
- Filter: You can create planning filters on selected aggregation levels on this tab page (❸).
- Planning Functions: This tab page is used to define different planning functions based on the selected aggregation level (❹).
- Planning Sequences: This tab page allows you to create different planning sequences, where you can define an execution sequence for different planning functions (❺).

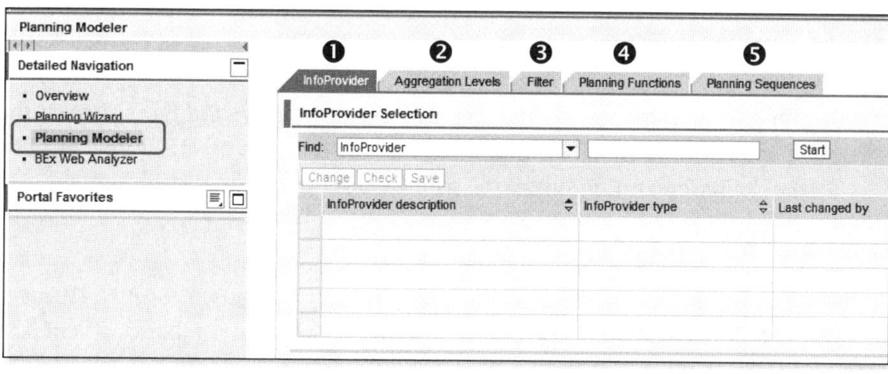

Figure 12.7 Planning Modeler Tabs

The Planning Wizard has an interface similar to the Planning Modeler, but the Planning Wizard shows you the step-by-step procedure for creating a simple planning model based on a single InfoProvider (Figure 12.8).

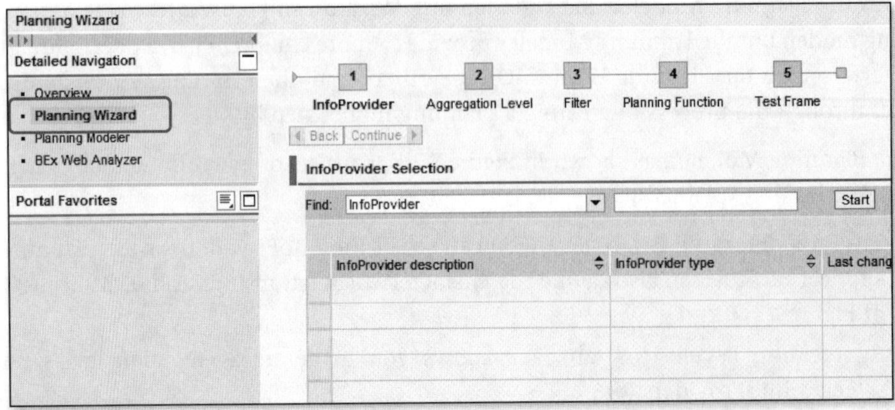

Figure 12.8 Planning Wizard

It helps you create a planning model in five different steps (Figure 12.8).

- Select InfoProvider [1]: Select an InfoProvider over which you want to define the planning model. Unlike the Planning Modeler, you can't create characteristic relationships or define data slices and other InfoProvider settings.
- Aggregation Level [2]: Create the aggregation level.
- Create Filter [3]: Create planning filter(s) based on the selected InfoProvider.
- Define Planning Function [4]: Define planning functions for automatic data processing.
- Test Frame [5]: In the last and final step in the Planning Wizard, you can test the planning model you've built using a default test input template. Also, you can debug the defined planning functions with a trace on the data.

12.3.2 Real-Time InfoCube

A real-time InfoCube forms the base for planning applications in SAP NetWeaver BW. The procedure to create a real-time InfoCube is the same as that of a standard InfoCube, as discussed in Chapter 5. The only difference is that while specifying the cube setting, you have to select the REAL-TIME checkbox (Figure 12.9).

You can decide on the characteristics and key figures to be included in the real-time cube based on the planning requirements. The primary factors that influence this decision are listed here:

- The entities that are needed to plan the data.
- The entities that are needed for further analysis of the plan data.

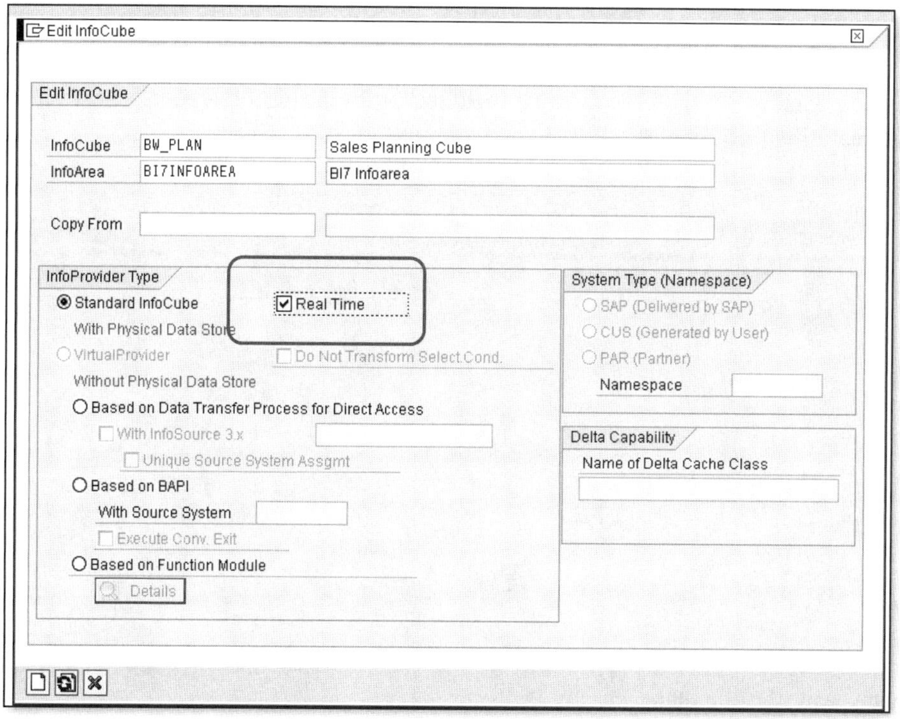

Figure 12.9 Creating a Real-Time InfoCube

In the example scenario explained in Section 12.2, Planning Requirements for ABCD Corp., these are the entities against which the ABCD Corp. plans the data:

- Sales organization
- Product range
- Product
- Calendar quarter
- Net value

Further, let's assume that ABCD Corp. needs the plan data to be analyzed by calendar year and also by the current and historical values of product group and product range. To address this requirement, the real-time InfoCube should include the following:

- Calendar year
- Product group as a characteristic for historical values

- Product group as a navigation attribute of product for current values
- Product range as a navigation attribute of product for current values

Having decided on the objects to be included in the InfoCube, you can now create the real-time InfoCube BW_PLAN, as shown in Figure 12.10.

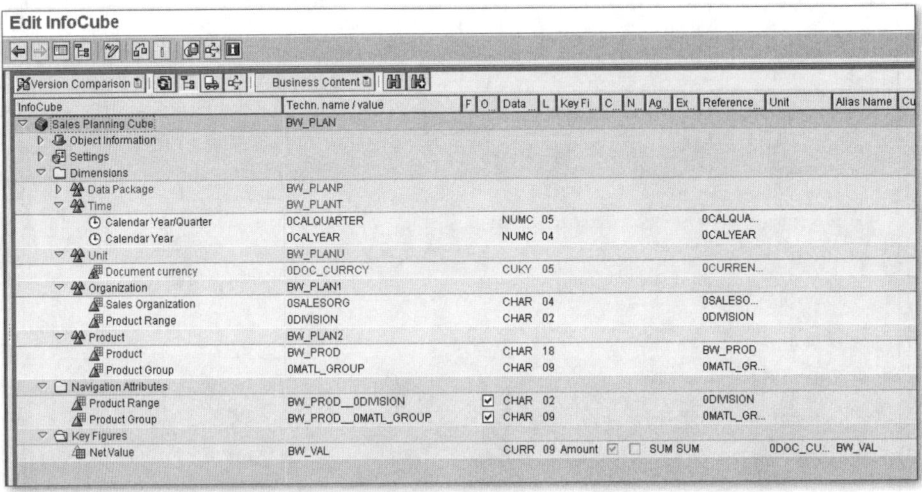

Figure 12.10 Real-Time InfoCube: BW_PLAN

A standard InfoCube is optimized for reading data in a way that considers reporting performance. A real-time InfoCube, on the other hand, is optimized for writing data into it. The data generated or modified in a planning application is written to the cube using an API. In a practical planning scenario, more than one user can work simultaneously in the same planning application, meaning that multiple users can attempt to write the data in the same real-time InfoCube. The API for real-time InfoCubes allows parallel writes to support multiple users simultaneously.

A real-time InfoCube can't be used for data loads using standard SAP NetWeaver BW data flow; however, the real-time behavior of a real-time InfoCube can be changed to enable data loads to it. In other words, a real-time InfoCube can switch between the real-time mode and data load mode.

In the Data Warehousing Workbench (DWW) (Transaction RSA1), you can see the option Change Real-Time Load Behavior in the context menu of the real-time InfoCube (❶ of Figure 12.11). Selecting this option displays a pop-up screen where you can set the real-time load behavior of the InfoCube (❷).

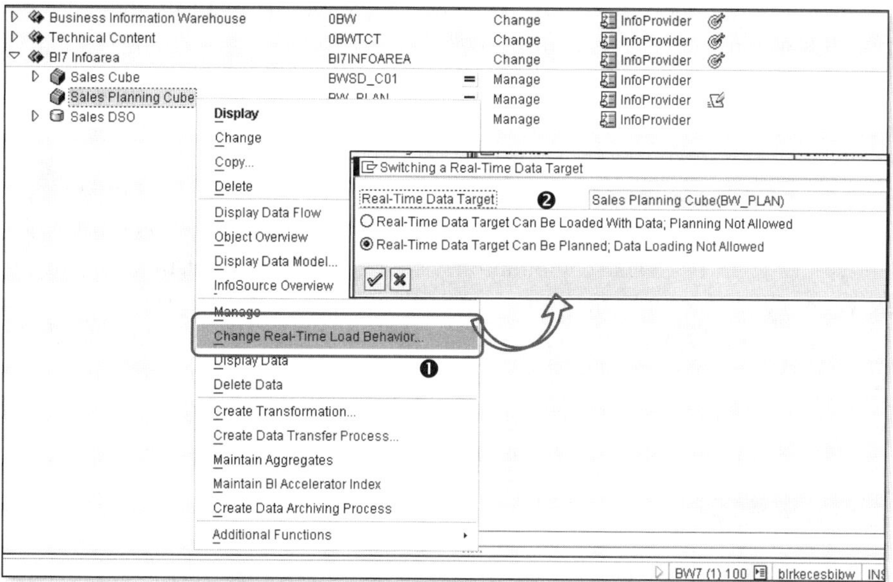

Figure 12.11 Changing Real-Time Load Behavior

If you select the Real-Time Data Target Can Be Loaded With Data; Planning Not Allowed radio button, the real-time InfoCube is switched to the read-only mode, and you can load the data to this InfoCube using regular SAP NetWeaver BW data load options. On the other hand, if you select the Real-Time Data Target Can Be Planned; Data Loading Not Allowed radio button, the InfoCube is switched back to the write mode where the planning can be performed. Data can't be loaded to the InfoCube in this mode using the data flow.

InfoProviders Used in Planning

Planning can be performed only on the real-time InfoCube, but standard InfoCubes can be used in a planning application for reading data.

After you have the real-time InfoCube ready, you can start building the planning components on this InfoCube.

12.3.3 Characteristic Relationships

Characteristic relationships are used to build logic that checks, proposes, and derives valid combinations of characteristic values in a planning application. This is one of the most important features to consider when building a planning model. Before we show you how to create characteristic relationships, let's first explain their usage in a practical scenario.

Consider a planning scenario where you first select a region and then enter the plan values for the countries under that region. As shown in Figure 12.12, when you select a region, you can technically create a record for any country under that region. For example, as a planner for region NA, you could create a record for GERMANY — even though this is an invalid combination. On the other hand, region NA and country CANADA *is* a valid combination. If the characteristic relationship for this scenario is defined, every time you enter a value for a country, the system validates and accepts it, or displays an error based on the validation result (Figure 12.12).

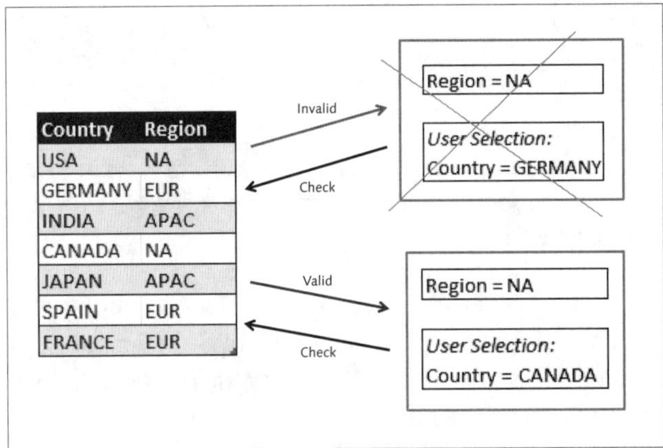

Figure 12.12 Characteristic Relationship: Check

The other use of characteristic relationships is to generate valid proposals based on business logic for planning applications. To explain this, let's have a look at the example shown in Figure 12.13, where the product range master data and the product master data both have three different values. You decide to provide the planning users with all possible combinations of product ranges and products to enter the plan values.

If you look at the technical combinations, nine different possible values can be generated for the given data but not all make functional sense. For example, the combination of *Product = Camera and Product Range = Domestic Appliances* is an invalid combination from a functional point of view. In this case, the logic defined in the characteristic relationship for product master data allows the system to *propose* only the valid combinations for data entry.

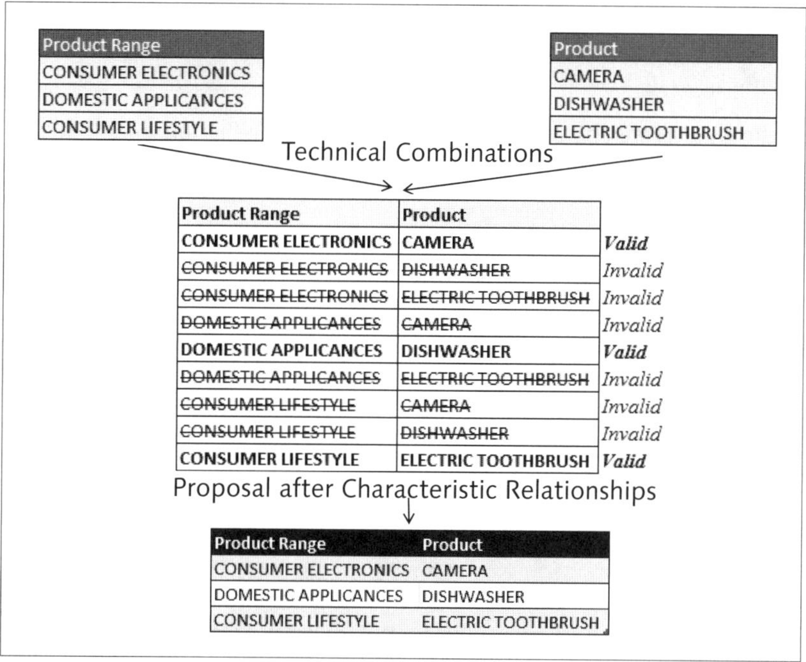

Figure 12.13 Characteristic Relationship: Propose

Finally, you can also use the characteristic relationships to derive values of a characteristic based on values of another characteristic. For example, if the requirement is to maintain the plan values for products and their corresponding product group, you can avoid entering both the products and the product groups during planning (Figure 12.14).

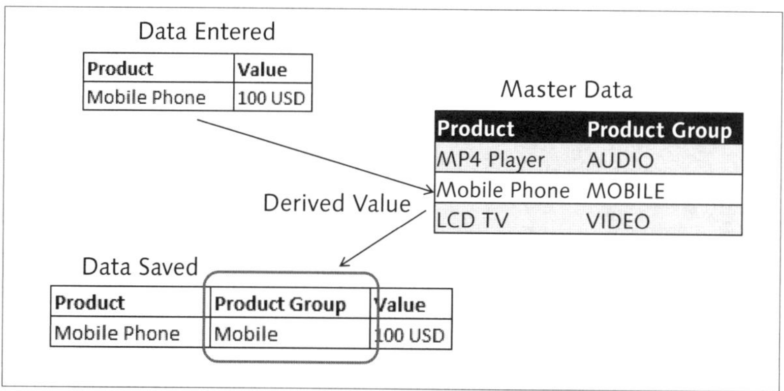

Figure 12.14 Characteristic Relationship: Derive

Using characteristic relationships, you can derive the value of a product group from product master data, if you know the product. So, the data saved in the cube contains the derived value as well.

Let's now see how to create characteristic relationships in the Planning Modeler.

1. You can create characteristic relationships in the InfoProvider tab of the Planning Modeler (❶ of Figure 12.15).

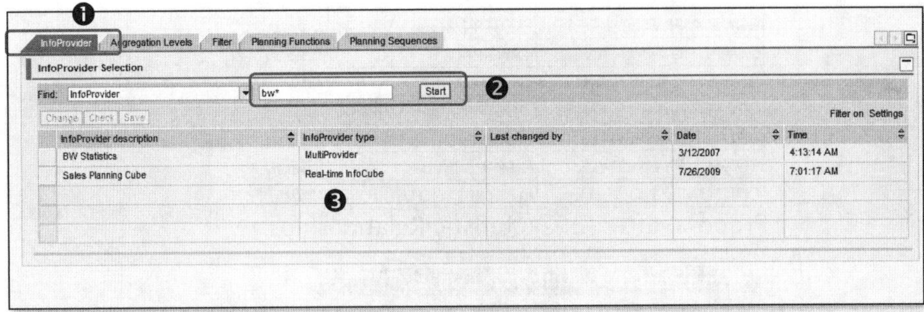

Figure 12.15 Search InfoProvider in Planning Modeler

2. You can locate the InfoProvider by using the search function, as shown in Figure 12.15 (❷). The list of all relevant InfoProviders is displayed based on the search criteria (❸).
3. Select the InfoProvider from the list. In this case, we select the Sales Planning Cube (BW_PLAN), which we created earlier (❶ of Figure 12.16). As soon as you select the InfoProvider, the definition of the InfoProvider is displayed on the screen (see Figure 12.16).

InfoProvider description	InfoProvider type	Last changed by	Date	Time
BW Statistics	MultiProvider		3/12/2007	4:13:14 AM
Sales Planning Cube	Real-time InfoCube		8/13/2009	12:44:08 PM

Display InfoProvider Sales Planning Cube

Dimension	Characteristic	With master data	With texts	With hierarchies	Compounding
Organization	Product Range	☐	☑	☐	
Organization	Sales Organization	☑	☑	☐	
Product	Product Group	☑	☑	☑	
Product	Product	☑	☑	☑	
Time	Calendar Year/Quarter	☑	☑	☐	
Time	Calendar Year	☑	☐	☐	
Unit	Document currency	☑	☑	☐	

Figure 12.16 Go to Characteristic Relationships Tab

4. The other three tabs that are displayed are CHARACTERISTIC RELATIONSHIPS, DATA SLICES, and SETTINGS. Click on the CHARACTERISTIC RELATIONSHIPS tab to create a characteristic relationship (❷ of Figure 12.16).

Note

If the InfoProvider is available in Display mode, click on the CHANGE button to set the InfoProvider definition to edit mode (❸).

5. Click on the Create button to create a new characteristic relationship (Figure 12.17).

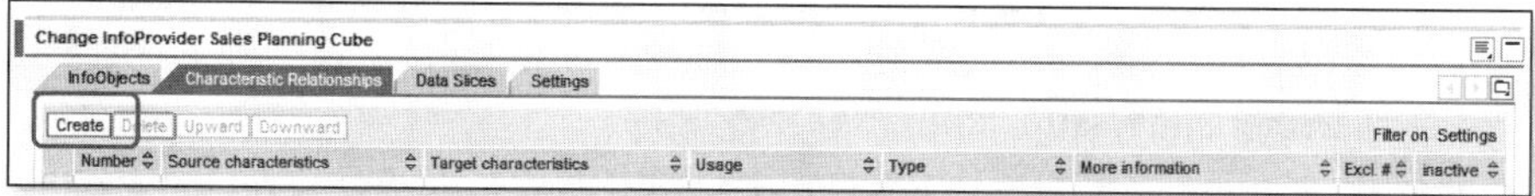

Figure 12.17 Create New Characteristic Relationship

6. Now you must select the type of characteristic relationship you want to create. The options here are Without Derivation, which is used only for check and proposal needs, or With Derivation, which is used if you want to derive values. In this case, we create a characteristic relationship to check the valid combinations of product (defined using InfoObject Material BW_PROD) and product range (defined using InfoObject Division 0DIVISION). Select WITHOUT DERIVATION, as shown in ❶ of Figure 12.18.

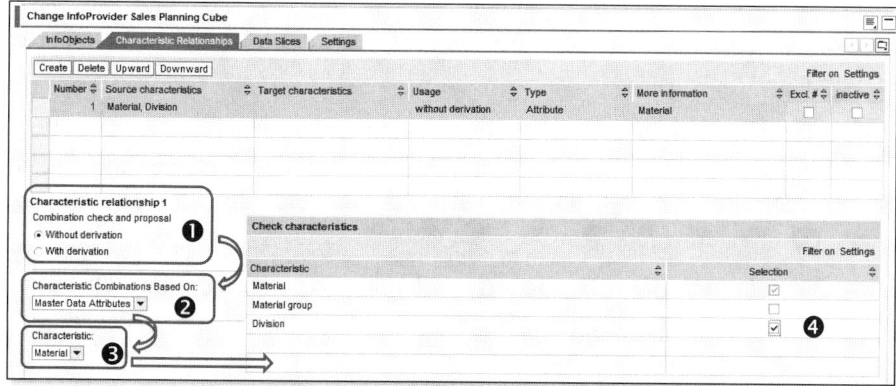

Figure 12.18 Define Characteristic Relationship Without Derivation

7. The next step is to select the base for the characteristic relationship (❷). The drop-down list provides four different options on which you can build the characteristic relationship:
   - Master Data Attributes: The validity of the data is based on the data existing in the selected master data. The characteristic and attribute values that are present in the master data are treated as valid for characteristic relationships.
   - DataStore Object: In this case, the base for the characteristic relationship is the data loaded in a DataStore Object (DSO). All of the records that exist in the DSO are treated as valid for characteristic relationships.
   - Hierarchy: The validity of the characteristic values is based on the definition of the hierarchy structure. Only those characteristic hierarchies that contain external characteristics other than the main characteristic can be used as the base for the characteristic relationship.
   - Exit class: If none of the preceding three types can be used to meet the requirements, you can use the characteristic relationships based on your own custom logic built using ABAP code. To build this, you have to implement the interface IF_RSPLS_CR_EXIT, or you can use the sample class CL_RSPLS_CR_EXIT_BASE as the template to create one.

   In this example, we select MASTER DATA ATTRIBUTES as the base for the characteristic relationship (❷ of Figure 12.18).
8. Select the master data characteristic to be the base for the characteristic relationship (❸).
9. The right side of the screen displays all of the attributes of the selected master data. Select the characteristic attributes that need to be validated under this characteristic relationship (❹). Note that the base master data characteristic material is selected by default.

In this example, we want to check and propose the valid combinations of product (defined using InfoObject Material BW_PROD) and product range (defined using InfoObject Division 0DIVISION). Select Division under the SELECTION column, as shown in ❹ of Figure 12.18.

1. Save this definition of the characteristic relationship by clicking the SAVE button on the INFOPROVIDER tab (Figure 12.19).

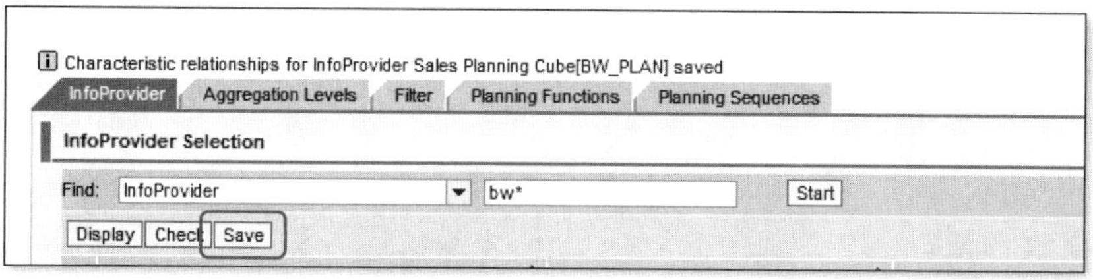

Figure 12.19 Save Characteristic Relationship

This characteristic relationship allows and proposes only those combinations that exist in the master data BW_PROD. You can further set this characteristic relationship as inactive by using the INACTIVE checkbox shown in ❶ of Figure 12.20.

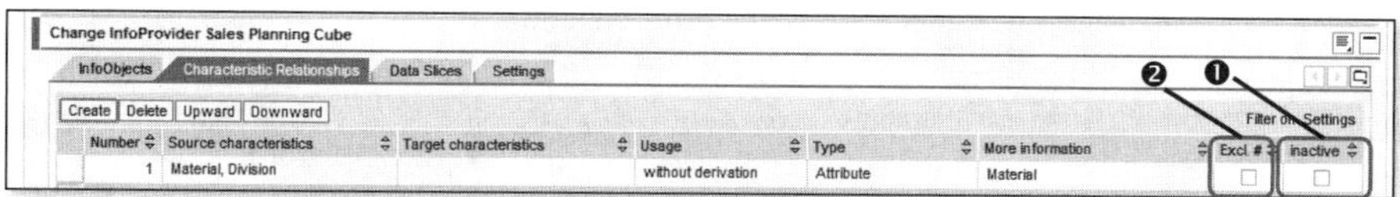

Figure 12.20 Additional Settings for Characteristic Relationships

Also, you can decide if the characteristic relationship has to exclude the blank values (i.e., records with value = "#"), by checking the checkbox EXCL. #, as shown in ❷ of Figure 12.20.

The DERIVE type of characteristic relationships can also be defined in a similar way. For our example scenario, the requirement is to allow users to enter the plan values for products (represented with InfoObject Material), and then derive the corresponding values of product groups (represented with InfoObject Material Group) while saving the data into the real-time InfoCube. The procedure to create this specific characteristic relationship is explained next and illustrated in Figure 12.21.

1. Select the type of characteristic relationship as WITH DERIVATION by selecting the radio button shown in ❶ of Figure 12.21.
2. Select MASTER DATA ATTRIBUTES as the base for the characteristic relationship (❷).
3. Select the characteristic that is used to derive the values for other characteristics (❸). This characteristic is marked as source characteristic.
4. Select the characteristics that are to be derived from the source characteristic. These characteristics are called *derived characteristics*. For our example, select Material Group as the derived characteristic, as shown in Figure 12.21.

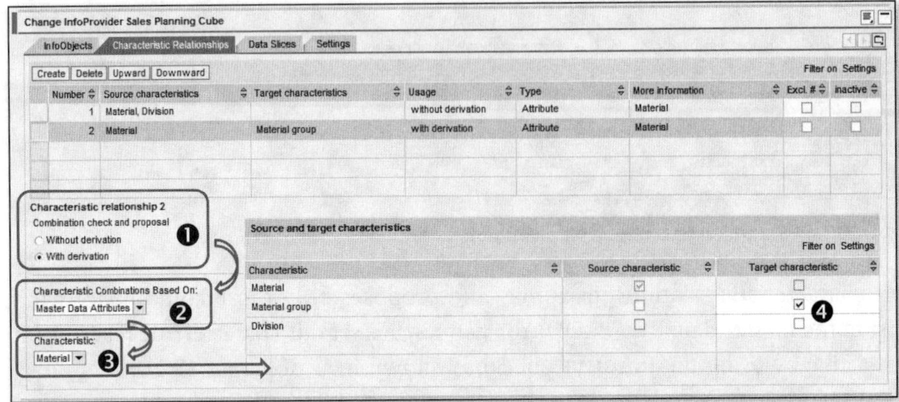

Figure 12.21 Create Characteristic Relationship with Derivation

Characteristic Relationship for Time Characteristics

The characteristic relationships for time characteristics are already built in BW-IP, so they don't need to be explicitly defined in the Planning Modeler.

12.3.4 Data Slices

Data slices are used to protect a specific set of data in the real-time InfoCube from changes. In a data slice, you can define restrictions on characteristics of the real-time InfoCube, and the data contained in those restrictions is then locked from any changes that could happen, either due to planning functions or due to manual planning.

To explain the use of data slices, let's take an example planning scenario in which you have both actual and plan data stored in the same cube, and you don't want users to change the actual data. This can be achieved by creating a data slice where the planning version characteristic is restricted to actuals to protect actual data from changes (❶ of Figure 12.22).

Figure 12.22 also illustrates how restrictions defined in a data slice change the data locked for planning (❷ and ❸ of Figure 12.22). The condition formed for the locks is based on the AND logical condition between the values defined. For example, in ❸, all those records are locked where Planning Version = ACTUALS AND Year = 2008.

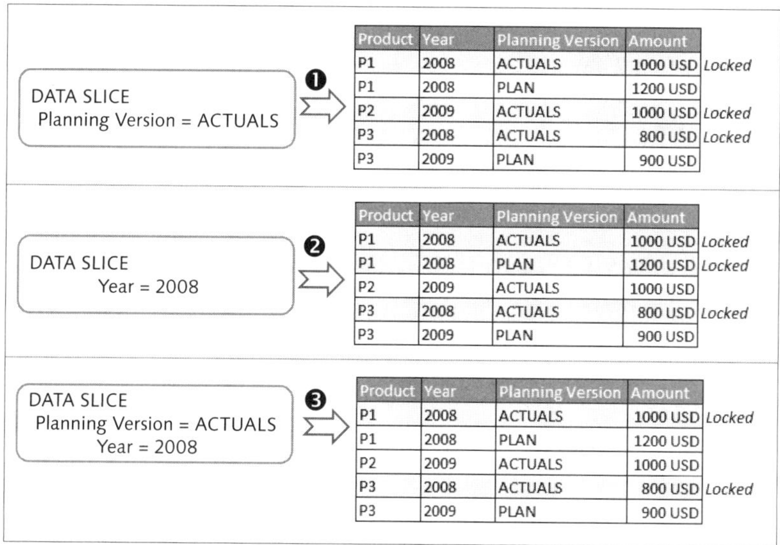

Figure 12.22 Data Slices

Let's see how to create data slices on a real-time InfoCube using the Planning Modeler:

1. Data slices are created on the INFOPROVIDER tab of the Planning Modeler. Click on the DATA SLICES tab page of the selected InfoProvider, as shown in ❶ of Figure 12.23.

Figure 12.23 Creating Data Slices

2. Click on the CREATE button to create a new data slice (❷ of Figure 12.23)
3. Maintain the description of the data slice, as shown in ❶ of Figure 12.24.
4. In the DATA SLICE BASED ON dropdown list, select FOR A SELECTION (❷ of Figure 12.24). This option allows you to maintain selections for different characteristic values that can be locked. If you want to define a custom and complicated logic for locking the plan data, you can define the data slice based on ABAP exits.

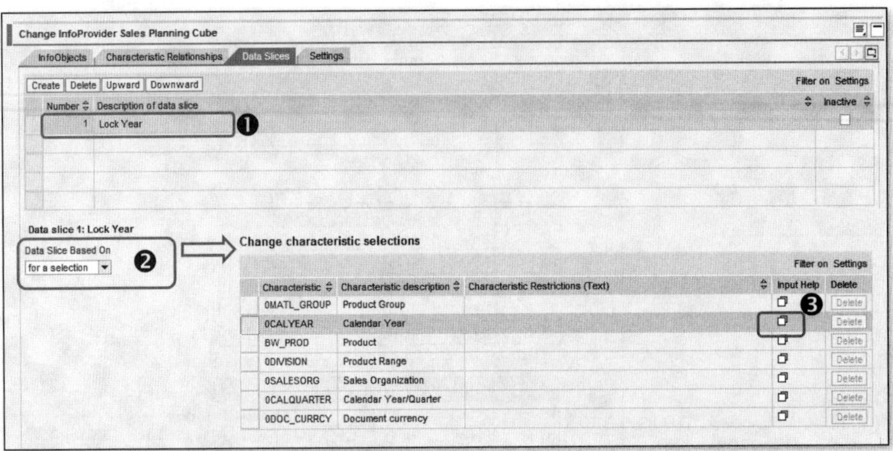

Figure 12.24 Define Data Slice

5. In the CHANGE CHARACTERISTIC SELECTIONS section, you can see a list of all characteristics included in the cube. Here is where you specify the selections that need to be locked. For example, if you want to protect the data for Calendar Year = 2009, lock this selection. To do this, select the characteristic 0CALYEAR, and click on INPUT HELP (see ❸ of Figure 12.24).
6. From the input help screen, select the value 2009 (❶ of Figure 12.25), and click on Add (❷) to include it in the chosen selections. Click OK (❸).

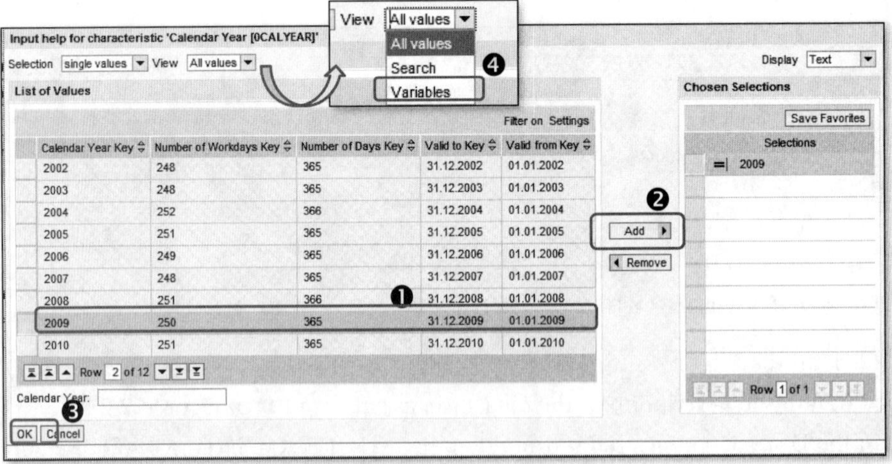

Figure 12.25 Define Selections for Data Slice

Note

This is an example of defining a data slice with fixed selection, but you can also use BEx variables to define a data slice. This option can be selected by selecting VARIABLES from the VIEW dropdown (❹ of Figure 12.25).

7. After you've defined all of the necessary selections for the data slice, click SAVE on the INFOPROVIDER tab (Figure 12.26).

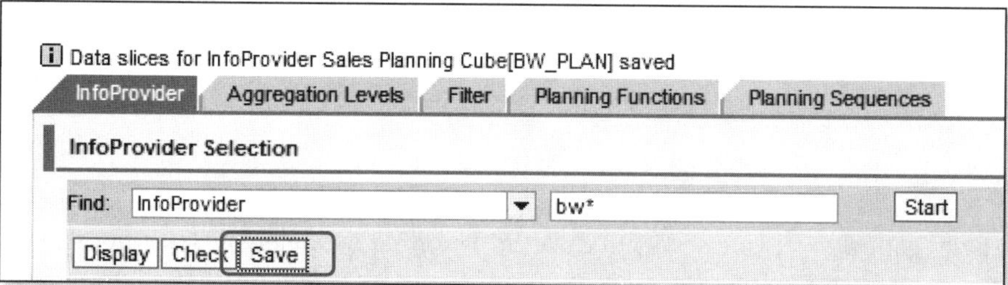

Figure 12.26 Saving Data Slices

If you're using the checkbox shown in Figure 12.27, you can create multiple data slices on an InfoProvider and toggle between the active and inactive modes.

Figure 12.27 Set Data Slices as Active/Inactive

Data Slice Without Any Selection

If you define a data slice on a real-time InfoProvider and then don't define any restrictions on any of the characteristic, the data slice blocks *all* values for the characteristics. In other words, the data slice locks the entire data set in the real-time InfoCube.

12.3.5 Aggregation Level

Aggregation levels (indicated by the [symbol] symbol) are InfoProviders specific to planning and are built as a subset of an underlying InfoProvider. In a simple scenario, an aggregation level can be built directly on a real-time InfoCube. In more complex situations, it's also possible to build an aggregation level on a MultiProvider. The prerequisite of the complex aggregation level is that the MultiProvider is based on at least one real-time InfoCube (see Figure 12.28).

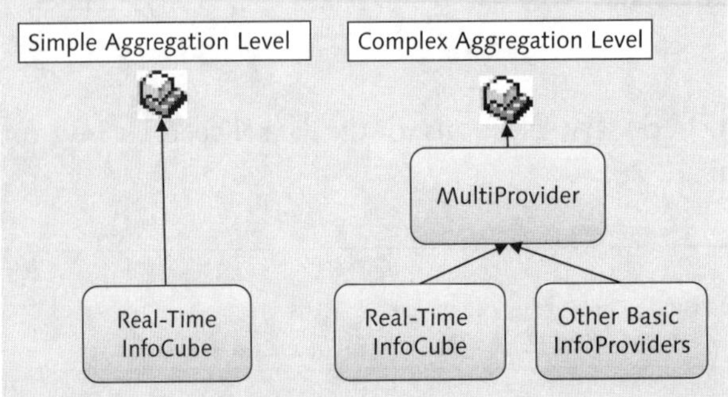

Figure 12.28 Types of Aggregation Levels

An aggregation level can be defined in the Planning Modeler by selecting specific characteristics and key figures from the underlying InfoProvider that are to be used for planning. The selected key figure values are aggregated for characteristics selected in an aggregation level, thus ignoring the characteristics that are not part of the aggregation level.

If some data is changed or edited for an aggregation level, the record is stored in the cube as # (i.e., not assigned) for all characteristics that aren't included in the aggregation level. We explain this concept with the help of Figure 12.29.

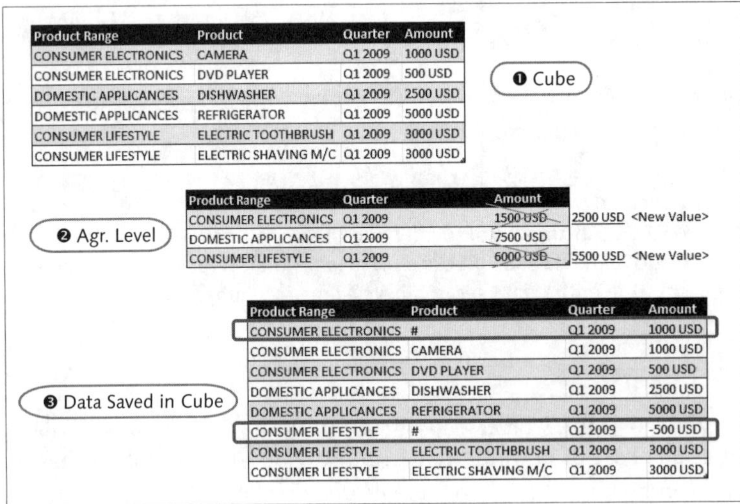

Product Range	Product	Quarter	Amount
CONSUMER ELECTRONICS	CAMERA	Q1 2009	1000 USD
CONSUMER ELECTRONICS	DVD PLAYER	Q1 2009	500 USD
DOMESTIC APPLICANCES	DISHWASHER	Q1 2009	2500 USD
DOMESTIC APPLICANCES	REFRIGERATOR	Q1 2009	5000 USD
CONSUMER LIFESTYLE	ELECTRIC TOOTHBRUSH	Q1 2009	3000 USD
CONSUMER LIFESTYLE	ELECTRIC SHAVING M/C	Q1 2009	3000 USD

Product Range	Quarter	Amount	
CONSUMER ELECTRONICS	Q1 2009	1500 USD	2500 USD <New Value>
DOMESTIC APPLICANCES	Q1 2009	7500 USD	
CONSUMER LIFESTYLE	Q1 2009	6000 USD	5500 USD <New Value>

Product Range	Product	Quarter	Amount
CONSUMER ELECTRONICS	#	Q1 2009	1000 USD
CONSUMER ELECTRONICS	CAMERA	Q1 2009	1000 USD
CONSUMER ELECTRONICS	DVD PLAYER	Q1 2009	500 USD
DOMESTIC APPLICANCES	DISHWASHER	Q1 2009	2500 USD
DOMESTIC APPLICANCES	REFRIGERATOR	Q1 2009	5000 USD
CONSUMER LIFESTYLE	#	Q1 2009	-500 USD
CONSUMER LIFESTYLE	ELECTRIC TOOTHBRUSH	Q1 2009	3000 USD
CONSUMER LIFESTYLE	ELECTRIC SHAVING M/C	Q1 2009	3000 USD

Figure 12.29 Not Assigned (#) Values

The InfoCube stores the data for the following characteristics: product range, product, and quarter (❶ of Figure 12.29). The aggregation level is defined at the product range and quarter level, so the data is aggregated for the characteristics that are included in the aggregation level (❷). Now, if the data is changed at this level, the changes to the data are saved in the cube (❸). The values for the product characteristic are saved as Not Assigned (#).

Let's explain how to create an aggregation level on a real-time InfoCube using the Planning Modeler. For the example scenario explained earlier in this chapter, the planning is done at two different levels, the product range level and the product level, so we must create these two aggregation levels as described next:

1. Go to the AGGREGATION LEVEL tab of the Planning Modeler, and click on CREATE to create a new aggregation level. (Figure 12.30). A pop-up screen appears.

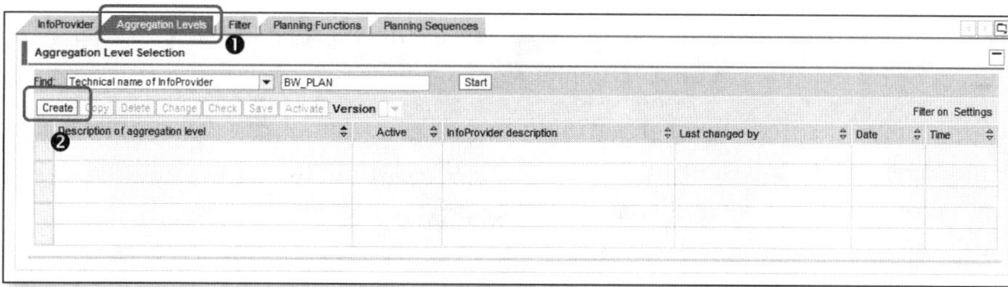

Figure 12.30 Create a New Aggregation Level

2. Enter the TECHNICAL NAME and DESCRIPTION of the aggregation level, as shown in ❶ of Figure 12.31. Select the InfoProvider over which you want to build the aggregation level (❷), and click on TRANSFER (❸).

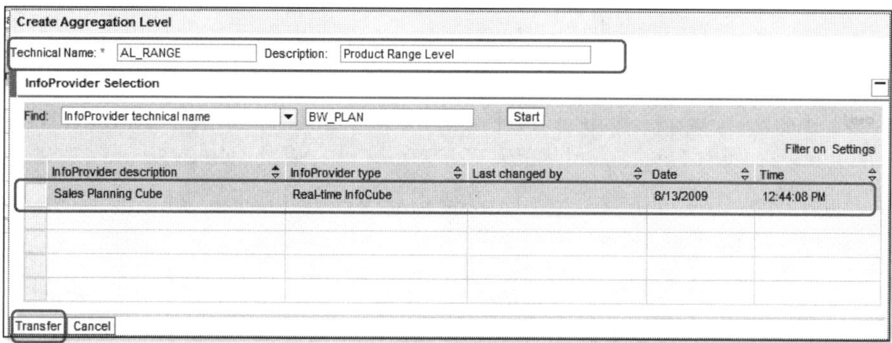

Figure 12.31 InfoProvider Selection

3. A list of all of the characteristics and key figures is displayed. You can define the aggregation level by selecting the specific characteristics and key figures, as shown in Figure 12.32.

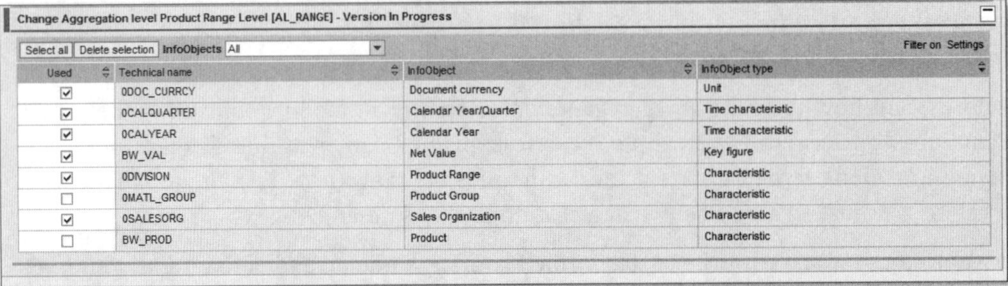

Figure 12.32 Define Aggregation Level

Note that the Product InfoObject isn't selected in the aggregation level because the planning is done at the product range level.

4. After you've defined the aggregation level, save it. You also have to activate the level to be able to use it for further planning development. Use the buttons shown in Figure 12.33 to save and activate the aggregation level.

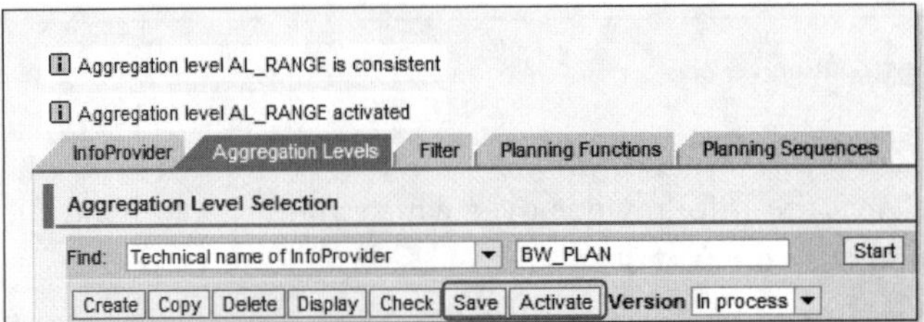

Figure 12.33 Save and Activate the Aggregation Level

A similar procedure can be followed to build different aggregation levels. For example, you can create a new aggregation level with the technical name "AL_PROD" and the description "Product Level" on the BW_PLAN InfoCube, as shown in Figure 12.34.

This level can be used to build the planning functions and layout, which will enable planning at the product level.

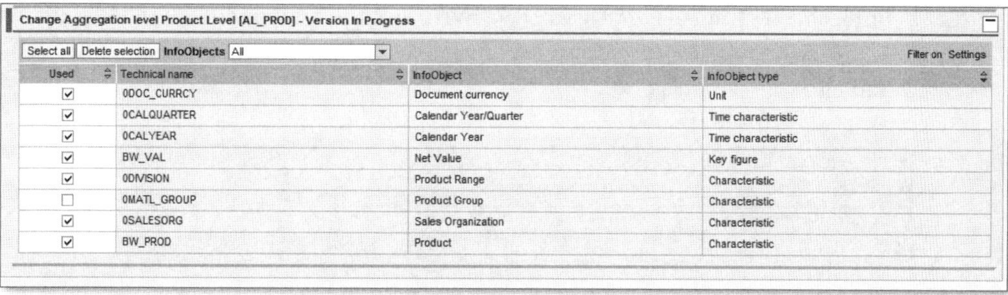

Used	Technical name	InfoObject	InfoObject type
☑	0DOC_CURRCY	Document currency	Unit
☑	0CALQUARTER	Calendar Year/Quarter	Time characteristic
☑	0CALYEAR	Calendar Year	Time characteristic
☑	BW_VAL	Net Value	Key figure
☑	0DIVISION	Product Range	Characteristic
☐	0MATL_GROUP	Product Group	Characteristic
☑	0SALESORG	Sales Organization	Characteristic
☑	BW_PROD	Product	Characteristic

Figure 12.34 Create Aggregation Level for Product Level Planning

12.3.6 Planning Filter

Planning filters are the subset of data contained in an aggregation level and are defined by putting specific selections on characteristics from the aggregation level. These filters can either be used in the input-ready queries to restrict data or to execute a planning function. An aggregation level can have multiple planning filters, whereas a planning filter can relate to one and only one aggregation level.

When you execute a planning function on a planning filter, it's executed for only the data that is selected in the planning filter. For example, if you enter Year = 2009 in the filter and execute the delete planning function, only those records with the year listed as 2009 are deleted.

The procedure to create planning filters is explained next:

1. To create planning filters, go to the FILTER tab in the Planning Modeler (❶ of Figure 12.35), and click on CREATE (❷). This gives you a pop-up screen where you define the filter.

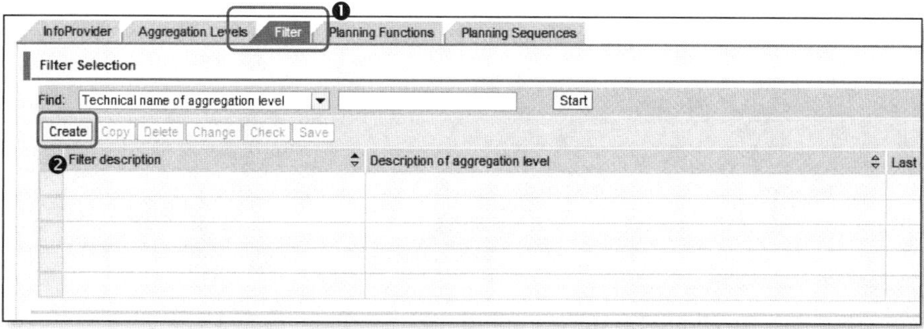

Figure 12.35 Create Filter

2. Enter the TECHNICAL NAME and DESCRIPTION of the filter as shown in ❶ of Figure 12.36. Select the Aggregation Level over which you want to build the filter (❷), and click on TRANSFER (❸).

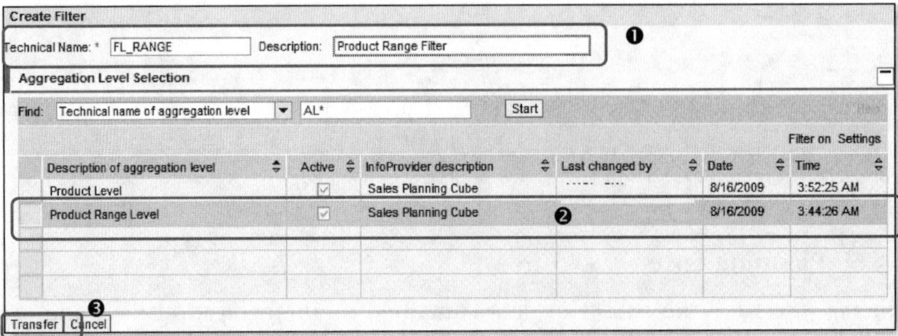

Figure 12.36 Select Aggregation Level

3. When you click on TRANSFER, the screen shown in Figure 12.37 is displayed. You can maintain the filter here. Add the characteristics that need to be included in the filter by selecting them from the dropdown list (❶) and clicking on the ADD button. You can use ADD ALL (❷) to include all of the characteristics from the aggregation level. Similarly, the buttons REMOVE and REMOVE ALL (❸) can be used to remove the characteristics from the filter.

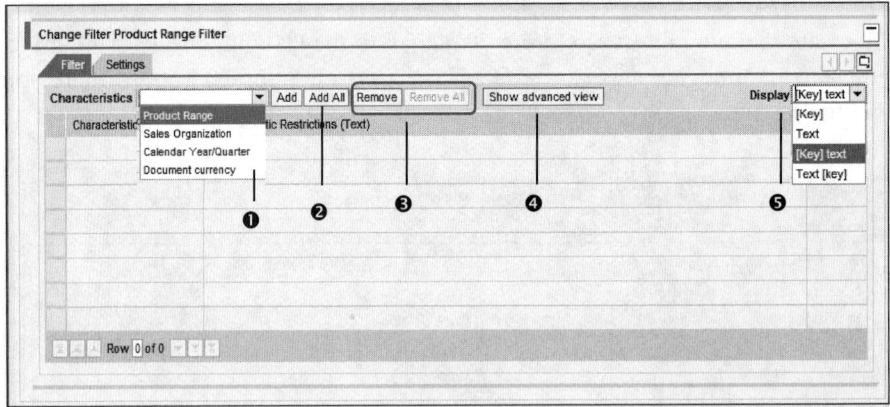

Figure 12.37 Change Filter Screen

A detailed view of the filter can be displayed using the SHOW ADVANCED VIEW button (❹). Also, the display of the Test and/or Key characteristics can be selected from the dropdown list on the right (❺).

Add all of the characteristics from the aggregation level using Add All, and set the display of the Filter to [Key] Text.

4. The next step is to restrict the characteristics in the filter. Use Input Help to define the characteristic restrictions (see Figure 12.38).

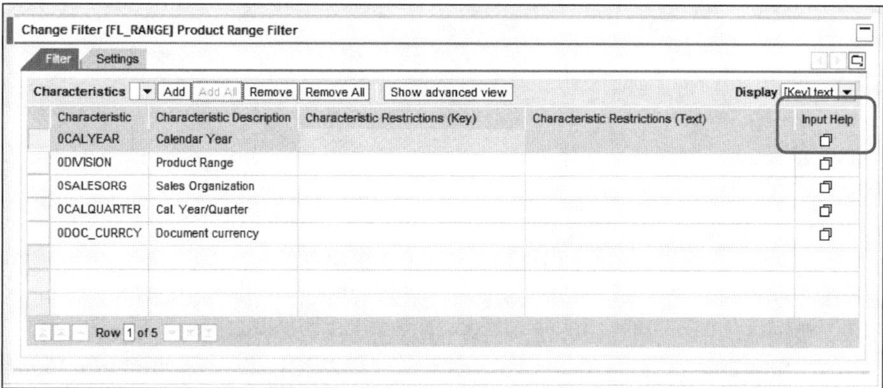

Figure 12.38 Input Help for Filter Characteristic

You can restrict the characteristic either with some fixed values or with characteristic variables. The OLAP characteristic variables built on the selected characteristic are available for restriction. In this example, we restrict the calendar year characteristic (0CALYEAR) with a variable.

5. Select the Variables view from the dropdown list (❶ of Figure 12.39), and the list of variables built on the characteristic is displayed. Select the variable with which you want to restrict the characteristic (❷). Click on ADD to add the selected variable to the selections (❸). Finally, click OK to get back to the main filter definition screen (❹).

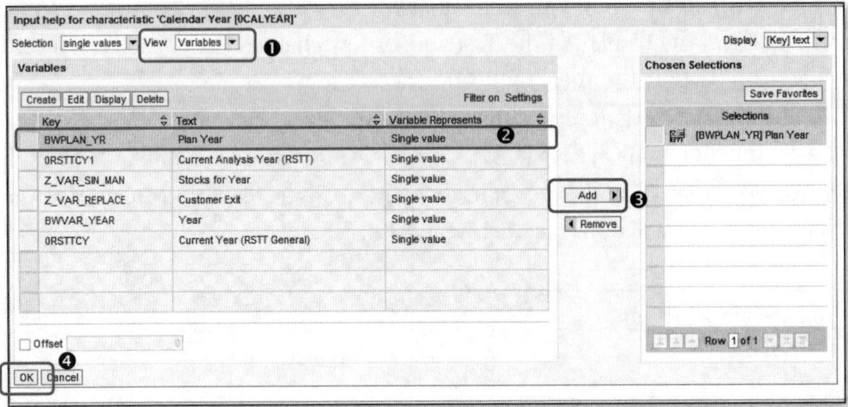

Figure 12.39 Restrict Characteristic with a Variable

In this case (Figure 12.39), the characteristic 0CALYEAR is restricted with a user entry variable BWPLAN_YR that has a single mandatory entry. The use of variables in filters increases the flexibility of the planning application, as the filters — and the data for the planning — are determined at runtime.

6. Restrict the remaining characteristics of the FL_RANGE filter as shown in Figure 12.40.

Change Filter [FL_RANGE] Product Range Filter

Filter | Settings

Characteristics | Add | Add All | Remove | Remove All | Show advanced view — Display [Key] text

Characteristic	Characteristic Description	Characteristic Restrictions (Key)	Characteristic Restrictions (Text)	Input Help
0CALYEAR	Calendar Year	BWPLAN_YR	Plan Year	
0DIVISION	Product Range	CL;CE;DA	CL; CE; DA	
0SALESORG	Sales Organization	BW_SORG	Sales Organization	
0CALQUARTER	Cal. Year/Quarter	!#	!Not assigned	
0DOC_CURRCY	Document currency	USD	United States Dollar	

Row 1 of 5

Figure 12.40 Define Filter Restrictions

Note that the characteristic sales organization (0SALESORG) is also restricted with a user entry variable, BW_SORG, which has a single mandatory entry. Also note that the value for 0CALQUARTER is set to !# (which means it isn't equal to not assigned).

7. After you've maintained all of the necessary restrictions to the filter, save it using the SAVE button available under the Filter tab (see Figure 12.41).

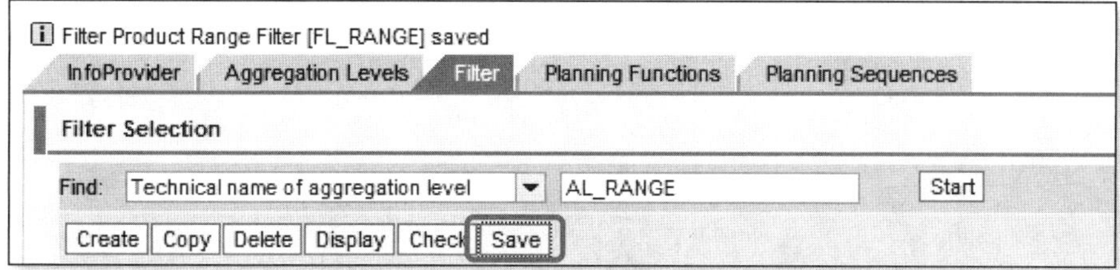

Figure 12.41 Save Planning Filter

You can now build another planning filter, FL_PROD (product filter), on the product level aggregation level. The restriction is shown in Figure 12.42.

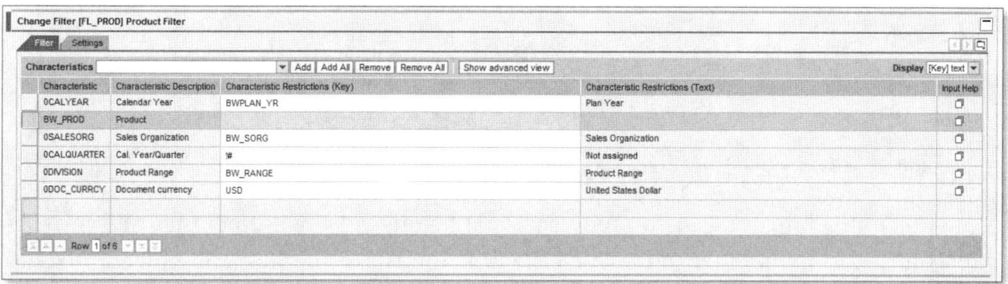

Figure 12.42 Create Product Filter

Here the product range (0DIVISION) characteristic is restricted with the BW_RANGE user entry variable, which has a single mandatory entry. Also, note that there is no restriction defined for the product (BW_PROD) characteristic. This means that all of the values of the product characteristic are available for planning. During planning, we'll be using characteristic relationships for the validation and proposal of product values.

Creating Planning Filters from BEx query designer

The planning filters are the same as the filters built on queries using BEx query designer. Planning filters can be created using the Planning Modeler, Planning Wizard, or the BEx query designer. If you're using BEx query designer for creating planning filters, the aggregation level should be selected as the InfoProvider.

12.3.7 Planning Functions

To facilitate automatic create/change/delete on the plan data, Integrated Planning delivers some prebuilt functions (standard functions) for use in the planning model. It also provides you an option to create/define your own custom planning function using ABAP, if needed. A planning function is built on an aggregation level but is always executed with a filter, so a planning function can be used by multiple planning filters based on the same aggregation level (see Figure 12.43).

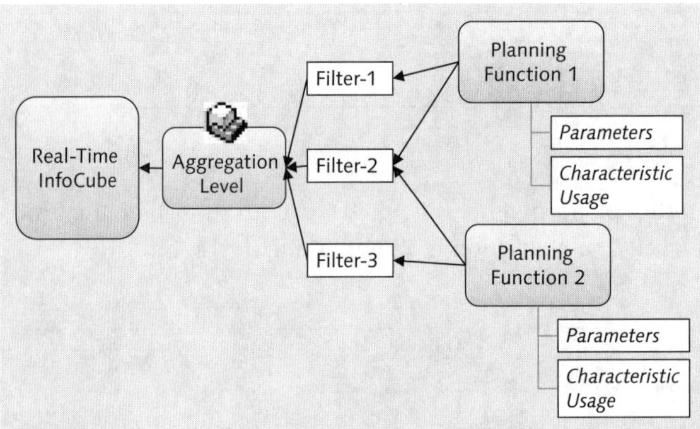

Figure 12.43 Planning Functions

A planning function can edit only data that belongs to a real-time InfoCube and that is included in the filter over which the function is executed, often known as data to be changed. However, a planning function can also read data from other types of InfoProviders or data that is out of the filter selection, just for reference. This is often known as *reference data.*

Before we explain each of the available standard functions, let's learn how to create a planning function based on an available standard function type. To create a planning function, go to the PLANNING FUNCTIONS tab in the Planning Modeler, and click on CREATE, as shown in Figure 12.44. A pop-up entry screen appears.

In the pop-up screen, select one of the available planning function types from the dropdown list (❶ of Figure 12.45). (We'll discuss each of these standard planning function types in subsequent sections.)

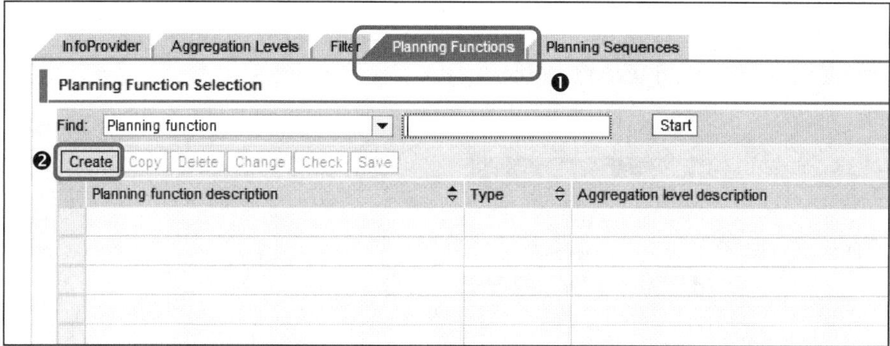

Figure 12.44 Planning Functions Tab Page

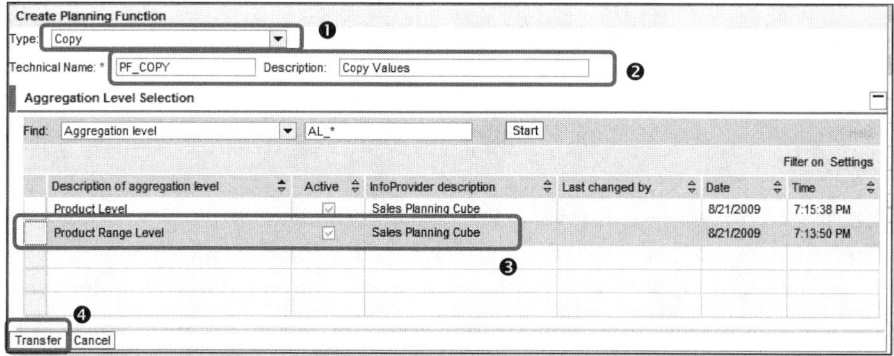

Figure 12.45 Create Planning Function

Enter the technical name and description for the planning function (❷ of Figure 12.45). Select an aggregation level over which the planning function has to be created (❸). After you define all of these settings, click on TRANSFER to create the planning function (❹).

A planning function is created in two steps:

- Define characteristic usage
- Define parameter values

Under Characteristic Usage, you can select different characteristics from the aggregation level that will be used in the planning function. A characteristic can be classified as a field to be changed or as a field to be used in conditions. The characteristics that aren't selected to be changed remain constant and aren't used and affected by the execution of the planning function.

To determine the fields to be changed, you have to first determine the characteristics for which the values are to be created/updated/deleted in a planning function. Let's look at the example shown in Figure 12.46.

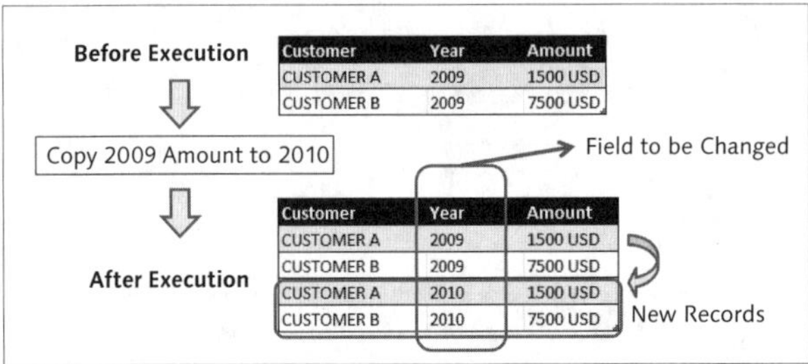

Figure 12.46 Field to Be Changed

Assume you want to copy the amount key figure from the year 2009 to 2010 for all customers. In this case, if you compare the records before and after the execution of the planning function, the value of the year characteristic changes from 2009 to 2010. So, for the Copy function in this example, the year is selected as a field to be changed.

Using characteristics as fields for conditions, you can define distinct processing for different characteristic values of the field selected. For the example shown in Figure 12.47, you want to copy the year 2009 key figure values to the year 2010 values with a *revaluation*. However, you also want to define different processing logic for Customer A and Customer B. So, in this case (Figure 12.47), the customer characteristic is the field for condition, and the year characteristic is the field to be changed.

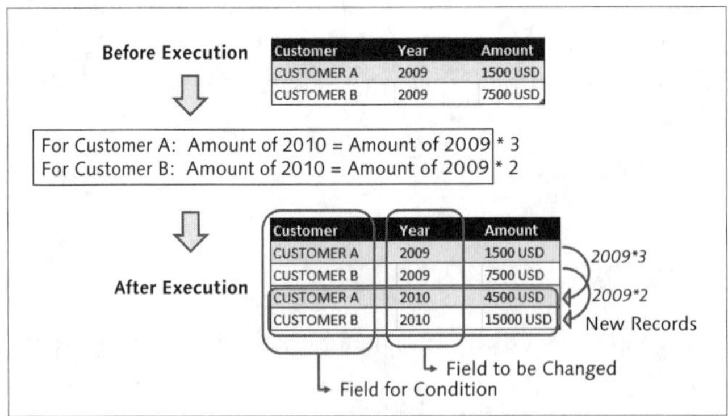

Figure 12.47 Field for Conditions

After the characteristics to be used in a planning function are identified, you can define the specific conditions and rules under Parameters. You can define multiple parameters for different values of characteristics selected as fields for conditions. However, if no characteristic is selected for conditions, only one parameter is sufficient. In this case, the entire data in the selection is processed with the same parameters.

In the following sections, we explain the different types of standard planning functions available and their use in a planning model.

Copy

The Copy function is used to copy the key figure values from one characteristic combination to other combination. In this function, you can define the From values as the source for copying and the To values as the target.

The From values are treated as reference data and are accessed only for reads by the Copy function; so it isn't necessary to include the From values in the filter over which the planning function is executed. On the other hand, upon execution of the copy planning function, the data in the To values changes. So, it's necessary to include the To values of the data in the filter over which the function has to be executed.

Let's build a Copy function for our example scenario, assuming you want to copy the values from the previous year to the current year (Figure 12.48). The current year is entered by the user, and the previous year is derived from the current year.

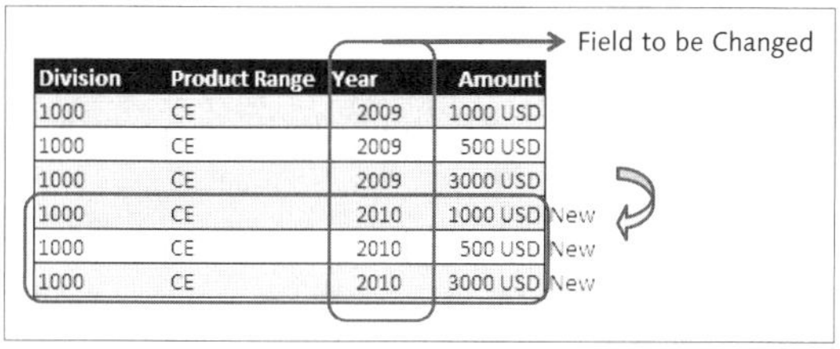

Field to be Changed

Division	Product Range	Year	Amount	
1000	CE	2009	1000 USD	
1000	CE	2009	500 USD	
1000	CE	2009	3000 USD	
1000	CE	2010	1000 USD	New
1000	CE	2010	500 USD	New
1000	CE	2010	3000 USD	New

Figure 12.48 Copy Function Example

As shown in Figure 12.48, the field to be changed is Year. By specifying fields in conditions, you can also define different parameters for different values of characteristics chosen for a condition. The procedure to define the copy planning function is explained here:

1. Create a copy planning function by following the procedure mentioned in the beginning of section 12.3.7. Use the technical name "PF_COPY" and description

"Copy from Previous Year" on the aggregation level for product range planning (AL_RANGE).

2. Select Calendar Year as the field to changed, as shown in ❶ of Figure 12.49. Then click on *To Parameters* (❷).

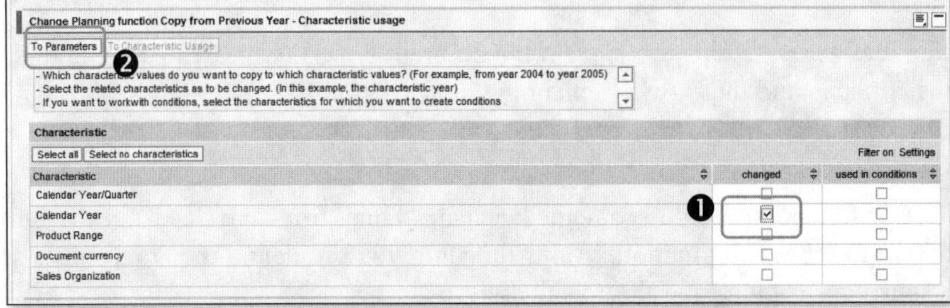

Figure 12.49 Characteristic Usage for Copy Function

3. On the Parameter screen, first select the key figures that need to be copied. For our example, select Net Value (BW_VAL), as shown in ❶ of Figure 12.50.

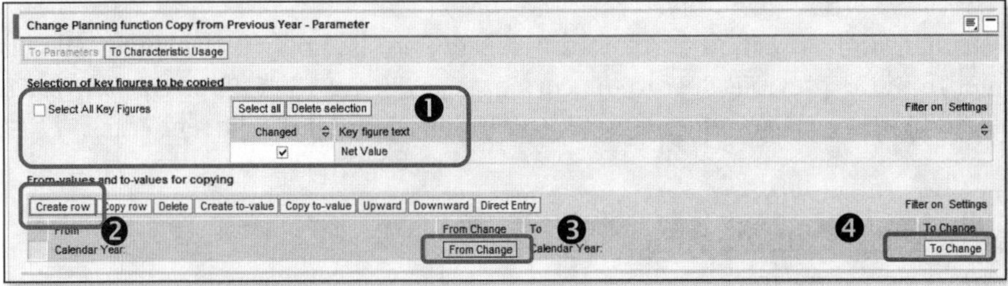

Figure 12.50 Define Parameters for Copy Function

4. To define the copy logic, you must specify the From and To values for the Copy function. Click on CREATE ROW (❷) to create the first row where you can specify From and To values.
5. Click on FROM CHANGE (❸) to specify the From values for copying.
6. As mentioned earlier in this section, you must copy the values from the previous year based on the variable value entered by the user. The variable used here is BWPLAN_YR (refer to Figure 12.39 earlier in this chapter). We use the same variable to derive the From values for the Copy function. As shown in ❶ of Figure 12.51, select the VARIABLES view from the dropdown list, and select Plan Year (❷).

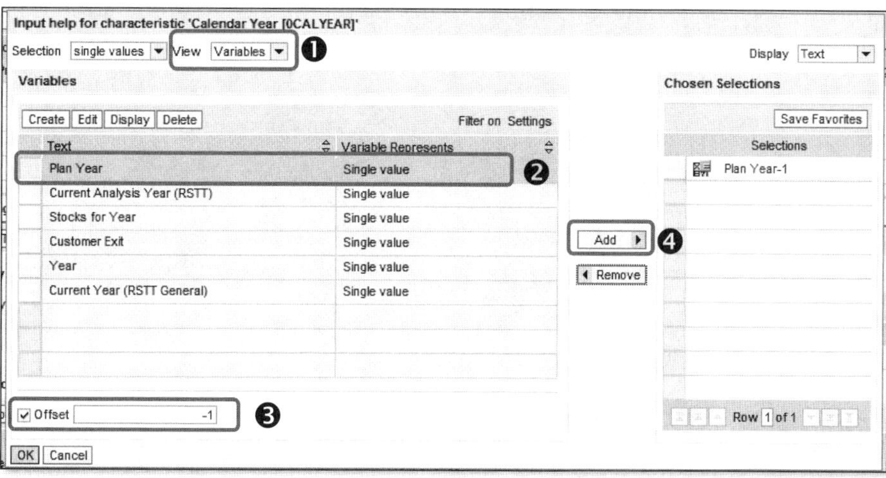

Figure 12.51 Use of Variable in Copy Planning Function

The logic to derive the previous year can be built by setting an offset on the value of user entry variable. Select the OFFSET checkbox (❸), and specify an offset of -1. Finally, click on ADD (❹) to choose the From value, and click OK to return to the main planning function definition screen. You can see that the From value is listed as Plan Year -1, that is, the previous year.

7. Similarly, restrict the To values for the Copy function by clicking on *To Change* (❹ of Figure 12.50, earlier in this chapter). Select PLAN YEAR without offset, as shown in Figure 12.52.

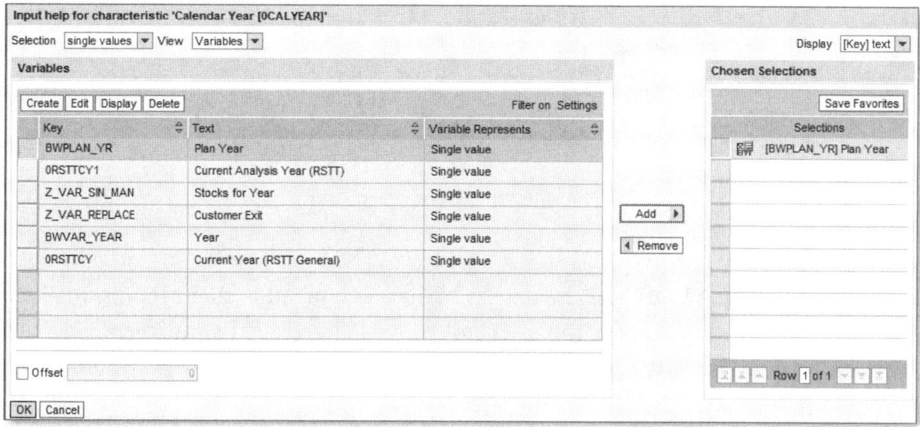

Figure 12.52 Define To Values for Copy Function

8. Finally, save the planning function by clicking on the SAVE button on the Planning Functions tab (Figure 12.53).

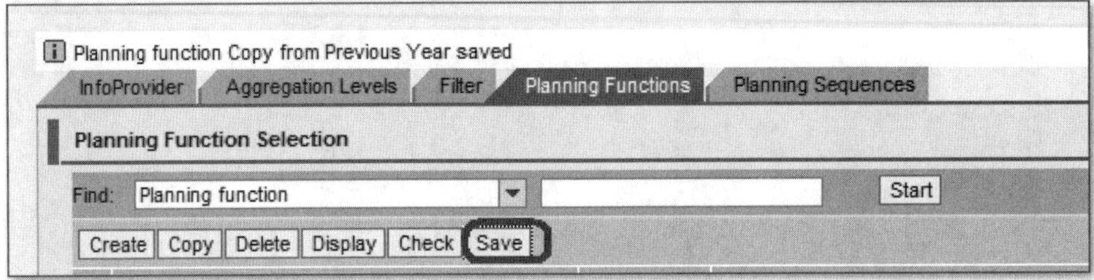

Figure 12.53 Save Planning Function

Note

When you use the copy planning function, the To values always get overwritten with the From values. This happens even when the From values are zero. The Copy function will set the To values to zero in this specific case.

Repost

The Repost function is used to change the characteristic values of existing plan data included in the selection of planning functions. For example, assume client representative CR1 has some sales target for a customer in his sales area, but now the target has to be shifted to client representative CR2 because the customer served by CR1 has now moved to the sales area where CR2 is responsible (Figure 12.54). The Repost function is useful in such a scenario.

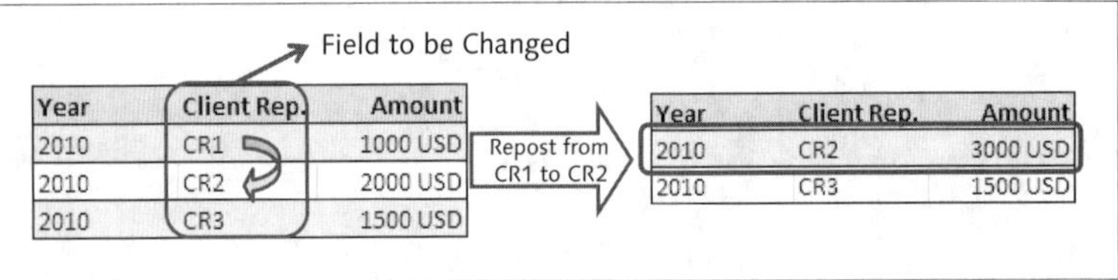

Figure 12.54 Example of Repost Function

In this case (Figure 12.54), the characteristic that is changed is client representative. You define the parameters for the selected to be changed field(s) by specifying the From and To values. This means that From values will be replaced by To values.

Upon execution, the reposted values are "added" to the existing To values. As shown in Figure 12.54, when CR1 is reposted as CR2, the value $1000 USD from CR1 is "added" to CR2, making the total of CR2 $3000.

The Repost function is defined and works in a way similar to that of the Copy function (see Figure 12.55). In this case, the From values are copied to the To values for the existing records in the given selection, and then the records with From values are deleted.

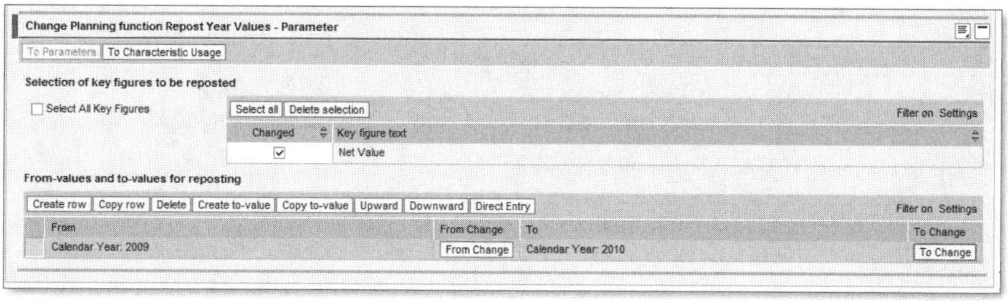

Figure 12.55 Define Repost Function

The Repost function shown in Figure 12.55 replaces Calendar Year = 2010 for all those records in the selection where Calendar Year = 2009.

Note

For a Repost function, the From and To values are always single values.

We've seen that the Repost function actually affects the data that is included in both From and To values. This means that for the Repost function to work, both From and To values must be included in the filter on which the function is executed.

Repost by Characteristic Relationships

This standard planning function reposts values from characteristics based on the characteristic relationships. This function is particularly useful when you want to correct already-entered data and make it consistent with the characteristic relationship.

For example, consider a situation where you've defined a characteristic relationship that derives the value of product group from product. Data is entered at the product level, and product group is derived based on this characteristic relationship (Figure 12.56). So, if you enter a record for Product = LCD TV, the value Product Group = Video is derived.

Now assume that, due to some organizational restructuring in 2010, a new product group called "Entertainment" is introduced, and now Product = LCD TV belongs to Product Group = Entertainment. A new planning record that gets posted in 2010 for Product = LCD TV will get saved with Product Group = Entertainment in the cube, as shown in Figure 12.56. This new relationship makes the record 1 from Figure 12.56

invalid. To correct the previously entered records, you must define the Repost by Characteristic Relationships planning function.

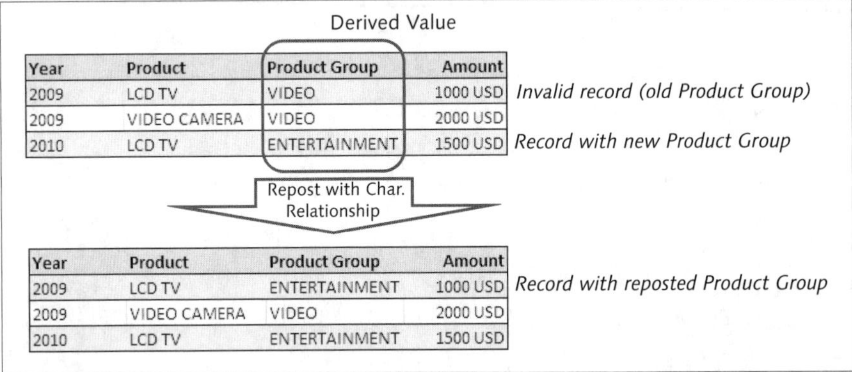

Figure 12.56 Repost with Characteristic Relationship

> **Note**
>
> This function is relevant only for those characteristics that are "derived" using characteristic relationships.

To define this function on an aggregation level, the aggregation level should *include all* of the InfoObjects from the real-time InfoCube. Also, you can create this function only on an aggregation level that is built directly on a real-time InfoCube.

You can define the characteristic use for this planning function by selecting the fields that need to be reposted as fields to be changed (Figure 12.57).

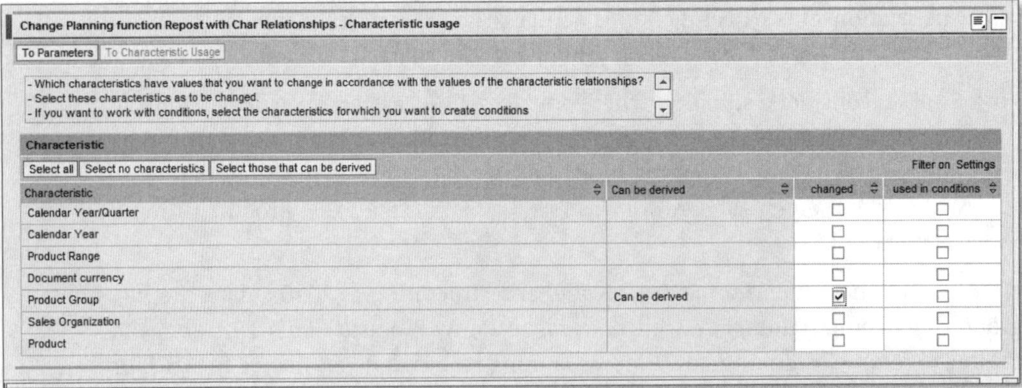

Figure 12.57 Define Function: Repost with Characteristic Relationship

You have to define only define the characteristic usage for creating this planning function. Because the values are reposted based on the logic defined in characteristic relationships, this planning function doesn't have any parameters.

Delete

This standard planning function is used to delete the key figure values of the data included in the selection. In the definition of the Delete function, you have to specify the key figures that need to be deleted for selected records (Figure 12.58).

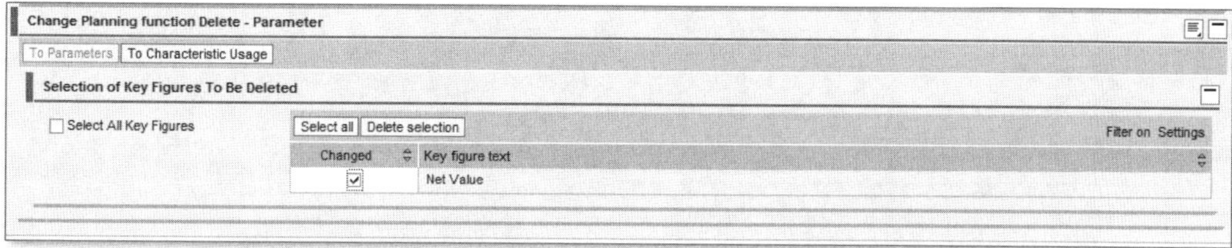

Figure 12.58 Define Delete Function

> **Note**
>
> When you delete a particular record using this planning function, it actually sets the key figures values to zero for that characteristic combination.

Generate Combinations

The *Generate Combinations* function type is used to generate blank records for an aggregation level. This function is dependent on characteristic relationships defined on the real-time InfoCube. The blank records are created for those combinations that are valid per the master data and characteristic relationship.

You don't have to define any parameters for this planning function. All valid combinations of characteristic values are generated based on characteristic restrictions defined at the filter over which this planning function is executed.

Delete Invalid Combinations

If you want to delete the key figure values for all of those records whose characteristic combinations aren't valid (as per characteristic relationships), you can use the *Delete Invalid Combinations* standard planning function type. This function is based on the characteristic relationships defined on the real-time InfoCube.

This function is dependent on characteristic relationships and can be executed only on an aggregation level that includes all InfoObjects of the real-time InfoCube.

Forecasting

Forecasting is one of the advanced planning functions available in Integrated Planning. This planning function uses different statistical forecasting methods to derive the plan values based on already-existing data (Figure 12.59).

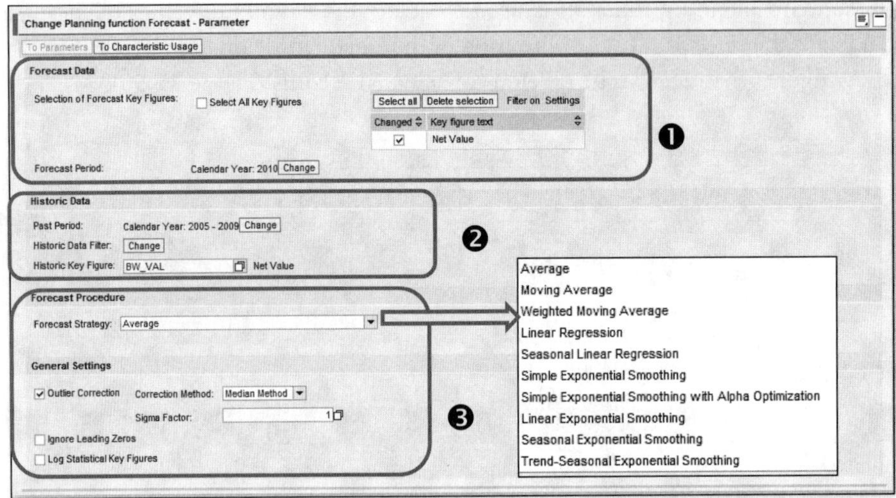

Figure 12.59 Forecasting Planning Function

To define a Forecasting planning function, you first have to specify the key figure and the period for which you want to generate the forecast data (❶ of Figure 12.59). The next step is to define the set of historical data that should be used to derive the forecast values (❷). For this, you have to set the data range and selection for the historical data, and also the key figure to which should be referred.

Finally, you have to define the forecasting settings for the planning function (❸). Here you can select the FORECAST STRATEGY from the available set of standard forecasting methods.

Revaluation

As the name suggests, the Revaluation planning function type is used to recalculate the key figure values for the records included in the selection. The key figure values can be increased or decreased by a percentage factor defined in the planning function. However, the characteristic values of data remain unchanged if this function is executed.

You can define a Revaluation planning function for all of the key figures in the selected set of data. Also, you can define each key figure to be revaluated separately with a different revaluation factor (❶ of Figure 12.60).

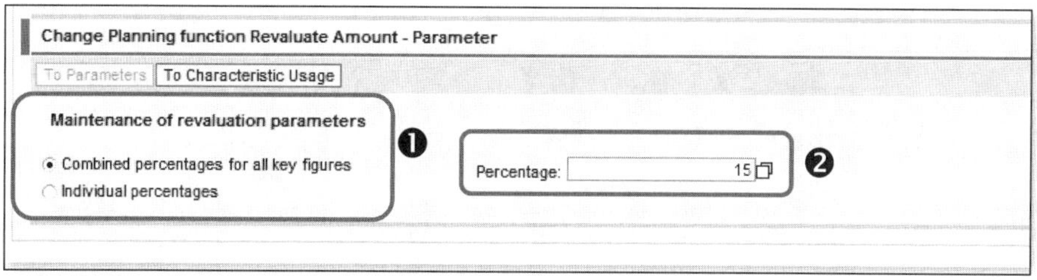

Change Planning function Revaluate Amount - Parameter
To Parameters | To Characteristic Usage
Maintenance of revaluation parameters
Combined percentages for all key figures
Individual percentages
❶
Percentage: 15
❷

Figure 12.60 Define Revaluation Planning Function

Define the revaluation factor as shown in ❷ of Figure 12.60. The revaluation logic with which the new value is calculated can be represented as follows:

```
New Value = {1 + (Revaluation Percentage/100)}* Existing Value
```

To add more flexibility to the planning application, you can use user entry variables for the revaluation factor. The key figure values will be revaluated dynamically based on the user input.

Distribution by Key

In a typical top-down planning scenario, the values planned at a higher level are transferred to a lower level for planning. The Distribution function is used to distribute the values from one level of planning to another level of planning. This distribution can happen either based on some already existing reference data, or by using a distribution key where the distribution weighting factors are defined.

We discussed the significance of Not Assigned (#) in SAP NetWeaver BW Integrated Planning in Section 12.3.5, Aggregation Level. The Distribution function can be used to bring consistency to the data between aggregation levels by eliminating the Not Assigned (#) values.

In the case of the Distribution by Key function, the characteristics that are used to distribute the data are selected as fields to be changed. You have to then define the distribution weight with respect to the characteristics values by which distribution should take place.

To define the parameters for Distribution by Key, you have to first select the key figures that need to be distributed (❶ of Figure 12.61).

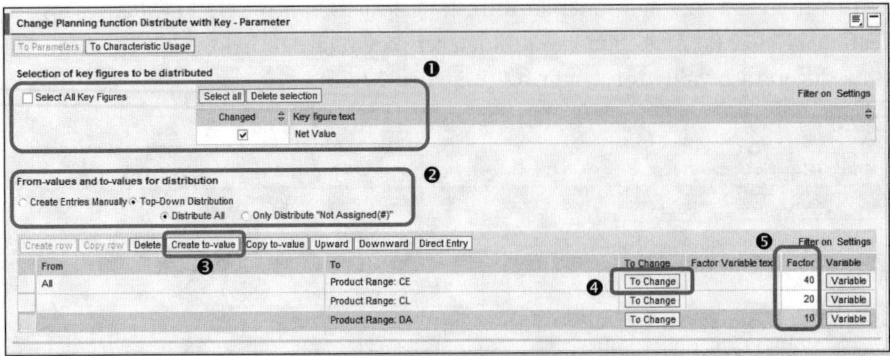

Figure 12.61 Define Planning Function Distribution with Key

Then you have to specify the source for the distribution function (❷). Following are the multiple options available.

- **Create Entries Manually:** This option can be used if you want to distribute data from a specific characteristic value to one or more specific characteristic values. In this case, you maintain the From and To values manually.
- **Top-Down Distribution:** This option follows the typical top-down distribution logic. The values for the records in selection are redistributed per the distribution key defined. There are two options for top-down distribution:
  - **Distribute All:** The total of the values in selection is redistributed per the distribution key defined.
  - **Only Distribute "Not Assigned (#)":** Only the record where characteristic value isn't Assigned (#) is distributed to other records in the selection where characteristic value exists. This option can be used to eliminate the # records by distributing its value to other records.

The next step is to maintain the distribution key. To create each new entry in the distribution key, you have to click CREATE TO-VALUE (❸). The specific To values can be selected by clicking on the TO CHANGE button (❹).

The distribution factors are maintained in the Factor column (❺). However, you can also use variables to determine the distribution factors.

Note that the distribution weight is calculated based on the relative weight of the factors, so it isn't necessary for the sum of the factors to be 100%. For the example shown in Figure 12.61, the product range CE will get a value that is double the value product range CL will get. Similarly, product range DA will get a value that is half the value CL will get.

Distribution by Reference Data

The Distribution by Reference function is defined the same way as you define the Distribution by Key planning function. Additionally, you have to select the characteristics that are used to define the reference data. The values included in the planning filter selection are distributed with respect to the mentioned reference data. The planning function parameter screen for distribution with reference data is explained in Figure 12.62.

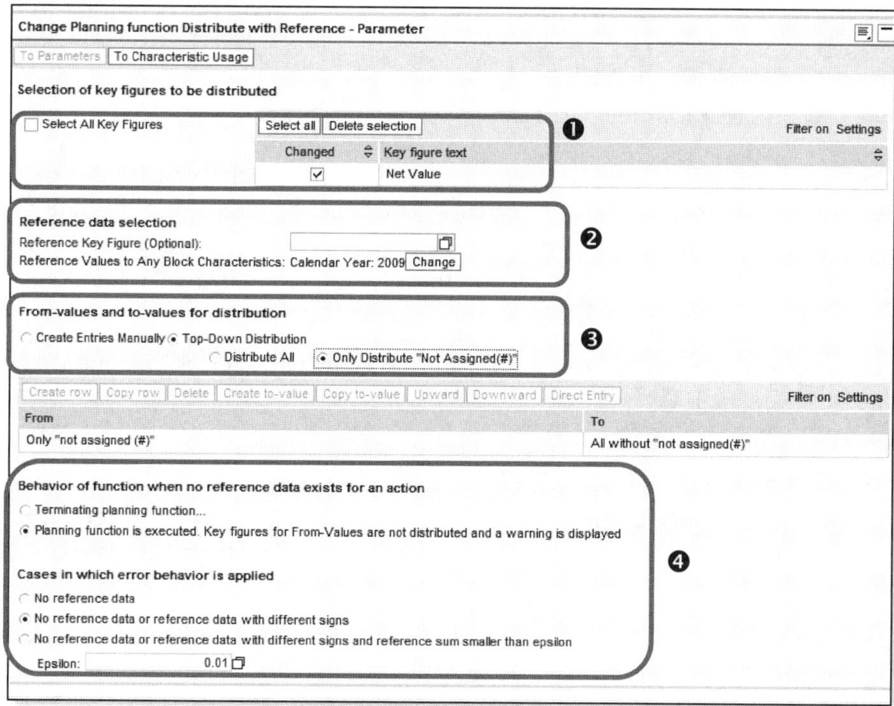

Figure 12.62 Distribution by Reference Data

Similar to the Distribution with Key function, you must select the key figure that needs to be distributed (❶). The next step is to define the reference data that should be used for distribution (❷). In the example shown in Figure 12.62, the Net Value key figure for the data in selection is distributed per the data for calendar year 2009. Further, select the method of distribution (❸) from the available options. You can also define the error handling for this function if there is no relevant reference data (❹).

Currency Translation

The Currency Translation planning function type is useful in a scenario where planning is performed in multiple currencies. The values entered in different currencies can be translated to a uniform currency using this function.

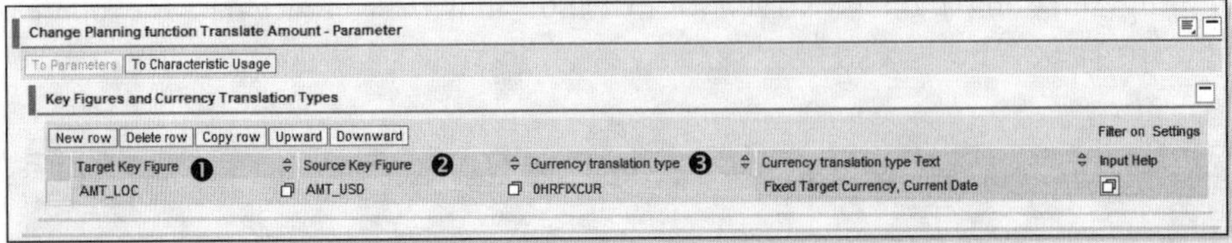

Figure 12.63 Currency Translation Function

To define the currency translation function, specify the key figure that needs to be translated in the column source key figure (❷ of Figure 12.63). Also, include the key figure where the translated values will be stored (❶). Both the source and target currency could be the same key figure; in this case, the translated values of the key figure overwrite the original values.

You must also specify the currency translation type, which decides how the values should be translated (❸).

Unit Conversion

This function is similar to the Currency Translation function discussed earlier. It's used when the planning is performed for a quantity involving multiple units of measure.

Similar to Currency Translation, to define the parameters of a Unit Conversion planning function, you have to specify the source unit, target unit, and the type for unit conversion.

Formula

This planning function is often referred to as the FOX (Formula Extension) function. The FOX function provides you with an enhanced formula editor that you can use to define your own processing logic.

The different options for building a function in the Formula Editor are listed here:

- Data access read, write, or reference
- Ability to read the values from BEx variables and master data attributes

- Use of internal programming components such as internal variables and constants
- Standard formula functions (logical, Boolean, data, string, etc.)
- Loop functions
- Calls to ABAP function modules

The parameter screen for the Formula planning function is shown in Figure 12.64.

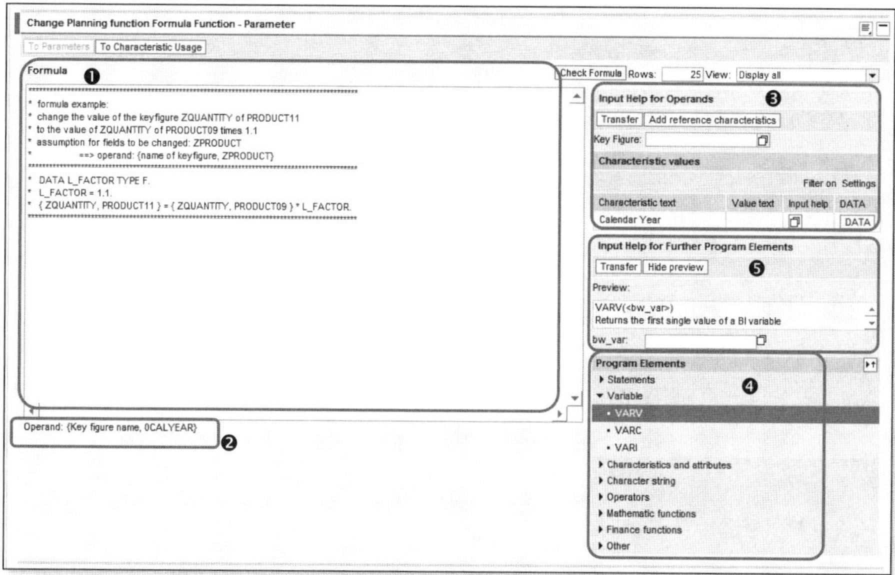

Figure 12.64 Formula Function Parameter Screen

You can write your planning function in the formula editor on the Parameter screen (❶ of Figure 12.64). The operands for writing the formula are based on the key figure and characteristic usage settings for the function. We've used 0CALYEAR as the field to be changed, so the operand is `{key figure name, 0CALYEAR}` (❷). You can also use the help available on operands when creating a formula (❸).

If you want to use additional programming elements to create the Formula function, you can choose from a variety of elements available under the PROGRAM ELEMENTS section (❹). The input help for the selected program element, its syntax, and a brief description is displayed under the PREVIEW section (❺).

An example of the formula with operand `{key figure name, 0CALYEAR}` is

```
{BW_VAL, 2010} = {BW_VAL, 2009}*1.25.
```

This formula calculates the values for key figure BW_VAL for the year 2010 by multiplying the corresponding 2009 values by a factor of 1.25.

For more complex formulas, you can use the available program elements (see Figure 12.65).

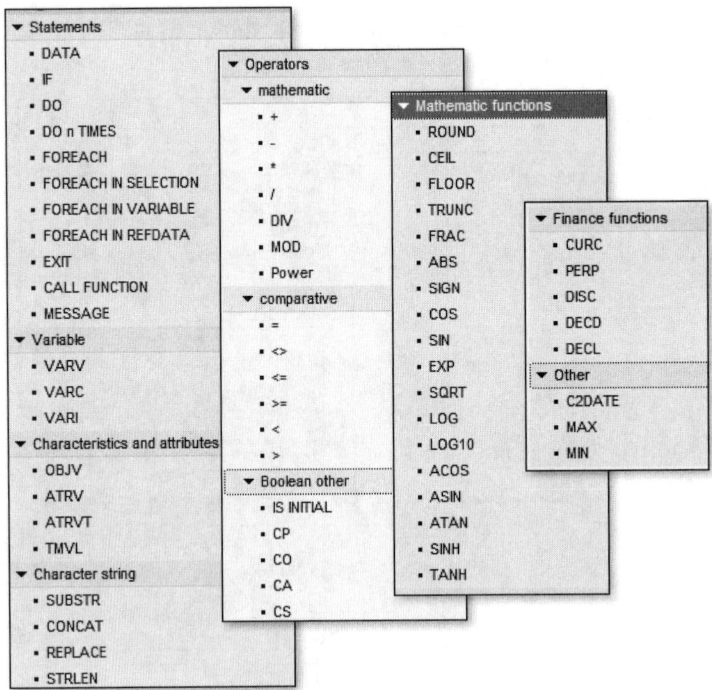

Figure 12.65 Program Elements for Formula Function

12.3.8 Planning Sequence

Planning sequences are used to compose execution plans for multiple planning functions, and the corresponding filter values over which those are to be executed. You can define the planning sequences in the Planning Modeler under the Planning Sequences tab. In this section, we explain how to create planning sequences. We'll also explain the use of this tab to test and debug one or more planning functions built in the planning model.

Create Planning Sequence

Follow these steps to create a planning sequence using the Planning Modeler:

1. Go to the Planning Sequences tab page, and click on CREATE (❶ of Figure 12.66). Enter the TECHNICAL NAME AND DESCRIPTION of the planning sequence, and click on TRANSFER (❷).

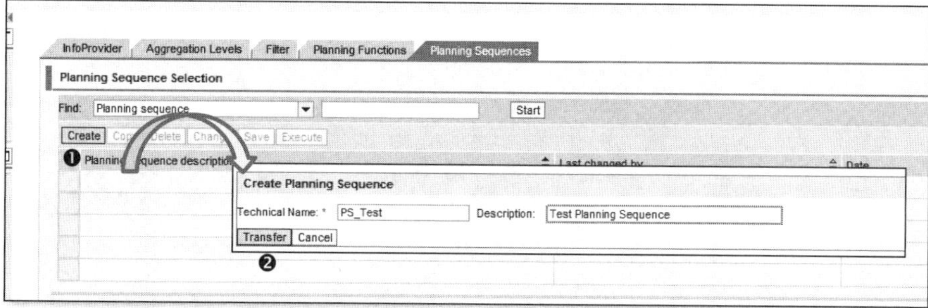

Figure 12.66 Create New Planning Sequence

2. In the next screen, define the planning sequence by adding different planning functions and defining the sequence of execution (Figure 12.67). By clicking on ADD STEP FOR PLANNING FUNCTION (❶), you create a new step in the planning sequence.

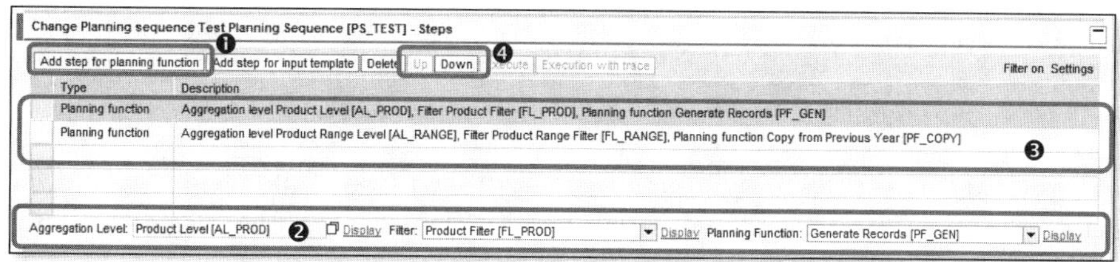

Figure 12.67 Defining Planning Sequence

3. Select the aggregation level, planning filter, and planning function to define the steps in the planning sequence (❷). This way, you can add multiple steps to the planning sequence (❸). You can also readjust the sequence of the planning functions with the help of the UP AND DOWN buttons (❹).
4. Finally, save the planning sequence by clicking the Save button on the tab page.

Testing Planning Functions and Planning Sequence

When you save a planning sequence, the Execute and Execution with Trace buttons are enabled (❶ of Figure 12.68). You can test and validate the complete planning sequence or a selected planning function using this option.

When you click on Execute, the selected function (or complete planning sequence, if no individual step is selected) is executed. When you click on Execution with Trace, the planning function is executed and all of the actions performed by the planning function on the data can be traced.

Before you execute any function or sequence, you have to first maintain the variable values involved in the planning function (❷).

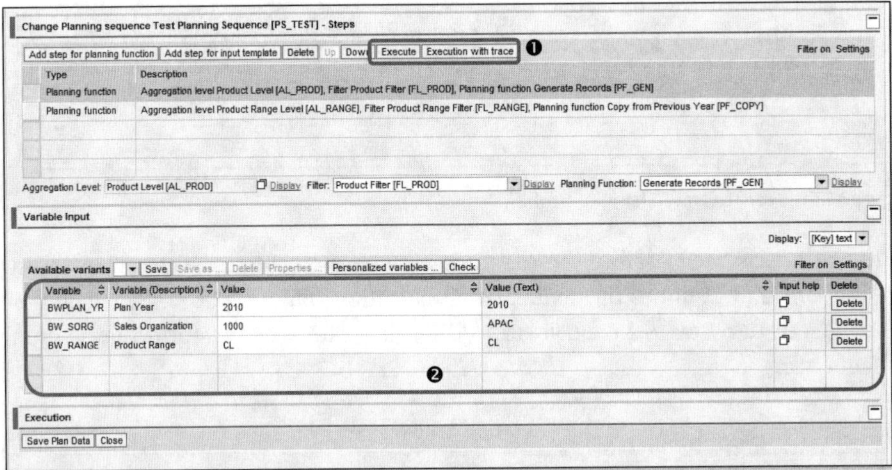

Figure 12.68 Executing Planning Function/Sequence

After you execute the planning function, you can see the system messages displayed on the top (see Figure 12.69). This will let you know if the planning function is executed successfully or not.

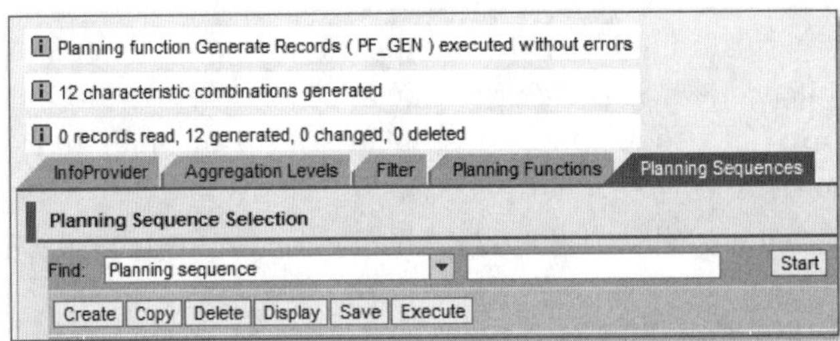

Figure 12.69 System Messages

If you execute the planning function with trace, then the trace information is available under the Execution section (Figure 12.70) on the bottom part of the screen.

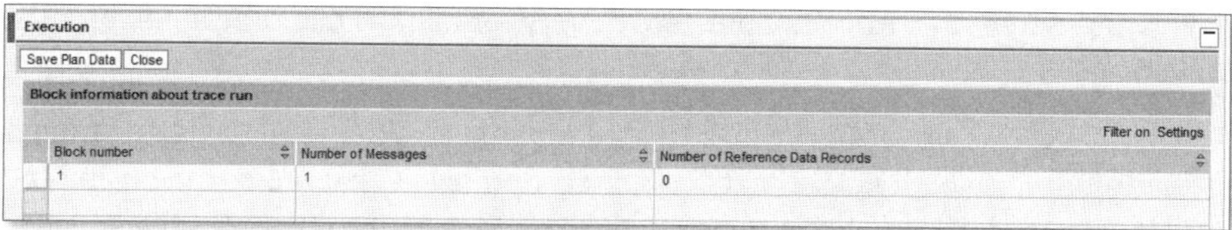

Block number	Number of Messages	Number of Reference Data Records
1	1	0

Figure 12.70 Information About Trace Run

Select the block row and the detailed trace information and data will be displayed below. The system displays the state of a data record before and after change. Also, the new records that are created can be identified using the Change Indicator (Figure 12.71).

Details for Block Number 1

Filter on Settings

Series	Data	Change Indicator	Cal. Year/Quarter	Calendar Year	Sales Organization	Product Range	Product	Net Value	Document currency
1	After	New	20101	2010	1000	CL	#	0.00	USD
2	After	New	20101	2010	1000	CL	92000	0.00	USD
3	After	New	20101	2010	1000	CL	92500	0.00	USD
4	After	New	20102	2010	1000	CL	#	0.00	USD
5	After	New	20102	2010	1000	CL	92000	0.00	USD
6	After	New	20102	2010	1000	CL	92500	0.00	USD
7	After	New	20103	2010	1000	CL	#	0.00	USD
8	After	New	20103	2010	1000	CL	92000	0.00	USD
9	After	New	20103	2010	1000	CL	92500	0.00	USD
10	After	New	20104	2010	1000	CL	#	0.00	USD
11	After	New	20104	2010	1000	CL	92000	0.00	USD
12	After	New	20104	2010	1000	CL	92500	0.00	USD

Figure 12.71 Trace Details

Execution with trace is a very important option available to debug and trace the planning functions and planning sequences.

12.3.9 Input-Ready Query

As we've seen in earlier sections, planning functions and planning sequences enable the automatic processing of data. Apart from this automatic processing, planning users also need an interface to manually edit the data. This process is called manual planning. A planning application that includes manual planning can be built using either the web application designer or BEx analyzer, but the base for all manual planning is an input-ready query.

An input-ready query is built in BEx query designer and is created the same way as a regular BEx query used for reporting. However, unlike a regular reporting query, an input-ready query can be built only on an aggregation level or a MultiProvider that includes a simple aggregation level.

Follow these steps to create an input-ready query for manual planning at the product range level.

1. Open the BEx query designer, and create a new query. When you navigate through the InfoAreas, you'll notice that the aggregation levels that are created using the Planning Modeler are also available as InfoProviders in the Query Designer. Select the level AL_RANGE (Product Range Level) to create the query (Figure 12.72).

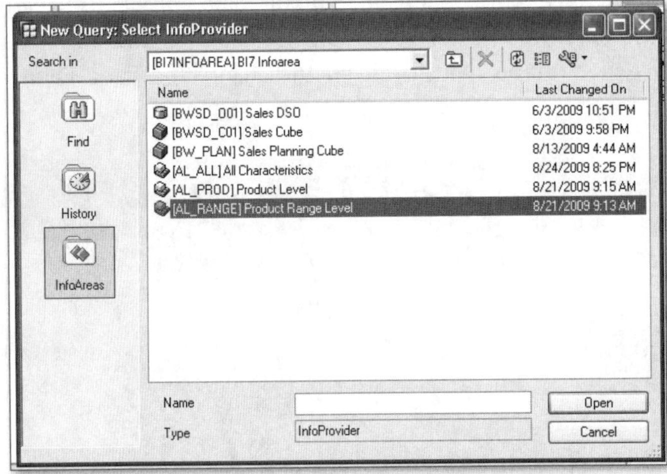

Figure 12.72 Create Query on Aggregation Level

2. In the query definition screen, you can see that the planning filters defined in the Planning Modeler are available under the Filter folder (Figure 12.73). Drag and drop the filter in the query definition.

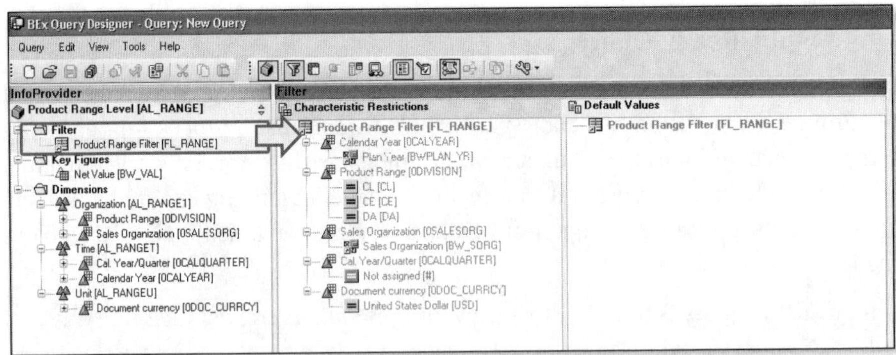

Figure 12.73 Filter for Input Ready Query

3. Drag and drop all of the necessary characteristics and key figures from the aggregation level in the query definition (Figure 12.74)

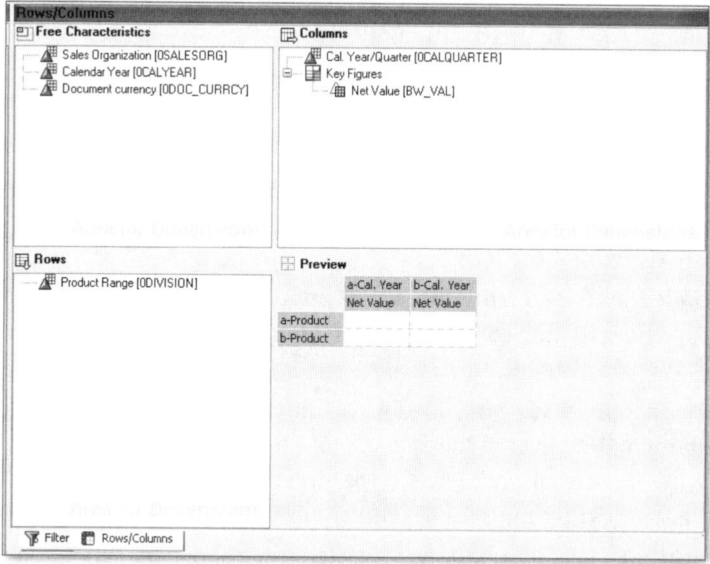

Figure 12.74 Define Input-Ready Query

4. For the user to be able to edit the key figure values, the key figure needs to be enabled for planning. Go to the key figure properties, and click on the Planning tab (Figure 12.75).

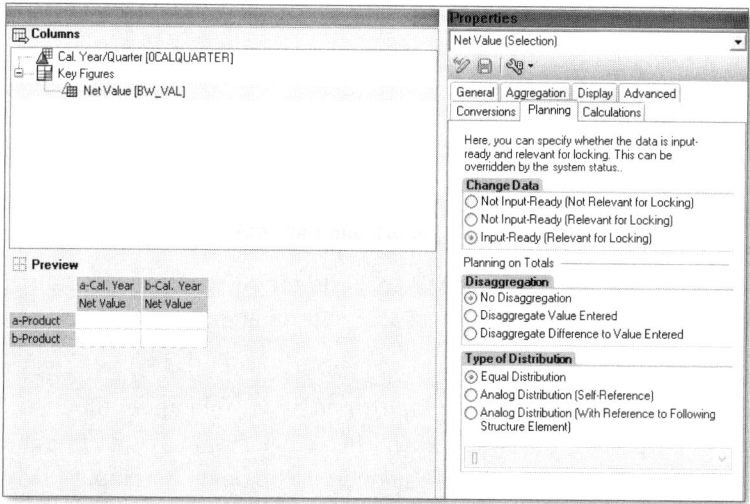

Figure 12.75 Key Figure Planning Properties

Different planning-related settings for the selected key figure are available on this tab:

- **Change Data:** Under this section, you can specify if the selected key figure should be input ready or not. There are three options available:
  - **Not Input-Ready (Not Relevant for Locking):** This option disables the input-ready property of the selected key figure; the data for that key figure won't be locked.
  - **Not Input-Ready (Relevant for Locking):** This option disables the input-ready property of the selected key figure, but the data will be locked. This data can be changed using planning functions.
  - **Input-Ready (Relevant for Locking):** With this option, the selected key figure is made input-ready, and the corresponding plan data is locked for other users.
- **Disaggregation:** In an input-ready planning layout, the data is entered only at the lowest level of drilldown. However, if the data is entered at result rows (i.e., at the aggregated level), the new result value has to be distributed to the lower-level records. This top-down distribution setting can be selected under this section.
  - **No Disaggregation:** If this radio button is selected, the change of values at an aggregated level is disabled.
  - **Disaggregate Value Entered:** For this setting, the new value entered at the aggregated level is disaggregated to lower records based on the type of distribution selected in the next section.
  - **Disaggregate Difference to Value Entered:** For this setting, only the change between the new and the old value is distributed.
- **Type of Distribution:** In this section, you can specify the type of top-down distribution by using the following settings:
  - **Equal Distribution:** The aggregated value is equally distributed across all of the records at the lower level.
  - **Analog Distribution (Self-Reference):** The value is distributed in the same proportion as that of the existing data for the same key figure.
  - **Analog Distribution (With Reference to Following Structure Element):** With this option, you can distribute the value with reference to the data for a specific structure element.

5. Also, you need to set the query property Startup View (visible under the Planning tab in Query Properties) to start the query in change mode. By selecting the checkbox shown in Figure 12.76, you set the query to be opened in input-ready mode when executed.

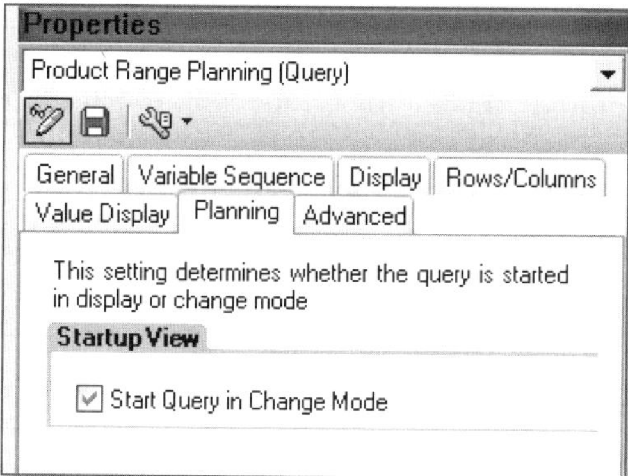

Figure 12.76 Start Query in Change Mode

6. Also, you can define some additional settings for the characteristics involved in the query definition. For example, if you want to list all of the possible values of product range in the default view of the query, you set the Access Type of Result Values property for the product range characteristic as Master Data (Figure 12.77).

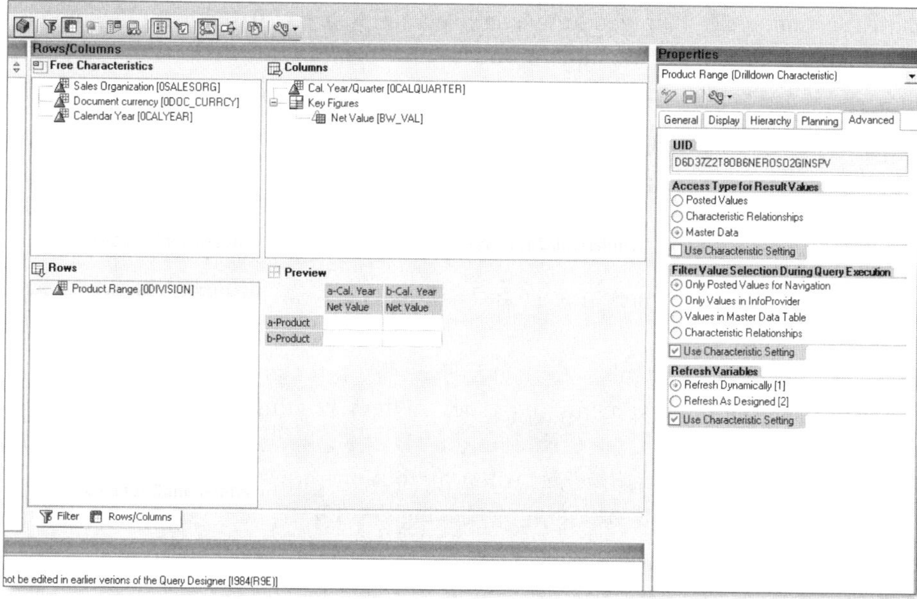

Figure 12.77 Characteristic Properties for Planning

7. Finally, save the query with technical name BW_PLAN_Q001 and description "Product Range Planning."

12.4 Planning Applications

A *planning application* is built by putting different planning components together so that you can perform manual planning as well as execute different planning functions. This can involve input-ready queries as well as read-only BEx queries. Different planning functions and planning sequences can also be included in planning applications. An Excel-based planning application is built using BEx analyzer, and a Web-based planning application is built using the web application designer. We discuss both of these in more detail in the following sections.

12.4.1 Excel-Based Planning Application

In the sections covered so far in this chapter, we've seen how to create different elements involved in building a planning application. The most important activity is to assemble these planning components together to form a user interface of the planning application. A planning application can include different planning objects, such as input-ready queries, planning functions, and planning sequences. Other than the planning object, a planning application can also include regular reporting queries based on InfoProviders other than real-time InfoCubes.

In this section, we explain you how to create a simple Excel-based planning application with the help of our example product range planning scenario. The procedure to create this is explained next:

1. Open BEx analyzer: START MENU • PROGRAMS • BUSINESS EXPLORER • ANALYZER.
2. Open a new Excel workbook, and switch to design mode by clicking on the button shown in ❶ of Figure 12.78.
3. Maintain the heading for this application by editing the Excel cells (❷).
4. For the input-ready query, insert an analysis grid from the BEx design toolbar (❸).
5. Assign the input-ready query to the analysis grid in the properties (accessed from the analysis grid context menu) of the design item. For this, first create a new data provider by clicking on the Create button (❶ of Figure 12.79). Assign the input-ready query to the data provider using the button shown in ❷. Assign this data provider to the analysis grid item by clicking OK (❸).

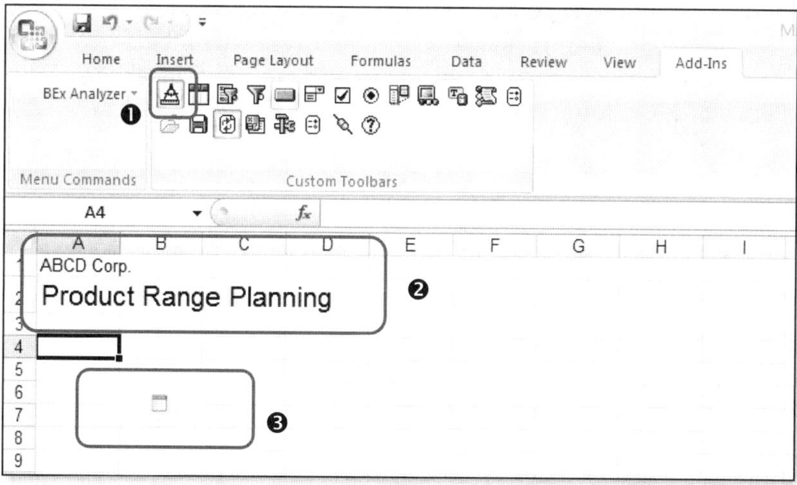

Figure 12.78 Create New Planning Application in BEx analyzer

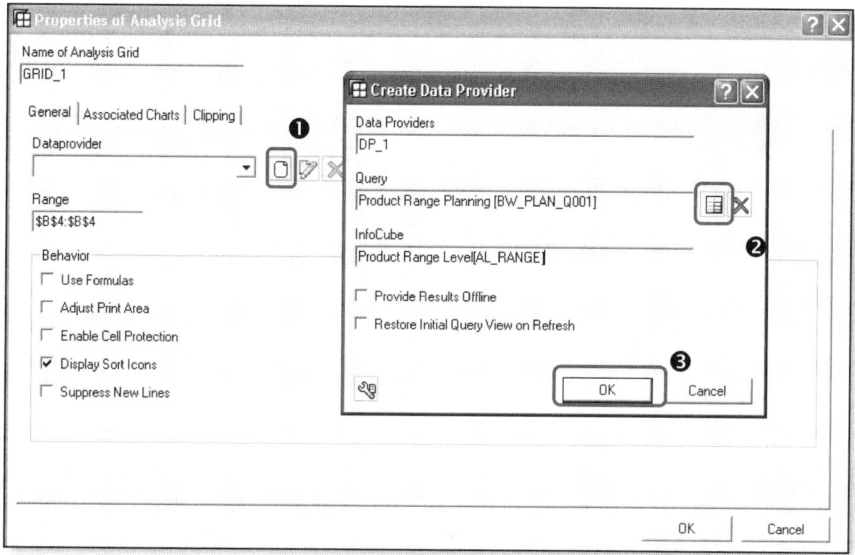

Figure 12.79 Assign Input Ready Query to Analysis Grid Item

6. With the previous step, the manual entry layout is made available in the application. Now, let's build some command buttons in this planning application. The first command button used in almost all planning applications is the Save command. Insert a button design item from the BEx design toolbar into the layout (❶

of Figure 12.80). We can assign the command to this button in the item properties. Go to the design item properties from the context menu of the newly inserted button, and select the Planning-Specific Command radio button (❷). Then click Next to define further settings (❸).

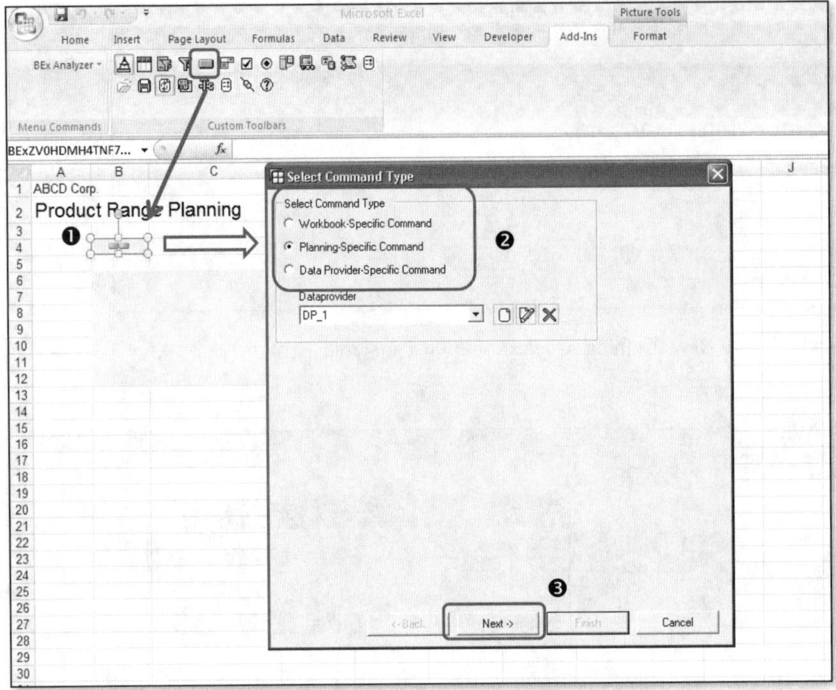

Figure 12.80 Assign a Planning-Specific Command to Button Design Item

7. The next screen shows the different planning commands that can be assigned to the button (Figure 12.81). Select the radio button for the Save command, and click on FINISH. This assigns the Save function to the button added.
8. You can further maintain the properties for this Save function assignment, as shown in Figure 12.82. You can define the cell range in the workbook to which the planning function will be applied (❶). The display text for the button can be maintained in the Button Text field (❷). The static parameters for the function are visible on the right side (❸). for the Save command, no additional parameters need to be defined. Maintain the properties for the button, and click OK to complete the command assignment.

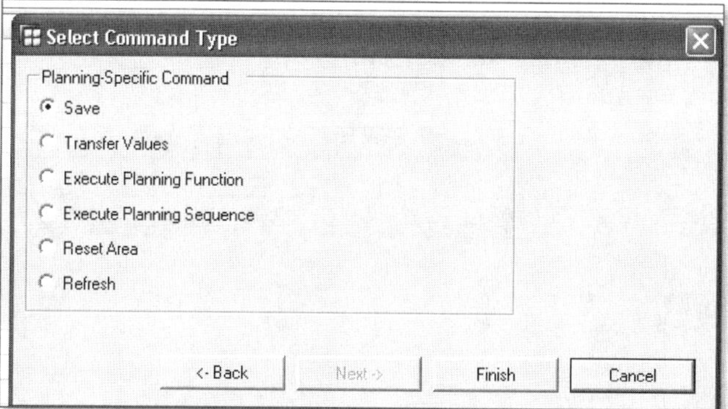

Figure 12.81 Select Command Type

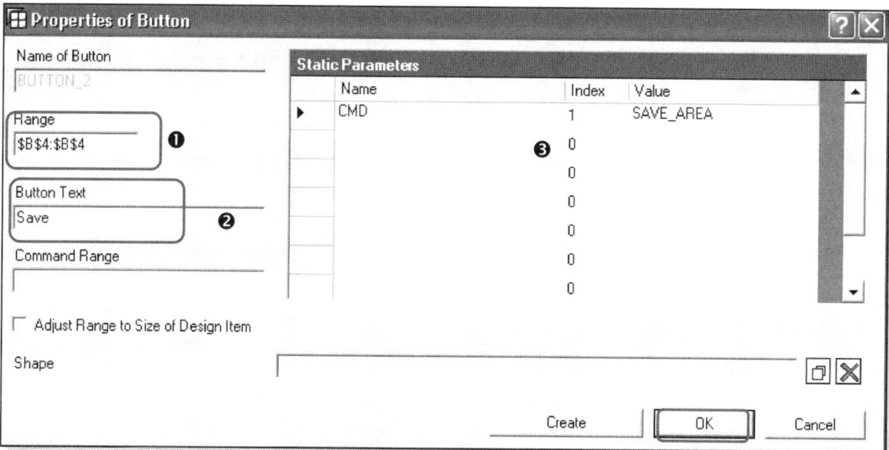

Figure 12.82 Properties for the Save Button

9. Let's now try to add another command button that will execute a planning function to copy the plan values from the previous year. The procedure is the same as shown in Figure 12.80 and Figure 12.81. First insert the button design item in the workbook, and then select the Execute Planning Function command type from the Design Item Properties screen. Click Next to further customize the properties.
10. On the next screen, first select the planning function and the data provider on which the planning function has to be executed. Select the planning function that needs to be assigned to the button, as shown in ❶ of Figure 12.83. Also select the data provider from the dropdown list on which the selected planning function should be executed; alternatively, you can create a new one if needed

(❷). If the planning function includes variables, the list of those variables are displayed after you select the planning function (❸).

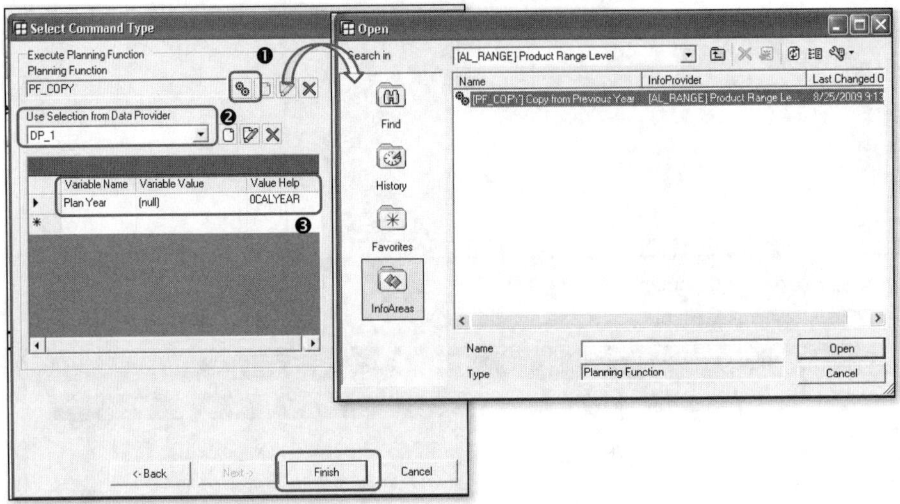

Figure 12.83 Select Planning Function

11. After you've defined the planning function and the data provider, click the Finish button to move to the next screen. This is where you can set the button properties and other parameters related to the planning function (Figure 12.84).
12. Maintain the button text as shown in ❶ of Figure 12.84.
13. You'll notice the list of static parameters on the right side of the screen. This lists all of the parameters associated with the planning function that you've selected earlier; you can maintain the values for those parameters that will remain static throughout. Also note that there are parameter entries for the variables used in the function. The parameter VAR_NAME_1 corresponds to the name of the variable, and the parameter VAR_VALUE_1 corresponds to the value that this variable will store. The planning function PF_COPY, which we've selected here, used the variable BWPLAN_YR (refer to this planning function definition in the section where we explain the Copy function). This is a user entry variable, so it isn't needed to define the static parameter for the variable value. Delete the entry VAR_VALUE_1 from the static parameters (❷), and click on OK to complete the planning function assignment to the button.

    You can also assign the planning sequence and other planning-specific commands to the button in the same way.

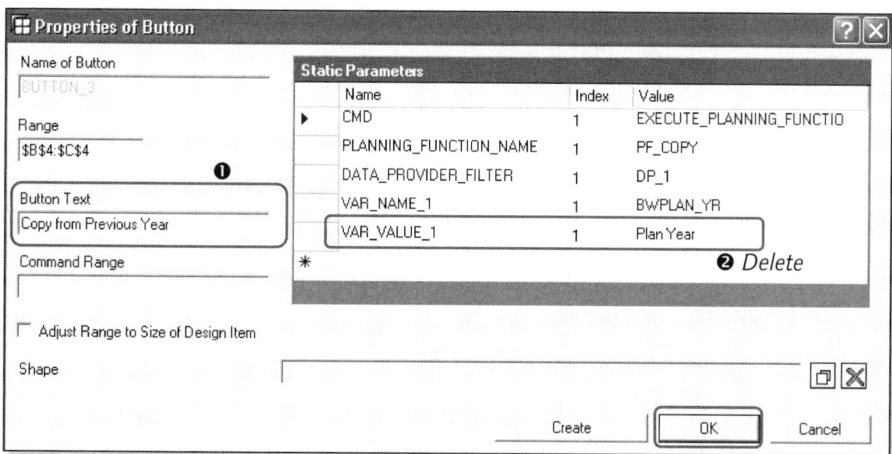

Figure 12.84 Maintain Properties of the Button

14. Your simple application for product range planning at the divisional level is ready. Save the workbook, as shown in Figure 12.85.

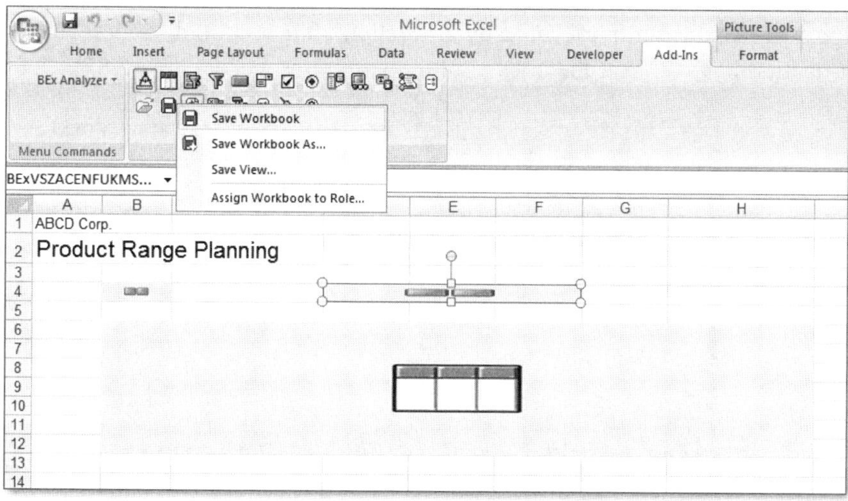

Figure 12.85 Save the Planning Application as a Workbook

When this workbook is opened for planning, the application will appear as shown in Figure 12.86.

You can enter/edit the plan values for the product ranges by calendar quarter (❶) for the plan year and sales organization entered in the variable screen of the query. Also, you can execute the planning function by clicking on the Copy from Previous Year button (❷). Clicking on the Save button (❸) saves the changed data and refreshes the totals.

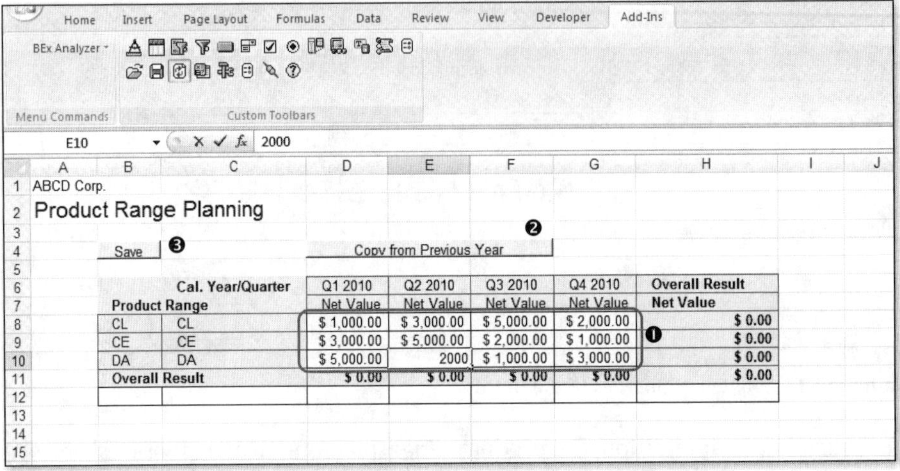

Figure 12.86 Working with Excel-Based Planning Applications

You can see the action performed by a function after you double-click on the information bar visible at the bottom of the workbook (see Figure 12.87).

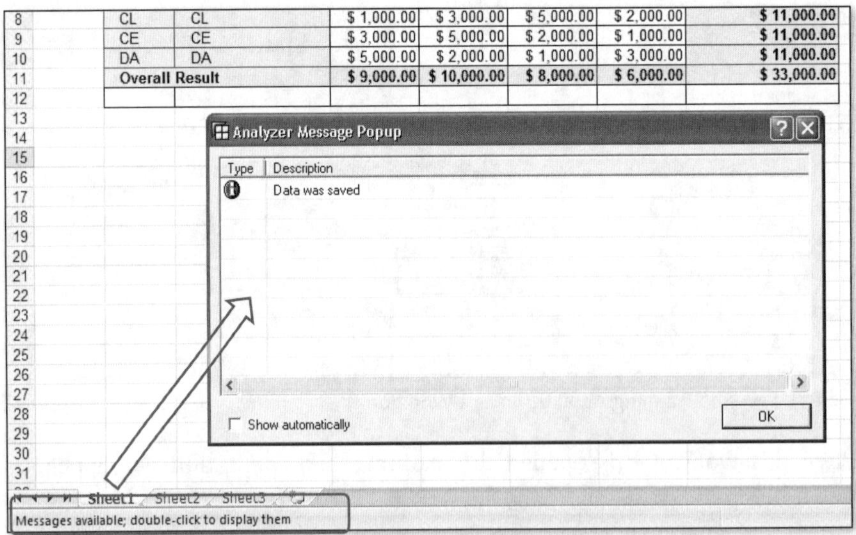

Figure 12.87 Display Messages

In this manner, you can create Excel-based planning applications in SAP NetWeaver BW Integrated Planning. You can, of course, add more input-ready queries and functions. You can also build more complex planning applications by combining the planning components with the regular BEx analysis components — such as charts, exceptions, filters, navigation blocks, and so on — available in BEx analyzer.

12.4.2 Web-Based Planning Applications

The web-based planning interface is built using BEx web application designer, and users can access this planning interface from the portal or by using a direct URL. In this section, we explain the different aspects of this development with the help of our example scenario, where the product range level planning happens through a web interface. The procedure to create this interface is explained next:

1. Open BEx analyzer from START MENU • PROGRAMS • BUSINESS EXPLORER • WEB APPLICATION DESIGNER, and open a new web template.
2. Create the heading for the planning application using the font options available in the web template (❶ of Figure 12.88).

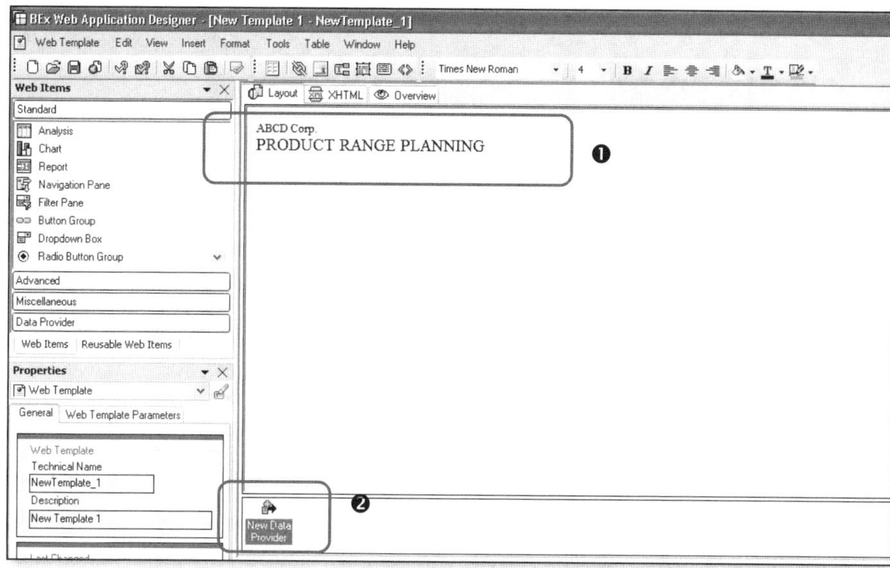

Figure 12.88 Create Heading for Planning Application

3. Define a new data provider based on the input-ready query. Click on the New Data Provider icon shown in ❷ of Figure 12.88. In the pop-up screen, give a description to the data provider (❶ of Figure 12.89). Select the type of data pro-

vider as Query View (❷), and assign the query to the data provider using the selection help (❸). Click on OK to complete the data provider creation. Generally, this type of data provider is based on the input-ready queries that are used to provide manual planning layouts in the planning application.

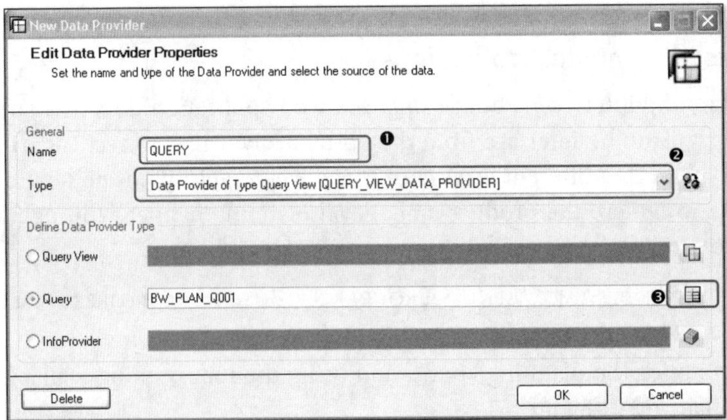

Figure 12.89 Define the Data Provider for Input-Ready Query

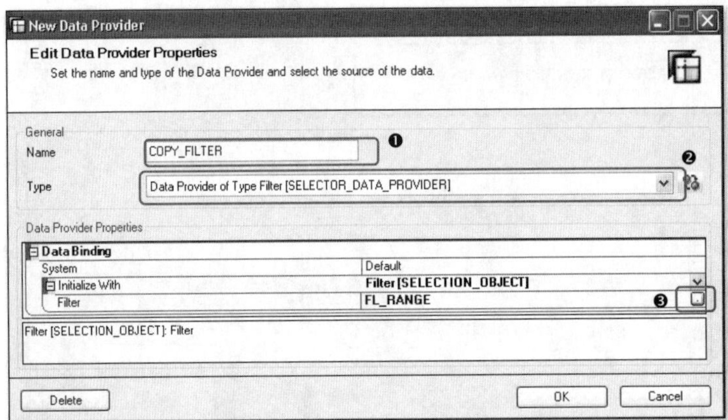

Figure 12.90 Define Filter Data Provider

4. Another type of data provider needed in building a planning application is the filter type. This type of data provider is used in the execution of planning functions because planning functions are always executed on some filter. Create a new data provider, as shown in Figure 12.90. Give a description to the data provider

(❶). Select the type of data provider as Filter (❷), and assign the required filter to the data provider using the selection help (❸). Click on OK to complete the data provider creation.

5. Drag and drop the Analysis web item into the web template (❶ of Figure 12.91). We'll use this web item to create the manual planning layout based on the input-ready query in the application. Assign the QUERY data provider, which you created in previous steps, to the Analysis item (❷).

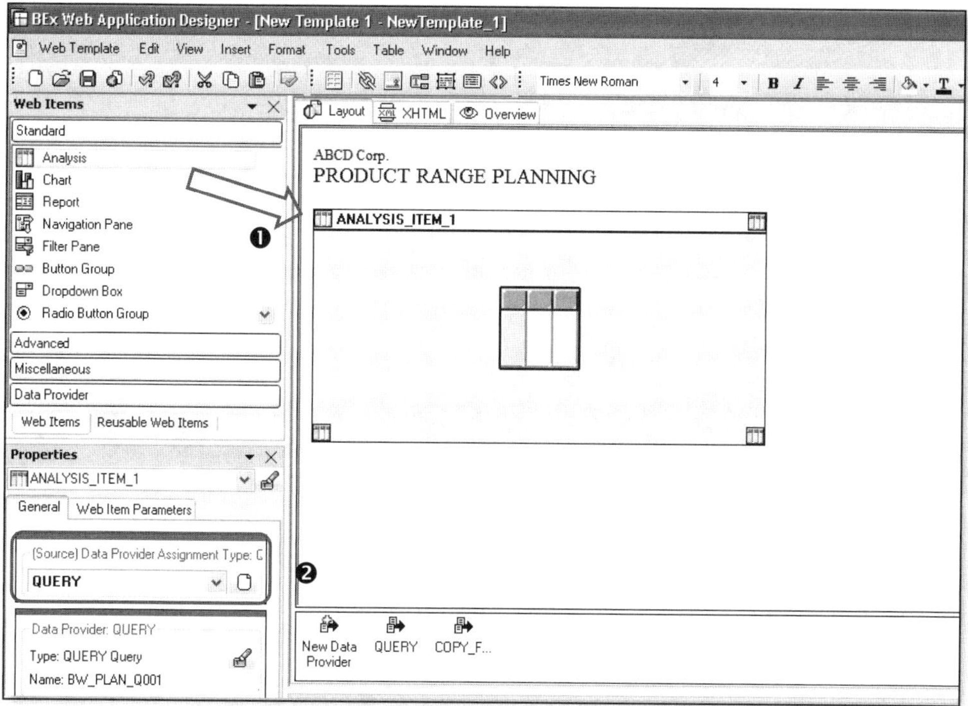

Figure 12.91 Add Analysis Web Item

6. Drag and drop the Button Group web item into the web template to add command buttons to the planning application (Figure 12.92).

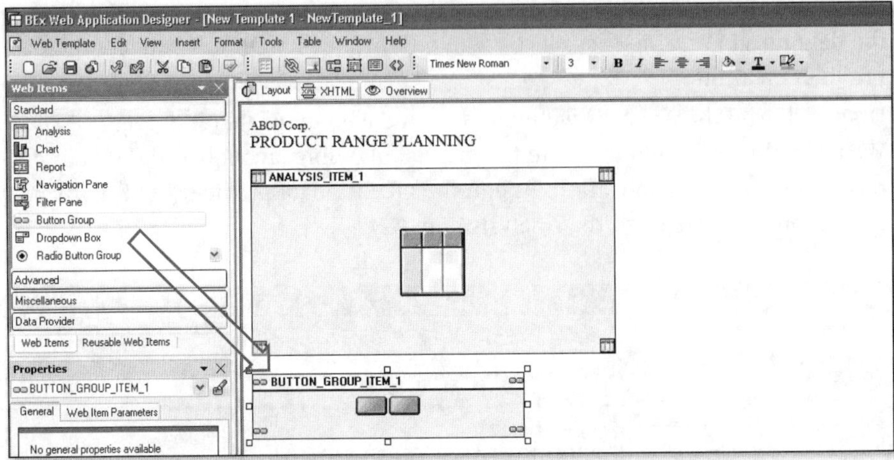

Figure 12.92 Add Button Group Web Item

7. The buttons for this button group are defined in the properties of the button group. Click on the button shown in Figure 12.93 to add a new button to the button group.

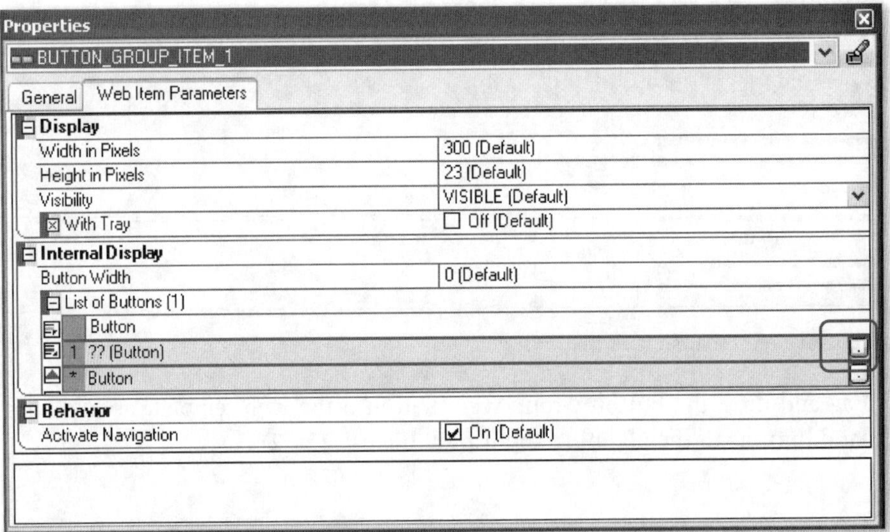

Figure 12.93 Add a Button to the Button Group

8. Define the new button by maintaining the display caption and other button parameters, as shown in Figure 12.94. The most important part of button config-

uration is to assign an action to the button. This can be done using the commands from the Command Wizard available in the web application designer. Select Command via Command Wizard as the action for the button (❶), and then click on the button shown in ❷ of Figure 12.94 to define the command settings.

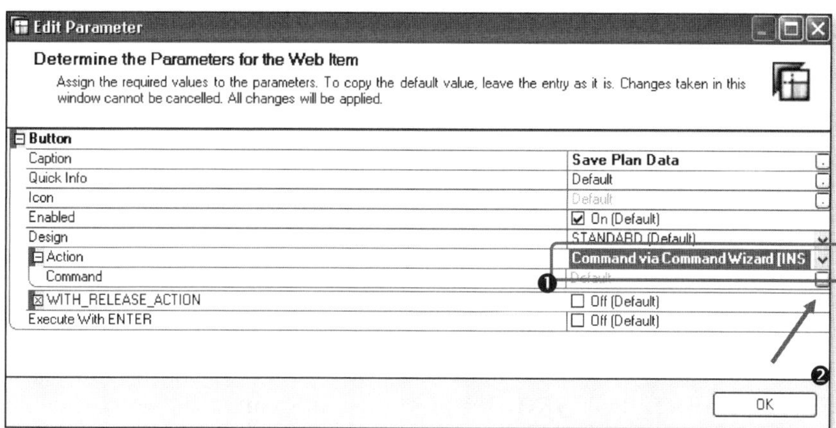

Figure 12.94 Define Button Parameters

9. You will see a list of all of the available commands in the Command Wizard under the All Commands tab (Figure 12.95).

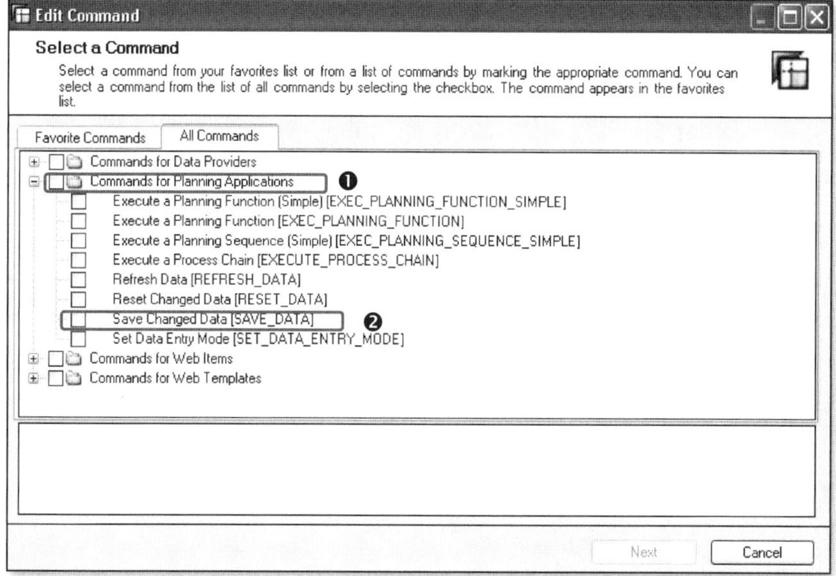

Figure 12.95 Planning Commands

All of the planning-related commands are grouped under the folder titled Commands for Planning Applications (❶ of Figure 12.95). These commands are explained here:

- **Execute a Planning Function (Simple) (EXEC_PLANNING_FUNCTION_SIMPLE):** You can use this command to execute a planning function that can be based on the filter from a single data provider.
- **Execute a Planning Function (EXEC_PLANNING_FUNCTION):** You can use this command if you want to execute a planning function and derive the filter for the planning function from multiple sources and data providers. You can independently define the source for each characteristic in the filter.
- **Execute a Planning Sequence (Simple) (EXEC_PLANNING_SEQUENCE_SIMPLE):** You can use this command to execute a planning sequence in the planning application.
- **Execute a Process Chain (EXECUTE_PROCESS CHAIN):** You can execute a process chain with planning-related process steps using this command.
- **Refresh Data (REFRESH_DATA):** You can use this command to transfer the changed values to the buffer after checking the entries.
- **Reset Changed Data (RESET_DATA):** You can undo the changes to the data using this command.
- **Save Changed Data (SAVE_DATA):** You can save the changes to the data to the InfoCube after validation of the entries.
- **Set Data Entry Mode (SET_DATA_ENTRY_MODE):** You can switch between Display and Change mode for a data provider based on an input-ready query.

For our example scenario, select the command Save Changed Data (SAVE_DATA) (❷ of Figure 12.95), and then click on the NEXT button.

10. The parameters for the selected command can be defined on the subsequent screen (Figure 12.96). Because there are no parameters to define for the Save command, click OK.
11. This takes you back to the button definition screen, where you can see the command assigned to the button under the Action settings (Figure 12.97). Click on OK to return to the button group web item properties screen.

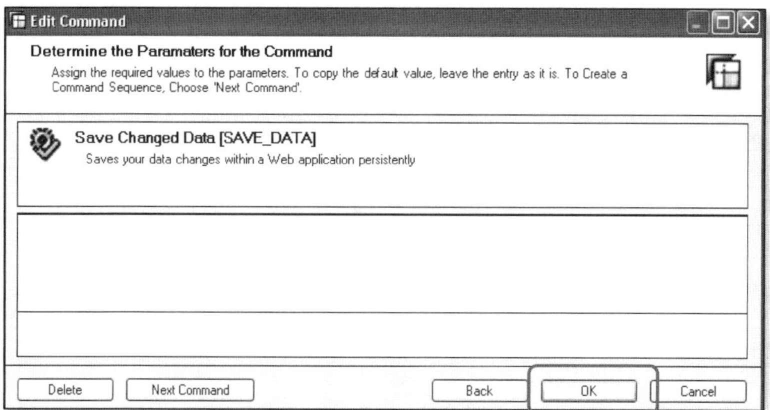

Figure 12.96 Parameter Screen for Save Command

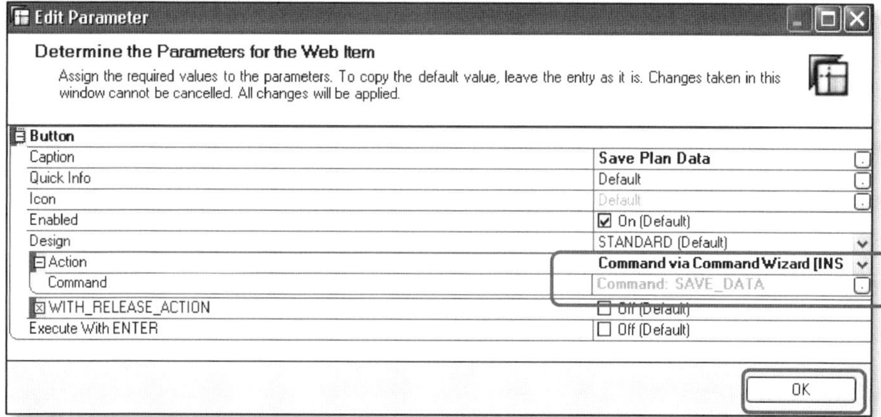

Figure 12.97 Save Button Definition

12. On the web item properties screen, the first button to save the data is defined. Let's now add a button to execute a planning function to copy values from a previous year. Click the button shown in Figure 12.98 to create another button.

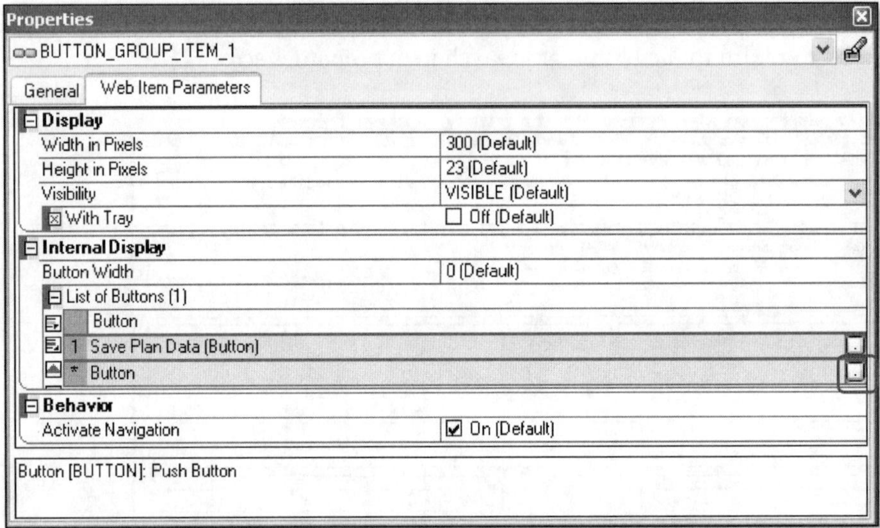

Figure 12.98 Add New Button

13. Define the parameters for the button, and click the button shown in Figure 12.99 to go to the Command Wizard.
14. Select the Execute a Planning Function (Simple) (EXEC_PLANNING_FUNCTION_SIMPLE) command (❶ of Figure 12.100), and then click on the NEXT button (❷)

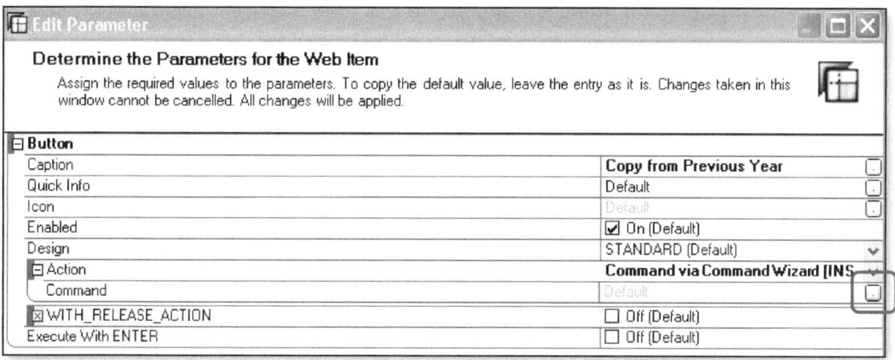

Figure 12.99 Define Parameters for the Copy Button

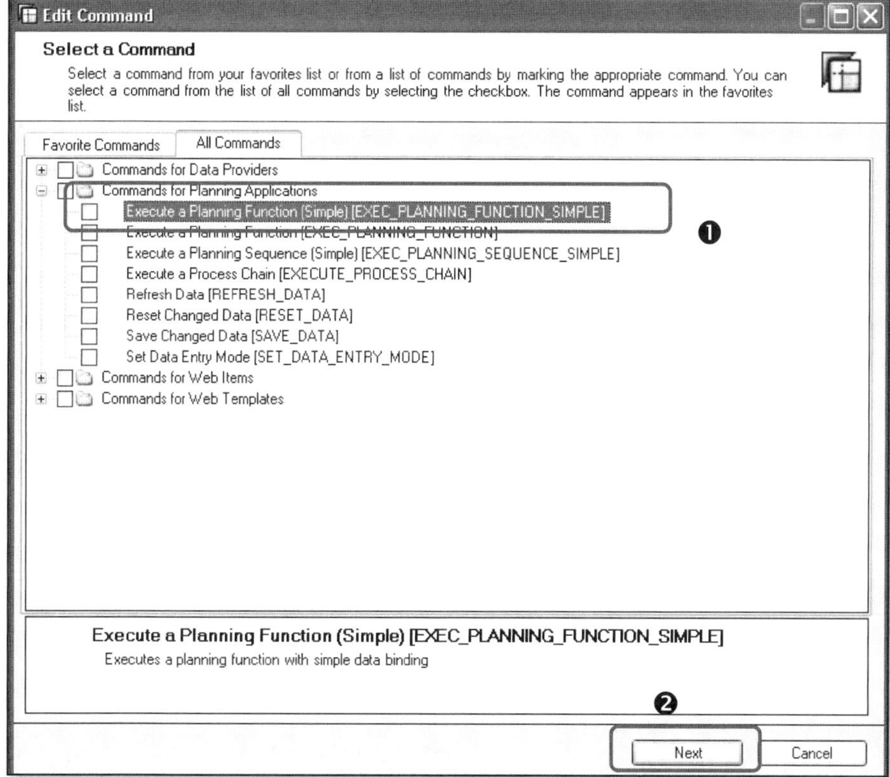

Figure 12.100 Select Command to for the Copy Button

15. Define the parameters for the planning function command on the next screen (Figure 12.101). The most important setting is to define the filter for the planning function. Select the COPY_FILTER data provider, which is based on a filter (❶). You can also maintain any default values for the variables used in the planning function under the Variant area of the screen (❷). Finally, assign the required planning function to the command using the selection help (❸). Click OK to complete the command setting, and then click OK on the button definition screen to confirm the definition.

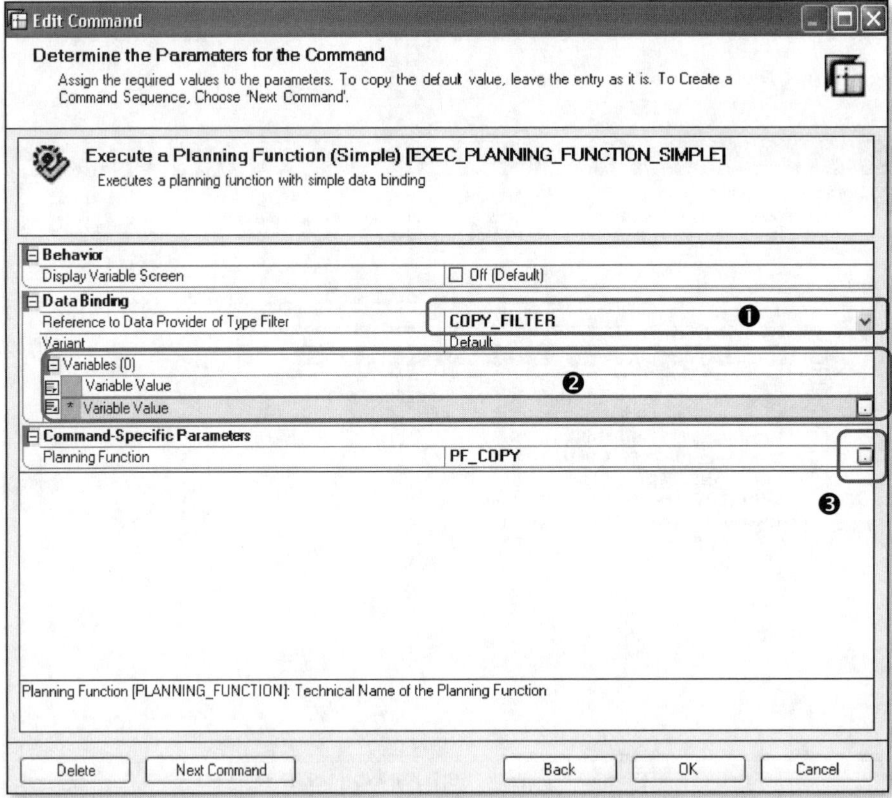

Figure 12.101 Define Parameters for the Command

16. You can see both the defined commands visible in the button group properties screen (refer Figure 12.102).

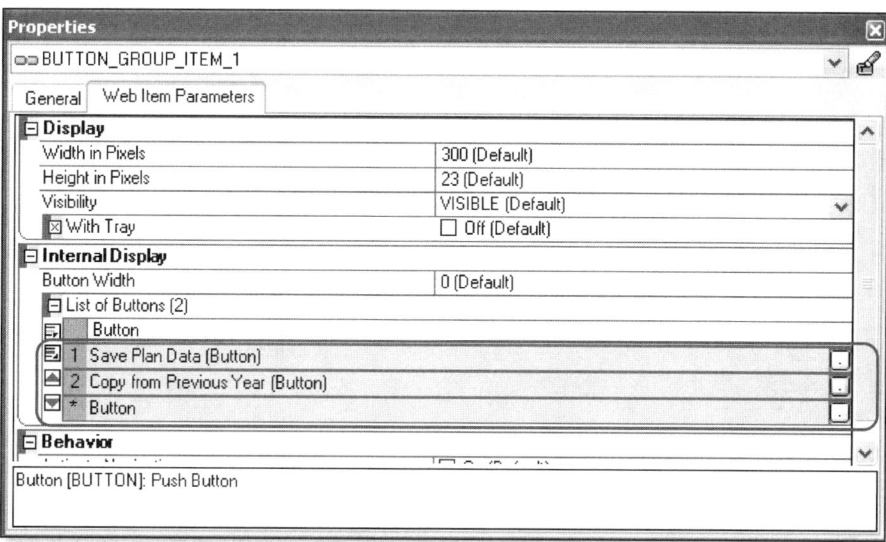

Figure 12.102 Button Group Properties

17. Your web-based application for product range planning at the divisional level is ready. Save the application by saving the web template (Figure 12.103).

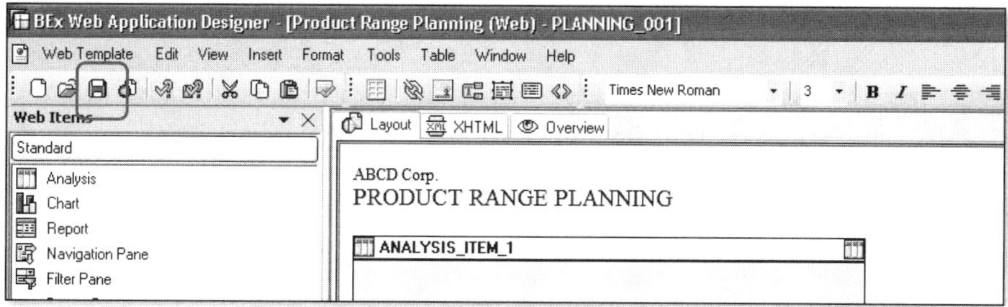

Figure 12.103 Save the Planning Application

When you execute this web-based planning application, the variable entry screen is invoked if variables are used in the application. Enter the variable selection, and click on OK to run the planning application (Figure 12.104).

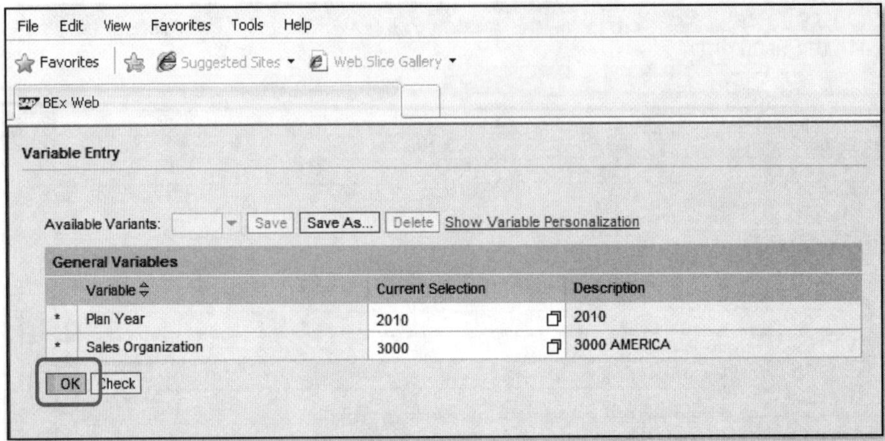

Figure 12.104 Enter Variables to Execute the Planning Application

The planning application is executed for the given selection, as shown in Figure 12.105. You can enter/edit the plan values for the product ranges by calendar quarter (❶ of Figure 12.105) for the plan year and sales organization entered earlier in the variable screen. Also, you can save the changed data or execute the planning function by clicking on the available buttons (❷).

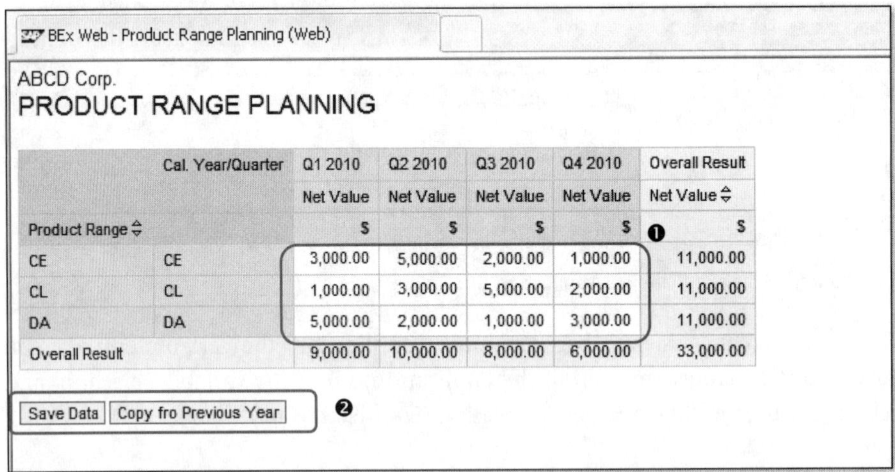

Figure 12.105 Working with the Web-Based Planning Application

A message is displayed based on the action performed in the planning application (Figure 12.106).

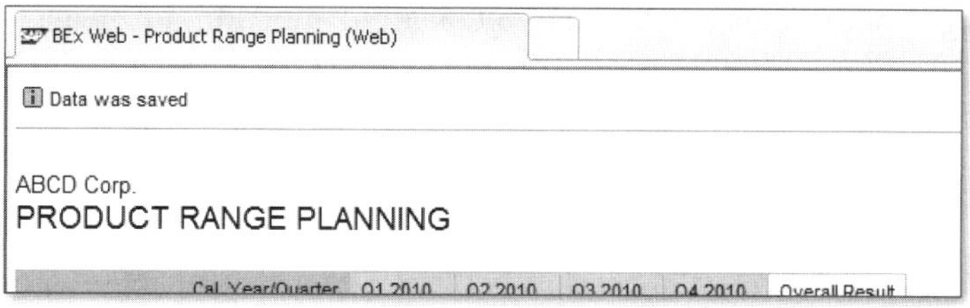

Data was saved

ABCD Corp.
PRODUCT RANGE PLANNING

Figure 12.106 System Messages for Action Performed

When you execute a planning function, the system messages are displayed showing the execution results for the planning function (Figure 12.107).

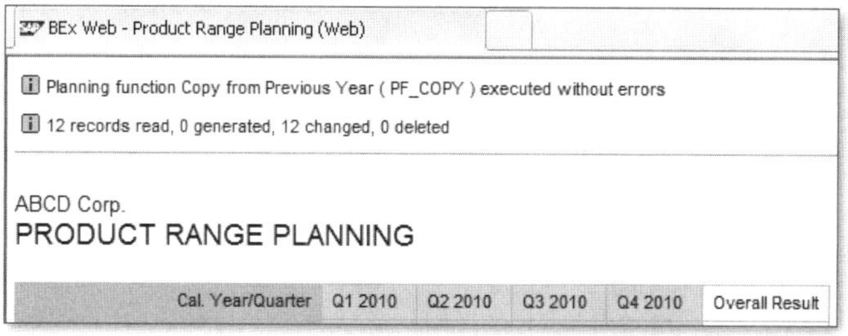

Planning function Copy from Previous Year (PF_COPY) executed without errors
12 records read, 0 generated, 12 changed, 0 deleted

ABCD Corp.
PRODUCT RANGE PLANNING

Cal. Year/Quarter	Q1 2010	Q2 2010	Q3 2010	Q4 2010	Overall Result

Figure 12.107 Execution Result for the Planning Function

In this manner, you can create and work with a web-based planning application created in SAP NetWeaver BW. You can add more manual planning layouts to the web template and add more functions and commands to the same. Also, you can build some more complex planning applications by combining the planning components with the regular BEx analysis components available in the web application designer, such as charts, exceptions, filters, navigation blocks, and so on.

12.5 Planning Locks

SAP NetWeaver BW Integrated Planning allows you to build an application that can support the planning operations in an organization. With this planning application, users can create and edit plan data. In a real-life scenario, multiple planners often are working on the same set of data at the same time, resulting in a conflict that can lead to data integrity issues. To address this situation, Integrated Planning uses the concept of planning locks. Using planning locks, the data selected by a user for editing is locked and made unavailable to all others who try to access the data with overlapping selections.

The data in a planning application is edited either by planning functions or by manual planning. In the case of planning functions, the entire data selection over which the planning function is executed is locked. In the case of manual planning, all of the data contained in the filter of the input-ready query used in the application is locked.

For two planners to work without locking each other, the data sets they are editing should be completely distinct; there will be a locking conflict even in the case of a slight overlap between the two data sets. This is illustrated in Figure 12.108.

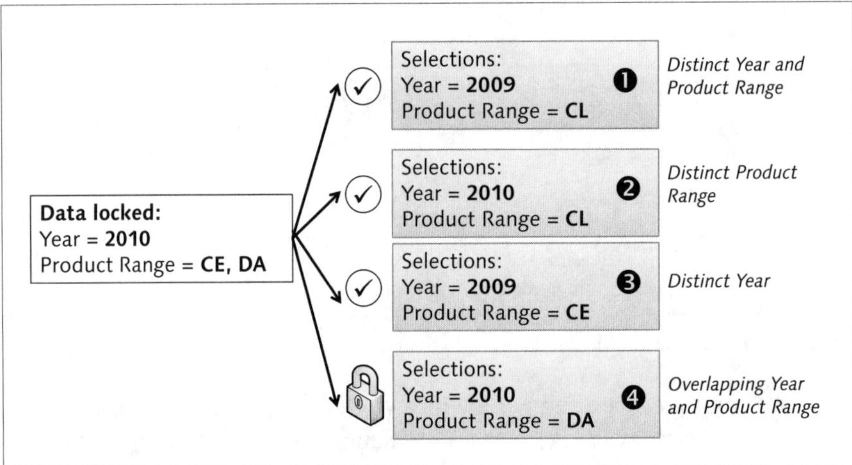

Figure 12.108 Examples of Planning Locks

Note

Data selections are locked regardless of whether there is already a data record in the cube for the given selection. This is done so that another planner can't create a new record and change the data for the given selection.

In most of the planning scenarios, the planning data is accessed from different aggregation levels. These aggregation levels can use different characteristics, so the data can be aggregated differently than the other aggregation level. In such a scenario, if a characteristic isn't included in one aggregation level, all of the values for that characteristic are locked. We'll explain this situation with an example in which we have two different aggregation levels: product range and product. In the product range level, you don't have the product characteristic, so the data is aggregated without it.

Now let's assume that a user, Planner A, starts planning the data for division 1000 for all three product ranges (CE, DA, and CL) using the product range level. Because the product characteristic isn't included in the level, all values for product are locked (Figure 12.109). At the same time, Planner B is trying to access the data from the product level for division 1000, the CE product range, and Product = Camera. In this situation, Planner B gets a lock because there isn't a single characteristic without any overlap.

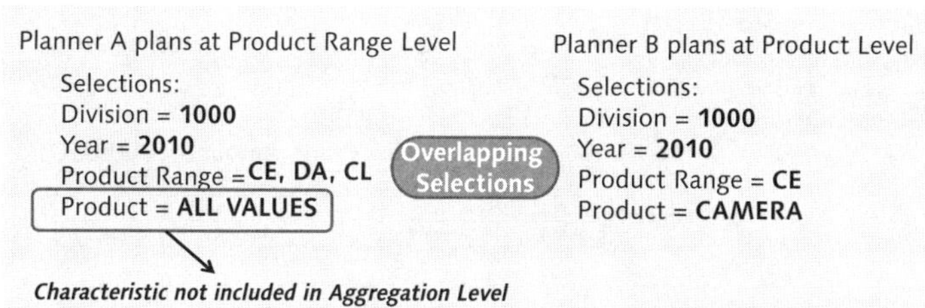

Figure 12.109 Locks on Different Aggregation Levels

Planning locks can be administered from Transaction RSLPLSE.

12.6 Changes to Data in Real-Time InfoCubes

In the previous sections, we explained the different ways in which you can automatically and manually change data using both planning functions and manual planning. This data, which is changed, created, or deleted, is stored in a real-time data cube; in fact, no record in an InfoCube is really changed or deleted. Instead, the changes to the plan data are managed by creating *additive delta* for the changes.

This is explained with an example in Figure 12.110.

If a record is deleted from the plan data, the deletion is actually stored by creating an additional record with the selected key figure value reversed (❶ of Figure 12.110). If the key figure value for a record is increased (e.g., from \$1000 to \$1500), the change is stored in the cube by creating an additional record for the increased value, that is, \$500 (❷). Similarly, if the key figure value for a record is decreased (e.g., from \$1000 to \$800), the change is stored in the cube by creating an additional record for the decreased value, that is, -\$200 (❸).

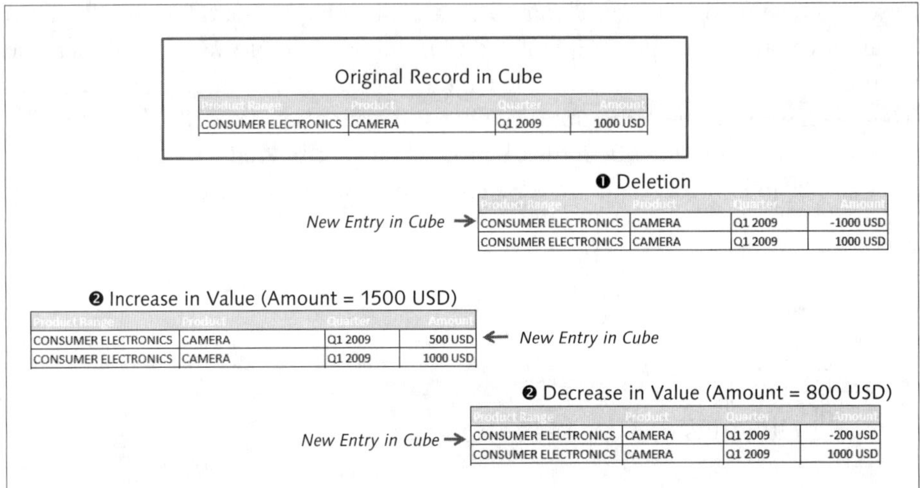

Figure 12.110 Data Changes in Planning Cube

12.7 Summary

In the beginning of this chapter, we provided an overview of the planning process in an organization and discussed the significance of SAP NetWeaver BW Integrated Planning to address the closed-loop planning requirements. We then explained the different planning components involved in building a planning application, and how these components are related to each other; including a discussion about the significance of each planning component and the procedure for creating them using the Planning Modeler. These planning components can be put together to build a planning application that can be accessed by the end user, and we explained the two different ways to create these planning application (Excel-based and web-based). Finally, we discussed the concept of locks in planning and how edited plan data is handled in a real-time InfoCube.

In the next chapter, we discuss reporting on SAP NetWeaver BW InfoProviders and queries using SAP BusinessObjects.

The integration of SAP NetWeaver BW and SAP BusinessObjects has provided more ways for users to present information. In this chapter, we help you understand how reporting can be done using SAP BusinessObjects on top of SAP NetWeaver BW.

13 Reporting with SAP BusinessObjects

The tools and products offered by SAP BusinessObjects have a variety of options relating to queries, reporting, and analysis of enterprise data, all of which can be used to analyze data that resides in SAP NetWeaver BW. One of the key elements in SAP BusinessObjects is the *universe*, which constitutes the semantic layer of the architecture and forms the base for reporting in SAP BusinessObjects. Another important tool from the set of offerings is *Web Intelligence* (WebI), which is an end-user reporting and analysis tool enabled with powerful and easy-to-use query features. WebI reports are built on top of the semantic layer, or, in other words, on top of the universe layer.

The integration of SAP NetWeaver BW and SAP BusinessObjects is made simple by using the Integration Kit for SAP NetWeaver BI reporting. This is an add-on kit installed to enable SAP BusinessObjects reporting and analysis on top of SAP NetWeaver BW components, such as SAP NetWeaver BW queries or SAP NetWeaver BW InfoProviders. The SAP Connectivity component of the kit provides different drivers that enable SAP integration, and includes the following:

- Open SQL driver
- InfoSet driver
- BW query driver
- BW MDX driver
- ODS driver
- OLAP BAPI driver

Among these drivers, you can use the BW query driver for integrating specifically with SAP NetWeaver BW queries, while BW MDX driver connects with SAP NetWeaver BW cubes as well as SAP NetWeaver BW queries.

Reporting from SAP BusinessObjects can be completed in two steps.

1. Create an OLAP universe on top of a SAP NetWeaver BW query, InfoCube, or MultiProvider.
2. Create a WebI report on top of the universe.

The conversion of metadata (InfoObjects and schema definitions) from SAP NetWeaver BW to a universe is facilitated by the Integration Kit. You must first create an OLAP universe before WebI can access data from SAP NetWeaver BW. This flow is illustrated in Figure 13.1.

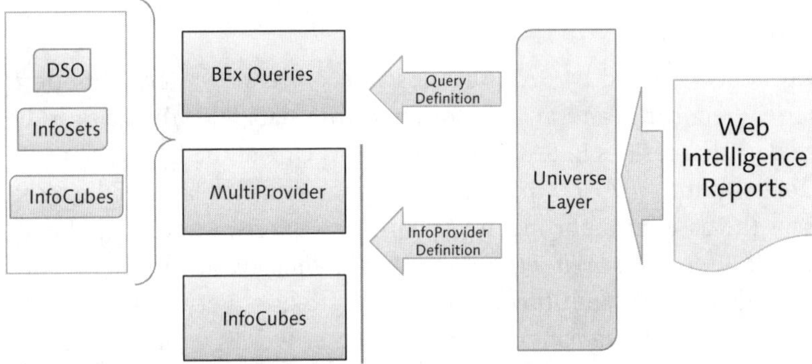

Figure 13.1 Data Access: Web Intelligence Reports from SAP NetWeaver BW Components

As Figure 13.1 shows, you can create the universe either on BEx queries, InfoCubes, or MultiProviders. As you've seen in earlier chapters of the book, you can build MultiProviders or BEx queries on all types of InfoProviders in SAP NetWeaver BW, which means that almost all InfoProviders can be accessed through WebI.

In this chapter, we explain the basic elements of an SAP BusinessObjects universe, how to create a universe, and how to create a WebI report based on this universe.

13.1 Basic Elements of a SAP BusinessObjects Universe

As mentioned earlier, Web Intelligence reports can access data from SAP NetWeaver BW through a semantic layer called the universe. This semantic layer keeps the report users away from the technical development at the backend DataSource (InfoCubes, BEx queries, etc.) and allows them to work with the represented entities in business language. Additionally, a universe can possess additional components such as calculated/restricted key figures for reporting without changing the SAP NetWeaver BW InfoCube or a BEx Query.

Before we get into the technical details, let's first understand some basic elements of the SAP BusinessObjects universe:

- **Classes:** A class within a universe represents a logical grouping of objects together. This can be compared with an InfoProvider dimension in SAP NetWeaver BW. Typically, classes constitute a group of objects that together makes some business sense. These appear as a folder icon () on the screen.
- **Objects:** An object is a detailed level component and a building block in a universe. It maps to data or a derivation of data in the universe DataSource. It can be compared with an InfoObject in SAP NetWeaver BW and is similar to an SAP NetWeaver BW InfoObject. An object in a universe represents a meaningful entity, fact, or calculation used in an end user's business environment. The objects are the basic data elements used to construct a query. For the purpose of analysis, objects are defined in three different categories:
  - **Dimension objects:** Dimension objects are the entities against which the analysis is performed. Dimensions relate to the characteristics included in an SAP InfoCube dimension. These objects are displayed as a blue diamond () on the screen. Some examples of dimension objects are material, sold-to party, country, year, and so on.
  - **Measure objects:** Measures are the measurable entities that either represent numeric data retrieved from the source or represent a result of calculations on the data from the source. They can be compared with key figures in SAP NetWeaver BW. A measure object is denoted by an orange bar () on the screen. For example, stock quantity could be a measure object corresponding to a universe that is built on inventory data.
  - **Detail objects:** Detail objects provide additional information to the dimension entity. The focus of detail objects isn't on analysis; rather, they focus on giving more information on an entity. A detail object is always attached to a dimension for which it provides additional information. This can be compared with display master data attributes and texts in SAP NetWeaver BW. A detail object is denoted by a green pyramid () on the screen. A phone number is an example of a detail object, and it belongs to the customer dimension.

Table 13.1 summarizes the mapping of these universe components with SAP NetWeaver BW elements.

Universe Element	Corresponding SAP NetWeaver BW Element
Classes	▶ Dimension
Dimensions	▶ Characteristics ▶ Navigational Attributes
Detail Objects	▶ Texts ▶ Master Data Display Attributes
Measures	▶ Basic Key Figures ▶ Calculated Key Figures ▶ Restricted Key Figures

Table 13.1 Mapping of Universe Elements with SAP NetWeaver BW Elements

Universes can establish a connection with the following SAP NetWeaver BW objects:

- **InfoCubes and MultiProviders:** A MultiProvider can include any of the available basic InfoProviders, such as a cube, DSO, InfoSet, or master data. The universe will pick up the schema definition of the InfoCube/MultiProvider as a base.
- **BEx queries:** There is no restriction on the queries that can be used as a DataSource to a universe. This means that a universe can connect to any BEx query, independent of the InfoProvider over which the query is built. However, for any query to be accessed by a universe, it needs to be released for external access (Figure 13.2).

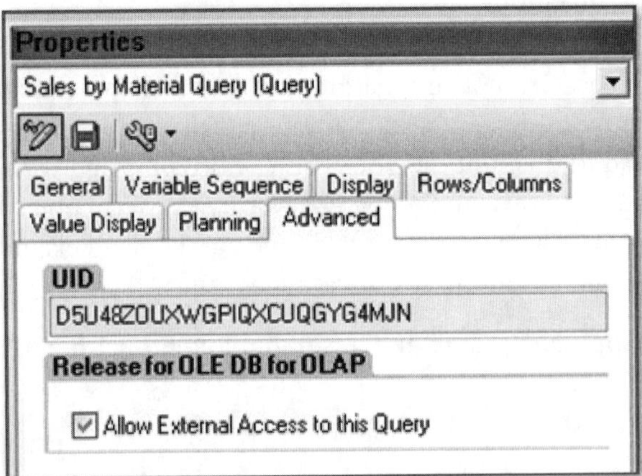

Figure 13.2 Release Query for External Access

To do this, you must ensure that the *Allow External Access to the Query (Release for OLE DB for OLAP)* checkbox is checked. This setting is available on the Advanced tab of query properties.

13.2 Creating a Universe

In this section, we explain how to create a universe — first on an InfoCube and then on a BEx query.

13.2.1 Based on an InfoCube

Follow these steps to create a universe based on an InfoCube:

1. Open the Universe Designer from the Start menu, and log on by entering the requested details. In the Authentication field, select SAP from the dropdown (Figure 13.3).

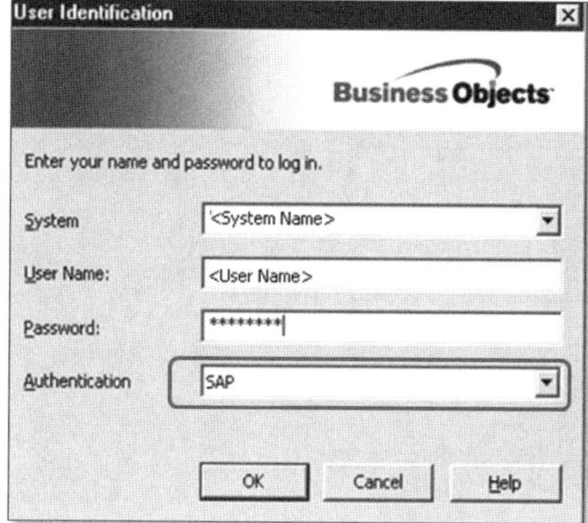

Figure 13.3 Log On to Universe Designer

2. Upon successful login, follow the menu path File • New to create a new universe (Figure 13.4). The next screen asks for universe parameters.
3. Define the basic universe parameters, such as Name (which, in our example, is Sales Universe — ❶ of Figure 13.5). If you want to enter additional information related to the universe, you can enter that in the Description field (❷). Next, fill the Connection field (❸) for the universe you're going to create. To do this, either select one of the existing connections from the dropdown, or create a new connection. To create a new connection, click on the New button.

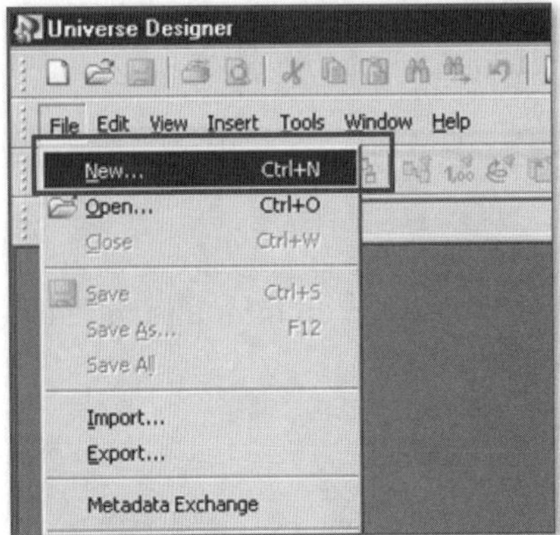

Figure 13.4 Create a New Universe

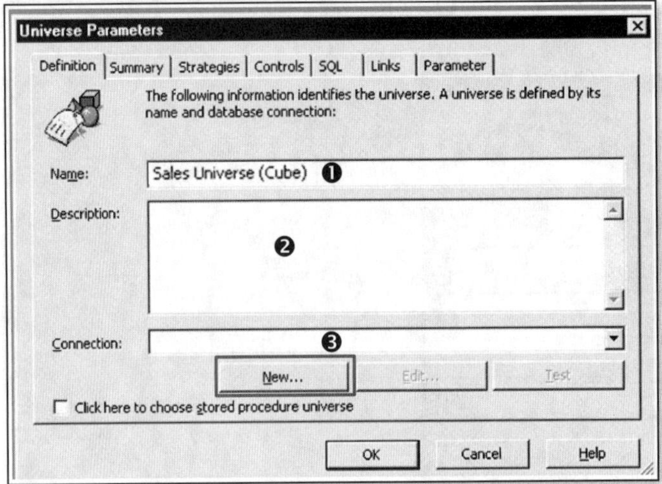

Figure 13.5 Supply Universe Parameters and Create New Connection

4. To define a new connection, enter the connection name "BW Cube Connection" (❶ of Figure 13.6), and then browse through the list of available data access drivers (❷). Select SAP • SAP BUSINESS WAREHOUSE 3.X • SAP CLIENT, and move to the next screen by clicking the Next button.
5. On the next screen, maintain the login parameters for the SAP NetWeaver BW system. The Authentication Mode can be based on single sign-on (SSO), or you can maintain a specific user name and password for the system (Figure 13.7). Go to the next screen after all of the relevant details are entered in this screen.

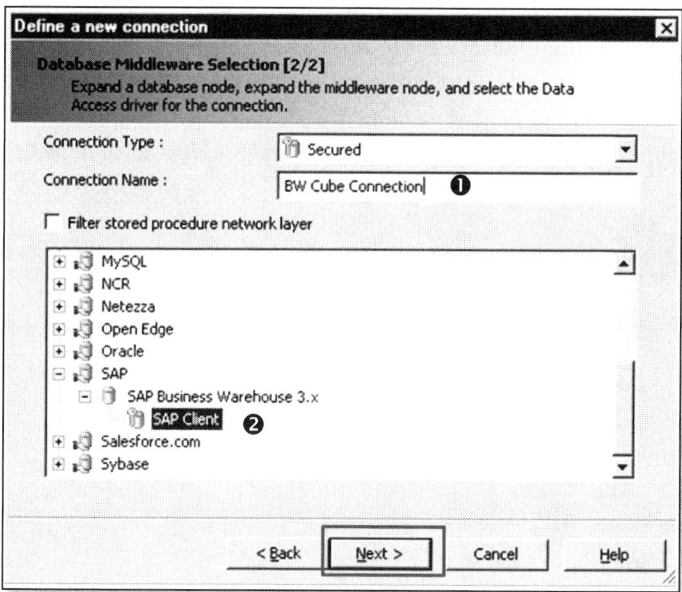

Figure 13.6 Select Data Access Driver

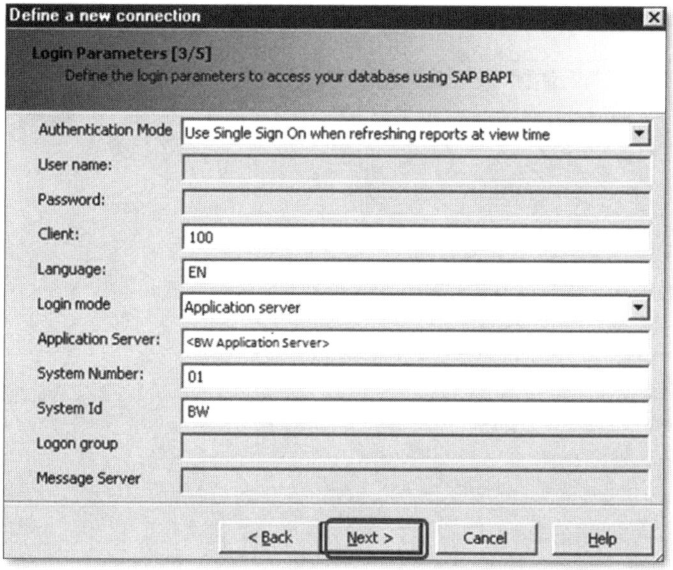

Define a new connection

Login Parameters [3/5]

Define the login parameters to access your database using SAP BAPI

Authentication Mode: Use Single Sign On when refreshing reports at view time

User name:

Password:

Client: 100

Language: EN

Login mode: Application server

Application Server: <BW Application Server>

System Number: 01

System Id: BW

Logon group

Message Server

< Back | Next > | Cancel | Help

Figure 13.7 Maintain Login Parameters

6. After the connection is validated, the screen displays a list of all of the available data providers (cubes and queries) under the OLAP Cubes folder in the SAP NetWeaver BW system. All of the InfoCubes are stored in one folder, $INFOCUBE. To select a cube (for our example, BWSD_C01), follow the path OLAP CUBES • ($INFOCUBE) • BWSD_C01 (Figure 13.8). Click on Next after selecting the cube.

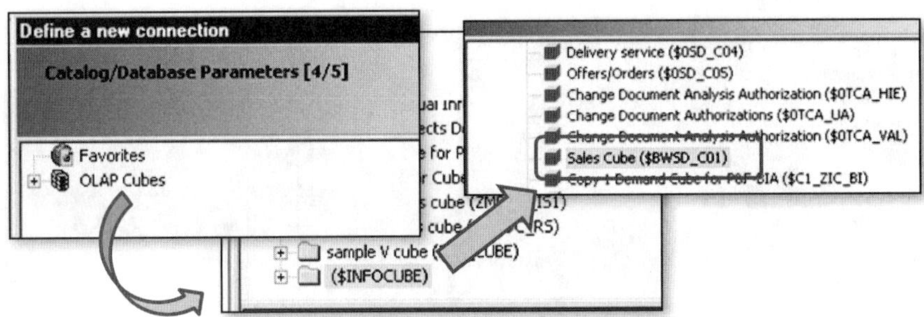

Figure 13.8 Select DataSource

7. The next screen gives you the option to define some advanced parameters for the universe connection (Figure 13.9). For this example, we retain the default values. Click on FINISH to complete the creation of a new connection.

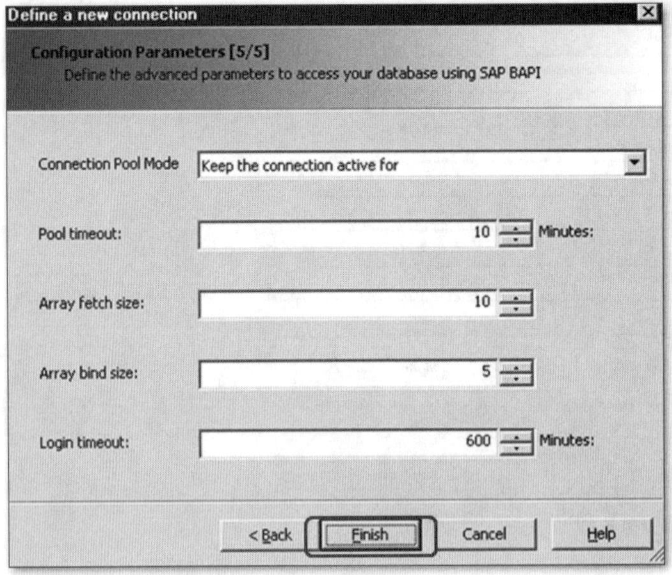

Figure 13.9 Finish the Connection Definition

8. After the connection is defined correctly, we're ready to create our new universe based on the sales cube (Figure 13.10). Click on OK to create the universe.

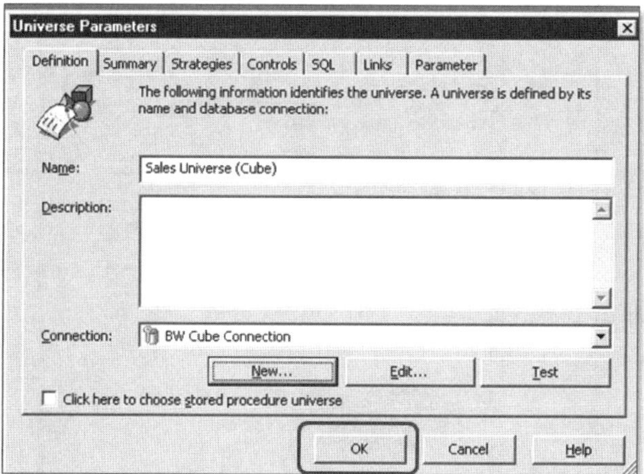

Figure 13.10 Create the Universe Based on a Cube

Based on the connection definition and the data provider selected, the Universe Designer automatically generates the universe by converting the metadata from SAP NetWeaver BW to SAP BusinessObjects. Different OLAP components are mapped to corresponding universe elements, and the generated universe is displayed (Figure 13.11). This figure also shows a mapping of the SAP NetWeaver BW cube elements to the converted universe elements.

All dimensions are converted to universe classes, and a separate key figures class is created for all of the key figures in the cube (❶ of Figure 13.11). A subclass is created for each of the characteristics contained in a SAP NetWeaver BW cube dimension. The subclass contains dimension objects L00 and L01, which further include the detail objects (e.g., L00 Material and L01 Material as shown in ❷). The L00 and L01 nodes correspond with the hierarchy on the characteristic. Level 00 or node 00 represents the root node of the hierarchy, which includes all of the values defined in the hierarchy as well as the values not assigned in the hierarchy. In simpler words, level 00 (L00) contains all values for a characteristic and is useful only if the reporting has to happen on the unassigned members as well. In a straightforward scenario, the L00 node can be removed from the universe, and level L01 behaves similar to a characteristic defined in the cube.

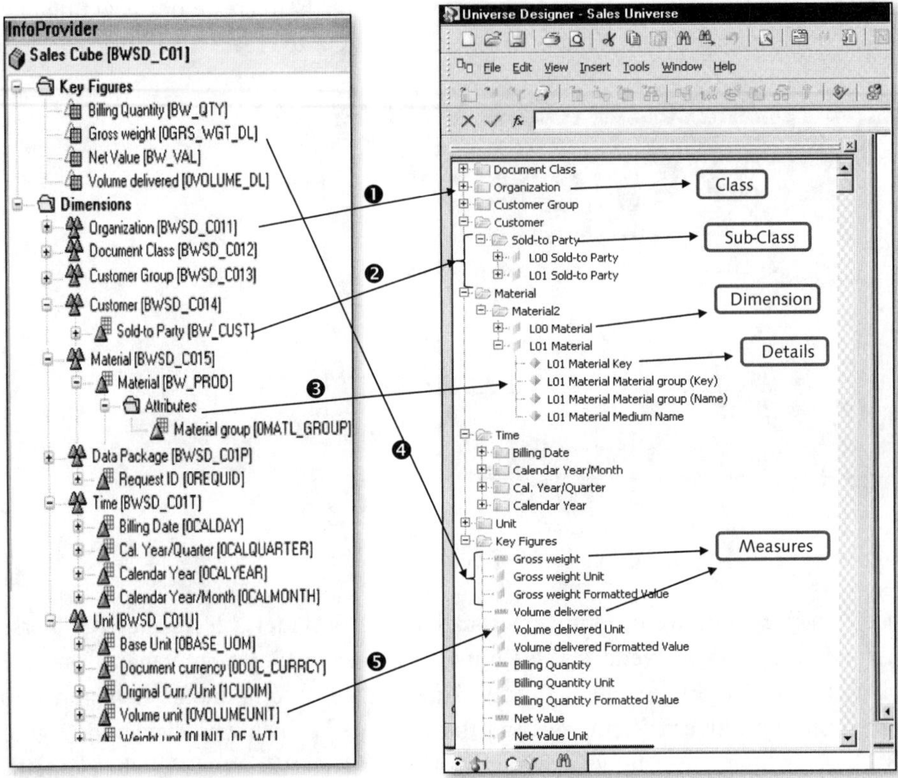

Figure 13.11 Mapping of InfoCube Elements and Generated Universe

The texts and attributes for a characteristic are converted into detail objects in a universe (❸). A separate object for characteristic keys and text is created. For example, if material master data has an attribute for material group, the detail objects created for the material universe dimension would include four detail objects:

- Material key
- Material text
- Material group key
- Material group text

All of the key figures from the cube are grouped under a key figures class in the universe (❹). For each key figure, there are three objects created in the universe:

- A measure object, representing only the numeric value of the key figure, without the unit. This is equivalent to a key figure with the `NODIM()` function in BEx Query

Designer. For example, the gross weight key figure value of 100 KG is shown as 100 only.

- A dimension object for a unit, representing the unit or currency of the key figure, such as KG, USD, and so on.
- A dimension object with a formatted value for the key figure, representing the value of the key figure with the unit, and displayed per the format of the key figure defined in the BEx query definition. For example, the gross weight key figure value of 100 KG formatted to display unit and two decimal places is shown as "100.00 KG".

After your universe is created, you can edit it further to suit your requirements. Editing the generated universe is discussed next:

1. **Remove unwanted L00 dimension nodes:** As discussed earlier, the L00 nodes are useful only when there is hierarchy-based reporting with unassigned members included in the root node of the hierarchy. To remove this from the universe definition, right-click on the L00 dimension node, and select CLEAR (Figure 13.12).

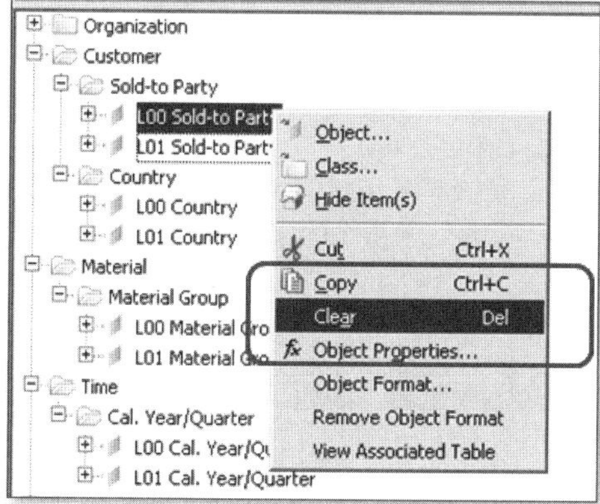

Figure 13.12 Remove Unwanted Elements from Universe Definition

2. **Edit Object Properties:** The properties of different objects in the generated universe can be changed if needed. To look into the properties, right-click on the selected object, and click on OBJECT PROPERTIES.

   Under the Definition tab, you can edit the name, type, and definition of the object. You can also see (and edit, if needed) the statement that defines the object.

   In the Properties tab, you set whether the object is a dimension, measure, or detail object (Figure 13.13). For measure objects, we can also define the aggregation property for the measure by picking up one of the values available in the dropdown.

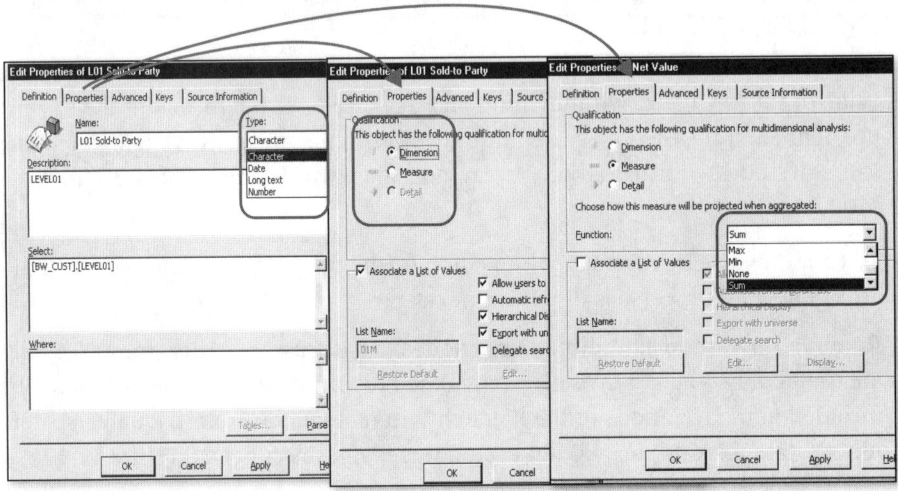

Figure 13.13 Maintain Object Properties

3. **Check the integrity:** After all of the changes to the universe are made, you can check the consistency of the universe by checking its integrity. Go to Tools, and select Check Integrity (Figure 13.14). Check all of the options in the following screen, and click OK. The integrity check results are displayed in the following screen.

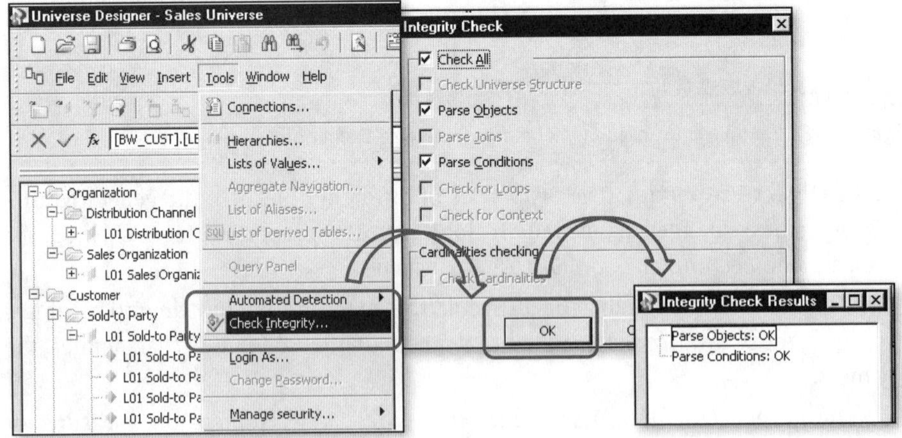

Figure 13.14 Check Integrity of the Universe

4. **Save the universe:** To save the universe, go to FILE • SAVE AS. Enter the universe name, and click the Save button (Figure 13.15).

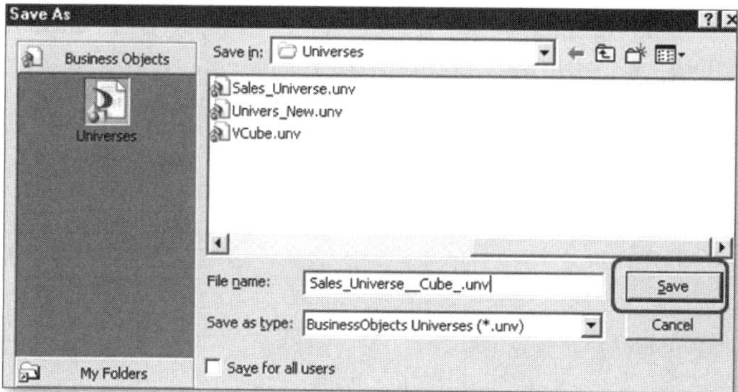

Figure 13.15 Save the Universe

After all of these steps are complete, you have a universe based on a SAP NetWeaver BW InfoCube ready for SAP BusinessObjects reporting.

13.2.2 Based on a BEx Query

One of the prerequisites for creating a universe on a BEx query is that the query has to be released for ODBO (as shown in Figure 13.2, earlier). The rest of the steps are similar to InfoCubes:

1. Define a new connection called "BW Query Connection" (refer to Steps 1-5 in the previous section).
2. Select a BEx query from the catalog, as shown in Figure 13.16.

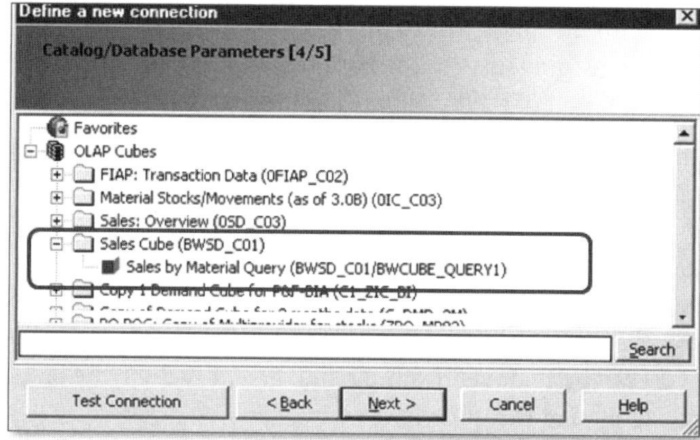

Figure 13.16 Select BEx Query from the Catalog

3. After the connection and universe parameters are defined correctly, create the universe. The Universe Designer automatically generates the universe by converting the metadata from the BEx query. Different query components are mapped to corresponding universe elements. The generated universe is displayed as shown in Figure 13.17. This figure also shows a mapping of BEx elements to the converted universe elements.
4. Save the universe definition with the name "Sales Universe." To save the universe, go to FILE • SAVE AS. Enter the universe name, and click the Save button.

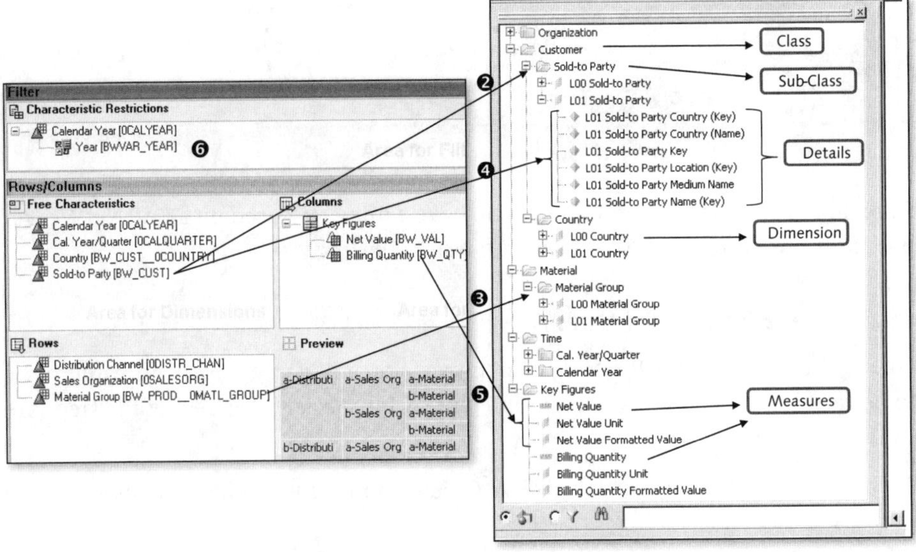

Figure 13.17 Mapping of BEx Query Elements with Generated Universe

All of the dimensions involved in the query (based on characteristics included in the query definition) are converted as universe classes (❶ of Figure 13.17). A separate key figures class is also created for all of the key figures in the query.

There is a subclass created for each of the characteristics included in the query definition. The subclass contains dimension objects L00 and L01, which further include the detail objects (e.g., L00 Sold-to Party and L01 Sold-to Party) in ❷ of Figure 13.17. Here again, the nodes L00 and L01 correspond to the hierarchy on the characteristic. Level 00 (L00) contains all values for a characteristic and is useful only if the reporting has to happen on the unassigned members as well. To make the universe definition simpler, node L00 can be removed from the universe. Level L01 behaves similarly to a characteristic defined in the query.

Navigational attributes used in the BEx query are treated as characteristics and are converted as a dimension in the universe. In ❸ of Figure 13.17, material group is a navigational attribute of material.

The texts and attributes for a characteristic are converted into detail objects in a universe (❹). A separate object for characteristic key and for text is created. For example, if sold-to master data has a country attribute, the detail objects created for a sold-to party universe dimension would include the following detail objects:

- Sold-to party key
- Sold-to party text
- Country key
- Country text

All of the key figures from the query are grouped under a key figures class in the universe (❺). For each key figure, there are three objects created in the universe.

- A measure object, representing only the numeric value equivalent to a key figure with the `NODIM()` function in the BEx query. For example, the net value key figure value of 100 USD is shown as 100 only.
- A dimension object for unit, representing the unit or currency of the key figure, such as KG, USD, and so on.
- A dimension object with a formatted value for the key figure, representing the formatted value of the key figure with the unit, and displayed per the format of the key figure defined in the BEx query definition. For example, the net value key figure value of 100 KG with a formatting of two decimal places and unit is shown as "100.00 USD".

Calculated Key Figures, Restricted Key Figures, Formulas, and Selections

Calculated key figures, restricted key figures, formulas, and selections are also converted into measure objects. The restrictions or calculations defined in the BEx query are applied to these measures but aren't visible in the universe.

The variables from the BEx query are converted to prompts in the universe. In the preceding figure, the restrictions imparted by the variable on the calendar year characteristic are treated as filters for the calendar year class (Figure 13.18). Select the radio button for filter ( ) from the pane at the bottom of the screen, and you see the list of all of the filters used in the universe.

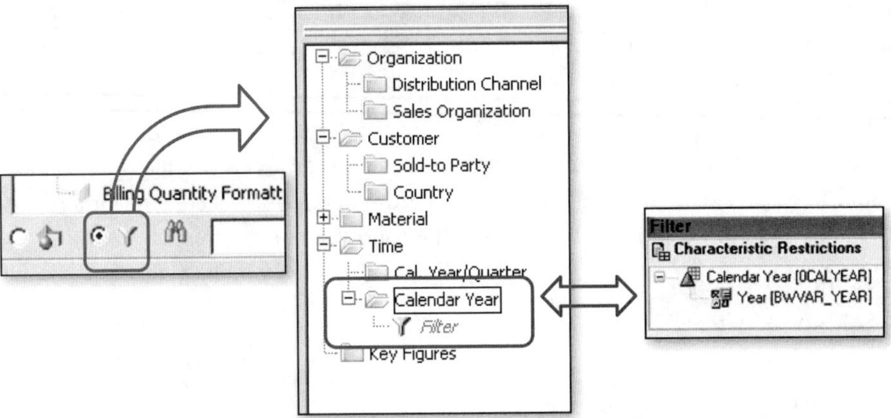

Figure 13.18 Mapping of BEx Query Variable to Universe Filter

The universe supports BEx variables built for characteristic values, hierarchies, hierarchy nodes, texts, and formula variables. However, certain restrictions apply to the variable conversion from a BEx query to a universe:

- Most of the variables of the user entry/default value processing type are supported, except the text variables.
- For text variables, only those of the replacement path processing type are supported.
- User entry/default value variables should be marked as ready for input.
- Variables of the customer exit and SAP exit processing type are supported without the user input option.
- For variables to be interpreted and visible in the universe, the characteristic should be included in the query as free characteristics/rows/columns.

The use of prompts in reporting is discussed in subsequent sections of the chapter, where we explain how to create a simple WebI report on top of a universe.

13.3 Web Intelligence

Web Intelligence (WebI) is an interface provided by SAP BusinessObjects that offers self-service access to data stored in data warehouses, data marts, and packaged business applications. Using WebI, you can autonomously access data, view reports, and perform query, reporting, and analysis tasks. It's a powerful tool that allows you to create reports (also known as WebI documents) on top of a SAP BusinessObjects universe to leverage the business-friendly semantic layer and keep the technical complexity away from the information consumer.

WebI makes reporting and analysis easy for casual users because they can create reports and analyze the data themselves via step-by-step report creation and intuitive data presentation. On the other hand, advanced users can fully leverage BI by creating complex reports with powerful calculations, filters, and drill-through analysis.

In the next section, we explain the following:

- Creating a WebI report based on a universe
- Editing and formatting WebI elements
- Performing local calculations in a WebI document

13.3.1 Creating a Web Intelligence Report Based on a Universe

Follow the steps given in this section to create a WebI report based on a universe:

1. Open Web Intelligence ( ) from the Start menu, and log on by entering the requested details. From the Authentication field dropdown list, select SAP. This opens the standalone version of WebI, which is installed on your computer (rich client). You can also open WebI from the Infoview. This doesn't need any installation on your computer (thin client).

Infoview

An Infoview is a BI portal for SAP BusinessObjects, which provides users with a single entry point to all of the reports and interfaces.

2. Upon successful login, go to File • New to create a new WebI document (Figure 1.19).

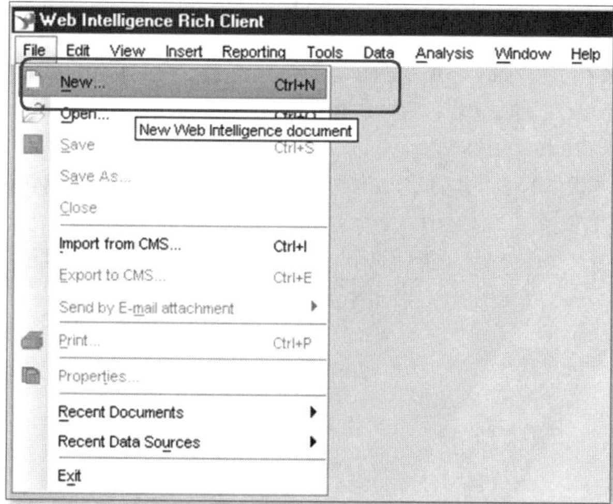

Figure 13.19 Create a New Web Intelligence Document

3. The next screen asks if the Web Intelligence document has to be based on a universe or on a local DataSource. Select Universe, and click NEXT. The following screen displays a list of all of the universes available to you. Select the universe (based on the BEx query), and click on OK (Figure 13.20).

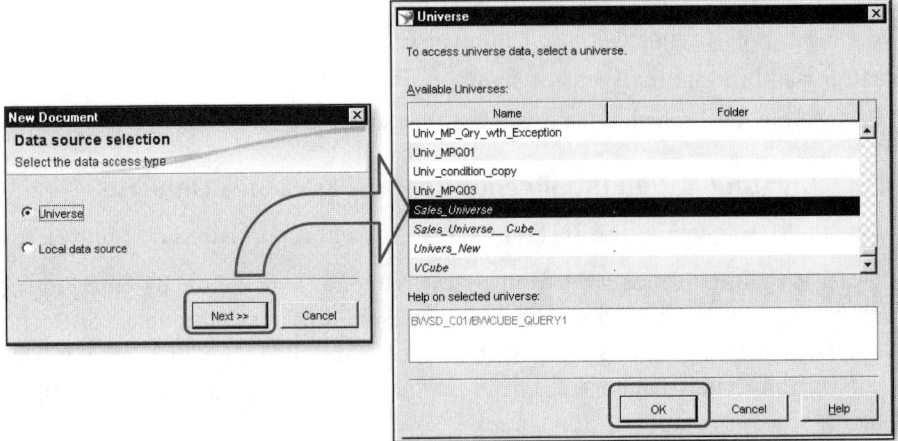

Figure 13.20 Select a Universe

The default layout screen where you create the query has three major sections (Figure 13.21).

The pane on the left side (❶ of Figure 13.21) displays all of the data elements from the universe over which the query had to be created. The structure in which the elements are displayed is similar to that of the universe, that is, following the class, subclass, dimension, and details. The Result Objects pane on the right side (❷) includes the objects that are displayed in the report. The Query Filters pane on the right side (❸) bears all of the filters or restrictions that are to be defined for a query. On this screen, you can create, edit, and format a WebI query. Let's build one for a business example, which shows yearly direct sales by material group for different sales organizations for the selected year, along with an additional column displaying sales per unit sold.

4. To address these requirements, let's first start with dragging all of the necessary objects from the Data section to the Result Objects pane (Figure 13.22).

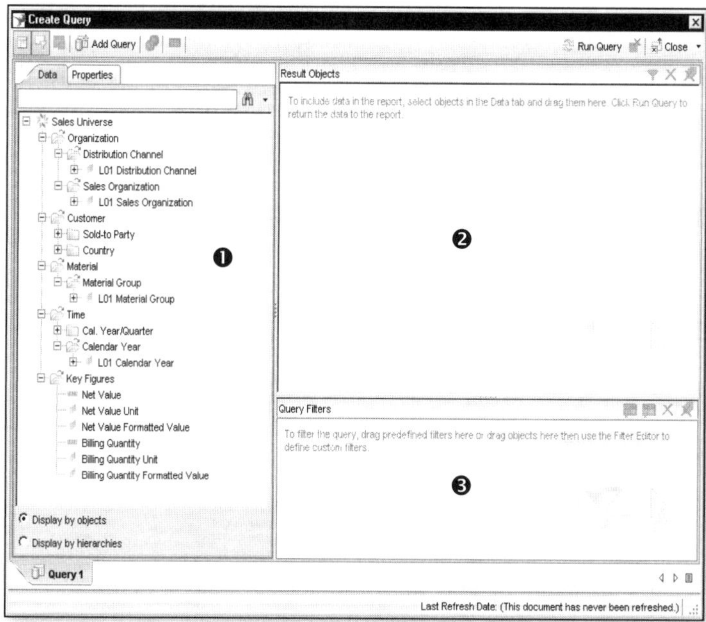

Figure 13.21 Create Query: Screen Layout

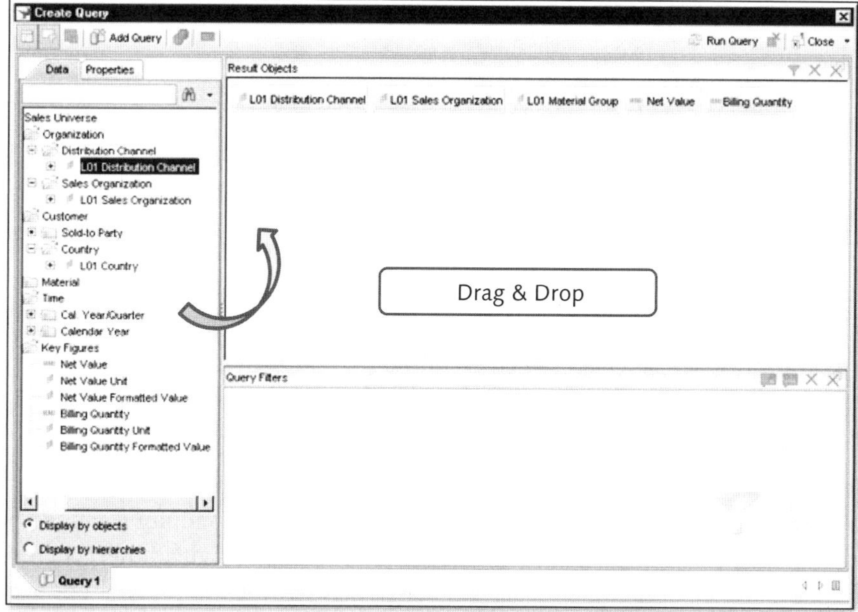

Figure 13.22 Select Result Objects for the Query

5. In the example scenario for ABCD Corp. used in this book, the sales are made through two different distribution channels: IT and direct sales. In this particular query, we need only the direct sales to be displayed in the result, so we need to restrict the query to Distribution Channel = Direct Sales. To achieve this, drag the distribution channel from the Data section to the Query Filters section (Figure 13.23).

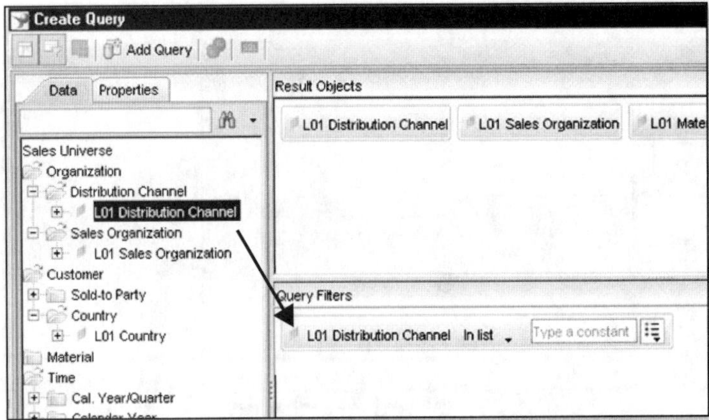

Figure 13.23 Add Query Filter

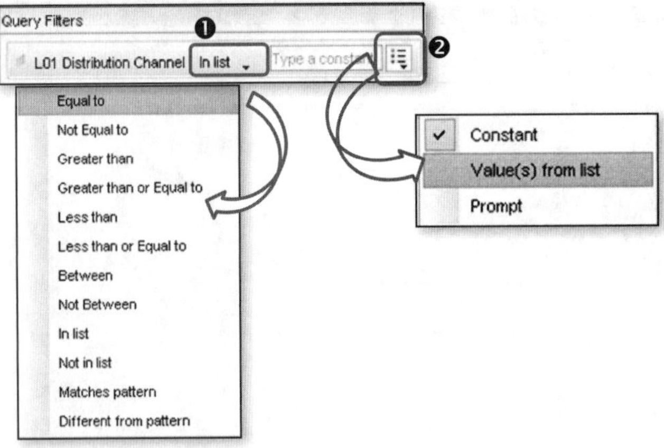

Figure 13.24 Filter Definition

A WebI query filter restricts the query result based on the conditions defined in the filter. There are different options available to define a particular filter; you can select its behavior from different conditional operators available in the dropdown list (❶ in Figure 13.24). Also, you can define the type of restriction for the data element dragged into the Filters section (❷). It can be a constant value defined at the query level, a set of values picked from a defined list, or a prompt for the user to enter a value during query execution. In our example, we chose the In List option and the Value(s) from List type.

After selecting Value(s) from List, a pop-up appears with values read from SAP NetWeaver BW for the distribution channel characteristic (Figure 13.25). Select the Direct Sales value (❶) and move it to the right pane by clicking on the arrow (❷). Return to the query definition by clicking OK (❸).

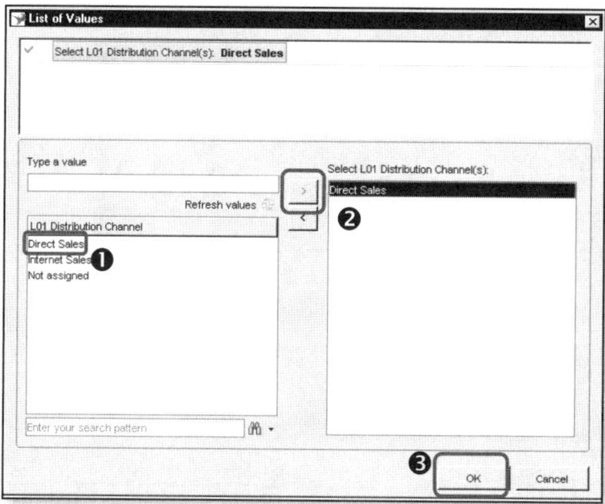

Figure 13.25 Restrict Filter with Values

6. You can see the filter with value direct sales in Figure 13.26. The query is now defined and ready to be executed. Click on the Run Query button to execute the query.
7. After you execute this query, you get a Prompts screen for year (Figure 13.27). This is due to the filter that is applied to calendar year in the universe. The filter in the universe is derived from the BEx variable that is a user entry, single value, or mandatory variable. As shown in Figure 13.27, select 2008 (❶), click on the arrow button to apply the value (❷), and then click on Run Query (❸) to submit the selected filter value and proceed with the execution of the query.

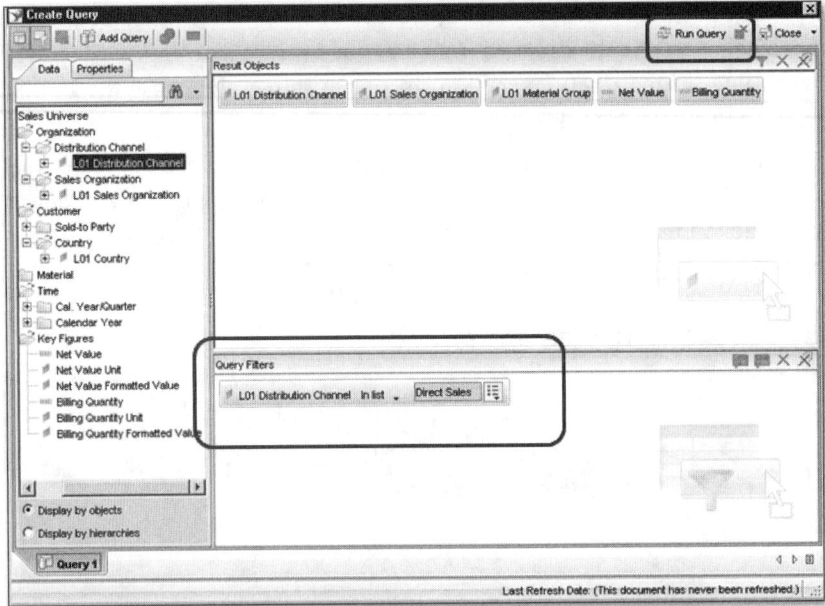

Figure 13.26 Execute Query

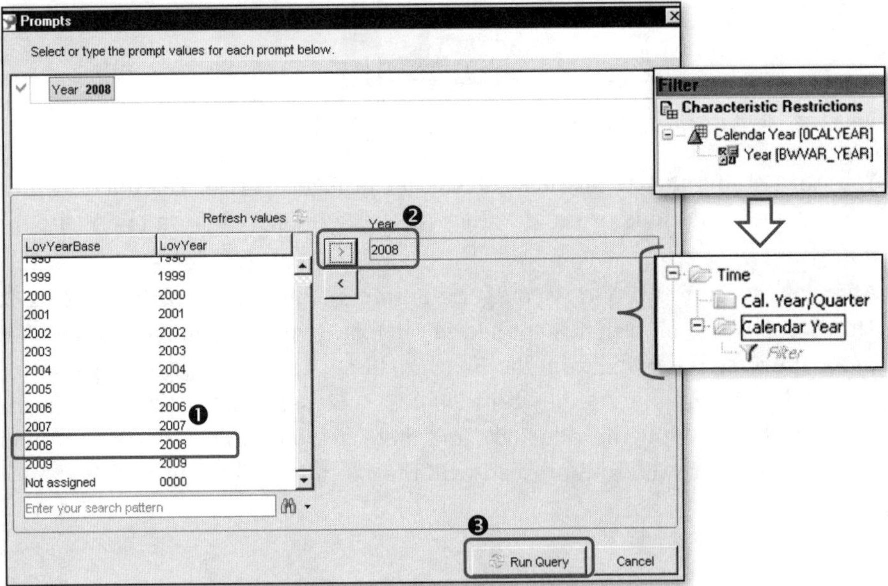

Figure 13.27 Prompts in WebI Query

8. The query result is displayed as shown in Figure 13.28. The left pane (❶) consists of all of the data elements that are selected to be in the report, and the right pane (❷) displays the query result.

   To go back to the query edit screen, click on the Edit Query button highlighted in Figure 13.28.

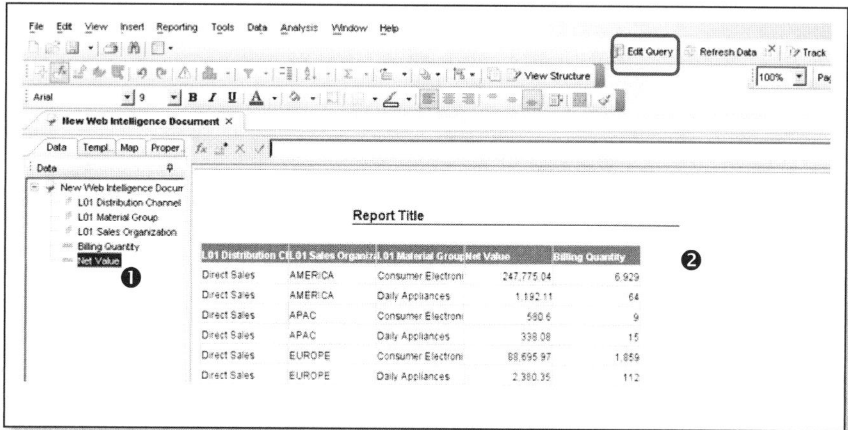

Figure 13.28 Default Report Layout

13.3.2 Editing and Formatting Web Intelligence Documents

In the previous section, we explained how to create a simple report from a WebI query. After a report is created, many options are available to further enhance it. Let's explore how we can use these options to attain the desired result, that is, to view the yearly direct sales by material group for different sales organizations, along with an additional column displaying sales per unit sold.

Let's begin by editing the report title. Right-click on Report Title, and select Edit Format from the context menu. The Properties pane on the left side of the screen displays the title properties (Figure 13.29). Here we can maintain the text for the report title and also control other appearance and display properties for the element. Maintain the text for the report title as "Yearly Direct Sales by Material Group."

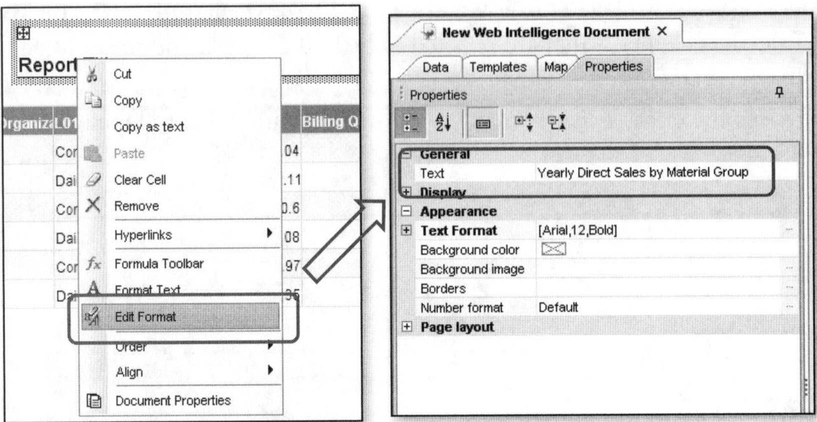

Figure 13.29 Change Report Title

This report currently displays columns such as Distribution Channel, Sales Organization, Material Group, Net Values, and Billing Quantity. We know that the query is restricted for Distribution Channel = Direct Sales, so, we don't need an explicit column for Distribution Channel, and this column can be removed. To remove a column from the layout, right-click on the column header, and select REMOVE • REMOVE COLUMN from the context menu (Figure 13.30). The selected column for Distribution Channel is removed from the report.

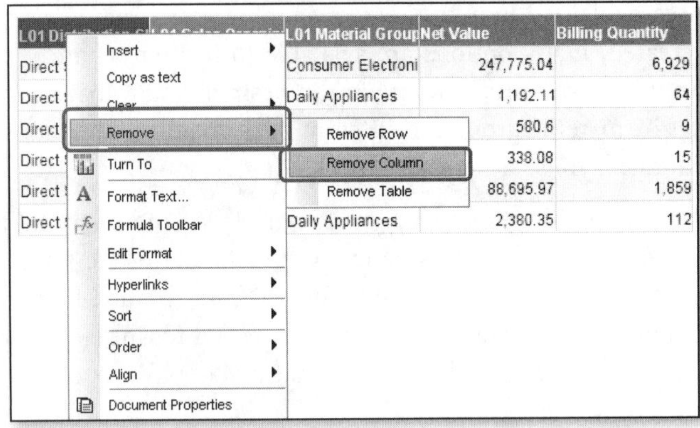

Figure 13.30 Removing Columns from Report Display

You can also include additional display elements in the WebI document. There are plenty of options available to represent the report data in different formats. The Templates tab on the left pane of the screen lists all of the report elements that can be added to the report (Figure 13.31). This includes tables, different types of charts, and so on.

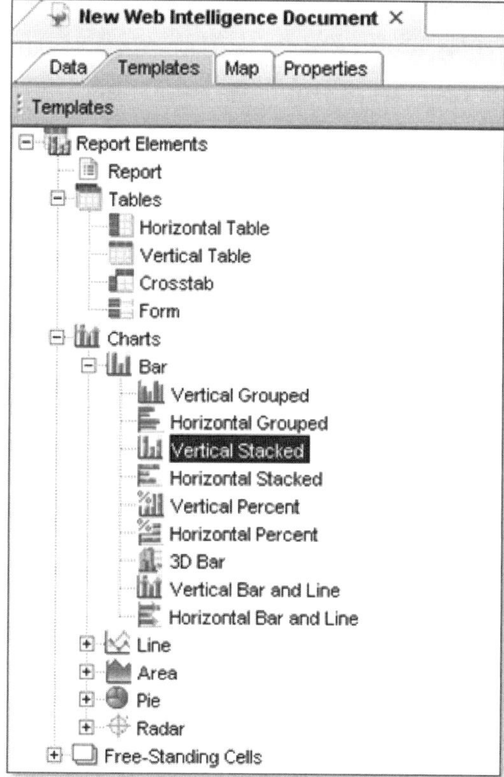

Figure 13.31 Templates for Adding Report Elements to WebI Documents

In our example, we build a bar chart to display net sales by different sales organizations. For this, drag Vertical Stacked Bar Chart from the Templates tab to the right pane, and go to REPORT ELEMENTS • CHARTS • BAR • VERTICAL STACKED (Figure 13.32).

To include the data elements in the chart, go to the Data tab on the left pane, and drag the net value and sales organization to the chart on the right side (Figure 13.32). After adding the bar chart to the layout, the report result will look like Figure 13.33.

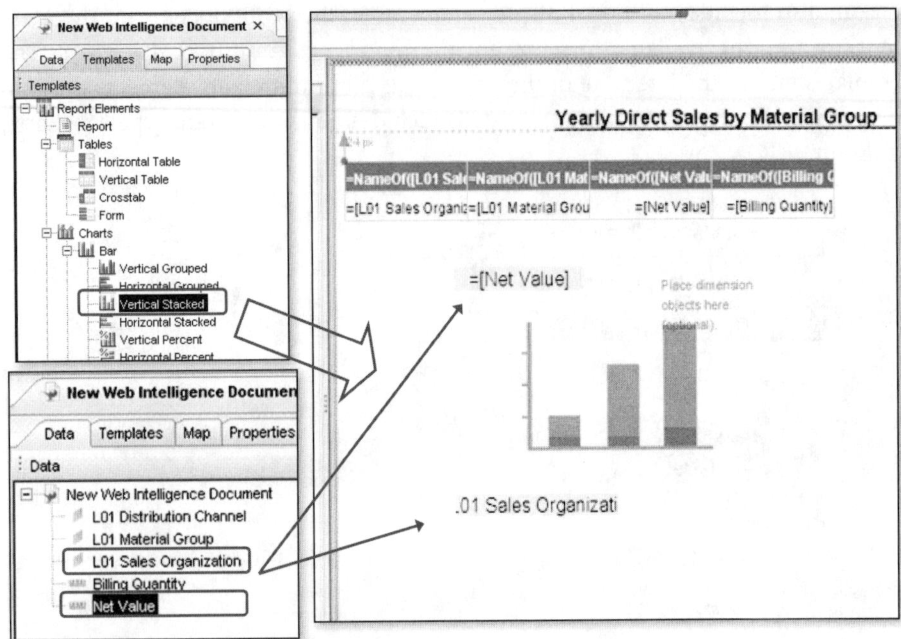

Figure 13.32 Add Charts to the WebI Document

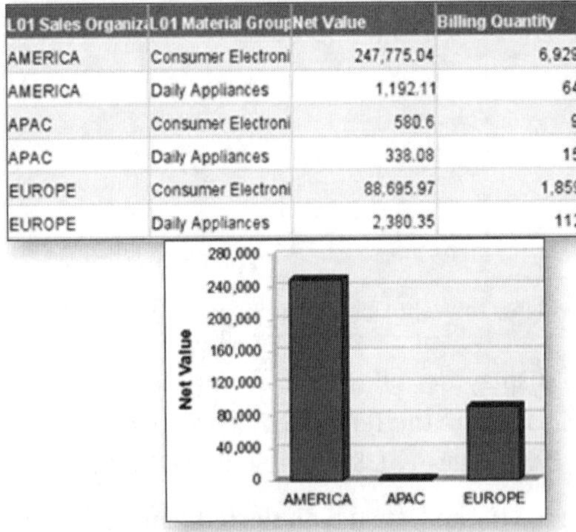

L01 Sales Organiz	L01 Material Group	Net Value	Billing Quantity
AMERICA	Consumer Electroni	247,775.04	6,92
AMERICA	Daily Appliances	1,192.11	64
APAC	Consumer Electroni	580.6	9
APAC	Daily Appliances	338.08	15
EUROPE	Consumer Electroni	88,695.97	1,85
EUROPE	Daily Appliances	2,380.35	11

Figure 13.33 Report Display with Chart

13.3.3 Performing Local Calculations in a WebI Document

Now let's again focus on the requirements. We need a report that displays yearly direct sales by material group for different sales organizations, along with an additional column displaying sales per unit sold. The additional column isn't visible in the report right now but can be calculated as net value divided by billing quantity. Now let's add this additional column to the report and then define a local calculation to derive the value of sales per unit sold.

On the report result screen, right-click on the Billing Quantity column, and select INSERT. There are options to insert either a row or a column. When you're working with measures, inserting rows is used when the measures are in rows, and inserting columns is used when the measures are in columns. In our example, you insert a column to the right of the existing column, Billing Quantity. Select INSERT COLUMN TO THE RIGHT, as shown in Figure 13.34.

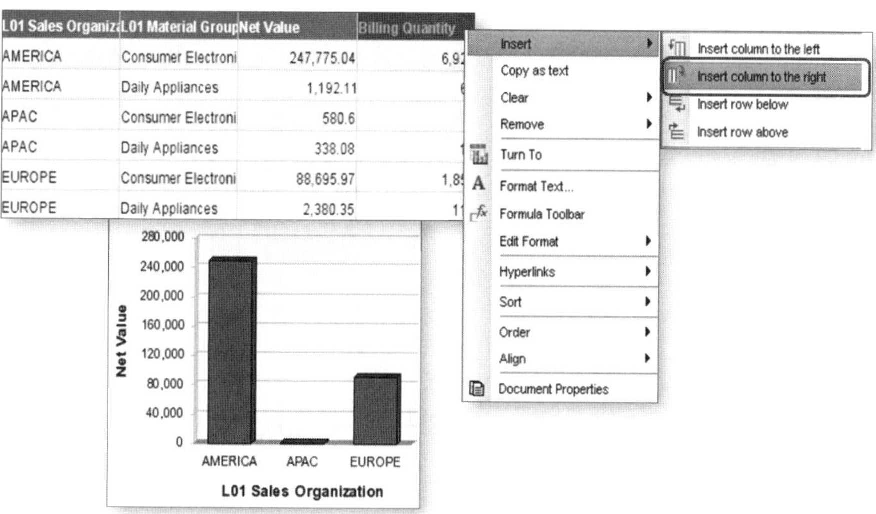

Figure 13.34 Insert a New Column in WebI Report

Enter the column header description as "Sales per Unit Sold." You now must define the formula for the newly created column. The Formula Editor can be accessed by pressing Ctrl-Enter, or from the context menu (right-click on the new column, and select Formula Toolbar) (Figure 13.35).

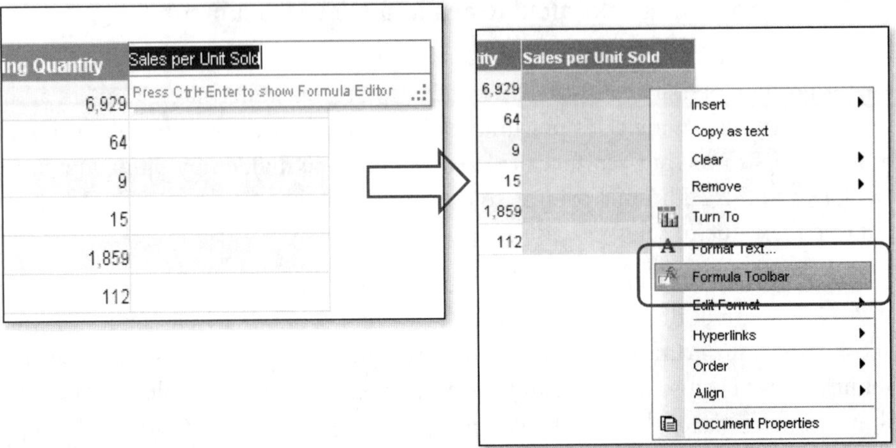

Figure 13.35 Show Formula Toolbar

The formula toolbar appears on the top part of the screen, as shown in Figure 13.36. You can enter the formula directly in the toolbar or define one by clicking the button highlighted in Figure 13.36.

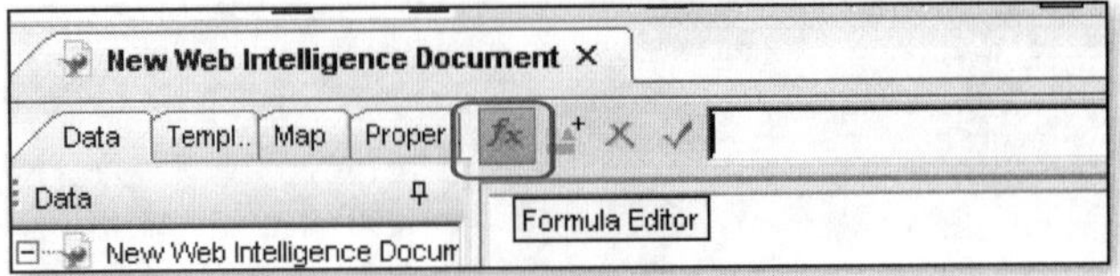

Figure 13.36 Open Formula Editor

The Formula Editor opens in a separate window, which provides options to build a formula for the newly created column (Figure 13.37).

On the Formula Editor screen, there are four sections (Figure 13.37):

- Data: This section lists all of the fields that are available in the report layout. These are the fields that can be used to build the formula.
- Functions: This section enlists different prebuilt functions that can be used to create formulas. The available functions include numeric functions such as Abs, Average, Count, and so on, as well as nonnumeric functions such as Concatenate Strings, and so on. It also includes system functions such as Current User, Current Date/Time, and others.

- Operators: Different operators that are needed to build a formula are listed in this section.
- Formula: The formula definition is visible in this section.

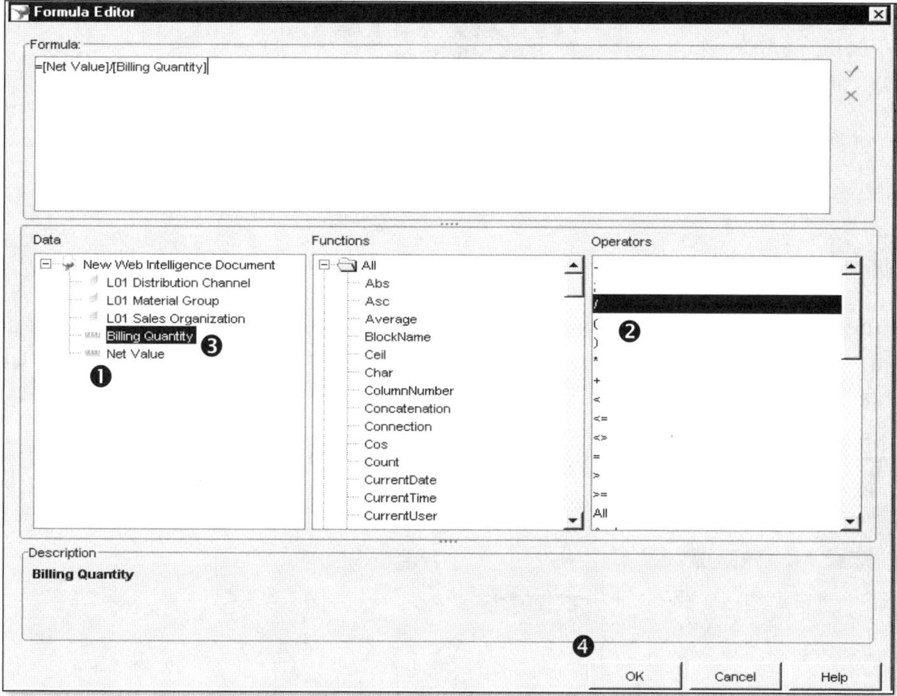

Figure 13.37 Working with the Formula Editor

To calculate sales per unit sold, we must build a formula where the Net Sales column is divided by the Billing Quantity column. To do this, first select Net Sales from the Data section (❶ of Figure 13.37), select the divided by operator (/) from the Operators section (❷), and then select Billing Quantity from the Data section (❸). Finally, click on the OK button to confirm the formula definition (❹).

The new column, Sales per Unit Sold, is now populated based on the defined formula (Figure 13.38). You can further edit the format for this column to alter the display of the values shown. Right-click on the column, and select FORMAT TEXT from the context menu (Figure 13.38).

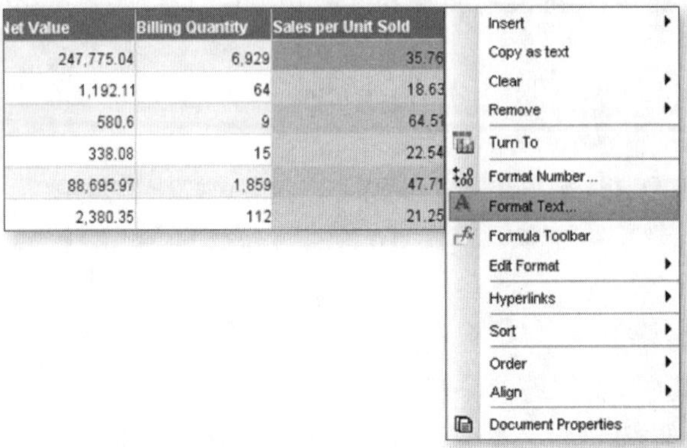

Figure 13.38 Format Text for Column Data

In the Format Text window that appears next, you can change parameters such as font, font style, size, font color, alignment, and other settings (Figure 13.39). Click OK after you're through with the format settings.

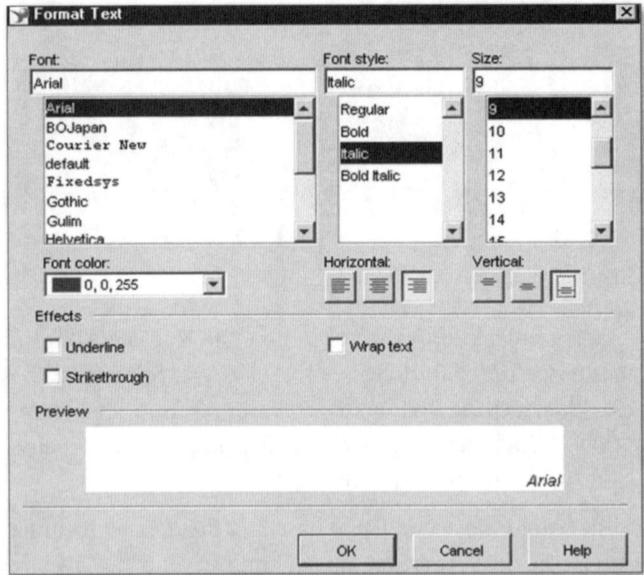

Figure 13.39 Format Text Options

Finally, we have a report that shows direct sales by sales organization, and a calculated column showing sales per unit price (Figure 13.40). The next step is to save the report. Follow menu path File • Save, or click on the button highlighted in Figure 13.40.

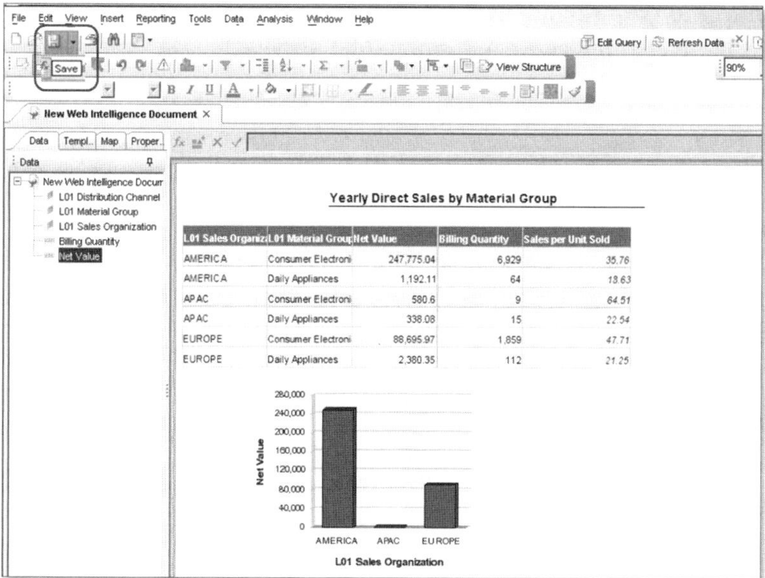

Figure 13.40 Save the Web Intelligence Report

Save the final WebI document as shown in Figure 13.41.

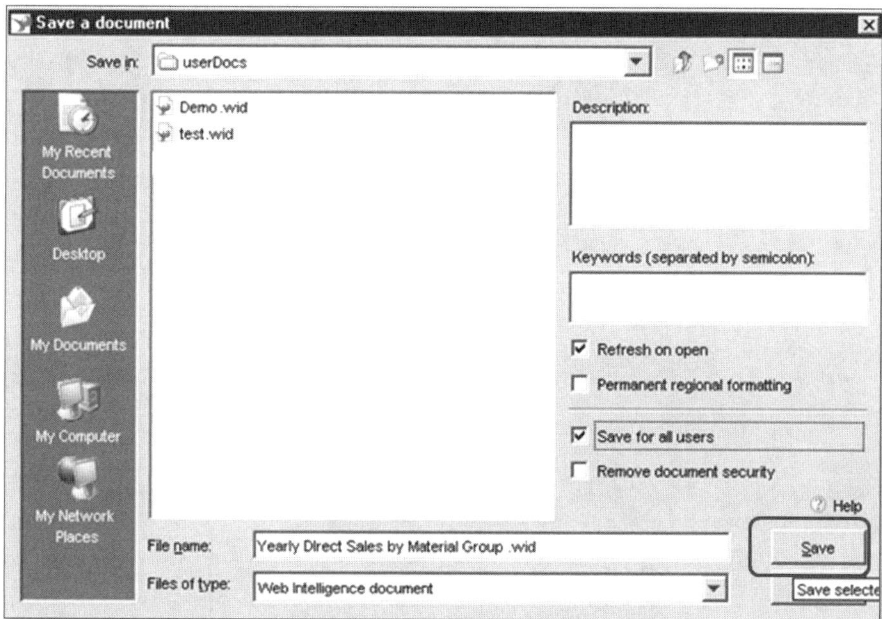

Figure 13.41 Saving the Web Intelligence Document

You now know how to create an ad-hoc report based on the universe using a user-friendly and flexible Web Intelligence tool from SAP BusinessObjects.

13.4 Summary

In this chapter, we explained how you can perform reporting from SAP BusinessObjects on top of SAP NetWeaver BW. All of the BEx queries, InfoCubes, and MultiProviders can be used in the universe semantic layer for reporting in SAP BusinessObjects. Web Intelligence is a simple and intuitive reporting tool that accesses the universe layer as a DataSource and allows you to create your own WebI documents.

The next chapter will explain some of the common administration and monitoring tasks performed in SAP NetWeaver BW.

In this chapter, we introduce some of the basic administration and maintenance aspects of SAP NetWeaver BW. Understanding these concepts will help you maximize your efficiency when using the SAP NetWeaver BW solution.

14 Administration and Monitoring

A BI solution is only successful when it lives up to its purpose of delivering the right information at the right time by consuming the right amount of resources — consistently. Administration and maintenance activities ensure that a solution lives up to its purpose with minimal total cost of ownership (TCO) and high reliability in data quality and information security.

In this chapter, we cover the following topics related to administration and maintenance of SAP NetWeaver BW:

- DSO administration and maintenance
- InfoCube administration and maintenance
- Aggregates
- Compression
- Process chains
- Analysis authorizations
- Other administration and maintenance tasks

We recommend that you read the reference material listed in the Preface to this book on each of the above topics while executing them in the solution to enhance your understanding of the solution.

14.1 DSO Administration and Maintenance

Administration and maintenance tasks for data targets (both DSOs and InfoCubes) are well organized in DWW by the buttons, icons, and tabs on the screen. This section provides an overview of the main tasks involved in DSO maintenance and performance improvement.

14.1.1 InfoProvider Administration Screen Tasks — DSO

Use Transaction RSA1 to reach the DWW screen, and choose InfoProviders within the Modeling tab on the left panel. Then choose DSO Object on the right panel (❶ of Figure 14.1).

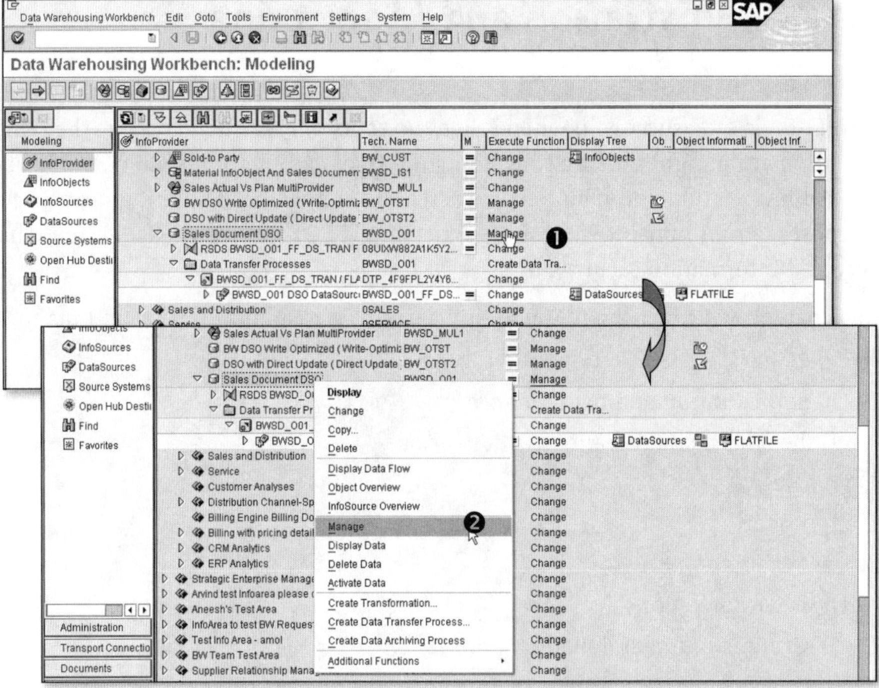

Figure 14.1 Managing a DSO

Click the Manage option in the context menu (❷), and the InfoProvider Administration screen appears (Figure 14.2). The upper part has the details of the InfoProvider, and the lower part has three tabs: Contents, Requests, and Reconstruction (❷ Figure 14.2). The lowest part of the screen in each tab has relevant options for executing the administration and maintenance tasks (❸).

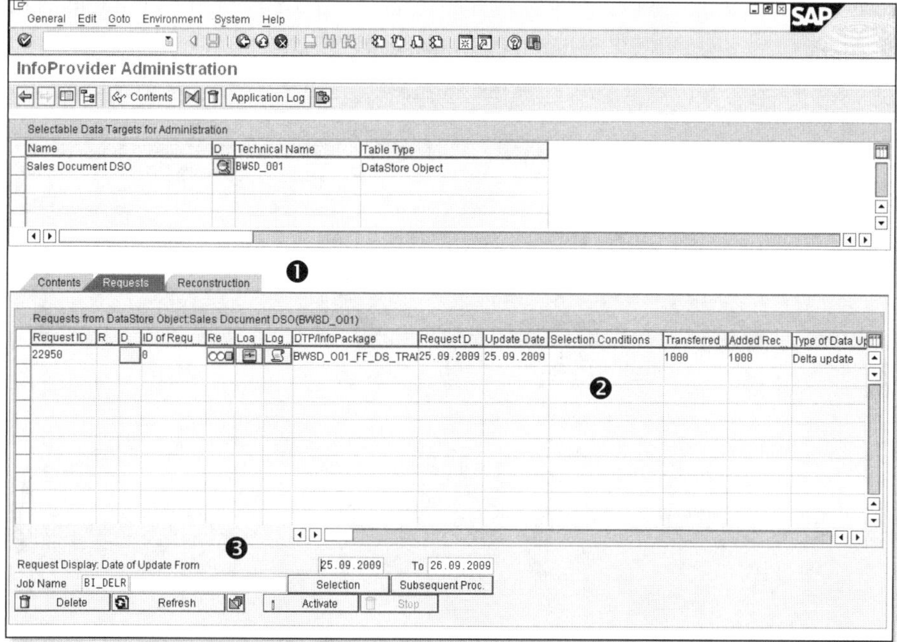

Figure 14.2 Administration Tasks for a DSO

We explain each of the three tabs next.

Contents Tab

Viewing the contents of a DSO figures fairly regularly in the administration of a DSO. As you know, a standard DSO has three different tables: the Activation Queue table, the Active Data table, and the Change Log table. The contents in these vary, and viewing their content helps in the reconciliation of any reporting errors.

The lower part of the Contents tab (❶ of Figure 14.3). provides buttons that allow you to view different types of content (❷ of Figure 14.3). Click on the button for the chosen table (the New Data button refers to the Activation Queue), and the system takes you to the Data Browser: Table <Technical Name> screen (❸). The selection screen contains fields for each of the InfoObjects in the DSO, along with the technical field value options relevant to the type of table. Click on the Number of Entries button, and the system provides information about the number of entries. To make a complex selection, use the icon. Make a selection for different InfoObjects on this screen, and click on the Execute icon () to view the contents of the Activation Queue table (❹).

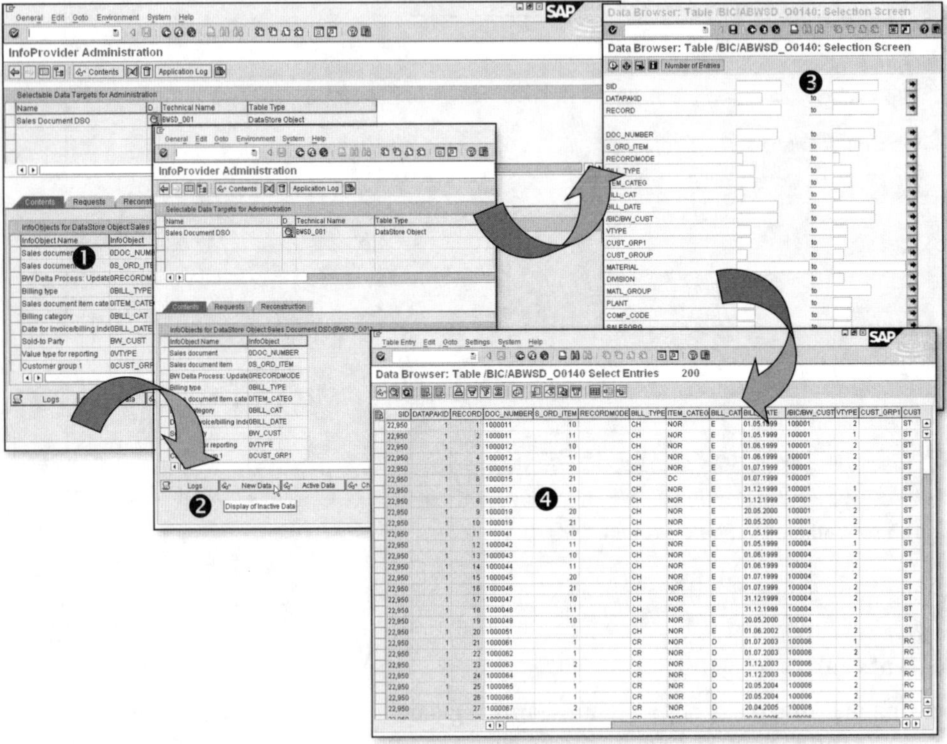

Figure 14.3 View Content of DSO – Active Data Table

The contents of the Change Log table can be viewed by following the same process (❶ to ❸ in Figure 14.4).

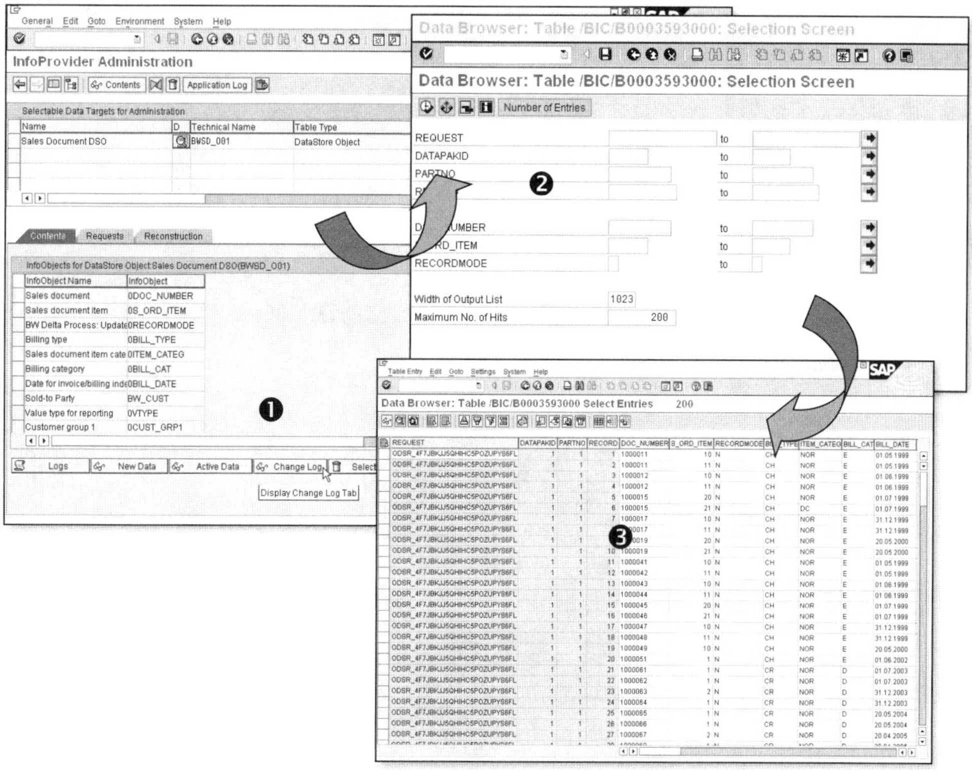

Figure 14.4 View Content of DSO — Change Log Table

Requests Tab

In Section 4.2.2, Activation Process for a Standard DSO, in Chapter 4, DataStore Object, we explained the process of activating requests in the system at the conceptual level. In this section, we explain the actual execution of the activation of a request in DSO, as this is a regular maintenance task that you perform using the Requests tab (❶ of Figure 14.5).

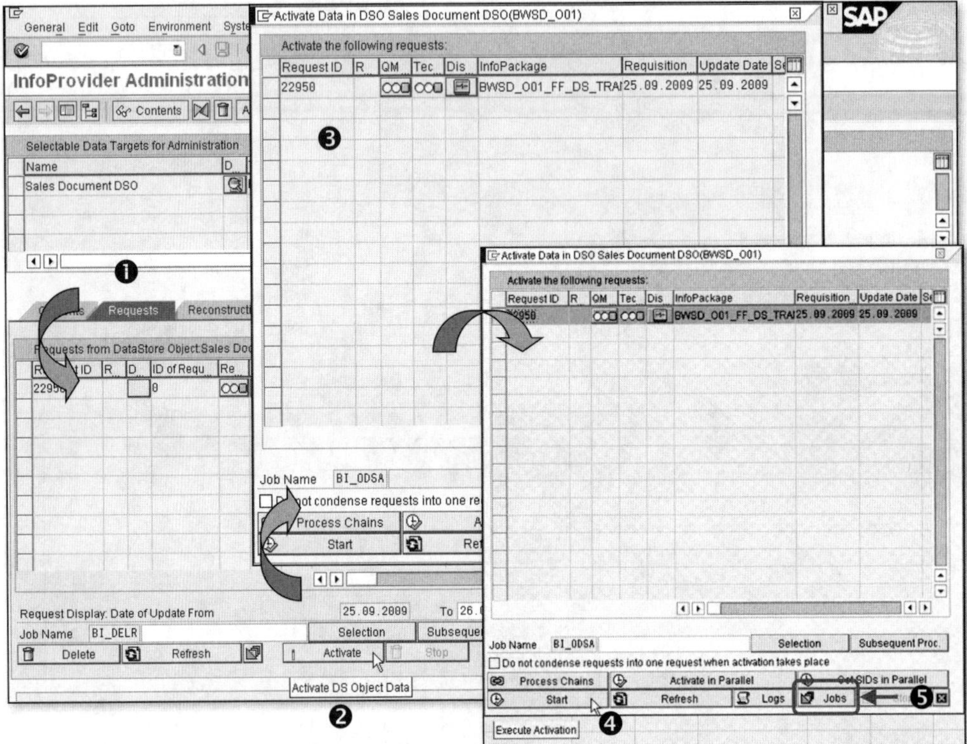

Figure 14.5 Activation of a New Request in a DSO

The lower part of the Requests tab has options relevant to executing the activation of requests (❷). Clicking the Activate button opens the Activate Data in DSO <Text Name of DSO> screen, with a list and details of the requests to be activated (❸). In our example, the screen shows request 22950, including its QM and technical status. Select the request, and click the Start button (❹).

The Jobs button (❺ of Figure 14.5) takes you to the Simple Job Selection screen (❶ of Figure 14.6), and the system prepopulates the entry box for the job name with a typical naming convention starting with BI_ODS <long technical name>.

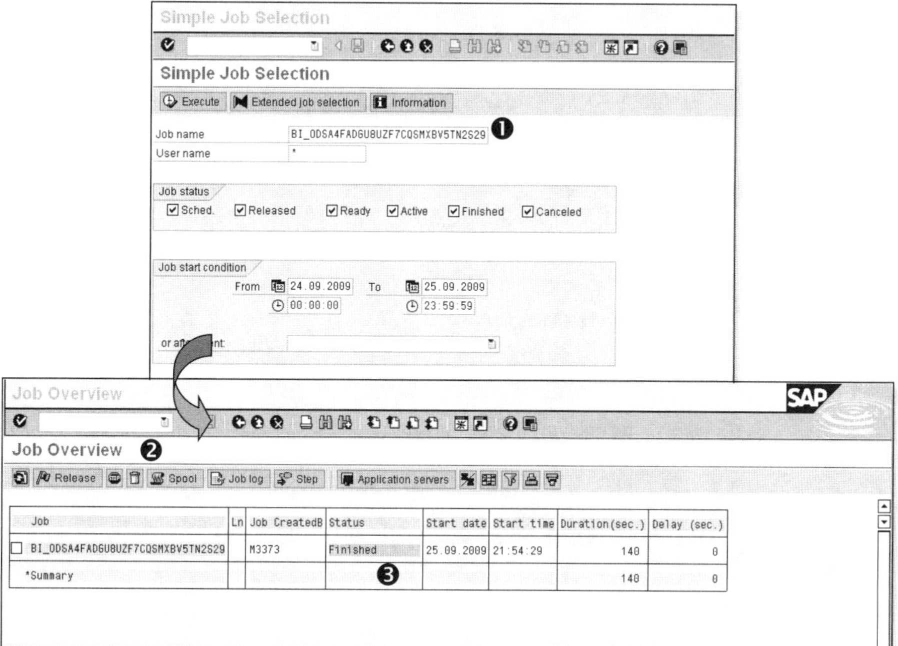

Figure 14.6 Activation Job Overview

To see the status of the activation job, click on the Execute button, which takes you to the Job Overview screen (❷). The status of the job can be monitored under the Status column of the table. The Refresh button (on the extreme left of the dynamic menu bar) is used to refresh the status of the job. Jobs that are finished are labeled as such and highlighted in green (❸). A Finished status indicates that the requests have been successfully activated.

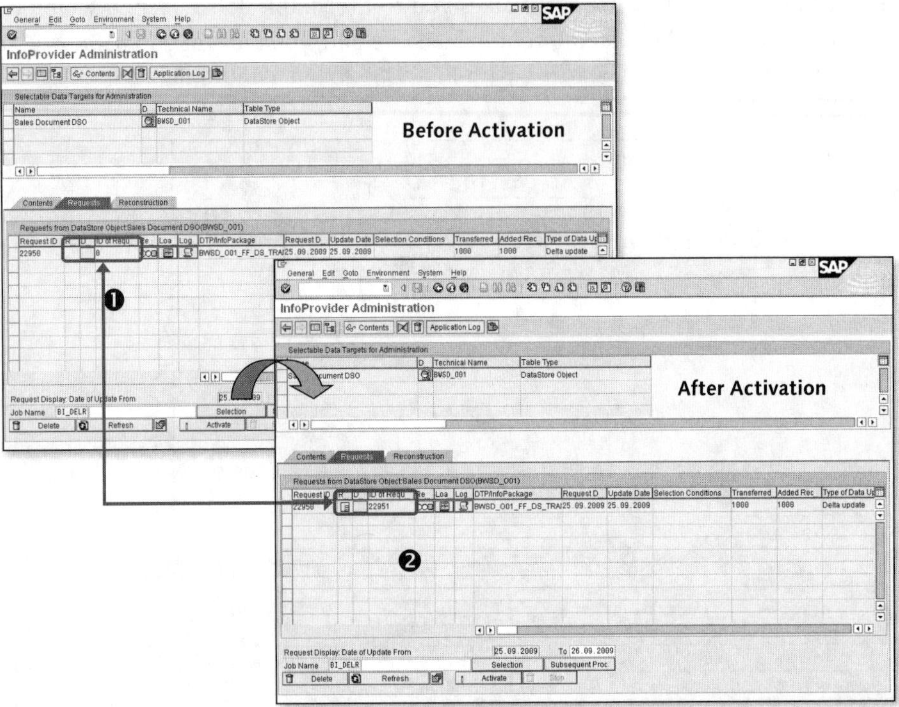

Figure 14.7 Activated Request in DSO

Upon successful activation, the status of the request in the Requests tab is reported with changes; see ❶ and ❷ of Figure 14.7 to view the status of request 22950 before and after activation, respectively. The request is now available for reporting.

You also have the option to activate multiple requests in one job (❶ of Figure 14.8). To do this, make sure the Do Not Condense Requests into One Request When Activation Takes Place checkbox is deselected. This causes the system to compress multiple requests into one.

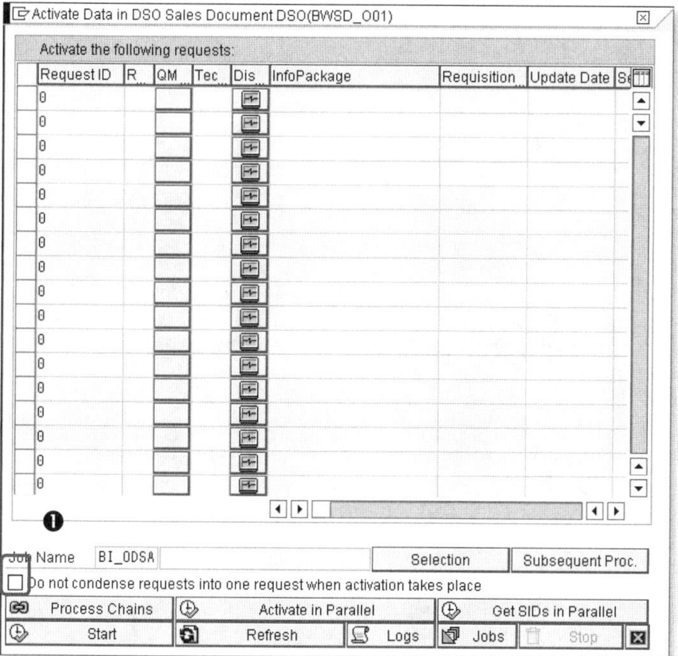

Figure 14.8 Condensing Option for Activation of Multiple Requests

When multiple requests are combined into one change log request, their individual request identifier (a separate request ID) is removed, and they appear as one request in the Change Log table. This necessitates that you must delete all of the requests from the DSO that were condensed and activated as one to delete a single request from the DSO. Check the flag (❶ of Figure 14.8) if you require deletion of a single request from the DSO.

Reconstruction Tab

> **Note**
>
> This tab is only relevant for data targets that use the ETL processes of SAP NetWeaver BW Version 3.X It isn't relevant for those using the DTP for data load.

Some requests involve data that requires manual modification or cleansing. To maintain data integrity and consistency, the system doesn't allow any such changes for a single record; instead, the entire request must be deleted from the DSO. Once this is done, you can perform the data maintenance in the PSA. Reloading the corrected request from the PSA to the data target is known as reconstruction and is managed using the Reconstruction tab (❶ of Figure 14.9).

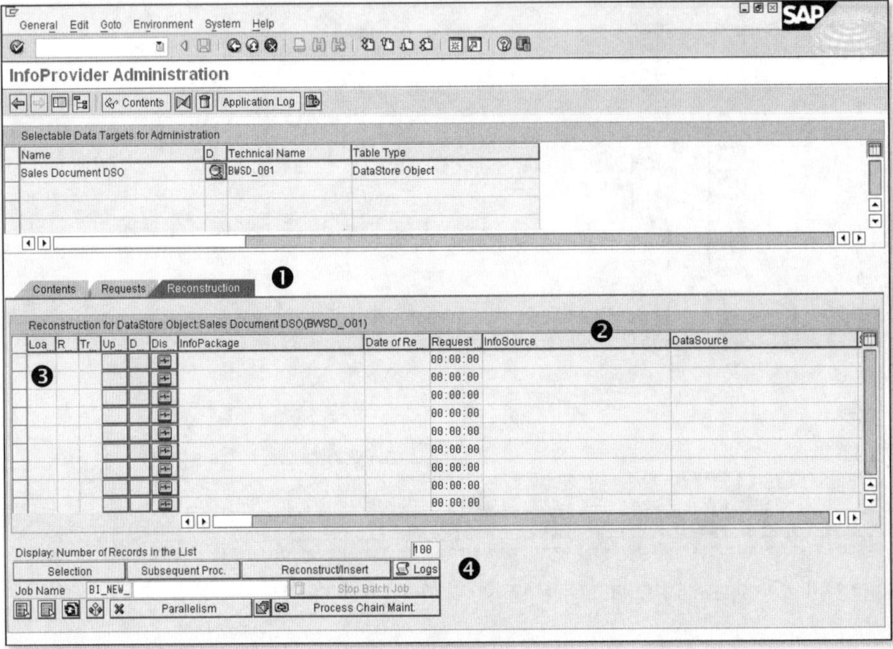

Figure 14.9 Reconstruction of a Request for a DSO

A request is only visible as a row item (❷) in the Reconstruction tab if it's deleted from the DSO. After deleting the request and making changes in the PSA, select the request (❸), and click the Reconstruction/Insert button (❹).

14.1.2 Performance Improvement Tasks

Next we discuss some tasks that will help you improve the performance of your SAP NetWeaver BW system.

Delete Change Log Data

As time goes by, data in the Change Log table builds up, negatively impacting activation processes in the system. To delete change log data, follow this menu path: Environment • Delete Change Log Data (❶ & ❷ of Figure 14.10).

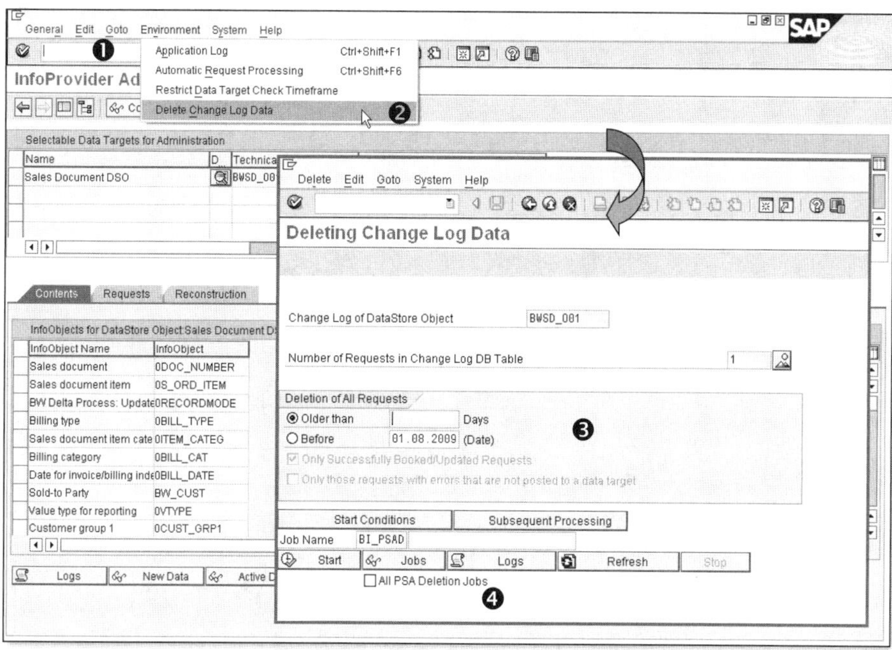

Figure 14.10 Delete Change Log Data

The Deleting Change Log Data screen opens where you can select what data should be deleted based on how old it is or when it was loaded (❸). After making the selection and starting the conditions for the job, click the Start button (❹).

Automatic Processing of Requests in a DSO

To configure the system to process requests automatically, use the following menu path in the Administration screen of the DSO: ENVIRONMENT Ð AUTOMATIC REQUEST PROCESSING (❶ & ❷ of Figure 14.11).

The resulting screen (❸) provides options for automatic request processing in the form of flags about data quality, request activation, and loading data to the data target above the DSO (❹). After making your choices, save your changes (❺).

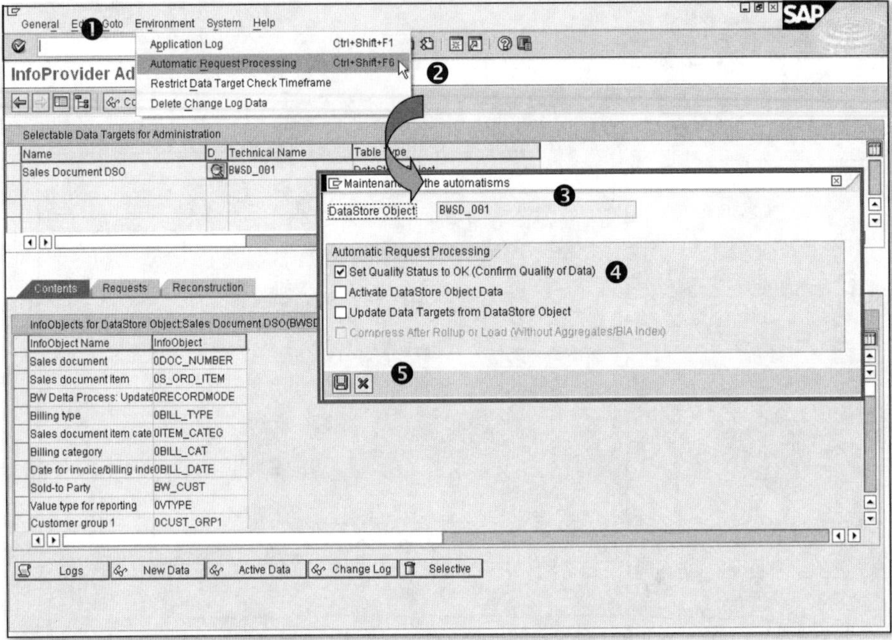

Figure 14.11 Automatic Request Processing Options for a DSO

Note

The administration of a DSO can vary based on its type. We explained the different types of DSOs in Section 4.1.2, Types of DSOs, in Chapter 4.

14.2 InfoCube Administration and Maintenance

Some of the administration tasks performed for an InfoCube are similar to those performed for a DSO, but there are also tasks that are unique to an InfoCube. In this section, we discuss some basic administration and maintenance tasks contained in the InfoProvider Administration screen, and then some performance improvement tasks.

14.2.1 InfoProvider Administration Screen Tasks — InfoCube

To open the InfoProvider Administration screen, click on the Manage option from the context menu of the InfoCube in DWW (Transaction RSA1) (in sequence ❶, ❷ and ❸ of Figure 14.12).

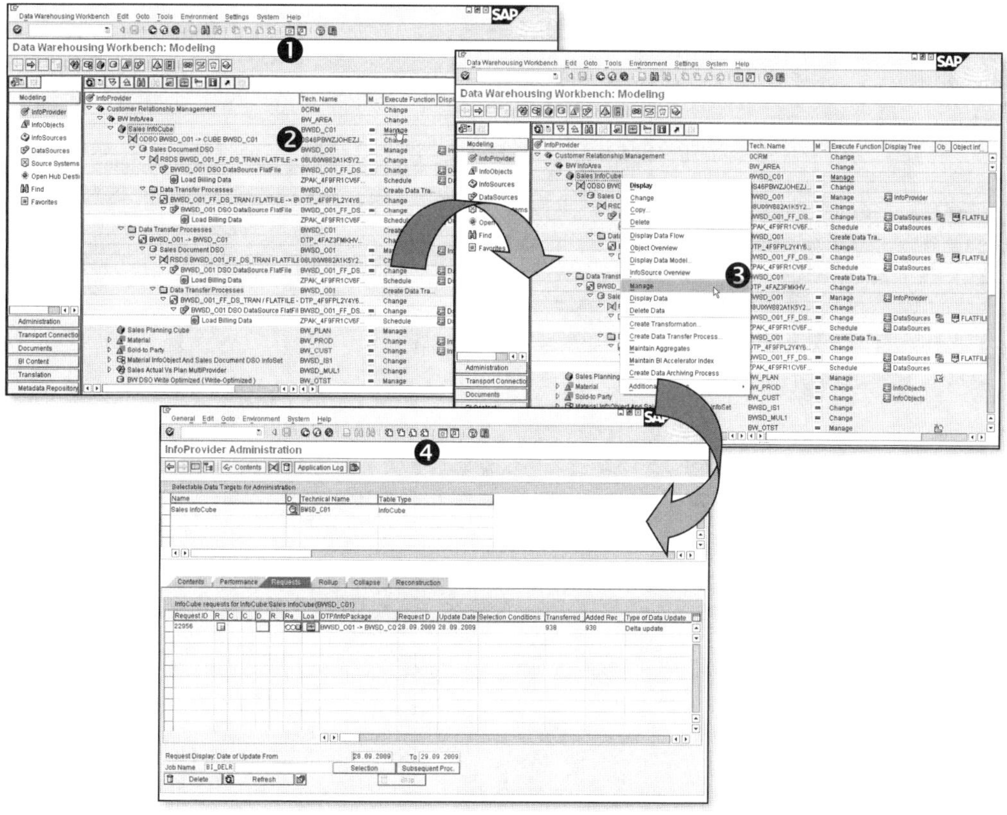

Figure 14.12 InfoCube Administration

The InfoProvider Administration screen for InfoCube has two parts (❹); the upper part contains the details of the InfoCube, and the lower part has six tabs: Contents, Performance, Requests, Rollup, Collapse, and Reconstruction. We explain each of these tabs next.

Contents Tab

The Contents tab (❶ of Figure 14.13) on the administration screen allows you to view the contents of the InfoProvider. This can be helpful in investigation and reconciliation of inaccurate data in the reports (Figure 14.13). You can choose to see contents of the entire InfoCube or only the fact table of the InfoCube by clicking on the appropriate button (❷).

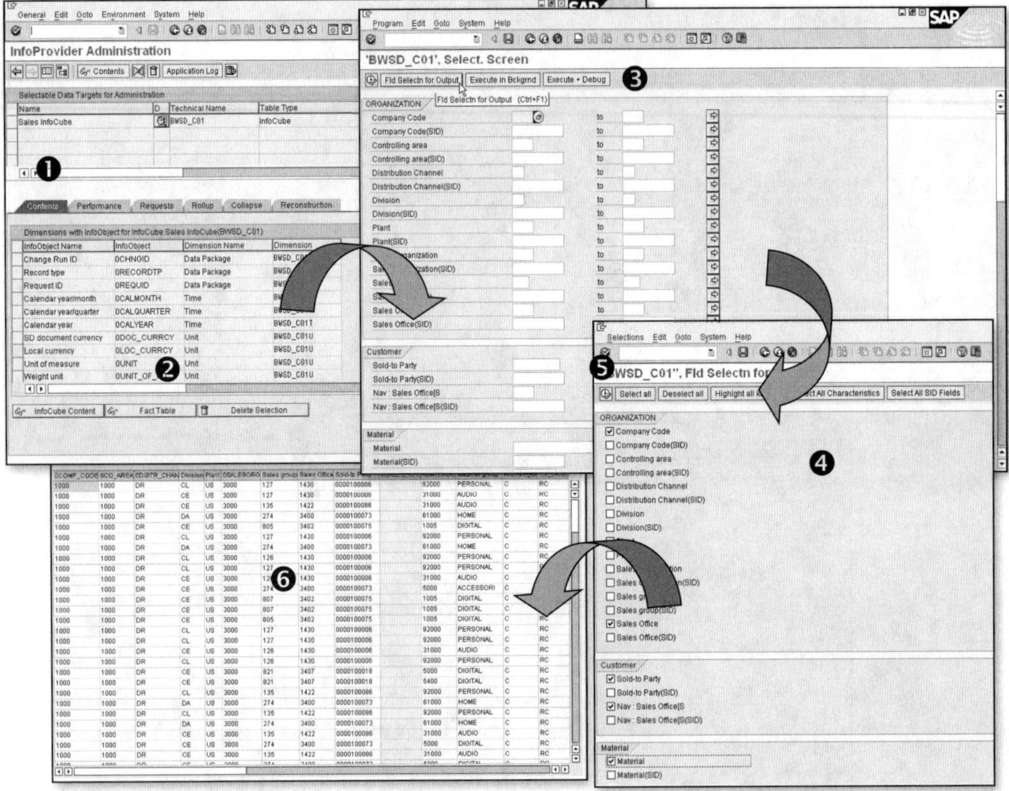

Figure 14.13 View Contents of InfoCube

When you click on the button for contents, the system takes you to a selection screen (❸) that has entry options for values of InfoObjects for each of the characteristics in the InfoCube. You have the option to choose the details in the output by flagging the appropriate characteristics and key figures (❹ and ❺). After the selection is made, click the Execute icon; the contents of the InfoCube/Fact Table are displayed (❻).

Performance Tab

The performance-related settings and actions for an InfoCube are maintained on the Performance tab (❶ of Figure 14.14). The upper part of the Performance tab (❷) provides tools to maintain DB indexes; the lower part (❹) provides tools for managing DB statistics. Optimal performance of an InfoCube is achieved by regular maintenance and updating of the indexes and statistics in a database. We discuss both of these topics next.

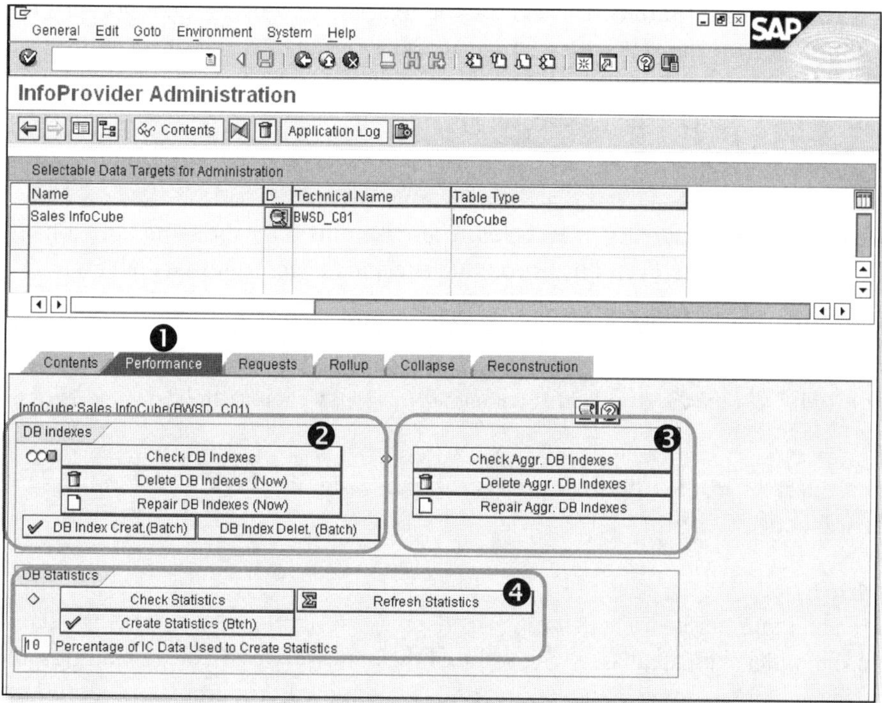

Figure 14.14 Performance Tab for InfoCube Administration

DB Indexes

Building DB indexes on an InfoCube helps improve the performance of the queries built on that InfoCube. Within this tab, there are various options (❷ and ❸) that allows you to check and control the status of indexes for the fact tables of both the InfoCube and its aggregates:

- **Check DB Indexes:** This checks the status of the indexes on the database and compares it with the index definitions in the dictionary.
  - Green light: This indicates that indexes exist and are correctly defined.
  - Yellow light: This indicates that indexes exist but are the wrong type.
  - Red light: This indicates that either (a) there are no indexes or (b) there are indexes but are incorrectly defined.
- **Delete DB Indexes (Now):** This allows you to delete the available indexes.
- **Repair DB Indexes (Now):** This allows you to create missing indexes and repair faulty indexes.

- **DB Index Creat. (Batch):** This allows you to schedule a background job that creates indexes on the fact table of the InfoCube. You can specify that indexes are deleted/rebuilt with each data load; however, the recommended approach is to manage this through the process chain.
- **DB Index Delet (Batch):** This allows you to schedule a background job that deletes the indexes.
- **Check/Delete/Repair Aggr. Indexes:** These buttons offer the same functionality as the preceding items in this list but are specific to aggregates fact tables.

> **Note**
>
> It's a best practice to delete the indexes before loading the data to an InfoCube and then recreate those after the data load is complete. This helps improve the data load performance to that InfoCube.

When query or loading performance is sub par, a simple check of the indexes can help solve the problem.

DB Statistics

There are a number of ways in which the database system can read data for a query from the underlying database table; some of these are very costly (e.g., reading a big database table sequentially and getting only a few records as output), and others are less so (e.g., using indexes to read the required data very quickly). Because there may be a number of indexes available on the same table, database statistics can help the database optimizer get the optimal execution path for a query. On the other hand, if the statistics aren't up to date, the database optimizer may decide on the wrong path, costing time and resources. As such, one of the important tasks of a SAP NetWeaver BW administrator is to keep the database statistics up to date.

Using the Check Statistics button (❹ of Figure 14.14), you can check whether the database system has statistics for the InfoCube, and whether they are up to date:

- Green light: Indicates that database statistics are available and up to date.
- Yellow light: Indicates that database statistics are available but not up to date.
- Red light: Indicates that database statistics are missing.

You can also control what percentage of the InfoCube data should be used to create statistics; normally, it's sufficient to specify only 10% (❹ of Figure 14.14) because this job takes a lot of time.

Requests Tab

In the Requests tab (❶ of Figure 4.15), the lower part of the screen shows administration and maintenance task buttons for requests (❷), and the lowest part of the screen provides buttons for execution of these tasks (❸).

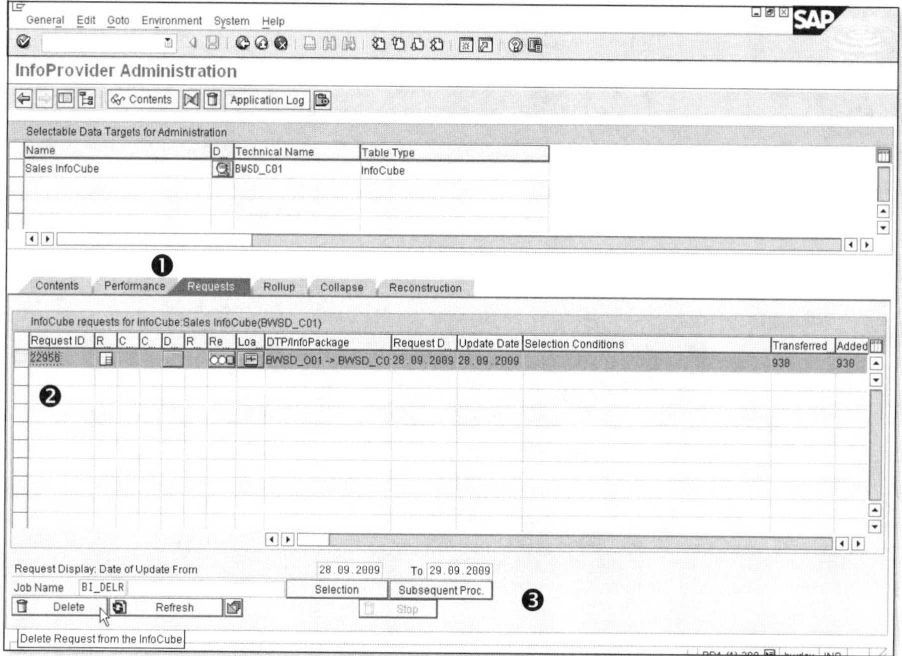

Figure 14.15 Request Tab for InfoCube Administration

The From and To fields help in limiting the display of requests to a specific period (❸). As you can see, this screen shows request 22956; the green light indicates that it's loaded and available for reporting. In the middle of the screen, columns report the details of the DTP and the date of loading into the InfoCube. The columns on the right report the number of records transferred and added to the InfoCube (938 and 930, respectively).

Rollup Tab

The Rollup tab (❶ of Figure 14.16) has buttons that replicate part of the InfoCube data into a summarized subset called an aggregate. We explain the concept of aggregates in more detail in Section 14.3, Aggregates.

The lower part of the Rollup tab now shows options related to rolling up requests into aggregates, and other relevant tasks (❷).

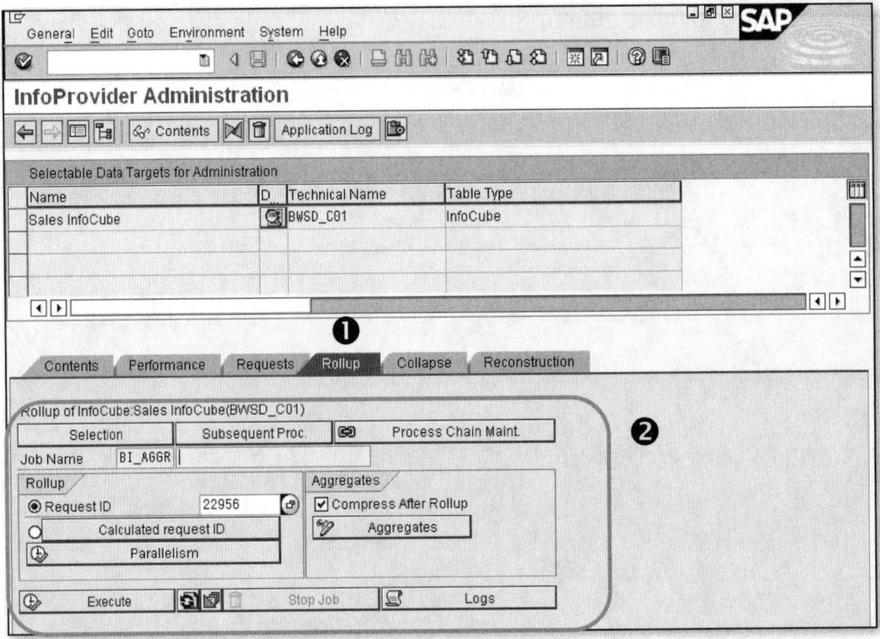

Figure 14.16 Rollup Tab for InfoCube Administration

The lowest part of the screen provides buttons to execute the rollup tasks and monitor the job, or analyze the job log for the rollup activity.

Collapse Tab

The Collapse tab (❶ of Figure 14.17) has buttons that perform compression activities, which move InfoCube data into a summarized table (i.e., moving data from an F table to an E table) and aids in improving loading and reporting performance. We explain the concept of compression in more detail in Section 14.4, Compression.

The lower part of the Collapse tab (❷) shows options for carrying out the collapse task, from calculating the request I.D. to selecting a job and its maintenance in the process chain (see Section 14.5, Process Chain).

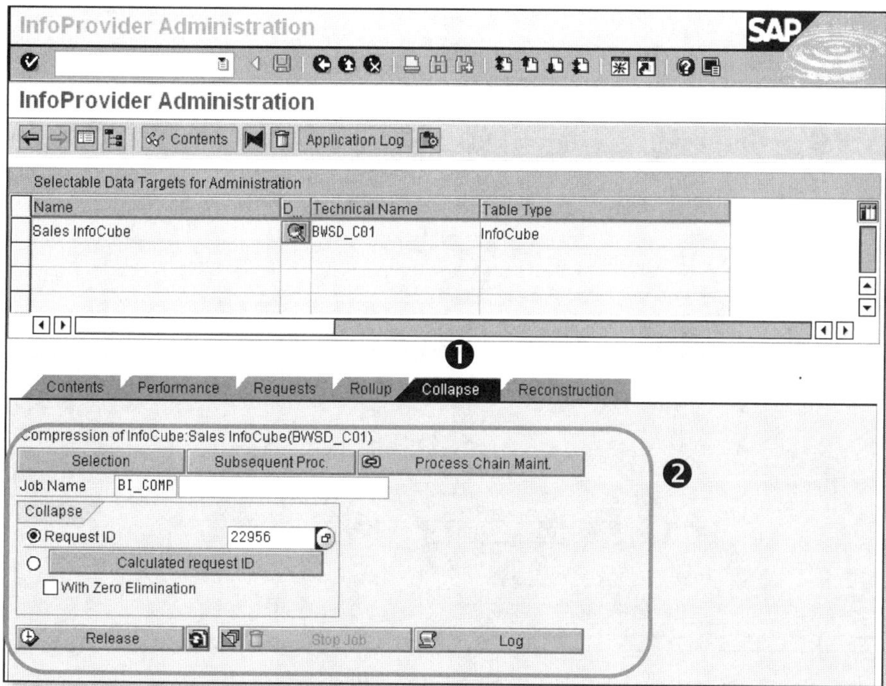

Figure 14.17 Collapse Tab for InfoCube Administration

The lowest part of the screen provides buttons to execute and schedule the job for releasing the collapse activity, to monitor the collapse job, and to analyze the job log for compression activity.

Reconstruction Tab

The Reconstruction tab (❶ of Figure 14.18) in the InfoProvider Maintenance screen of an InfoCube offers exactly the same options and functions as in a DSO. As a reminder, this tab is relevant for those data targets that use ETL processes of SAP NetWeaver Version 3.x. It isn't relevant for ETL elements such as the DTP process.

A request is only visible as a row item (❷) in the Reconstruction tab if it's deleted from the InfoCube. After deleting the request and making changes in the PSA, select the request (❷), and click the Reconstruction/Insert button (❸).

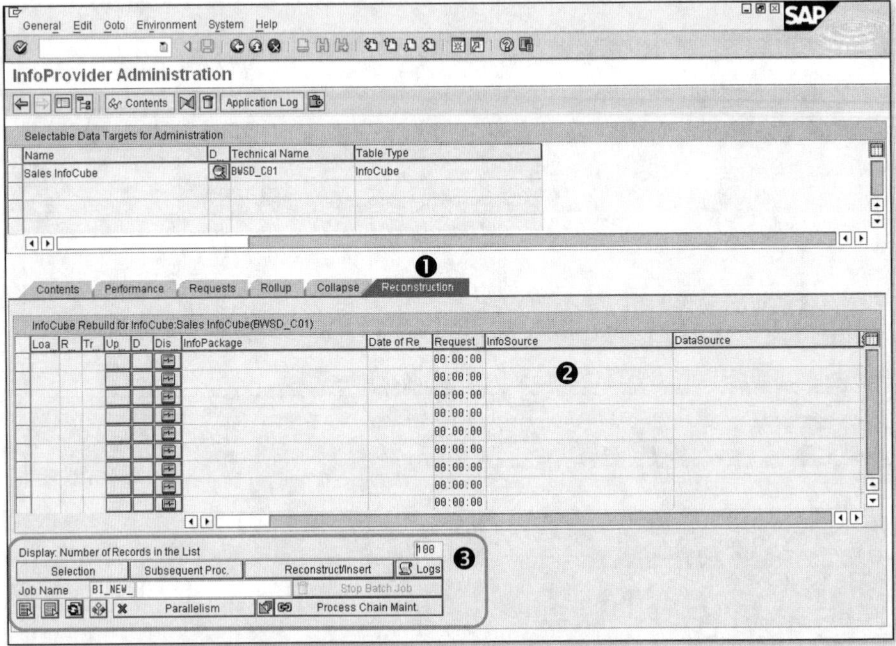

Figure 14.18 Reconstruction Tab for InfoCube Administration

14.2.2 Performance Improvement Tasks

One of the main ways to improve performance in InfoCubes is to automate request processing. Choose the following menu path within the administration screen of the InfoCube: ENVIRONMENT • AUTOMATIC REQUEST PROCESSING (❶ and ❷ of Figure 14.19).

The resulting pop-up box (❸) allows you to set flags related to data quality, rollup, and compression of requests (❹).

In Table 14.1, we summarize the main administration and maintenance tasks and their applicability to the specific data targets.

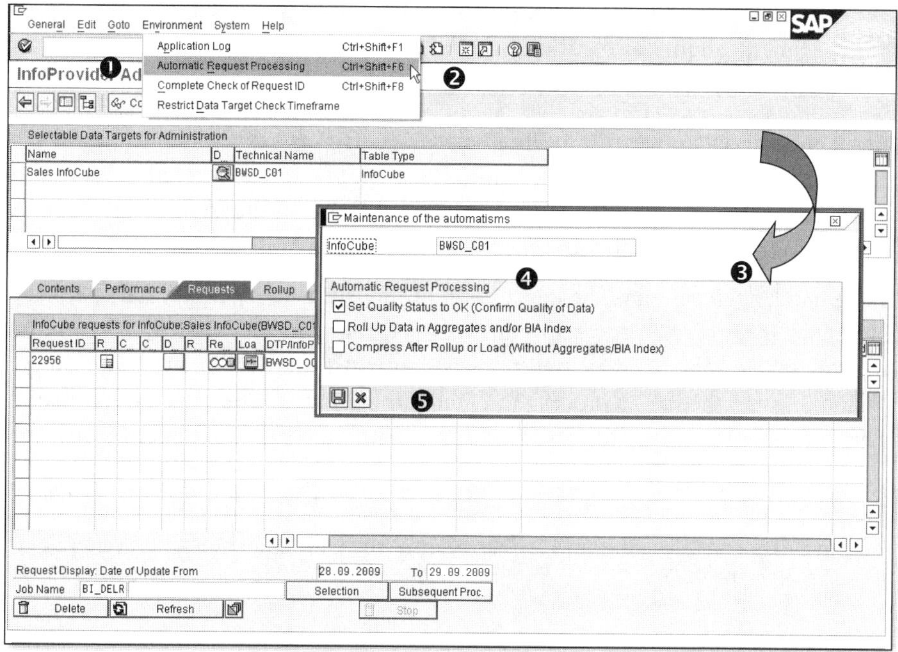

Figure 14.19 InfoCube – Automatic Request Processing

	Contents	Performance	Requests	Rollup	Collapse	Reconstruction
DSO	✓		✓			✓
InfoCube	✓	✓	✓	✓	✓	✓

Table 14.1 Summary of Administration and Maintenance Tasks for DSOs and InfoCubes

Now that we've covered administration and maintenance tasks for DSO and InfoCube, let's move on to the concept of aggregates, their relevance to performance improvement, and their management.

14.3 Aggregates

An *aggregate* is an object that stores a summarized subset of data in an InfoCube, grouped by a specific set of selected characteristics. When an appropriate aggregate for an InfoCube exists, summarized data can be read directly from the database during query execution, instead of having to perform this summarization during runtime. Aggregates generate the following direct benefits:

- Reduction in the volume of data to be read from the database
- Improvement of query execution time
- Reduction of overall load on the database during query execution

When you load data into an InfoCube, you must also load the data into aggregates; this is known as the *rollup* process. Without rollup, the data loaded in the InfoCube isn't available for reporting. The OLAP processor ignores requests that aren't rolled up into an aggregate to maintain reporting integrity.

On one hand, aggregates are the best option for boosting query performance because they reduce most of the processing time needed for aggregating the data read from the database. However, if they aren't created correctly, they can actually inhibit performance, due to the rollup process and realignment run (see Section 14.7.1, Executing an Attribute Hierarchy Change Run, for more details on realignment runs).

> **Note**
>
> You can create multiple aggregates for BasicCubes. You can't create them for MultiCubes, VirtualProvider, or DSOs.

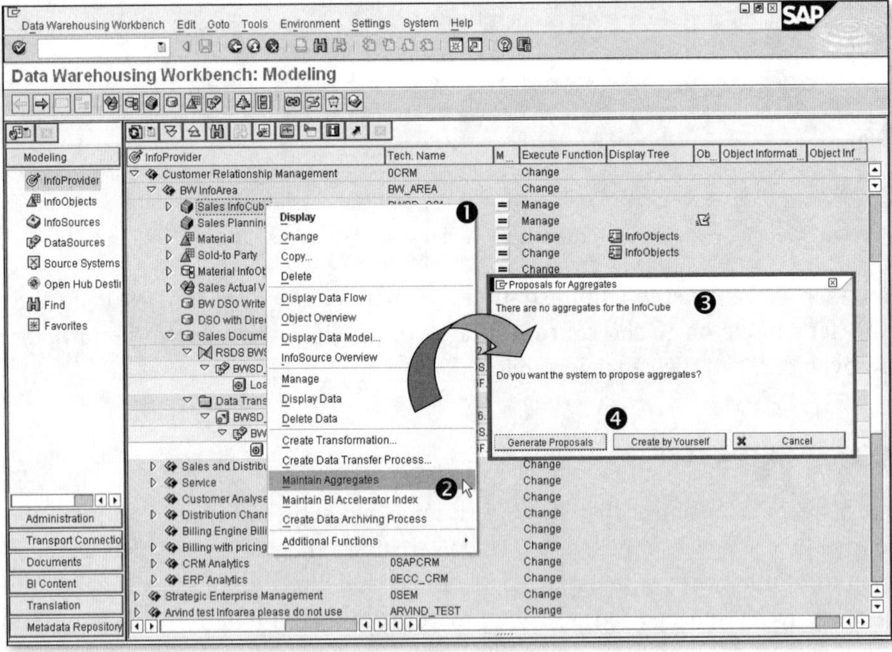

Figure 14.20 Maintain Aggregates for InfoCubes

There are multiple options for identifying and creating aggregates, such as manual creation or the use of the Aggregate button (which is found in the Rollup tab in the InfoProvider Administration screen of an InfoCube; refer to Figure 14.16). In this section, we focus on manual creation of aggregates. To begin, choose Maintain Aggregates from the context menu of the InfoCube (❶ and ❷ of Figure 14.20). If there are no aggregates defined for this InfoCube, the Proposals for Aggregates pop-up box appears (❸). You can select Generate Proposals for the system to propose aggregates or click on the option Create By Yourself to manually create the aggregate (❹).

The system takes you to the maintenance screen for aggregates, which has two panels; the left panel shows the dimensions, characteristics, and navigation attributes of the selected InfoCube (❶ of Figure 14.21). From the dynamic menu bar, click on the Create New Aggregate icon (🗋). A pop-up box appears, where you can enter the short and long text description for the aggregate (❷). Enter the description (❸), and click on the Continue icon (❹) to return to the Maintain Aggregates screen (❺).

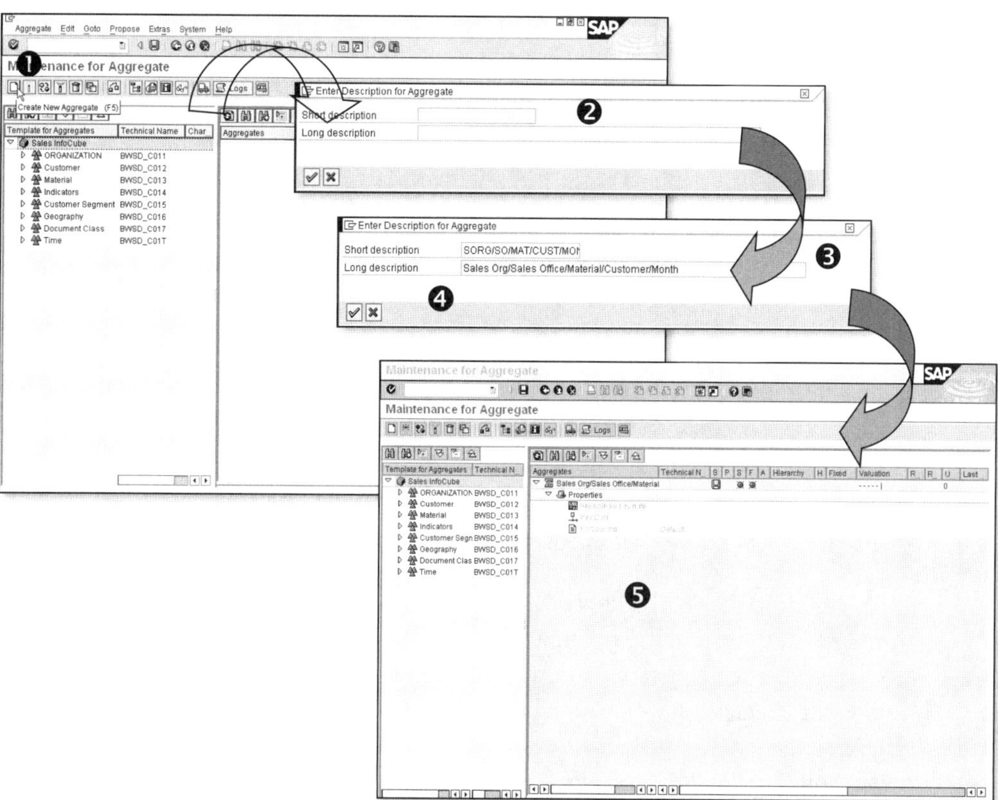

Figure 14.21 Create Aggregate

By clicking the Expand icon (▷) to the left of the aggregate name (on the right panel), the properties for the aggregate are visible (❶ Figure 14.22). On the left panel, all characteristics are available within their respective dimensions. For the purpose of explanation, we select the Organization dimension; click the Expand icon to open the Organization dimension, and all of the characteristics that are part of this dimension for InfoCube BWSD_C01 are listed (❷).

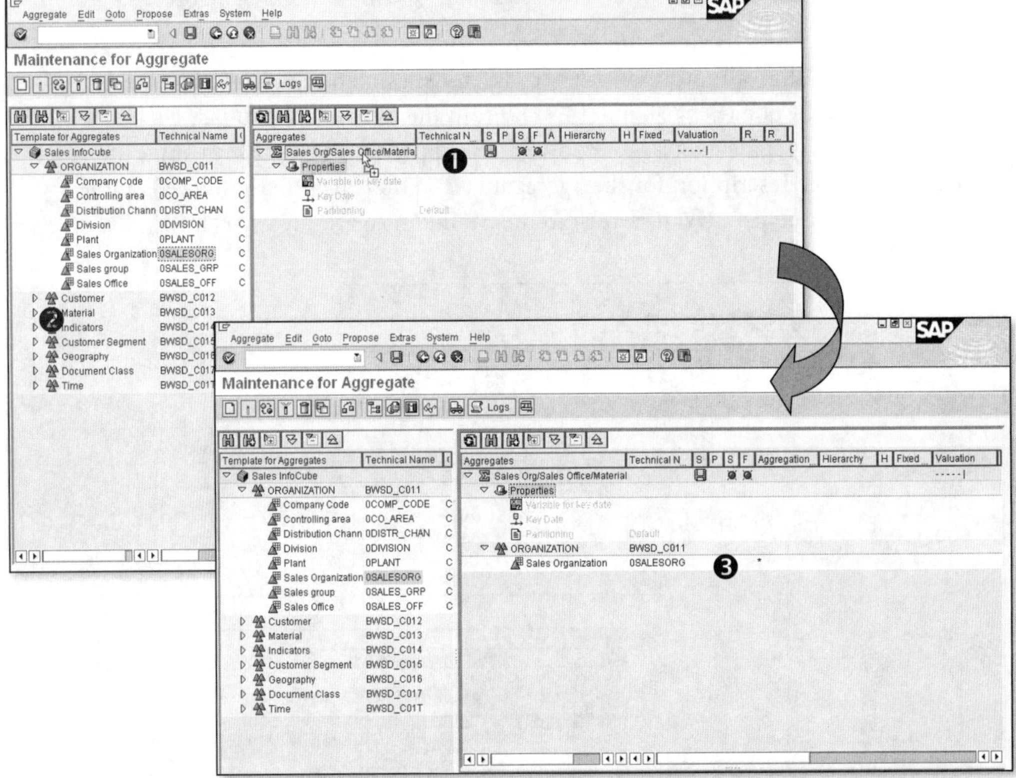

Figure 14.22 Add Characteristics to the Aggregate

Drag and drop the 0SALESORG characteristic (in the left panel) into the Summation icon (Σ) at the top of the right panel. 0SALESORG and the Organization dimension are added to the aggregate definition (❸). Repeat the drag and drop process for the remaining characteristics: 0SALES_OFF, 0MATERIAL, BW_CUST, and 0CALMONTH. These characteristics, and their respective dimensions, are added to the aggregate definition.

Business requirements might require analysis to determine the need of an aggregate for specific values of characteristics. For example, assume a specific group of users always runs the query for Sales Organization = Europe. In this case, the sales organization characteristic should be restricted to a fixed value of Europe in the aggregate. To do this, choose the option Fixed Value from the context menu of the characteristic in the aggregate definition (❶ of Figure 14.23) and select Europe from the list in the pop-up box. However, our scenario doesn't need to have a fixed value, thus we don't use the option.

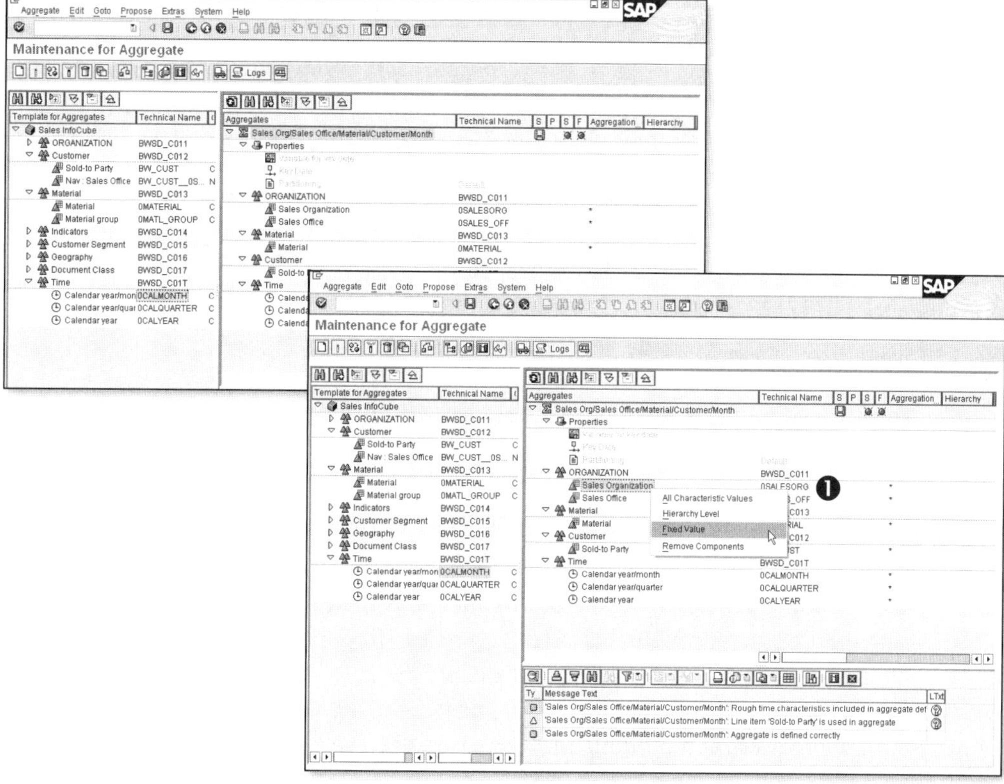

Figure 14.23 Define Fixed Value for a Characteristic in an Aggregate

Having defined the aggregate, you now need to check the definition of the aggregate for accuracy. Click on the Check icon (❶ of Figure 14.24).

Figure 14.24 Check Aggregate Definition

The lower-right panel reports any messages that result from the process; a green light indicates that the aggregate has been defined correctly (❷). A correctly defined aggregate is like an empty box and isn't used by queries because it's just the definition for summarizing the subset of an InfoCube, and there's no data inside it.

Activation of the aggregate fills the aggregate with data from the InfoCube. To do this, click the aggregate on the right panel, and then click on the Activate and Fill icon on the dynamic menu bar (❶ of Figure 14.25). A pop-up box appears (❷); place the cursor on the row with the text definition of the aggregate (❸), and click the Start icon (❹). Another pop-up box appears, which gives you the options for when to time the execution of filling the aggregate (❺). The aggregation job can be started immediately by clicking the Immediate button, or it can be started later by clicking the Later button (❻). In our example, we choose Immediate. After the job is complete, the status bar and log section indicate this with a message. An aggregate (with a technical name allocated by the system) is created for InfoCube BWSD_C01; as you can see, the resulting screen shows green boxes (❶ of Figure 14.26) as well as details about the valuation of the aggregate.

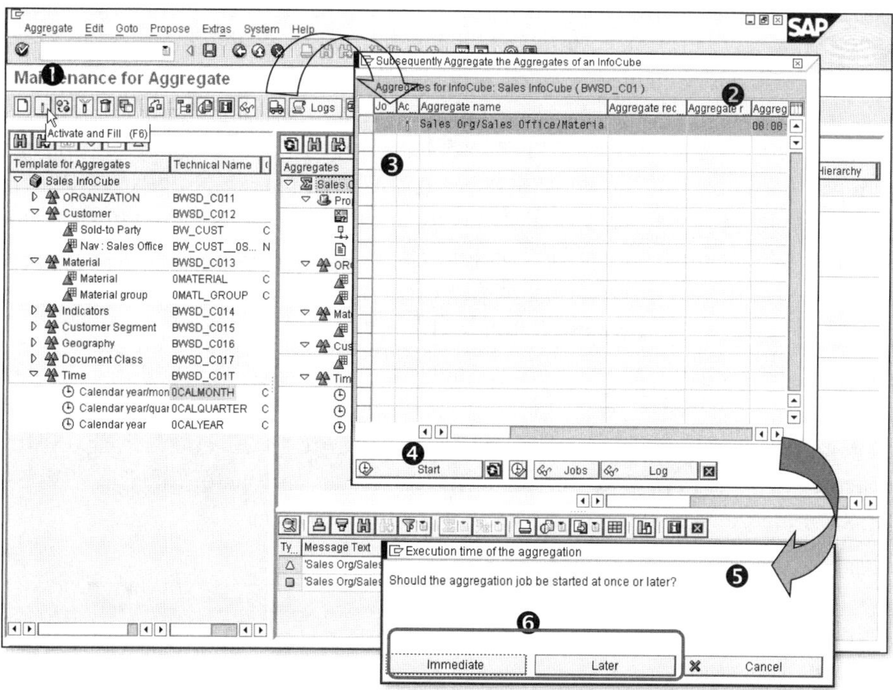

Figure 14.25 Activate an Aggregate

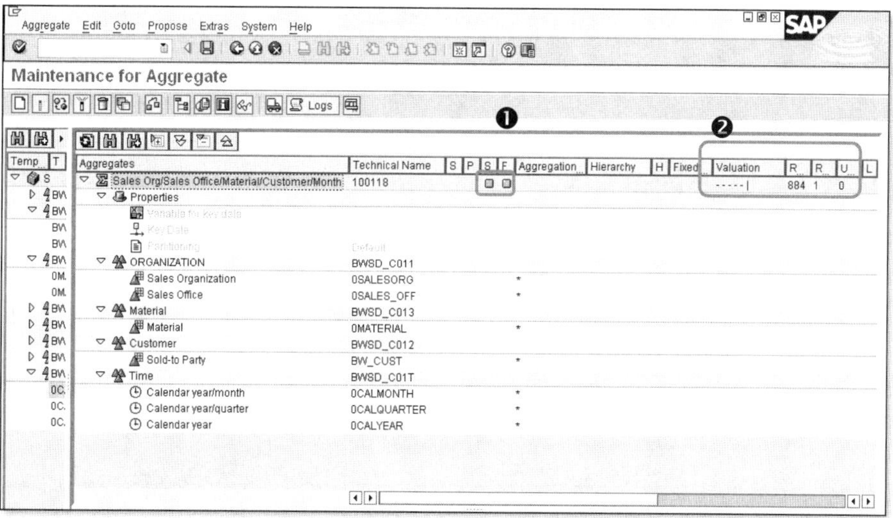

Figure 14.26 Valuation of Aggregates

The system evaluates aggregates using plus and minus signs (❷ Figure 14.26); five plus signs (+++++) indicates the highest valuation, whereas five minus signs (-----) indicates the lowest valuation. Valuation is a good indicator for whether an aggregate is likely to serve its purpose in performance improvement, but it should not be the only factor affecting whether you keep or delete an aggregate. (For more information on this, we recommend the book *SAP BW Performance Tuning [SAP PRESS, 2007]*.) One of the parameters for this valuation is the level of summarization, which can be checked in the Record Summarizes column. The value here indicates how many BasicCube records (on average) correspond to the number of records in that aggregate. For a good aggregate, this value should be 10 or more.

After the aggregate is created and activated, the information for the InfoCube gets added to it. Compare the details in the Object Information for the InfoCube BWSD_C01 both before the aggregate is created (refer to Figure 14.20) and then again after the aggregate is created. Note that the SUM icon is now visible for InfoCube BWSD_C01 (❶ of Figure 14.27).

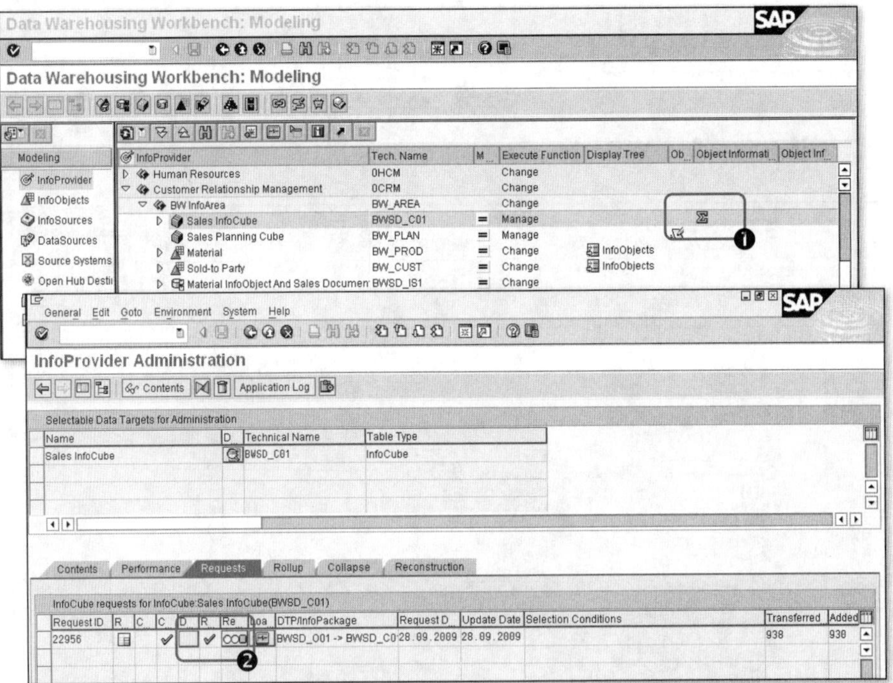

Figure 14.27 InfoCube with Aggregate

Now compare the Request tab of the InfoCube for BWSD_C01 (refer to Figure 14.15) with the same tab in Figure 14.27, and you'll notice that there are additional details reported (❷). To maintain integrity in reporting, the new InfoCube data isn't available for reporting until the request is successfully rolled up into all of the aggregates for the cube. After this happens, the request record in the Requests tab for the InfoCube will be marked with the OK icon (✔).

14.4 Compression

The process of consolidating the data loaded in the InfoCube after removing the request ID dimension is called *compression.* As the technical identifier is removed, multiple records are consolidated (or compressed) together. On the other hand, because request ID is the technical identifier for the data loaded, its removal in the compression process results in loss of the ability to identify individual requests in an InfoCube. Compression makes it impossible to delete individual requests from the compressed data in the InfoCube.

Request ID

The SAP NetWeaver BW system creates a new request ID whenever new data is loaded into an InfoCube. If all data in a previously loaded request must be deleted, you can identify the data from an InfoCube with the help of the request ID. Although the request ID is helpful in identifying data, it also hampers the performance of a query.

The request ID is part of the data packet dimension, which is automatically created by the system when you create a BasicCube. The key of the fact table is a combination of all of the dimension keys; so, in this way, the request ID is also a part of the fact table key. Request IDs are automatically generated by the system during extraction.

When new data is loaded into an InfoCube, it's first loaded into the F fact table of the InfoCube. Compressing the requests moves the data from the F fact table to the E fact table; in doing so, the system also sets the request ID to 0 and creates a single record from multiple records with the same combination of the remaining characteristics (Figure 14.28). When the request is successfully compressed, data for the compressed requests is deleted from the F fact table.

The advantage to compression is that a query has to read significantly less records; additionally, in RDBMSs that support physical partitioning, you can partition the E fact table according to time criteria. (For more information about partitioning, we recommend the book *SAP BW Performance Tuning [SAP PRESS, 2007].*) The disadvantage is that request identifiers are lost, and you no longer identify or delete data pertaining to a specific request.

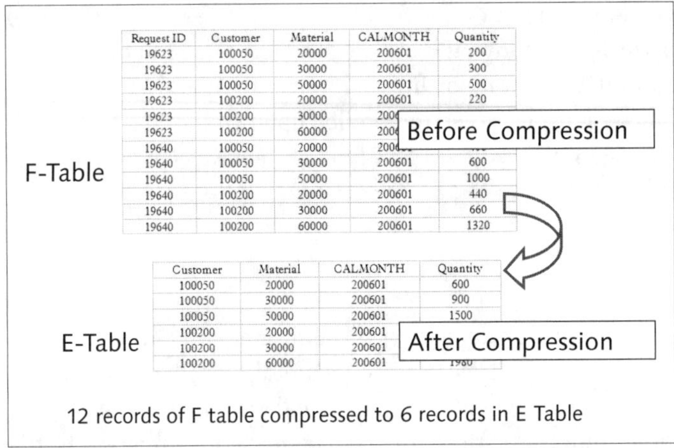

Request ID	Customer	Material	CALMONTH	Quantity
19623	100050	20000	200601	200
19623	100050	30000	200601	300
19623	100050	50000	200601	500
19623	100200	20000	200601	220
19623	100200	30000	[illegible]	[illegible]
19623	100200	60000	[illegible]	[illegible]
19640	100050	20000	[illegible]	[illegible]
19640	100050	30000	200601	600
19640	100050	50000	200601	1000
19640	100200	20000	200601	440
19640	100200	30000	200601	660
19640	100200	60000	200601	1320

Customer	Material	CALMONTH	Quantity
100050	20000	200601	600
100050	30000	200601	900
100050	50000	200601	1500
100200	20000	200601	[illegible]
100200	30000	200601	[illegible]
100200	60000	200601	[illegible]

Figure 14.28 Compression of Requests in an InfoCube

The data in an InfoCube can be compressed from the Collapse tab on the InfoProvider Administration screen (refer to Figure 14.17). Enter the request number in the Request ID field; all requests previous to this one (and including this one) will be compressed. Click on the Release button to start compression.

It isn't mandatory to compress all requests in an InfoCube, but we suggest doing so to improve performance and manage data storage space. You can also partially compress, depending on the frequency in which you delete data from the InfoCube. After a request is successfully loaded into an InfoCube and you know that it won't need to be deleted, you can compress it.

Compression improves loading performance and makes for faster aggregate rebuilding, although the reduction ratio between the number of records in the F and E tables depends on the granularity of data and the frequency of loading to the InfoCube. For example, if you've included characteristics such as document number, customer, material, and calendar day, the frequency of loading is once a day; so, there won't be much reduction in records.

14.5 Process Chain

Recall that one of ABCD Corp.'s BI requirements was to implement automated process control, including the establishment of email alerts for occurrences of successes or failures in systemic processes. In this section, we discuss how that can be done using *process chains*.

Process chains are used extensively to automate most administration and monitoring tasks, such as transactional and master data loads, or index and statistic rebuilds. A *process chain* is a group of processes or system jobs that are linked together; each process has a defined beginning point and end point, and the linkages between processes have a predetermined sequence that is governed by interdependent conditions assigned to a system-generated event. During execution, each process waits for the predecessor to complete based on the dependency assigned. Process chains can send email alerts based on events in the system, which makes management more efficient and eliminates mundane and manual efforts.

A typical process chain consists of a start process, individual application processes, and collectors. The *start process* defines the start of a process chain; other chain processes are scheduled to wait for a systemic event. *Application processes* refer to actual processes; they represent SAP NetWeaver BW activities that are typically performed as part of SAP NetWeaver BW operations. For example:

- Data load
- Attribute/hierarchy change run
- Aggregate rollup
- Reporting agent settings

Application processes also include custom ABAP programs that you can implement in your system; additionally, you can include process chains as processes in another process chain.

Finally, *collectors* are used to manage multiple processes that feed into one subsequent process. The collectors available for SAP NetWeaver BW are listed here:

- AND: All of the processes that are direct predecessors must send an event for subsequent processes to be executed.
- OR: At least one predecessor process must send an event. The first predecessor process that sends an event triggers the subsequent process.
- EXOR (Exclusive Or): Similar to regular OR, but there is only *one* execution of the successor processes, even if several predecessor processes raise an event.

In this section, we explain the creation of a simple process chain and then the creation of email alerts related to the process chain.

14.5.1 Creating a Process Chain

Here we explain the creation of a simple process chain for automating transactional data, from the extraction of billing data from an SAP source system, to the loading process culminating in the InfoCube BWSD_C01. To begin, you must first create the sequence of tasks you want the system to automatically process:

1. Start the process at 7:00 a.m.
2. Execute the InfoPackage for extracting the delta load for the billing data from the source system.
3. Execute the DTP for loading the data from the PSA into BWSD_O01.
4. Activate the newly loaded request in BWSD_O01.
5. Delete indexes for BWSD_C01.
6. Execute the DTP for loading the data from the DSO (BWSD_O01) to InfoCube (DSO BWSD_C01). Send an email alert if the data load fails.
7. Create indexes for BWSD_C01.
8. Roll up the request into the aggregate.

SAP has developed more than 50 predefined standard process variants that you can use to develop process chains. Table RSPROCESSTYPES provides a view of all process types and specific attributes important to understanding how process types work.

Process chains are created using the process chain configuration utility, which you can find via Transaction RSPC or by clicking on the chain-link icon that appears on the menu bar in the Data Warehouse Administrator Workbench. The process chain utility offers a planning view, a checking view, and a monitoring view, which allow you to build, check/test, and monitor process chains in real-time, respectively.

Choose the Process Chain Maintenance icon from the DWW toolbar, or use Transaction RSPC. The system takes you to the Process Chain Display Planning View screen (❶ of Figure 14.29).

Click on the Create icon (❷), and a New Process Chain pop-up box appears. There are two fields, Process Chain and Long Description (❸ of Figure 14.29). Use the following inputs (❹):

- Process Chain: "BW_LOAD_BWSD_C01"
- Long Description: "Load Data into BWSD_C01"

Click the Continue icon to confirm the entries (❺ of Figure 14.29), and the Process Chain Selection dialog box appears (❶ of Figure 14.30). The system automatically opens a pop-up box for inserting a start process (❷ of Figure 14.30).

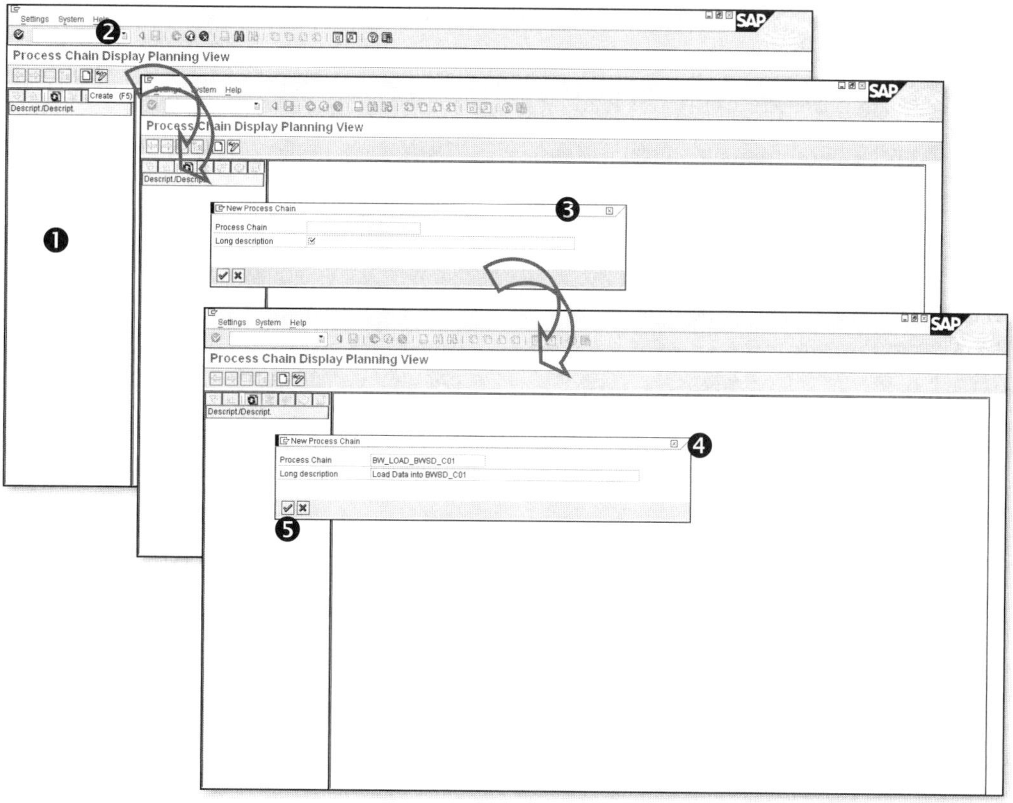

Figure 14.29 Create New Process Chain (Part I)

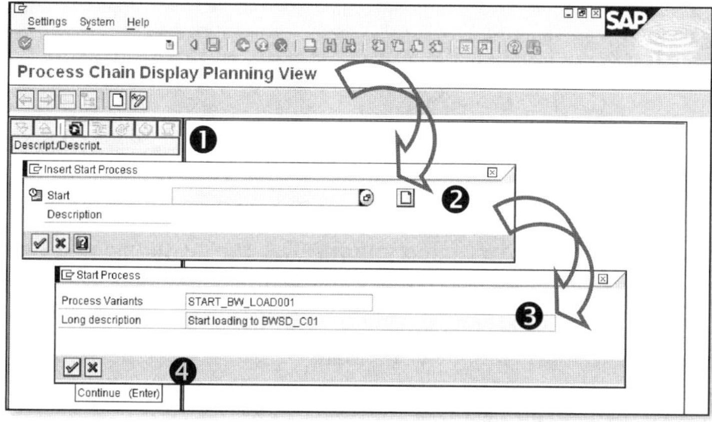

Figure 14.30 Process Chain — Create Start Variant

Click the Create icon (❷), and enter the following (❸):

- Start: "START_BW_LOAD001"
- Long Description: "Start loading to BWSD_C01"

Click the Continue icon (❹) to confirm the entries. The system takes to the Maintain Start Process screen (❶ of Figure 14.31).

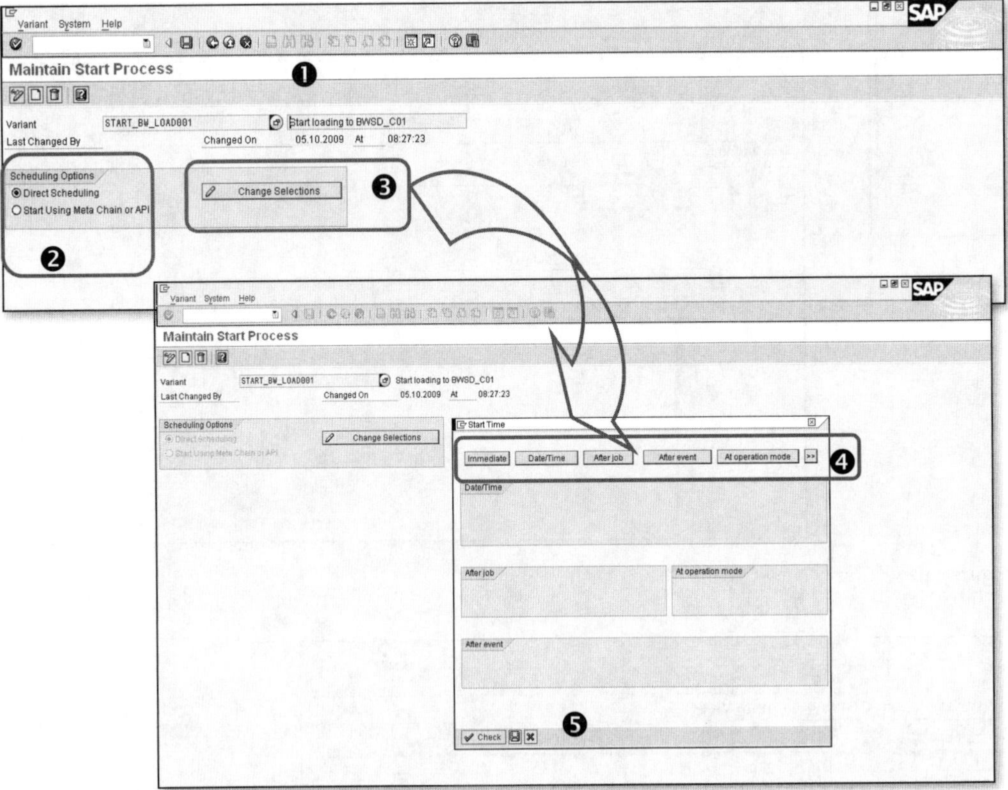

Figure 14.31 Process Chain – Maintain Start Process

The Maintain Start Process screen has two radio buttons: Direct Scheduling, and Start Using Meta Chain or API (❷). There are also buttons that help you in setting the start time(❸); like any typical system job, there are multiple options for this (❹). When finished choosing appropriate settings, save your changes, and use the Back icon to return to the Process Chain Maintenance screen. The panel on the right should now display the start process (Figure 14.32).

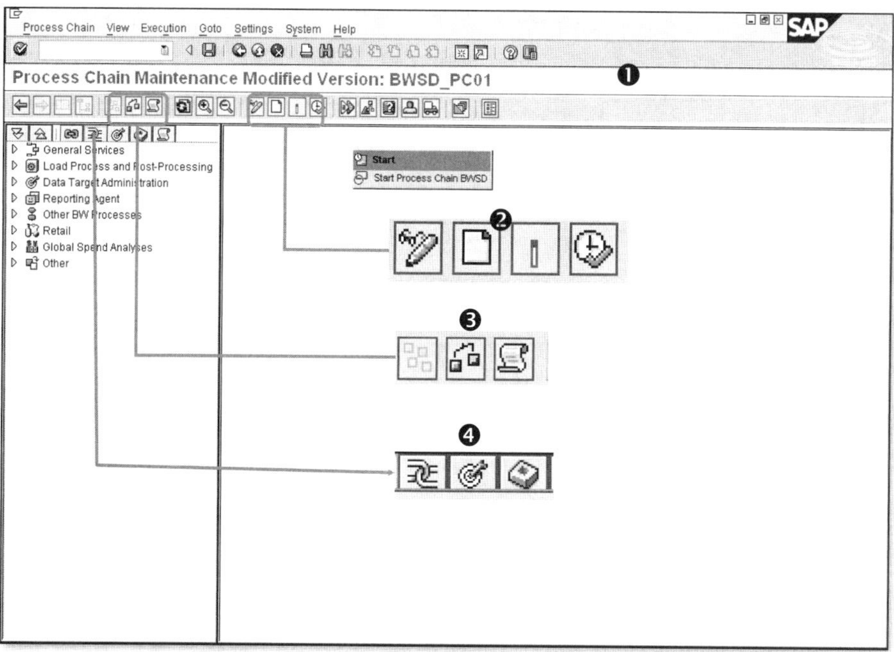

Figure 14.32 Icons and Buttons for Process Chain

Dynamic menu bar on the screen (❶) has icons for edit, create, activate & schedule a process chain (❷) and icons for choosing the view of a process chain(❸). Now click on the Process Types icon (❹ of Figure 14.32). The left panel unfolds the list of all process types. The first process we want to be executed by the system is for data extraction from a source system; so, from the left panel, choose the Execute InfoPackage process type (❶ of Figure 14.33).

Drag and drop this process to the right panel; the Insert Execute InfoPackage pop-up box appears (❷), as does another pop-up box with a list of all InfoPackages (❸). Select the billing data (delta) DataSource (❹), and click the Continue icon (❺) to confirm the selection. Insert Execute InfoPackage has an entry with the technical ID for the DataSource; confirm by clicking the Continue icon (❻). The right panel now has the start process item, and another item for the load data (Figure 14.34).

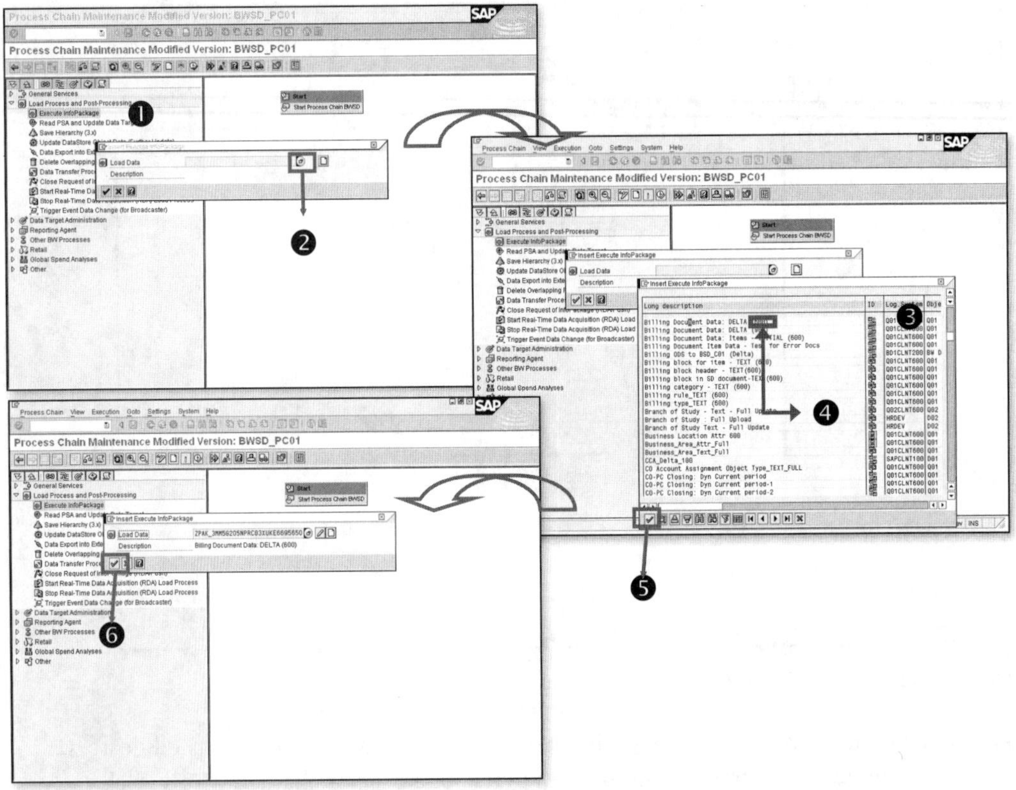

Figure 14.33 Add Process Type in Process Chain

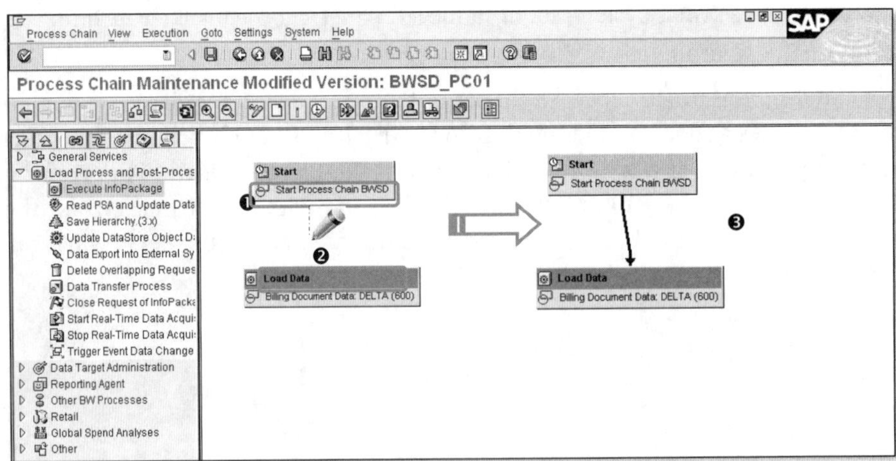

Figure 14.34 Establish a Linkage Between Elements of the Process Chain

To link the two processes for establishing the sequence, click on Start Process Chain (❶ of Figure 14.34), and drag the cursor down. A pencil with a dotted line appears on the screen (❷); drag the cursor to the Load Data box, and the system establishes a sequence (❸).

Repeat this process for all of the steps we listed at the beginning of this section.

14.5.2 Setting Email Alerts

We must also set up emails that alert solution administrator on failure of a data load between the DSO and InfoCube. To do this, select the DTP item in the process chain that is responsible for loading the data from DSO BWSD_O01 to InfoCube BWSD_C01 (❶ of Figure 14.35). Open the context menu, and select Create Message (❷).

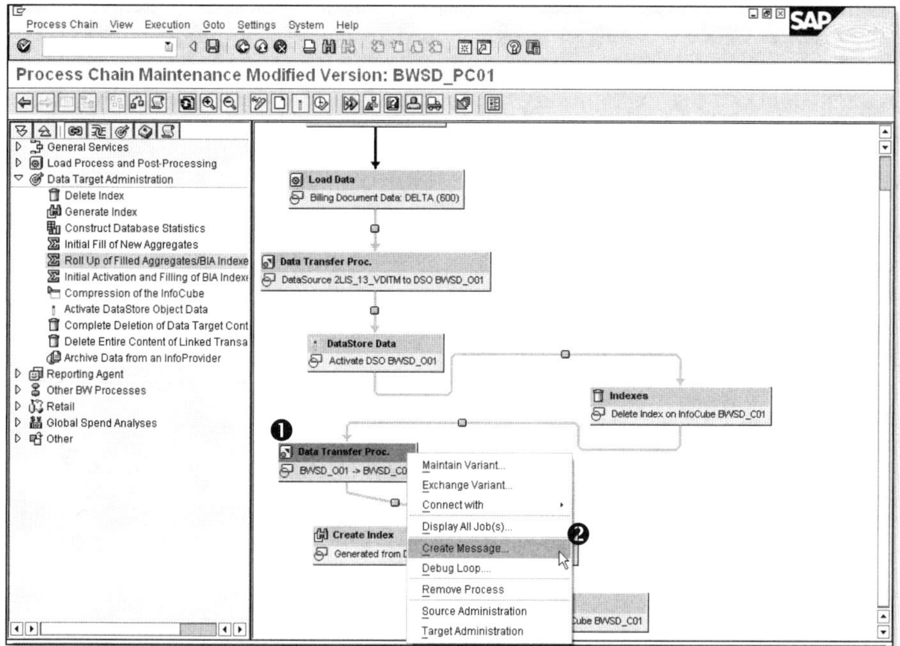

Figure 14.35 Setting Alert Message in Process Chains

In the Action For pop-up box, select the Errors radio button (❷ of Figure 14.36), and click the Continue icon. In the Insert Send Message box (❸), you can choose an existing message from the dropdown list, or create a new one by clicking the Create icon (❸). Now a Send Message box appears, which has two fields. Enter the following:

- Processes Variant: "ERROR MSG_BWSD_O01_C01"
- Long Description: "Error message loading from DSO BWSD_O01 to InfoCube BWSD_C01" (❹)

Confirm the entries by clicking the Continue icon. The system opens the Process Maintenance: Send Message screen (❺).

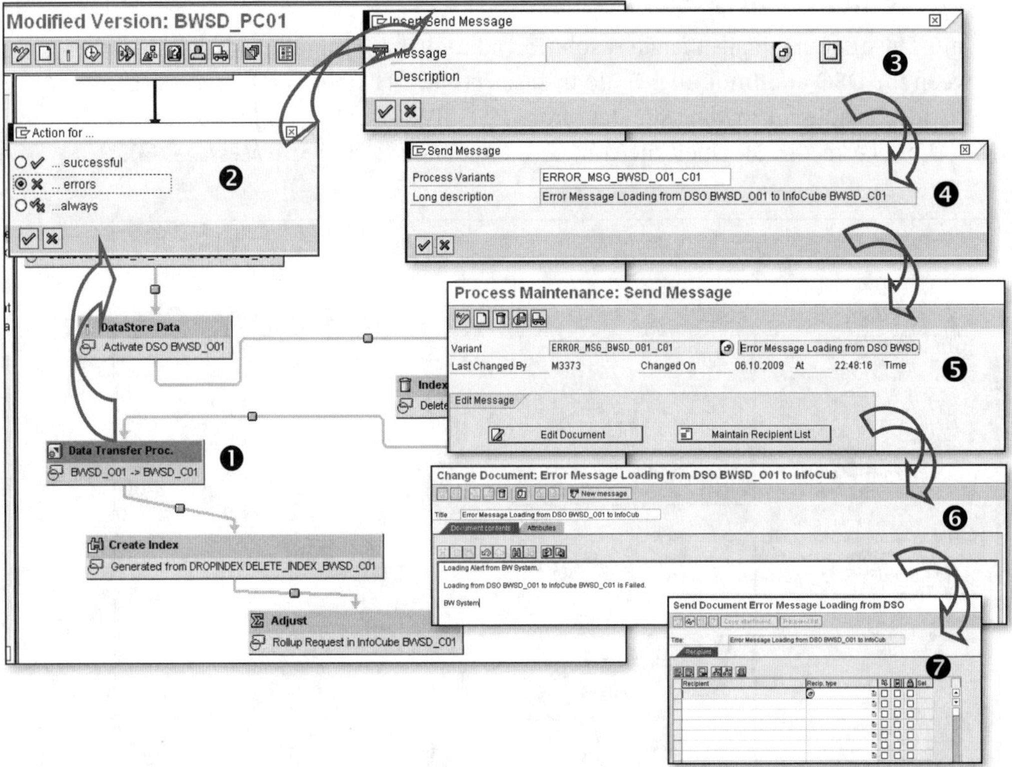

Figure 14.36 Process Maintenance – Send Message

The screen has two buttons: Edit Document and Maintain Recipient List. Click Edit Document; the next screen has two tabs: Document Contents and Attributes. In the Document Contents tab, type the text of the message (❻).

Save your changes, and use the Back icon to return to Process Maintenance: Send Message (❺). Clink on Maintain Recipients List, and the system opens a box where you can enter recipient email addresses and recipient types (❼). Click the Save icon and the Back icon; your email alert is now configured.

Check your process chain using the Check icon (), and make any necessary corrections (i.e., any changes suggested by the system in the log). If there are no errors, save the process chain, and click the Activate icon. A new process chain (technical name: BW_LOAD_BWSD_C01; text description: "Load data into BWSD_C01") is ready to be scheduled. As you can see, the active process chain matches the steps stated in the beginning of the section (Figure 14.37).

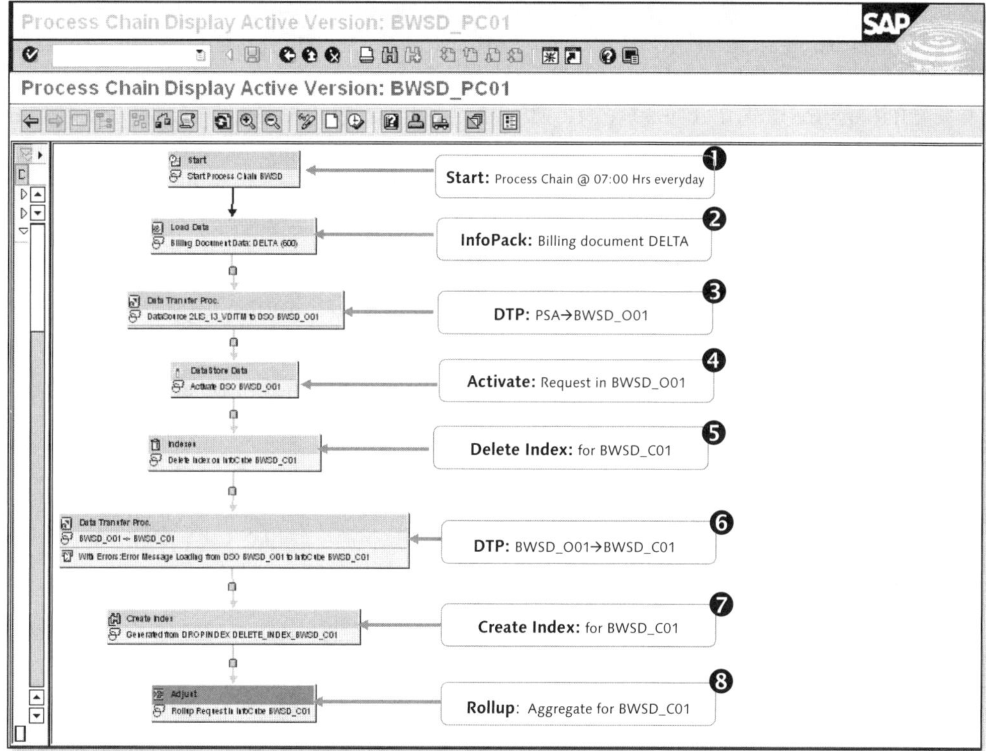

Figure 14.37 Overview of the Process Chain

Now schedule the process chain using the Schedule icon (), which will automate the process of data extraction from the SAP R3 system every day at 7:00 a.m (❶ through ❽ of Figure 14.37).

14.6 Analysis Authorizations

The ABCD Corp.'s IT team requires that users have access to information relevant to their roles and that other users can't access privileged information without specific approval. Information security and authorization in SAP NetWeaver BW is a vast subject, and a full discussion is beyond the scope of this book. In this section, we specifically focus on creating an analysis authorization to meet the specific IT business requirement.

The latest version of SAP NetWeaver BW offers extremely refined information security governance. In general, authorizations relate to a set of authorization objects that ensure information security. There are primarily two classes of authorization in SAP NetWeaver BW: reporting and administration. *Reporting authorization objects* are used for field-level security, and *administration authorization objects* are used to secure administration functions such as the creation of InfoObjects, the creation of queries, and so on.

For this basic introduction to reporting and analysis authorization, we explain how to do the following:

- Restrict access at a specific InfoCube level, so users will not be able to access any reports based on other objects (e.g., the DSO object).
- Restrict access to the characteristics within an InfoCube. This feature ensures that users will be able to analyze data in a report that is based on a specific characteristic; for example, Sales Manager with user-ID SM01 for 0SALES_OFF value 1422 (Figure 14.38).

Sales Manager	Sales Office	Sales 2009	Sales 2008	YoY Comparison (%)
SM00	1000	[illegible]	[illegible]	24.11
SM00	1002	[illegible]	[illegible]	145.13
SM01	1422	$30,855.50	$14,072.42	119.26
SM01	1422	$22,618.81	$28,826.48	-21.53
SM01	1422	$18,974.66	$21,661.73	-12.40
SM03	1421	[illegible]	[illegible]	1,086.37
SM03	1421	[illegible]	$0.00	0.00

Figure 14.38 Analysis Authorization Restriction by Characteristics

- Restrict access to a specific node of a hierarchy of a characteristic within an InfoCube, so that users will not be able to view the information/data for any other node or set of nodes (Figure 14.39).

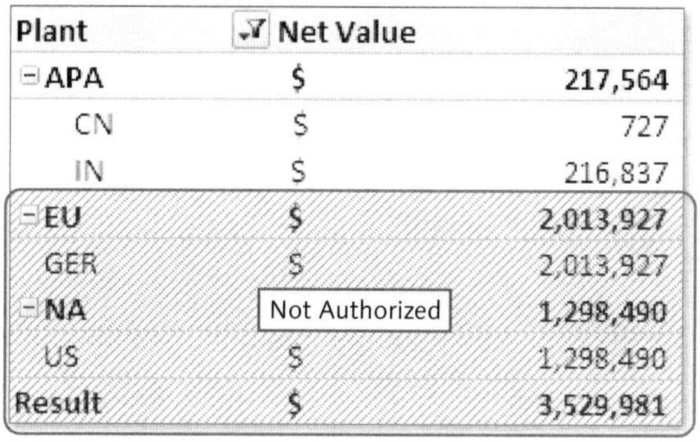

Plant	Net Value	
APA	$	217,564
CN	$	727
IN	$	216,837
EU	$	2,013,927
GER	$	2,013,927
NA		1,298,490
US	$	1,298,490
Result	$	3,529,981

Not Authorized

Figure 14.39 Analysis Authorization Restriction by Hierarchy and Hierarchy Node Figure

- Restrict access to specific key figures within an InfoCube, so that users will not be able to view the information/data on a row (or column) that has this specific key figure (Figure 14.40).

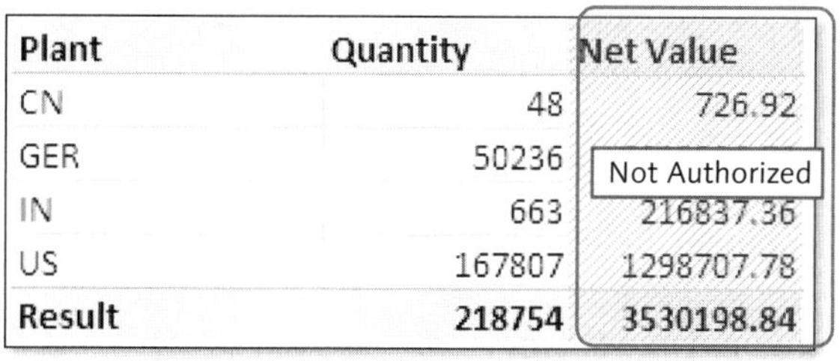

Plant	Quantity	Net Value
CN	48	726.92
GER	50236	
IN	663	216837.36
US	167807	1298707.78
Result	218754	3530198.84

Not Authorized

Figure 14.40 Analysis Authorization Restriction by Key Figure

The following steps provide a quick overview of the process of creating an analysis authorization.

14.6.1 Step 1: Define the InfoObject

The first step is to define the InfoObject as relevant for authorization. Use Transaction RSD1, and go to the InfoObject maintenance screen in the Business Explorer tab. Define the authorization-relevant characteristics. This will enable authorizations on characteristic values, for example, 0SALES_OFF (❶ of Figure 14.41).

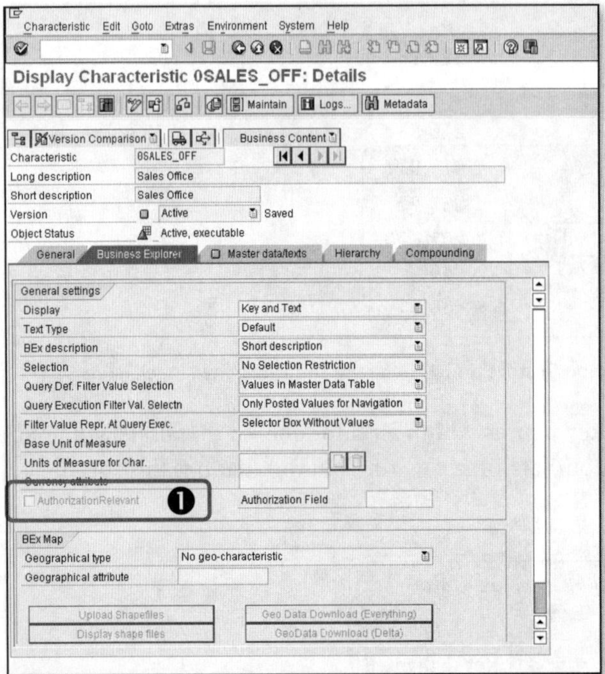

Figure 14.41 Authorization Relevant InfoObject

14.6.2 Step 2: Create an Authorization Object

The second step is to create an authorization object. Use Transaction RSECADMIN. The system takes you to the Management of Analysis Authorizations screen (Figure 14.42).

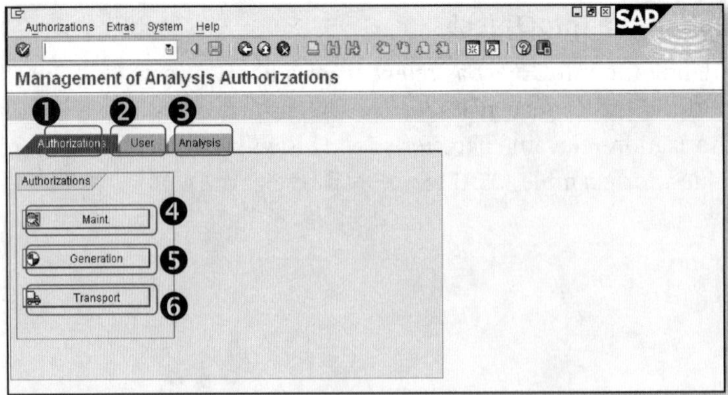

Figure 14.42 Management of Analysis Authorization

This screen has three tabs for carrying out the management of analysis authorizations: Authorizations (❶), User (❷), and Analysis (❸). In the following steps, we deal with the Authorization and User tabs (the Analysis tab is beyond the scope of this book).

The Authorization tab has three buttons for carrying out authorization-related tasks: Maintenance (❹), Generation (❺), and Transport (❻). The Maintenance button is the one relevant for our discussion; click it and the Maintain Authorizations: Initial screen appears (Figure 14.43).

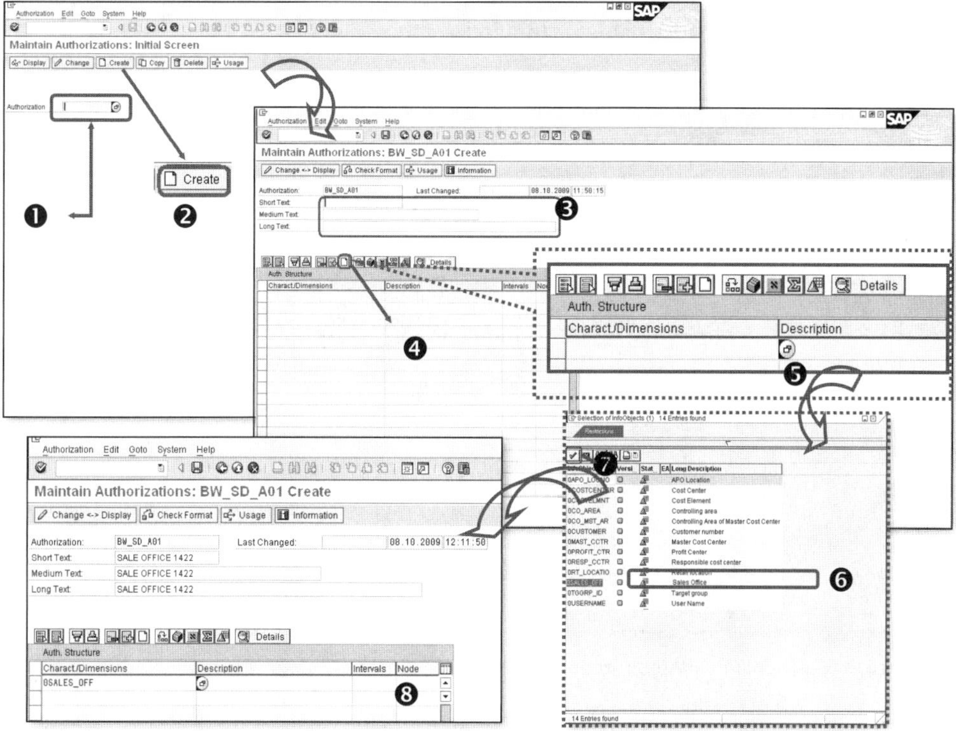

Figure 14.43 Create Analysis Authorization Object

In the Authorization field, enter "BW_SD_A01" (❶ of Figure 14.43), and click the Create button (❷). The next screen is Maintain Authorization: BW_SD_A01 Create. The screen has three fields for the authorization object's short, medium, and long descriptions (❸). Enter the following:

- Short Text: "SALES OFFICE 1422"
- Medium Text: "SALES OFFICE 1422"
- Long Text: "SALES OFFICE 1422"

Click on the Create Row icon (❹). The screen below now has a row open for entry; on the extreme right of the field, there is a dropdown list (❺) that lists all InfoObjects defined as relevant for the authorization (❻). Select 0SALES_OFF row, and then click the Copy icon (❼). The row in the screen now has an entry for InfoObject 0SALES_OFF (❽).

Double-click the 0SALES_OFF row. The system takes you to a screen where you can enter the characteristics value or hierarchy value (Figure 14.44).

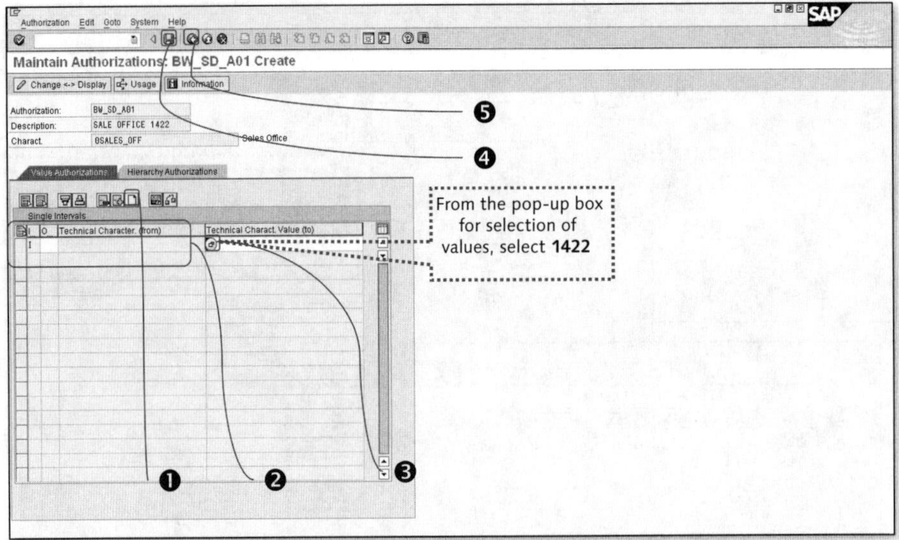

Figure 14.44 Maintain Authorization Values

Now choose the Value Authorizations tab, and click the Create Row icon (❶ of Figure 14.44), which opens a row editable in the table (❷). From the dropdown list (❸), choose a value to which to restrict the information in sales office reports (in our example, we use 1422). Click the Save and Back icons, respectively. Authorization object BW_SD_A01 is created, which allow analysis only for sales office 1422.

Table 14.2 gives authorization value options and the resulting behavior, with examples.

Authorization Value	Authorization Behavior
* (asterisk)	Denotes a set of arbitrary characters Used alone to grant access to all values Used at the end of a value to specify a simple pattern (example: SAP*)
: (colon)	Allows access only to aggregated data (e.g., allows information on all sales areas only on aggregated level — not on particular sales areas)
+ (plus)	Denotes exactly one character Used at the end of a value to specify a simple pattern
# (hash)	Stands for the initial or unassigned value

Table 14.2 Authorization Value Options and Their Influence on Access Behavior

14.6.3 Step 3: Assign a User ID

The third step is to assign the authorization object to a user ID. Use Transaction RSECADMIN, and the system opens Management of Analysis Authorizations. Click on the User tab (Figure 14.45). You're now assigning the authorization object to a user ID for providing access to analysis on reports for sales office 1422.

The screen has two separate boxes: Analysis Authorizations and NetWeaver Transactions (❶ of Figure 14.45). Click on the Assign button (❷), and the system takes you to BI Reporting: Init. Screen Assignment of User Authorizations. Use the user ID SM01 (A in Figure 14.45) for the sales manager (for Sales Office 1422), and click on the Change button (B in Figure 14.45). The system brings you to Assignment of User Authorizations: Edit (❸). The following screen has 2 tabs; Manual or generated and Role Based (❹). System by default takes you to Manual or generated tab, note at this instance, there is no row in the table of Assigned Authorization. In the entry box for Name (Techn.) field (❺), enter the name of the authorization object you created (BW_SD_A01, in our example), and click Insert. The authorization object is assigned to the user referred to in ❻. Click the Save icon, and the system displays a message indicating successful assignment at the bottom of the screen. Use the Back icon to return to Management of Analysis Authorizations.

Click the Analysis tab to check the authorization restriction for the user ID based on the authorization object. Authorization object BW_SD_A01 should be assigned to the user ID SM01 for the sales manager responsible for sales office 1422.

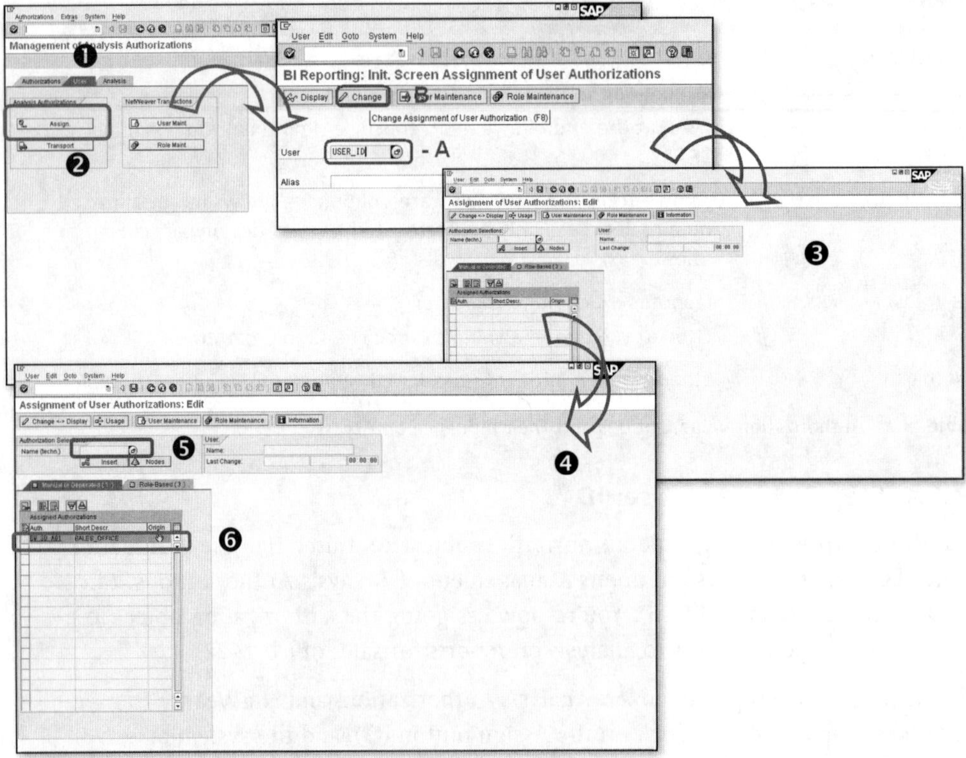

Figure 14.45 Assign Analysis Authorization

14.7 Other Administration and Maintenance Tasks

In this section, we briefly introduce some other administration and maintenance tasks without going into too much detail.

14.7.1 Executing an Attribute Hierarchy Change Run

The changes to the master data can also result in changes to navigational attributes or hierarchies. Recall from Section 14.3 that aggregates can be built using navigational attributes and hierarchies, so it's absolutely essential that you adjust data in the aggregates after you load master data. So that reporting delivers consistent results, master data and hierarchies are kept in two versions: the active version (which you can see in the query), and the modified version (which at some point becomes the active version).

The *attribute hierarchy change run* (also called the *realignment run)* adjusts the data in aggregates and turns the modified version of the navigational attributes and hierarchies into the active version. If there are any changes to master data, they aren't available for reporting until the change run is executed and finished.

Let's understand this important concept with the help of an example. Assume that InfoObject BW_CUST represents customers and has a navigational attribute 0SALESEMPLY, which represents the sale employee responsible for those customers (recall that we've used BW_CUST in InfoCube BWSD_C01). Sales employee 67679999 is responsible for customer 100086 for a certain period of time, but eventually the sales employee is changed to 6768000. Meanwhile, you've designed an aggregate based on 0SALESEMPLY, the purpose of which is to boost the query performance of queries with this characteristic. Although employee 6768000 is responsible for customer 100086 currently, the aggregate built using 0SALESEMPLY will have sales figures for the previous sales employee associated with that customer, 67679999. So if the system activates new master data without adjusting the aggregate, there will be data inconsistency.

To avoid this, the system doesn't activate newly loaded master data before the attribute hierarchy change run has adjusted the aggregate. After the attribute hierarchy change run is finished, all of the new relationships are also adjusted in the aggregates. So, in our example, all of the sales figures pertaining to customer 100086 now correctly fall under employee # 6768000.

The attribute hierarchy change run is a very important process. By executing it, not only do you activate newly loaded master data in the system, but you also adjust the aggregates.

14.7.2 Deleting Extra Aggregates

The Aggregates Maintenance function should be called regularly to delete unused aggregates. This improves load performance because the rollup process and realignment runs consume system resources. We explained earlier how the realignment run is essential to maintain information integrity.

An aggregate might be unnecessary for several reasons:

- There are similar aggregates that could be combined into one new aggregate.
- There are aggregates that are never used and aren't base aggregates.
- There are aggregates with an insufficient reduction factor compared to the InfoCube.

Aggregates are created especially for performance reasons, but unnecessary aggregates waste disk space and have to be regularly maintained via rollup and change runs, so it's important to regularly check your usage of your aggregates.

14.7.3 Deleting PSA Data

You need to determine a defined data retention period for data in PSA tables; the exact period depends on the type of data involved and your data uploading strategy. As part of this policy, establish a safe method to periodically delete data. If the PSA data isn't deleted on a regular basis, the PSA tables grow unrestricted. Very large tables increase the cost of data storage, the downtime for maintenance tasks, and the time required for uploading data. PSA deletion can be easily integrated in process chains.

14.7.4 Deleting DTP Temporary Storage

The deletion of DTP temporary storage is another action that can improve the performance of your system. This can be accomplished via DTP • DISPLAY • GOTO • SETTINGS FOR DTP TEMPORARY STORAGE. Based on the retention time frame for the temporary storage, choose the appropriate option within Delete Temporary Storage.

14.7.5 Using Report SAP_INFOCUBE_DESIGNS

Use Transaction SA37 to execute the SAP_INFOCUBE_DESIGNS report. The result shows the database tables of an InfoCube, the number of records in these tables, and the ratio of the dimension table size to the fact table size. If dimension tables are too large, they can cause badly performing table joins on the database level. As data volume grows and data allocation changes over time, this check should be executed regularly. Based on the results from this report, you can use the settings such as Line Item dimension or High Cardinality dimension to improve performance of the InfoCube. These settings are explained in Chapter 5, InfoCubes.

14.7.6 Checking Data Consistency

Use Transaction RSRV to analyze the important objects in the SAP NetWeaver BW system; this transaction also provides repair functionality for some tests. These tests only check the intrinsic technical consistency of objects such as foreign key relations of the underlying tables, missing indexes, and so on; they don't analyze any business logic or semantic accuracy of data. Missing table indexes or inconsistencies in master data or transactional data can have a negative impact on your system performance or lead to missing information in your SAP NetWeaver BW reporting.

Again, as a reminder, we recommend reading the reference material mentioned in the Preface to the book, which will teach you the techniques for optimizing your use of SAP NetWeaver BW.

14.8 Summary

In this chapter, we introduced the fundamental idea behind administration and maintenance tasks: ensuring your system lives up to its purpose of delivering the right information at the right time by consuming the right amount of resources – consistently. We began the chapter with a discussion of managing data targets (DSOs and InfoCubes), briefly explained the ideas of aggregates of compression, and then moved on to a discussion of process chains and analysis authorizations. We concluded the chapter with a summary of other important administration and maintenance tasks. In the next chapter, we explain some of the advanced features and functionality offered by SAP NetWeaver BW.

In this chapter, we introduce you to some of the advanced features of SAP NetWeaver BW. The content discussed here is meant to get you started toward gaining advanced technical understanding of SAP NetWeaver BW as a data warehousing, reporting, and analysis tool.

15 Advanced Features

The previous chapters were designed to give you a basic understanding of SAP NetWeaver BW. In this chapter, we introduce you to some of the more advanced features offered by SAP NetWeaver BW, which are used to address complex and high-end analysis requirements and to maintain scalability of the solution. The topics covered in this chapter are

- Open hub
- Analysis Process Designer (APD)
- Remodeling

15.1 Open Hub

In this section, we briefly explain the open hub concept and then explain how to create an open hub destination.

15.1.1 The Open Hub Concept

As a data warehouse, SAP NetWeaver BW can acquire data from a variety of sources and then store this data in data targets. SAP NetWeaver BW can also act as a source for the data that is acquired from other systems (SAP or non-SAP) (Figure 15.1). In such a scenario, SAP NetWeaver BW acts as a *hub* that is *open* for the distribution of data to different destination systems.

15.1.2 Creating an Open Hub Destination

Using the open hub service, you can transfer data from SAP NetWeaver BW InfoProviders to different destinations in either *full mode* or *delta mode*. The destination from where data is extracted is known as the *open hub destination (OHD)*. An OHD is created and maintained in the Data Warehousing Workbench (DWW), under the Modeling section (❶ of Figure 15.2). The InfoArea tree is displayed on the right panel of the screen.

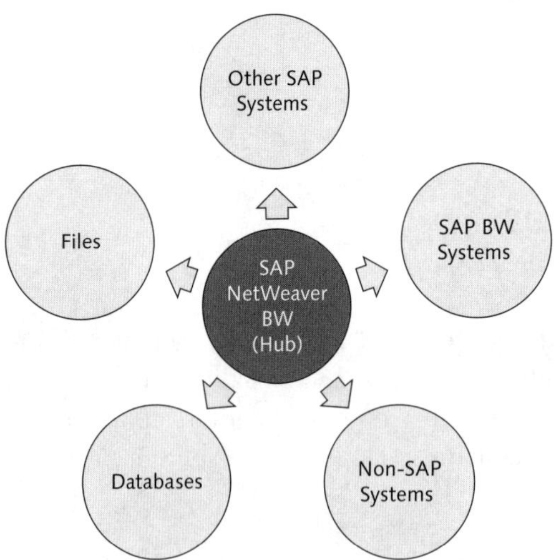

Figure 15.1 SAP NetWeaver BW as an Open Hub

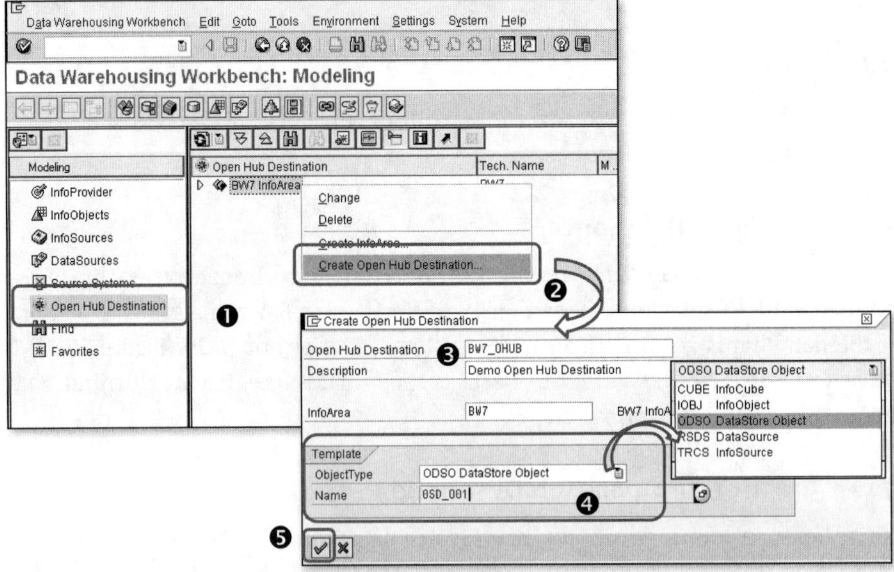

Figure 15.2 Create Open Hub Destination

To create an OHD, select Create Open Hub Destination from the context menu of the InfoArea where you want to create it (❷ of Figure 15.2). A pop-up box appears for entering the technical name and description of the OHD (❸). To reduce development time, you can also use the object from which you are going to load data as a template to create the OHD definition (❹). Click on OK to continue with the OHD creation (❺). The detailed OHD definition is maintained on the screen shown in Figure 15.3.

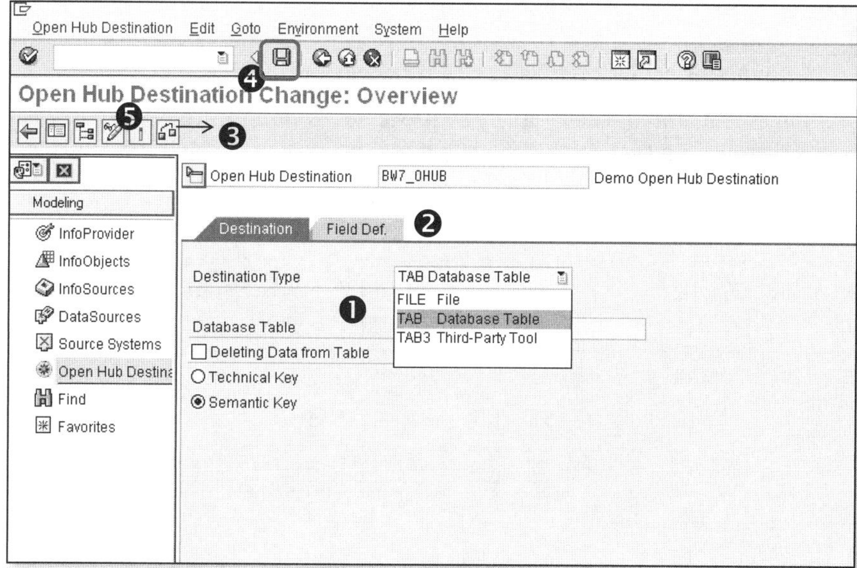

Figure 15.3 Define OHD

The two tabs on the OHD definition screen are explained here:

- Destination: The open hub service allows you to transmit data to various destinations. On the Destination tab (❶ of Figure 15.3), you can define the destination where the data needs to be sent.
- Field Definition: The fields and format in which the data has to be sent to the destination is defined in the Field Definition tab (❷).

After the OHD is defined, check the definition (❸), save the definition (❹), and, finally, activate the definition (❺).

After the OHD is active, you can create a *transformation* and *data transfer process (DTP)* from the source to this OHD to transfer the data. The DTP for an open hub is the same as the regular DTP and can be scheduled the same way.

15.2 Analysis Process Designer

The Analysis Process Designer (APD) provides advanced analysis options in SAP NetWeaver BW. Data from a variety of InfoProviders (DSOs, InfoCubes, InfoObjects, as well as data providers such as BEx queries, etc.) can be linked together with logic and transformations to create additional information needed for business analysts. APD also supports data mining operations based on the data stored in SAP NetWeaver BW. In this section, we discuss the Analysis Workbench used in APD and also explain how to create an analysis process.

15.2.1 Analysis Workbench

The creation and maintenance of analysis processes is done in the *Analysis Workbench*, which is accessed using Transaction *RSANWB*. You can also access this from DWW by clicking the APD icon shown in Figure 15.4.

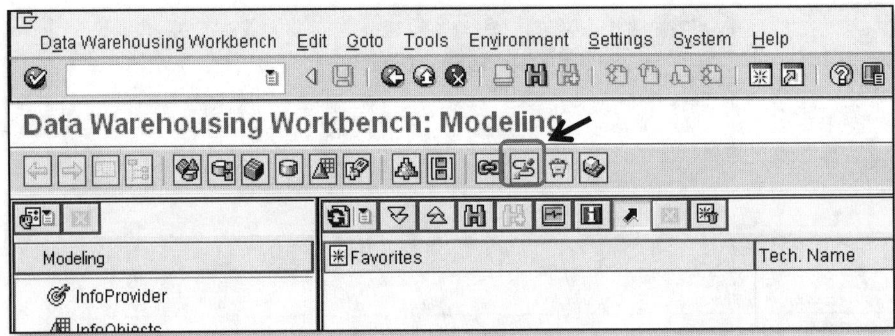

Figure 15.4 Accessing Analysis Workbench

The Analysis Workbench has a default layout, as shown in Figure 15.5. To create a new analysis process, click on the Create icon (Figure 15.5), and select GENERIC General as the application.

This displays the Analysis Process Designer – Create screen (Figure 15.6). The left panel of the screen displays all of the components that can be used to build an analysis process, and the right panel displays the design area where the analysis process is built.

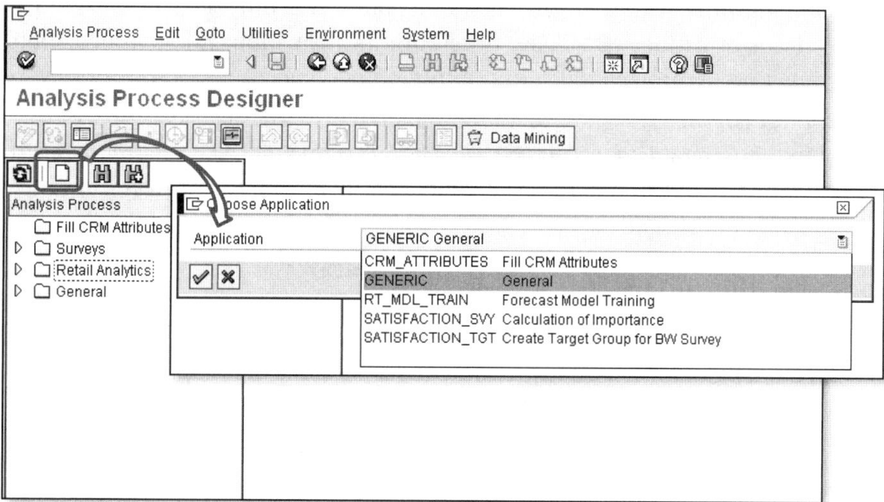

Figure 15.5 Create Analysis Process

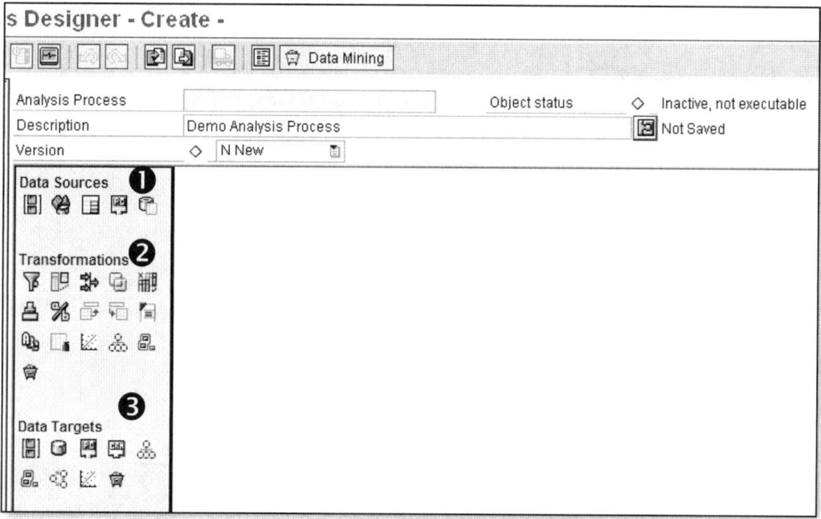

Figure 15.6 Components of Analysis Process

There are three types of components used in an analysis process:

- **Data source:** The components from which data is read for further processing in an analysis process are categorized as data sources (❶ of Figure 15.6). An analysis process can use master data, BEx queries, InfoProviders, flat files, or database tables as a data source.

- **Transformations:** Different analysis functions used on the data are grouped under Transformations (❷). These different transformations range from a simple filter function to more complex data mining functions.
- **Data targets:** The data processed and generated in an analysis process can be saved into different data targets (❸), such as direct update DSOs, master data attributes, flat files, and so on. The data generated in an analysis process can also be fed to data mining models.

15.2.2 Creating an Analysis Process

Let's take a simple example where you want to perform some advanced analysis based on a query and master data. Assume that you want the output of the analysis to be stored in a direct update DSO. Follow these steps to create an APD:

1. Drag the Query icon from the Data Sources area to the design area (❶ of Figure 15.7), and assign a query to this data source using the Choose Query button in the pop-up box (❷). Press Enter, or click on the icon shown in ❸ of Figure 15.7 to return to the design screen.

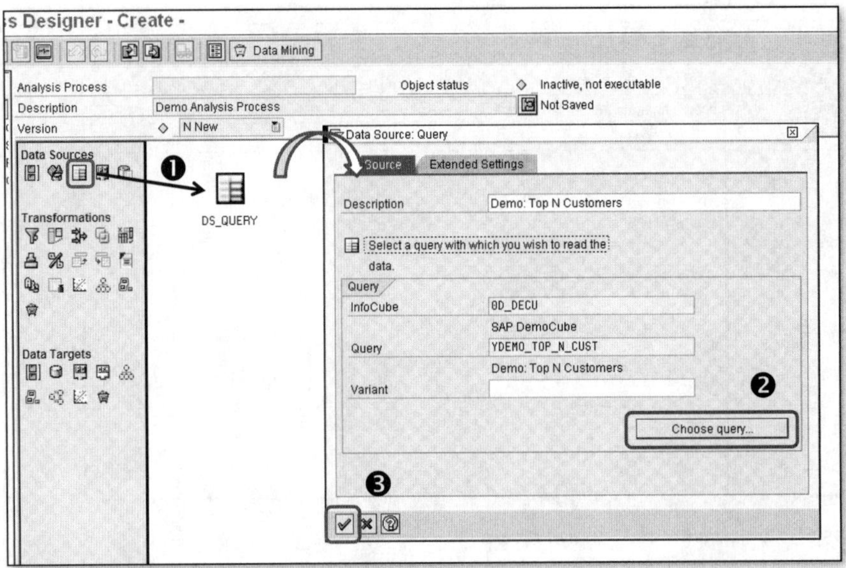

Figure 15.7 Add Data Source - Query

2. Drag another data source, master data, in the design area (❶ of Figure 15.8), and assign the master data characteristic that is needed to perform the analysis (❷). Press Enter, or click on the icon shown in ❸ of Figure 15.8 to return to the design screen.

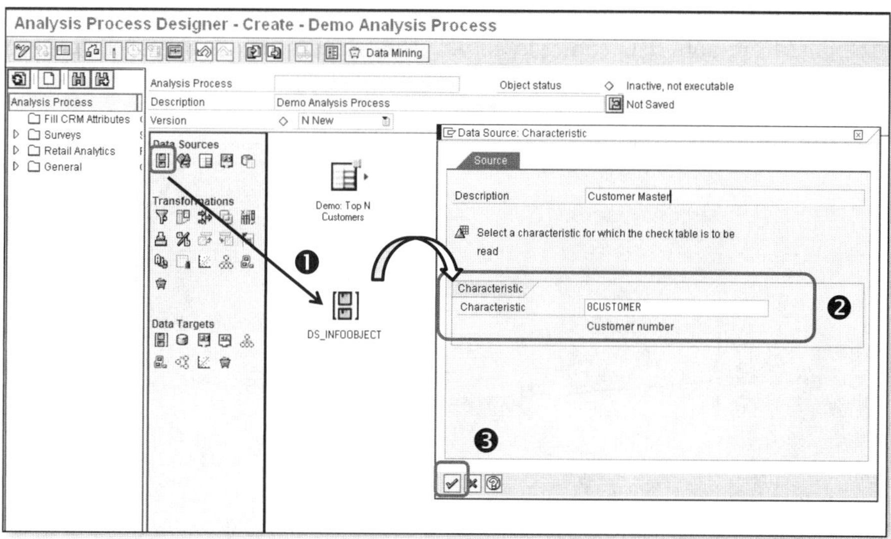

Figure 15.8 Add Data Source – Master Data

3. Drag the Direct Update DSO icon from the Data Targets area to the design area (❶ of Figure 15.9), and select the direct update DSO to where the data from the analysis process should be saved (❷). Press Enter to return to the design screen.

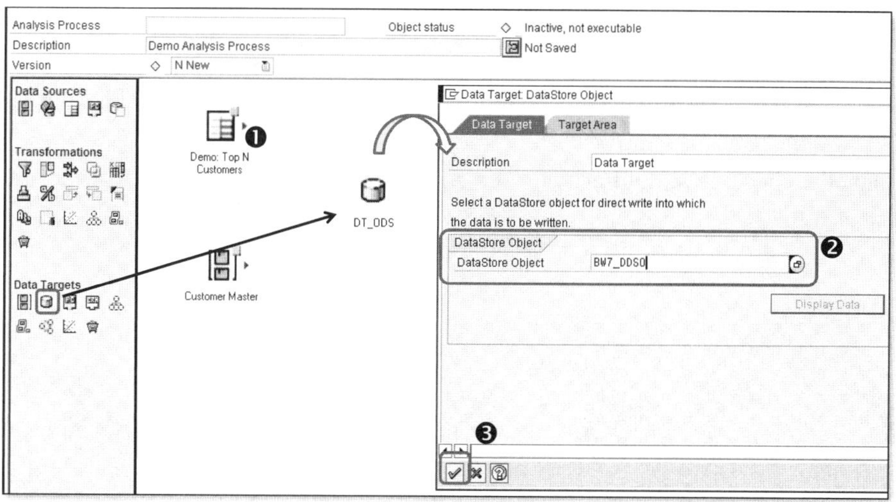

Figure 15.9 Add Data Target – Direct Update DSO

4. Drag the Join icon from the Transformations area to the design area (Figure 15.10). The data from both data sources will pass though this transformation before getting saved to the data target.

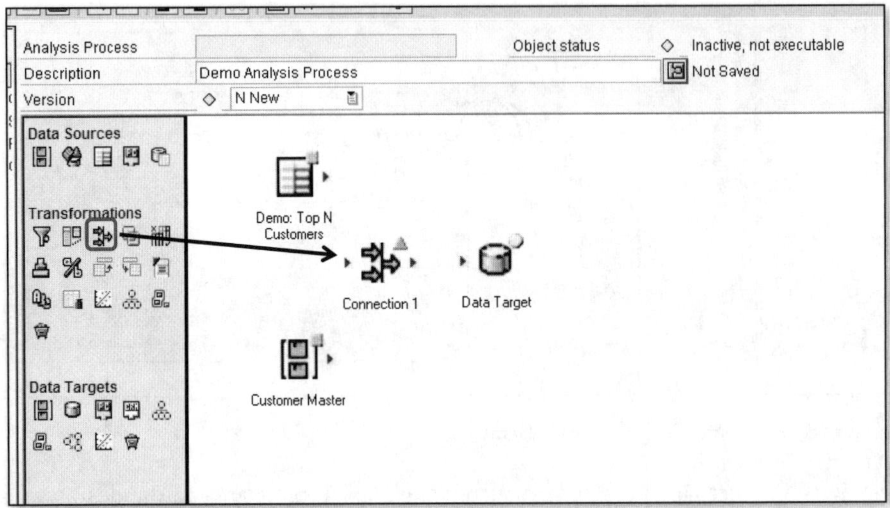

Figure 15.10 Add Transformation – Join

5. Create links between the components by dragging the mouse from one component to the other (❶ of Figure 15.11).
6. You can now maintain the join conditions for both data sources (❷ of Figure 15.11), as well as the rules for mapping the transformed data to the fields in the data target (❸).
7. Finally, check, save, and activate the analysis process. You can now execute the active analysis process.

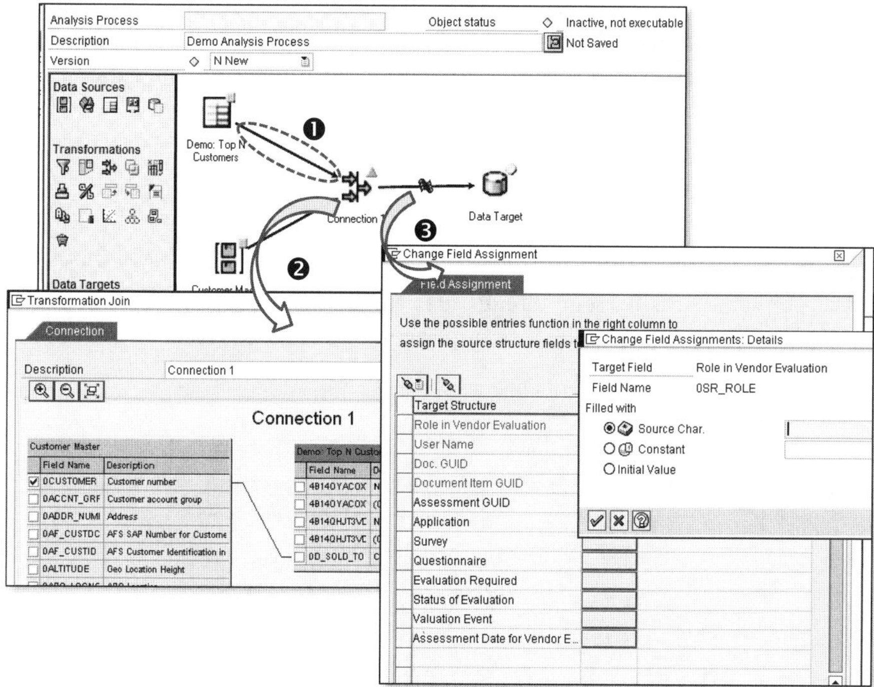

Figure 15.11 Define Transformations

15.3 Remodeling

In this section, we explain the remodeling feature offered by SAP NetWeaver BW, briefly discussing the need for remodeling, and how to create remodeling rules.

15.3.1 Need for Remodeling

When an InfoCube is in use for a long period (and therefore has a large quantity of data), it needs to be enhanced to meet new analysis requirements. Such enhancements might include the following:

- Adding a new characteristic and populating it with new values.
- Replacing an existing characteristic with a new one.
- Deleting a characteristic.
- Adding a new key figure and populating it with new values.
- Replacing an existing key figure with a new one.
- Deleting a key figure.

Because these enhancements result in structural changes to an InfoCube, you must delete data from the InfoCube before implementing and then reload the data. This process can be cumbersome if a large amount of data must be deleted and then reloaded. The *remodeling* feature available in SAP NetWeaver BW allows you to build remodeling rules that define logic behind the enhancement and then execute these rules to make changes without deleting the data.

15.3.2 Creating Remodeling Rules

To create or maintain the remodeling rules for an InfoCube, select ADDITIONAL FUNCTIONS • REMODELING from the context menu of the InfoCube in Transaction RSA1 (❶ of Figure 15.12).

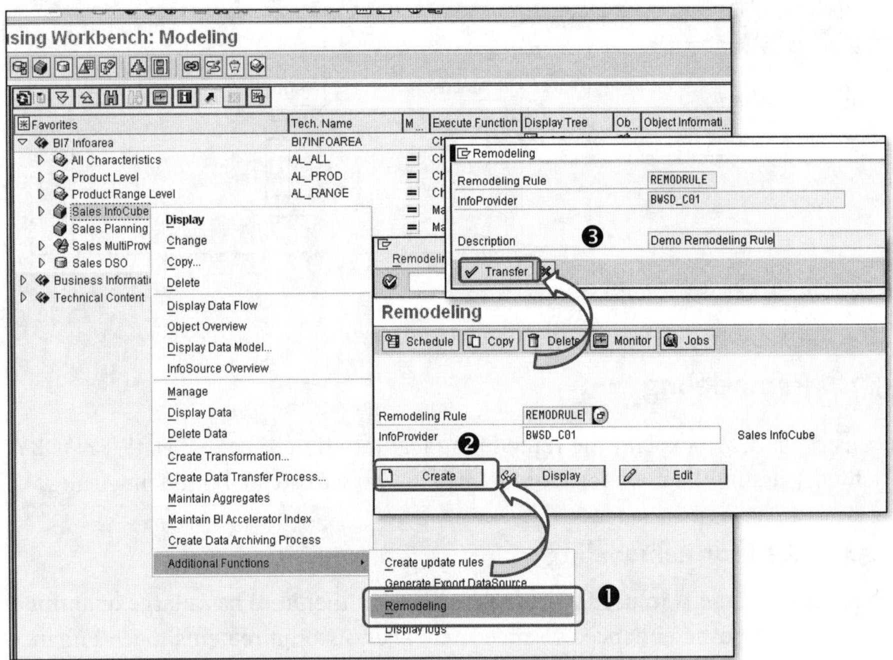

Figure 15.12 Create Remodeling Rules

This takes you to a screen where you can specify the name of the rule and the InfoProvider. To create a new rule, click on the Create button (❷ of Figure 15.12). A pop-up box appears to enter the description of the rule. Enter the description, and then click the Transfer button (❸). On the next screen, you can define the rule for the selected InfoCube (Figure 15.13).

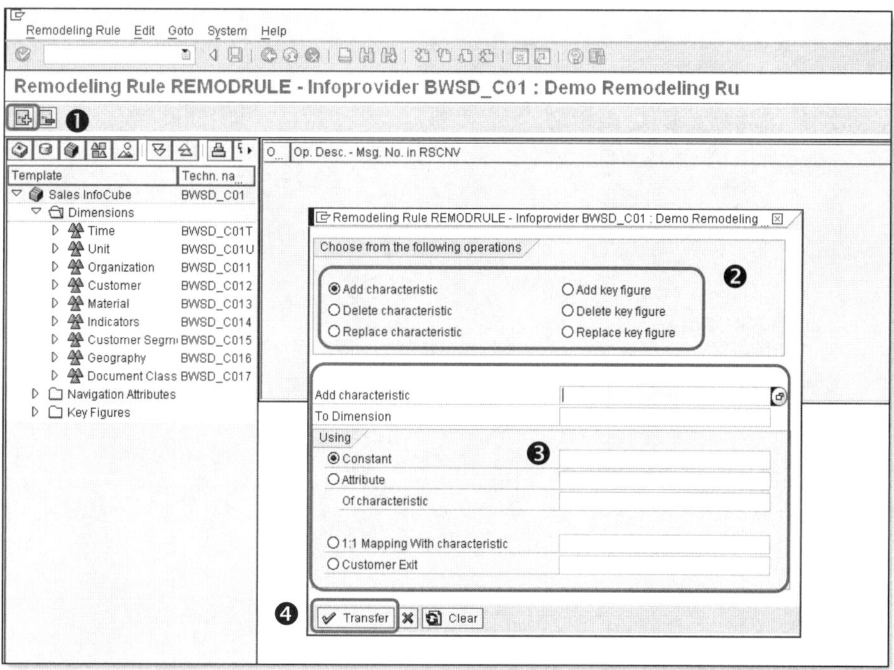

Figure 15.13 Define Operations

Click on the icon shown in ❶ of Figure 15.13 to add an *operation* to the rule. A pop-up box appears in which you can select the type of operation you want to perform (❷); maintain the parameters and logic for the operation in the bottom part of the pop-up box (❸).

Finally, click the Transfer button to add the defined operation to the remodeling rule. If you want to perform multiple operations on the InfoProvider, you can add these operations in the same remodeling rule.

Once it's completely defined, save the remodeling rule, and return to the previous screen. You can execute this rule by using the Schedule button shown earlier in Figure 15.12.

15.4 Summary

This chapter explained three advanced features of SAP NetWeaver BW: open hubs, analysis process designer, and remodeling. The intention of this chapter was to get you started with your advanced technical understanding of SAP NetWeaver BW.

Appendices

A Case Study: ABCD Corp.

Marketing Region	Country	Market Code
AMERICA	USA	NA
AMERICA	Canada	NA
EUROPE	UK	EU
EUROPE	Germany	EU
EUROPE	France	EU
ASIA-PACIFIC	China	APAC
ASIA-PACIFIC	India	APAC
ASIA-PACIFIC	Singapore	APAC
ASIA-PACIFIC	Australia	APAC
ASIA-PACIFIC	Japan	APAC
ASIA-PACIFIC	Saudi Arabia	APAC
ASIA-PACIFIC	South Africa	APAC
AMERICA	Mexico	NA

Table A.1 Countries in the Marketing Regions

Plant Location	Plant Code
USA	US
Germany	GR
China	CN
India	IN

Table A.2 Plants

Customer Code	Customer Name	Customer Group	City	Contact Name	Country
100017	Consumer Electronic Store	Store	Adeleaide	Georg Pipps	Australia
100071	Sound Systems	Store	Perth	Roland Mendel	Australia
100042	James	Store	Charleroi	Pascale Cartrain	Belgium
100051	Mike	Store	Bruxelles	Catherine Dewey	Belgium
100015	Comércio Mineiro	Store	São Paulo	Pedro Afonso	Brazil
100023	Familia Arquibaldo	Store	São Paulo	Aria Cruz	Brazil
100033	Gourmet Lanchonetes	Store	Campinas	André Fonseca	Brazil
100037	Hanari Carnes	Store	Rio de Janeiro	Mario Pontes	Brazil
100059	Que Delícia	Store	Rio de Janeiro	Bernardo Batista	Brazil
100060	Queen Cozinha	Store	São Paulo	Lúcia Carvalho	Brazil
100064	Ricardo Adocicados	Store	Rio de Janeiro	Janete Limeira	Brazil
100080	Tradição Hipermercados	Store	São Paulo	Anabela Domingues	Brazil
100088	Wellington Importadora	Store	Resende	Paula Parente	Brazil
100035	Great Eastern	Store	Tsawassen	Elizabeth Lincoln	Canada
100050	Mère Paillarde	Store	Montréal	Jean Fresnière	Canada
100082	Trans Canada	Store	Vancouver	Yoshi Tannamuri	Canada
100070	Simons	Store	København	Jytte Petersen	Denmark
100083	Vaffeljernet	Store	Århus	Palle Ibsen	Denmark
100087	Wartian Herkku	Store	Oulu	Pirkko Koskitalo	Finland
100090	Wilman Kala	Store	Helsinki	Matti Karttunen	Finland
100009	Blondel père et fils	Store	Strasbourg	Frédérique Citeaux	France

Table A.3 Customers

Customer Code	Customer Name	Customer Group	City	Contact Name	Country
100011	Bon app'	Store	Marseille	Laurence Lebihan	France
100021	Du monde entier	Store	Nantes	Janine Labrune	France
100025	Folies gourmandes	Store	Lille	Martine Rancé	France
100027	France restauration	Store	Nantes	Carine Schmitt	France
100044	La corne d'abondance	Store	Versailles	Daniel Tonini	France
100045	La maison d'Asie	Store	Toulouse	Annette Roulet	France
100056	Paris spécialités	Store	Paris	Marie Bertrand	France
100072	Spécialités du monde	Store	Paris	Dominique Perrier	France
100084	Victuailles en stock	Store	Lyon	Mary Saveley	France
100085	Vins et alcools Chevalier	Store	Reims	Paul Henriot	France
100001	Alfreds Futterkiste	Store	Berlin	Maria Anders	Germany
100008	Blauer See Delikatessen	Store	Mannheim	Hanna Moos	Germany
100019	Die Wandernde Kuh	Store	Stuttgart	Rita Müller	Germany
100020	Drachenblut Delikatessen	Store	Aachen	Sven Ottlieb	Germany
100029	Frankenversand	Store	München	Peter Franken	Germany
100043	Königlich Essen	Store	Brandenburg	Philip Cramer	Germany
100046	Lehmanns Marktstand	Store	Frankfurt a.M.	Renate Messner	Germany
100052	Morgenstern Gesundkost	Store	Leipzig	Alexander Feuer	Germany

Table A.3 Customers (Cont.)

Customer Code	Customer Name	Customer Group	City	Contact Name	Country
100054	Ottilies Käseladen	Store	Köln	Henriette Pfalzheim	Germany
100061	QUICK-Stop	Store	Cunewalde	Horst Kloss	Germany
100078	Toms Spezialitäten	Store	Münster	Karin Josephs	Germany
100007	Bharat Electronics Ltd.	Retail Chain	Mumbai	Bharat Patel	India
100055	Palekar & Sons	Store	Delhi	Amol Palekar	India
100074	SWS Associates	Store	Bangalore	S W Shiralkar	India
100040	Hungry Owl All-Night Grocers	Store	Cork	Patricia McKenna	Ireland
100028	Franchi S.p.A.	Store	Torino	Paolo Accorti	Italy
100049	Magazzini Alimentari Riuniti	Store	Bergamo	Giovanni Rovelli	Italy
100063	Reggiani Caseifici	Store	Reggio Emilia	Maurizio Moroni	Italy
100002	Ana Trujillo Emparedados y helados	Store	México D.F.	Ana Trujillo	Mexico
100003	Antonio Moreno Taquería	Store	México D.F.	Antonio Moreno	Mexico
100013	Centro comercial Moctezuma	Store	México D.F.	Francisco Chang	Mexico
100036	GROSELLA-Restaurante	Store	México D.F.	Manuel Pereira	Mexico
100038	HILARIÓN-Abastos	Store	México D.F.	Carlos Hernández	Mexico
100047	LILA-Supermercado	Store	México D.F.	Carlos González	Mexico
100048	LINO-Delicateses	Store	México D.F.	Felipe Izquierdo	Mexico

Table A.3 Customers (Cont.)

Customer Code	Customer Name	Customer Group	City	Contact Name	Country
100057	Pericles Comidas clásicas	Store	México D.F.	Guillermo Fernández	Mexico
100079	Tortuga Restaurante	Store	México D.F.	Miguel Angel Paolino	Mexico
100067	Santé Gourmet	Store	Stavern	Jonas Bergulfsen	Norway
100091	Wolski Zajazd	Store	Warszawa	Zbyszek Piestrzeniewicz	Poland
100030	Furia Bacalhau e Frutos do Mar	Store	Lisboa	Lino Rodriguez	Portugal
100058	Princesa Isabel Vinhos	Store	Lisboa	Isabel de Castro	Portugal
100010	Bólido Comidas preparadas	Store	Madrid	Martín Sommer	Spain
100024	FISSA Fabrica Inter. Salchichas S.A.	Store	Madrid	Diego Roel	Spain
100031	Galería del gastrónomo	Store	Barcelona	Eduardo Saavedra	Spain
100032	Godos Cocina Típica	Store	Sevilla	José Pedro Freyre	Spain
100066	Romero y tomillo	Store	Madrid	Alejandra Camino	Spain
100005	Berglunds snabbköp	Store	Luleå	Christina Berglund	Sweden
100026	Folk och fä HB	Store	Bräcke	Maria Larsson	Sweden
100014	Chop-suey Chinese	Store	Bern	Yang Wang	Switzerland
100065	Richter Supermarket	Store	Genève	Michael Holz	Switzerland
100004	Around the Horn	Store	London	Thomas Hardy	UK
100012	B's Beverages	Store	London	Victoria Ashworth	UK

Table A.3 Customers (Cont.)

Customer Code	Customer Name	Customer Group	City	Contact Name	Country
100016	Consolidated Holdings	Store	London	Elizabeth Brown	UK
100022	Eastern Connection	Store	London	Ann Devon	UK
100041	Island Trading	Store	Cowes	Helen Bennett	UK
100053	North/South	Store	London	Simon Crowther	UK
100069	Seven Seas Imports	Store	London	Hari Kumar	UK
100006	Best Buy	Retail Chain	Portland	Fran Wilson	USA
100018	Cosco	Retail Chain	Anchorage	Rene Phillips	USA
100034	Great Audio Systems	Store	Eugene	Howard Snyder	USA
100039	Hungry Coyote Import Store	Store	Elgin	Yoshi Latimer	USA
100062	Rattlesnake Canyon Grocery	Store	Albuquerque	Paula Wilson	USA
100068	Save-a-lot Markets	Store	Boise	Jose Pavarotti	USA
100073	Home Depot	Retail Chain	Washington	Abraham Lincoln	USA
100075	Target	Retail Chain	Walla Walla	John Steel	USA
100076	The Big Cheese	Store	Portland	Liz Nixon	USA
100077	The Cracker Box	Store	Butte	Liu Wong	USA
100081	Trail's Head Gourmet Provisioners	Store	Kirkland	Helvetius Nagy	USA
100086	Wal-Mart	Retail Chain	San Francisco	Jaime Yorres	USA
100089	White Clover Markets	Store	Seattle	Karl Jablonski	USA

Table A.3 Customers (Cont.)

Customer Group Code	Customer Group Name
ST	Store
RC	Retail Chain

Table A.4 Customer Groups

Product Code	Product Name	Product Range Name (Code)	Product Group Code
31000	Compact Cassette	Consumer Electronics	AUDIO
31500	DVD Player	Consumer Electronics	AUDIO
5200	Cassette - Answering Mc	Consumer Electronics	AUDIO
38000	MP4 Player	Consumer Electronics	AUDIO
37500	Home Theatre	Consumer Electronics	AUDIO
37800	Personal Stereo	Consumer Electronics	AUDIO
31300	Compact Disc	Consumer Electronics	AUDIO
31400	DVD	Consumer Electronics	AUDIO
5000	Answering Machine	Consumer Electronics	DIGITAL
5400	Answering Machine Battery	Consumer Electronics	DIGITAL
5300	Answering Machine Charger	Consumer Electronics	DIGITAL
5450	Answering Machine Stand	Consumer Electronics	DIGITAL
2008	Answering Machine Extra Cassette	Consumer Electronics	DIGITAL
5500	Answering Machine Extra Cord	Consumer Electronics	DIGITAL

Table A.5 Products

Product Code	Product Name	Product Range Name (Code)	Product Group Code
5510	Answering Machine Extra handset	Consumer Electronics	DIGITAL
1009	Dictaphone Battery	Consumer Electronics	DIGITAL
1000	Dictaphone Pouch	Consumer Electronics	DIGITAL
1005	Dictaphone Charger	Consumer Electronics	DIGITAL
93000	Desktop PC	Consumer Electronics	PC
93500	Laptop PC	Consumer Electronics	PC
38300	Mobile Phone	Consumer Electronics	MOBILE
8148055	Color TV	Domestic Appliances	HOME
42000	LCD TV	Domestic Appliances	HOME
81460	Air Conditioner	Domestic Appliances	HOME
61000	Refrigerator	Domestic Appliances	HOME
21000	Video Camera	Domestic Appliances	HOME
63000	Dish Washer	Domestic Appliances	HOME
92000	Electric Shaving Machine	Consumer Lifestyle	PERSONAL
92500	Electric Toothbrushes	Consumer Lifestyle	PERSONAL
2009	Answering Machine Cord	Consumer Electronics	ACC
5000	Battery	Consumer Electronics	ACC

Table A.5 Products (Cont.)

Product Group Code	Product Group Name
AUDIO	Audio Systems and Equipments
DIGITAL	Digital Audio/Video Systems
HOME	Home Appliances
PERSONAL	Personal Systems
ACC	Accessories

Table A.6 Product Groups

Product Range Group Code	Product Range Group Name
CE	Consumer Electronics
DA	Domestic Appliances
CL	Consumer Lifestyle

Table A.7 Product Range Groups

Selling Channel Code	Selling Channel Name
DR	Direct
IT	Internet

Table A.8 Selling Channels

Billing Document Code	Type of Transaction
CR	On Credit
CH	On Cash

Table A.9 Types of Transactions

Billing Document Category Code	Type of Billing Transaction
DOM	Customer within USA
EX	Customer outside USA

Table A.10 Billing Types

Billing Value Limit	Billing Value Indicator Codes
Item without any cost	XX
Item value < 10000 USD	
Item value > 10000 USD	HV

Table A.11 Billing Value Indicators

B Glossary

Aggregate Aggregate is a summarized subset of the data in an InfoCube. In spite of the additional cost of storage, these objects help improve performance of analysis and reporting.

Aggregate rollup Aggregate rollup is a process of updating aggregates with new data.

Application component Application components are sets of InfoSources grouped logically. They are similar to the InfoAreas for InfoCubes.

Authorization An authorization defines what a user can do and to which SAP objects. For example, a user with an authorization can display and execute, but not change, a query. Authorizations are defined using authorization objects.

Authorization object An authorization object is used to define user authorizations. It has fields with values to specify authorized activities, such as display and execution, on authorized business objects, such as queries.

Authorization profile An authorization profile is made up of multiple authorizations.

Bitmap index Bitmap indexes are very effective for Boolean operations of the WHERE clause of a SELECT statement. When the cardinality of a column is low, a bitmap index size will be small, thereby reducing I/O volume.

BW Statistics BW Statistics is a tool for recording and reporting system activity and performance information.

Change run Change run is a procedure used to activate characteristic master data changes.

Characteristic A characteristic defines a business entity that is being evaluated or measured by a key figure in SAP NetWeaver BW. Customers and companies, for example, are both characteristics.

Client A client is a subset of data in an SAP system. Data shared by all clients is called client-independent data, as compared with client-dependent data. When logging on to an SAP system, a user must specify which client to use. Once in the system, the user has access to both client-dependent data and client-independent data.

Communication structure The communication structure is the structure underlying the InfoSource.

Compound attribute A compound attribute differentiates a characteristic to make the characteristic uniquely identifiable. For example, if the same characteristic data from different source systems means different things, then we can add the compound attribute 0SOURSYSTEM (source system ID) to the characteristic; 0SOURSYSTEM is provided with the SAP Business Content.

Compression Compression is an activity of reducing the data quantity in the InfoCube into another summarized multidimensional table (F table to E Table). Compression help improve performance both for loading as well as reporting.

Data packet size For the same amount of data, the data packet size determines how work processes will be used in data loading. The smaller the data packet size, the more work processes are needed.

Data Warehouse Data Warehouse is a dedicated reporting and analysis environment based on the star schema database design technique and requiring special attention to the data ETL process.

DataSource A DataSource is not only a structure in which source system fields are logically grouped together, but it's also an object that contains ETL-related information. Four types of DataSources exist: DataSources for transaction data, DataSources for characteristic attributes, DataSources for characteristic texts, and DataSources for characteristic hierarchies. If the source system is R/3, replicating DataSources from a source system will create identical DataSource structures in the SAP NetWeaver BW system.

Delta update The Delta update option in the InfoPackage definition requests SAP NetWeaver BW to load only the data accumulated since the last update. Before a delta update occurs, the delta process must be initialized.

Development class A development class is a group of objects that are logically related.

Display attribute A display attribute provides supplemental information to a characteristic.

Drilldown Drilldown is a user navigation step intended to get further detailed information.

DSO SAP NetWeaver BW's technical architecture has the DataStore Object (DSO), which stores data at a detailed level, tracks changes to data, and stores master data.

DTP Data Transfer Process (DTP) controls the distribution of data within SAP NetWeaver BW.

ETL The entire process of data acquisition from the sources, transformation of acquired data to the requisite format and then adding to the data target is called extraction, transformation, and loading or ETL.

Free characteristic A free characteristic is a characteristic in a query used for drilldowns. It isn't displayed in the initial result of a query run.

Full update The full update option in the InfoPackage definition requests SAP NetWeaver BW to load all data that meet the selection criteria specified via the Select Data tab.

Generic data extraction Generic data extraction is a function in SAP Business Content that allows you to create DataSources based on database views or InfoSet queries. InfoSet is similar to a view but allows outer joins between tables.

Granularity Granularity describes the level of detail in a data warehouse. It's determined by business requirements and technology capabilities.

IDoc IDoc (Intermediate Document) is used in SAP to transfer data between two systems. It's a specific instance of a data structure called the IDoc Type, whose processing logic is defined in the IDoc Interface.

Index An index is a technique used to locate needed records in a database table quickly. SAP NetWeaver BW uses two types of indices: B-tree indices for regular database tables, and bitmap indices for fact tables and aggregate tables.

InfoArea InfoArea is a logical group that is required for managing and designing the Data Warehouse; the InfoObjects are grouped in an InfoObject Catalog.

InfoCube SAP NetWeaver BW uses the extended star schema model. The InfoCube is based on this model and is one of the data targets (objects that physically store data) in SAP NetWeaver BW; in fact, it's the central object of SAP NetWeaver BW. An InfoCube is a fact table and its associated dimension tables in the star schema.

InfoObject In SAP NetWeaver BW, an InfoObject is the smallest building block. You use InfoObjects to design other objects such as InfoCubes, DSOs, MultiProviders, queries, InfoSets, and so on.

InfoObject Catalog InfoObject catalogs organize InfoObjects. Two types of InfoObject catalogs exist: one for characteristics, and one for key figures.

InfoPackage An InfoPackage specifies when and how to load data from a given source system. SAP NetWeaver BW generates a 30-digit code starting with ZPAK as an InfoPackage's technical name.

InfoSource An InfoSource is a structure in which InfoObjects are logically grouped together. InfoCubes and characteristics interact with InfoSources to get source system data.

Key figure Key figures are numeric values or quantities, such as Per Unit Sales Price, Quantity Sold, and Sales Revenue.

Line item dimension A line item dimension in a fact table connects directly with the SID table of its sole characteristic.

Logical system A logical system is the name of a client in an SAP system.

Monitor Monitor displays data loading status and provides assistance in troubleshooting if errors occur in the SAP NetWeaver BW system.

MultiCube A MultiCube is a union of basic cubes. The MultiCube itself does not contain any data; rather, data resides in the BasicCubes. To a user, the MultiCube is similar to a BasicCube. When creating a query, the user can select characteristics and key figures from different BasicCubes.

Navigational attribute A navigational attribute indicates a characteristic-to-characteristic relationship between two characteristics. It provides supplemental information about a characteristic and enables navigation from characteristic to characteristic during a query.

Number range A number range is a range of numbers that resides in application server memory for quick number assignments.

Parallel query A parallel query uses multiple database processes, when available, to execute a query.

Partition A partition is a piece of physical storage for database tables and indices. If the needed data resides in one or a few partitions, then only those partitions will be selected and examined by an SQL statement, thereby significantly reducing I/O volume.

PSA Persistent staging area (PSA) is a data staging area in SAP NetWeaver BW that allows you to store the data in an intermediate location before the data is sent to its destinations in SAP NetWeaver BW.

Query A SAP NetWeaver BW query is a selection of characteristics and key figures for the analysis of the data in an InfoCube. A query refers to only one InfoCube, and its results are presented in an BEx Excel sheet.

Read mode Read mode for a query determines the size and frequency of data retrievals from a database: all data at once, as needed per navigation step, or as needed per hierarchy node.

Reconstruct Reconstruction is the process of pulling back loaded data and reloading it.

Request A request is a data load request from SAP NetWeaver BW Scheduler. Each time SAP NetWeaver BW Scheduler loads data into an InfoCube, a unique request ID is created in the data packet dimension table of the InfoCube.

RFC RFC (Remote Function Call) is a call to a function module in a system different from the caller's – usually another SAP system on the local network.

Role In the Profile Generator, an authorization profile corresponds to a role. A user assigned to that role also has the corresponding authorization profile. A user can be assigned to multiple roles.

SAP Business Content SAP Business Content is a collection of all of the preconfigured scenarios and their components that are provided as part of the solution by SAP.

SAP NetWeaver BW SAP NetWeaver BW is the current business warehouse component from SAP.

Scheduler Scheduler specifies when to load data. It's based on the same techniques used for scheduling R/3 background jobs in the SAP NetWeaver BW system.

SID SID (Surrogate-ID) translates a potentially long key for an InfoObject into a short four-byte integer, which saves I/O and memory during OLAP.

Source system Source system is System that is available to SAP NetWeaver BW for data extraction. SAP as well as NON-SAP system can be configured as source system in SAP NetWeaver BW.

Star schema A star schema is a technique used in the Data Warehouse database design to help data retrieval for OLAP.

Statistics For a SQL statement, many execution plans are possible. The database optimizer generates the most efficient execution plan based on either the heuristic ranking of available execution plans or the cost calculation of available execution plans. Statistics is the information that the cost-based optimizer uses to calculate the cost of available execution plans and select the most appropriate one for execution. SAP NetWeaver BW uses the cost-base optimizer for Oracle databases.

System Administration Assistant The System Administration Assistant is a collection of tools used to monitor and analyze general system operation conditions.

System landscape The system landscape specifies the role of each system and the paths used in transporting objects among the various systems.

Time-dependent entire hierarchy A time-dependent entire hierarchy is a time-dependent hierarchy whose nodes and leaves are not time-dependent.

Time-dependent hierarchy structure A time-dependent hierarchy structure consists of nodes or leaves that are time-dependent, but the hierarchy itself is not time-dependent.

Transfer rule Transfer rules specify how DataSource fields are mapped to InfoSource InfoObjects.

Transfer structure A transfer structure maps DataSource fields to InfoSource InfoObjects.

Transformation Transformation is the process of converting the data format acquired from a variety of sources to the desired data format for the data target.

Update rule An update rule specifies how data will be updated into their targets. The data target can be an InfoCube or an ODS object. If the update rule is applied to data from an InfoSource, the update rule's technical name will match the InfoSource's technical name.

Variable A variable is a query parameter that gets its value from user input or takes a default value set by the variable creator.

Workbook A SAP NetWeaver BW workbook is an Excel file with a BEx query result saved in BDS.

C Important OSS Notes

SAP offers online support applications, one of which is SAP Notes. These help you avoid and correct errors in the SAP system. We have listed the SAP Notes we find most relevant for you in the context of the case study in the book and the overall context of your learning SAP NetWeaver BW.

OSS Note Number	Short description of the OSS Note
984229	F4 modes for input help as of SAP NetWeaver 2004s BI
350024	BW-OLTP-APCO: Frequently asked questions (FAQ)
1013140	BI Frontend / BW Add-on - General Information & Limitations
1013201	Hardware and Software requirement for BI Standalone frontend
955990	BI in SAP NetWeaver 7.0: Incompatibilities with SAP BW 3.x
160317	Customer namespace for objects in the Business Warehouse
1056259	Collective note: Performance of BI planning
1009497	UD Connect: How to update JDBC driver
919694	UD Connect - JDBC Limitations and performance
1050618	Problem analysis when you use a DTP to load master data
130253	General tips on uploading transaction data to BW
928044	BI lock server
396647	FAQ: V3 update: Questions and answers
380078	FAQ: BW delta queue (RSA7): Questions and answers
873694	Consulting: Delta repeat and status in monitor/data target
1335058	BexAnalyzer: F4 Help, Read Mode Setting Value
121291	Tips and tricks for the use of variables
1053310	Report-report interface: Application rules
124662	Description of the aggregation
152638	Aggregation settings in calculated key figures
460255	Information about aggregation, cumulation, results row
917950	SAP NetWeaver 2004s: Setting Up BEx Web
407260	FAQs: Compression of InfoCubes

OSS Note Number	Short description of the OSS Note
1117724	Change run and condensing (BW 7.X)
903886	Hierarchy and attribute change run
820183	New authorization concept in BI
846839	Types of Authorizations in BW
177875	Authorizations for analyzing OLAP problems
934848	Collective note: (FAQ) BI Administration Cockpit
1025307	Composite Note for NW2004s performance: Reporting
130696	Performance trace in BW
309955	BW statistics - Questions, answers and errors
731682	Backup in BW and OLTP: Experiences, risks & recommendations

D The Authors

Bharat Patel has extensive experience, spanning more than 16 years of IT and managing data warehouse technology. His experience covers the entire lifecycle management of data warehousing solution from evaluation and identification of the solution to its upgrade and retirement. He is a regular faculty at SAP Partner academy and SAP Labs in India. He has published a book and many technical articles on SAP NetWeaver BW. He has presented papers at many international conferences. He currently manages a large and complex SAP NetWeaver BW system at Bharat Petroleum Corp. ltd., a Fortune 500 Oil company. Bharat is a post-graduate in computer applications and a certified consultant for SAP NetWeaver BW, Supply Chain, and ABAP. You can contact him at *bkpatel67@yahoo.com*.

Amol Palekar has been engaged in BI consulting for eight years and has worked on a variety of SAP NetWeaver BW implementations for customers in manufacturing, automotive, CPG, and telecom domains across geographies. His recent work focuses on expanding the BI footprint within an enterprise to help the business achieve maximum value from analytics and planning capabilities offered by information technology. Amol has made significant contribution in competency building for the organizations he has worked for or served. He has trained many IT professionals on SAP NetWeaver BW and regularly publishes articles and blogs on the subject. He is currently Lead Consultant for business analytics in a major IT services company. You can reach Amol at *amolpp@yahoo.com*.

Shreekant Shiralkar's career, spanning more than 22 years, reflects his ability to manage transformation and innovation for growth. Currently he is a Senior Executive at Accenture India and part of their SAP leadership team. Previously, he held various leadership roles at another leading IT organization their Energy, and SAP Practice, where he grew its business, acquiring new clients in new geographies and adding new service offerings. Earlier, he made significant contributions in varying capacities such as the launch of the "Shell Gas" business in India, leading major transformation projects, and development of a supply chain strategy generating high-value cost optimization for a Fortune 500 oil company. Shreekant has published many technical articles on SAP APO, SAP NetWeaver BW, and RFID, including a book on SAP NetWeaver BW. He has presented papers at many international conferences. You can contact him at *S_Shiralkar@yahoo.com*.

Index

D

E

F

G

H

I

J

K

L

O

P

Q

R

S

T

U

V

W

X

Z

Provides an easy-to-read overview of all Business Objects client tools in an SAP environment

Explains which tools to use for which types of reporting

Offers simple and practical hands-on examples that leve-rage robust sample scenarios and case studies

Ingo Hilgefort

Reporting and Analytics with SAP BusinessObjects

This book provides comprehensive coverage of the major business intelligence tools in the SAP/BO toolset with a practical focus on the user experience and integration with SAP. Coverage includes detailed application features and functionality, as well as practical, how-to content geared toward end users hoping to maximize the benefits their BI investment by creating actionable, easy to read and disseminate reports, analytics and other business process metrics. The author will present the content in an easy to read, step-by-step fashion.

approx. 500700 pp., 79,95 Euro / US$ 79.95
ISBN 978-1-59229-310-0, Jan 2010

>> www.sap-press.com

Learn the essentials of MDX as implemented in NetWeaver BI and Business Objects

Explore examples of common business problems solved with MDX using Business Objects, and other third-party tools

Design MDX-friendly InfoCubes

Larry Sackett

MDX Reporting and Analytics with SAP NetWeaver BW

An Up-to-Date Guide for Business Intelligence Reporting and Analytics with SAP

This is the first book to provide a detailed guide of how MDX works in the SAP NetWeaver BW and Business Objects environments. Readers will learn the concepts behind MDX querying, how to design MDX-friendly InfoCubes, and how to apply the knowledge in solving business problems and creating reports efficiently.

383 pp., 2009, 69,95 Euro / US$ 69.95
ISBN 978-1-59229-249-3

>> www.sap-press.com